KU-581-724

Industrial Psychology 7/e

7th edition

Industrial

Psychology

Ernest J. McCormick

Professor Emeritus
Purdue University

Daniel R. Ilgen

Purdue University

London
GEORGE ALLEN & UNWIN
Boston   Sydney

© 1980, 1974, 1965, 1958, 1952, 1947, 1942 by Prentice-Hall Inc., Englewood Cliffs, N.J. 07632

This book is copyright under the Berne Convention. No reproduction without permission. All rights reserved.

George Allen & Unwin (Publishers) Ltd,
40 Museum Street, London WC1A 1LU, UK

George Allen & Unwin (Publishers) Ltd,
Park Lane, Hemel Hempstead, Herts HP2 4TE, UK

George Allen & Unwin Australia Pty Ltd,
8 Napier Street, North Sydney, NSW 2060, Australia

First published in Great Britain in 1942
Seventh edition 1981
Third impression 1983

British Library Cataloguing in Publication Data

McCormick, Ernest J.
    Industrial psychology.—7th ed.
1. Psychology, Industrial
I. Title   II. Ilgen, Daniel
158.7   HF5548.8
ISBN 0-04-150078-4

Printed in Great Britain by
Hazell Watson & Viney Ltd, Aylesbury, Bucks

contents

INTRODUCTION   1

JOB - RELATED BEHAVIOR AND ITS MEASUREMENT
35

PERSONNEL SELECTION   101

IV

THE ORGANIZATIONAL
AND SOCIAL CONTEXT OF HUMAN WORK   225

THE JOB AND WORK ENVIRONMENT   335

preface

This text is intended as a survey of the field of industrial organizational psychology. This field addresses itself to the wide spectrum of human problems that arise in the production and distribution of the goods and services of the economy. The dynamic nature of the technology involved in these processes and of the cultural and economic environment in which they take place has tended to bring about changes in the nature, importance, and priorities of the human problems associated with these processes, and in turn, in chain-reaction manner, has stimulated changes in the field of industrial psychology. These shifts in industrial psychology have been reflected in a broadening of the entire field, changing emphasis on certain areas, the development of new methods and techniques for the measurement and analysis of relevant variables, and increased attention to the development of theories that might serve as generalized bases for "explaining" human behavior in the industrial context.

The seventh edition of *Industrial Psychology,* has been written to keep abreast of the changes in this field. This edition incorporates a substantial amount of material from the most current research in the field. Increased attention has been given to the area of organizational psychology, to the treatment of relevant theories, and to certain new methods, techniques, and procedures that relate to industrial organizational psychology. Since it is not possible within the scope of a single text to bring together the bulk of available research, it has been the intent to include, as examples of research in various areas, what are some of the most important and significant research investigations.

The field of industrial/organizational psychology includes both the "science" of psychology (as rooted in research) and the "profession" or "practice" of psychology. The latter deals specifically with the application of the knowledge from the theories and methods of psychology to the practical human problems in organizations. In the writing of this text it has been the objective of the authors to bridge the theoretical and applied aspects of industrial/organizational psychology.

The body of research data that comprises substantial portions of this text reflect the efforts of many researchers in industry, universities, and other organizations. We take this opportunity to express our appreciation to them collectively. Acknowledgement of their individual contributions is given in the body of the text, with complete references at the end of each chapter.

Much of this revision was carried out when the second author was on sabbatical leave from Purdue University at the University of Washington, Seattle, Washington. This temporary location in a different city required much of the United States mails and of Barbara Ilgen. In addition to her responsibilities as wife and mother she provided much needed support, typing, and editing. Her efforts have been greatly appreciated.

We would like to acknowledge the following reviewers for their contributions: Dr. Jan L. Ditzian, State University of New York at Buffalo; Professor Richard J. Klimoski, Ohio State University; Professor Ben B. Morgan, Jr., Old Dominion University; Professor Paul M. Muchinsky; Professor Denise M. Rousseau, University of Michigan; Professor James R. Terbourg, University of Houston; Professor John R. Wakeley, Michigan State University.

Ernest J. McCormick

Daniel R. Ilgen

Dedication
to
DR. JOSEPH TIFFIN

The history of every discipline is punctuated with the names of individuals who have made significant contributions to the development of the discipline, through research, writing, teaching, and related activities. In the field of industrial/organizational psychology, Dr. Joseph Tiffin is such an individual. One could not adequately review the early stages of the development of the field of industrial psychology without reference to his work.

A highly respected experimental psychologist whose early work focused upon physiological and psychological factors related to vision, Joseph Tiffin backed into the field of industrial/organizational psychology when he began to apply his research on vision to visual concerns of industrial workers. This work led him into the area of personnel testing which at that time was the major thrust of industrial psychology.

From his entry into the field in the late 1930s up to the time of his retirement from Purdue University in 1971, Joseph Tiffin made major contributions in several areas. He actively developed and shaped the field of industrial psychology as a discipline through his participation in the division of the American Psychological Association that is devoted to industrial psychology: this participation was culminated by his election to the presidency of that division in 1958.

He strongly influenced the field through his writing of one of the first major texts in the area. Finding the field of industrial psychology to be rather barren of textbooks, he brought out the first edition of *Industrial Psychology* in 1942. Dr. Tiffin wrote the second and third editions in 1947 and 1952. Professor McCormick co-authored with him the fourth and fifth editions in 1958 and 1965, and revised the work for the 6th edition in 1974. Various editions of the text have been published in eight foreign countries, in six different languages.

Although research and writing may have provided the greatest breadth of Joseph Tiffin's influence, it was his teaching that gave it its depth. When he came in 1938 Purdue University had no industrial psychology program. When he retired, the program was internationally known as one of the top in the field. Joseph Tiffin was primarily responsible for the development of the program and he contributed significantly to its international reputation. Furthermore, in this process, he trained a wide variety of well known psychologists who have developed outstanding reputations as industrial psychologists in industry, government, consulting firms, and universities. Through his students he has had an unmeasurable but nonetheless profound influence on the field of industrial/organizational psychology, just as he has influenced his former students directly by becoming for them a friend and a mentor in the truest sense of the word.

Because of his significant contribution to industrial/organizational psychology in general and this textbook in particular, we respectfully dedicate the seventh edition of *Industrial Psychology* to Joseph Tiffin and we want to express our sincere appreciation for the privilege of sharing in the continuation of the text.

Ernest J. McCormick

Daniel R. Ilgen

Test of solar collectors. *(Courtesy the Boeing Company)*

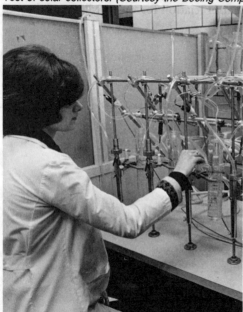

Observing effects of new drug.
(Courtesy Eli Lilly and Company)

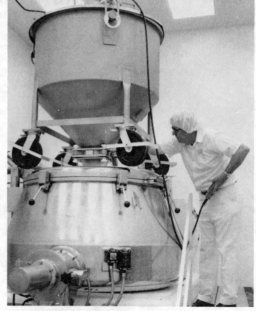

Bulk powder granulations.
(Courtesy Eli Lilly and Company)

introduction

Psychology is the study of human behavior, but in contrast to most disciplines, it has two faces. One face is the discovery through research, of information about human behavior. The other face is the application of such knowledge to various practical problems. The research face is sometimes called the *science* of psychology, and the application side is sometimes called the *profession* of psychology. The profession is similar to those of physicians, engineers, and others concerned with the application of knowledge of some field to the practical problems of the real world.

Industrial psychology includes both these faces. Its scientific aspect is rooted in research that provides the knowledge that is a prerequisite for any practical applications. This knowledge can be in the form of theories or in the form of empirically determined relationships. In either case, such knowledge frequently can be applied by organizations to minimize some of the human problems that inevitably arise in the operations of all kinds of organizations.

The first part of the text includes as an overall introduction to industrial psychology, a discussion of some of the factors that influence job-related behavior (the "bases" of such behavior), and an overview of behavioral research.

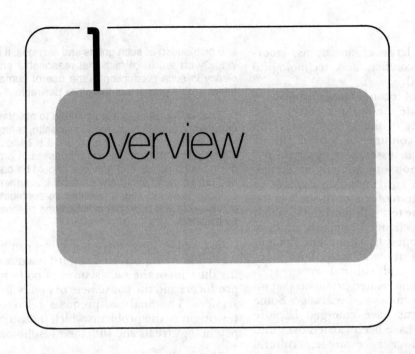

overview

Human work is concerned with the production and distribution of the goods and services of the economy. During and since the industrial revolution the world has witnessed major changes in work, triggered by technological developments that have resulted in virtually millions of new products and services and in methods for producing such products and services. In the developed countries of the world, in particular, these technologies have served as the basis for the creation of organizations to provide such goods and services, such as those in manufacturing, transportation, utilities, extraction of raw materials, wholesale and retail trade, services, business and professional services of many kinds, education, and entertainment and leisure services. In addition, government agencies have been created at various levels, either to provide certain services (such as police and fire protection, trash collection, and assistance to

the needy) or to monitor the organizations producing goods and services.

The technological developments of the past hundred or two hundred years thus have brought about major changes in the nature and organization of human work. For example, some of the functions formerly carried out exclusively by hand or with hand tools have become mechanized, thereby creating jobs in the operation and maintenance of machines. The continuing trend toward automation is further altering the nature of many jobs. These technological developments and the accompanying changes in the nature of human work have been accompanied not only by certain human benefits (such as the reduction of human labor, improvement in working conditions, and higher income), but also by certain costs (such as the routinization of some work processes, the sense of "meaninglessness" in some work, the sense of being "lost" in large organizations, labor-management conflict, and technological unemployment).

The effects of technological change have been felt outside the workplace itself. The entire economy of the United States and certain other countries has been altered from that of an essentially agrarian and handcraft economy to a highly industrialized one, with corresponding changes in the overall pattern of life for the bulk of the population. The technological changes that have markedly changed human work have been accompanied by significant changes in such aspects of life as the political, economic, social, and cultural areas, such changes spawning related problems that we could not have envisioned years ago. Some of the problems have emerged because these changes have been carried over into human work. For example, cultural changes in the recent decades have brought about somewhat different attitudes toward work and have resulted in different value systems. In addition, the increased concern for equal opportunity (in part emphasized in the United States by the Equal Employment Opportunity Act of 1964) has brought about several practical problems in managing business and industrial organizations.

Industrial psychology is the study of human behavior in the work-related aspects of life and the application of knowledge of human behavior to the minimization of human problems in this context.

INDUSTRIAL PSYCHOLOGY: ITS PREMISES

Industrial psychology has certain premises, the first three of which may be viewed as desirable objectives of industry:

1. That industry should produce those goods and services that fulfill the reasonable needs of people, considering both their physical welfare and personal values.

2. That it is desirable to increase the effectiveness of human involvement in the production

and distribution of such goods and services. It is virtually an article of faith that reasonable efficiency in such production in the use of human talent in this process is therefore desirable.

3. That in this process it is desirable to maintain or enhance certain human values (health, safety, job satisfaction, etc.). In this regard it is becoming an article of faith that the processes of producing such goods and services should be carried out so as to avoid any physical impairment of those involved and, if possible, to contribute positively to the personal satisfactions of those so involved.

In a sense, these three objectives can be viewed as being directed toward maximizing the sum of the satisfactions of both the producers and the consumers of goods and services. The final two premises relate to the origin of the problems which industrial psychology treats and with their resolution:

4. That marked disparities between the above objectives and their reasonable fulfillment are the sources of most of the human problems in industry.

5. That knowledge of and insight into human behavior gained through psychological research and through experience can help minimize such problems.

In sum, then, the *raison d'être* of industrial psychology is the existence of human problems in organizations, and its objective is somehow to resolve these problems or, more realistically, to minimize them.

The Development of Industrial Psychology

Industrial psychology grew to its present maturity against the backdrop of these major changes in our economy. This field of psychology has developed largely since the turn of the century. One of the first major books in the area was Hugo Münsterberg's *Psychology of Industrial Efficiency* (1913). The early industrial psychologists were concerned particularly with problems of personnel selection, but their interests also embraced other applied areas, such as advertising and selling, accidents, and employee rating processes.

A very significant early step in the application of psychological techniques to personnel problems was the use of personnel tests by the Army during World War I. In particular, tests were developed and used by the Army for the classification and assignment of Army personnel. In Great Britain the Industrial Fatigue Research Board (later called the Industrial Health Research Board) was organized at this time to investigate problems associated with fatigue, hours of work, conditions of work, and related matters. (During and since World War II these and other activities have been carried out by the Applied Psychology Research Unit of the Medical Research Council of Great Britain.)

For several years after the war, the interest in psychology as applied to the human problems of industry was relatively sporadic, but by the 1930s the field of industrial psychology had been established as a reasonably distinct phase of psychology. Its major development and expansion, however, have occurred since then. In the intervening years the field has developed in countries all over the world, with the primary development being in certain countries in Western Europe and in the United States.

Changes in Emphasis in Industrial Psychology

The last four decades have seen various changes in emphasis on the kinds of problems with which industrial psychologists have been concerned. Probably the dominant emphasis during the early years, continuing through the 1930s and 1940s, was on personnel selection and placement. This has continued to be important to industrial psychology and probably will continue to be in the years to come. But recent years have brought about a critical reevaluation of the use of tests for such purposes

in the United States according to the provisions of the Equal Employment Opportunity Act of 1964 and the Uniform Guidelines on Employee Selection Procedures (1978), along with various related court decisions relating to alleged discriminatory practices in the use of personnel tests. (The main object of the federal regulations in this area is to require that employers demonstrate the "job-relatedness" of such tests.)

During the 1940s and 1950s there was considerable interest in the human relations aspects of personnel management, with particular concern for group interaction, supervision and leadership processes, communications, and job satisfaction. This increased emphasis on human relations in industry led to greater attention to human relations training of supervisory and management personnel and to management development programs generally. What is more, interest in the social aspects of human work has led logically to the crystallization of what is now referred to as organizational psychology; in this discipline the dominant focus is on human motivation, and efforts are made to understand the effects of the organizational setting on motivation, job satisfaction, and work effectiveness. The development of organizational psychology has entailed a growing interest in leadership styles, management philosophies, organizational policies and structures, incentive systems, and other aspects of organizations as they relate to both human satisfactions and organizational effectiveness.

Paralleling these developments during the past three or four decades or so has been the development of human factors engineering (or *ergonomics,* as it is called in most other countries). The objective of this field is to design physical equipment and facilities tailored to human abilities and limitations. Although this field is interdisciplinary, psychologists have been important to it over the years; the segment of this domain to which psychologists have contributed is sometimes called *engineering psychology* or simply *human factors*.

Looking Ahead

To date, the efforts of industrial psychologists have been directed largely toward the study of the independent relationships between specific variables on the one hand, and various aspects of work-related behavior on the other. There have been scads of independent investigations of such specific variables as individual differences, organizational characteristics, incentives, group structure, equipment design, and working conditions. But studies of *combinations* of these and other variables are relatively few and far between, as was pointed out by Uhlaner (1970). According to Uhlaner, effective behavior and work performance are not always the *additive* effects of whatever variables may be involved, for the different variables *interact* in this process and may be complicated by different types of jobs. For example, one type of incentive might be appropriate to some kinds of people and

jobs but not to others. Uhlaner's argument is that more behavioral research relating to human work should be carried out in the framework of its total context in order to explore the possible interactions. His own generalized conceptualization of the various possible interactions is illustrated in Figure 1.1, in which he depicts the various sets of variables that may interact to contribute to effective work and work performance. It seems reasonable to expect that the same illustration can be applied to criteria of various human values (such as health, safety, and satisfactions) as well as to criteria of effective work and work performance. For this reason one should not view system "design," personnel selection, and training as separate, isolated facets of work-related functions but rather, as an integrated package. Related research should be approached accordingly.

THE SYSTEMS CONCEPT. Although, as Uhlaner implied, this multifaceted, interactive approach is not commonly used, it has not been entirely neglected. In fact, paralleling the development of human factors

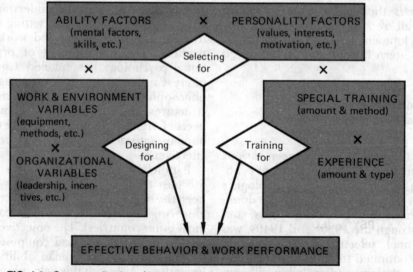

FIG. 1.1 Conceptualization of interactions of human factor system variables as related to human performance effectiveness. These kinds of data provide a "measurement bed" for analyzing interactions of variables as related to effective behavior and work performance. (*Adapted from Uhlaner 1970, Schema 1.*)

engineering has been the development of the *systems concept*. In this specific frame of reference, the intent is to develop a "system" that provides an optimum blend of people, equipment, procedures, and operations in order to capitalize on the relative capabilities of human beings and of physical equipment in performing different functions. Although the systems concept is most obviously applicable to circumstances in which human beings are to interact with items of physical equipment, it is also applicable to processes or operations in which little physical equipment is used, such as office operations, service and distribution processes, and communication processes. Even a complete organization can be viewed as a system.

In the past, most of the behavioral research related to systems has been carried out in connection with military man-machine operations, as discussed by Parson (1972). Some of this work has employed the type of integrated framework discussed above, and some of it has been carried out in laboratory settings, in some instances using very elaborate experimental facilities and procedures.

DISCUSSION. We have no instant insight into the future direction of industrial psychology, but we agree with Uhlaner that industrial psychology needs to shift somewhat from the investigation of individual variables and factors relating to human behavior to the study of behavior within various industrial contexts, including whatever interactions there may be in such contexts. It is hoped that research in this direction will be rewarded by greater understanding of and insight into human behavior.

THE MODUS OPERANDI OF INDUSTRIAL PSYCHOLOGY

As stated earlier, the objective of industrial psychology is to provide the basis for minimizing some of the human problems in industry. The *modus operandi* of industrial psychology in this process has a sequence of four phases or stages: (1) the identification of the problems to be treated; (2) the use of various methods of collection and analysis of relevant data; (3) the findings resulting from these methods and associated analyses; and (4) the application of such findings to the problems at hand.

Identification of the Problems

The problems relevant to industrial psychology are manifest in various ways and at various levels of abstraction—most of them being manifestations of the disparities between the objectives referred to above and the reasonable fulfillment of these in practice. An illustrative inventory of these problems might include the following: indications of organizational ineffectiveness and of inadequate job performance of people; high personnel turnover rates; injuries; poor employee morale; dissatisfaction; controversy and occasional conflict; and failure to fulfill the reasonable needs of consumers.

For the reasonable fulfillment of the goals of the people involved, we need to recognize that there are different groups of participants in this total process, such as owners or stockholders, managers, supervisors, employees, unions, consumers, the government, and the general public. The opposing interests of some of these groups frequently (and in certain circumstances almost inevitably) lead to controversy and conflict. We must recognize that—almost by definition—the interests of some of the participants cannot be entirely fulfilled.

The realities of life characteristically impose constraints on the achievement of the legitimate objectives of industry discussed earlier. Some trade offs are required, such as settling for something less than topnotch efficiency in order to reduce accident liability or imposing restrictions on earnings in the interest of maintaining a competitive position (and thus enhance future security). In the best of all possible worlds the potentially conflicting facets would be dealt with in such a manner as to achieve reasonable balance.

Methods

The primary aim of industrial psychologists in treating human problems in the industrial arena is to apply knowledge and insight that can be used to resolve these problems. Because this is essentially a research function, the methods used in this process are central to the development of such knowledge and insight. A number of the methods used will be described or illustrated throughout this book with the specific topics to which they are relevant, so that for the moment we will mention only a few of them. By and large, they fall into three classes: (1) experimental design (methods of investigation), (2) data collection (the use of such methods as tests, questionnaires, ratings, performance appraisal, observation, and job analysis), and (3) statistical analysis methods.

Findings

The results from statistical methods are the basis of the "findings" of psychological research. More will be said about this later; here we will observe only that they tend to fall into at least two predominant categories: (1) theories or generalizations (such as the usefulness of feedback in learning); and (2) empirically derived research findings (findings that are specific to certain situations, such as the times required to learn a job by different training methods).

Application of Findings

The "application" of research findings implies the adoption of certain practices, procedures, policies, or actions predicated on the findings in question. Examples of such practical steps include: using certain tests or other predictors as the basis for personnel selection; developing training programs that incorporate certain learning principles; training supervisors and managers in personnel relations practices; establishing financial and other incentives compatible with human needs; and creating physical working conditions satisfactory in terms of appropriate health and safety standards.

The findings of psychological research can be (and often are) used by people other than psychologists, such as personnel managers, supervisors, managers, and advertising personnel. In some cases, however, research findings need to be applied by, or under the supervision of, professional psychologists who serve in a consulting or advising capacity. In this role a psychologist serves essentially as a professional practitioner.

It should be added that sometimes the area of "application" is by no means apparent at the time the "problem" is identified. A single type of problem (such as poor performance) conceivably could be the consequence of any of several precipitating factors, such as improper personnel selections, inadequate training, improper incentives, poor working conditions, or poorly designed equipment. In fact, one of the primary purposes of this problem-methods-findings-applications sequence is to track down these sometimes elusive relationships.

THE TWO FACES OF INDUSTRIAL PSYCHOLOGY

Industrial psychologists become involved in a variety of activities, but in a sense their responsibilities can be viewed as relating either to the *science* of psychology (with an emphasis on research) or to the *profession* of psychology (with an emphasis on the application of knowledge and insight to practical problems). In this regard it should be emphasized that the profession of psychology needs to be rooted in psychological research; indeed, in many instances practitioners themselves do research relating to the problems with which they are dealing, such as analyzing the factors associated with accidents, conducting an attitude survey, or studying the buying habits of consumers. Even psychologists who are serving primarily as professionals usually need to be well versed in research methodology.

Industrial Psychology as a Science

The solution to most of the human problems in industry requires knowledge of human behavior. Such knowledge can be derived in part through experience, and it would be a poor observer of human behavior who did not, through observation and experience, develop some useful insights. The insight into human behavior derived from "experience," however, has its limitations. Hence the value of research, for it can provide the basis for developing information about many aspects of human behavior that cannot be inferred from experience.

All scientific endeavor is predicated upon the assumption that events and phenomena are the consequences of precipitating factors. As applied to the study of human behavior in industry or elsewhere, this means that we must assume that behavior is based on complex assortments of variables, both individual and situational. It is the intent of psychological research to identify the variables associated with different aspects of behavior, such as the relationship between aptitudes and job performance or between illumination and the ability of people to make visual discriminations.

Beyond the objective of identifying such relationships, some psychological research is aimed at determining the underlying reasons for the behavior of people—at "explaining" such behavior on the basis of theories. Such research typically is initiated after the development of speculations about the cause of some aspect of behavior, leading to the formulation of a theory. Ultimately the accumulation of research evidence may tend to support the theory in question. Of course, in a sense one can never statistically "prove" a theory, or a cause-and-effect relationship, or "why" people behave in a given manner. But, it is sometimes possible to build up such a persuasive body of evidence that one is willing to accept a theory as being "true" or to conclude that a cause-and-effect relationship does in fact exist.

Certain aspects of behavioral research are discussed in chapter 3, and examples are scattered throughout the text.

INDUSTRIAL PSYCHOLOGY AS A PROFESSION. Psychology as a profession is concerned with the "application" of knowledge to some practical problem. Industrial psychologists who perform such functions are serving as professional practitioners— they are practicing the profession. In industry this can include consulting, program development, and individual evaluation. Typically, a psychologist in consulting activities advises in some area of expertise, such as management development, equipment design, or training methods. A psychologist in program development would be responsible for developing and installing some program, such as a training program or a personnel selection program. In individual evaluation, psychologists function much like a clinician in assessing the potentialities of individuals for specific positions, promotions, and so forth, or in counseling individuals themselves. In this capacity they typically use interviewing techniques, tests, and related techniques as the basis for evaluation. Psychologists in industry may also use their psychological background in dealing with individuals in connection with other functions in an organization, such as in helping to resolve individual or organizational conflicts. In other functions they treat human behavior in conceptual terms rather than on an individual basis.

THEORETICAL VERSUS EMPIRICAL BASES OF APPLICATIONS

As indicated earlier, the primary findings of behavioral research are of two general types. One of these is theories or generalizations (such as a theory of motivation). The other is empirically determined relationships (such as the relationships between training methods and learning). There are differences of opinion of the appropriateness or utility of these two types of research bases in the practice of psychology. For example, some people take it for granted that "applications" of research must necessarily follow the acceptance of some theory. Snijders accurately characterized this assumption as the belief that "pure or fundamental research must firstly lay the theoretical foundations, on which secondly a technology is erected; only after that can a start be made with applications to practical problems"(1969, p.13–19). Snijders hastened to point out that contemporary psychology refutes the idea that such a logical and temporal relationship between theory and application must universally apply. To support this he stated that there can be "practice without a theory" (such as the widescale use of mental tests) and also "theory without practice" (such as the extensive research relating to learning theory that to date has been "applied" very nominally if at all). In the relationship between theory and applications, Chapanis (1971) stated that the best basic work in psychology starts not with psychological theory but with attempts to solve questions posed by the world around us.

Certainly in industrial psychology much of the research has been directed toward solving practical problems and thus has an applied, empirical nature unaccompanied by much related theory. Although empirically determined relationships do not explain *why* people behave in some given manner, such relationships nonetheless can serve as the basis for achieving certain practical objectives. For example, we might find, in general, that employees with a given constellation of personal background experiences (that is, hobbies, family relationships, education, and so forth) tend to remain longer on jobs in an organization than do other employees. Although we may not know why this is so, this information can be useful in selecting personnel.

The fact that applied, empirical research can be useful in practice should not lead us to neglect the sorts of understanding that can be gained through theory formulation. But such objectives should not become a fetish that blinds us to the potential practical usefulness of empirical research. We agree with Viteles:

> I have become increasingly concerned about a growing tendency on the part of applied psychologists to subordinate empiricism, in the form of attachment to facts, to a concept of science that gives the latter, especially as represented by its theories, an aura of inner and transcendental perfection—a quality of the *précieux* that sometimes achieves the quality of the absurd. (1969)

Thus, an industrial psychologist might find it more useful to carry a study to find which of two or three wage incentive systems are liked best by the employees than to select some theory of "motivation" (of which there are many) as the basis for deciding which incentive system to use.

When the results of psychological research are to be "applied," it is clear that the objective is some form of control of behavior of the people in question. This control can range from forms widely held to be desirable (such as vocational counseling, training, education, and the like) to forms that are at odds with commonly accepted values, such as brainwashing. The types of control implicit in psychological research essentially are ethically oriented toward the objectives of basic human welfare.

TREATMENT OF INDUSTRIAL PSYCHOLOGY IN THIS BOOK

This book is intended to be a survey of industrial psychology. As such, it will be concerned with the spectrum of its problems, the methods used in investigating these problems, and illustrative findings from such research. Because of the extensive material available, the content of this book must be selective and illustrative rather than inclusive. In the selection of the problems, methods, and findings, it has been our intent to include as illustrations at least some of the more important examples.

Aside from the introductory chapters, the book is organized into certain major "content" areas of industrial psychology, generally the primary areas of application:

Introduction

Measurement of Job-related Behavior

Personnel Selection

The Organization and Social Context of Work

The Job and Work Environment

Inasmuch as industrial psychology is directed toward resolving practical problems, this organization was suggested in large part because it reflects the main areas of practice in this field. We should keep in mind, however, that the various areas do not exist in isolation but are indeed interrelated—so much so that, as noted before, any given "problem" might lead one into any of the several areas of application.

A special comment should be made about the discussion of methods. Some of the methods of collection and analysis of data are relevant to various content areas. Here they generally will be brought up in the first context to which they are relevant, even though their potential use may well extend to other areas.

REFERENCES

CHAPANIS, A. Prelude to 2001: Exploration in human communication. *American Psychologist,* 1971, *26* (11), 949–961.

PARSONS, H. M. *Man-machine systems experiments.* Baltimore: Johns Hopkins Press, 1972.

SNIJDERS, J. T. Interaction of theory and practice. *Revue Internationale de Psychologie Appliquée,* April 1969, *18* (1), 13–19.

UHLANER, J. E. *Human performance, jobs, and systems psychology: The systems measurement bed.* U.S. Army, Behavior and Systems Research Laboratory, Technical Report S-2 (AD 716 346), October 1970.

Uniform guidelines on employee selection procedures. *Federal Register,* Vol. 43, No. 166, Friday, August 25, 1978, pp. 38290–38309.

VITELES, M. S. The two faces of applied psychology. *Revue Internationale de Psychologie Appliquée,* April 1969, *18* (1), 5–10.

2
bases of job-related behavior

The world of human work consists of individuals performing jobs in some setting, usually in some organization. The fact that there are tremendous differences among individuals and among jobs is the basis of the frequently expressed notion of "matching" people and jobs and of the expression "round pegs in square holes" when the "match" is not a good one. Mismatches can occur in any setting. The business of matching becomes particularly complicated when the job setting is taken into account. The same "types" of people in essentially the same jobs but in different organizations or with different work groups may perform quite differently because of the different settings.

The fact that many matches are far from perfect is obvious to the individuals as well as to the organizations and is reflected in any of many different ways, such as differences in how well people perform their

jobs, differences in how long people stay on their jobs, how often they are late for work, variations in how well people like their jobs, differences in the number and severity of injuries people experience on their jobs, and differences in how well people can "take" their jobs physically and psychologically. Since there is no one word in the English language that adequately describes these (and other) job-related factors, let us use the word "behavior." The usual notion of behavior as an overt action, that is, observable, certainly applies to many job activities, such as when a person shows up for work, how well someone does his job, and even when someone hits one's thumb with a hammer. We will simply stretch the word "behavior" to cover covert, less observable manifestations of work, such as the attitudes toward and opinions of people about their jobs and job situations, as well as the physiological or physical effects of work.

FACTORS ASSOCIATED WITH DIFFERENCES IN BEHAVIOR

Behaviors generally can be construed as varying along two dimensions. The first of these is *quantitative*. Most job-related behaviors can be quantified (that is, they can be measured) in some units appropriate to the behavior under consideration. For example, by hook or by crook we usually can measure such behaviors as job performance (such as quantity, number of errors, accuracy, and so forth), tenure on the job, number of absences, attitudes (as reflected by scores on an attitude scale), time required to complete a particular task, heart rate, energy expenditure, and job satisfaction (as measured by job satisfaction questionnaires). These examples and measurements of other types of behaviors serve to classify and quantify various types of job-related behaviors.

The other dimension on which behaviors can be characterized is *qualitative,* which is essentially evaluative in that the behavior is viewed as being somewhere along a scale of "goodness-badness" or "desirable-undesirable." Given the measurement of some behavior on a *quantitative* scale, one then can make an evaluation on a *qualitative* scale as to whether the behavior is good, bad, or indifferent. For example, the per hour production of widgets by a worker (a quantitative measure) then can be evaluated as to whether it is up to standard, how it compares with that of other workers, and so forth. In this regard, a given level of production might be very good for a beginner, but not for an experienced worker. Similarly, other behavioral measures can be evaluated along a qualitative continuum, variables such as job satisfaction, heart rate, absenteeism, and so forth. Such evaluation frequently is based on comparison with measurements of the behavior of other people, rather like comparing a person's score on a test with others' scores.

Causation in Human Behavior

For any given type of behavior, the variability along the quantitative continuum is assumed to be the consequence of some combination of factors. To illustrate this point, let us take the hypothetical case of employees on a particular type of job and concern ourselves with the differences in performance of the individual employees. Job performance almost inevitably varies among employees (and from time to time for the same employee). The differences in performance sometimes (but not invariably) form a distribution something like a normal distribution, as illustrated in Figure 2.1. Assuming some criterion (such as productivity in units per day or sales in dollars), one would find that individuals fall at different points (A, B, and C) along the performance continuum. If our assumption of multiple causation is valid, then we must infer that individuals A, B, and C fall at their respective positions of below average, average, and above average for some combination of reasons.

If we were to speculate about some of the factors that might be associated with the relative performances of these three individuals, and workers in general, there are certain kinds of factors that almost inevitably would be suggested. This list would include a variety of *individual variables,* such as aptitudes, personality characteristics, physical characteristics, interests and motivation, age and sex, education, experience, and other personal variables. In addition, it would also include a number of *situational variables.* These, in turn, tend to fall into two general classes. In the first are those we might call the *job and working conditions variables* that include methods of work, the design and condition of work equipment, work space and arrangement, and the physical work environment (including illumination, noise, temperature, etc.). In the second place are what we might call *organizational and social variables,* including

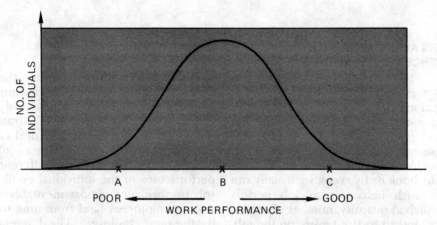

FIG. 2.1 Distribution of differences in work performance of a hypothetical group of workers in a job. Positions A, B, and C represent three hypothetical individuals within the distribution, these being generally below average (A), average (B), and above average (C).

the character of the organization, type of training and supervision received, types of incentives, the "social" environment, and union relations. Some of these variables are represented in Figure 2.2. Each of the categories shown is itself a class of variables. Within each one there might be several more specific variables, such as specific aptitudes, specific physical characteristics, specific aspects of the physical work environment, and specific aspects of the social environment.

Thus, we see that there are many kinds of variables that can influence the work performance or behavior of people. Figure 2.2 is a generalized one. Theoretically, one could construct such a chart for every type of job. The chart for any given type of job could differ from others in two ways. First, it could be different in its *combination* of specific variables, and second, it could be different in the relative *importance* of the variables. It can be seen that for some types of jobs certain variables simply might not be pertinent to performance on the job; for example, eye-hand coordination presumably would have no bearing on the performance of executives.

The generalized picture presented in Figure 2.2 is applicable to any given type of job on something of an across-the-board basis—wherever the job exists. It should be

pointed out that in any *specific* situation such as a given job in a given department of a company, there may be no variability on some of the *situational* variables. For example, if all employees on the job are subject to the same physical working conditions (say illumination), in *that situation* working conditions usually would not operate *differentially* to cause some people to perform better than others. Conversely, if the same job were performed under *other* illumination conditions, as might happen in another department or in another company, one might find a difference in the performance level of employees in the two departments or plants that would be associated with the different illumination.

Although Figures 2.1 and 2.2 are presented as illustrations of variables that might affect performance on a job, the same general model also could be applied to other aspects of job-related behavior of people. This would mean relabeling the criterion in Figure 2.1 to reflect the type of behavior in mind (such as differences in attitudes, job attendance, accident rates, and heart rates.).

Combining Variables Related to Behavior

In general, then, we can postulate that the "quantitative" behavior of whatever

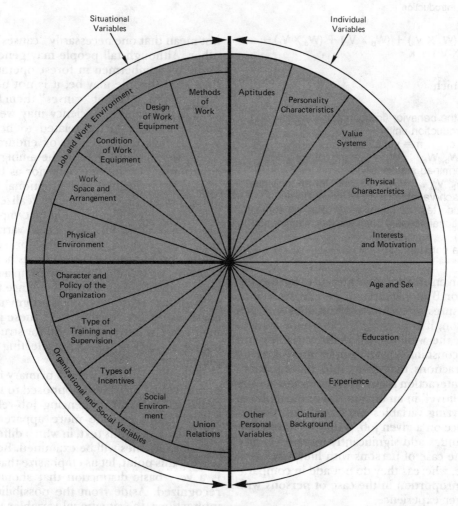

Situational Variables

Individual Variables

Job and Work Environment

Methods of Work

Design of Work Equipment

Condition of Work Equipment

Work Space and Arrangement

Physical Environment

Aptitudes

Personality Characteristics

Value Systems

Physical Characteristics

Interests and Motivation

Organizational and Social Variables

Character and Policy of the Organization

Type of Training and Supervision

Types of Incentives

Social Environment

Union Relations

Other Personal Variables

Cultural Background

Experience

Education

Age and Sex

FIG. 2.2 Graphic representation of some of the individual and situational variables that may be associated with job performance. This is a generalized representation. The representation for any given job might include only some of these variables, and their relative importance as influencing factors might be unique to the job in question.

form (job performance, attitudes, automobile driving, and so forth) is the consequence of the total effects of several variables—individual and situational. If one can somehow measure both the behavior and the specific variables that might be related to it, then it would be possible, at least in theory, to quantify the effects of the several variables as related to the behavior in question and to express this as an equation. For example, performance on a particular

job might be measured as units of production. In turn, the individual variables might include such variables as test scores and years of education, and the situational variables might include such values as footcandles of illumination and number of people in the work group. Assuming we could obtain a "value" on each variable pertinent to each individual in such a case, the equation to predict behavior (in this case job performance) might look like this:

$$B = (W_a \times V_a) + (W_b \times V_b) + (W_c \times V_c) + \ldots (W_n \times V_n) + k$$

in which

B = the behavior (in quantitative terms such as production units)
$a, b, c, \ldots n$ = variables
$W_a, W_b, W_c \ldots W_n$ = weights of variables (determined statistically)
$V_a, V_b, V_c, \ldots V_n$ = "values" for an individual on each variable (such as score on an aptitude test, or quantitative value on some situational variable such as, say, illumination level)
k = a constant

Given quantitative measures of the behavior B in a sample of people, as well as measures of each of the variables for each person, it is possible to determine statistically the weights (w) of the variables and the constant (k). Of course, there may be interactions that enter into the equation. An interaction is an effect that is not strictly "additive" in an equation. For example, in analyzing variables associated with performance on a given job, it may be found that aptitudes add significantly to performance in the case of persons with limited experience, whereas they do not add in comparable proportion in the case of persons with longer experience.

Although it is not possible to predict behavior perfectly in this manner, nonetheless there have been many situations in which behavior (such as job performance) has been predicted to a practically useful degree by such a scheme.

Discussion

As we think about causation of human behavior, we need to be wary of saying that any *specific* human attribute or characteristic of the job setting "causes" a particular form of behavior. Because there is a statistical relationship between two variables does not mean that one necessarily "causes" the other. Although tall people may generally be better lumbermen in forest operations than short people may be, it is not necessarily their height that "causes" them to be so. Their greater proficiency may well be due to another factor related to height, such as muscular strength or endurance. Thus, we find ourselves in the ambiguous situation of considering behavior as being caused by individual and situational variables, but at the same time we realize that it is extremely difficult and in fact impossible to nail down all the specific variables that do produce such behavior. Even though proof positive is sometimes hard to come by, we frequently can build up a sufficient body of circumstantial evidence to be able to make reasonably good judgments of cause and effect. Furthermore, these judgments can be extremely useful for structuring job settings as well as for selecting people for jobs.

The difference between a primary focus on individual variables as opposed to situational variables in influencing job-related behavior will become more apparent in later chapters of this text, in which different types of variables will be examined. Before leaving this point, let us emphasize that this is a very basic distinction that should be recognized. Aside from the possibility of interactions, the situational variables (such as equipment, environment, social work groups, and procedures) may be viewed as aspects of the "system," if you will, within which individuals function. If there is evidence that situational factors may influence behavior (such as job performance), then it *may* be possible to modify these factors in order to create a situation (a "system") reasonably conducive to more acceptable behavior. But let us keep in mind that, in one sense, we are not here looking strictly at human performance as such but rather, at "system" performance. As Taylor (1957) pointed out in his discussion of physical equipment, one system (A) might have greater output than another (B), even though system B might make greater demands on human performance than system A. On the other hand, the *individual,* as opposed to *situational,* variables take on importance *within* any given system or situation, such as in the context of a given job or of a given organization.

INDIVIDUAL VARIABLES IN JOB-RELATED BEHAVIOR

The evidence that quantitative differences in job-related behavior can be attributed in part to individual differences is abundant and pervasive. This is the case with virtually all types of job-related behavior but is perhaps especially so with respect to different aspects of job performance. Typical examples of such evidence are data for incumbents in individual jobs on the relationship between scores on some type

of personnel test and some measure of job performance. (In data for incumbents on a particular job in a given organization, the job situation usually is the same for all incumbents.) Some examples of such relationships will be given in later chapters.

In some jobs the differences in job performance of different incumbents are of appreciable magnitude and of considerable practical importance in terms of productive efficiency, earnings of individuals, and other considerations.

Figure 2.3 shows the performance of employees on three jobs—cablers, mechanical assemblers, and unit wirers—in a company manufacturing electronic equipment. The first two jobs are preparing parts for the wiring operation. The wirer then assembles a component of the finished product. His task includes soldering of the connections, and he may take several hours on a difficult component. Production on all

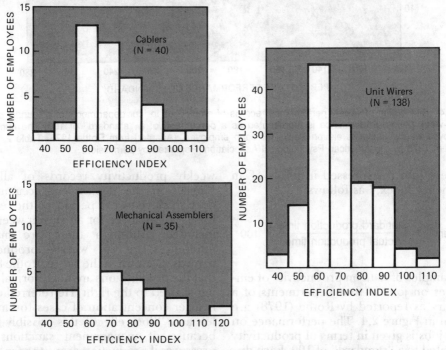

FIG. 2.3 Distribution of efficiency indexes of employees on three production jobs in an electronics company. (*Courtesy Tetronix, Inc. and Dr. Guyot Frazier.*)

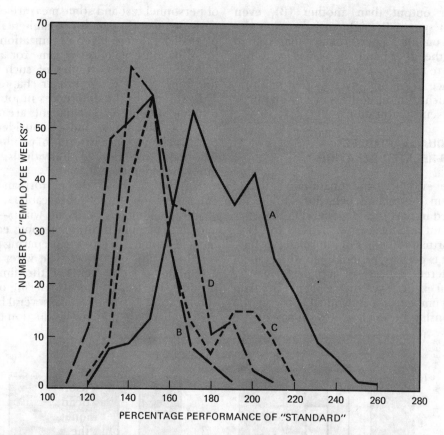

FIG. 2.4 Distribution of weekly performance records of employees in four departments of a foundry over an eleven-week period. Performance is represented as a percentage of a "standard" of 100. The number of "employee weeks" includes eleven weeks for each employee. (Adapted from Rothe 1978, Table 2, p. 43.) Copyright 1978 by the American Psychological Association. Reprinted by permission.

of these jobs is expressed in terms of an "efficiency index," as follows:

$$\text{Efficiency} = \frac{\text{Standard production time}}{\text{Actual production time}} \times 100$$

Examples of data on productivity of employees on jobs in four departments of a foundry as reported by Rothe (1978) are shown in Figure 2.4. The performance on these jobs is given in terms of productivity as related to a "standard" of 100. Each distribution in that figure represents the weekly productivity records of all employees in the department accumulated over an eleven-week period, so the records for each employee for all eleven weeks are included. Although there are marked differences in the weekly productivity records as shown in the figure, Rothe found that the distributions are not "normal," being skewed to the right. He referred to the heavier concentration of cases toward the left as a "floor effect," this possibly being because of management sanctions and pressures if production drops too far below some standard, to internal group pressures to achieve some desirable standard of "premium" pay, or to the existence of "tight" rates since the employees were being paid on an incentive basis. ("Tight" incentive rates are those that do not permit as wide ranges in earnings among individuals as "loose" rates.) The "floor effect" mentioned by Rothe probably can be viewed as a situational factor. The differences between the departments, especially department A as contrasted to departments B, C, and D also can be considered as being associated with the job situations in question.

In analyzing the variability of performance of employees on individual jobs, it is sometimes the practice to express such differences as a ratio of the productivity of the least productive employee to that of the most productive. For the employees in these four departments, these ratios, obtained by dividing the output of the highest employee by that of the lowest for each week, were: (A) 1:1.73; (B) 1:1.42; (C) 1:1.49; and (C) 1:1.46. The ratios for the three jobs represented by Figure 2.3 ranged from about 1:2.7 to 1:3. For ninety-nine employees with the job of looping in a hosiery mill, the productivity of employees ranged from about 2.5 dozen hose per hour to about 7 dozen pair, a ratio of almost 1:3. Such ratios frequently are about 1:2 and on some jobs may be as much as 1:5 or more.

Aside from differences in job productivity as such, differences in the suitability of individuals to various jobs are reflected in other ways, such as in the quality of work, piece-rate earnings, job tenure, accidents, and performance appraisals. A distribution of performance appraisals for 710 men from one department of a steel mill is shown in Figure 2.5. Many cautions should be observed in interpreting the significance of these values inasmuch as they reflect subjective judgments, but it is safe to conclude that the spread from 240 to 450 points suggests definite differences in the quantity and quality of service rendered by the different employees.

SITUATIONAL VARIABLES IN JOB-RELATED BEHAVIOR

As discussed earlier, the situational factors which may influence job-related behavior fall generally into two classes, namely, (1) job and working condition variables and (2) organizational and social variables. It might be added that the organizational and social variables in particular tend to fall into a couple of subclasses. On the one hand, certain such variables can be characterized in reasonably objective terms, such as the size of an organization or work group, or the monetary value of an incentive system. On the other hand, certain organizational and social variables must be characterized as the subjective *perceptions* of people. Schneider (1977), for example, based on responses of people in one organization, reported that the people tended to "think" of their organization in

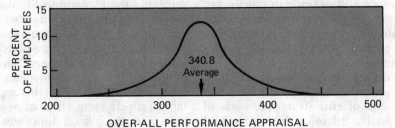

FIG. 2.5 Distribution of overall performance appraisal ratings of 710 men from one department of a steel mill.

terms of such dimensions as the nature of the company management, the nature of supervision, equal employment opportunity, and job challenge.

Differences in the physical environment (such as temperature, noise, and illumination) and the job can be associated with (and presumably can influence) differences in most of the types of behavior we have referred to, such as job performance, attitudes, and other subjective reactions of workers, accidents, and physiological conditions (such as heart rate). On the other hand, differences in the organizational and social variables tend to have their dominant impact on people's attitudes and other subjective reactions. Such attitudinal variables may sometimes indirectly influence other behaviors, such as job performance and job attendance. Their impact on physiological conditions and accidents is undoubtedly very limited.

Examples of the relationships between the situational variables and different aspects of job-related behavior will be given in later chapters.

DISCUSSION

A primary objective of research in industrial psychology is to determine the relationship between specific individual and situational variables on the one hand, and relevant job-related behaviors of people on the other hand. The results of such research, in turn and in some instances, can be used as the basis for taking some action to bring about improvement, as in the case of those behaviors whose levels are considered undesirable.

In this regard, the practice of matching people to jobs probably has been based on generally one of two strategies, each of which is predicated on a different set of assumptions. One is predicated on the assumption that jobs (and other situational factors) are "fixed"—set in concrete—and that the variability in relevant job-related behaviors on any given job therefore arises mainly from differences among the individuals on the job. The strategy followed in such a case would focus on personnel selection of those individuals most suitable to the job, considering relevant personal characteristics (aptitudes, physical characteristics, personality factors, education, experience, and so forth). In selecting individuals without the specific job-related experience or training that would be required, the selection would focus on identifying individuals who seem to have the potential for learning the particular job.

The second strategy followed in many circumstances is predicated on the general assumption that the primary source of variability in relevant job-related behaviors is more a function of the job (and other "situational" factors). The strategy based on such an assumption leads to designing jobs and job situations so they are in some respect suitable to people on an across-the-board basis, or at least to large numbers of people. Perhaps the most common application of such a strategy is reflected in job simplification which, carried to the extreme, would result in jobs that virtually anyone would be able to perform. The stereotype of this approach is the repetitive assembly job. Reaction against job simplification has contributed to developing job enlargement or job enrichment programs aimed at creating jobs more intrinsically satisfying than "simplified" jobs are. Even these programs are predicated on the assumption that people are relatively constant (that most people are pretty much the same), but that the assumed "constancy" is people's need for "involvement" in their work activities. Although this approach certainly reflects a more human view of people than does the job simplification approach, it nonetheless is directed toward changing jobs to "fit" people in general.

We have intentionally exaggerated the distinction between the two sets of assumptions underlying these two strategies to make a point. In practice the distinctions between the assumptions and their associated strategies are by no means clear-cut. At the same time they do represent somewhat different frames of reference in approaching the person-job matching process, one tending to emphasize the selection of people (considering job situations as being relatively fixed or constant), the other tending to emphasize the adaptation of job situations to people (considering people as being relatively fixed or constant).

We would like to suggest that the world of human work cannot be viewed exclusively from either of these points of view but rather, that there are interactions between people and their job situations and that, within reasonable bounds, both people and job situations are amenable to change. The implied strategy of such a frame of reference would be to seek to optimize the combination of people and jobs so as to increase effectiveness of human involvement in producing goods and services and of enhancing desirable human values in the process. Actually, current theory tends to emphasize such an interactive frame of reference. The practical implementation of such a point of view on a broad scale is still in the future, if for no other reason that at present there are no navigation charts available for such uncharted waters. The best that can be hoped at present is that researchers and practitioners will become better at "reading" situations and will be able to emphasize the strategies considered best for individual situations.

For behaviors substantially influenced by individual variables, the major focus of action certainly should be to improve personnel selection procedures. For example, if one finds through research that there are marked individual differences in the job performance of cloth inspectors and in turn finds that the cloth inspectors who do the best job are those who have high scores on a perception test, in the future one could select applicants with higher scores on that test, with the expectation that those so selected generally would be better on the job than an unselected group of applicants.

Conversely, if one can find through research that certain behaviors are substantially influenced by situational variables, the major focus of action should be to improve the situational circumstances. For example, if workers performing a job by method A make fewer errors than those using method B, one might well adopt method A. Or if one finds out that the job performance of, say, cloth inspectors is influenced by illumination, the obvious decision should be that of selecting that illumination found to be best. If one finds that people on "enlarged jobs" tend to stay longer than those on "simplified" jobs—and perform equally well—one could argue for a job enlargement program. And if one finds that the job satisfaction of people being paid on an hourly basis is higher than those on the same job being paid on a piece-work basis, one might well consider adopting an hourly pay system, especially if productivity under the two methods is the same.

In any given situation, therefore, one should adopt the strategy (or combination of strategies) supported by whatever research evidence is available or can be generated. Job design (which may very well be involved) will be discussed more extensively in a later chapter.

Much of this text will deal with research methods and examples of the results of such research that might be the basis for administrative decisions that could contribute toward fulfilling the objectives mentioned in the first chapter, namely, improving the effectiveness of human involvement in producing the goods and services of the economy and maintaining or enhancing the welfare of those workers.

REFERENCES

ROTHE, H. F. Output rates among industrial employees. *Journal of Applied Psychology,* 1978, *63* (1), 40–46.

SCHNEIDER, B. Person/situation selection research: The problem of identifying salient situational dimensions. College Park, Md.: University of Maryland, Department of Psychology, Research Report No. 13, February 1977.

TAYLOR, F. V. Psychology and the design of machines. *American Psychologist,* 1957, *15,* 249–258.

3
behavioral research

We have said before that in this text we will be dealing with research relating to the behavior of people in their work relationships. The various topics will include examples of such research, with implications for applying relevant research findings to certain practical personnel and organizational problems. Although this text is not intended as a study of research methods, it will be helpful to the reader who is not already familiar with such methods to have at least a brief overview of some of the relatively basic research methods, statistical concepts, and procedures used in behavioral research. This is the aim of this chapter.

TYPES OF VARIABLES USED IN BEHAVIORAL RESEARCH

Most behavioral research is aimed at making "predictions" of relevant behavior.

Such predictions typically require the use (including the measurement) of two types of variables. One type of variable, that which is being predicted, usually is called the *criterion*, and most typically characterizes some type of "behavior" (such as job performance, job satisfaction, absenteeism, or heart rate). The other type of variable is the one used in predicting the criterion and usually is called simply the *predictor*. In some instances predictors are individual variables (such as test scores, measures of physical characterisitics, or measures of other personal characteristics); in other instances they are measures of situational characteristics (such as size of the work group, method of training, or noise level).

Frequently the criterion is also called the *dependent variable* or the *measured variable*, and the predictor is also called the *independent variable* or *controlled variable*. These terms are used especially in those studies in which there is some possible "control" of the predictor and in which the measure of the criterion (the dependent variable) is viewed as being attributed to the "effects" of the predictor (the independent variable). Thus, one might study the "effects" of noise on hearing, of work schedules on production, of organizational climate on employees' attitudes, and of intensity of sound signals on reaction time.

In some research investigations the investigator is primarily interested in the criterion as it reflects the "problem" at hand, such as work performance, poor employee morale, or high accident rates. In such instances the investigator is concerned with trying to identify possible causative factors (that is, predictors) of the criterion values. The predictors that might be investigated could be either individual or situational variables, or both. In other circumstances, however, the primary interest of the investigator might be that of the predictor (the independent variable), as in studying the effects of noise, of work schedules, of organizational climate, or of the aging process.

We should hasten to add that there are circumstances, like the chicken-and-the-egg conundrum, in which one variable can be used either as the predictor or as the criterion. For example, job satisfaction might be used to predict work performance, or work performance might be used to predict job satisfaction. (Such an example reinforces the point made earlier that we need to be cautious in inferring cause-and-effect from the fact of a relationship between two variables.)

TYPES OF MEASUREMENT OF VARIABLES

Virtually any type of behavioral research requires that the variables, both the predictors and the criteria, be measured. Measurement is basic to any statistical treatment of research data. In this regard there are four basic types of measurement, or "scales," as described below.

Nominal Scale

A nominal (or categorical) scale is one that has two or more mutually exclusive classes or categories of the general type of variable in question, such as male and female, rural and urban (as places of residence), and job classification (carpenter, plumber, and electrician). Some types of variables that vary in "level" are occasionally treated as nominal scales. In educational level, for example, individuals might be categorized according to their highest diploma or degree, such as elementary school, high school, or bachelor's degree.

Ordinal Scale

An ordinal scale is used to characterize the rank order on some variable of individual cases in a sample, such as the rankings of a group of employees according to job performance or the ranking of jobs according to pay level. A rank order tell us nothing about how *much* difference there is between adjacent ranks. For example, the first, second, and third prizes awarded to Afghan Hounds in a dog show tell us nothing about whether the differences between first and second, and between second and third, were very slight or very marked.

Interval Scale

In an interval scale the individual cases have numbers associated with them, and these numbers are significant in that any given numerical difference, anywhere along the scale, theoretically represents an equal difference in the underlying variable. The scale has no absolute zero. Many tests of human attributes and abilities, at least theoretically, are examples of interval scales. With a properly developed test of arithmetic ability, for example, the difference between a score of 70 and 75 presumably would represent the same "difference" in arithmetic ability as the difference between 80 and 85 would. We would be hard pressed to think of a person having absolutely *no* arithmetic ability. Furthermore, we could not say that someone with an IQ of 70 is only half as smart as someone with an IQ of 140.

It should be added that various types of tests often are treated *as if* their scores represented interval scales, although the assumption that equal differences in score values represent equal differences in the variable measured by the test frequently is not fulfilled.

Ratio Scale

A ratio scale is one in which the individual cases have numerical values that, as with the interval scale, represent equal differences in the variable being measured. In contrast with the interval scale, the ratio scale does have an absolute zero. These scales are best illustrated by variables of physical measurements. For people, for example, one could think of height and weight, or of energy expenditure (in calories) in carrying out various types of job activities. Since there is an absolute zero for a ratio scale, one can characterize various cases as ratios, such as Mortimer weighing twice as much as Archibald, or Geraldine taking half the time to assemble an electric toaster as it takes Suzie.

BASIC RESEARCH STRATEGIES

The most important fact to remember is that research is conducted in order to answer some question. The question can be very simple—"What is the *real* length of the fish he caught?"—or it can be very complex —"Why do some executives turn down important promotions?" The next most important fact about research is that no matter what method is used there is always some possible alternative explanation for the results obtained. This is not to say that

some ways to answer the question are not better than others. Obviously they are. For example, our best check on the angler's honesty would be to measure the fish with a ruler. Even this might be in error if the measurer or the ruler were not very accurate. We could also "measure" the fish from a photograph by comparing the ratio of the size of the fisherman's hand in the picture to the fish's length and then multiplying this by our measurement of the actual length of the angler's hand. Obviously this approach is less suitable than the former, *unless* at the time the question was asked, we have nothing but an old photograph and a plateful of bones!

The need for research arises because some questions need to be answered. The first step for any research is to structure the question or questions so that some data can be gathered to answer the question. This seems so basic that we really should not need to bring it up. Unfortunately, many research projects are undertaken before the questions are clearly stated. As a result, hours and hours of time of both the researchers and the people who provided the data are wasted because of a failure to outline the question of interest so that it could be answered adequately.

As a starting point, we shall assume that a thoughtful question has been formulated and that we want to select a research strategy to answer it. From this point the research strategy selected can be developed on the basis of the answers to three basic questions:

1. What variables need to be studied?

2. How should these variables be treated?

3. In what setting should the research be undertaken?

Once all three of these are answered, the research design is quite well formulated. The questions are complicated, however, because they are not independent. Therefore, the selection of a given variable of interest may severely limit the treatments available and/or the selection of settings. Nevertheless, it is instructive to consider these three as classes of questions to be asked. As we treat each set below, we should point out that a heavy debt is owed to the work of Runkel and McGrath (1972) for our thinking on these issues.

Selection of Variables

The variables to be considered in the research depend on *theoretical* and *practical* issues. By theory we simply mean that they depend on the construct(s) outlined in the questions to be answered. Consider, for example, the question of why some people turn down important promotions. Obviously, one of the variables that must be considered is the behavior of accepting or not accepting a promotion. Yet even the decision about how to deal with this very obvious variable has some problems associated with it. One could offer promotions and see who does or does not accept them, or one could describe a promotion and ask people if they would or would not accept it. Conceptually, these may be very similar, although the former may be closer to what is actually of interest. From a practical standpoint, these two methods are widely discrepant. It is almost always easier, and it costs less, to ask the people than it does to offer promotions and observe their subsequent behavior. Therefore, the choice of the variable would be affected by practical as well as by theoretical concerns.

Treatment of Variables

Table 3.1 describes several ways in which variables can be treated. These descriptions closely resemble those used by Runkel and McGrath (1972) with some modifications in description and labels. Let us consider each one.

For both practical and theoretical rea-

TABLE 3.1 TREATMENTS OF VARIABLES IN RESEARCH

I. Do not measure:
   a. Ignore (Treatment 1)
   b. Randomization (Treatment 2)
II. Measure under the following conditions:
   a. With no manipulation (Treatment 3)
   b. Manipulated by:
      1. Holding constant (Treatment 4)
      2. Matching (Treatment 5)
      3. Creating specific levels or categories (Treatment 6)

sons there is an indefinite number of variables which are not of interest in any given research. If there is no reason to believe these variables are interesting or could affect the results, they are usually *ignored* (Treatment 1). There is always the chance, however, that a particular variable may have an effect even though the researchers can think of no reason for such an effect. If the variable is simply ignored under such conditions, its effect still will show up. For example, let us assume that a person was interested in comparing two dentists' chairs in terms of their judged comfort. The person may very legitimately consider the chair's color to be unimportant. Yet, if it did happen to influence people's judgments of comfort, ignoring it and comparing two chairs of different colors would be a problem. Therefore, a better way to deal with such an uncontrolled variable would be to use *randomization* (Treatment 2). In this way, the ignored variables are assumed to affect only the variable(s) of interest, by chance alone. Over many observations the chance effects should cancel each other out.

For those variables of interest to the research, it is necessary first to measure them in some fashion and to decide on whether or not to manipulate them in some fashion. The simplest strategy is to measure the variables as they exist *with no manipulation* (Treatment 3). The variable is allowed to vary freely and is observed. For example, we might be interested in the relationship between age and job satisfaction. In this case both variables probably would be measured and allowed to take on whatever value the respondents had for them.

It should be pointed out that in any research, one may treat one or more variables in this fashion, but *at least one* variable must be allowed to vary freely. If all were controlled, there would be no gain in information. For example, if we want to see how age is related to job satisfaction and choose only older people who were satisfied and younger people who were dissatisfied for our study, we will find out nothing about the relationship between age and job satisfaction; all we will be able to say is that we selected the people as we wanted. Variables treated according to Treatment 3 are called *dependent variables* when related to variables using Treatment 6 to be explained below.

Treatments 4 and 5 represent ways of control so that the variable cannot have an effect on the observed conditions. The first, *holding constant* (Treatment 4) is making every case of interest the same on the variable. The effect of color in the dental chair study could have been controlled by using chairs of only one color. In this case, color may still affect the judgment of comfort, but if chair *A* is compared to chair *B* for comfort and both are the same color, then color is "controlled" and does not affect the difference between them.

Variables can also be controlled by *matching* (Treatment 5) to eliminate possible effects of the variable. Here we might have dental chairs of type *x* and type *y* and for each have one red, one white, and one blue chair. Color is not constant for each type, but within each type all are represented, so differences in type are the same. Another example might be to compare two training programs and to control for the sex of the participants. Sex could be controlled not to have an effect by using only women in the study (Treatment 4) or by keeping the percentage of women (for ex-

ample, 75 percent) the same in each group (Treatment 5).

The final method of control is by *creating specific levels or categories* of the variable (Treatment 6). Thus, we could vary the levels of illumination or noise or the size of work groups, and we could set up different categories (that is, different "types") of training programs or of work design, and so forth. (Whether the variable lends itself to variations in quantitative level or only to the identification of different categories or types, it is frequently the practice to refer to such differences as "levels.") As indicated before, the variable that is so varied sometimes is called the independent variable. In any "true" experiment, one or more variables are manipulated, and their effects on another (treated by Treatment 3) are observed.

Research Settings

Research settings vary along a continuum from contrived to natural. Usually we refer to studies done in very contrived and artificial settings created by the researcher as *laboratory* studies and those done in natural settings as *field* studies. Although within these settings, variables can be treated in any of the six ways already described, the treatment of variables tends to be associated with the setting used. In the laboratory, variables with unknown effects or that are of no interest are treated by randomization (Treatment 2), and specific levels are created on some variables (Treatment 6) to observe their effects on the dependent variable (Treatment 3). Field research tends to ignore (Treatment 1) many variables because of the difficulty of being able to obtain randomization, and field research typically requires collecting data that makes it possible to analyze the covariation of several unmanipulated variables (Treatment 3). We call the latter a *field study*.

When variables are manipulated by creating specific levels on the variable (Treatment 6), it is seldom possible to have randomization. This kind of field research is called a *field experiment,* but it is not a true experiment because the lack of randomization means that many other ignored variables may affect our results. For example, we might want to compare the effects of a new company policy using flexible work schedules on absenteeism. Assume we institute the new policy in Plant *A* and keep the old one in Plant *B,* then observe absenteeism for a three-month period. The policy change (change or no change) is Treatment 6, and absenteeism receives Treatment 3. We can hardly randomly assign people to the two plants. If it turns out that Plant *A* workers are less frequently absent than those in Plant *B,* we can never be sure the difference was due to our policy change or to other differences between the plants.

Experimental and Correlational Strategies

In research strategies there sometimes is a distinction between experimental and correlational strategies. The experimental approach usually involves some form of "manipulation" of the predictor (that is, the independent) variables(s), as by holding it (or them) constant (Treatment 4), by matching (Treatment 5), or by creating specific levels or categories (Treatment 6). The experimental strategy is used most commonly in laboratory studies but sometimes is used in field studies when some form of manipulation or control of predictors is feasible. It lends itself most readily to investigating situational variables, such as the effects of incentive systems, leadership style, temperature, and work methods.

In the correlational strategy, data are obtained on the predictor and criterion variables for each "case" in the sample (each case usually being an individual), without any experimental manipulation or control. For example, for each person (a case) the investigator might obtain information on age (the predictor) and job satisfaction (the criterion). Although this strategy is used mostly for investigating individual variables as predictors of behavior, it is also used occasionally for investigating situational variables. This approach is used when the investigator's intent is to determine the relationship between some predictor and criterion variables, this relationship usually being measured by a *coefficient of correlation.* (The coefficient of correlation, usually called a correlation, will be discussed later in this chapter.) The correlational strategy is used most frequently in field studies but is also used in laboratory studies.

With the correlational approach, one can determine the strength of the relationship between reaction time and number of accidents, between attitudes toward one's supervisor and productivity, or between educational level and time to learn a particular job. The research data for the correlational approach can be obtained at places of work (as for employees of an organization), from available records (as for automobile drivers), by surveys (as for public opinion polling), or in other appropriate ways.

Discussion

As indicated earlier, decisions about research strategies need to be based on consideration of the combination of the variables to be investigated, the treatment of those variables, and the setting in which the research is to be carried out.

Various advantages and disadvantages have been attributed to laboratory versus field setting for conducting behavioral research. For example it is usually easier to control experimental variables in a laboratory study than in a field study; however it has been argued that laboratory studies lack the reality of field studies. In part because of the the aspect of reality of field studies there is a rather common belief that such settings provide for more generalizations of research findings than laboratory settings do. On the basis of an analysis of numerous studies from both types of settings, however, Dipboye and Flanagan (1979) concluded that this is not necessarily true. In part, however, it is probable that the extent to which one can generalize from studies in laboratory versus field settings would depend upon the nature of the subject of the research. For example, laboratory experiments usually would be particularly relevant to investigations of sensory, perceptual, and psychomotor skills. Thus, if one were interested in the effects of various colors of light on a visual inspection task, a laboratory setting probably would be most suitable. The laboratory setting also has been used rather extensively for a variety of other topics, however, such as supervisory style, the effects of participation in task performance, group interactions, communication networks, and the effects of incentives on performance. The results of some such studies have had rather direct implications for application to industrial situations, and in other instances have provided hypotheses for subsequent testing in field settings.

In very general terms, laboratory experiments are most relevant in circumstances in which the results of short periods of experimentation would be reasonably predictive of long-term performance or behavior. If the investigation deals more with problems in which *long-term* motivational and attitudinal variables would be important, however, the real-life field setting usually will be preferable, or in some instances, virtually mandatory. Then the results of a short laboratory experiment would not necessarily predict the long-term results of a day-in-day-out routine. You might find from a laboratory study that people report that they like a particular type of music while performing a laboratory task. But in practice, such music might drive them up the wall if they listened to it month after month. Or

the interest in a challenging laboratory task might make it possible to perform the task well in that setting, whereas the same task might be so boring over a period of months that performance (and interest) might wane.

Although there are certain types of behavioral research projects that most reasonably should be conducted in laboratory settings, and others in field settings, there are others that might lend themselves to either. In this regard Dipboye and Flanagan (1979) argue for coordinated strategies in both types of settings (when appropriate) on the grounds that laboratory and field research may be viewed as complementary rather than conflicting strategies.

In carrying out experiments either in the laboratory or field setting, one should follow professionally accepted research practices, if at all possible. But there are circumstances in which it is simply not possible or practical to conform rigorously to ideal experimental design practices. This is especially so in field settings, as in industrial or business organizations. For example, there may not be enough eligible subjects to use in both experimental and control groups. In this regard, Cook and Campbell (1976) discussed what they called quasi-experiments. Quasi-experiments depart in some manner from the ideal experimental practices characterizing "true" experiments. Cook and Campbell asserted that, although quasi-experiments do not provide as positive results as true experiments do, in some cases they still can provide useful information. Needless to say, such experiments should be planned so as to provide as sound a basis as possible for producing relevant information, and the results should be interpreted with appropriate caution. (Cook's and Campbell's discussion would be helpful to individuals planning quasi-experiments.)

We should add a comment about inferences from data obtained through the correlational versus the experimental strategies. The correlational approach often is not good for supporting very strong inferences about cause-and-effect relationships, for in any given circumstances a correlation between two variables might be caused by the relationship of the two variables to a third variable. Although the experimental approach cannot really "prove" any cause-and-effect relationship, it is appropriate to somewhat more confident inferences of this type, for (at least under ideal conditions) the effects of "other" variables can be minimized or eliminated by appropriate "control" of such variables.

STATISTICAL ANALYSES IN RESEARCH

Although this text does not require understanding or using very complex statistical concepts or methods, the reader should have at least passing acquaintance with certain basic concepts and methods. Certain statistical concepts are discussed in Appendix A, including graphic representations of data (such as frequency distributions and frequency polygons), measures of central tendency (the mean, median, and made), measures of variability (particularly the standard deviation), correlations, standard scores, and percentiles. The reader who is not already familiar with these should begin to develop such familiarity by referring to Appendix A. For now it is suggested that the reader become familiar with graphic representations of data, and measures of central tendency.

When the text first refers to the other concepts, we will make another reference to the Appendix. One statistic, however, the correlation, is so commonly used that it is described here.

Correlations

A coefficient of correlation (usually called a correlation) is a statistical index of the degree of linear relationship between two variables. It ranges from +1.00 (a per-

fect postive relationship) through intermediate positive values down to 0.00 (the absence of any relationship), through intermediate negative values to –1.00 (a perfect negative relationship). Figure 3.1 illustrates the concept of correlations, showing different *scattergrams* that reflect varying degrees of relationship.

It takes a bit of experience to be able to evaluate the magnitude of correlations, since such evaluation depends in part on the nature of the data. (For one type of data, a correlation of, say, .60 might be considered to be exceptionally encouraging, whereas for another type of data it might be considered as being very poor.) We should add that a coefficient of correlation cannot be interpreted directly as a proportion. In statistical terms, a correlation of a given magnitude accounts for the percentage of "variance" represented by the squared value of the correlation; thus, a correlation of .60 can account for 36 percent of the variance (.60 x .60 =.36 or 36 percent). This means that one can predict the percentage of the "variability" of one of the variables by knowing the value of the other (in this case 36 percent).

Statistical Significance

A discussion of statistical methods should include reference to the concept of *statistical significance.* In a general sense it deals with the possible error associated with individual "statistics." (In the results of political polls, for example, you may have heard that a given candidate was preferred by 53 percent of the respondents and that this was "accurate" within ± 3 points.) The notion of statistical significance can be applied to virtually any type of "statistic," such as percentages (as in the case of political polls), means, percentiles, and correlation coefficients, or to differences between them. The concept as related to the difference between two arithmetic means can be shown with

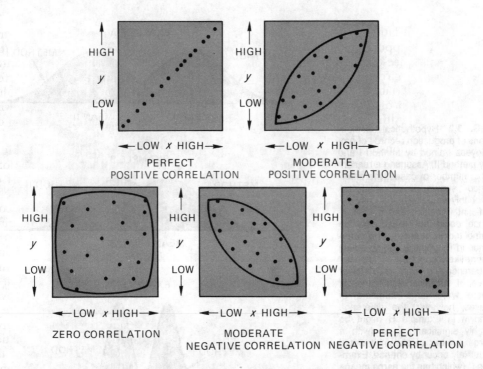

FIG. 3.1 Illustration of scattergrams of several hypothetical correlations between two variables, ranging from a perfect positive correlation ($r = +1.00$) through a zero correlation ($r = 0.00$) to a perfect negative correlation ($r = -1.00$). Lines around dots depict the scatter or concentration of cases. Each dot represents one case.

hypothetical data from a study of the effects of two methods of training employees on a particular job. The independent variable is the training method. Let us call the two variations methods I and II. Let us assume that the dependent variable (what we will call the criterion) is the production of employees during a specified week (say, the eighth week of training). We might obtain the results shown in Example A of Figure 3.2. The difference between these two methods is very clear; assuming a reasonable number of subjects in each group, such differences undoubtedly should be statistically significant. Although the formula for determining the level of statistical significance will not be discussed here, it is sufficient for our purposes to know that it depends upon the *number* of cases, the statistical *variability* of the cases, and the *nu-*

merical values in question (in this case the difference between the means of methods I and II). Typically, the level of statistical significance is expressed in such terms as the ".01" or "05" level (or whatever the actual value turns out to be). The statement that a finding "is significant at the .01 level" would be interpreted as follows: The obtained difference (in this case the difference between the means) is of such a magnitude that it would occur *by chance* in only one case out of a hundred replications of such an experiment *if there were no true difference in the methods*. (For the .05 level, such a difference would be expected to occur by chance in five out of a hundred similar experiments.) When we refer to statistically significant relationships, then, we are referring to the "odds." If a relationship is found to be significant at a sufficiently low

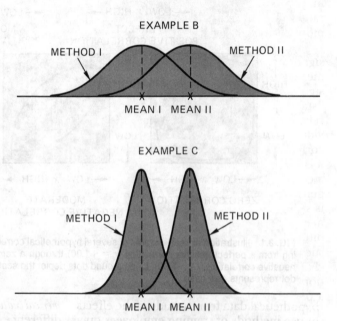

FIG. 3.2 Hypothetical distributions of production records of employees trained by method I and by method II. Assuming a reasonable number of cases, the difference shown in Example A probably would be statistically significant (meaning that the difference could not reasonably be attributed to chance). The difference in Example B (being small) more likely could be a "chance" difference and would have a lower level of statistical significance; if there were large numbers of cases, however, the difference shown in Example B might be highly significant since (with a large number of cases) it would not likely occur by chance. Example C (which has the same means as Example B) would be statistically significant with a smaller number of cases, since there is less variability in the two distributions (and less "overlap" between the two).

level (say at the .01 level), we infer that the relationship is not likely to be attributable to chance. (Note that we never can *prove* a relationship; we can only say that the likelihood of the relationship being caused by chance is extremely small.)

In the case of Example B from Figure 3.2, there is a difference between methods I and II, but this difference is not great, and there is considerable overlap in the production records of the two groups. With a small number of cases this difference probably would not be statistically significant; with a large number of cases, it could be. In Example C, the means for the two methods are the same as in Example B, but there is less variability in the performance of the individuals in the two groups—there is less

"overlap" between them. This difference could be statistically significant with a smaller number of cases than would be required for statistical significance in Example B.

Statistical significance should not be confused with practical significance. When we say that a relationship is statistically significant we claim merely that the relationship cannot reasonably be attributed to chance. However, the relationship may well be trivial and unimportant, of little or no consequence. On the other hand, practical significance refers to the extent to which (statistically significant) results have possible practical utility, taking into account whatever practical considerations are pertinent, such as cost, amount of possible benefit, and so forth. The possible advantage of method II over method I in Example A (Fig. 3.2) would be much greater than in Example B or C. (In Example B or C, assuming that the differences were statistically significant, there might be some question as to whether it would be worthwhile, in practical terms, to adopt method II rather than I, especially if method II were more costly.)

Just as we can determine the statistical significance of the difference between two means, we also can determine the statistical significance of the difference between two "statistics" of some other type, such as correlation coefficients. As we talk about individual statistics, such as a single mean or correlation, we can determine the odds that it is "not zero." If, for example, we find that a correlation between scores on an intelligence test and those on an arithmetic test is significant at the .01 level, we are saying in effect that the correlation is of such magnitude that, with the given sample size, such a correlation could have occurred by chance in only one of a hundred replications of the study. (The implication, but not a proven point, is that there is some relationship between the variables measured by the two tests.)

As another twist on the concept of statistical significance, we can establish "confidence" limits around any given individual statistic. This indicates the possible limits of error at a specified probability level. Thus, for the political poll, the ± 3 points represents the range of possible error in the poll at some specified probability level, such as .01.

DISCUSSION

The result of any behavioral research consists of data. These data then may be used as the basis for formulating theories (which in turn might be applied to the resolution of some behavioral problem), or they might be used directly for some specific problem, as in a given organization. In any event, the data from a research investigation (usually coughed up by a computer) are simply data. The interpretation and application of research findings depend on the sound judgment of investigators and on those who are in a position to apply such findings.

REFERENCES

COOK, T. D., & CAMPBELL, D. T. The design and conduct of quasi-experiments and true experiments. In M. D. Dunnette (Ed.), *Handbook of industrial and organizational psychology* (chap. 7). Chicago: Rand McNally, 1976.

DIPBOYE, R. L., & FLANAGAN, M. F. Research settings in industrial and organizational psychology. *American Psychologist*, 1979, *34* (2), 141–150.

RUNKEL, P. J., & McGRATH, J. E. *Research on human behavior: A systematic guide to method.* New York: Holt, Rinehart & Winston, 1972.

The Lakeside Press
R·R·DONNELLEY & SONS COMPANY

JOB DESCRIPTION

SECTION 1–IDENTIFICATION INFORMATION

JOB TITLE—

DIVISION—   DATE—

DEPARTMENT—   SECTION—

SECTION 2–STATEMENT OF PURPOSE

THE PURPOSE OF THIS JOB IS—

The Lakeside Press
R·R·DONNELLEY & SONS COMPANY

PERFORMANCE APPRAISAL   OD-12

SECTION 1–IDENTIFICATION INFORMATION

EMPLOYEE NAME—   EMP. NO.—

JOB TITLE—

DIVISION—   DATE—

DEPARTMENT—   SECTION—

SUPERVISOR—

CURRENT REVIEW PERIOD: FROM   TO

SECTION 2–JOB PERFORMANCE RATING CATEGORIES

O —Outstanding	—	Exceeds all job standards and greatly exceeds standards in key areas.
SH —Satisfactory high	—	Meets all job standards and exceeds standards in key areas.
S —Satisfactory	—	Meets job standards in a fully satisfactory manner.
SL —Satisfactory low	—	Generally does not meet job standards in key areas.
BDS—Below desired standard	—	Does not meet most required job standards.
TRE—Too recent to evaluate	—	Has been on current assignment for less than 3 months.

SECTION 3–JOB PERFORMANCE RESPONSIBILITIES AND RATINGS

JOB RESPONSIBILITIES KEY PHRASE & NUMBER IN ORDER OF IMPORTANCE	RATING CATEGORIES						DOCUMENTING COMMENTS AND SPECIFIC INSTANCES OF JOB PERFORMANCE
	TRE	BDS − +	SL − +	S − +	SH − +	O − +	
1.							
2.							

Portions of job description and performance appraisal forms. *(Courtesy R. R. Donnelley & Sons Company)*

job-related behavior
and its measurement

There are two primary purposes for the "measurement" of what we will call job-related behavior. First, virtually all psychological research in industrial psychology depends on the measurement of various aspects of behavior in the working environment. Second, certain personnel management functions (such as personnel evaluation) require the measurement in quantitative terms of work-related behavior, such as job performance.

The measurement of job-related behavior of course has its roots in the nature of the work activities that people perform on their jobs. The first chapter of this part, therefore, consists of an overview of the field of job analysis. The remaining two chapters deal with the circumstances in which the measurement of job-related behavior is useful, the types of job-related behaviors for which measurements can be developed, the methods of developing or obtaining such measurements, and some of the pitfalls that can be encountered in their development and use.

job-related behavior
and its measurement

4

jobs and job analysis

People's jobs represent the manner in which they contribute to the production of the goods and services of the economy. Jobs also are the means by which people earn their daily bread and represent how they spend a major portion of their lives. In many instances jobs influence life style, "status" in a community, and even where people live. Jobs then, have important implications for the individuals themselves, for the organization of which they are a part, for the economy, and even for society at large.

This text deals directly or indirectly with people's jobs, both from the point of view of individuals and from that of their organizations.

For some personnel research purposes and for carrying out certain management functions, job information is useful or even necessary. This leads us into the field of *job analysis*, which is the process by which one obtains information about jobs. This chapter presents an overview of the field of job analysis, with particular reference to certain recent developments in this field that provide for quantification of job information.

TERMINOLOGY

Although the terminology of jobs is fairly loosely used in practice it may be useful here to define certain terms according to McCormick (1979):

Position. A *position* consists of the tasks and duties for an individual. A position exists, whether occupied or not. There are as many occupied positions as there are individuals in an organization.

Job. A *job* is a group of positions which are identical with respect to their major or significant tasks and sufficiently alike to justify their being covered by a single analysis. There may be one or many persons employed for the same job.

Occupation. The term *occupation* usually refers to jobs of a general class, on an across-the-board basis, without regard to organization. Thus, one can refer to the occupation of an accountant, machinist, or tight-rope walker wherever people engage in the activities implied.

JOB DETERMINANTS

As we look at jobs, we might ask ourselves two questions: (1) How do jobs come into being? (2) What factors cause jobs to be what they are (in terms of content or other characteristics)? The answer to the first question relates to the objectives of the organization; presumably any job is created in order to fulfill certain functions considered necessary to achieve the objectives of the organization.

Although a job derives its reason for being and its primary characteristics from its relevance to organizational goals, there seem to be two types of factors that determine the nature of individual jobs. First, there are factors that, in effect, are fixed as far as the incumbent is concerned, these being "givens." These include one or more of the following: the design of any physical equipment used; the physical arrangement; specified procedures, methods, and job standards; division of labor; traditional practices; organizational structure and policy; legal requirements; and work environment.

It should be noted that in recent years there has been considerable interest in the notion of job enlargement, that is , the "enlargement" of jobs in various ways so as to increase job incumbents' job satisfaction. More will be said about this in a later chapter, but to the extent that jobs are enlarged, the "fixed" or "given" characteristics of jobs are altered from what they otherwise would have been.

Second, both experience and experimental evidence indicate that, in *some* positions, the incumbent can have some influence, moderate or major, on the activities that make up the position and on how the activities are performed. Such latitude is, of course, greater in managerial, professional, and technical jobs than in production jobs.

In sum, various factors can be considered "determinants" of the work activities of jobs. The combination of the actual work activities that comprise a job, the physical and social environment, and perhaps other job-related factors collectively predetermine the nature of "job requirements"— that is, the demands imposed on the incumbent. These requirements have implications both for the personal characteristics that presumably contribute to successful job performance and for the training that should be provided to job incumbents.

USES OF JOB INFORMATION

In the many phases of operating an organization there is no substitute for having relevant information available to contribute to decision making. It is inevitable that, in the various circumstances in which some decisions are to be made that affect jobs on the one hand, and with applicants or workers on the other, relevant information about the jobs and individuals in question usually can increase the odds of making good decisions. Although much information about jobs resides in people's memories, documented information usually can be obtained through some form of job analysis. Job analysis can be considered as embracing the collection and analysis of any type of job-related information, by any method, for any purpose. Perhaps it can be defined more generally as the study of human work. The information obtained by job analysis can serve a variety of purposes, including certain personnel decision-making purposes, such as those shown in Figure 4.1.

USES OF JOB ANALYSIS			
Personnel Administration	Work and Equipment Design	Administrative Control	Other Uses
Personnel recruitment, selection, and placement Training and personnel development Performance measurement and rating Wage and salary administration Labor relations	Engineering design Methods design Job design	Organizational planning Manpower planning and control	Planning educational curricula Vocational counseling Job classification systems

FIG. 4.1 Some of the uses of information obtained through job analysis.

JOB ANALYSIS

McCormick (1979) proposed that we study human work from at least four different angles, depending upon (1) the type(s) of information to be obtained; (2) the form in which the information is obtained and/or presented (referring particularly to the extent to which it is qualitative versus quantitative); (3) the method of analysis; and (4) the agent (usually the individual who makes the analysis, such as a job analyst, but in isolated instances, a device such as a camera).

Types of Job Analysis Information

Among the types of information sometimes obtained by job analysis are the following: job-oriented work activities (descriptions of work in "job" terms, such as galvanizing, weaving, cleaning); worker-oriented work activities (human behaviors, such as sensing, decision making, performing physical actions, communicating); ma-

chines, tools, work aids, and the like; materials processed; knowledge covered; working conditions; and personnel requirements.

Form of Job Analysis Information

The form of job analysis information refers essentially to the distinction between qualitative and quantitative features. Qualitative information is typically descriptive (such as narrative descriptions of work or general statements about working conditions, social context, personnel requirements, and so forth), whereas quantitative information is typically characterized by the use of "units" of job information expressed in numerical terms (such as ratings of job characteristics, time required, or oxygen consumption).

Methods of Collecting Job Information

Job information can be obtained by various methods such as observation of a worker by a job analyst; interview of a worker by a job analyst; technical conferences employing several "experts" on the job; structured questionnaires consisting of lists of job activities and other aspects of jobs to be used in checking or rating each item as it applies to a job; work diaries that workers use in recording what they do during a work day; records (such as maintenance records); mechanical recordings (such as of heart rate); films; and analysis of blueprints of equipment to be used for inferring what workers will have to do in operating the equipment.

Agent Used in Collecting Job Information

Typically, job analysts are the "agents" used in collecting job information, but sometimes a supervisor or the incumbent does this, and in special circumstances some device, such as a camera or automatic recording mechanism, may "collect" job-related data.

Discussion of Job Analysis Procedures

Job analysis was characterized years ago as "a sort of handmaiden serving in various ways a variety of needs and all the while floundering in a morass of semantic confusion" (Kershner 1955). This castigation, which applies mainly to conventional essay job descriptions, is probably fairly well deserved. We should hasten to point out, however, that well-written job descriptions can, and do, serve certain useful purposes, especially in providing personnel people, applicants, counselees, and other interested people with an organized overview of individual jobs or positions.

If one is to discuss job-related information more systematically, however, a more quantitative approach must be followed. This means that one must identify and if pertinent, measure relevant aspects or characteristics of jobs. Thus, we have to think in terms of "units" of work (or of

other job features) that can be reliably identified, measured, or rated. We could, for example, measure the physiological cost of operating a punch press or the time spent by an automobile mechanic removing a carburetor. We also could ask job incumbents or their supervisors to estimate the time spent or the importance of various job activities, such as preparing balance sheets, performing laboratory blood tests, or telephoning prospective customers. Although such estimates would be somewhat subjective, the use of rating scales in giving such estimates would make it possible to "quantify" the job information derived from them.

STRUCTURED JOB ANALYSIS QUESTIONNAIRES

For at least certain purposes the structured job analysis questionaire has been demonstrated to be the most useful instrument for shifting job analysis processes in the direction of quantification. Such questionnaires consist of lists of job activities or other characteristics (such as working conditions), with provision either for *checking* an item if it applies to a given job, or for *rating* an item, using an appropriate rating scale, in terms of its relevance to the job. The structured questionnaire approach lends itself to the collection of various types of job-related information. Certain examples will be discussed briefly.

Task Inventories

Task inventories (also referred to as job inventories) typically consist of lists of the tasks pertinent to some occupational area. In completing an inventory for any given position within the occupational area, each task is either checked or rated as it applies to the position. The rating may be in accordance with any of several possible rating factors, such as the *frequency* with which a task is performed, the *time* spent on the

1. Check tasks you perform now (√). 2. On the back of the book, write in any unlisted tasks which you do now. 3. In the "Time Spent" column, rate all checked (√) tasks on time spent in present job.	Check	TIME SPENT Present Job
	√ IF DONE NOW	1. Very small amount. 2. Much below average. 3. Below average. 4. Slightly below average. 5. About average. 6. Slightly above average. 7. Above average. 8. Much above average. 9. Very large amount.
DUTY H. REPAIRING AND MAINTAINING JET ENGINES		
1. Adjust afterburner nozzles		
2. Adjust maintenance trailers		
3. Apply safety wire to engine components		
4. Assemble engine sub-assemblies		
5. Assemble inner races of bearings on mating shafts		
6. Assemble main engine sections		
7. Clean engine parts and flush out cleaning fluids		
8. Clean or inspect oil filters		
9. Collect and forward oil samples for lab testing		

FIG. 4.2 Portion of United States Air Force task inventory for Jet Engine Mechanic. The basic inventory was developed for the Air Force by Lifson, Wilson, Ferguson, and Winick, Houston, Texas. The "time spent" scale is one currently used by the Air Force.

task, its judged *importance* or *significance*, its judged *difficulty*, the degree of *delegation* to others, or the estimated *time to learn*.

Task inventories have been used extensively by the U.S. Air Force, as described by Christal (1974). The Air Force method typically has the inventories completed by the incumbents themselves, either airmen or officers. A part of one inventory is shown in Figure 4.2 to illustrate the nature of the tasks, a typical format, and one type of rating scale. Jobs based on task inventories can be described statistically—for example, by summarizing the number of people in the occupation who perform each task—or by grouping positions together that have the same basic combinations of tasks—for example, grouping hospital attendants into groups that largely do patient care tasks

and groups that largely do housekeeping tasks.

Position Analysis Questionnaire (PAQ)

A task inventory contains essentially "job-oriented" tasks, and thus its use is restricted to positions that fall within the occupational area for which it was developed. In contrast, a questionnaire that lists more "worker-oriented" job elements can be used more broadly, inasmuch as it tends to cover more generalized worker behaviors. One such questionnaire is the Position Analysis Questionnaire (PAQ), developed by McCormick, Jeanneret, and Mecham.[1]

[1]The Position Analysis Questionnaire (PAQ) is available from the University Bookstore, 360 West State Street, West Lafayette, Indiana 47906.

The PAQ consists of 194 job elements in the following divisions:

The first three divisions of the PAQ parallel a conventional model of behavior in which behavior is viewed as consisting of a stimulus (S) acting upon an organism (O) to bring about a response (R). Human work is one manifestation of this model but might be expressed in different terms, as follows:

Information → Information → Action or
input   processing   response
               and
               decision

The individual job elements within each of the six classes can either be checked if they apply to the position being analyzed or rated on an appropriate rating scale (such as importance, time, or difficulty). Although some of the job elements are not, strictly speaking, behavioral items, it is nonetheless believed that these elements have strong implications in terms of human behaviors. In practice the PAQ can be used in analyzing jobs by job analysts, by supervisors, and in some instances by the incumbents themselves. (Some applications of data based on the PAQ will be discussed later).

In discussing the PAQ as a job analysis instrument, it may be helpful to refer to a study by Arvey and others (1977) of PAQ analyses as possibly influenced by the sex of the job incumbents and the sex of the analysts. In this study, PAQ analyses were carried out with twenty-two male and thirty-five female college students serving as job analysts. The "job" that was analyzed was depicted on film as a white-collar, salaried job in which the kinds of incumbent responsibilities and activities were such things as writing affirmative-action summary reports, making representations to company personnel, supervising two employees, preparing budgets, and handling irate employees. Actually, there were six films depicting this job, three presenting males and three presenting females as the job incumbents. They all were named "Pat Watson" and had been matched for age and ratings of physical attractiveness. The analysts first were trained in using the PAQ and then were assigned to the job analysis. Half the analysts saw and heard a female "Pat Watson" portraying the job, and half saw and heard a male "Pat Watson." The script used by all the "Pat Watsons" was the same.

It is encouraging that in the analysis of the results, it was found that there was no systematic tendency for either male or female analysts to devalue or to inflate their PAQ descriptions of the job as a function of whether the incumbent was a male or female. This finding is especially relevant in

Division	No. of Job Elements
1. Information input (Where and how does the worker get the information used in the job?) Example: Use of written material	35
2. Mental processes (What reasoning, decision making, planning, etc., are involved in the job?) Example: Coding/decoding	14
3. Work output (What physical activities does the worker perform and what tools or devices does he use?) Example: Use of keyboard devices	49
4. Relationships with other persons (What relationships with other people are required in the job?) Example: Interviewing	36
5. Job context (In what physical and social contexts is the work performed?) Example: Working in high temperatures	19
6. Other job characteristics Example: Irregular hours	41

the light of the current concern about equal pay for equal work and the implications of the analysis of jobs with female versus male incumbents as such analyses might influence rates of pay. (Comparison of the analyses' results of the male and female "Pat Watsons" was based on the "job dimension scores" that resulted from the analyses. The derivation of such scores is discussed below.) It was found, however, that female analysts tended to rate jobs a bit lower on the job elements than male analysts did as reflected by the job dimension scores based on the analyses. Such findings, if confirmed by other studies, might suggest that both male and female analysts might be necessary for job analysis.

JOB DIMENSIONS

Even though we can describe a job in terms of the dozens or hundreds of tasks or job elements contained in a structured questionnaire, such an ensemble of bits and pieces of job information can be rather uninformative. It would be handy if we could somehow boil down and consolidate such information into several more basic job features. Fortunately, certain job activities or other characteristics do tend to go together or to coexist in jobs. In a statistical sense they are correlated, which means that certain statistical procedures, such as factor and cluster analysis, can be used to identify these combinations. Such combinations, or groups, or clusters, or bundles of interrelated job elements can be called *job dimensions*. What is more, by subsequent statistical manipulations we can, for any given job, add together (with appropriate statistical weights) the data on the individual job elements that characterize each job dimension so that we have, for that job, a job dimension score for each of the several dimensions. We now have a more comprehensible description of each job in terms of a more basic profile—namely, a set of job dimension scores.

One example of the process of identifying job dimensions involves the use of the Position Analysis Questionnaire described above. In a study carried out by Mecham (1977), a relatively representative sample of 2,200 jobs that had been analyzed with the PAQ was subjected to a series of factor analyses (technically, principal components analyses). Analyses of the data for the job elements within each of the six PAQ divisions resulted in the identification of thirty-two "divisional" job dimensions. In another analysis, the job elements from all divisions were pooled together, resulting in thirteen "overall" dimensions. Twelve of these are listed and defined below (the thirteenth was not very well crystallized and was left unnamed). The title and definition of any given dimension are based on the nature of the job elements that tend to "dominate" the dimension, particularly in what seems to be the "common denominator" of these job elements.

Overall PAQ Job Dimensions

1. *Having decision, communicating, and general responsibilities*

This dimension is the most inclusive of all the dimensions, having significant correlations with many of the job elements in the PAQ. The dimension reflects activities with considerable amounts of responsibility for decision making, communicating, and general responsibilities.

2. *Operating machines/equipment*

This dimension tends to characterize activities in which individuals are responsible for operating machines, equipment, tools, and other types of mechanical and related devices.

3. *Performing clerical/related activities*

The dominant feature of this dimension is involvement in the performance of typical clerical, office, and related activities.

4. *Performing technical/related activities*

This dimension covers a variety of activities that, in general, can be characterized as involvement in the use of various technical and related devices, or performing technical work without such devices.

5. *Performing service/related activities*

The common theme of the job activities covered by this dimension is associated with performing some service, generally for others, although such services often are also accompanied by various sensory and manual activities.

6. *Working regular day versus other work schedules*

The primary distinction represented by this dimension is between working the typical day schedule and working nontypical day schedules (such as shift work) and irregular work schedules.

7. *Performing routine/repetitive/activities*

This dimension is characterized by routine, repetitive work activities, in some instances performed at predetermined work paces.

8. *Being aware of work environment*

This dimension typically involves continuing awareness of, or sensitiveness to, the individual's environment, such awareness being based on the various senses, such as vision or hearing. In addition, the dimension usually requires some kind of response to the changing environmental conditions, such as the use of various kinds of control mechanisms or the operation of vehicles.

9. *Engaging in physical activities*

The dominant feature of this dimension is involvement in general body or physical activities such as walking, stooping, standing, or handling. Implicit in these activities in some instances is the possibility of physical hazards and associated physical impairment.

10. *Supervising/coordinating other personnel*

This dimension is characterized by responsibility for the supervision and direction of other individuals or coordinating their activities.

11. *Public/customer/related contacts*

This dimension is characterized dominantly by the need for personal contacts with the public, customers, or other individuals such as clients or patients.

12. *Working in an unpleasant/hazardous/demanding environment*

This dimension is characterized by any of various types of job environments that usually would be considered as unpleasant, potentially hazardous, or personally demanding.

Although in some instances the nature of job dimensions identified by statistical analyses may seem simply to confirm "common sense" impressions of the dominant features of jobs, a couple of points should be made. First, because "common sense" is not necessarily valid, statistical confirmation is certainly comforting. Second (and more important), by using statistically identified job dimensions, it is possible to convert job information into quantitative terms, such as job dimension scores. Such quantification not only facilitates the evaluation and interpretation of job information but also makes it possible to carry out further statistical manipulations and analyses, some of which will be illustrated later .

DISCUSSION

Notebooks with conventional job descriptions have for some years been standard items on the desks of job interviewers, placement officials, and others in the personnel offices of many organizations. They have been used for such management purposes as personnel selection, training, and job evaluation (that is, the establishment of wage and salary scales for jobs). Because of their "descriptive" nature, they have not been used extensively in personnel and organizational research undertakings.

The more recent development and use of structured job analysis questionnaires, however, has contributed significantly to various research projects. Most research efforts require the "measurement" of the variables of concern, and structured job analysis questionnaires make it possible to "quantify" information about jobs and thus to "hang numbers" on jobs, such as the average time taken by job incumbents to repair a tire, to take an x-ray of a patient, or the scores on various job dimensions for a particular job. The ability to quantify job information, in turn, has made possible more systematic approaches to such functions as establishing personnel requirements for jobs, grouping jobs into job families, and setting wage or salary rates for jobs. Certain applications of such job data will be illustrated in later chapters.

REFERENCES

ARVEY, R. D., PASSINO, E. M., & LOUNSBURY, J. W. Job analysis results as influenced by sex of incumbent and sex of analyst. *Journal of Applied Psychology*, 1977, *62* (4), 411–416.

CHRISTAL, R. E. The United States Air Force Occupational Research Project. AFHRL, Occupational Research Division, Lackland Air Force Base, Texas, AFHRL-TR-73-75, January 1974.

KERSHNER, A. M. A report on job analysis. Washington D.C.: Office of Naval Research, 1955.

MCCORMICK, E. J. *Job analysis: Methods and applications*. New York: American Management Association, 1979.

MECHAM, R. C. Unpublished study. PAQ Services, Inc., P.O. Box 3337, Logan, Utah 84321, February 1977.

MORSH, J. E. Job analysis in the United States Air Force. *Personnel Psychology*, 1962, *37*, 7–17.

5
behavioral measurement: general considerations

In the preceding chapters we referred to the need for criteria in behavioral research. In work situations, these are job-related "behaviors" (using the term *behavior* in the broad sense mentioned earlier). In research such criteria are the variables that one often is interested in predicting from some other set or sets of variables (the latter often being termed predictors or independent variables). For administrative, as opposed to research, purposes there also is sometimes the need to measure job-related behaviors. For example, in personnel management various measures of job performance may be used for such personnel actions as pay raises, promotions, and separations. Attendance records also may be used for such purposes. Likewise, results of attitude and opinion surveys may be used for revising organizational policies. The analysis of errors made by individuals might point to the need for changing work

methods or modifying the equipment used, or it might indicate the need for improved employee selection or further job training. Accident and related injury records may be used to improve the safety conditions of a work situation. Thus, measures of some job-related behaviors can and often do serve two objectives, administrative and research. Although there may be some differences in the specific measures of the same aspect of behavior for these two purposes, the basic problems of measurement for these two purposes are much the same, and the approaches or methods of measurement that might be used also may have much in common.

In this chapter we discuss various types of behaviors for which measures might be developed and some considerations important to deciding on such measures. Although we discuss these in terms of the use of such measures as research "criteria," remember that at least some of the same measures also might be used for administrative purposes. (The next chapter covers performance evaluation, and a later chapter deals with measures of attitudes and opinions.)

TYPES OF CRITERIA

We already mentioned certain types of job-related behaviors for which criterion measures might be developed. Here these are grouped into six classes: performance criteria, job attendance criteria, accident and injury criteria, physiological criteria, status criteria, and subjective criteria.

Performance Criteria

In job situations these criteria typically represent some aspect of job performance such as productivity or quality of work and might be based on available records or on the ratings of persons familiar with the work of the individuals in question. In general, performance criteria vary along two dimensions—quantity and quality. The quantity dimension is based on the number of "units" produced, in terms relevant to the job. Thus, we can talk about the number of zippers produced, the dollar volume of a salesperson's sales, or the number of classes taught by a teacher. The quality of work usually is more difficult to measure or judge. Very frequently quality is related to some type of human error. In fact, what we might think of as good performance is performance characterized by few or no errors. Human error is such a pervasive fact of life that it has given rise to such literary expressions as "to err is human, to forgive divine." Although the consequences of some human errors in job situations are of minor importance, with little more than nuisance value, the consequences of others may be of major proportions in terms of human safety, effectiveness of operations, time, physical damage, economic loss, and oth-

ers. Although the notions of "error-free" performance and zero defects are probably will-o'-the-wisps, efforts to reduce errors usually can be justified, especially when the possible consequences of error are major.

THE NATURE OF HUMAN ERROR. Human error obviously takes many forms, but it was characterized by Meister (1967) and by Rook (1962) in the framework of poor workmanship. Some workmanship errors can be perceived readily either by direct observation or by subsequent consequences. But the quality of many types of workmanship varies along a continuum from good to poor; in such instances the line between acceptable and unacceptable workmanship needs to be delineated. An operational definition of human error was proposed by Peters: "Any deviation from a previously established, required, or expected standard of human performance that results in an unwanted or undesirable time delay, difficulty, problem, incident, malfunction, or failure" (1962).

ERROR ANALYSIS. The interest in the systematic analysis of errors as a criterion has come mainly from the ranks of engineers and others concerned with the human aspects of equipment and systems design. The focus of this concern has been the design or modification of physical equipment and facilities so as to reduce the possibility of errors when used. Although design engineers and others in the human factors aspects of equipment design have been primarily responsible for developing what is called error analysis, human errors are (or at least should be) of concern to industrial psychologists, managers, and others who are involved in personnel-related affairs, and in the day-to-day performance of people in their jobs. Let us review some aspects of error analysis as developed to date.

VARIABLES THAT CONTRIBUTE TO ERRORS. Because job-related behavior generally is the result of individual or situational variables, errors (theoretically) also can be attributed to one or the other of these sources, or to a combination thereof. The situational variables that can contribute to errors are to a large extent specific to the situation, but Meister (1967) indicated that in general they may be related to the following: work space and equipment layout; environment; design of machinery, hand tools, and other equipment; methods of handling, transporting, storing, and inspecting equipment; job planning information and its transmission; and operating instructions. Ware (1964) described these categories in somewhat different terms, referring to them as task characteristics, system organization, test characteristics, and physical environment.

The individual variables that might be associated with high error rates in each of various types of jobs cover virtually the entire range of human characteristics discussed in chapter 2. In arguing for greater recognition of the difference between situational and individual variables as sources of error, Ware showed that both types of variables *mediate* human performance (that is, they act as intervening variables), but they do not directly "control" performance. He suggested that the difference between them is the degree of *directness* with which they

influence human performance. The situational variables "set the stage" or provide a framework within which the individual variables operate. In effect, they influence the probabilities of successful performance. In turn, the individual variables can be viewed as the basis for predisposing individuals toward behaviors that, in turn, increase the odds of successful (error-free) performance or its obverse. An overly simplified and generalized representation of the relationship between situational and individual variables as related to error rate is shown in Figure 5.1. In particular, this illustrates how these two sets of variables might interact to affect the probability of errors.

ERROR CLASSIFICATION SYSTEMS. Our primary interest in errors is in those areas in which there is some element of human culpability or involvement. In such areas our all-too-human tendency toward error-producing behavior may not always produce errors, but it has the effect of increasing the probabilities thereof. Payne and Altman (1962) proposed that errors be characterized in terms of "behavior components" that reflect the basic type of human behavior generating them. These components, as subsequently incorporated into

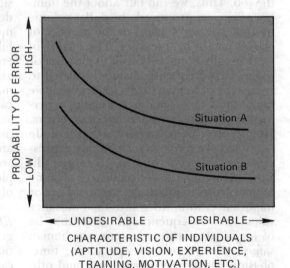

FIG. 5.1 Generalized relationship of situational variables and of individual characteristics as related to error rate (probability of error). Situations A and B might be differences in equipment design, methods, work periods, environments, and so on. (*Adapted from Rook, 1962, Figure 1.*)

an error classification developed by Rook (1962), are: input behaviors (errors of sensory or perceptual input), mediation errors (errors of mediation or information processing), and output errors (errors in making physical responses). These behavior components were combined by Rook into a two-way classification scheme, the other dimension of the system describing the "conscious level or intent" in performing the action that resulted in the error. This classification scheme is as follows:

Conscious level or intent in performing act	Behavior component		
	Input *I*	*Mediation* *M*	*Output* *O*
A Intentional	AI	AM	AO
B Unintentional	BI	BM	BO
C Omission	CI	CM	CO

Individual errors are classified into one of the nine cells. For example, misreading the altitude of an aircraft altimeter would be classified as AI, punching the wrong key on a typewriter would be BO, and failing to figure the sales tax on a purchase would be CM. (Note that category A, intentional, refers to the intent in performing the act that resulted in the error, *not* to the intent of actually making the error.)

The purpose of using error classification systems like this in actual work situations is to accumulate data that can provide inferences about the sources of errors, in order that some corrective action can be taken. Many errors in any given cell might provide such cues, such as finding out (as has actually been the case) that many aircraft accidents have occurred because of misreading the altimeters (in which case the "solution" is to design the instruments so they can be read more accurately) or finding many instances in which the sales tax of purchases has not been included (in which case the solution may be to improve sales training

or to add a specific place on sales slips for sales tax entries, as "reminders").

METHODS OF IDENTIFYING SOURCES OF ERROR. Peters (1962) suggested that there are four principal methods of identifying sources of error. These methods, in somewhat modified form, are described below.

One of these is *data collection and analysis.* For ongoing operations error, data can be obtained from reported malfunctions, system failures, quality control and inspection reports, equipment logs, accident records, personal injury records, and other sources. Such data can be summarized in various ways, including using some type of classification scheme such as the one discussed above.

Another method is *direct observation.* The observation of work in process either on a continuous or sampling basis sometimes can aid in identifying actual or potential error-producing factors. In this regard, Meister (1967) suggested a number of questions that can serve as cues in the observation process, such as questions relating to the design of equipment, work area, materials handling, and environmental factors.

When a new or modified system is being planned, a *systems analysis* method may be used to analyze job operations and operation sequences in order to identify potential sources of error. Such analyses sometimes are made on the basis of design drawings or blueprints, with the view toward finding potential sources of error before the system is actually produced. *Simulation* is still another method. The experimental use of prototypes, mockups, or other forms of simulating systems or components being developed, frequently can help to identify potential sources of error.

RELIABILITY IN ERROR ANALYSIS. In some error analysis programs, the "reliability" of performance is measured. In other sections of this text, including the later discussion in this chapter of the reliability of criterion measure, the term *reliability* refers to the reliability of *measurement* of variables (as of a criterion or a test). In the framework of error analysis, reliability refers to the consistency of "performance," either of an item of equipment or an individual. Since this usage comes from engineering, let us call it *engineering reliability*.

In this framework there are two basic indexes of reliability. One of these is the probability of successful performance. This index is used for activities that represent separate, independent (that is, "discrete") events (such as starting an automobile, inspecting individual bottles on a conveyor, or sorting letters into alphabetical piles). In such instances reliability is stated as the probability of successful performance expressed as a proportion, such as .92 or .99, or in some instances as more precise values, such as .9936 or .9974. Such values are the *obverse* of the probabilities of errors and in effect represent the "odds" of successful or satisfactory performance. The other index of engineering reliability applies to *continuous* (as opposed to *discrete*) activities and is called the mean time to failure (MTF), the mean time until the component in question performs satisfactorily before it fails to perform. This concept applies particularly to physical components (such as the mean life of light bulbs, or the mean time of aircraft engine performance before they give up the ghost). In certain special circumstances it could apply to continuous human activities such as driving a car (in which case one might measure the mean time people can drive before their performance falls below a given level, or even before they fall asleep). Or, in a hand steadiness test in a laboratory one could measure the mean time people can maintain the posture of holding a stylus in a hole without the stylus touching the sides of the hole.

DISCUSSION OF JOB PERFORMANCE CRITERIA. For job performance criteria it should be noted that, at least in some circumstances, such criteria are "dynamic"

(Ghiselli & Haire 1960; Bass 1962). This means that job performance may continue to change over time as the result of the experience of the individuals in question. Ghiselli and Haire reported, for example, that with a group of investment salesmen, performance continued to change (generally to improve) ten years after initial employment. During that period, average production in sales increased 650 percent, and there was still no evidence of leveling off. In numerous studies it has been found that although most individuals generally show continuous improvement, they change somewhat in terms of their relative performance. In this connection it has been proposed that *rate* of change in performance can serve as a possible criterion. This criterion generally was considered more appropriate for a group of taxicab drivers, for example, than was "productivity" during any given period of the first eighteen weeks of employment.

Because job performance levels of individuals change over time, this implies that the criterion measures obtained at one time will not necessarily be closely related to those obtained at some other time in the job career of the individuals in question. Therefore, criterion information about employees obtained early in their employment on a given job will not necessarily be indicative of later criterion information.

Some measures of job performance criteria are quite objective in that they are based on some method of measurement minimizing human judgment or involvement. Thus, in actual job situations, measures of units produced per hour or per day might be obtained, or in laboratory experiments one might measure reaction time to a given stimulus or time to complete a given task. In many, if not most, circumstances, however, one must use ratings of performance, either because it would be difficult or impossible to obtain objective measures, or because the performance criterion in question is essentially subjective (as in the case of persons in most artistic activities, in certain types of interpersonal-relations activities, etc.). The next chapter covers various types of rating systems, some of which are relevant for rating work performance.

Job Attendance Criteria

At least three kinds of criteria can be lumped together under the heading of job attendance criteria, inasmuch as they all relate to some aspect of the tendency of employees to "attend" to their jobs. These are: (1) job tenure (how long people remain on their jobs), (2) absenteeism, and (3) tardiness. The problem of measurement of such criteria, especially absenteeism is not as simple as it might at first appear to be. For absenteeism, for example, one could consider number of absences, duration of absences, absences for cause (such as illness) and without cause, as well as other aspects. In fact it has been estimated that there are over forty different ways of deriving indexes of absenteeism. Because of some of these problems, Latham and Purcell (1975) proposed using "attendance" as a substitute for absenteeism, indicating that the reliability of attendance records is higher than the reliability of typical absenteeism records. However, as Ilgen (1977) found, there are some logical and statistical arguments against the general use of attendance as a substitute for absenteeism criteria (although there may well be some circumstances in which this might be appropriate). The moral of all this is that, in developing a criterion of absenteeism, one should carefully consider the possible variations on this theme and choose the particular basis for the criterion that would best serve the purpose at hand.

Accident and Injury Criteria

These criteria are used when the inquiry in question is concerned with matters of safety, such as in industry or in driving. Such criteria can be useful either in analyzing the relative safety of two or more circumstances (such as different designs of equipment) or in analyzing the personal variables related to accident or injury occurrence.

Physiological Criteria

Physiological criteria include such measures as heart rate, blood pressure, electrical resistance of the skin, and oxygen consumption. Such criteria typically are used in studying the effects of environmental variables, physical work load, work periods, methods of work, and so forth.

Status Criteria

Occasionally the "status" of individuals with respect to some factor is used as a criterion. This "status" may be some indication of group "membership," such as individual's occupation, position, or education level. In other instances the "status" may be based on relevant recorded information about individuals, such as number of promotions received or duration of job tenure.

Subjective Criteria

As discussed above, many performance criteria are based on subjective judgments of raters. Other types of subjective criteria used in industrial psychology include measures of attitudes and opinions obtained by questionnaires. In addition, in certain special circumstances other types of subjective responses are used as criteria, such as the ratings of jobs, the ratings of job applicants, or preferences of people for different types of work equipment or working conditions. (The subjective judgments of the previously discussed types of criteria, especially job performance, should be considered as falling in their appropriate categories.)

Discussion

Of the various criteria used in personnel research, it is probable that, for better or worse, supervisory ratings of job performance are used most frequently. This is evident from the results of an analysis by Lent and others (1971) of 406 studies published in *Personnel Psychology*. Of 1,506 criteria used in those studies, 897 were supervisory ratings of the job performance of their subordinates.

SELECTION OF CRITERIA

The selection and development of behavioral measures (that is, criteria) are critical to whatever pupose they may be used, either a research program or for some administrative purpose. In this connection, three basic considerations should be taken into account: *relevance, freedom from contamination,* and *reliability.*

Relevance of Criteria

The relevance of a criterion refers to the extent to which criterion measures of different individuals are meaningful in terms of the objectives for which such measures are derived. Every job exists for some purpose, or complex of purposes, whether formally stated or not. Relevance, then, relates to the adequacy of criterion measures as indices of the relative abilities of individuals in fulfilling such purposes. Because most jobs have various objectives (rather than just one), there is an issue as to whether it is best to use a single overall criterion, or to use separate criteria (subcriteria) for the individual objectives. This question will be discussed later.

It has been postulated that there is, theoretically, an ultimate criterion that would serve as the basis for characterizing performance of individuals along a "true" scale (Thorndike 1949). Typically, this "ultimate" criterion has been viewed in the context of long-range overall performance, as, for example, "the total worth of a man to a company—in the final analysis," as suggested by Guion (1961, p. 141). If there were some yardstick by which ultimate performance could be measured, it would be possible to use it to characterize the position along such a scale where each individual on any given job would fall. Although such a yardstick of the ultimate criterion is more theoretical than actual, the more closely any actual criterion approximates this theoretical ultimate standard, the more *relevant* it is.

In practical situations, it usually is necessary to select or develop a criterion that is in some respects short of this goal. Such criteria are sometimes referred to as intermediate and immediate criteria, depending upon how close they come (even in point of time) to approximating the ultimate criterion. To illustrate, let us take the case of individuals selected for apprentice training in some craft. The ultimate criterion of performance of a craftsman might be based on long-range considerations of the extent to which he fulfills the variety of work activities expected of craftsmen, including work he accomplishes, how well he is able to plan and organize his work, how well he adapts to changing requirements of the work to be done, and how dependable he is. A criterion of such a nature would be hard to come by, but an intermediate criterion might consist of ratings by craft supervisors of the performance of the craftsmen. In turn, an immediate criterion might consist of grades in apprentice training courses. Both of these would be relevant criteria for the construct under consideration.

Freedom from Contamination

As indicated earlier, the behavior of individuals is a function of both individual and situational variables. When one is concerned with criteria that reflect *individual* differences, any influence of differences in *situational* variables can "contaminate" criterion measures for individuals. A couple of examples will illustrate this. Let us suppose that we have two employees operating looms for weaving textiles, but that each has a different type of loom. The production records of such employees probably would *not* be an appropriate index of their *relative* abilities, for each individual's production is in part influenced by the productive capabilities of his own loom. Similarly, criterion contamination can occur in the case of salespersons assigned to sales territories differing in sales potential. In using production indices as criteria, one has to be wary of the possibility that the production of individuals might have been differentially affected by factors not under the control of the individuals, such as variation in the quality of the material handled, the working conditions, or the conditions of machines and equipment used.

Other sources of possible contamination might include the extent of training or experience different individuals have had, differences in the incentive systems used with different individuals (such as hourly versus piece-rate pay), and possible pressures upon individuals to restrict their output.

The ever-present possibility of many forms of criterion contamination should not cause us to throw up our hands in despair, for there are ways of minimizing if not eliminating their influence. One approach is selecting those individuals for whom the contaminating variables are equal or nearly so. Another method is making statistical adjustments for the influence of the contaminating variables. These adjustments can be made, for example, by using what are called partial correlations that can statistically "partial out" the influence of the contaminating variable. Another scheme is adjusting for differences in the mean values (and the distributions of values) of individuals in groups known to be different in terms of contaminating vari-

able, such as individuals working on different types of machines or individuals with different lengths of experience. This sometimes can be done by converting the original criterion values of individuals in each such group to some type of "standard score." (More will be said about this in the next chapter.)

It should be pointed out that these various schemes do not necessarily eliminate the influence of the contaminating variable on the criterion, although they would at least tend to reduce its effects.

Reliability of the Criterion

Earlier in this chapter we discussed the concept of reliability in the frame of reference of error analysis, referring to it as *engineering reliability*. As we now discuss the reliability of criteria, we will be concerned with the *reliability of measurement*. As we now use the term reliability, we will be talking about reliability of measurement. Reliability of measurement can be viewed as applying to the measurement of virtually any type of variable, such as criteria, tests, and ratings. Unfortunately there is no simple, pat definition of such reliability, but in a very general sense we can think of it as the stability or consistency of measures of whatever variables we are using.

The measures of different variables, such as performance ratings to be used as criteria, can be influenced by different factors *other* than the "true" performance of the individuals being rated, such as the raters who make the ratings, when the ratings are made, the opportunities for the raters to have observed the performance of the ratees on various tasks, and the format and instructions of the rating forms. For criterion measures we would like to have, for each individual in question, a good, solid, stable index of the criterion as applied to that person, independent of the extraneous factors that can influence such an index. Actually achieving such an objective is pretty tricky, but in any event one should have some inkling of the reliability of whatever criterion is used in any research undertaking. There are certain rather sophisticated statistical procedures that can be used in reliability analysis, but for our purposes we will generally use coefficients of correlation.

For most job-related criteria (such as job performance) a rather straightforward approach to the measurement of reliability is determining the extent to which individuals tend to maintain the same level on the criterion over time. Sometimes such a time-related measure of reliability is determined by comparing the criterion values for individuals for two periods of time, as illus-

trated in Figure 5.2, which shows the consistency (in other words, the reliability) of production records of seventy-nine unit wirers for two five-week time periods. The correlation between these two sets of data is .87, which reflects a fairly high degree of stability. The figure shows along the base line the efficiency index of the wirers during the five even-numbered weeks of the ten-week period (that is, weeks 2, 4, 6, 8, and 10), and on the vertical axis the index for the odd-numbered weeks (1, 3, 5, 7, and 9). Each point represents the two values for a given individual, that is, the index for the even- and for the odd-numbered weeks. The similarity between these is quite apparent.

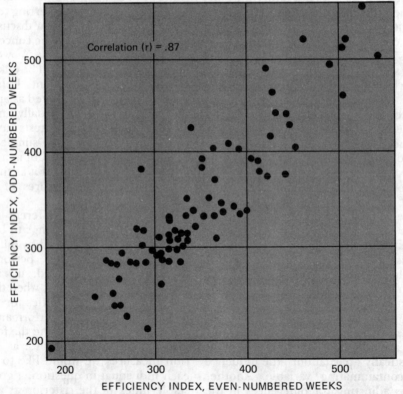

FIG. 5.2 Scattergram showing the relationship between efficiency indexes of a group of seventy-nine unit wirers for two five-week periods (five even-numbered weeks and five odd-numbered weeks). (*Courtesy Tetronix, Inc. and Dr. Guyot Frazier.*)

The reliability of ratings for a group of employees could be determined by correlating two sets of ratings made by a single rater at different times or by correlating two sets of ratings of the same employees made by two different raters. Similarly, one can determine the reliability of the heart rate of individuals, or the reaction time of people to given stimuli. Most commonly, reliability is expressed as a correlation coefficient. Generally speaking, a reliability coefficient of .90 or higher would be considered exceptionally good, and those between .80 and .90 normally would be very acceptable. It is unfortunate that one frequently has to tolerate the use of criteria whose reliabilities are lower than such values.

STABILITY OF JOB PERFORMANCE.
In connection with the reliability of criteria of various aspects of job performance, we should raise the question as to the stability of such differences in actual practice. In other words, to what extent do people actually maintain consistently their own "levels" of performance over time? A categorical response to this question is not in the cards. Although there are circumstances in which individuals tend to maintain over time an approximately stable level of performance, as illustrated in Figure 5.2, there are some job situations in which there is considerable variability in the performance of individuals. This was found to be the case, in a series of studies summarized by Rothe (1978). In these studies the output rates of employees on each job for each week were correlated with those for the following week covered by the study in question. Any given correlation reflects the extent to which the production rates of the employees in one week were related to their production rates in the following week. There were 164 correlations in all, these representing data from ten studies. The median of the several correlations for each study was derived, the ten medians ranging from .48 to .85. An examination of

these ten medians indicated, however, that there was a systematic difference in the correlations, depending on whether the employees were paid on the basis of an incentive system or not, as shown below:

Incentive system?	Correlations
No	.48; .52; .53; .64
Yes	.67; .68; .72; .78; .82; .85

One of Rothe's conclusions was to the effect that the consistency of production, as measured by week-to-week consistency, may indicate the influence of the incentives operating in the situation in question, since workers in jobs paid on an incentive basis were more consistent in their production than those in non-incentive pay jobs. In addition his studies indicated that output rates on at least some industrial jobs are quite inconsistent from week to week, and that short work periods of a few days or even weeks may not be sufficient to produce reliable criterion measures. In the case of jobs for which relatively short periods of time are found to reflect relatively high levels of consistency from week to week, however, extended periods of data collection would not be necessary.

Instability of job performance level can occur in part as the consequence of any of a number of situational factors that influence the performance of individuals at different times, such as differences in the quality of materials being worked on, the condition of machines, and differences in supervisory pressure. But further, Ronan (1971) suggested that there are individual differences in "performance stability" itself —in other words, that some people tend to remain on an even keel in terms of job performance whereas others tend generally to wobble around, sometimes performing well and at other times performing poorly. An analysis by Klemmer and Lockhead (1962) somewhat supported this contention. In analyzing about a billion responses by more than a thousand card punch and bank proof machine operators, Klemmer and Lockhead found that errors made by such operators varied from day to day to a much greater extent for some operators than for others.

In circumstances in which it is necessary to be concerned about individual differences in job behavior (as in some research projects), one should indeed go out of the way to determine the pattern of stability (or instability) of performance of the individuals in question.

PROBLEMS IN OBTAINING CRITERION DATA

The process of obtaining criterion data about individuals sometimes is a bit ticklish since the individuals in question may not understand the reason for obtaining such data and may in any event be queasy about having such data made available to whoever would be handling it. Regardless of the purpose in mind, such data should be regarded as strictly confidential, to be made available only to "authorized" individuals, and the persons about whom such data are obtained should be given these positive assurances. They also should be fully informed about the uses to be made of the data. If the data are being obtained only for research purposes, the individuals should be so advised and given assurances that the data will be used only for such purposes and will in no way influence their future status in the organization. If, on the other hand, "criterion" data (such as personnel appraisals) are to be used for some administrative purpose (such as for personnel development or promotion decisions), the individuals should be fully advised of the intended use and usually should be provided feedback of the results. (More will be said about this in the next chapter on personnel appraisal.)

The development of criteria and the development of appropriate criterion data

about individuals frequently present serious obstacles for researchers. Relevant criteria seldom "grow on trees," and the investigator may have to stretch his ingeniousness to the limit in order to have appropriate criterion data. Yet, results of any research investigation largely hinges on the adequacy of such data.

CRITERION DIMENSIONS

In many contexts in which criteria are to be used, there may be no single criterion that is obviously the one and only one to use. Rather, two or more possible criteria might be relevant. In human work, for example, most jobs have various facets that typically give rise to what one might call criterion dimensions. When this is the case, an individual might do well in one aspect of a job (such as producing a large quantity of items) but less well on another aspect (such as the quality of the items produced).

Examples of Multiple Dimensions of Criteria

To illustrate the multidimensional nature of criteria, a couple of examples will be given. One example comes from a study by Seashore, Indik, and Georgopoulos (1960) of 975 delivery men for whom several different criteria were available, including productivity (based on established time standards), effectiveness (ratings on overall quality of performance), accidents, absences, and errors (based on "nondeliveries" of packages). The correlations of these five criteria are given in Table 5.1. The generally low correlations indicate that these five aspects of job performance are relatively independent; the highest correlations (.28, .26, and .32) are among the variables of productivity, effectiveness, and errors. These and other results were interpreted by the investigators as contradicting the validity of "overall job performance" as a unidimensional construct and as a refutation of the practice of combining job per-

TABLE 5.1 INTERCORRELATIONS AMONG FIVE CRITERION VARIABLES FOR 975 DELIVERY MEN

	Effectiveness	Accidents	Absences	Errors
Productivity	+.28	−.12	+.01	+.26
Effectiveness		+.02	+.08	+.32
Accidents			+.03	−.18
Absences				+.15
Errors				

Source: Adapted from S. E. Seashore, B. P. Indik, & B. S. Georgopoulos, "Relationship among Criteria of Job Performance," *Journal of Applied Psychology*, 44 (1960), 195–202. The signs of certain correlations (+ or −) have been changed so that a + sign indicates a positive correlation between "desirable" values of the two variables, and a − sign indicates a negative correlation between the "desirable" values. Copyright 1960 by the American Psychological Association and adapted with permission.

formance variables into a single measure having general validity.

A second example comes from study by Tornow and Pinto (1976) in which they dealt with managerial jobs. They developed what they called the Management Position Description Questionnaire (PMDQ) that consisted of 208 items describing various position activities, responsibilities, demands, and other position characteristics. Some examples of items are: uses accounting procedures in analyzing financial information, decides in what business activities the company is to be engaged, phases out unprofitable products or services, and develops high-level management talent. This questionnaire was used by 433 executives in several companies to describe their jobs, and the resulting descriptions were subjected to factor analysis (technically a principal components analysis) to identify the broader "factors" into which the 208 items of job characteristics tended to be grouped across the 433 positions. The resulting factors are: 1. Product, marketing, and financial strategy planning; 2. Coordination of other organizational units and personnel; 3. Internal business control; 4. Products and services responsibility; 5. Public and customer relations; 6. Advanced consulting; 7. Autonomy of action; 8. Approval of financial commitments; 9. Staff service; 10. Supervision; 11. Complexity and stress; 12.

Advanced financial responsibility; and 13. Broad personnel responsibility.

Each of these factors is dominated by a combination of certain of the basic items, and the name given to each factor generally characterizes the "common denominator" of those dominant items. Such an assortment of factors can be considered as representing the basic criterion "dimensions" of executive and managerial positions as described by the PMDQ items.

Possible Treatment of Multidimensional Job Criteria

From these and other studies, it is evident that in many circumstances various criterion dimensions can be used. When such criteria are highly intercorrelated, there is no particular problem selecting which criterion to use; in such a circumstance any given criterion, or an "overall" criterion, could be used for the purpose at hand inasmuch as the other criteria are highly related to it. The snag comes when the two or more criteria are not highly correlated. In such instances the investigator is faced with various alternatives, such as:

1. To select one of the criteria and use it;

2. To use each criterion independently;

3. To combine the various criterion dimensions

into a single "composite" criterion, using some weighting scheme;

4. To develop an "overall" criterion, usually ratings (such as supervisors' ratings of overall job performance).

Since this question has generated quite a bit of controversy, we should explore at least certain aspects of the issues in using either separate (independent) criterion dimensions or some composite or overall criterion.

ARGUMENTS FOR MULTIPLE CRITERIA. On the one hand, Guion (1961) expressed the opinion that when various criteria are clearly independent, they should be used independently and should not be combined. (When they are shown to be related, however, he suggested that it may be useful to combine them into a composite.) Dunnette also argued for using multiple criterion dimensions and suggested that we "cease searching for single or composite measures of job success and proceed to undertake research which accepts the world of success dimensionality as it really exists" (1963, p. 252). Based on a study of criteria of performance of skilled tradesmen, Ronan (1963) took the position that a criterion of overall job performance, or any other single criterion, is of limited usefulness in evaluating the performance of such personnel.

The advocates of multiple job criteria prefer criteria such as Schmidt's and Kaplan's (1971) "*behavioral* constructs" for they reflect essentially different facets of job behavior. They pointed out that the personal characteristics of individuals who perform well on one criterion may be very different from the characteristics of those who perform well on another criterion; for this reason the use of separate criteria contributes to the understanding and to the prediction of the different aspects of job performance. In turn, they argued that the use of a single composite or overall criterion muddies the waters inasmuch as any

given value on a composite or overall criterion scale can be produced by different *combinations* of performance. Thus, two or more individuals might have equal criterion values on a composite or overall criterion, but they could have those same values for different reasons. For example, one person could be high on a quantity criterion dimension and low on a quality criterion dimension, a second person could have the reverse pattern, and a third person might be intermediate on both. Continuing with this line of argument, one could not reasonably expect to identify a common set of personal factors that would aid in identifying (predicting) individuals who might have the same composite criterion level but who achieve it by highly varied job behavior patterns. Rather, one might reasonably expect to identify a combination of factors associated with one subcriterion (say, quantity) and another combination associated with another subcriterion (say, quality).

ARGUMENTS FOR COMPOSITE OR OVERALL CRITERIA. The basic contention of the advocates of a composite or overall criterion of job performance is that such a criterion should provide a measure of the individual's overall "success" or "value-to-the-organization." Insofar as this is so, such a criterion is more an *economic* construct than a behavioral construct. In this connection, a significant concept was proposed by Brogden and Taylor (1950). If one is interested in criteria for individuals within an organization, they suggested that the criterion should measure the overall contribution of the individual to the organization. Toward this end, they proposed the construction of criterion measures in cost-accounting terms—the "dollar criterion." This proposal is predicated on the proposition that (when possible) the dollar provides a common denominator or a common metric for combining quite different subcriterion measures. To illustrate the concept, they referred to an earlier situation mentioned by Otis (1940) in which it was found that in a key-punching operation thirteen cards could be key-punched in the same time required to correct one error. Therefore, one could say that the personnel costs of correcting one error are the same as for punching thirteen cards. For those jobs for which performance on different subcriteria could be expressed in terms of dollar costs, it would be possible to add the dollar cost values of subcriteria together for each individual, thus providing an economic index of the relative value of different individuals.

Although very few composite or overall criteria actually are expressed in dollar terms, most composite or overall criteria probably do have implications in terms of some concept of total worth or contribution to the organization. The conventional "supervisory rating" probably reflects some such frame of reference.

DISCUSSION. In the final analysis to combine or not to combine criteria is an unanswerable question. The fact remains that there are almost no jobs where a single criterion is sufficient to describe. A salesperson may be excellent in interpersonal relationships with customers, but poor in handling paper work in connection with sales. A plant manager may do very well in scheduling production, but may be inept in dealing with subordinates. In addition, equally effective performance of many jobs can be accomplished in many different ways. If the multiple criteria are combined into a single measure, two things will be lost. First, information about the behavior on each criterion which may be valuable is lost. To look only at dollar volume per month tells you nothing about how well a salesperson makes new contacts, maintains old accounts, keeps accurate records, and so forth. Second, a single index may simply be inaccurate because it often cannot reflect the fact that jobs can be accomplished in different ways.

Nevertheless, many personnel decisions require that a single index be constructed in order to make a unidimensional decision. Promotion decisions, salary decisions, and hiring decisions are judgments which require that all those being considered be evaluated on some overall criterion dimension. Therefore, like it or not, some combination of criteria is necessary. On the other hand, some decisions may be better if criteria are not combined. For example, to decide who should receive some training would require a comparison of the specific skills of the individuals in the specific areas to which the training was directed. Overall, general, evaluations may not be useful for such decisions.

Let us consider the initial use of multiple criterion dimensions, such as in a validation study directed toward establishing a set of personnel specifications for a given job. Although we might be able to determine the personal characteristics that contribute to performance on each criterion dimension, if we wanted to be able to apply the results of such a study we would have to weight the different dimensions and add these weighted values together to arrive at some relative index of "overall" potentialities of each candidate. Such a weighting might be done subjectively or on other bases (to be discussed later), but no matter how it is done, one cannot avoid some consolidation of criterion dimensions in such a situation.

In the initial use of an overall criterion such as supervisory ratings, the combining (and the associated weighting) of different dimensions of performance usually is done "intuitively" by raters as they rate the various individuals. Often the raters may not be aware that they are in fact weighing the different aspects of performance, thus creating a composite criterion, which is a consolidation of several separate criterion dimensions that necessarily have to be given some individual weights.

The resolution of the dilemma of using single versus multiple criteria in part is implied by the objectives at hand. To reiterate a point made above, psychological understanding of predictor-criterion relationships is best achieved by using individual criterion dimensions, as pointed out by Schmidt and Kaplan (1971). For the practical goals of prediction (as in making personnel decisions about individuals), Schmidt and Kaplan suggested that the ideal approach is to weight the several criterion dimensions and to add the weighted values together to derive a composite value representing the "economic" or practical construct of overall worth. But in the same breath, they urged the simultaneous analysis of predictors and criterion dimensions in order to achieve understanding of these relationships. This approach offers a fairly reasonable resolution to this otherwise controversial issue. With respect to their proposal, it should be pointed out that although equal composite criterion values can arise from various combinations of the separate dimensions, does not in fact constrain the identification of relevant predictors of personal characteristics. The prediction of such a composite criterion can be made statistically.

Weighting of Multiple Criteria

When two or more criterion dimensions are to be consolidated into a single composite criterion, some weighting of the separate dimensions or subcriteria is necessary. But the weighting systems used can affect the relative "composite" values for different individuals, as shown in the illustration in Table 5.2. This shows, for the three hypothetical individuals (X, Y, and Z), their "ratings" (on a ten-point scale) on each of two dimensions (A and B, which might represent quantity and quality of work). The composite ratings (C) are based on the combinations of the "weights" assigned to the individual dimensions and the ratings given to the individuals on the dimensions. The table shows the effects of three weighting systems: (1) A = 50, B = 50; (2) A=25, B=75; and (3) A=75, B=25. In the case of the equal weighting system, the three individuals end up in a dead heat, with each having a composite value of 500. For the two differential weighting systems, however, the rank order of the three individuals as based on their composite ratings (C) is reversed. This particular illustration is "rigged" to amplify the effects of the different weighting systems. Although the effects of different weighting systems in actual circumstances usually would not be as marked as they are in this illustration, they still can have some influence on the composite ratings that are developed.

The weighting system selected should be one that results in criterion values for individuals that represent reasonably valid relative positions for the individuals along a scale of overall worth. The weighting can be done either on the basis of judgment by knowledgeable persons or on the basis of

TABLE 5.2 ILLUSTRATION OF THE DEVELOPMENT OF COMPOSITE CRITERION VALUES (C) FROM DIFFERENT WEIGHTING VALUES FOR TWO CRITERION DIMENSIONS (A AND B) FOR THREE INDIVIDUALS (X, Y, AND Z)

Individuals	Ratings Given on Criterion Dimensions		Values of Weighted Dimensions and of Composite								
			1. Equal Weights			2. Different Weights			3. Different Weights		
	A	B	A(50)	B(50)	C	A(25)	B(75)	C	A(75)	B(25)	C
X	8	2	400	100	500	20	150	350	600	50	650
Y	2	8	100	400	500	50	600	650	150	200	350
Z	5	5	250	250	500	125	375	500	375	175	500

some statistical procedure. Probably the most valid basis is a statistical procedure (specifically, regression analysis) that results in the statistical determination of optimum weights as related to some "overall" criterion. This procedure requires that a sample of individuals be "ordered" along a predetermined overall criterion scale, that values on the various specific subcriteria or criterion dimensions be derived for each individual, and that a statistical operation be performed to determine the appropriate weights for each of the subcriteria.

Criteria in Evaluating Situational Variables

So far, our discussion of the use of separate criterion dimensions versus composite or overall criteria has been in the framework of understanding and predicting the relationship between individual characteristics and the criteria. When using criteria as the basis for evaluating situational variables (such as working conditions or equipment design), somewhat the same considerations are pertinent. Here again, however, one can make a strong case for using all relevant criteria (as well as composite or overall criteria) in order to gain as much knowledge as possible of the interrelationships among the variables in question. It is sometimes the case, however, that certain independent criteria are incompatible with each other. For example, in designing a machine, it might be that a design conducive to a high rate of productivity by the employees also might be conducive to a high incidence of accidents. In such cases some trade off must be made—that is, some degree of one advantage must be given up for the other. In such a case, one would try to develop a design that would be most nearly optimum in terms of the two or more criteria in question. Such an optimum incorporates a weighting of the relative importance of the separate criteria in terms of the overall objectives.

DISCUSSION

In large part industrial psychology is directed toward exploring and understanding the "sources" of variation in different aspects of job-related behavior, in order to take appropriate action, when relevant, to improve such behavior. In this regard, both research and appropriate administrative actions critically depend on developing and using appropriate criteria of the behavior in question.

REFERENCES

BASS, B. M. Further evidence on the dynamic character of criteria. *Personnel Psychology,* 1962, *12,* 93–97.

BROGDEN, H. E., & TAYLOR, E. K. The dollar criterion—Applying the cost accounting concept to criterion construction. *Personnel Psychology,* 1950, *3,* 133–154.

DUNNETTE, M. D. A note on the criterion. *Journal of Applied Psychology,* 1963, *47,* 251–254.

GHISELLI, E. E., & HAIRE, M. The validation of selection tests in the light of the dynamic character of criteria. *Personnel Psychology,* 1960, *13,* 225–231.

GUION, R. M. Criterion measurement and personnel judgments. *Personnel Psychology,* 1961, *14,* 141–149.

ILGEN, D. R. Attendance behavior: A reevaluation of Latham and Purcell's conclusions. *Journal of Applied Psychology,* 1977, *62* (2), 230–233.

KLEMMER, E. J., & LOCKHEAD, G. R. Productivity and errors in two keying tasks: A field study. *Journal of Applied Psychology,* 1962, *46* (6), 401–408.

LATHAM, G. P., & PURSELL, E. D. Measuring absenteeism from the opposite side of the coin. *Journal of Applied Psychology,* 1975, *60* (3), 369–371.

LENT, R. H., AURBACH, H. H., & LEVIN, L. S. Predictors, criteria, and significant results. *Personnel Psychology,* 1971, *24*, 519–533.

MEISTER, D. Applications of human reliability to the production process. In W. B. Askren (Ed.), *Symposium on reliability of human performance in work.* USAF, Aerospace Medical Research Laboratory, Report AMRL—TR-67-88, May 1967.

OTIS, J. (Chapter V, The criterion, in W. H. Stead & C. L. Shartle (Eds.), *Occupational counseling techniques.* New York: American Book Company, 1940.

PAYNE, D., & ALTMAN, J. W. *An index of electronic equipment operability.* American Institutes for Research, Report AIR-C-43-1/62, 1962.

PETERS, G. A. Human error and "goof proofing." Paper presented at Product Assurance Symposium, American Society for Quality Control, San Fernando Valley Section, Glendale, California, October 20, 1962.

RONAN, W. W. Personal communication to the authors, April 26, 1971.

———. A factor analysis of eleven job performance measures. *Personnel Psychology,* 1963, *16*, 255–267.

ROOK, L. W., Jr. *Reduction in human error in industrial production.* Albuquerque, N.M.: Sandia Corporation. Technical Memorandum SCTM 93-62 (14), June 1962.

ROTHE, H. F. Output rates among industrial workers. *Journal of Applied Psychology,* 1978, *63* (1), 40–46.

SCHMIDT, F. L., & KAPLAN, L. B. Composite vs. multiple criteria: A review and resolution of the controversy. *Personnel Psychology,* 1971, *24* (3), 419–434.

SEASHORE, S. E., INDIK, B. P., & GEORGOPOULOS, B. S. Relationships among criteria of job performance. *Journal of Applied Psychology,* 1960, *44*, 195–202.

THORNDIKE, R. L. *Personnel selection: Test and measurement technique.* New York: Wiley, 1949.

TORNOW, W. W., & PINTO, P. R. The development of a managerial job taxonomy: A system for describing, classifying, and evaluating executive positions. *Journal of Applied Psychology,* 1976, *61* (4), 410–418.

WARE, C. T., Jr. Individual and situational variables affecting human performance. *Human Factors,* 1964, *6* (6), 673–674.

6 personnel evaluation and assessment

In the last chapter we discussed some general considerations relating to the measurement of job-related behavior and indicated that such measurement can be used either as criteria for research or for some administrative purpose. In this chapter we will deal more specifically with measurement as it relates personnel evaluation and assessment.

Informal judgments of subordinates by their superiors (and vice versa) have always been a part of superior-subordinate relationships. More formal, systematic procedures for making such judgments, however, are of relatively recent origin. Such judgmental processes have been labeled *merit rating, employee appraisal, employee evaluation, personnel evaluation, personnel rating, performance evaluation, performance rating, performance appraisal, performance review,* and the like. Lopez (1968) distinguished between what he called *performance evaluation*

(that is, evaluation of employees' actual work performance) and *employee assessment* (that is, the assessment of an employee's strengths and weaknesses in specific areas, especially for personnel development purposes).

In this text, we make the basic distinction proposed by Lopez with slight modifications of terminology and meaning. We use the term *personnel evaluation* (instead of *performance evaluation*) to refer to judgments of employees' behavior and certain related personal characteristics as manifested in their work, although the primary focus of such judgments usually is on job performance as such. These personnel evaluations are sometimes used as criteria in research, but they are used more typically for various administrative purposes such as the basis for granting wage or salary increases, determining training needs, personnel development, or certain personnel actions such as promotions, transfers, and discharges.

We use the term *personnel assessment* for the assessment of people's abilities, personal characteristics, and other attributes as might be relevant in considering the *potentialities* of individuals for some "new" type of work. These assessments most typically apply to current employees who might be considered for promotion to other positions or to their development in their current positions. However, essentially the same kinds of assessments frequently are made of candidates being considered for employment in some capacity.

The line between personnel evaluation and personnel assessment is very thin, especially since the same types of judgments, or at least of judgmental ratings, may well be involved in both. The critical distinction between them relates to purpose, the distinction being between evaluation of *present or past* behavior or of certain personal qualities, as contrasted with *potential for future performance*. The demonstrated ability to perform a given job, for example, provides no assurance of the potential to perform at a higher level or in a different type of job. The "Peter principle" certainly is relevant to this frame of reference. The Peter principle, enunciated by Peter (1969) in his light-hearted book, characterized the unfortunately rather common practice of promoting people to their "level of incompetence." The "confirmation" of the principle is demonstrated by many examples of individuals who have been promoted from time to time because of their satisfactory performance in their *past* positions and who then are promoted to positions *exceeding* their level of ability—in other words to positions matching their "level of incompetence." At this level, individuals are beyond their depth and flub the jobs to which they have been promoted. They may remain in such positions for a long time, prohibited by formal rules from being promoted and prohibited by common practice from being demoted. The moral of this is that in considering individuals for promotion one needs to assess *future potential,* although this assessment may take into account demonstrated past performance in areas relevant to the positions for which they are being considered.

TYPES OF RATING SYSTEMS

Personnel evaluations and assessments typically are based on the use of some type of rating system requiring some individual or individuals (usually supervisors) to evaluate the behavior and/or personal qualities of others. Most of these rating systems also are used in other contexts, such as evaluating students in schools, in public opinion polling, in consumer research, and in social psychology. Certain types of rating systems, however, have been developed specifically for personnel evaluation and assessment. Most of the rating systems used for personnel evaluation and assessment are listed below:

1. Rating scales

2. Personnel comparison systems
   a. Rank-order system
   b. Paired comparison system
   c. Forced distribution system
   d. Point allocation technique (PAT)

3. Critical incident technique

4. Behavioral checklists and scales
   a. Weighted checklist
   b. Forced-choice checklist
   c. Behavioral expectation scale (BES)
   d. Behavioral observation scale (BOS)
   e. Mixed standard scale

5. Other methods

These five categories all are based on essentially different rating procedures. Because each of the various methods has certain inherent advantages and disadvantages, there is no single "best" method; rather, one method may best serve one purpose, and another method may best serve a different purpose. Some of the specific plans used in organizations have features of two or more types of rating systems. Each of these systems will be considered.

Rating Scales

Rating scales are undoubtedly the most widely used rating system for personnel evaluation and assessment. Such scales provide for rating individuals on each of a number of traits or factors. For each trait or factor the rater judges "how much" of the trait or factor applies to the individual. Such judgments are, in effect, *absolute* since they reflect estimates of the degree to which the trait or factor applies. There are two primary variations in how the ratings may be made. In the *graphic* rating scale, a line represents the range of the factor, and the raters place a check mark at the position along this line that they consider to represent the degree of the factor possessed by the individual being rated. The *multiple-step* rating scale provides for rating on each factor in terms of any one of a number of "degree" categories, usually from five to nine. Some examples of typical rating scales are shown in Figure 6.1 for a few different rating factors.

RATING FACTORS. Rating scales used by different organizations differ widely in the number of traits or factors to be rated and in the particular factors. For personnel evaluation plans, the more common factors are quantity, quality, judgment, dependability, initiative, cooperation, leadership, and job knowledge. It should be noted that some of the traits or factors used in rating scales do not really represent different dimensions of behavior. In one study, for example, the ratings of a random sample of 1,100 employees out of a work force of 9,000 were analyzed. The ratings for each employee were made on twelve separate traits. The ratings on each of these twelve traits were correlated with those on every other trait and then were subjected to factor analysis. As discussed earlier, factor analysis is a statistical technique that reduces a set of measurements (such as test scores or ratings) to the minimum number of basic variables or factors that will account for the variations in the original data. The factor analysis of the ratings revealed that for practical purposes there were only two basic factors—ability to do the present job (a very general factor) and quality of performance.

Personnel Comparison Systems

Whereas the rating scales provide for rating against some defined standard, personnel comparison systems allow individuals to be rated in comparison with each other. With conventional rating scales there is a tendency for the raters to pile up the ratings at one end of the scale, frequently at the higher end. If this occurs, the results have limited value, for they do not differentiate adequately among the individuals. Personnel comparison systems avoid this problem completely, for individuals are rated relative to each other. There are three principal variations in the methods of comparing people with each other.

RANK-ORDER SYSTEM. With this method the rater simply ranks the individuals. Each person's rating is then determined by position in rank. If a system using several traits is used, the ranking should be made separately for each trait.

PAIRED COMPARISON SYSTEM. Some work on the application of a standard psychological method, paired comparisons, to the problem of personnel rating has shown very favorable results. This method ordinarily provides for rating individuals on only a single general trait—overall ability to do their present job—but it can be applied separately to more traits or characteristics if it is desirable to do so. Cards or

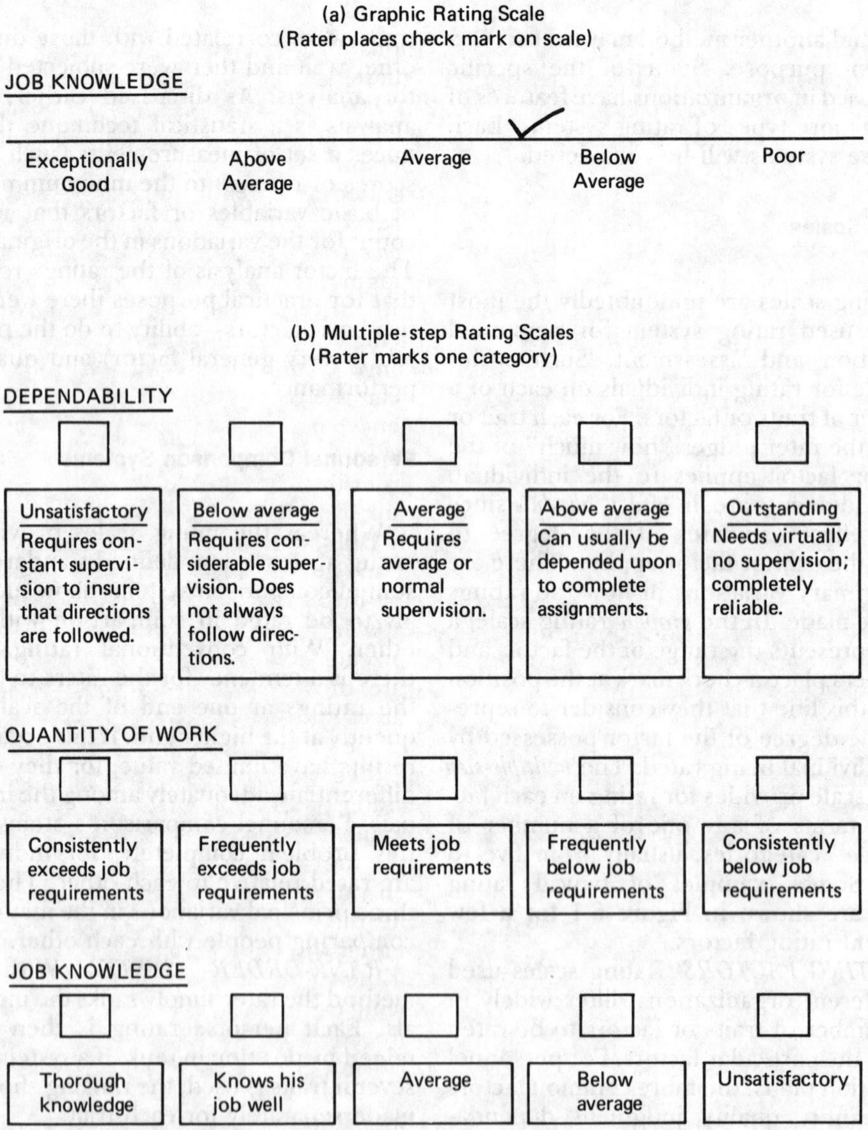

(a) Graphic Rating Scale
(Rater places check mark on scale)

JOB KNOWLEDGE

| Exceptionally Good | Above Average | Average ✓ | Below Average | Poor |

(b) Multiple-step Rating Scales
(Rater marks one category)

DEPENDABILITY

☐ ☐ ☐ ☐ ☐

| Unsatisfactory | Below average | Average | Above average | Outstanding |
| Requires constant supervision to insure that directions are followed. | Requires considerable supervision. Does not always follow directions. | Requires average or normal supervision. | Can usually be depended upon to complete assignments. | Needs virtually no supervision; completely reliable. |

QUANTITY OF WORK

☐ ☐ ☐ ☐ ☐

| Consistently exceeds job requirements | Frequently exceeds job requirements | Meets job requirements | Frequently below job requirements | Consistently below job requirements |

JOB KNOWLEDGE

☐ ☐ ☐ ☐ ☐

| Thorough knowledge | Knows his job well | Average | Below average | Unsatisfactory |

FIG. 6.1 Examples of typical rating scales for certain rating factors. Multiple-step scales usually have anywhere from five to nine categories.

slips of paper are prepared so that each contains the names of two of the persons who are to be rated. In this manner, each ratee is paired with every other one. The rater then simply checks the name of the person who is considered better on the characteristic on which they are being compared. The number of pairs of names when this sytem is used in the form described is given by the equation:

$$\text{No. of Pairs} = \frac{N(N-1)}{2}$$

in which N is the number of individuals to be rated. If there are 20 ratees the number of pairs is thus $20(20-1)/2$, or 190. But if there are 100 ratees, the number of pairs, $100(100-1)/2$, or 4,950, is obviously far too great for expedient use of the system. Two solutions have been proposed for when the number of pairs becomes too unwieldy to handle. One method is to divide the original group into a number of smaller groups and set up the pairs for the smaller groups (Lawshe, Kephart, & McCormick, 1949). Scales have been developed so that ratings of those in several subgroups, which may not be equal in size, can be converted to a common base.

A second procedure that may be used if division into smaller groups is not practicable and if there is good reason to believe that the rater is sufficiently familiar with the work of each ratee on the job so that the rating will be reasonably valid, is to extract from the table of all possible pairs of ratees a patterned sample of pairs. It has been shown that the ratings obtained from such a patterned sample correlate approximately .93 with ratings obtained from the complete matrix of pairs (McCormick & Bachus, 1952).

FORCED DISTRIBUTION SYSTEM. This method is particularly useful when a large number of individuals is to be evaluated by the same rater. This scheme is used most often for rating overall job performance but is equally good for rating specific factors or traits. In either case the rater is asked to distribute the individuals into a limited number of categories (usually five) according to a predetermined and specified percentage distribution, such as the following:

Lowest	Next	Middle	Next	Highest
10%	20%	40%	20%	10%
□	□	□	□	□

This procedure reduces the tendency to concentrate the ratings in one or a limited number of rating categories. In some situations the percentages are used more as guideposts than as rigid requirements.

POINT ALLOCATION TECHNIQUE (PAT). A rather interesting variation of personnel comparison procedures was described by Duffy and Webber (1974). This procedure, called the *point allocation technique* (PAT), combines *relative* and *absolute* judgments. One of the possible problems with absolute rating systems is the tendency for the ratings to be concentrated in some section of the rating scale, usually near the top (this is the "leniency" tendency). The personnel comparison systems avoid this problem by forcing the rater to order the ratees from high to low (as in the rank order method). The scheme described by Duffy and Webber had been suggested at an Air Force workshop dealing with officer rating systems. With this system the rater is given a specified number of points for each ratee (such as 100) and can allocate the points given to him for all the ratees to the individuals in whatever manner he wishes, except that no two ratees can receive the same number of points. Thus, if a rater has ten ratees, he would have 1,000 points to allocate to the ten individuals. The rank order of the points he gives to the ten ratees reflects the *relative* ratings, and the differences between the point values (either slight or great) reflect his judgments of the differences between the ratees, this being essentially an *absolute* judgment. This procedure probably should not be used with fewer than four or five ratees.

Critical Incident Technique

This method of performance evaluation, developed by Flanagan and Burns (1955), provides for the recording by supervisors of employees' critical "behaviors." This preferably should be done on a current basis. Whenever an employee does something especially noteworthy or especially undesirable ("critical" to either good or poor performance), a notation is made in the employee's record. These "critical behaviors" usually are classified into certain categories, such as judgment and comprehension, productivity, dependability, and initiative. The number of positive and negative incidents recorded in each category can be tallied. Although it is preferable that critical incidents be recorded as they occur, it is probable that in most circumstances such records are made after the fact, on the basis of the "recall" of the rater.

The use of the critical incident method to evaluate salespeople was discussed by Kirchner and Dunnette (1957). Each of eighty-five sales managers was asked to report as many critical incidents as possible illustrating both effective and noneffective behavior among the group of salesmen. Sixty-one usable instances were obtained. For these instances, a rating form was prepared which the authors felt to be very promising.

Another use of critical incidents, this time in training salesmen, was reported by Bridgman and others (1958). In this investigation, critical incidents of effective and ineffective behavior among salesmen were utilized with good results in a training program for new salesmen in the field.

Although the critical incident method does not readily lend itself to objective quantification, it offers a strong advantage for purposes of employee counseling because it provides the supervisor with a record of "specifics" to discuss with the employee.

Behavioral Checklists and Scales

Another basic method of personnel rating uses some type of behavioral checklist or rating scale. The rater is given descriptive statements of job-related "behavior" and is asked to indicate, in one way or another, those statements which are (or might be expected to be) descriptive of the individual in question. Thus, the rater tends to be more a *reporter* of *the work behavior* of

individuals than an evaluator of their performance or of their personal characteristics.

Because these methods are difficult and time-consuming to develop, they usually can be justified only if they are to be used widely. They offer some advantages, however, that warrant their serious consideration for circumstances in which they would be widely used.

WEIGHTED CHECKLIST. This rating system consists of a list of statements of work behavior such as those shown in Table 6.1. The weighted checklist is based on the Thurstone scaling procedure (Thurstone & Chave, 1929). The checklist in Table 6.1, reported by Knauft (1948), was prepared for rating bake shop managers. In rating an employee, the rater simply checks each statement that describes the work behavior of the individual. (The scale values shown are *not* on the rating form but are used later in deriving the person's rating.)

The procedures used in developing such a checklist will be described. First, many statements are written that describe, in relatively objective terms, various aspects of work behavior, ranging from desirable to undesirable. Next, these statements are "judged" by a number of "experts" on the *degree* to which they are considered to indicate favorable or unfavorable behavior. This is done by the method of "equal-appearing intervals" in which the judges classify the statements in categories ranging from those they consider extremely favorable to those they consider extremely unfavorable.

These judgments then are summarized and analyzed in order to identify the statements that are most reliably judged. Table 6.2 illustrates three hypothetical examples as "judged" by ten judges. Statement A was placed in the same category (4) by all ten judges and is therefore a highly stable item. Statement B, for which the judgments are quite variable, is a very unstable item. Statement C has moderate stability.

TABLE 6.1 EXAMPLES OF ITEMS FROM WEIGHTED CHECK LIST PERFOR-
MANCE RATING FOR BAKE SHOP MANAGER

Item	Scale Value
Window display always has customer appeal.	8.5
Encourages employees to show initiative.	8.1
Seldom forgets what has once been told.	7.6
Sales per customer are relatively high.	7.4
Has originated one or more workable new formulas.	6.4
Belongs to a local merchants' association.	4.9
Weekly and monthly reports are sometimes inaccurate.	4.2
Does not anticipate probable emergencies.	2.4
Is slow to discipline employees even when needed.	1.9
Rarely figures the costs of products.	1.0
Often has vermin and insects in the shop.	0.8

Source: Adapted from Knauft, (1948). Copyright 1948 by the American Psychological Association, and adapted by permission.

The scale value assigned to an item usually is the mean or median of the categories
in which the statement has been classified
by the several judges. A possible fallacy in
the use of the median for this was pointed
out by Jurgensen (1949). The fallacy is that
for some individuals many more items are
checked by the rater in the top half of the
scale than in the lower half. Jurgensen
proposed that median values be replaced
by positive and negative values obtained by
subtracting the mid-value of the scale (4, 5,
or 6 depending on whether there are 7, 9,
or 11 categories in the scale) from each
median. The rating score for each individual then would be the algebraic sum of
these revised weights for the items checked
by the rater.

This scale also can be used for a more
generally applicable rating procedure, as
illustrated by the results of a study by Uhrbrock (1950) in which 724 behavioral statements were scaled in this manner. A few
examples are given in Table 6.3, along with
their scale values based on the judgments
of twenty foremen. The "variability" column has an index of the variability of the
judgments (the smaller this value, the
greater the degree of consistency in the
judgments).

FORCED-CHOICE CHECKLIST. In
forced-choice rating systems, two or more

TABLE 6.2 HYPOTHETICAL EXAMPLES OF JUDGMENTS BY TEN JUDGES
ON THREE CHECKLIST RATING STATEMENTS*

	Rating Category								
	Unfavorable							Favorable	
Statement	1	2	3	4	5	6	7	8	9
A				10					
B		1	2		1	3	2	1	
C	2	5	3						

*The number entered under each category is the number of judges who placed the
statement in that category.

69

TABLE 6.3 SCALE VALUES OF SELECTED CHECKLIST RATING SCALE
STATEMENTS AS DERIVED FROM JUDGMENTS OF TWENTY FOREMEN

Statement	Scale* Value	Variability†
6. Makes the same mistakes over and over.	14	33
34. Is a clock-watcher.	22	179
83. Can't seem to get the hang of things.	29	79
171. Conduct borders on insubordination.	36	535
238. Can do good work if he (she) tries.	49	79
257. Never quits ahead of time.	64	124
277. Is orderly in work habits.	69	219
377. Gets production out in less than average time.	79	109
498. Can concentrate under difficult conditions.	90	190
539. Merits the very highest recommendation.	107	51

*Scale values have been multiplied by 10 to avoid decimal values.
†The "variability" is the square of the standard deviation of the placements multiplied by 100. It can be interpreted as a relative index of the consistency of judgments.
Source: Uhrbrock (1950).

statements (typically statements of behavior) are grouped together, and the rater is asked to indicate which statement is most descriptive of the person being rated (and in some cases which is least descriptive). In practice there are a number of variations in the method, such as differences in the number of statements in a block and in the number and type of response required. Some variations studied by Berkshire and Highland (1953) included blocks with two, three, four, and five statements, with certain groups including only favorable or unfavorable statements, but not both. The example of a block of forced-choice statements given below was drawn from a rating form used for rating Air Force instructors; all of these statements are "favorable."

a. Patient with slow learners.

b. Lectures with confidence.

c. Keeps interest and attention of class.

d. Acquaints classes in advance with objectives for each class.

The selection of the statements for each block is based on extensive preliminary research to determine the *degree* to which each statement is considered by raters generally to be "favorable" or "unfavorable" (favorability index) and the extent to which the statement, when used in a rating situation, tends to *discriminate* between above-average and below-average individuals (discrimination index). The statements are then grouped together on the basis of relatively comparable favorability indexes; the statements above, for example, have been placed in the same block because they have approximately *equal favorability* indexes. The items placed in a block, however, *differ* in their *discrimination* indexes. Usually only one item in a block is a discriminative item.

A major advantage of this method is that the rater, who may attempt (consciously or unconsciously) to rate a person higher or lower than the person's "true" worth, has no way of knowing which of the statements to check to raise (or lower) the rating from what it should be. There are, however, certain disadvantages to the method. First, because the rater does not (and should not) know how the final rating values are derived, he may resent the system as a whole and therefore may not give it whole-hearted support. In addition, the method does not lend itself readily to counseling the employee.

Of the various versions of this method, Berkshire and Highland found that the form with four favorable statements from which the rater was to select the two most like the ratee had advantages over other forms. It was the most resistant to bias; it yielded consistently high validities under various conditions; it had adequate reliability; and it was one of the two forms preferred by the raters.

In some situations, the forced-choice method is used in combination with other rating procedures. This has the advantage of making the combined rating procedure useful for more purposes.

BEHAVIORAL EXPECTATION SCALES (BES). Most types of rating scales have been around for many years in one form or another. More recently, there has been a flurry of interest in what are called behavioral expectation scales (BES). (They also

are called scaled expectancy rating scales and behaviorally anchored rating scales.) The original scales were developed by Smith and Kendall (1963) for use with nurses. These scales typically are developed for the evaluation of incumbents in a specific type of job and provide for rating the incumbents on each of several "dimensions." A typical example is one developed for department store managers (Dunnette, Campbell, & Hellervic 1968). The scale for one of the dimensions is shown in Table 6.4. Each scale consists of a list of "scaled expectancies," each one describing a job-related "behavior" that a job incumbent might possibly be "expected" to demonstrate in his work. Note that these are ordered from low (very undesirable behaviors) to high (very desirable behaviors), the numbers from 1 to 9 representing the "scale." The rater is asked to indicate the behavior that the person being rated would be "expected" to demonstrate. In this par-

TABLE 6.4 BEHAVIORAL EXPECTATION SCALE, FOR USE WITH DEPARTMENT STORE MANAGERS ON DIMENSION OF "MEETING DAY-TO-DAY DEADLINES"

Meeting Day-to-Day Deadlines

Instructions to rater: In the job as department manager how well are the day-to-day deadlines met? Consider not only *typical* job behavior but also the *best* job performance. Write BEST on the scale opposite the action that seems to fit most closely when the manager is doing the best in meeting day-to-day deadlines. Write TYPICAL opposite that action that seems to fit most closely when doing the usual or typical job in meeting day-to-day deadlines.

9. Could be expected *never* to be late in meeting deadlines, no matter how unusual the circumstances.

8. Could be expected to meet deadlines comfortably by delegating the writing of an unusually high number of orders to two highly rated selling associates.

7. Could be expected always to get associates' work schedules made out on time.

6. Could be expected to meet seasonal ordering deadlines within a reasonable length of time.

5. Could be expected to offer to do the orders at home after failing to get them out on the deadline day.

4. Could be expected to fail to schedule additional help to complete orders on time.

3. Could be expected to be late all the time on weekly buys for his department.

2. Could be expected to disregard due dates in ordering and run out of a major line in his department.

1. Could be expected to leave order forms in the desk drawer for several weeks even when they had been given to the manager by the buyer after calling attention to short supplies and due dates for orders.

Source: Adapted from Dunnette, M.D., Campbell, J.P., & Hellervic, L.W. Job behavior scales for Penney Company Department Managers, Figure 5.2. Minneapolis: Personnel Decisions, 1968.

ticular example the rater marks two statements for the ratee, one representing the "best" behavior he would expect of the individual, and the other representing the "typical" behavior he would expect, such expectations being based on observation of the individual in the past. The development of such scales is admittedly time consuming and rather difficult. One does not simply pull them out of one's sleeve. We will summarize the procedures in their development, as adapted from Schwab and others (1975).

1. *Obtaining critical incidents.* First, individuals familiar with the job in question (like job holders or supervisors) are asked to write statements illustrating specific, observed effective and ineffective job performance. These are "critical incidents." This step is patterned after the critical incident technique that was described above.

2. These critical incidents then are *clustered into sets* of tentative performance dimensions based on judgments of those developing the scale of similarity of content, each dimension then being defined.

3. Another group of persons familiar with the job usually is then asked to *"retranslate" (or reallocate) the incidents* to the dimensions that have been developed. In effect they are asked to assign each incident to the dimension that they think it best describes. Typically an incident is retained in its original dimension if some specified percentage (usually 50 percent to 80 percent) of the group assigns it to the dimension in question.

4. *Scaling incidents.* A number of job-knowledgeable individuals (usually those in the second group in step 3) are asked to rate the behaviors described by the statements as to how effectively or ineffectively they represent performance on the appropriate dimensions. This usually is done using a seven- or nine-point rating scale. The procedures here are essentially the same as those for the weighted checklist rating

scale. As in the weighted checklist scale, the retained behavior statements are those that represent various positions along the scale from unfavorable to favorable (that is, poor to good performance) and in addition are statements for which there has been reasonable agreement in the ratings assigned by the different raters.

5. *Final instrument.* The final instrument consists of a subset of incidents that represent various positions along each performance dimension. Most typically one is selected to represent each scale position such as 1, 2, 3, etc., to 7 or 9). They are worded as illustrated in Table 6.4, each starting with "Could be expected to. . . ." The final instrument then consists of a series of vertical scales, one for each dimension, anchored by the incidents retained. Each statement is located on the scale at the position established by its rating.

Certain variations of these procedures have been used in some circumstances and have been subjected to experimental analysis. For example Bernardin, LaShells, and others (1976) compared two scoring methods. One of these (a procedure originally proposed by Smith and Kendall) was based on the practice of having the rater record, for each ratee, at least three critical incidents applicable to the ratee, assigning scale values to them on the basis of the judgment as to where they "fitted in" with the other incidents on the dimension in question. These newly scaled items then were averaged for the ratee, this average being the score for the dimension in question. The other scoring procedure, the most commonly used, was a "summary" rating reflected by the single scale value checked for the ratee on the dimension. The first of these methods (based on averaging of scale values of incidents specifically applicable to the ratees) was found to be somewhat superior in that it reduced the tendency toward leniency in ratings and increased discrimination across raters.

The usual development of such scales provides for the active participation of job incumbents and/or supervisors in various stages of the process, as in the development of the critical incidents at the beginning, the development of the dimensions, and the "scaling" (that is, the rating) of the incidents used in the final selection of incidents for the dimension scales. The collective knowledge and judgments of such participants aids in developing the scales. One of the major arguments for behavioral expectation scales is that such participation contributes significantly to the acceptance of the scales so developed.

Research and experience with behavioral expectation scales represent something of a mixed bag. Schwab and others (1975, p. 557), for example, commented that, despite the intuitive appeal of such scales, " . . . findings from research have not been very encouraging". On the basis of their review of relevant research they expressed the opinion that there is little reason to believe that such scales were superior to other types of scales. Although such scales have not yet been found to "solve" the problem of personnel evaluation, it probably can be said that they deserve a place in the repertoire of rating methods available for industry, in those circumstances to which they might be especially relevant. In any event, they should be studied further, possibly to improve them.

We should add one more comment. In their typical applications, behavioral expectation scales are developed and used within the framework of specific jobs. In this regard Goodale and Burke (1975) suggested that the procedure may well lend itself to use across a number of jobs and provided some evidence to support this contention. This broader application would require the use of "dimensions" applicable to various jobs and examples of incidents with rather general applicability. The dimensions they used experimentally were: interpersonal relationships, organizing and planning, reaction to problems, reliability, communicating, adaptability, growth, productivity, quality of work, and teaching.

BEHAVIORAL OBSERVATION SCALES (BOS). Behavioral observation scales (BOS) are a rather recently developed approach to personnel rating and have been used in only a limited number of circumstances. Like behavioral expectation scales (BES), they are based on critical incidents (discussed above). Although the BES scales provide for rating in terms of how the ratee would be "expected" to perform relative to the scaled examples of each dimension, the BOS scales provide for rating by the rater of the frequency of the "incidents" listed on the rating scale that he actually observed in the ratees over a period of time (such as a month). An example of a behavioral item for appraising salespeople, as given by Latham and Wexley (1977), is given below:

"Knows the price of competitive products."
Never Seldom Sometimes Generally Always
 1   2   3   4   5

The rater simply records the frequency of observing the employee engaging in the behavior in question, usually using frequency categories such as 0%-19%, 20%-39%, 40%-59%, 60%-79%, and 80%-100%.

Another variation of behavioral observation scales was given by Dunnette (1970, p. 16), this also dealing with sales activities, particularly of department store managers. Examples of a few items are given below:

The behaviors used can be grouped into categories based on subjective judgments of the similarity of their content, or based on a factor analysis of ratings of frequencies of observed occurrences. These two procedures result in what Latham and Wexley called, respectively, qualitative and quantitative BOS scales.

	Almost Always	Usually	Sometimes	Very Rarely
Re-evaluates sales trends and takes them into account in maintaining up-to-date merchandising position in the department.	___	___	___	___
Is acutely attuned to merchandising trends related to competitor's merchandising activities.	___	___	___	___
Shops competitors' stores, when appropriate, to gather information about sales trends and customer preferences.	___	___	___	___
Is flexible and quick in changing the ordering, stocking, and merchandising procedures to reflect accurately the assessments of sales trends.	___	___	___	___
Takes quick action to gather more information in response to customer requests for new or different items.	___	___	___	___

In one instance in which such scales were used in rating three hundred supervisors of logging crews (that is, "producers") Latham and Wexley (1977) used scales consisting of seventy-eight statements of job behavior. Based on rating data obtained from "dealers" (who dealt continuously with the supervisor-producers) they carried out a factor analysis that identified ten factors. The results from this scale (a quantitative BOS scale) then were compared with the results from a previous study (Latham, Wexley, & Rand 1975) in which an eight-factor qualitative scale had been used in similar circumstances. Although the interrater reliability coefficients for the two types of BOS scales were about the same (.80), they differed in their correlations with three relatively objective cost-related criteria of performance of the supervisor—producers being rated, namely, productivity, absenteeism, and attendance on the part of the logging crews being supervised. These correlations are given below:

These and other data suggest that the quantitative BOS scales may have some advantage over the qualitative BOS scales. It should be added, however, that the development of the quantitative type of scale requires rating data for a large sample of individuals for the factor analysis phase. When such a sample is not available, the qualitative variety should be used. It should also be added that BOS scales are most effective when the raters have a continuous opportunity over a period of time to observe those to be rated, in order to be able to estimate the frequency of the behaviors in question.

MIXED STANDARD SCALE. Another somewhat experimental personnel rating method is the mixed standard scale, originally developed in Finland by Blanz and later used in a study of managers by Blanz and Ghiselli (1972). The rating system consists of a description of three degrees of each trait or factor for which ratings are to be obtained, one characterizing a high degree of the factor, one a moderate degree,

		Criterion	
Type of BOS scale	Productivity	Absenteeism	Attendance
Qualitative	.37	.31	.45
Quantitative	.50	.46	.66

and one a low degree. These three descriptions for each rating factor are randomized, so the rater is not presented with "identifiable" scales for the various rating factors. Neither is the order of merit of the descriptions of the three degrees of the various factors apparent in the format of the rating materials.

Raters are asked to rate each ratee in terms of whether they consider the ratee "better than," "worse than," or the "same as" each "description" in the randomized list. It is postulated that the "mixed" nature of the rating form helps to minimize the tendency toward leniency in the ratings and toward giving somewhat equal ratings for each of the several rating factors (the "halo" effect). It is also believed that the system would make it possible to identify less competent raters by determining how inconsistent the raters are in their ratings (as reflected, for example, in giving a "better than" rating for the "high" degree description of a factor and a "worse than" rating for the "moderate" or "low" degree description). This type of rating has not been used much, but in one study of the rating of police officers, Saal and Landy (1977) found that it did tend to reduce the leniency and halo effect, although its reliability was not particularly good.

Other Rating Methods

Other methods of personnel rating are sometimes used. One is a group evaluation plan in which each person is evaluated by a group of supervisors during a conference. In certain situations a "free written" rating procedure is used; in this procedure the evaluator (usually a supervisor) "describes" the person in question by writing a "word picture" of that person. In other circumstances those being evaluated participate in some type of group problem, discussion, or "game," and the evaluation is made by observers.

RELIABILITY AND VALIDITY OF PERSONNEL RATINGS

The potential utility of personnel evaluations and assessments depends in large part on their *reliability* and *validity*.

Reliability

The reliability of ratings refers to the consistency with which the ratings are made. There are two bases for determining the reliability of ratings. One of these is interrater reliability, the consistency of two or more raters who rate the same individuals. The other is consistency over time (sometimes called rate-rerate reliability), the extent to which the same rater in rating the same individuals on two or more occasions several days apart gives about the same rating to any given ratee at different times. Reliability frequently is measured with a coefficient of correlation between two sets of ratings for the same individuals (either ratings by two different raters or two ratings by the same rater). In using ratings either for research or for administration, the reliability of the ratings usually should be determined.

The reliability of ratings can be influenced by several factors, such as the type of rating system being used, the dimensions or "factors" on which the ratings are being made, the familiarity of the raters with the ratee, and the ability of the raters to make the required judgments. Although it is impossible to make very definite generalizations about the reliability of personnel ratings, a few examples may at least show the variability of reliabilities that have been reported and demonstrate that in some circumstances the reliabilities are, unfortunately, rather poor.

In one comparison of the interrater reliability of behavioral expectation scales with a couple of more conventional rating scales, Bernardin (1977) reported the following correlations: behavioral expectation scale, .74 and conventional rating scales, .72 and .70. This particular study was based on the ratings of instructors by students. In the analysis of ratings of 342 police officers by their supervisors in eleven cities, Landy and others (1976) reported median reliability coefficients for pairs of raters ranging from .57 to .74 for the eight rating scale dimensions used. (The rating scales were behavioral expectation scales.) As other examples of rater reliability, Borman and Vallon (1974) reported interrater reliability coefficients of the ratings of hospital nurses as follows: behavioral expectation scale, .61, conventional scale, .56. In still another study of the interrater reliability of ratings on the twelve factors of a conventional rating scale for industrial workers, the reliablity coefficients ranged from a low of .35 to .55.

Although overall comparisons of the reliability of various types of rating scales are admittedly risky, there are some hints that the reliability of personnel comparison systems generally seems to be reasonably respectable. For example, the reliability coefficients of rank order ratings reported by Taylor (undated) ranged from .85 to .95. In a study of the paired comparison ratings of three groups of employees by two raters, the correlations between the various pairs of raters ranged from .81 to .86, with an average of .83 (Lawshe and others, 1949).

The reliability of forced-choice ratings is also quite respectable, as reflected by the results of the study by Berkshire and Highland (1953). The split-half and rate-rerate reliability coefficients for different variations of numbers and types of item within the "blocks" were:

Split-half (6 variations): .74, .82, .85, .90, .95, .96

Test-retest (4 variations): .59, .72, .72, .74

To the extent that ratings are unreliable, one cannot regard small differences (as for the same person at different times or for different persons) as reflections of "real" differences in the attribute being rated. (By a simple statistical procedure it is possible to compute what is called the standard error of measurement of a set of ratings. Unless two ratings differ by more than three standard errors of measurement, it is unsafe to assume that they reflect true differences.)

Validity of Ratings

The validity of ratings is associated with the extent to which they reflect the "true" variable being evaluated—such as a human attribute, some aspect of behavior, or job performance. It must be said, however, that determining the validity of ratings is difficult and often impossible. By all odds, the best way of doing this is to obtain an independent, external "true" criterion for a sample of ratees and then to determine the relationship (such as with a correlation) between the ratings and the criterion. The problem here is that "true" criteria are hard to come by; in fact they rarely exist. In the few reported studies in which ratings have been correlated with some type of separate criterion, the resulting correlations tended to have only moderate magnitude, as reported by Barrett (1966). Although such results are not very encouraging, it should be noted that the evidence here is quite sparse.

An alternative to the possible use of the seldom available external "true" criteria to evaluate ratings systems was suggested by Borman (1978). In particular he proposed using videotapes that depict the "performance" of individuals. In the study in which this technique was used, there were sixteen scripts, each depicting either a manager talking with a problem subordinate or a recruiter interviewing a prospective employee. The scripts reflected as closely as possible the performance levels defined by the intended true scores. Actors were selected to play each role. The same actor played the recruitee in all eight recruiter performances, and another actor played the disgruntled employee in all eight manager performances. Sixteen different actors played the various recruiter and manager roles. Each actor conformed closely to the script during the videotaping session.

With this technique, the "criterion" values are "built in" to the scripts, with the various scripts reflecting varying degrees of performance on the job in question. The raters then are asked to rate the "performance" of the employees so depicted. In turn, the ratings given by the raters (using whatever rating scales are provided) then are analyzed in relation to the "criterion" values associated with the performance depicted in the various scripts. Although this scheme uses a simulated situation (and does not use ratings such as those obtained in real-world circumstances), it probably does offer the advantage of being able to compare different rating practices or procedures and of trying to identify sources of rater error.

A less direct scheme for evaluating the validity of ratings is to analyze the variability and dispersion of the ratings on the various factors in the rating system being used. Considering any *given* rating factor, it is assumed that variability of the ratings given to the various ratees reflects discrimination by the raters in evaluating different individuals on the factor in question. Considering the ratings on *different* factors, it is assumed that substantial dispersion of the ratings given to individuals reflects discrimination by the raters in evaluating each individual on the various rating factors. Dispersion alludes to the halo effect mentioned briefly before, and that will be discussed further a bit later.

Although variability and dispersion of ratings do not furnish proof positive of the validity of ratings, they can at least be considered as hints in that direction. In addi-tion, respectable reliability of the ratings (particularly interrater reliability) can add confidence in the ratings.

SOURCES OF POSSIBLE DISTORTIONS IN RATINGS

In our previous discussion of personnel ratings, there have been some suggestions of undesirable distortions in the ratings. These possible distortions can arise from various sources, including certain raters' tendencies, contamination from extraneous sources, and inappropriate weighting of factors.

Raters' Tendencies

Some of the distortions in personnel evaluation arise from rather common tendencies by raters, in particular the halo effect, the constant error, and what we will call rating restriction, and raters' stereotypes.

THE HALO EFFECT. The halo effect already has been mentioned, in the discussion of the dispersion of ratings. Many years ago Thorndike (1920) pointed out that on the basis of experimental evidence, some raters have a tendency to rate an individual either high or low on many factors because the rater knows (or thinks) the individual to be high or low on some specific factor. Thorndike called this tendency the "halo" effect. Applied to the industrial situation, this means that if a supervisor regards an employee as very satisfactory in one factor (such as general personality or tact), the supervisor is likely to rate the employee high also on other factors (such as productivity, ingenuity, inventiveness, and adaptability). In general, the result of the halo effect is that ratings on various factors tend to have higher correlations with each other than would otherwise be the case.

Some evidence of the halo effect comes from a study by DeCotiis (1977) in which he had twenty-eight police supervisors rate police officers in a somewhat simulated context, using three types of rating scales, as follows: a behavioral expectation scale with six dimensions; a "trait" rating scale providing for rating police officers on each of eleven undefined personal traits or performance characteristics (such as knowledge of assigned duties, initiative, and reaction to stress); and a numerically anchored rating scale providing for rating on each of ten job performance factors (such as judgment, quality of work, and cooperation). For each of the three rating scales, correlations were computed between the ratings of each pair of factors in the scale in question. (Recalling the reference to the number of pairs in the paired comparison method, the number of correlations for each of the scales would be based on the number of rating factors and would be 15, 55, and 45, respectively.) The median and range of these correlations for each of the three scales are given below:

Scale	Correlations Median	Range
Behavioral expectation scale	.73	.27
Trait rating scale	.91	.15
Numerically anchored rating scale	.85	.28

These correlations are all quite high, reflecting a strong tendency by the raters to assign ratings to individuals across the several rating factors at somewhat corresponding levels, thus suggesting the possible influence of the halo effect.

In another study of the ratings of police officers (but rating "real" officers rather than "simulated" officers) Landy and others (1976) made a similar analysis of ratings of all pairs of eight dimensions of a behavioral expectation scale. The medians of the intercorrelations for the eight dimensions ranged from .54 to .67, which probably still reflect a fairly high degree of halo. In another investigation in which students rated university instructors (Bernardin, Alvares, and Cranny 1976), corresponding types of correlations were somewhat lower: .49, .39, and .36 for three types of rating scales. (The first two scales were conventional scales, and the third was a behavioral expectation scale.)

The halo effect is indeed a problem in ratings, in part because one seldom can know what the "true" correlations are between rating factors. It is undoubtedly true that many desirable traits and job-related behaviors are in fact correlated with each other. Everyday observation of friends, acquaintances, and others tends to support, in common-sense fashion, the tendency for "desirable" (and undesirable) human qualities to "go together" in individuals. At the same time, one should take a somewhat jaundiced view regarding, highly correlated factors. In any event, the organization using a personnel rating system should have information on the correlation between and among the various rating factors in order to evaluate better the ratings of their employees.

CONSTANT ERROR. The constant error is a tendency to concentrate the ratings in one section of the rating scale, such as toward the upper end of the scale (sometimes referred to as the *leniency tendency*), in the center of the scale (the *error of central tendency*), or toward the lower end of the scale. These tendencies all were reflected in the ratings obtained from different raters in one company in which the ratings made by one supervisor averaged 405 points out of a possible 600, whereas those of another supervisor averaged 295 points. Probably the most common type of constant error is the leniency tendency, the tendency to concentrate the ratings toward the upper end of the scale. If various raters within an organization do demonstrate different raters' tendencies (as reflected by significant differences in their average ratings), and if the purpose of the ratings requires the comparison of ratings across raters, one cannot compare equitably the actual rating values of individuals rated by different raters. Rather, it is necessary to convert the different sets of ratings to a common numerical scale, in particular, some type of standard score system. Such procedures will be discussed later.

RATING RESTRICTION. Another type of raters' tendency, somewhat tied to the constant error, is that of rating restriction. This is the tendency to use only a restrict-range of the rating scale when assigning ratings to individuals. This restriction sometimes occurs in combination with the leniency tendency since the leniency tendency frequently is characterized by a clustering of most of the ratings near the top of the scale. Rating restriction usually is reflected by a small standard deviation of the ratings or by a narrow range of ratings across those who are rated.

RATERS' STEREOTYPES. Another factor associated with raters that can adversely influence personnel ratings is that of some raters' stereotypes. Attitudinal stereotypes typically characterize biases associated with persons of various groups, perhaps most commonly sex and race. The biases in many aspects of life prompted the establishment of the Equal Employment Opportunity Commission (EEOC), that is charged with helping to ensure equal employment opportunities for all individuals. A number of studies have demonstrated that there are influences on the ratings as given by some individuals by reason of certain personal characteristics of the ratees such as sex, race, and age (Bigoness 1976; Rosen & Jerdee 1976; and Terborg & Ilgen 1975). Most such studies, however, have been carried out in simulated laboratory settings rather than in actual work situations. There is relatively little good data available from actual work situations on the nature or extent of the influence of stereotypes by raters as related to the personnel ratings given. In this regard, sometimes field research has implied that the job and group membership of job incumbents are confounded. For example, some studies that purport to demon-

strate that stereotopic biases in ratings of women are based on samples of employees in which the women generally hold lower status jobs than men do. Regardless of the reason for the differences in the job distributions of men and women in such samples, it is not possible to tell if the differences in the ratings of men and women are due to stereotyping in ratings, to differences in their jobs, or to actual differences in their job performance.

Before we obtain more adequate data based on ratings from actual work situations, it is probable that the best strategy for personnel administrators is to provide adequate training for raters, emphasizing the desirability of minimizing the influence of personal biases when rating individuals.

Contamination of Ratings

In the previous chapter the possible contamination of various types of criteria was mentioned. Contamination can likewise occur in personnel ratings, as when raters are influenced, perhaps unknowingly, by various factors extraneous to whatever is being rated. Among such extraneous factors are the organizational unit, the job of the ratee, and length of experience of the ratee. These and other factors can be sources of contamination of ratings.

ORGANIZATIONAL UNIT. Frequently the ratings reported from one organizational unit (such as a department) are different from those from other units. Although such differences may be due in part to "true" differences in the performance of individuals in the various units, it is also possible that they may result from differences in the standards or rating "policies" of raters in the different units. Illustrations of the actual differences in ratings of three departments in one company are shown in Figure 6.2. From this we can see that a rating of 350 would be very low for a man in the engineering department, approxi-

Job level:	A (low)	B	C	D	E	F (high)
Mean rating (1 = high; 5 = low):	4.0	3.6	3.4	2.3	2.3	2.5

mately average for a man in the maintenance department, and very high for a man in the plant-protection department.

JOB DIFFERENCES. There sometimes are somewhat similar differences in the ratings of people on various jobs. In a steel mill, for example, the average ratings of people on various jobs ranged from about 385 for tinners to about 275 for openers and examiners. The same tendency was reported by Klores (1966, p. 416) for professional personnel in various job levels, as shown below.

DISCUSSION. Data could be given to illustrate the relationship between ratings and various other factors. For example, a summarization of the ratings of the nine thousand personnel in the steel mill mentioned before showed that the average rat-

ings decreased from those with less than five years of service to those with twenty-five or more years. Referring to the discussion of stereotypes based on age, the data also showed that personnel between the ages of thirty and thirty-five had higher average ratings than those who were younger or older.

The existence of differences in ratings between groups does not necessarily imply contamination of the ratings. In part such differences may be valid. For example, it is possible that the higher average ratings mentioned above for personnel between thirty and thirty-five years of age could be valid, perhaps because younger workers are less experienced and older members are "slowing down." Thus, such differences need to be interpreted with caution.

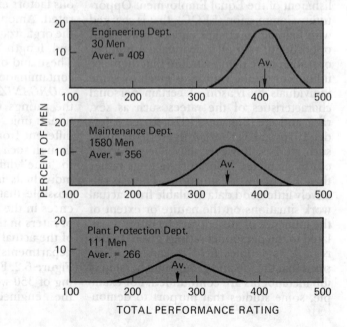

FIG. 6.2 Differences in performance ratings among departments in a steel mill.

Engineering Dept.
30 Men
Aver. = 409
Av.

Maintenance Dept.
1580 Men
Aver. = 356
Av.

Plant Protection Dept.
111 Men
Aver. = 266
Av.

PERCENT OF MEN

TOTAL PERFORMANCE RATING

Some of the relationships mentioned in our illustrations, it should be noted, will not necessarily be found in other organizations. Indeed, obverse relationships might be found in other organizations. The point to keep in mind is that the organization should know what these relationships are and should try to figure out the basis for them in order to judge whether they are "true" differences or whether they represent some form of contamination.

WEIGHTING FACTORS IN RATING SCALES

Certain types of rating systems provide for ratings to be made on each of several factors or dimensions, especially conventional rating scales, behavioral rating scales, and behavioral observation scales. Different dimensions of performance also can be measured with other types of rating systems. For example, it would be possible with personnel comparison systems to provide for ratings on different factors, although this is not commonly done. (One could, for instance, have individuals ranked first on one factor and then on another.)

When different factors are to be rated (as with conventional rating scales), it is often necessary to combine the ratings on the various factors to derive a total rating for each individual. This immediately raises the question of how to combine or weight the factors. The simplest way is simply to add the rating values for each individual on all the factors to derive a total score for each individual. If the scale for each factor had the same number of scale values (such as from 1 to 50), the intent of such addition would be to give *equal weighting* to each factor. As discussed later, however, this does not necessarily result in equal weighting of the factors.

The equal weighting of factors (even if it is achieved) may not be appropriate to some jobs because different factors may differ in their importance to different jobs. For example, technical competence and interpersonal skills may be needed for a com-

puter programmer who works as an internal consultant to an organization. If a programmer were highly competent technically, however, the organization probably could tolerate a few rough edges in the programmer's interpersonal skills. In other words, ratings on technical competence should be weighted more heavily than ratings on interpersonal skills. In such a job, then, the factors should have differential weighting. Differential weights assigned to different factors usually are based on the judgment of those responsible for the personnel rating program, but there are methods available by which weightings can be based on statistical analyses. (One such procedure involves a large number of cases, the availability of a very good "overall" criterion, and the use of regression analysis procedures.) If a decision is made to apply differential weights to the factors in a rating system, it is usually implemented by setting up scales value ranges that reflect the intended weights (such as assigning a range from 1–10 for one factor and from 1–20 for a factor intended to have twice the weight of the first one). In some instances in which the scale value ranges of the different factors are the same, the ratings assigned to individuals are multiplied by the intended weights for the specific factors.

If the *intended* weights of individual factors are appropriate (whether they be differential or equal), the *actual* weights of the various factors can differ from the *intended* weights. This effect arises from the fact that, when one combines scores, the scores in part weight themselves *automatically* in proportion to their *respective variability*. In statistical terms they weight themselves in proportion to their respective standard deviations. Let us take the hypothetical case of two factors, each of which can be rated on a fifty-point scale. If the variability of the ratings of all employees on one of the factors—say judgment—is two times as large as the variability on the other factor—say initiative—and assuming reasonably normal distributions, the addition of the ratings for each employee on these two factors results in the *actual* weighting of the "judgment" ratings being twice that of the "initiative" weightings. If they are to have equal weights or differential weights (other than 2 to 1), some statistical adjustment must be made. The statistical explanation for this effect is discussed in Appendix A.

Continuing with this example, let us suppose that, using the fifty-point scale for each of the two factors, the ratings of all the employees on initiative range from 20 to 30 and on judgment range from 10 to 40. Any person's combined rating would be the sum of the ratings on these two factors. It has often been assumed that in such instances the two factors would be weighted equally because both originally were rated on the same scale. Under these circumstances, however, the factors are not weighted equally at all. The judgment ratings, which vary over a range of 30 points —from 10 to 40—will have approximately three times as much effect on the combined ratings as the ratings on initiative do, which vary over a range of only ten points—from 20 to 30.

The simple adding of ratings for several factors not only can fail to weight the factors equally (if equal weights are intended) but also can fail to give them any preassigned weights. Suppose, for example, that management has decided that accuracy is twice as important as production is, and therefore has adopted a rating system in which accuracy is rated on a forty-point scale and production on a twenty-point scale. This arrangement will not necessarily result in accuracy being weighted twice as heavily as production, for the relative weights of the factors are determined by the *variability* or *spread* of the actual ratings on each, and *not* by the maximum values or by the range of values assigned to each.

Adjusting Ratings for Raters' Tendencies or Distortion

When there is evidence, or even strong suspicion, that ratings have been distorted by raters' tendencies or by contamination, the ratings cannot be accepted as actual reflections of "true" evaluations of the individuals in question. In this case, there is a question about how one can use these ratings or, indeed, whether one can use them at all. Of course, the distortions are not important *if* there is reasonable validity among the ratings, and *if* the ratings are to be used *entirely within the context of the group.* But if the ratings are to be compared *between or among* groups of ratees, they should *not* be used *unless* they are adjusted for whatever distortions may exist. There are at least two ways of doing this.

ADJUSTING FOR DIFFERENCES IN MEANS. Let us use, as an example, the situation in which the ratings given by different raters differ significantly. Then, one solution is to determine the average of the ratings given by each rater and compute the difference between *each rater's* average and the average of *all raters*. This difference then can be added to or subtracted from the ratings given by a particular rater, in order to bring them into alignment with those of other raters. This simple adjustment is satisfactory if the *variabilities* of the ratings given by the different raters are about the same. The variability in the distributions of ratings can be compared by comparing their *standard deviations.* (See Appendix A, pp. 426–442 for a discussion of the standard deviation.)

ADJUSTING FOR DIFFERENCES BY STANDARD SCORES. A more systematic method of adjusting for such differences is to convert all ratings to a common numerical scale. Some type of *standard score* (comparable score) may be used for this. There are various types of standard scores, such as z-scores. Standard scores, including z-scores, indicate the *relative* position of individual cases in a distribution. Such scores are based on deviations of individual cases from the mean and are expressed in *standard deviation units*. A "standard deviation" is a statistical index of the degree of variability of the cases within a distribution. It is expressed in terms of the numerical values of the original distribution. In a relatively normal distribution, two-thirds of the cases fall within one standard deviation above and below the mean, about 95 percent are within two standard deviations above and below the mean, and about 99 percent fall within three standard deviations. Thus, regardless of what the mean of a distribution is, or what the magnitude of its standard deviation is, it is possible to express the deviation of any given numerical value in terms of the number of standard deviation units it is above or below the mean. A z-score is simply the deviation of a given raw score from the mean expressed in standard deviation units.

Let us now see how this helps us in comparing the ratings produced by a "tough" rater with those produced by a "lenient" rater. Let us suppose that the distributions A and B of Figure 6.3 represent, respec-tively, the total ratings given to their respective groups by rater A and rater B. We can see clearly that a rating of 110 by itself is meaningless unless we relate it to the distribution of which it is a part. (It means a very high rating by rater A and a very low rating by rater B.) These two distributions can both be converted to z-scores, as illus-trated at certain points on the distributions by the broken lines and dotted lines from the basic rating scale to the z-score scale below it. We can now see that a rating of 110 by rater A would mean a z-score of *plus* 2, but by rater B would mean a z-score of *minus* 2, and that a rating of 100 from rater A would correspond to a rating of 125 from rater B, since both convert to z-scores of plus 1. Similar conversions can be made with other groups of ratees for which some form of contamination is apparent, as for employees on different jobs or in different departments.

Adjusting for Unintended Weights of Factors

We have seen that the actual or effective weights of different factors will be different from the intended weights if the *variabilities*

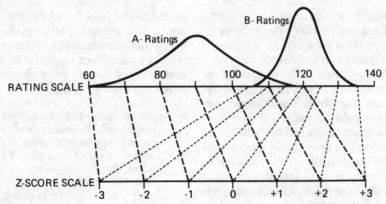

FIG. 6.3 Illustration of conversion of two sets of ratings (A and B) to a common scale of z-scores.

of the ratings for the various factors are markedly different. When this is the case, one solution to the problem caused by such differential variabilities is to convert the ratings on the different factors to standard scores (such as z-scores), to multiply these by their desired weights, and to sum up or average these weighted values.

ASSESSMENT CENTERS

Recently there has been a great deal of interest in what are called assessment centers. The typical objective of assessment centers is the evaluation of individuals for future development and growth. In most instances the individuals are current employees of organizations, most typically individuals in supervisory and management positions or those who are possible candidates for such positions. In certain instances, assessment centers are organized for applicants for employment (to assess their potential for employment) or for new employees (to provide assessments of their future assignments or development).

In part the interest in developing assessment centers has come from some of the problems in obtaining evaluations of employees by others in regular on-the-job situations, usually ratings made by supervisors. As discussed earlier, the ratings of employees on their jobs can be influenced by various factors extraneous to the "true" qualities being rated. Thus, ratings of different individuals might be distorted because they are rated by different raters, because of their jobs, because of their personal characteristics, and so on. Thus, one of the objectives in developing assessment centers is to "standardize" the situation in which people are assessed in order to gain more control of ratings by eliminating possible effect on the ratings caused by raters and by different situational variables.

The typical scheme used in assessment centers is to have a few or several "candidates" or "assessees" (those going through assessment) organized as a group which undergoes several types of individual and group activities or exercises over a period of one or more days, guided by a small staff of assessors. The activities and exercises include such things as management games, group discussions, tests, interviews, self-ratings, and problem-solving exercises. The final assessments by the staff are based on the "data" resulting from these activities (test scores, self-ratings, and so forth) and on the observations of the participants by the staff. In arriving at their judgments the staff can use a variety of specific assessment methods. The staff typically prepares a report on each individual; this report is then made available to certain managerial personnel as input for personnel development and promotion.

Methods and Techniques of Assessment

The specific programs used in various organizations obviously vary, but generally the methods and techniques of assessment greatly rely on the observations of behavior in contrived situations, designed to simulate the situations that would be experienced in the jobs for which the candidates are being assessed. For assessment centers for management types of personnel the typical procedures included in the assessment center battery were characterized by MacKinnon as follows:

An *In-Basket Test* which must be quickly completed. In-basket tests will be discussed in a later chapter, but in general terms consist of examples of memoranda, notes, letters, etc. such as typically are found in "in baskets," and provide for individuals to "do" something with these. Individuals are scored on the adequacy of their "actions" with these.

A *Leaderless Group Discussion of a Cooper-*

ative Nature in which, for example, a candidate assumes the role of a business consultant who—with five other consultants—receives data on a particular company and has the task of helping the group to decide whether to recommend that the company continue to operate or to sell out.

A *Leaderless Group Discussion of a Competitive Nature* in which, for example, each candidate is assigned the role of vice-president (Public Relations, Personnel, Manufacturing, and the like) of a company which, in a period of expansion, is considering the purchase of one of three new sites. The six "vice-presidents" are meeting to decide which of the sites should be selected. The conflict for each assessee is obvious: to win selection of the site he favors vs. selection of the best possible site for the company.

Dyadic situations are also employed in which, for example, the assessee is interviewed by his supervisor (played by a member of the assessment staff) concerning the actions he took in clearing his In-Basket; or the assessee (playing the role of a manager), interviews a capable but troublesome employee, a standardized role played by a staff member.

Individual exercises are frequently also included, such as a *Writing Exercise* as an example of written communication skills or a *Speaking Exercise* as an example of oral communication skills.

Other procedures sometimes used are a *Life-History Interview* with the assessee, which frequently builds upon a *Biographical Inventory Blank* which the candidate has filled out. The interview typically covers an assessee's personal history, work history, and the history of his goals and values. *Peer Ratings* and *Sociometric Ratings* as well as *Self-Ratings* are often collected. *Projective Tests,* most often the *Thematic Apperception Test* and a *Sentence Completion Test,* may be used to reveal the quality and strengths of the assessee's motivations, especially for a career in management.

Finally, *Psychometric Tests* of mental ability, interests, values, and personality are administered in some centers, but typically test scores are not used in making decisions or recommendations concerning candidates. They are used as a check upon decisions or recommendations already agreed upon, and are sometimes retained for later research. The time may come when psychometric tests may indeed be demonstrated to be efficient predictors of managerial behavior.

Assessment centers bring assessees and assessors together for varying periods of time. During that period, at meals, at coffee breaks, and at cocktail hours (if they are included in the program), a large variety of behaviors may be observed. Some assessment centers believe all these casual observations are grist for the assessment mill and they are so used; others believe that assessment and recommendations should be based solely upon behaviors and responses revealed in the formal exercises. (1975, pp. 6, 7)

In assessment centers for assessing individuals for nonmanagement positions, there usually would be other activities.

Operation of Assessment Centers

Assessment centers are scheduled for periods of from one day to a week and may be administered by staff members of the organization itself or by consultants. The "assessors" are sometimes psychologists and sometimes members of management. Usually the assessors receive some training.

In assessment centers for current employees of an organization, the candidates may be nominated by their supervisors or they may nominate themselves. If nominated by supervisors, the individuals are free to accept or reject the nominations. For applicants for employment, the assessment center usually is considered as one of the stages of the application process (although there presumably are very few instances in which assessment centers are used in the employment process).

After the assessment center activities, the staff typically discusses each candidate in the light of the data obtained. In turn, they usually prepare a report of the evaluations of the staff for management. Mac-Kinnon (1975) indicated that these reports are of two types, depending on the purpose of the assessment program. Most typically they describe the performance of the candidate in the assessment center and include ratings of the candidate on the rated variables, with an overall rating of the candidate's potential (such as managerial potential if selected or promoted). For companies that use the assessment findings in creating tailor-made programs for the development of their personnel, a second report, or a second part of a single report, has development recommendations. It also is usual to provide oral feedback to the candidates, sometimes accompanied by a written report to them.

In a very few instances assessment centers have been operated only for research. In these instances there have been no reports to management or feedback to the candidates.

Assessment Variables

The variables on which candidates are evaluated vary from organization to organization. The American Telephone and Telegraph Company (A.T.&T.) assessment program is an example (Bray and others 1974). Some of the dimensions on which their assessments are made are oral communication skill, human relations skill, creativity, self-objectivity, behavior flexibility, realism of expectations, energy, and decision making.

Reliability of Assessments

Since the assessments resulting from assessment center programs are essentially the judgments of the assessors, we should recognize that any indications of reliability reflect the reliability of judgments (albeit in certain cases they are based partially on somewhat objective measures). In a review of the reliability of such assessments Hinrichs and Haanperä (1976) reported the average interrater reliability across all rating dimensions for each of fifteen sets of ratings. These "average" reliability coefficients ranged from .23 to .92, with the median being .52.

They also reported the "internal consistency" reliability of assessment ratings on each of fourteen dimensions as used in assessment centers as operated by a large manufacturing company in eight countries. (The internal consistency reliability is a measure of the extent to which independent ratings in several exercises measured the overall "construct" of the dimension in question.) There were clear-cut differences in the reliability coefficients for various dimensions, varying from virtually zero for administrative ability to .73 for oral communications, with a median of .49. They concluded with good reason that the reliability of assessment center ratings left something to be desired and urged that assessment centers should focus on assessing those variables that can be reliably rated.

In some circumstances the reliability of assessments has not been quite as dismal as the "average" reliability data reported by Hinrichs and Haanperä. In summarizing data from the assessment center of a large midwestern utility company, for example, Schmitt (1977) reported interrater reliability coefficients for seventeen rating dimensions as ranging from .46 to .88, with most being in the .60s and .70s. These ratings were made by the assessors before discussing the candidates. Ratings made after discussing the candidates were systematically higher, ranging from .74 to .95.

In reflecting on the matter of reliability, it seems apparent that there are differences in the reliability of ratings on different dimensions and also for the same dimensions from one circumstance to another. The moral of all this is that the managers of assessment centers should analyze the obtained ratings in terms of reliability and should try to increase the reliability with which assessors can make ratings, by careful selection and training of assessors, developing or selecting exercises providing the most adequate ratings of the dimensions in question, and using rating procedures that enhance the reliability of ratings. For rating dimensions with poor reliability, such dimensions should not be used for final assessments or should be used with extreme caution.

Validity of Assessments

The validity of assessments usually is determined by comparing the evaluations (usually ratings) made by the assessors with some criterion of success or job performance. In this regard Huck (1973) distinguished between "external" and "internal" criteria. External criteria are based on some indication of later job success, usually as reflected by promotions, pay increases, and so forth. Thus, the assessments would be considered as predictors of later achievement. In turn, internal criteria are indications of current job proficiency or status, frequently such criteria consisting of ratings of performance on the individuals' present jobs. Of these two types of criteria, the external variety would usually be preferred, since the assessment center evaluations in real life would be used to predict future achievement.

However, there is a problem in using external criteria, namely the possibility of contaminating the criterion measures from the assessment ratings. If those responsible for making promotion decisions have access to the assessment center results, they might use those assessments (good or bad)

in making decisions to promote or not to promote the individuals in question. In fact, one of the long-range objectives of assessment evaluations *is* to use them to help make such personnel decisions.

In view of this, the only way in which the *uncontaminated* validity of assessment center ratings can be determined is by ensuring that the ratings are *not* available to the personnel decision makers, in other words, are only for assessment center research. MacKinnon (1975), from an extensive review of reports on assessment centers, found only two "pure" validity studies, these having been carried out some years ago by A.T.&T.'s Bell Telephone companies. One of these (Bray & Grant 1966) dealt with 269 men who had been through assessment centers from 1956–1960. At that time the men were evaluated by the staff as to whether they could be expected to reach the "middle management" level (the level to which college graduates usually are expected to advance within from five to ten years). The follow-up study was done to see what had happened to the 269 men compared with the original assessment center predictions. These results are summarized in Figure 6.4.

Somewhat similar results for the second "pure" validation study are reported by Bray and Campbell (1968) on assessment center operations for sales (rather than for managerial) personnel. The assessments made by the assessment center staff were compared six months later with evaluations at the time of their sales performance. These results are summarized below:

Staff assessment	Percent Meeting Sales Standards
More than acceptable	100
Acceptable	60
Less than acceptable	44
Unacceptable	10

Most other studies of the "validity" of assessment center evaluations are at least a

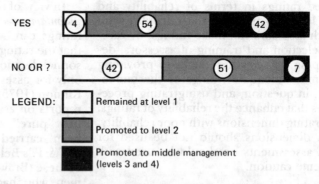

Assessment Center Predictions
(will make middle management:
levels 3 or 4)

Managerial Level Actually Achieved
Five or More Years Later: %

YES 4 54 42

NO OR ? 42 51 7

LEGEND:

☐ Remained at level 1

▨ Promoted to level 2

■ Promoted to middle management
(levels 3 and 4)

FIG. 6.4 Percentage of men evaluated by assessment center staff in terms of expectation of being promoted to middle management. Five years later, these men were at three levels of management. (*Adapted from Bray & Grant 1966, Table 12, p. 17.*) Copyright 1966 by the American Psychological Association. Reprinted by permission.

bit suspect because of the possibility of criterion contamination. In this regard Moses (1971) analyzed data for 5,943 employees of A.T.&T. who had been through assessment centers over a seven-year period. In this case the individuals were given feedback, but it was felt that the influence of this on the criterion of subsequent promotions would be "minor." Although assessment results were available for making promotional decisions, reliance on the assessment data varied in different locations (as shown by the fact that some persons with high assessments were not promoted). The results are given in Figure 6.5.

Some more general hints of the effectiveness of assessment centers are reported by Byham (1970), who summarized the results of several studies (some unpublished) about assessment centers. In six studies, assessment center evaluations of managerial personnel were correlated with subsequent performance as rated by superiors. These correlations ranged from .27 to .64. In twenty-three studies, Byham was able to compare assessment center evaluations with other methods (including conventional personnel tests) in their effectiveness for spotting potentially superior personnel. In these studies various criteria were used,

such as performance ratings, subsequent advancements, and salary. A review of these studies shows how the assessment center evaluation compared with other methods:

	No. of Studies
Assessment center *more* effective	22
Assessment center *equally* effective	1
Assessment center *less* effective	0

These results could be partially influenced by possible criterion contamination. Admitting the possible criterion contamination effects in many studies, MacKinnon stated: "The findings of both the pure and operational validity research studies lead to the conclusion that assessment centers can be remarkably effective in identifying managerial potential—but precisely how effective, one cannot say" (1975, p. 19).

Although the candidates in most assessment centers have been males, Moses and Boehm (1975) made an analysis of the results of an assessment center study of

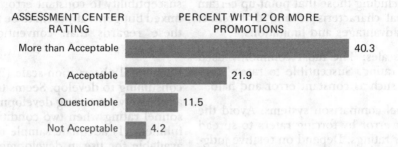

ASSESSMENT CENTER RATING	PERCENT WITH 2 OR MORE PROMOTIONS
More than Acceptable	40.3
Acceptable	21.9
Questionable	11.5
Not Acceptable	4.2

FIG. 6.5 Percent of managerial personnel in various rating categories (as based on assessment center results) who subsequently received two or more promotions. (*Adapted from Moses 1971, Table 2.*)

females and concluded that the assessment center predicted the future performance of women as accurately as it did that of males.

Discussion

The general impression from the studies and discussions of assessment centers is euphoric—that assessment centers have substantial potential utility for identifying those who have the greatest potential for the jobs in question. But if one jumps to the conclusion that assessment centers are just what the doctor ordered, we should listen to the words of caution of Klimoski and Strickland (1977). The central theme of their paper centered on the question of whether assessment centers "work" simply because assessment center staffs are able to predict how (and on what bases) operating managers will make their decisions in the areas of promotions. If managers tend to promote people who are "like themselves," the long-term effect could be to develop a staff of people who are like clones—mirror images of each other—thereby minimizing the possibility of getting creative, imaginative people, or even odd-balls, into responsible positions. Klimoski and Strickland did not seriously propose dismantling all assessment centers, but they did urge serious consideration of the criterion problem, suggesting that we be on the lookout for

other, perhaps better criteria than the ones used so far.

DEVELOPING AND ADMINISTERING PERSONNEL RATING SYSTEMS

The development of effective personnel evaluation systems and the effective administration of personnel evaluation programs depend on several important aspects: the selection or development of an appropriate type of rating system for the purpose(s) in mind; the selection of raters; the training of raters; in some instances the "conversion" of the original ratings given by the raters into summated ratings; and, in most situations, provision for feedback of the ratings to the ratees.

Selection of Type of Rating System

The first step in establishing a personnel evaluation program, or for carrying out any type of program for which ratings are to obtained, is to select the rating system that would best serve the intended purpose. The various types of rating systems have their own advantages and limitations. The pros and cons for the various systems, in turn, influence their suitabilities to various uses. To begin, let us toss in a few general comments about the various types of systems, including those that point up certain individual characteristics and that reflect certain advantages and limitations:

Rating scales: The most commonly used type of rating. Susceptible to raters' tendencies such as constant error and halo.

Personnel comparison systems: Avoid the constant error by forcing raters to spread out their ratings. Depend on relative judgments rather than on absolute judgments and tend to have respectable reliability. Limited in some uses (such as personnel counseling) since they reflect only order of merit and are not "analytical" in showing specific strengths and weaknesses of ratees. The point allocation technique (PAT), basically a personnel comparison system, still is in the experimental stage but may offer some promise of combining the advantages of absolute and relative judgments.

Critical incident technique: Tends to be burdensome for routine use. Does not lend itself readily to quantification. Its major strength: provides a record of specific incidents for use in employee counseling.

Weighted checklists: Time consuming to develop. Interpretation of results may be difficult. Relatively simple for raters to use because of job-related nature. Are not commonly used.

Forced-choice checklist: Time consuming to develop. Not readily accepted by raters as they do not know what responses are used to derive a person's final rating. Tend to minimize the constant error. Probably should be used only when it is feasible to hide final ratings from raters.

Behavioral expectation scale (BES): Time consuming to develop. Probably relatively simple for raters to use because of job-related nature. Participation by employees in their development probably contributes

to their acceptability in use. Evidence of susceptibility to constant error and halo is mixed but generally seem to be no better in these regards than conventional rating scales are.

Behavioral observation scale (BOS): Time consuming to develop. Seems to represent a relatively promising development in personnel rating when two conditions can be fulfilled: (1) adequate sample of ratings is available for use in development, and (2) continuous opportunity for raters to observe ratees in order to rate frequency of behaviors. Reliability seems satisfactory.

Mixed standard scale: Still experimental but may be less susceptible to constant error and halo effects. May help identify less competent raters (who could then be given special training). Time consuming to develop.

On the basis of an evaluation of certain types of rating systems Barrett (1966) worked up a table reflecting his judgment of the possible practical uses of the various types of systems. His evaluations are given in Table 6.5. The table indicates by a "yes" or "no" whether he considered a particular type of system to be appropriate to each of the eight uses listed. We generally concur in his evaluations, although in special circumstances one might depart from his specific recommendations.

Development of Rating Materials

With a particular type of rating scale selected, the particular rating system then must be developed. The first stage is to develop the specific scales to be used. For scales in which different factors are to be used (as in conventional rating scales), this means deciding what factors to use, defining or describing the factors, and deciding what form of scale to use (graphic, numeri-

TABLE 6.5 SUGGESTED USES OF CERTAIN TYPES OF PERSONNEL RATING SYSTEMS

Type of System	Rating Scale	Personnel Comparison Systems	Weighted Check List	Forced Choice Check List	Critical Incident
Wage and salary administration	Yes	No	Yes	No	No
Personnel promotion	Yes	Yes	Yes	No	No
Personnel transfer	Yes	No	Yes	Yes	No
Personnel layoff	Yes	Yes	No	No	No
Discharge or demotion	Yes	No	No	No	No
Administrative control	Yes	Yes	No	No	Yes
Personnel development	Yes	No	Yes	No	Yes
Research	Yes	Yes	Yes	Yes	Yes

Source: Barrett (1966), Table 5, p. 61.

cal, etc.). For the behavioral checklists and scales, the first step is to develop the statements of behavior to use experimentally. These are then used experimentally with a sample of people, leading up to the selection of the statements to be incorporated in the final scale.

Once the basic scales have been developed, they need to be worked into a format that would be readily understandable to the raters, with clear, unambiguous accompanying instructions. Regarding the format of rating scales, especially conventional rating scales, there is much lore about the scale features that purport to reduce the influence of the halo effect and of constant errors. Particular emphasis has been placed on the practice of alternating the "good" and "bad" ends of scales and of rating all individuals on the same attribute at the same time. In addition, there have been proponents of graphic rating scales, on which rating variables are represented by continuous lines, and proponents of categorical scales, which use several—usually from five to nine—distinct rating categories. Data to support or reject these and other practices are fairly skimpy, but a study by Blumberg, DeSoto, and Kuethe (1966) suggested that such variations in

format have no appreciable effect on ratings.

Selection of Raters

In the typical administration of personnel evaluation programs it is customary for supervisors to serve as the raters of their own subordinates, such ratings sometimes being subject to review by the individuals to whom the supervisors report. In certain circumstances, peers and subordinates of ratees are asked to serve as raters. The operational situations in which this is done most often are in organizations in which employees frequently participate in managerial affairs. Experience with such ratings suggests that in some circumstances the ratings of peers are preferable to those of subordinates. The ratings of peers and subordinates also have been used in various research undertakings, as contrasted with operational circumstances.

The raters used in assessment centers usually are the "observers." Observers in such programs may be members of the personnel staff, psychologists, members of management, consultants, or staff members of organizations hired for the assessment program.

Training Raters

Training of raters clearly pays off in the improvement in the ratings they later provide. This training should cover such subjects as the sources of distortion of ratings, the desirability of focusing on the ratees' observable behaviors (as contrasted with their personal traits), and the desirability of spreading the ratings over the whole range of possible ratings (but doing so discriminantly).

As one example of the effectiveness of the training of raters Latham and others (1975) reported a well controlled experiment carried out in a large corporation in which sixty managers who were to serve as raters were used as subjects. They were divided randomly into three groups as follows:

Workshop group. This group was given videotapes on the rating of individuals, discussed rating procedures and problems, and made practice ratings, the objective being to reduce certain common raters' tendencies.

Discussion group. This group received training similar in content to the workshop group, but the training method was basically discussion.

Control group. This group received no training.

Six months later the three groups were "tested" by presenting them with videotapes of several "job candidates" along with job descriptions and statements of job requirements and were asked to rate the individuals in terms of their suitability to the jobs in question. The raters were scored according to the extent to which they committed four types of rating errors (the halo effect and three other types we need not describe). A comparison of the ratings made by the three groups revealed significant errors in the four "error types" on which they were scored, as shown below:

Group	No. of error types
Workshop	0
Discussion	1
Control	3

As another example, it was reported that a seven-hour training program for raters in a petroleum company had reduced the halo effect as measured by subsequent reductions in the intercorrelations among the rating factors.

Conversion of Ratings

The procedures for converting the original rating responses to some type of "summated" rating for each individual depend on the type of scale being used. For ratings of different factors or dimensions this usually consists of adding up the ratings on the individual factors; if differential weights are to be given, this may involve the multiplication of the original ratings by the designated weights before adding them up. As indicated in the earlier discussion of weighting, if there is any evidence of some form of distortion one should either correct for the distortion if it is feasible to do so or use the ratings in an extremely guarded manner that fully considers the distortion.

In some circumstances ratings for the same individuals are obtained from two or more raters and then pooled. There is evidence from a study by Bayroff, Haggerty, and Rundquist (1954) to support the contention that pooled ratings *by competent raters* generally are better than single ratings. Frequently the most *competent* raters available are the supervisors of the individuals being rated. This was reflected, for example, in the results of a study by Whitla and Tirrell (1954) which indicated that the raters closest to the ratees (in terms of organizational level) were able to rate the ratees better than raters at higher levels of organization could. These findings suggest that the ratings of competent raters can be safely combined but that one should avoid the pooling of ratings of poor raters with those of competent raters.

FEEDBACK OF EVALUATIONS

Personnel evaluations serve two primary functions. First, they provide data necessary for making staffing decisions. Second, the information from a personnel evaluation can be fed back to the individual.

The information about performance is essential to the individual for learning and improving on the job. It is also essential to planning one's career realistically. For the most part, our discussion of personnel evaluation has emphasized organizational functions. Now let us turn to the individual with the feedback function.

The Nature of Feedback

Feedback on performance on the job influences the individual in two ways; it can provide information, and it can motivate the individual. As information (or knowledge of results) feedback can facilitate performance by making the individual aware of his errors and by providing directions for correcting them. Feedback can affect the individual's desire to put forth the effort needed to perform well.

The feedback from personnel evaluation originates from some source, usually the individual's immediate supervisor. As a result, the feedback message to the individual is not merely information about his or her past performance but information *from a certain person or persons* about past performance. The latter cannot be stressed

enough, for the extent to which the individual accepts the feedback is a function not only of the information per se but of the individual's reaction to the person who provides the feedback.

Ilgen, Fisher, and Taylor (1979) found that *credibility* and *power* are the two most important characteristics of feedback sources. Credibility is the extent to which the recipient of the feedback believes that the source can legitimately evaluate the recipient's past performance. Factors such as the supervisor's expertise and the extent to which he is able to observe the subordinate's performance affect the supervisor's credibility. Power is the formal power to control valued rewards of the subordinate. The authors hypothesize that both the credibility and the power of the source influence the extent to which feedback recipients (1) accurately perceive the feedback, (2) believe the feedback is accurate, and (3) desire to respond according to the feedback.

The Role of Supervisors in Feedback

It is logical to view supervisors as the individuals who should assume the role not only of evaluating their subordinates but also of providing feedback to them of the results. However, qualms have been expressed about the role of supervisors in this regard. McGregor (1957), for example, expressed the opinion that conventional evaluation places the supervisor in the untenable position of judging the subordinate and then acting on this judgment. It is probably true that many supervisors do not feel comfortable in performing these functions and, indeed, are not very adept at it; this is especially true of the feedback role. At the same time, displacing responsibility for the evaluation of subordinates and the subsequent feedback of information to them would seem to evade supervisory responsibilities.

Perhaps the primary focus here should be on trying to provide guidance (including training) for supervisors in the most effective approaches in counseling subordinates.

THE EVALUATION INTERVIEW. Some organizations have supervisors arrange for scheduled evaluation interviews with their subordinates once a year or at some other stated interval. In reflecting on the evaluation interview, Burke and Wilcox (1969) suggested that three outcomes appear important—(1) the satisfaction of the subordinate with the interview; (2) the motivation of the subordinate to improve job performance; and (3) subsequent actual improvement on job performance. For 323 female telephone operators, it was found (through responses to anonymous questionnaires) that these three outcomes were correlated as follows:

Variables	Correlation
Satisfaction with the interview and desire to improve	.43
Satisfaction with the interview and actual improvement	.32
Desire to improve and actual improvement	.57

Although we cannot positively attribute these correlations to a cause-and-effect relationship, they at least suggest that the desire to improve oneself and actual improvement may be a function of how satisfying the interview process is to the individual.

Some clues to the characteristics of interviews associated with more positive outcomes come from a series of studies in a plant of the General Electric Company. These studies by Meyer and his associates probably are the most comprehensive studies of the evaluation interview.

In one of these studies (Meyer, Kay, & French 1965), ninety-two salaried employees were interviewed by research personnel; they also completed questionnaires before and after their regular salary action

interview with their supervisory managers and were interviewed again after a later second discussion with their managers dealing with subsequent performance improvement. Half of the managers were instructed to use a high participation approach during the salary action interview, in which the manager asked the subordinate to prepare a set of goals for improved job performance and to submit them for the manager's review and approval. The other managers were instructed to use a more traditional low participation approach in which the manager formulated a set of goals for the subordinate; these goals were later reviewed in the performance improvement session. In general, those subordinates in the high participation group reacted more favorably to their interviews and to the appraisal system than did those in the low participation group. What is more, they achieved a somewhat higher percentage of their predetermined "improvement goals."

In another part of the General Electric Company studies, Kay, Meyer, and French (1965) investigated the relationship between "threats" during the appraisal interview and subsequent goal achievement. The "threats" during the interview were statements made by the managers about the subordinate which were interpreted by trained observers to be critical and to threaten the subordinate's self-esteem. (The subordinates in all cases had agreed to the presence of an outside observer.) The relationship between the number of threats (categorized as above or below average) and later estimates of goal achievement is shown in Figure 6.6. This figure also differentiates between those who had been characterized, on the basis of a questionnaire, as having high or low "occupational self-esteem." It can be seen that the number of "threats" during the interviews had no appreciable effect on those subordinates who were high on occupational self-esteem. But for those who were low on oc-

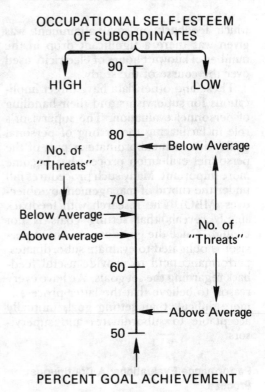

OCCUPATIONAL SELF-ESTEEM
OF SUBORDINATES

HIGH   90   LOW

              80
No. of   ← Below Average
"Threats"

              70
Below Average →
                          No. of
Above Average →   "Threats"

              60

                          ← Above Average

              50

PERCENT GOAL ACHIEVEMENT

FIG. 6.6 Relationship between number of "threats" during evaluation interviews and subsequent goal achievement for subordinates with high and low occupational self-esteem. (*Adapted from Kay, Meyer, & French 1965, Table 2.*)

cupational self-esteem, a high level of threat can have a distinctly dampening effect. These and other results led the investigators to conclude that:

1. Comprehensive annual performance appraisals are of questionable value.

2. Coaching should be a day-to-day, not a once-a-year activity.

3. Goal setting, not criticism, should be used to improve performance.

4. Separate appraisals should be made for different purposes.

The upshot of all this was that the company developed a new appraisal program, the work-planning-and-review method, the basic features of which departed from the more traditional evaluation programs in that (1) there are more frequent discussions of performance, (2) there are no sum-mary judgments or ratings, (3) there are separate salary action discussions, and (4) mutual goal planning and problem solving are emphasized.

GOAL SETTING AND FEEDBACK. Recently, there has been much emphasis on goal setting and the supervisor's role in it. An extensive review by Latham and Yukl (1975) showed quite clearly that goal setting in organizations can significantly influence individual performance. Feedback is important to goal setting. In fact, recent evidence indicates that feedback is necessary for goal setting to affect performance (Becker 1978; Erez 1977). For example, Becker (1978) set goals (either difficult or easy) and either gave or did not give feedback on electrical energy consumption to residents in a New Jersey community. Only in those households to which difficult goals were assigned (to reduce electrical energy consumption by 20 percent) and also to which feedback on goal attainment was given was there a significant drop in the number of kilowatt hours of electricity used over the course of the study.

These and other data have direct implications for supervisors and their handling of personnel evaluation. The supervisor's role in facilitating the setting of personal goals with each subordinate as part of the personnel evaluation process has become more important. Many such procedures fall under the rubric of management by objectives (MBO). The research with feedback simply reveals that setting goals is not enough. Once the goals are set, the supervisor is obligated to evaluate subordinates' performance and to provide useful feedback regarding the set goals. We have every reason to believe that the latter process is more difficult than setting goals mutually acceptable to subordinates and supervisors.

Performance Evaluations: A Continuous Process

Although for administrative purposes periodic performance appraisals are useful, they are not sufficient to meet individuals' needs for performance feedback. The experience of the General Electric Company suggested that more continuous, day-to-day feedback was needed for counseling subordinates and providing them with the information needed to improve their performance. The goal-setting research implies the same need for more frequent feedback. The personnel evaluation process, if it is to be effective, must never stop. Supervisors must recognize subordinates' strengths and shortcomings and make constructive criticisms as soon as possible after the behaviors have been observed. Once a year or even once every four to six months is not sufficient for the feedback requirements of many employees.

DISCUSSION

In all aspects of life, including the work world, people make judgments about other people. There are indeed many circumstances in which the behavior or performance of others can be measured objectively by some method, by production records, errors, and the like. But often the work-related behavior of individuals cannot be measured objectively. In such instances the behavior must be evaluated by other people. (To be a bit philosophical, we might add that life would be a bit dull if all human evaluations and judgments were removed.) Many judgments of others are made informally on a day-to-day basis in continuing operations of one sort or another. In many operations and in research, however, there is a need for more formal or systematic judgments of people in work situations, either to evaluate their actual work performance or to assess their potential for other types of activities. It is in these circumstances that the use of various types of rating systems can be used to improve judgments for the purposes in question.

REFERENCES

BARRETT, R. S. *Performance rating.* Chicago: Chicago Science Research Associates, 1966.

BAYROFF, A. G., HAGGERTY, H. R., & RUNDQUIST, E. A. Validity of ratings as related to rating techniques and conditions. *Personnel Psychology,* 1954, *7,* 93–113.

BECKER, L. J. Joint effect of feedback and goal setting on performance: A field study of residental energy conservation. *Journal of Applied Psychology,* 1978, *63,* 428–433.

BERKSHIRE, J. R., & HIGHLAND, R. W. Forced-choice performance rating—A methodological study. *Personnel Psychology*, 1953, *6*, 355–378.

BERNARDIN, J. H. Behavioral expectation scales versus summated scales: A fairer comparison. *Journal of Applied Psychology*, 1977, *62*(4), 422–427.

BERNARDIN, J. H., ALVARES, K. M., & CRANNY, C. J. A recomparison of behavioral expectation scales to summated scales. *Journal of Applied Psychology*, 1976, *61*(5), 564–570.

BERNARDIN, J. H., LA SHELLS, M. B., SMITH, P. C., & ALVARES, K. M. Behavioral expectation scales: Effects of developmental procedures and formats. *Journal of Applied Psychology*, 1976, *61* (1), 75–79.

BIGONESS, W. J. Effect of applicant's sex, race and performance on employers' performance ratings: Some additional findings. *Journal of Applied Psychology*, 1976, *61*(1), 80–84.

BLANZ, F., & GHISELLI, E. E. The mixed standard scale: A new rating system. *Personnel Psychology*, 1972, *25*, 185–199.

BLUMBERG, H. H., DESOTO, C. B., & KUETHE, J. L. Evaluation of rating scale formats. *Personnel Psychology*, 1966, *19*(3), 243–259.

BORMAN, W. C. Exploring upper limits of reliability and validity in performance ratings. *Journal of Applied Psychology*, 1978, *63*(2), 135–144.

BORMAN, W. C., & VALLON, W. R. A view of what can happen when behavioral expectation scales are developed in one setting and used in another. *Journal of Applied Psychology*, 1974, *59*(2), 197–201.

BRAY, D. W., & CAMPBELL, R. J. Selection of salesmen by means of an assessment center. *Journal of Applied Psychology*, 1968, *52*, 36–41.

BRAY, D. W., CAMPBELL, R. J., & GRANT, D. L. *Formative years in business: A long-term AT&T study of management lives.* New York: Wiley-Interscience, 1974.

BRAY, D. W., & GRANT, D. L. The assessment centers in the measurement of potential for business management. *Psychological Monographs: General and Applied.* Whole No. 625, 1966, *80*(17), 1–27.

BRIDGMAN, C. S., SPAETH, J., DRISCOLL, P., & FANNING, J. Salesmen helped by bringing out jobs' critical incidents. *Personnel Journal*, 1958, *36*, 411–414.

BURKE, R. J., & WILCOX, D. S. Characteristics of effective performance review and development interviews. *Personnel Psychology*, 1969, *22*(3), 291–305.

BYHAM, W. C. Assessment centers for spotting future managers. *Harvard Business Review*, July-August 1970, *48*(4), 150–167.

DECOTIIS, T. A. An analysis of the external validity and applied relevance of three rating formats. *Organizational Behavior and Human Performance*, 1977, *19*(2), 247–266.

DUFFY, K. E., & WEBBER, R. E. On "relative" rating systems. *Personnel Psychology*, 1974, *27*(2), 307–311.

DUNNETTE, M. D. Managerial effectiveness: Its definition and measurement. *Studies in Personnel Psychology*, 1970, *2*(2), 6–20.

DUNNETTE, M. D., CAMPBELL, J. P., & HELLERVIC, L. W. Job behavior scales for Penney Company department managers. Minneapolis: Personnel Decisions, 1968.

EREZ, M. Feedback: A necessary condition for the goal-setting performance relationship. *Journal of Applied Psychology.* 1977, *62*, 624–627.

FLANAGAN, J. C., & BURNS, R. K. The employee performance record: A new appraisal and development tool. *Harvard Business Review,* 1955, *33*(5), 95–102.

GOODALE, J. G., & BURKE, R. J. Behaviorally based rating scales need not be job specific. *Journal of Applied Psychology,* 1975, *60*(3), 389–391.

HINRICHS, J. R., & HAANPERÄ, S. Reliability of measurement in situational exercises: An assessment of the assessment center method. *Personnel Psychology,* 1976, *28*(1), 31–40.

HUCK, J. R. Assessment centers: A review of the external and internal validities. *Personnel Psychology,* 1973, *26*(2), 191–212.

ILGEN, D. R., FISHER, C. D., & TAYLOR, M. S. Motivational consequences of individual feedback on behavior in organizations. *Journal of Applied Psychology,* 1979, *64*(4), 349–371.

JURGENSEN, C. E. A fallacy in the use of median scale values in employee checklists. *Journal of Applied Psychology,* 1949, *33*, 56–58.

KAY, E., MEYER, H. H., & FRENCH, J. R. P., Jr. Effects of threat in a performance appraisal interview. *Journal of Applied Psychology,* 1965, *49*(5), 311–317.

KIRCHNER, W. K., & DUNNETTE, M. D. Identifying the critical factors in successful salesmanship. *Personnel,* 1957, *34*(2), 54–59.

KLIMOSKI, R. J., STRICKLAND, W. J. Assessment centers—Valid or merely prescient? *Personnel Psychology,* 1977, *30*(3), 353–361.

KLORES, M. S. Rater bias in forced-distribution performance ratings *Personnel Psychology,* 1966, *4*, 411–421.

KNAUFT, E. B. Construction and use of weighted checklist rating scales for two industrial situations. *Journal of Applied Psychology,* 1948, *32*, 63–70.

LANDY, F. J., FARR, J. L., SAAL, F. E., & FRENTAG, W. R. Behaviorally anchored scales for rating the performance of police officers. *Journal of Applied Psychology,* 1976, *61*(6), 750–758.

LATHAM, G. P., & WEXLEY, K. N. Behavioral observation scales for performance appraisal purposes. *Personnel Psychology,* 1977, *30*(2), 255–268.

LATHAM, G. P., WEXLEY, K. N., & PURSELL, E. D. Training managers to minimize rating errors in the observation of behavior. *Journal of Applied Psychology,* 1975, *60*(5), 550–555.

LATHAM, G. P., WEXLEY, K. N., & RAND, T. M. The relevance of behavioral criteria developed from the critical incident technique. *Canadian Journal of Behavioral Science,* 1975, *7*, 349–358.

LATHAM, G. P., & YUKL, G. A. A review of research on the application of goal setting in organizations. *Academy of Management Journal,* 1975, *60*, 299–302.

LAWSHE, C. H., KEPHART, N. C., & MC-CORMICK, E. J. The paired comparison technique for rating performance of industrial employees. *Journal of Applied Psychology,* 1949, *33*, 69–77.

LOPEZ, F. M. *Evaluating employee performance.* Chicago: Public Personnel Association, 1968.

MACKINNON, D. W. An overview of assessment centers. CCL Technical Report No. 1. Greensboro, N.C.: Center for Creative Leadership, May 1975.

McCormick, E. J., & Bachus, J. A. Paired comparison ratings: I. The effect on ratings of reductions in the number of pairs. *Journal of Applied Psychology*, 1952, *36*, 123–127.

McGregor, D. M. The human side of enterprise. *Management Review*, November 1957, *46* (11), 22–29, 88–92.

Meyer, H. H., Kay, E., & French, J. R. P., Jr. Split roles in performance appraisal. *Harvard Business Review*, 1965, *43*, 123–129.

Moses, J. L. Assessment center performance and management progress. Paper given at meetings of American Psychological Association, Washington, D.C., September 1971.

Moses, J. L., & Boehm, V. R. Relationship of assessment center performance to management progress of women. *Journal of Applied Psychology*, 1975, *60*(4) 527–529.

Peter, L. J. *The Peter principle.* New York: William Morrow, 1969.

Rosen, B., & Jerdee, T. H. The nature of job-related age stereotypes. *Journal of Applied Psychology*, 1976, *61*(2), 180–183.

Saal, F. E., & Landy, F. J. The mixed standard rating scale: An evaluation. *Organizational Behavior and Human Performance*, 1977, *18*(1), 18–35.

Schmitt, N. Interrater agreement in dimensionality and combination of assessment center judgments. *Journal of Applied Psychology*, 1977, *62*(2), 171–176.

Schwab, D. P., Heneman, H. G., III, & DeCotiis, J. D. Behaviorally anchored rating scales: A review of the literature. *Personnel Psychology*, 1975, *28*(4), 549–562.

Smith, P. C., & Kendall, L. M. Retranslation of expectations: An approach to the construction of unambiguous anchors for rating scales. *Journal of Applied Psychology*, 1963, *47*(2), 149–155.

Taylor, H. C. Upjohn Foundation for Community Research. Personal communication.

Terborg, J. R., & Ilgen, D. R. A theoretical approach to sex discrimination in traditionally masculine occupations. *Organizational Behavior and Human Performances*, 1975, *13*, 352–376.

Thorndike, E. L. A constant error in psychological ratings. *Journal of Applied Psychology*, 1920, *4*, 25–29.

Thurstone, E. L. & Chave, E. J. *The measurement of attitude.* University of Chicago Press, 1929.

Uhrbrock, R. S. Standardization of 724 rating scale statements. *Personnel Psychology*, 1950, *3*, 285–316.

Whitla, D. K., & Tirrell, J. E. The validity of ratings of several levels of supervisors. *Personnel Psychology*, 1954, *6*, 461–466.

Application For Employment
an equal opportunity employer—M/F

The heading of an employment application form.

An employment interview.

An applicant taking dexterity test.

personnel selection

One of the important roles of some industrial psychologists is that relating to personnel selection. Although some industrial psychologists become directly involved in day-to-day personnel selection operations (including interviewing, personnel testing, and personnel appraisal), usually they are behind the scenes carrying out research to establish personnel selection standards, developing and validating personnel tests, and providing related consulting services to those responsible for personnel selection operations.

This part of the text deals with the various aspects of personnel selection with which industrial psychologists become involved, including general practices in personnel selection, using personnel tests, biographical data, and the interview in personnel selection, and the implications of the Equal Employment Opportunity Act as related to personnel selection.

7
general practices in personnel selection

A critical function of personnel management is that of making decisions about assigning individuals to specific jobs or positions or about training individuals for specific jobs. This function basically is "matching" individuals to jobs, considering on the one hand the actual or potential qualifications of individuals and on the other hand the requirements of jobs.

TYPES OF PERSONNEL ACTIONS

This function includes various personnel "actions," so let us digress for a few moments to discuss certain distinctions sometimes made among such actions. Personnel *selection,* in a technical sense, refers to choosing, from a number of available candidates, one or more who are to be employed; typically the selection decision is made with the view of assigning an individ-

ual to a given job or to training for a job. Such decisions are based on data or on judgments of the various candidates' qualifications as related to the requirements of the job. In turn, *placement* is viewed more from the individual's viewpoint and focuses on choosing from a number of possible jobs the one presumably best suited to a given candidate. In such instances the individual is already "employed," and the placement decision is then made to assign the employee to the job for which he is considered to be best qualified. The term *classification* is rather closely related to placement but has a slightly different twist. It applies to a situation in which there is a pool of individuals and a pool of jobs and refers to the assignment of the individuals to the jobs in order to optimize, collectively, the "matches" between the two. It might be that many individuals would not be assigned to their own "best" jobs nor that all jobs are filled by the "best" candidates. But the composite assignments collectively are optimum. Classification is perhaps best represented by the handling of recruits in the military services.

Promotions are advancement of individuals to higher-level jobs, *transfers*, shifting people to jobs on a similar level, and *demotion*, the assignment of individuals to lower-level jobs. Although there are these different functions, or stages, in the alignment of individuals with specific jobs or training programs, most of them have much in common, in that they require matching individuals with jobs (or training for jobs). Because of the common bases for these various personnel actions and for the sake of semantic simplicity, we will generally refer to them all as *personnel selection* (although this term also has its own specific meaning).

JOB REQUIREMENTS AND PERSONNEL SPECIFICATIONS

Personnel selection should be directed toward identifying those individuals who stand the best chance of success in the job in question. This means that one should try to identify those characteristics most likely to contribute to job success. In selecting individuals for any given job, then, there is (or should be) some set of what are variously called *personnel specifications* or *job specifications*. These frequently are written, although sometimes they exist partly or entirely in the minds of those responsible for personnel selection.

For the characteristics associated with success on any given job (and that may be set forth in the personnel specifications), we would like to make a possibly important distinction, albeit one based more on logic than on empirical evidence. We would like to suggest that the requirements in personnel specifications fall into two classes.

The first class are those specifications that are reasonably *intrinsic* to the job and are required for effective performance as such (for example, the visual acuity and hand steadiness in sawing lumber, as mentioned above). These intrinsic requirements generally include aptitudes and sensory and physical abilities. Such requirements presume reasonable similarity of job content and of acceptable standards of performance.

The second class are other specific requirements associated with *labor market conditions;* the implications of this class are shown in the types of candidates who make themselves available for work. Thus, in an actual example, the case of long distance telephone operators, it was found that married women remained on the job longer than single women did in one town, whereas in a town in an adjoining state the reverse was found to be the case.

To the extent that labor market conditions change, the kinds of people available as job candidates also may be expected to change, thus suggesting the need to modify the personnel specifications accordingly, as far as the aspects related to the "labor market" are concerned. Some further distinctions can be made, especially with regard to personal background data, but we will defer further discussion until later.

The "intrinsic" requirements of course vary from job to job, some being rather clear-cut and obvious, and others being rather vague and hard to pin down. For a bookkeeper, for example, it is clear that the job requires basic arithmetic abilities such as adding and subtracting. A warehouse loader certainly has to have a fair amount of physical strength and endurance. On the other hand, the requirements for laboratory technician, city planner, or detective are not quite as obvious. Even for the bookkeeper or warehouse loader one might wonder how *much* arithmetic ability or physical strength and endurance would be required. In other words, we can see that there might be a fair amount of ambiguity in determining job requirements.

In a sense, then, job requirements are not absolute and inviolate; rather, they "depend." They depend, for example, upon value judgments of acceptable standards of performance and the extent to which certain values can be sacrificed for others. Granting this, however, the realities of personnel administration processes necessitate some sort of guidelines for personnel selection.

Objectives in Establishing Personnel Specifications

The objective of setting up personnel specifications is to state those items of personal data that are "valid" for selecting individuals for the job. We will discuss validity later in this chapter, but for the moment let us say that a set of personnel specifications would be valid (they would have validity) to the extent that those individuals who meet that specification have a significantly better chance of performing effectively than those who do not. Referring to the example of the warehouse loader above, if individuals who *meet* some minimum height and weight specifications are generally better at performing the physical activities of the job than those who *do not meet* those standards, it could be said that these specifications are valid. Actually, the personnel selection process essentially is predicting job success on the basis of relevant information about the candidates. Some of the methods for establishing personnel specifications will be discussed later in this and the following chapters.

Personnel Specifications

Personnel specifications, whether formally written or just in the minds of personnel decision makers, essentially are predictors (that is, independent variables) of whatever criterion is in mind, the criterion usually being some measure (s) of job-related behavior such as job performance.

TYPES OF PERSONNEL SPECIFICATIONS (PREDICTORS). The specific possible predictors of job-related criteria for various jobs would almost fill the remaining pages of this book, but we at least will indicate a few of the basic types, as follows:

Work experience

Education

Training

Biographical data (such as given on application forms)

Physical data (such as height, weight, age, visual and hearing ability)

Information on various abilities, personality, interests, and other characteristics.

Specifications for Trained versus Untrained Personnel

Personnel selection practice is roughly divided into a two-track system. For some jobs, for example, the intent is to select candidates who are already trained or experienced in the jobs, whereas for other jobs the intent is to select untrained candidates who have the potential to learn the jobs in question.

SPECIFICATIONS FOR TRAINED PERSONNEL. First, if trained or experienced individuals are sought for the job, the focus of the specifications will be primarily on the nature, length, and quality of any relevant training, education, or experience required for the job. The definition of such specifications is essentially the result of a logical process, coupled with experience in personnel selection and tempered by value considerations, including, in some cases, compromises that may be indicated by the practical realities of the labor market.

SPECIFICATIONS FOR UNTRAINED PERSONNEL. Second, if untrained individuals are being sought for the job (usually for training on the job), the focus will be primarily on those qualities presumed to reflect their potentialities for the job. Such qualities might include various specific aptitudes, sensory skills, physical characteristics, personality, and interests, as illustrated in Figure 2.2 (in chapter 2). In such instances the personnel specifications usually are a step removed from the more basic requirements. For example, the physical activities of a job might require handling heavy loads for extended periods of time. It is probable, however, that the personnel specifications of this activity would be expressed in terms from which one could *infer* the ability to do this work, such as height and weight, a minimum score on some physical strength test, or previous work experience involving heavy physical activity, albeit of a different sort. In like manner, specifications expressed in terms of test scores, vision tests, age, general education, and so forth are not statements of "intrinsic" job requirement; rather, they *imply* the potentialities to perform (or to learn to perform) the job activity in question.

DISCUSSION. It is usually more straightforward to establish personnel specifications for selecting trained personnel (as discussed above) than for selecting untrained personnel. For trained personnel the specifications usually are set forth in terms of the nature, length, and quality of any relevant work experience, training, or education, that would imply the *present ability* to do the job, whereas for untrained personnel one needs to specify qualities that imply *potentialities* to be able to do the job after training.

Sources of Relevant Personnel Data

In matching individuals and jobs it is necessary to obtain, for individual candidates, personnel data relevant to the specifications of the job. Some of the more commonly used sources of such information are given below:

Personnel tests and inventories

Application forms and other personal data questionnaires

Physical examinations

Interviews

Letters of reference

Most of these will be discussed later.

Discussion

We want to discuss the various methods of establishing personnel specifications and the associated use of different sources of personnel data, but let us delay that and bring up now the important issues of *reliability* and *validity* as they apply to the person-job matching process. Generally, reliability is concerned with the stability or consistency of "measurement" of variables (most typically measurements of individuals, such as test scores, criterion indexes, and ratings). Validity is an extremely complex concept and is discussed in a later section. For the moment, however, let us say that it pertains to inferences that can be drawn from tests or other variables. These inferences may be about the individuals in question, or about predictions that can be made on the basis of measures relating to individuals or to groups of people.

RELIABILITY

We already have discussed the notion of reliability, as related to criteria and performance evaluations. In our interest in person-job matching, reliability is relevant to at least three contexts, namely, the reliability of criteria, of judgments of personnel specifications, and of measurements of individuals. In all of these, it refers to the consistency or stability of whatever measurements are in question.

For measurements of human variables, the American Psychological Association has published a set of *Standards for Educational and Psychological Tests* that sets forth guidelines for the use of "tests," in which various types of test reliability are described. We should hasten to point out that the term *test* is used in a very broad sense, as follows:

> It is intended that these standards apply to any assessment procedure, assessment device, or assessment aid; that is, to any systematic basis for making inferences about people. A test is a special case of an assessment procedure. It may be thought of as a set of tasks or questions intended to elicit particular types of behavior when presented under standardized conditions and to yield scores that will have desirable psychometric properties such as high reliability and validity. Tests include standardized aptitude and achievement instruments, diagnostic and evaluative devices, interest inventories, personality inventories, projective instruments and related clinical techniques, and many kinds of personal history forms. These standards . . . should in principle also apply to the judgments (assessments) of the employment interviewer. It may not be possible to apply the standards with the same rigor, but the kind of judgments the interviewer is to make can be identified; the time and procedures for developing and recording them can be standardized, and they can be validated in the same way that scores are validated. (1974, pp. 2, 3)

Types of Reliability Coefficients

Now, to get back to the types of reliability, the American Psychological Association standards recognize three classes, these being expressed in terms of different types of "coefficients" associated with them: coefficient of stability, coefficient of equivalence, and coefficient of internal consistency.

COEFFICIENT OF STABILITY. A coefficient of stability is based on the use of the same type of measurement instrument administered at two points in time to a sample of people, the results of these two adminis-

trations usually being correlated; the resulting correlation is called a *coefficient of stability.* This approach is frequently called the *test-retest method.*

For conventional types of tests the same test is administered twice to the same subjects at different times. This method should not be used for tests in which practice or memory associated with the first administration might influence performance on the second. This influence might apply, for example, to tests of knowledge (with questions such as "who commanded the French forces at the battle of Waterloo?), or tests that require practice in some task (such as converting yards to meters). This method can be used with tests of sensory, psychomotor, or cognitive skills that cannot be improved with brief practice, nor influenced appreciably by memory from the first administration. For example, if a person takes a test consisting of one hundred items of multiplication of, say five-digit numbers, it is doubtful if, on a second administration, the person would "remember" the specific problems or would have improved his multiplication skills by having taken it once before.

A coefficient of stability is sometimes used to estimate the reliability of various types of ratings, such as performance evaluations or ratings of job requirements. The possibility of remembering the first ratings could influence the second ratings, however, especially if the intervening time is short, such as a few days or even a few weeks. Thus, a fairly long time interval usually should be planned when using this method. However, in connection with performance ratings, it is possible that the performance of the individuals might have changed during the intervening time.

A coefficient of stability also can be used with other sets of data (such as criterion data) obtained at different times. For example, in one company injury indexes of employees in a given department were derived for two periods, one based on injuries during odd-numbered weeks and the other on even-numbered weeks. These two indexes were correlated. (In this instance the correlation was.69).

COEFFICIENT OF EQUIVALENCE. A coefficient of equivalence index of reliability is based on data from two "samples" of the "universe" of the behaviors or events being measured. The most clear-cut circumstance to which this applies is a conventional test for which alternate and comparable forms are available. This approach to reliability is sometimes called the *alternate forms method.* The two alternate forms should be developed so that they are virtually matched in style, content, and statistical characteristics. In effect, each form should have about the same number of each kind of item, the means of the two forms should be about the same, and the standard deviations of the scores of the two forms should be about the same. The use of alternate forms of tests evades the problem associated with the test-retest approach that can arise from the influence of practice or memory from the first administration on performance on the second administration.

The coefficient of equivalence sometimes can be used with ratings made by supervisors or interviewers. In such an instance it would be necessary to have two "equivalent" rating forms, each with many different items that provide collectively for ratings on the same attributes or qualities but that are worded differently.

The same approach sometimes can also be used with certain other types of personal or personnel data, such as measures of learning during training, productivity, and absenteeism, by viewing data obtained at different times as being "equivalent forms" of the basic measure in question. However, this approach gets us into a bit of a twilight zone with the test-retest approach, since it also deals with measures obtained at different times.

COEFFICIENT OF INTERNAL CONSISTENCY. Generally the various parts or items of a test of some behavior or attribute all should measure essentially the same thing. In other words, the various parts or items should be internally consistent. There are two methods for deriving coefficients of internal consistency. Both are based on data obtained from a single administration of the measuring instrument. One of the methods is called the *split-half method.* When the test is "scored," two scoring keys are used, each covering only half of the items. The two halves may be chosen randomly or may consist of alternate items, with one scoring key used on all the even-numbered items and the other used on all the odd-numbered items. The correlation between scores made on the two halves is then computed. This provides a reliability measure of a test half as long as the original test. By using a commonly accepted statistical procedure, the correlation is corrected by the Spearman-Brown prophecy formula (Guilford 1956) to provide an estimate of the reliability of the total test.

The other method is based on some type of *analysis of variance,* the results of which reflect estimates of the average of the correlations between and among the items of the test. Probably the most common example of this method is Kuder-Richardson formula 20 (K-R 20). This formula yields essentially an average of all the split-half correlations that could have been obtained using all possible ways of dividing the test.

It should be pointed out that a coefficient of internal consistency is *not* appropriate for what are called speed tests. A speed test is one in which all of the items are the same or virtually the same, such as a finger dexterity test putting pegs into holes. The scoring of such tests is based on how many "items" a person completes within a stated time period or how long it takes to complete a specified number of items.

A coefficient of internal consistency approach can be used with ratings if the various items in a rating system deal with basically the same construct. It can be used with various types of criterion measures if there are data available for several similar "units" of work (such as the number of items produced or time required to complete specified units of work). When performance measures for individual units of time are available as criterion indexes, the reliability could be viewed in the frame of reference of coefficients of stability or equivalence as well as that of a coefficient of internal consistency, although for any given situation one of these might be more appropriate.

Discussion

There are variations and refinements of the reliability theme that we will not discuss here (Campbell 1976). The appropriateness of the three basic approaches discussed will depend upon the circumstances in question and on the type of "data" in question (such as data from conventional types of tests, performance ratings, interviewer ratings, productivity measures, other types of criteria, or clinical assessments).

It should also be remembered that there is no such thing as *the* reliability of any test or other measurement instrument. Rather, reliability is in part a function of the individuals or events (or of whatever units of measurements are used) and of the approach used in deriving the reliability estimate. When using virtually any measurement instrument, however, it is desirable to determine the reliability in the situation in question unless there already are substantial reliability data that would provide reasonable confidence and comfort in using the instrument. For many published tests at least some reliability data usually are reported in the accompanying manuals.

How important is the reliability of a test or other measurement instrument? This question can be answered by saying that respectable reliability does lend confidence

in the use of the measures or scores in question. Conversely, low reliability virtually precludes the possibility of obtaining any meaningful results from using the data. For example, a criterion with poor reliability is not worth trying to predict, and a predictor with poor reliability cannot predict any criterion.

VALIDITY

Validity is difficult to define in a single statement. The American Psychological Association in its *Standards for Educational and Psychological Tests* stated that questions of (test) validity are "questions of what may properly be inferred from a test score" and that validity refers to the "appropriateness of inferences from test scores or other forms of assessment" (1974, p. 25). In a similar vein Guion stated that test validity "is concerned with how relevant test scores are to something else" (1965, p. 123). In an overly simplified way one can think of test validity as being represented by a correlation between test scores and that "something else." In some instances that "something else" might be some human quality (in which case validity would refer to the extent to which the test or other measurement actually measures the quality it is intended to measure). In other instances that "something else" might be a separate criterion such as job performance (in which case validity would refer to the degree of relationship with that criterion, such as measured by a correlation).

The American Psychological Association in its *Standards for Educational and Psychological Tests* set forth three basic types of validity of tests. (Remember that the concept of a "test" in this frame of reference is a very broad one.) These include *criterion-related validity*, *construct validity*, and *content validity*. In this regard, however, Dunnette and Borman (1979) believe that the implication that validities come in different types is confusing and thus leads to oversimplification. Although the many variations on the validity theme do defy classification into clear-cut, mutually exclusive categories, such categories at least help to simplify the concept of validity by illustrating the many variations in validity. Further, the official recognition of various types of validity argues for familiarity with them. Let us now describe these three types of validity.

Criterion-Related Validity

Criterion-related validity is determined by comparing test scores with one or more independent criteria. In personnel selection the criterion usually is a measure of job performance of individuals, but it also may consist of "membership" in different groups, such as occupational groups. There are two kinds of criterion-related validity, concurrent validity and predictive validity.

Concurrent validity is established by relating test scores with the criterion values or categories available at the same time. Usually this involves the correlation of test scores with currently available criteria of job performance of the individuals in question. (The procedures used in this process are covered a bit later in the discussion of the present-employee method of test validation.)

As related to the use of personnel tests, *predictive validity* is determined by relating test scores obtained at one time (such as at the time of employment) with criterion measures (such as job performance) obtained at a later time. (The procedures used in determining predictive validity are covered later in the discussion of the follow-up method of test validation.)

Construct Validity

Construct validity is concerned with the extent to which a test measures the "construct" it is intended to measure. Cronbach and Meehl (1955) originally defined a construct as a postulated (that is, assumed or hypothetical) attribute of people that underlies and determines their overt behavior. Cronbach expressed it this way: "Construct validity is evaluated by investigating what psychological qualities a test measures; i.e., by determining the degree to which explanatory concepts or constructs account for performance on the test" (1971, p. 444). If some form of behavior can be directly observed, or if some trait can be operationally defined, it would not be considered a construct in this sense. There is some difference of opinion, however, on the nature of constructs. Some investigators have proposed that there are a number of relatively distinct, discrete, identifiable human attributes and that individuals vary in how much of each attribute they possess. The efforts of such investigators have been directed toward the identification of the specific attributes that comprise a total inventory. The "existence" of possible constructs typically is inferred from the results of factor analyses of data from several or many tests. Each factor that results from such an analysis is characterized by a combination of tests that are correlated with each other. Each factor can be viewed as a construct, the nature of which is inferred from the common denominator that is interpreted as being the attribute common to the tests in question and that presumably gave rise to the correlations between and among the tests that dominate the factor.

Ebel (1977), however, considered such efforts as a will-of-the-wisp, stating that no finite number of traits had been discovered and predicted that none will be, since, as he said, he sees no reason to believe that the complexities of human behavior can be explained to any substantial extent as the outward manifestations of the interactions of a few internal forces of personality.

We cannot resolve the question as to whether the "constructs" identified by factor analysis actually are discrete underlying human attributes or whether they simply represent postulated concepts that can be attributed to people (in other words our "conceptualization" of human attributes). We are inclined toward the second of these interpretations. In either case they can help us to describe people and to measure the dimensions that we use in such description. (In later references to constructs in this text they should be considered in terms of such descriptions.)

The construct validity of a test or other measuring instrument refers to the extent to which it measures the construct it is supposed to measure. Although construct validity applies most neatly to conventional tests of human attributes, it can also be viewed as applying, for example, to ratings of the behavior or characteristics of people or even to the ratings of job characteristics.

Content Validity

The *content validity* of tests or other measurement instruments traditionally has been viewed as referring to the extent to which the instrument provides for the measurement of a reasonably representative sample of the behaviors or other kinds of responses considered to comprise the "domain" the test is supposed to cover. In the most straightforward examples, it applies to various types of achievement tests, that is, tests that measure the level of achievement in some relatively definitive domain of knowledge or performance. The validity of job knowledge tests or job performance tests typically would be considered to be content validity. Such validity usually is based on the judgments of experts as to the extent to which the sample of questions, problems, or tasks (the "content" of the test) are representative of whatever the test is supposed to measure.

However, questions have been raised about this concept of content validity. Tenopyr (1977), for example, made the point that content validity usually has been considered to be an indication of how well the content of a test samples a larger universe of content, and that it therefore is based on inferences about test *construction* and not about test *scores.* Since validity typically is concerned with inferences about test scores (that is, with making predictions on the basis of test scores) she stated that that which has been called content validity is not validity at all. Guion (1978) echoed this view, commenting that when one is constructing an ability test by content sampling, we may speak of the validity of the *sample,* or its representativeness of the defined job content domain. But to describe the validity of the test as the basis for drawing inferences one needs to deal with test *scores,* as these might be relevant to making predictions. As Tenopyr said, it is difficult, if not impossible, to establish a meaningful (cutoff) score on an employment test unless one uses a predictive framework.

Referring to the relationship between content validity and construct validity, Tenopyr observed that, reduced to its simplest terms, traditional content validity is based on the results of a comparison of the representativeness of test tasks as related to the universe of tasks of which the test is a sample and says nothing about the processes of accomplishing the tasks. The "processes" about which she speaks are rooted in constructs underlying performances of both the test tasks and the job tasks.

Although Guion and Tenopyr argued that there is no such thing as content validity, the American Psychological Association and the *Uniform Guidelines on Employee Selection Procedures* both recognize such validity for personnel selection purposes. In light of this disparity, it is suggested that those who tread the murky waters of content validity try to establish the predictability of any test in question by determining the relationship betweeen test scores and relevant criteria.

Job Component Validity

Aside from the three types of validity set forth by the American Psychological Association, another validity term is introduced here, namely, job component validity. (This concept has most frequently been called synthetic validity, but for various reasons it is believed that the term job component validity is more descriptive.) It has also been called generalized validity. The concept of job component validity is predicated on the assumption that the human requirements of any given job activity or "component" would be comparable in any job in which that activity or component occurred in equal degree. The development of a procedure for establishing the job-component validity for jobs would consist of the following: (1) some method for identifying or quantifying the various constituent components of jobs; (2) a method for determining, for an experimental sample of jobs, the human attribute(s) required for successful job performance when a given job component is common to several jobs; and (3) some method of combining the estimates of human attributes required for individual job components into an overall estimate of the human attribute requirements for an entire job. Such a procedure would make it possible to "build up" the aptitude requirement for any given job by: (1) know-

ing what job components occur in the job in question, (2) knowing what aptitudes are required for each such component, and (3) having a procedure for "summating" the attribute requirements relevant to the individual job components.

This notion is reflected in Table 7.1, in which certain hypothetical job components are listed (A, B, C, D, . . . , N), along with the human "attribute" required to perform each (a, b, c, d, . . . , n). Each of three jobs (X, Y, and Z) is "described" in terms of the importance of each component to the job. The level of the requirement for each *attribute* for a given job is a function of the *importance* of the *component* for which the attribute is required. The total job requirement, in turn, is the summation of the requirements for the individual attributes. This is an overly simplified model; in practice, the "building-up" of total job requirements is not this straightforward.

The job component validity concept does not fit neatly into any one of the three types of validity recognized by the American Psychological Association. In a very general sense job component validity can be viewed in the frame of reference of content validity, if the test in question measures some specific job content (such as job-related knowledges or skills) or of construct validity if the test in question measures some basic attribute (that is, construct).

TABLE 7.1 SIMPLIFIED HYPOTHETICAL EXAMPLE OF APPLICATION OF THE CONCEPT OF JOB COMPONENT VALIDITY

Job Component	Attribute Required for Component	Importance of Component to Given Jobs			Total Attribute Requirements for Jobs		
		Job X	Job Y	Job Z	Job X	Job Y	Job Z
A	a	5	1	0	5a	1a	—
B	b	1	0	5	1b	—	5b
C	c	0	4	1	—	4c	1c
D	d	3	0	2	3d	—	2d
N	n	0	3	1	—	3n	1n

Source: McCormick (1979, Figure 10–1)

Discussion

In personnel selection the most "approved" validity is criterion-related validity, particularly the predictive variety. For reasons that will be discussed later, it is frequently not possible, or at least not practical, to use this tack, so the concurrent validity approach has been used more commonly. Even this approach is often not practical, as for example, when there are not enough incumbents on a job to serve as an adequate sample. In more recent years there has been greater interest in the possible use of content and construct validity, this being in part the consequence of the concern for equal employment opportunity, which will be discussed in a later chapter. To date, however, these types of validity have not been used very much in personnel selection processes.

METHODS OF ESTABLISHING PERSONNEL SPECIFICATIONS

As indicated before, the personnel specifications for the selection of *experienced* versus *inexperienced* candidates differ. In selecting experienced candidates—those who have had or claim to have had, experience or training for the job in question—the personnel specifications should be based on a sound job analysis describing the job activities. Individual candidates would then be evaluated in terms of the adequacy of their experience or training in those activities. In some instances the qualifications of the candidates are evaluated by job sample or achievement tests.

The more difficult procedure in establishing personnel specifications is for the selection of inexperienced candidates. In such instances one is interested in predicting the suitability of candidates for learning and adapting to the jobs in question. This must be done by determining the basic abilities (that is, aptitudes), personality and interests, and other attributes presumably required for learning or adapting to the job.

Any statements of such personnel specifications certainly need to be valid.

There are various ways of setting such personnel specifications. We will discuss these under three categories, those based on judgments, on structured job analysis procedures, and on statistical analysis. In practice, however, these sometimes are mixed together.

Specifications Based on Judgment

In some instances personnel specifications are established on the basis of judgments, considering each job as a complete entity. In discussing such judgments Barrett (1963) differentiated between what he called the "patent medicine" approach and the "man-position matching" approach. It must be stated that in past years (and probably even today) many personnel specifications have been pulled out of the hat or based on off-the-cuff guesses. This is the patent medicine approach. Such guesswork does not necessarily mean that the "judgments" are invalid, but simply that one does not know whether they are valid or not. At the least, this approach questions the validity of any resulting specifications and also, professional ethics.

Judgments of personnel specifications need not be willy-nilly; they can be based on knowledge and understanding of the job activities. This is essentially an inferential process, since the "requirement" (typically some ability) must be "inferred" from the work activity. Establishing personnel specifications in this manner implies the use of Barrett's man-position matching approach. As he pointed out, however, this approach receives mixed blessings from the psychological fraternity, in part because there are so many variations on this theme and in part because of the varied backgrounds of the practitioners of this art. In the hands of a professional who is familiar with a given job, however, the method can result in personnel specifications in which one can place reasonable confidence. Such inferences can be fairly straightforward. For example, the requirement for a reasonable level of arithmetic computation ability can be inferred with considerable confidence for an account clerk who needs to add and subtract numbers. The inferences of the requirements for many job activities, however, are not at all obvious, such as the requirements for learning to perform a complicated chemical laboratory task. At the same time inferences frequently must be made in such circumstances.

Various procedures have been used for judging the specifications of jobs, ranging from completely unsystematic schemes to those using standardized systematic procedures. One such procedure is used by the United States Training and Employment Service for setting forth the worker trait requirements of jobs as given in the Dictionary of Occupational Titles (1977). For the various jobs in the Dictionary, ratings are made by job analysts on each of the following worker traits: G (Intelligence); V (Verbal); N (Numerical); S (Spatial); P (Form perception); Q (Clerical perception); K (Motor coordination); F (Finger dexterity); M (Manual dexterity); E (Eye-hand-foot coordination); and C (Color discrimination). The ratings are made according to a rating scale which expresses the amount of each trait possessed by various segments of the working population, as follows:

1. The top 10 percent of the population.

2. The highest third exclusive of the top 10 percent of the population.

3. The middle third of the population.

4. The lowest third exclusive of the bottom 10 percent of the population.

5. The lowest 10 percent of the population.

RELIABILITY OF JUDGMENTS. Some indication of the reliability of ratings of jobs in terms of aptitudes comes from a study by Trattner, Fine, and Kubis (1955) in which they had ten jobs rated on ten different aptitudes by two groups of job analysts. One group of eight analysts rated the ten jobs on the basis of their job descriptions, and the other group rated corresponding jobs by direct observation. In each instance the analysts estimated the degree of the aptitude required by the job. The reliability coefficients of the ratings (as based on all eight raters) were very respectable, especially for the "mental" aptitudes (intelligence, verbal, and numerical) and the "perceptual" aptitudes (spatial, form perception, and clerical perception), the coefficients ranging from .87 to .96. In the case of the "physical" aptitudes (eye-hand coordination, motor coordination, finger dexterity, and manual dexterity), the reliability coefficients were generally lower, ranging from .08 to .87 (with most of them from .57 to .87).

Thus, we see that the reliability of judgments of job requirements made by trained raters is reasonably high, although some attributes can be rated more reliably than others. Interrater reliability by itself, however, is not necessarily an indication of the validity of such judgments.

VALIDITY OF JUDGMENTS. Even though personnel specifications have been established on the basis of judgments in millions of situations, there is actually little quantitative evidence on the validity of such judgments. Some data relating to the validity of such judgments comes from the study by Trattner, Fine, and Kubis. They had available test data for about sixty workers on each of the ten jobs; the data included a test score for each person on a test of each of the ten aptitudes. For those workers on each job the mean test score was computed for each of the ten aptitude tests. In turn, the mean aptitude rating was computed for each aptitude from the ratings given by the eight analysts in each of the two groups. Through a procedure that need not be described here, correlations were computed for the two "groups" of aptitudes, as follows:

The results of this rather modest study need to be accepted with some caution, but they tend to indicate that judgments of the mental and perceptual aptitude requirements of jobs may be better (that is, more valid) than judgments of physical aptitudes. This same indication can be found in the results of a study by Frank (1972) in which vocational counselors were asked to judge the minimum aptitude requirements for twenty-five occupations in terms of nine of the same ten aptitudes, following a somewhat parallel analysis.

	Based on Job Description	Based on Observation
Mental and perceptual aptitudes	.60	.71
Physical aptitudes	.01	.27

Specifications Based on Structured Job Analysis Procedures

Using judgments to establish personnel specifications for jobs as complete entities typically is (or at least should be!) based on knowledge of the job (Barrett's man-position approach). A somewhat more analytic approach is based on the use of job data from structured job analysis procedures. These procedures typically provide for the analysis of jobs in terms of specific "units" or components. The personnel requirements for these components then are established either on the basis of judgments or of statistical analysis. In turn, the total requirements for any individual job are derived by first analyzing the job in terms of these components and then "building up" the total requirements by consolidating the requirements of the individual components that apply to the job.

As one example of this approach, Marquardt and McCormick (1972) arranged for

judgments to be made of the "attribute requirements" of the job elements of the Position Analysis Questionnaire (PAQ). The ratings were obtained for seventy-six human attributes from psychologists, there being anywhere from eight to eighteen raters per attribute. The median of the ratings of these seventy-six attributes was .90, with only ten being below .80.

In an example of another variation on this general theme, Bouchard (1972) urged using the critical incident technique to identify "job dimensions" as discussed in chapter 4. Given such dimensions for a job, he suggested that they be used as the "units" of job behaviors about which inferences of job requirements can be made. Thus the ratings of the importance of the dimensions can give cues to the relative importance of the requirements inferred from them. Table 7.2 illustrates the concept of job dimensions based on critical incidents and the nature of the inferences about the abilities required for satisfactory performance of the behaviors associated with the dimensions and lists potential tests to measure those abilities.

An additional and rather different example of this general approach is the "generic skills" program of what is now the Canadian Employment and Immigration Commission (Kawala & Smith 1975). This study focused on identifying "generic skills" that would be relevant to training people for various occupations. For this purpose generic skills were considered to be those behaviors fundamental to the performance of many tasks performed in a wide range of occupations. Five classes of generic skills were covered in the study, these being listed below along with a few examples of specific skills within each class:

A total of 192 such skill items were identified, these being grouped into two "core" clusters, one at the nonsupervisory level and the other at the supervisory level.

Although the focus of the study was on developing broad-based occupational

TABLE 7.2 ILLUSTRATION OF JOB DIMENSIONS FOR A HYPOTHETICAL
JOB BASED ON THE CRITICAL INCIDENT TECHNIQUE AND THE ABILITY
REQUIREMENTS INFERRED FROM THEM.

Job Dimension	Importance Rating*	Abilities Inferred	Potential Tests
1. Planning (coordination of information and projection to future)	1.2	Intelligence	WAIS Watson-Glaser Wessman
		Verbal comprehension	Terman Concept Mastery Quick Word Test
2. Supervision of subordinates	1.6	Leadership Dominance	Fleishman Leadership Opinion Questionnaire CPI
3. Communication with higher level personnel and other agencies	2.5	Verbal fluency Self-confidence	SRA Verbal Fluency Guilford Fluency Test CPI

*The ratings in this illustration are based on a five-point scale of importance, with
1 = extremely important and 5 = hardly important at all.
Source: Adapted from Bouchard, 1972, Table 1.

Class	Examples
1. Mathematic skills	Multiplying whole numbers Adding fractions Solving single variable algebraic equations
2. Communication Skills	Reading to determine job requirements Recording data on forms Writing technical reports
3. Reasoning skills	Scheduling work Diagnosing problems Making decisions
4. Interpersonal skills	Giving rewards and discipline Using attending behaviors Using group maintenance skills
5. Manipulative skills	Using eye-hand coordination Using proper body posture for lifting and carrying

training programs, the study has interesting implications for some aspects of establishing job requirements. First, it provides a reasonably well formulated inventory of "generic" skills which could be considered "units" of job requirements. Second, the study included the use of a potentially useful procedure for determining the relevance of such "units" of job requirements, specifically an interview using employees and supervisors as respondents.

The survey by Kawula and Smith encompassed seventy-six occupations with 820 worker interviews and 1130 supervisor interviews; a major aspect of the interviews was identifying the specific skills judged to be required in individual positions. For each occupation it was possible to tally the frequency with which specific skills actually were used. These frequencies were converted to a common metric, specifically the "number of skill users out of 10." If this was 3 (out of 10) or more for a particular skill, that skill was considered to be "significant." One result was an occupational matrix that showed, for each occupation, the number of "significant" skill users (that is, the number of skill users of 3 out of 10, or above). A partial matrix is shown in Figure 7.1.

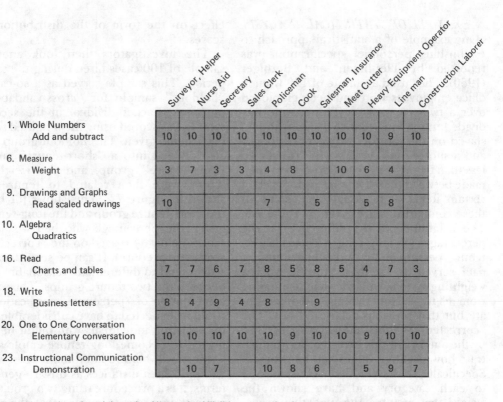

	Surveyor, Helper	Nurse Aid	Secretary	Sales Clerk	Policeman	Cook	Salesman, Insurance	Meat Cutter	Heavy Equipment Operator	Line man	Construction Laborer
1. Whole Numbers Add and subtract	10	10	10	10	10	10	10	10	10	9	10
6. Measure Weight	3	7	3	3	4	8		10	6	4	
9. Drawings and Graphs Read scaled drawings	10			7		5		5	8		
10. Algebra Quadratics											
16. Read Charts and tables	7	7	6	7	8	5	8	5	4	7	3
18. Write Business letters	8	4	9	4	8		9				
20. One to One Conversation Elementary conversation	10	10	10	10	10	9	10	10	9	10	10
23. Instructional Communication Demonstration		10	7		10	8	6		5	9	7

FIG. 7.1 Illustration of partial matrix of "generic skills" for a sample of nonsupervisory occupations. The numbers in the cells represent the "significant" skills, in particular the numbers of positions (out of ten) for which the skill was reported. (Adapted from Kawula & Smith 1975, Chart 6, pp. 120–125.)

Specifications Based on Statistical Analysis

The use of statistical analysis to establish personnel specifications is directed toward determining the relationship between measures or indications of differences in some human characteristic (that is, a predictor) and a measure of a relevant criterion (such as job performance). This is an oversimplification, as we shall see later, but for the moment let us look at this process in this oversimplified manner. The predictors used can represent individual differences of virtually any human characteristic or attribute that might be related to job effectiveness. In practice such indications include biographical data (age, marital status, education, work experience, etc.), test scores, ratings (such as by interviewers), and other data. The indications of job effectiveness can consist of any relevant criterion, such as those discussed in chapter 5. The methods for analyzing the data on the interrelationships between the predictor and the criterion will be elaborated later; they can range from very simple summarization and presentation of data to very sophisticated statistical analyses.

Such an analysis usually is carried out for a sample of people on a particular job in order to determine what predictors are significantly related to the criterion in that sample. In turn, these predictors then are used, in the case of candidates for the job, as the basis for predicting the criterion values of the candidates.

117

EXAMPLE OF STATISTICAL ANALYSIS. One example of a statistical approach to establishing personnel specifications was reported by Fleishman and Berniger (1960). They used a sample of 120 women office employees who had been employed over a two-year period. This sample was divided into a long-tenure group who had stayed on the job for two years or longer and a short-tenure group who had stayed less than two years. A comparison was then made between these two groups for each of certain items of personal data; some of these comparisons are given in Table 7.3. The magnitude of the differences in the percentages of long-tenure versus short-tenure personnel for individual items of data served as the basis for deriving a weighting system, with the weights ranging from +3 to –3. Note that age did differentiate but that previous salary did not. The "corrected" weights shown were derived by the authors of this text in order to illustrate how negative values can be avoided. Specifically, we have added a constant of 3 to each category and have shown the weight that results. Although this procedure increases the ultimate numerical values of all weighted scores (by 30), it has no

effect on the form of the distribution of scores.

The investigators then took another sample of 100 cases hired during the same period. This sample served as a so-called "holdout" sample for "cross-validation" purposes. Each individual in the second sample was scored using the weighted scoring scheme given. This holdout group was also divided into a "short-tenure" and a "long-tenure" group, and the weighted scores were then related to tenure, as shown in Figure 7.2. This shows for both the short-tenure group and the long-tenure group the percentage who had weighted scores below 34 (based on the "corrected" scoring procedure). It can be seen that the scores tend to differentiate reasonably well between the two tenure groups. Thus, this combination of "personnel specifications" could be expected to have considerable use for selecting individuals who might be expected to become long-tenure employees.

More will be said later about cross-validation in such instances as this. In general terms, it is a procedure using two groups of subjects in order to ensure that the relationships of predictors to the criterion are stable. The use of a second group provides

TABLE 7.3 EXAMPLE OF ANALYSIS OF TWO ITEMS OF PERSONAL DATA OF FEMALE CLERICAL EMPLOYEES AS RELATED TO JOB TENURE

	Criterion Groups*		Weight Assigned to Category	
	Short-Tenure Percent	Long-Tenure Percent	"Original"	"Corrected"
Age				
Under 20	35	8	–3	0
21–25	38	32	–1	2
26–30	8	2	–1	2
31–35	7	10	0	3
35+	11	48	+3	6
Previous salary				
Under $2,000	31	30	0	0
$2,000–$3,000	41	38	0	0
$3,000–$4,000	13	12	0	0
Over $4,000	4	4	0	0

*Some percents do not add up to 100 because of omissions, rounding, etc.
Source: Fleishman & Berniger, (1960).

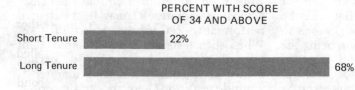

PERCENT WITH SCORE
OF 34 AND ABOVE

Short Tenure — 22%

Long Tenure — 68%

FIG. 7.2 Relationship between weighted scores based on several items of personal data and tenure of a sample of female office employees. One item scored was age, the "scores" for age being shown in Table 3.1. (*Adapted from Fleishman & Berniger* 1960.)

for a double check on the results obtained with the first group, thus minimizing the possibility that the results with the first group were due to chance.

Discussion

The use of statistical analysis is generally regarded as the most defensible method for developing personnel specifications, *if* it is feasible to use such procedures. Sometimes it can be used for confirming specifications based on judgments or on structured job analysis procedures. Conventional test validation procedures using criterion-related validity are based on statistical analysis. These validation procedures will be discussed later in this chapter. In chapter 10 we will deal with the use of statistical analysis of personnel data such as those available on application forms.

GENERAL CONSIDERATIONS IN USING PERSONNEL TESTS

Properly used personnel tests can serve as an integral part of an organization's personnel management program. In particular they should be used only when there is reasonable evidence that they can serve their purpose, that is, when they have reasonable validity. Many industrial psychologists have argued for years for adequate validation of personnel tests. Evidence of unfair discrimination against minority groups and females in the employment practices of many organizations led to the passage of the Civil Rights Act of 1964, administered by the Equal Employment Opportunity Commission (EEOC). In turn, the EEOC, the Civil Service Commission, the Depart-

ment of Justice, and the Department of Labor have promulgated a set of *Uniform Guidelines on Employee Selection Procedures* (1979) that impose certain legal requirements relating to personnel selection procedures (including tests) to minimize unfair discrimination. This issue will be discussed further in chapter 11.

Psychological Tests Are Not Infallible

Although personnel tests can be very useful for personnel selection (and other personnel management purposes), the advocate of such tests should never forget that they are not infallible; in personnel selection, for example, some persons who score high on a test that actually is valid, might not perform satisfactorily on the job. Any new procedure, whether in employment, production, or whatever, should be evaluated not as to whether it achieves perfection but as to whether it results in some improvement over methods that have preceded it. For example, let us take a company that has been selecting candidates for a particular job and finds that only 60 percent of those selected turn out to be successful on the job. If the company finds that by using tests, 70 percent of the applicants hired are successful, it might consider the test worthwhile even though 30 percent of the applicants hired do not turn out to be successful on the job.

Types of Tests[1]

Tests that have been and are being used for employee selection may be classified in

[1]A list of some commonly used tests is given in Appendix D.

several different ways. They may be *group* or *individual* tests. The group variety may be given to almost any number of persons simultaneously, the only limitation being the number that can be seated and provided with writing facilities and an adequate opportunity to hear the instructions given by the group examiner before the test is begun.

Individual tests, on the other hand, are given to one person at a time and usually call for the undivided, or nearly undivided, attention of the examiner while the test is being administered. The phrase "nearly undivided attention" is used because in certain cases, as with the Purdue Pegboard Test of Manual Dexterity, it is possible for an attentive examiner to test several persons simultaneously if the necessary sets of equipment are available.

In content, most of the tests used in industry are of three types. The first includes tests of basic human abilities, such as mental abilities and psychomotor skills. These tests generally are used as *aptitude* tests in that they are used to determine whether individuals have the capacity or latent ability to learn a given job if they are given adequate training. The second type of test measures job-specific abilities, such as typing skill and knowledge of machine-shop practices. Some such tests are called *achievement* tests because they measure the level of achievement in some job-related area. Usually they are used for such purposes as employing experienced workers and evaluating learning acquired during training. In some instances they also are used for employing inexperienced job candidates, but in these cases they are used more as aptitude tests, inasmuch as their purpose is to predict future performance. The third class of tests are measures of personality and interest; these are usually named *personality and interest inventories*. Personality and interest tests (or inventories) are intended to measure personality characteristics or patterns of interests of individuals, on the assumption that such characteristics or interests may be related to performance on various kinds of jobs. When such tests are used as employment tests, they are used to predict job performance in essentially the same manner as aptitude tests do. There are certain serious limitations to the usefulness for employment purposes of currently available personality and interest tests; these limitations will be discussed in chapter 9.

METHODS OF VALIDATING TESTS

As mentioned before, there are different types of test validity. As one would expect, the procedures for determining these different types of validity are different. Let us first make a distinction relevant to the three types of validity recognized by the American Psychological Association. *Criterion-related* validity is the validity of tests in specific situations (as for specific jobs), and is established by determining the relationship between test scores of job incumbents and some criterion of their job performance. *Content* and *construct* validity are viewed more in relation to the tests themselves. Guion (1976) labeled these as *descriptive* validity since they do pertain to the nature of the tests as such. Since criterion-related validity is the most relevant to personnel selection purposes, let us start with this, differentiating between the concurrent and predictive varieties.

Concurrent Validity

The concurrent validity of a test for a particular job is derived by what is sometimes called the *present-employee method* of test validation, since it is based on the use of a sample of incumbents who at the time in question are on the job. The procedures are as follows:

1. *Select battery of experimental tests.* An early step in a test validation project is the selection of

a battery of tests to be tried. These tests should be chosen in accordance with the extent to which they are considered to measure attributes judged to be important to job success. This selection should be made on the basis of information obtained from a job analysis.

2. *Administer tests to present employees.* The tests selected are then given to employees presently on the job. When an organization plans to carry out a test validation research project that will include the experimental testing of present employees, the organization should make such participation voluntary and should give full assurance that the tests are being given only for experimental purposes and that the results will not in any what affect the employees' relationships with the organization. It is usually desirable to distribute among the employees a sheet such as this: The Personnel Department is conducting a series of experiments. You have our assurance that this testing is being done to "test the tests" and that the results will *not* be used, now or later, in any way that will affect your standing with the company.

3. *Select appropriate criteria.* At some early phase of a test validation project it is necessary to determine what criterion of job performance to use. Criteria were discussed in chapter 5, so we need not repeat that discussion here; we only will remind you that the criterion or criteria used in any test validation study should be *relevant,* meaning that it should reflect the standards by which the performance of employees should be evaluated in terms of management's objectives.

4. *Obtain criterion information on present employees.* After determining what criterion or criteria to use, it is then in order to obtain criterion information on the individual employees now on the job. Depending on the criterion in question, this may involve the accumulation of available records (such as production records, sales volume, and the like), or it may consist of obtaining ratings from supervisors on job performance of the employees, or other appropriate processes.

Depending on how the results are to be analyzed, the criterion information may be used to divide the total employee group into two groups such as "high" (or above average) and "low" (or below average), or it may be expressed in quantitative terms, such as units of production or numerical ratings.

5. *Analyze results.* After the test scores and criterion information have been obtained, the results may be analyzed in several different ways. One method has three steps. First, the total group of employees is divided into a "high" criterion group and a "low" criterion group, as mentioned above. Next, the employees are divided on the basis of test scores into two test score groups, those scoring in the top half on the test and those scoring in the lower half. Then the percentage of "high" criterion employees in each test group is determined. If there is a higher percentage of high criterion employees among the employees in the top half on the test than there is among those in the lower half on the test, the difference is subjected to a statistical check to determine whether it is "significant." (This check is a common procedure in statistics and shows the probability that the obtained difference could have occurred by chance. If the analysis shows that the difference could have occurred by chance only one time in one hundred, the difference is said to be significant at the .01 confidence level. If the difference could have occurred by chance five times in one hundred, it is said to be significant at the .05 confidence level. It is standard practice in the field not to use tests when the confidence level is not at least at the .05 level.)

When a test has been found to be acceptable on this basis, employees are then split into smaller groups by test score, such as fifths—that is, the highest fifth on the test, the second fifth, the third fifth, the fourth fifth, and the lowest fifth. The percentage of "high" criterion employees is then computed for each of these test groups, and the resulting data are then plotted in an expectancy chart such as the one shown in Figure 7.3.[2] The chart shows the "odds" of being a superior employee for employees in each test score bracket.

An even more effective method of determining the relationship between test results and job performance is to compute a coefficient of correlation between the test scores of the employees and their criterion values. This has certain advantages over the expectancy chart method men-

[2]The procedure for constructing a five-bar expectancy chart such as the one shown in Figure 7.3 is given in detail in Lawshe, C. H., & Balma, M. J., *Principles of Personnel Testing.* New York: McGraw-Hill, 1966.

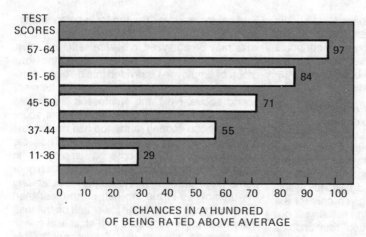

FIG. 7.3 Expectancy chart showing the relation between scores made on the Minnesota Paper Form Board and rated success of junior draftsmen in a steel company.

tioned above. First, it more accurately indicates the *amount* of the relationship between test scores and job performance. Second, it enables the employment manager to take advantage of the all-important selection ratio (see p. 000) in using the test. Third, it enables computation of the relative importance of several tests in an employment battery so that the tests may be "weighted" according to their importance. Finally, the use of the correlational method makes it possible to offset, statistically, whatever influence such factors as experience on the job or age may have had both on the test scores and on job performance of the employees. These possible influences will be mentioned later.

Although the correlational approach has certain advantages over the expectancy chart method, these are largely statistical advantages. In terms of understanding by nonstatisticians, the expectancy chart method probably is superior.

Predictive Validity

The predictive validity of a test is determined by what is called the *follow-up* method of test validation. It consists of administering tests to individuals at the time they are candidates for the job in question. The tests, however, are *not* used as the basis for selection. Rather, the individuals are selected just as they normally would have been selected if the test had not been administered, and the test scores are later re-

lated to whatever criterion is appropriate. The steps in this method are described below.

1. *Select battery of experimental tests.* This step is essentially the same as with the present-employee method.

2. *Administer tests to applicants.* The tests are administered to applicants who are to be employed for the job in question, but the applicants should not know at the time that a decision has been made to employ them. The test results are then filed until a later date.

3. *Select appropriate criterion.* This determination is made in the same way as with the present-employee method.

4. *Obtain criterion information on the new employees.* The criterion information on the new employees should not be obtained until after sufficient time has elapsed for them to demonstrate their actual abilities on the job. Usually this would be after completion of training, or at least after the completion of most of the training.

5. *Analyze results.* This step is carried out in the same manner as with the present-employee method.

Comparison of Concurrent and Predictive Validity

Both the concurrent and predictive test validation strategies have advantages and disadvantages. In using concurrent validity with aptitude tests, for example, it is possible that the test scores achieved by present employees may reflect in part the improvement in some ability resulting from experience on the job. In other words, the test scores may represent some combination of the original level of attribute measured by the test when the incumbents began work on the job plus whatever improvement the individuals have achieved through experience on the job. (Some abilities are more influenced by additional experience than others are.) In validating aptitude tests by this method, it is necessary to ensure that the tests, besides differentiating between employees according to a criterion of actual job performance, do *not* show a significant correlation with length of experience on the job, for an aptitude test should be one on which the employees who score high on the test do not score high simply because they have had the opportunity—on the job—to develop the ability which the test measures. If test scores *do* show some correlation with length of experience, the net relationship between test scores and job performance, after the effect of experience has been eliminated, can be determined by partial correlation. The procedure for computing partial correlations may be found in any standard textbook of statistics.

Although the influence of experience on test scores in such a situation can be eliminated by the use of partial correlations, a more direct manner of getting around such a problem is through using a predictive validity strategy. In this case the test scores are obtained *prior* to any experience on the job and therefore cannot be influenced by job experience.

The concurrent validity approach has certain other possible disadvantages. In some instances, the present employees on a job may be a highly select group, inasmuch as most of those who were *not* satisfactory either may have been dismissed or have left of their own accord. In such a case,

the correlation between test scores and criterion values would *not* represent the relationship that one would expect with the predictive validity approach.

Further, the "mental set" of present employees toward taking tests on a voluntary "experimental" basis may be different from the "mental set" of applicants. This difference can influence performance on some types of tests, especially personality and interest tests. When this influence is of some consequence, it would be preferable to use a predictive validity approach. If this is done, the test is then validated in the same type of situation as the one in which it will later be used.

Another disadvantage of the concurrent validity strategy is that the arrangements for testing present employees sometimes are difficult to work out, especially because it is necessary to take people away from their jobs in order to test them.

The predictive method is clearly preferable for validating tests, except for the possible disadvantage of the time required. Fortunately, it is possible in some cases to use the concurrent method for developing a battery of tests for immediate use and still plan on later "follow-up" of those selected. Although the range of test scores (and of criterion values) for those so selected usually would be restricted (thus bringing about a low correlation), it sometimes is possible to adjust for this restricted range statistically. Such an adjustment makes it possible to obtain an estimate of what the predictive validity coefficient *would* have been had the tests *not* been used for initial selection. This adjustment procedure would not be appropriate, however, if some nontest basis (for example, membership in a minority group) has been used for excluding some applicants.

Content Validity

As indicated earlier, content validity is controversial. Basically we believe that it should be viewed as an attribute of the test itself, in particular the extent to which the test consists of a representative sample of the tasks or knowledge domain it is intended to measure, such as knowledge of electrical practice, typing ability, driving ability, or law practice. Such validity frequently is based on a combination of thorough job analysis and the judgments of experts of the adequacy of the content sample of the test to the domain in question. There are, however, certain fairly systematic sampling procedures that can contribute to the development of a representative sample.

Given a test that is an adequate representative sample of the domain in mind, the question then is whether it predicts what one wants to predict, such as level of performance on a job. Here we need to determine the relationship between test scores and the criterion. Tenopyr (1977) proposed to do a thorough job of content-oriented test construction followed by a token criterion-related study, indicating that such an approach would support construct interpretations and would also solve the problem of setting a meaningful critical score to use in personnel selection. Such an approach would seem to offer a reasonable solution to what is otherwise a bit of an enigma.

Construct Validity

Construct validity is a bit like content validity in that it must considered from two aspects. The first deals with the extent to which a test measures the construct it is intended to measure. Although this usually starts with factor analyses of masses of test data, other procedures usually are also involved, all of this making a very complex process. The second aspect deals with the extent to which the construct is a requirement of whatever job is in question. This, the relevance of the construct to the job, must be supported by job analysis that

shows the work behavior(s) required for successful job performance, the critical or important work behaviors, and the construct(s) believed to underlie (or to be required for) successful performance of the behaviors in question. Such a demonstration is complicated and has not often been carried out in the field of personnel selection.

Job Status Method of Test Validation

This approach to test validation does not fall clearly into any of the above strategies, but it can be viewed in somewhat the same frame of reference as concurrent validity can. In conventional concurrent validity the criterion is a measure of job performance, whereas in the job status validity methodology the criterion is membership in some job or occupational group. The rationale for the use of such a criterion is that incumbents in a given job or occupation have "gravitated" into that type of work and presumably have performed at an acceptable level since they have "survived" on the job for a period of time.

When this method is used, the test scores of employees on each of two or several jobs are compared to ascertain whether there are significant differences. In one company the Bennett Test of Mechanical Comprehension was administered to employees on each of several jobs. Following are the mean test scores for those on certain jobs.

Job	Mean Test Score
Insulators	30.9
Pipefitters	33.8
Electricians	36.4
Welders	39.7
Instrument mechanics	42.4

If it can be assumed that, in general, most persons on a job are achieving a reasonable degree of success on that job, it is then possible to *compare* the employees on various jobs in order to ascertain what *differences* there are from job to job, as in the above example. It is then possible to select for initial placement or for promotion, those individuals whose test scores most nearly correspond to the test scores of individuals now on the job.

Job Component Validity

As indicated before, when criterion-related validity procedures are feasible and practical, they usually would be preferable. There are many circumstances in which such procedures cannot be used, however (such as when there are too few incumbents for an adequate sample), or when they may be too time consuming or costly. Thus one would wish for a generalized, simplified, and yet valid method that bypasses conventional test validation procedures for ascertaining what tests to use for selecting personnel for a given job.

In this regard, one could hypothesize that those jobs that have in common the same basic kind of human behavior or job characteristic or job component would require the same human attributes. In turn, it would seem that the same test(s) should be valid for personnel selection for all such jobs. If one could by some method identify a test valid for selecting individuals for a sample of jobs with a given human behavior or job characteristic in common, it would be reasonable to expect the test to be valid

for all jobs with that *same* behavior characteristic. These hypotheses give rise to the concept of job component validity.

JOB COMPONENT VALIDITY FOR CLERICAL JOBS. A few isolated studies have been made in which this concept has been tested in the case of specific jobs, with generally confirming results. These include one study by Lawshe and Steinberg (1955) on clerical jobs. They used the *Clerical Task Inventory* (originally called the *Job Description Check List of Clerical Operations*)[3] to identify the work activities of job incumbents in 262 clerical positions in twelve companies. The people in these positions were given the *Purdue Clerical Adaptability Test,* which results in several subscores. By a procedure that need not be discussed here, various operations had been determined to have "critical" requirements for each of the several subscores on this test, such as "spelling." In general, it was found that the larger the number of "critical" work operations in a job was, the higher the scores of individuals on such jobs were, as shown in Figure 7.4.

A GENERALIZED BASIS FOR JOB COMPONENT VALIDITY. A basic prerequisite for determining job component validity is a systematic scheme for identifying or measuring the job characteristics that might be the common denominators for comparing

[3]Copyright 1975, C. H. Lawshe. Available from Village Book Cellar, 308 West State Street, West Lafayette, Indiana 47906.

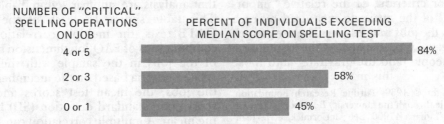

FIG. 7.4 Percent of individuals exceeding median score on spelling subtests by number of "critical" spelling operations in their jobs. (*Adapted from Lawshe & Steinberg,* 1955.)

or contrasting jobs. Probably the most generalized such basis uses the Position Analysis Questionnaire PAQ,[4] which was described in chapter 4. It will be recalled that the PAQ includes job elements that characterize the "human behaviors" in jobs, and that principal components analyses of PAQ data for a large sample of jobs resulted in identifying job dimensions that can be thought of as reflecting the "structure" of jobs.

The basic scheme in which the PAQ has been used in the job component validity context has consisted of using job dimension scores of jobs as the basis for identifying what would most likely be relevant aptitudes for selecting personnel for any given job and for estimating the aptitude- test scores that could be considered as possible cutoff scores for selecting candidates for the job. The basis for using job dimension scores for this purpose is rooted in data for a sample of jobs or the relationship between job dimension scores of those jobs and certain test data for the incumbents of those jobs. The primary analysis of this was done by Mecham (1977) with a sample of 163 jobs for which the United States Employment Service had published test data for job incumbents on each of the nine tests of the General Aptitude Test Battery (GATB). The test data for the incumbents on each job included the mean test score and the standard deviation of the test scores. The mean test scores of the incumbents of the jobs were used as an indication, or criterion, of the relative "importance" of the attribute measured by each test to the jobs in question. The use of such a criterion is predicated on the assumption that people tend to "gravitate" into those

jobs which are reasonably commensurate with their own levels of abilities. Thus, for any given test, jobs on which the incumbents have "high" mean test scores presumably require more of the attribute measured than do jobs on which the incumbents have "low" mean test scores.

The second criterion for each job was the score of the job incumbents on each test that was one standard deviation below their mean. Such a score in a reasonably normal distribution separates the lowest 16 percent of the sample from the upper 84 percent of the sample. Since only a small percentage of the actual incumbents on any given job have scores below one standard deviation, that score might be considered a very rough "lower bounds" score or possible cutoff score for candidates for the job, since most incumbents who have succeeded on the job have higher scores.

In his study Mecham used PAQ analyses for jobs that matched the 163 jobs for which the GATB test data were available. In the case of many of the 163 jobs there were several PAQ analyses; in such instances a single "composite" PAQ analysis was derived, the averages of the job dimension scores of the several analyses of the same job. These composite or averaged PAQ analyses (one for each of the 163 jobs) were then used in regression analyses (one for each of the GATB tests) as predictors of the two test-related criteria, the mean test scores and the scores one standard deviation (SD) below the mean. The results of that analysis are summarized in Table 7.4. This table shows, for each of the nine GATB tests, the multiple correlations of combinations of PAQ job dimension scores of the jobs in the sample with the test-related criteria based on the incumbents of the jobs, the mean test scores and the scores one standard deviation (SD) below the mean. A multiple correlation can be interpreted in much the same fashion as a regular correlation, except that it reflects the relationship between an optimally

[4]Copyright © 1969, Purdue Research Foundation. Available through the University Bookstore, West Lafayette, Indiana 47906. See McCormick, E. J., Jeanneret, P. R., & Mecham, R. C. A study of job characteristics and job dimensions as based on the Position Analysis Questionnaire (PAQ). *Journal of Applied Psychology*, 1972, 56(4), 347–368.

TABLE 7.4 SHRUNKEN MULTIPLE CORRELATIONS OF COMBINATIONS OF PAQ
DIVISION JOB DIMENSION SCORES AS PREDICTORS OF GATB TEST-RELATED
CRITERIA (NUMBER OF JOBS = 163)

GATB Test	Criterion	
	Mean Test Scores	1 SD Below the Mean
G: Intelligence	.79	.78
V: Verbal Aptitude	.83	.84
N: Numerical Aptitude	.77	.73
S: Spatial Aptitude	.69	.71
P: Form Perception	.61	.60
Q: Clerical Perception	.78	.75
K: Motor Coordination	.73	.67
F: Finger Dexterity	.41	.41
M: Manual Dexterity	.30	.24
Median	.73	.71

Source: Mecham 1977.

weighted *combination* of predictors (in this case job dimension scores of jobs) and the criterion (in this case mean test scores and scores one SD below the mean). It can be seen that most of these correlations are quite respectable, with the median correlations for the two criteria being .73 and .71. In only two of the tests were the correlations below .60, those being Finger Dexterity (F) and Manual Dexterity (M). The predictions for both criteria were relatively the same. These data strongly suggest that quantitative data from a structured job analysis procedure (as represented by the PAQ) can be used statistically to identify aptitudes relevant to selecting candidates for individual jobs (as such aptitudes are identified by predictions of high mean test scores) and to derive approximations of test cutoff scores that might be used (as predictions of scores one standard deviation below the mean).

Since GATB tests are not available for general use, another research exercise was required to bridge the gap between PAQ predictions of GATB test-related data and test data for job candidates that might be based on other (commercial) tests that normally would be used by most organizations.

Toward this end McCormick and others (1978) obtained test data on job incumbents on certain tests that were judged to measure the same constructs as those measured by five of the GATB tests. In turn, by a procedure that need not be described here, they converted scores on those tests to the same metric used with the GATB tests, namely, a standard score system with an arbitrary mean of 100 and a standard deviation of 20. They also obtained PAQ analyses for these jobs and derived job dimension scores for each job. As the next step they applied the regression equation as derived from the analysis of each of the five GATB tests to the PAQ job dimension scores for the jobs in question to derive predicted mean tests scores and scores one standard deviation below the mean of incumbents as based on the commercial tests that had been judged to measure the same construct as measured by each of the five GATB tests. For each of the five constructs the predicted test-related criterion values were correlated with the actual criterion values. These correlations are given in Table 7.5 with the number of jobs in each instance.

This study represents something of a

TABLE 7.5 CORRELATIONS BETWEEN PREDICTED AND ACTUAL CRITERIA
FOR FIVE CONSTRUCTS AS MEASURED BY VARIOUS COMMERCIAL TESTS

| Construct | Criterion | | Number of Jobs |
	Mean Test Scores	1 SD Below the Mean	
G: Intelligence	.74***	.66***	33
V: Verbal	.71***	.71***	50
N: Numerical	.67***	.63***	64
S: Spatial	.74***	.76***	26
Q: Clerical	.53*	.60**	15
Average	.66***	.68***	

*Significant, p < .05
**Significant, p < .01
***Significant, p < .001
Source: McCormick, DeNisi, & Shaw 1977.

cross-validation to test data based on commercial tests of PAQ-based test predictions as originally obtained from an analysis of job data in relation to GATB test data. The results of this also support the possibility of developing a generalized approach to the derivation of personnel test specifications on the basis of a job component validity model, since the resulting correlations are relatively satisfactory, with medians for the two criteria being .66 and .68. It might be pointed out that the lowest of the correlations (those for the clerical construct) are based on a rather small sample of fifteen jobs; this sample size might explain why these correlations were smaller than those for the other four constructs.

FACTORS DETERMINING THE FUNCTIONAL VALUE OF PERSONNEL TESTS

There are several practical and theoretical factors that determine the functional utility of personnel tests. These include the *reliability* and *validity* of the tests used, the *selection ratio,* and the *percentage of present employees who are "satisfactory" on the job.* Our discussion of these factors will be primarily in the frame of reference of criterion-related validity (concurrent and predictive

validity). In a general sense, the discussion also will apply to circumstances in which other types of validity are used.

Reliability

As stated earlier, a test must have an acceptable level of reliability if it is to be useful. The fact that a test has high reliability, however, provides no assurance of its criterion-related validity. A test might have *high reliability* but *low validity,* or even no validity at all. The converse is not true, for if a test has *low reliability* it cannot be expected to have any appreciable degree of validity as related to a criterion. (This is not only a rational conclusion but is also based on the principles of statistical theory. The coefficient of reliability of a test imposes a theoretical maximum on its possible coefficient of validity.)

Validity

Recognizing the potential "ceiling" of validity imposed on a test by its reliability, it is logical for us to ask: How high must the concurrent or predictive validity coefficient of a test be for the test to be worthwhile in actual use?

The answer to this question depends on

the use being made of the test. The user of tests is nearly always interested in one of two objectives but is seldom interested in both at the same time. He is interested in either making a careful and accurate analysis of *each person tested*, which is to be used for individual prediction or vocational guidance, or in selecting from a large group of individuals a smaller group that, *on the average,* will surpass the larger group in some particular respect. In individual counseling work, which deals with vocational aptitude and guidance, psychologists are interested in the former objective. Their work will stand or fall on the accuracy of their predictions of individual clients. They therefore have little use for tests that do not have a validity sufficiently high to justify their use in individual prediction. The exact value of the validity coefficient that meets this requirement is not completely agreed upon by all students of the subject, but it is uniformly agreed that the higher the validity of the test the better and that *there is no substitute for high validity for individual prediction.*

On the other hand, one may be interested in segregating from a large group of persons tested a smaller group that, on the average, will surpass the larger group in whatever trait is being tested. This is, in fact, the situation that confronts employment managers. They are willing to accept, on the basis of tests, a few individuals who will fail on a given job and to reject (or place upon some other job) a few who, had they been placed upon that job, would have succeeded, *if on the whole their percentage of successful placements is higher with the tests than it is without them.* In other words, although employment managers would like to have every swing result in a home run, they usually recognize that under normal circumstances this is not practical, and therefore are satisfied if they can improve their batting averages. Under these circumstances the acceptable validity of the tests can be much lower. But one may still ask: How low

can it be? A categorical answer to this question can be given, but the full significance of the answer will be clear only after a thorough study of the next section, which deals with the *selection ratio.* The answer is that a test probably will be valuable, no matter how low the coefficient of validity, if it indicates a *statistically significant* relationship between test scores and the criterion. Often this rule will admit tests whose validity is as low as .30 or even lower. The use of tests with such low validity is sufficiently contrary to much current thought among psychologists to warrant a fairly detailed justification for this conclusion

The Selection Ratio

Given a personnel test with a validity coefficient indicating *some* relationship with the criterion and given more candidates than can be placed on the job in question, the functional value of the test depends on the ratio of those placed to those tested who are available for placement. This has been referred to as the "selection ratio." An example will clarify the operation of this principle.

If a certain test is given to a large number of employees for whom a criterion of successfulness as employees is available and if the scattergram of test scores against the criterion is plotted, the points ordinarily will fall into an oval-shaped area somewhat similar to the oval in Figure 7.5. The higher the coefficient of validity, the narrower the oval will be; and the lower the validity, the more nearly the oval will approach a circle. A validity coefficient of approximately .60 will result in a scattering of scores approximately covering the oval area shown in Figure 7.5. Now, if candidates are placed without regard to test scores, their criterion scores usually will be the average of all individuals falling within the oval. If only those placed in this job have test scores as high as or higher than T_1, those not placed on the job will clearly

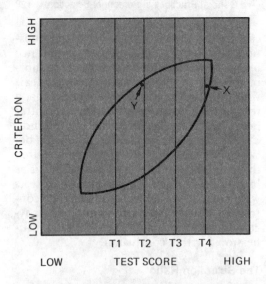

FIG. 7.5 Effect of shifting the critical score required of applicants on average criterion score of employees hired.

have, on the average, lower criterion scores than the group as a whole, and those placed will accordingly be higher in their criterion scores, on the average, than the group as a whole. A still higher average criterion score for the group placed can be achieved by setting the critical test score at T_2. By moving the critical score to T_3, T_4, or even higher, still more favorable placements, according to average criterion score, can be made.

If a given number of persons, say sixty, are to be placed, any one of the conditions mentioned above may exist. Which one exists will depend upon the selection ratio that is utilized, that is, the ratio of the number placed to the number tested. Suppose we work with a ratio of 1.00—that is, all those tested are placed. In this case, the distribution of test scores will be over the whole range of possible test scores; the criterion scores will be over the whole range of possible criterion scores, and the test will contribute nothing whatever to the efficiency of the placement procedure. Now suppose that we test eighty individuals and place the sixty who score highest on the

test, either not hiring the twenty who score lowest or placing them on some other job. We thus reduce those placed to 75 percent of those tested, or reduce the selection ratio to .75. Under these conditions, we will place on this job only individuals who test at least as high as T_1, and the average criterion scores of those so placed will clearly be higher than the average of the group as a whole. By testing 120 persons and placing the sixty who score highest on the test, the selection ratio will be reduced to .50 and only individuals to the right of T_2 will be placed. The average criterion score of this group not only will be higher than that of the whole group but also will be higher than that of the group placed when the critical test score was at T_1. Thus, by increasing the number tested before the sixty to be placed are identified, the selection ratio will be decreased with a continuous increase in the average criterion score for the group of sixty finally placed. If, for example, the organization is expanding so greatly that six hundred new employees can be tested before sixty are selected for this particular job (or if the labor market were such that six hundred applicants were tested before sixty were hired for this job), the selection ratio would be decreased to .10, only those testing at least as high as T_4 would be placed on the job, and the average criterion score of the group of sixty placed under these circumstances would be much higher than the score of sixty placed under any larger selection ratio.

The foregoing discussion is based on the assumption that the placement of employees is successful in proportion to the average success of the employees placed. Anyone can readily see that even working with a selection ratio of .10, some individuals (like X in Figure 7.5) will be placed who will be poorer according to the criterion than a few other individuals (like Y in Figure 7.5) who have not been allocated to this job. But if one is willing to measure the success of the testing program by average results rather than by individual cases, the results will be more and more favorable as the selection ratio is decreased.

The main argument of this discussion is that—in *group* testing—one can effectively use a test with a relatively low (statistically significant) validity coefficient by sufficiently reducing the selection ratio. In other words, in group testing, *a reduction in the selection ratio is a substitute for high validity.* This principle applies as well when only a few candidates are to be selected as when many are to be selected. (A selection ratio of .50 applies equally well when selecting five out of ten candidates as when selecting fifty out of one hundred.) The principle also applies under conditions of a tight labor market when virtually every applicant is to be employed, so long as the people employed are to be placed on two or more different jobs. In this regard, a *reduction* in the selection ratio can be utilized *whenever two or more candidates* are to be placed on *two or more different jobs,* if tests of some validity are available for each of the jobs.

Percentage of Present Employees Considered Satisfactory

Another factor that affects the efficiency of a personnel test in a given employment situation is the percentage of present employees who are considered satisfactory. This factor may be made clear by reference to Figure 7.6. Suppose we are working with a test having a validity coefficient such that the employees tested fall into the oval-shaped area. Suppose, further, that we are working with a selection ratio of .50—that is, only persons falling in the oval-shaped area to the right of T_2 will be placed on the job. If 50 percent of the present employees are satisfactory, any increase over this amount in the percentage of satisfactory employees placed that can be achieved by using the test is a gain. Under these conditions, the ratio of satisfactory employees among those placed to the total of those placed would be the ratio of the number of

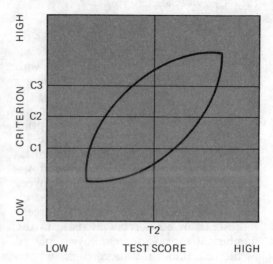

FIG. 7.6 Variation of efficiency of an employment test with differences in percentage of current employees considered satisfactory.

individuals falling to the right of line T_2 and above C_2 to all persons to the right of line T_2. This ratio would clearly be higher than .50, and the amount by which it exceeds .50 would be indicative of the functional value of the test under the conditions discussed.

If all conditions named above remain the same except that previous employment methods have resulted in 75 percent satisfactory employees, then the criterion separation line of the successful and unsuccessful employees would be C_1 and the percentage of satisfactory employees placed by means of the test would be the ratio of the individuals to the right of line T_2 and above C_1 to all persons to the right of line T_2. In the latter case, a larger percentage of employees hired will be satisfactory than in the former case, even though the test, selection ratio, and other controlling factors remain the same. In other words, if everything else is equal, the smaller the percentage of present employees who have been placed satisfactorily without tests is, the larger will be the percentage increase of satisfactory employees when employees are placed using test results. This may be illustrated by an example. Suppose we have available a test with a validity coefficient of .50 and are using a selection ratio of .50. Table 7.6 shows the increase, due to using the test, over the percentage of satisfactory employees prior to using the test. The values in Table 7.6 were obtained from the Taylor-Russell tables (Taylor & Russell 1939) shown in Appendix B. If only 5 percent of employees placed by traditional means are successful, then the expected increase to 9 percent represents an 80 percent increase in the number of satisfactory employees placed by the test, under the specified conditions of test validity and selection ratio. If larger percentages of satisfactory employees have been achieved without the test, the percentage of increase achieved by using the test will become increasingly smaller. If 90 percent of employees placed by traditional means have been successful, the increase of this percentage to 97 percent by the test, used under the specified conditions, results in an improvement of only 8 percent in the

number of employees satisfactorily placed.

The general conclusion is that, other things being equal, the more difficult it has been to find and place satisfactory employees without using test procedures, the greater the gain one may expect from a suitable testing program.

Use of Taylor-Russell Tables

The foregoing discussion was to point out that the four factors mentioned earlier —reliability, validity, percentage of present employees considered to be satisfactory, and selection ratio—operate to determine the functional value of a personnel selection test. Assuming that the reliability of a test is reasonably satisfactory and knowing the values of the other three factors, we can predict the improvement in personnel placement that would result from using the test. What is more, we also can estimate the further improvement that would result from reducing the selection ratio.

Figure 7.7 is a chart that shows how the percentage of employees selected who will

TABLE 7.6 INCREASES IN PERCENTAGE OF SATISFACTORY EMPLOYEES PLACED ON A JOB OVER VARIOUS ORIGINAL PERCENTAGES OF SATISFACTORY EMPLOYEES WHEN A TEST WITH A VALIDITY COEFFICIENT OF .50 IS USED WITH A SELECTION RATIO OF .50

A	B		
Percentage of Satisfactory Employees Placed on the Job without the Test	Percentage of Satisfactory Employees Placed on the Job with the Test	Difference in Percentage Between Columns A and B	Percentage of Increase of Values in (B) over Values in (A)
5	9	4	80
10	17	7	70
20	31	11	55
30	44	14	47
40	56	16	40
50	67	17	34
60	76	16	27
70	84	14	20
80	91	11	14
90	97	7	8

Source: Taylor-Russell Tables, Appendix B.

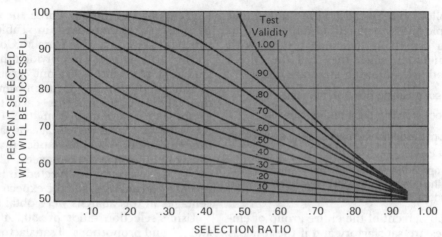

FIG. 7.7 Effect of test validity and the selection ratio on the working efficiency of an employee selection test.

be successful is determined by the validity of the test and the selection ratio. This chart represents an employment situation in which 50 percent of present employees are considered satisfactory. The base line in this figure gives the selection ratio, and each of the curves plotted indicates a different test validity. It will be seen that, by using a test with a validity of .90 and by reducing the selection ratio to .60, the percentage of satisfactory employees placed will be raised from 50 percent to 77 percent. It also will be noted that a corresponding increase to 77 percent in the number of satisfactory employees will be achieved by a test with a validity of only .50 if the selection ratio is decreased to .20.

The Taylor-Russell tables make it possible to determine what percentage of employees hired will be satisfactory under different combinations of test validity, selection ratio, and percentage of present employees considered satisfactory.

The use of these tables may be made clear by an example. Suppose an employment manager with a test with a validity coefficient of .40, has twice as many applicants available as there are jobs to be filled and is hiring for a department in which 30 percent of the present employees are considered satisfactory. Looking in the upper half of the table on p.445 (entitled "Proportion of present employees considered satisfactory = .30"), we find in the row representing a validity coefficient of .40 and in the column representing a selection ratio of .50, the value .41 where the indicated row and column cross. This means that under the conditions specified, 41 percent of the employees placed will be satisfactory, instead of the 30 percent attained without the test. If conditions are such that the selection ratio may be reduced still further, the same test will place a still higher percentage of successful employees. For example, if only the highest 10 percent of the persons tested are placed on the job, the percentage of satisfactory employees will be raised to 58 percent, or nearly double the percentage of satisfactory employees placed without the test.

The "Direct Method" of Estimating Test Effectiveness

In the foregoing discussion, the use of the selection ratio requires that test validity be expressed as a coefficient of correlation.

McCollom and Savard (1957) showed that a simple and direct method can be used to obtain essentially the same results. With this method, which they call the Direct Method, the following steps are taken:

1. Select a cutting point on the test.

2. Select a cutting point on the criterion.

3. Count the number of cases falling above both cutting points: test and criterion.

4. Compare the number of cases found in Step 3 with the number that would have been secured by random selection.

If 50 percent of the entire group of employees are satisfactory and if the test has no validity at all, 50 percent of the employees above *any* so called critical test score will be satisfactory. But if the test has *any* validity, more than 50 percent of employees above a critical test score will be satisfactory. The extent to which the satisfactory percentage of those above the critical test score exceeds the satisfactory percentage, without regard to the test score, indicates the validity of the test in the particular situation.

McCollom and Savard made several empirical comparisons between this Direct Method and results obtained with the Taylor-Russell tables, which require using co-efficients of correlation. Three such comparisons are summarized in Table 7.7, which is based on a table from McCollom's and Savard's article. They divided the data from each study into a "try-out" group and a "follow-up" group. They then computed the validity coefficient for each try-out group and determined from the Taylor-Russell tables what percentage of satisfactory employees would be expected among subsequent groups of employees. The try-out groups were then subjected to the Direct Method analysis, and the expected percentages in this analysis were obtained.

Using selection ratios of .30, .40, .50, and .60 and proportions of satisfactory employees of .50, .60, .70, and .80, the average percentage error for all three studies was 6.6 when the Taylor-Russell tables were used on the follow-up groups. The corresponding average error for the Direct Method was 5.6. These results strongly suggest that one can effectively use the selection ratio concept without computing a coefficient of correlation.

Possible Limitations of Taylor-Russell Tables

Smith (1948) made several warnings about using the Taylor-Russell tables. He pointed out that the tabled values do not

TABLE 7.7 COMPARISON OF AVERAGE ERROR (IN PERCENTAGES) OF PREDICTION FOR TAYLOR-RUSSELL METHOD AND DIRECT METHOD FOR THREE JOBS

Job and Data Source	Test	r	Average Error in Prediction	
			Taylor-Russell	Direct Method
Aircraft workers (50) (Aircraft Co.)	Wonderlic Personnel Test	.59	3.8	5.7
Clerical workers (60) (Bellows)	Clerical Aptitude Test	.57	9.0	2.2
Machine operators (46) (Tiffin)	Bennett Test of Mechanical Comprehension	.36	7.5	9.1
Averages of all three groups			6.6	5.6

Source: McCollom & Savard, 1957. Copyright 1957 by the American Psychological Association, and reproduced by permission.

apply to triangular distributions of test scores plotted against a criterion. Figures 7.5 and 7.6, which were used to explain the operation of the Taylor-Russell tables, assume that every increase in average test score is associated with an increase in average criterion measure. The tables further assume that the criterion measure in relation to test score is a linear function. Under certain conditions, however, neither of these assumptions is fulfilled. For example, it is sometimes found that success on a job increases with test scores up to a certain point, but that above this point, further increases in test scores have no relation or even (in rare cases) have a negative relation to job success. Guilford (1956) stated that an inspection of the scattergram between test scores and criterion is usually sufficient to determine whether the relation is essentially linear, but there are several methods available if it seems desirable to test the linearity of the plot. If it is decided that the scattergram represents a definitely nonlinear function, the Taylor-Russell tables should not be used to predict the proportion of successful employees that will be obtained by using the test.

Although there is a definite theoretical point to Smith's warning, some work by Tiffin and Vincent (1960) suggested that one usually can safely assume that the relationship shown by a correlation coefficient is sufficiently linear to justify the use of the Taylor-Russell tables. Using fifteen independent sets of predictor-criterion data, the theoretical expectancies obtained from modified Taylor-Russell tables (which are known as the Lawshe Expectancy Tables; see Appendix B)—were compared with the empirical expectancies determined directly from the raw data. The data of each sample were split into fifths on the test score continuum, and the percentage of satisfactory employees in each test score category was computed directly. These percentages were then compared with the theoretical percentages predicted from the Lawshe tables. In none of the fifteen sets of data did

the empirical percentages differ from the tabled percentages more than could be accounted for by chance, and in the majority of cases there was rather remarkable agreement between the empirical and the theoretical expectancies. Figure 7.8 (a) gives an example of one of the worst fits from the fifteen studies, and Figure 7.9 (b) gives an example of one of the better fits. On the basis of these results, the authors concluded that in the majority of instances it is advisable to use theoretical instead of empirical expectancies in constructing expectancy charts.

A second caution by Smith is on the source of the validity coefficient used with the Taylor-Russell tables. When, as is often the case, the validity coefficient of a test is based upon the present employee method of test validation, the validity coefficient obtained usually will be lower than what one would have obtained if the follow-up method had been used with a group of new employees. The reason for this difference is that many unsatisfactory employees have terminated their employment, and only those doing at least well enough to remain on the job are available for the determination of the validity coefficient of the test. This reduction in the range of the criterion measures reduces the validity coefficient. The difference between the available and the true validity coefficients tends to underestimate the increase in satisfactory employees that would be obtained by using the test as a part of employment procedures.

An example of the application of the Taylor-Russell tables to a set of data is shown in Figure 7.9. The validity coefficient of a battery of three dexterity tests (treated finally as a single measuring instrument) was found by Surgent (1947) to be .76. A tryout of this battery on a "hold-out" group of employees, who had not been used in determining the validity coefficient, gave the results that have been plotted in Figure 7.9. Interpolation from the Taylor-Russell tables gave expected theoretical

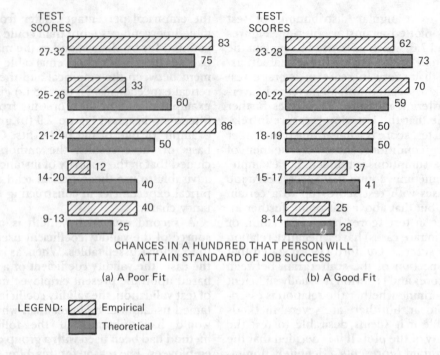

FIG. 7.8 An example of one of the poorest "fits" (a) and of one of the best "fits" (b) of empirical to theoretical expectancies. (*From Tiffin & Vincent* 1960.)

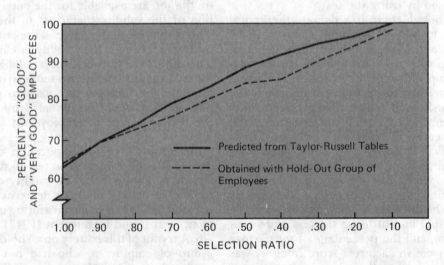

FIG. 7.9 Curves showing the percents of high criterion employees predicted from the Taylor-Russell tables and the empirical results obtained with a "hold out" group of employees not used in determining the validity of the tests.

percentages that also have been plotted in Figure 7.9. The two curves plotted do not differ significantly. It is therefore advisable, whenever possible, to make this kind of empirical check on the application of the Taylor-Russell tables to personnel test data.

INDIVIDUAL VERSUS INSTITUTIONAL EXPECTANCY CHARTS

The use of expectancy charts to show graphically the validity of a test was discussed on page 120 and illustrated in Figure 7.3. There are two types of such charts —the individual and the institutional. The individual chart (which is illustrated in Figure 7.3) shows what percentage of employees in *each test score bracket* will be superior on the job. Who is considered a "superior" employee (that is, the criterion) must be decided before the analysis can be made. Another example of an individual expectancy chart is shown in Figure 7.10(a). The employees tested in this study were maintenance men in an artificial ice plant. Each man was rated on a five-point scale by the supervisor, and men receiving a rating of 4 or 5 were considered "supe-

rior." As Figure 7.10(a) shows, if a man receives a test score between 103 and 120, there are ninety-four chances in one hundred that he will be given a rating that would classify him as superior. On the other hand, if he receives a test score between 60 and 86, he has only twenty-five chances in one hundred of being rated superior. The individual expectancy chart thus permits individual prediction—that is, the employing official can say what *each applicant's* chances are of being superior once he knows the applicant's test score on the test involved.

The primary task of employment officials is to be sure that, on the *average,* they are hiring individuals who will be most satisfactory on the job. They therefore ordinarily will be more concerned with the *institutional expectancy chart* than with the *individual expectancy chart.* The institutional chart shows the percentage of superior employees that will be obtained *if all applicants above a certain score are employed.* An example of an institutional chart constructed from the same data used in Figure 7.10(a) is shown in Figure 7.10(b)

If the labor market will permit doing so,

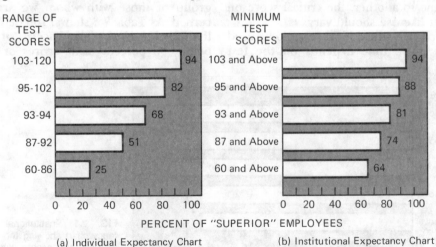

RANGE OF TEST SCORES		MINIMUM TEST SCORES	
103-120	94	103 and Above	94
95-102	82	95 and Above	88
93-94	68	93 and Above	81
87-92	51	87 and Above	74
60-86	25	60 and Above	64

PERCENT OF "SUPERIOR" EMPLOYEES

(a) Individual Expectancy Chart   (b) Institutional Expectancy Chart

FIG. 7.10 Illustration of (a) an individual expectancy chart and (b) an institutional expectancy chart as a function of scores on the Purdue Mechanical Adaptability Test for the same sample of job incumbents.

only those scoring 103 or above on the test should be employed. In this case, it can be expected that ninety-four out of every hundred persons employed, or 94 percent, will be superior. If it is impossible to get enough who make a score of 103, the hiring standard will need to be reduced. If it is necessary to employ individuals who score lower on the test, say down to 95, then only 88 percent of those employed will be "superior." With an institutional expectancy chart available, employment officers can be constantly aware of the chances they are taking as they reduce the hiring score when faced with a tight labor market.

HOW TO USE TESTS FOR EMPLOYMENT

When a test has been found to be valid for a certain job, the next question is how the test should be used in the employment situation. What critical score (cutoff score) on the test should be required? Is it necessary, or desirable, to change the critical score from time to time? The answer to all these questions is that the critical score should be as high as the labor market will permit. Because labor markets vary from one time to another, the critical score on the test likewise should vary.

Specifically, the critical score to be used at any given time depends on the test norms and the selection ratio used for the hiring. An example in which both of these data were used will clarify this point. First, the validity of the Adaptability Test for first-line supervisors was determined. This investigation resulted in the institutional expectancy chart shown in Figure 7.11. It is clear from Figure 7.11 that there were ninety-four chances in one hundred that individuals making scores of 18 or higher would survive as supervisors for a period of six months. Figure 7.11 also shows the percentages surviving among those making successively lower critical scores. Obviously, in placing individuals in the supervisory job, the higher the Adaptability Test score, the greater the chances are that those who are selected will be able to handle the new assignment. However, to decide without regard to the pool of eligible candidates that only those making a score of 18 or higher will be placed on the job is quite unrealistic. At this point, therefore, we should look at norms on the test derived from the eligible candidates. These norms are shown in Table 7.8. They show the percentile ranks (see Appendix A, p. 426) equivalent to various raw scores for the group of those with whom we are concerned. As Table 7.8 shows, 100 percent of the individuals who made scores of 27 or below, 95 percent made scores of 26 or

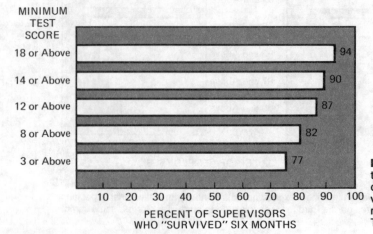

FIG. 7.11 Institutional expectancy chart showing the percent of new supervisors who "survived" six months as a function of minimum score on the Adaptibility Test.

TABLE 7.8 PERCENTILE NORMS ON THE ADAPT-ABILITY TEST FOR FOREMEN IN ONE PLANT

Percentile Rank	Score on Test
100	27
95	26
90	21
80	17
70	15
60	12
50	11
40	10
30	9
20	7
10	5
5	4
1	3

below, 90 percent made scores of 21 or below, 80 percent made scores of 17 or below, and so on down the table. In other words, with 80 percent of those making scores of 17 or below, only 20 percent made scores of 18 or above. This means that to find twenty individuals scoring 18 or above, we would need a pool of one hundred from which to select and we would therefore need to use a selection ratio of .20. Because a pool of one hundred individuals might not be available, we would have to reduce our critical score in order to fill the vacancies. If we needed twenty individuals and there were only fifty to choose among, we would be operating with a selection ratio of 20:50 or .40, which means that we would have to reduce the critical score to 13. The reason for this change in the critical score is that, as Table 7.8 shows, a score of 12 is at the sixtieth percentile, which means that 60 percent of the group made a score of 12 or below, with only 40 percent of the group scoring 13 or higher. Referring again to the expectancy chart shown in Figure 7.11, it will be seen that we will not have as high a percentage of individuals surviving on the supervisor's job for six months when we use the critical score of 13 as we had when the critical score of 18 was used.

The point is that the critical (cutoff) score on a test must be varied with the tightness or looseness of the labor market. The tighter the market, the lower the critical score. The looser the market, the higher the critical score can be.

COMBINING TESTS INTO A BATTERY

No single test will measure all of the capacities or abilities required on any job. Even the simplest of jobs is complex if one considers the combination of capacities or abilities required of a person who is to remain on the job and to do it well. The aptitudes for any job consist of a syndrome of abilities, and one needs all of these to be successful. This fact makes it desirable, and in some cases necessary, to use a battery of tests rather than a single test. There are two basic methods of using tests in a battery— the *multiple cutoff* method and the *composite score* method. With both methods, it is assumed that the validity of each test in the battery has been established for the job in question.

The multiple cutoff method involves the application of the tests one at a time and the elimination of applicants who do not score at a satisfactory level with each test. After the first test has been administered, certain low-scoring applicants are eliminated, and no further tests are administered to this group. In a similar way more applicants will be eliminated after the second test has been administered. This process is continued with all tests in the battery. After this has been completed, the only applicants remaining will be those who have made an acceptable minimum score on every test in the battery. Sometimes this method is used so that applicants (or candidates for promotion) are required to make a certain score on a stated number of tests in the battery but do not have to "pass" all of the tests.

The composite score method usually is based on the use of multiple correlations and regression analysis. A multiple correlation can be thought of as the correlation of a combination of two or more predictors (in this case tests) with another variable (in this case a criterion), with the predictors having their optimal weights. The basic data for a multiple correlation consist of correlations of all the tests with each other and with the criterion. By regression analysis it is possible to identify the combination of tests that has the highest multiple correlation with the criterion. In addition, regression analysis provides the basis for deriving the weights for the individual tests that are optimum for predicting the criterion. These weights, in turn, can be applied to the scores on the respective tests for any given individual, which are then added together to derive a composite score. (For the original sample of individuals used in the regression analysis, the "single" correlation between their composite scores and their criterion values would be about the same as the "multiple" correlation of the combination of tests and the criterion values.)

Although composite scores usually are based on the weights derived by regression analysis, in some instances the composite scores are based on the simple addition of the raw test scores. However, if the magnitudes of the scores on the seceral tests vary quite a bit, the scores should first be converted to some form of standard score (such as z-scores discussed in chapter 6) before they are added.

Quite a bit of sophisticated research work on the weighting of test scores has been published during the past twenty or thirty years. Theoretically, it seems that appropriate weighting would result in a more efficient (valid) predictor than by simply adding the raw scores made on the tests that are to be combined. The logic in favor of differentially weighting the scores seems unassailable, and therefore the method has been widely used for many years. Some empirical research on the topic was conducted by Lawshe (1959) and some of his students which makes it quite clear, however, that the differential weighting of test scores frequently does not result in a higher validity coefficient than the simple adding of raw scores does.

An example of the combination of test scores into a single composite score may be found in a set of tests worked out for placing menders in a hosiery mill. A number of tests were given to one hundred employees on this job. For each employee, data were obtained on age and experience as well as on average hourly earnings for the twelve-week period preceding the administration of the tests. The correlations between several of the tests and the earnings criterion are given below:

Test	Correlation
Purdue Hand Precision Test	.27
Finger Dexterity Test (Error Score)	.18
Hayes Pegboard	.16
Composite Score of Three Above Tests	.35

It will be noted that the maximum correlation of any individual test with earnings was .27, but that a battery made up of all three correlated at the .35 level with the same criterion. In obtaining the composite score the following formula was used: Composite Test Score = 12 (Hayes Pegboard) – 4 (Purdue Hand Precision Test) – 2 (Finger Dexterity Error Score). The constants by which the raw test scores are multiplied in this formula result in the theoretically best combination of the tests to predict job success for a combination of test scores. The usefulness of a test battery that correlates at the .35 level with a criterion may be inferred from Figure 7.12, which shows the percentage of employees placed by this battery, who will be above the average of present employees when different selection ratios are used in hiring or placement. For example, if the selection

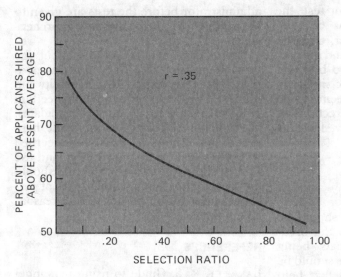

FIG. 7.12 Variation in percent of employees who will be above the present average of employees when different selection ratios are used with a test having a validity coefficient of .35.

ratio could be reduced to .10, approximately 74 percent of the employees placed would be above the current average. The value of the testing procedure in this case is enhanced by the use of several tests in combination, inasmuch as no single test, of those tried, gave as high a validity coefficient as did the battery as a whole.

In some cases the form of a scattergram itself of test scores and criterion values will indicate that a single test covers only one phase of the job requirements. This is indicated especially when a scattergram shows that persons scoring high on a test may be either high or low on the criterion, whereas virtually all of those testing low on the test are low on the criterion. The significance of this finding is that the test in question apparently is measuring one essential job requirement, but only one. An employee who lacks this requirement is almost certain to be low on the criterion, but an employee who tests high might also be low on the criterion because he lacks some other requirement not measured by the test. Those with high test scores who also are high on the criterion presumably also have the "other" requirement as well as that measured by the test in question. The

Taylor-Russell tables do not apply to tests with triangular scattergrams in relationship to the criteria.

Analyses of combinations of tests in predicting job performance criteria have led to some interesting implications for interactions among tests. In this connection, Ghiselli (1956) presented some evidence indicating that the performance of *some* individuals can be predicted from tests more accurately than the performance of *others* can. But beyond this, he found, in certain jobs, it is possible to use *one* test to identify those individuals for whom *another* test (or tests) *could* be used to predict their job performance. As he put it (1960), in certain cases it seems possible that one can predict predictability! In a study of executives, for example, Ghiselli (1963) reported that one test (called a "moderator" variable or moderator test) was used to differentiate those individuals whose job performance could be adequately predicted by another test (a "predictor" test). For the entire group, the validity coefficient of the predictor test was .41. For the 21 percent with lowest scores on the moderator test, however, the validity of the predictor test was only .10, whereas for the 26 percent with highest scores on the moderator test, the validity of the predictor test was .68.

It should be noted, however, that the identification of the moderator and the predictor test presumably needs to be done through research in the specific situation. Even though this interaction seems to be fairly situational, it suggests directions of research that may lead to improved prediction of job performance.

TEST ADMINISTRATION AND CONFIDENTIALITY

The use of personnel tests should be mutually advantageous both to the organization and to the individuals being tested. Toward this end, the tests should be administered under conditions that help place the individual at ease, for some people tend to become nervous and apprehensive at the prospect of being tested. Success in this area depends in large part on the test administrator and the manner of administering tests to job candidates. In order to ensure reasonably adequate test results, the following guidelines should be followed:

1. The test room should be light, roomy, and quiet.

2. Each person should have a comfortable chair and table or desk.

3. The test administrator should follow whatever instructions there are for administering the test, including adherence to any specified time limits.

Once tests have been administered to individuals, they should be used in a professionally ethical manner, which means that test scores of individuals should be available only to those persons who have a legitimate use for them and that the scores and tests should be considered entirely confidential by those persons who do have access to them. The fact that they will be kept in confidence should be stated by the test administrator before the tests are given to the candidates to help allay their apprehensions.

There have been questions about the possible invasion of privacy in asking people to take tests (especially personality and interest inventories) or in obtaining certain types of personal data on job candidates. We will not elaborate on this issue here other than to note that persons concerned with the selection, administration, and use of tests should be aware of this and should ensure that the tests and other types of personnel information do not violate reasonable bounds.

REFERENCES

BARRETT, R. S. Guide to using personnel tests. *Harvard Business Review,* September–October 1963, *41*(45), 138–146.

BOUCHARD, T. J. A manual for job analysis. Minneapolis: Minnesota Civil Service Commission, May 1972.

CAMPBELL, J. P. Psychometric theory. In M. D. Dunnette (Ed.), *Handbook of industrial and organizational psychology* (Chap. 6). Chicago: Rand McNally, 1976.

CRONBACH, L. J. Test validation. In R. L. Thorndike (Ed.), *Educational measurement* (2nd ed.). Washington: American Council on Education, 1971, pp. 443–507.

CRONBACH, L. J., & MEEHL, P. E. Construct validation in psychological tests. *Psychological Bulletin,* 1955, *52*, 281–302.

DUNNETTE, M. D., & BORMAN, W. C. Personnel selection and classification systems. *Annual Review of Psychology,* 1979, *30*, pp. 477–525.

EBEL, R. L. Comments on some problems of employment testing. *Personnel Psychology,* 1977, *30*(1), 55–63.

FLEISHMAN, E. A., & BERNIGER, J. One way to reduce turnover. *Personnel,* May–June 1960, *37*(3), 63–69.

FRANK, ELLEN J. A study of the reliability and validity of counselors' judgment of occupational aptitude requirements. Unpublished M.S. thesis, Purdue University, 1972.

GHISELLI, E. E. Differentiation of individuals in terms of their predictability. *Journal of Applied Psychology,* 1956, *40,* 374–377.

GHISELLI, E. E. The prediction of predictability. *Educational and Psychological Measurement,* 1960, *20*(1,) 1–8.

GHISELLI, E. E. Moderating effects and differential reliability and validity. *Journal of Applied Psychology,* 1963, *47,* 81–86.

GUILFORD, J. P. *Fundamental statistics in psychology and education* (3rd ed.) New York: McGraw-Hill, 1956.

GUION, R. M. *Personnel testing.* New York: McGraw-Hill, 1975.

GUION, R. M. Recruiting, selection, and job replacement. In M. D. Dunnette (Ed.), *Handbook of industrial and organizational psychology* (Chap. 18). Chicago: Rand McNally, 1976.

GUION, R. M. "Content validity" in moderation. *Personnel Psychology,* 1978, *31*(2), 205–213.

KAWULA, W. J., & SMITH, A. DE W. *Handbook of occupational information.* Prince Albert, Saskatchewan, Canada: Manpower and Immigration, Training Research Station, 1975. (Note: The generic skills program is now being carried out by the Occupational and Career Analysis Branch, Canadian Employment and Immigration Commission, Ottawa, Ontario.)

LAWSHE, C. H. Employee selection. *Personnel Psychology,* 1952, *5,* 31–34.

LAWSHE, C. H., Statistical theory and practice in applied psychology. *Personnel Psychology,* 1959, *22,* 117–124.

LAWSHE, C. H., & STEINBERG, M. D. Studies in synthetic validity. I: An exploratory investigation of clerical jobs. *Personnel Psychology,* 1955, *8,* 291–301.

McCOLLOM, I. N., & SAVARD, D. A. A simplified method of computing the effectiveness of tests in selection. *Journal of Applied Psychology,* 1957, *41,* 243–246.

McCORMICK, E. J. Job analysis: Methods and applications. New York: AMACOM, American Management Associations, 1979.

McCORMICK, E. J., DeNISI, A. S., & SHAW, J. B. Uses of Position Analysis Questionnaires in personnel administration. *The Personnel Administrator,* 1978, *23*(7), 50–55.

MARQUARDT, L. D., & McCORMICK, E. J. Attribute ratings and profiles of the job elements of the Position Analysis Questionnaire (PAQ). Department of Psychological Sciences, Purdue University, June 1972. ONR Contract NR 151–231.

MECHAM, R. C. Unpublished report. Logan, Utah: PAQ Services, Inc., P.O. Box 3337, February, 1977.

SMITH, M. Causations concerning the use of the Taylor-Russell tables in employee selection. *Journal of Applied Psychology,* 1948, *32,* 595–600.

Standards for educational and psychological tests. Washington, D.C.: American Psychological Association, 1974.

SURGENT, L. V. The use of aptitude tests in the selection of radio tube mounters.

Psychological Monographs, 1947, *61*(2), 1–40.

TAYLOR, H. C., & RUSSELL, J. T. The relationship of validity coefficients to the practical effectiveness of tests in selection: Discussion and tables. *Journal of Applied Psychology*, 1939, *22*, 565–578.

TENOPYR, M. L. Content-construct confusion. *Personnel Psychology*, 1977, *30*(1), 47–54.

TIFFIN, J., & VINCENT, N. L. Comparisons of empirical and theoretical expectancies. *Personnel Psychology*, 1960, *13*, 59–64.

TRATTNER, M. H., FINE, S. A., & KUBIS, J. F. A comparison of worker requirement ratings made by reading job descriptions and by direct job observation. *Personnel Psychology*, 1955, *8*, 183–194.

Uniform guidelines on employment selection procedures. *Federal Register,* vol. 43, no. 166, August 25, 1978, pp. 38290–38309.

U.S. Department of Labor, Employment and Training Administration. *Dictionary of occupational titles.* (4th ed.) Washington, D.C.: Superintendent of Documents, Government Printing Office, 1977.

8

human abilities and their measurement

The great assortment of jobs in the world requires a wide range of human qualities, some of which are called aptitudes, abilities, skills, attributes, traits, and characteristics. As we view the range of human qualities we can consider them as forming two somewhat separate classes, namely, human *abilities* and *personality and interest* factors. This chapter deals with abilities in human work, and the next chapter deals with personality and interest factors.

The gamut of human abilities can be considered as forming two general classes. The first of these includes what we will call basic abilities, those general abilities that most of us share, but in varying quantity, such as various mental abilities, perceptual skills, and psychomotor skills. These can be labeled constructs, as discussed in the last chapter. (Referring to that discussion it will be recalled that there is some question as to whether constructs are discrete, human

qualities, or whether they represent our conceptualization, that is, our assumption or hypotheses, of people's make-up. In any event they are useful concepts for describing people and job requirements. In the second group are those that we will call job-specific abilities, those possessed by individuals who have learned to perform particular activities, such as playing an oboe or programming a computer. We should add a couple of comments about these two groups. First, the line between them is admittedly fuzzy, and second, we can think of specific types of basic human abilities (the first type) as being necessary to learn specific types of job-related abilities (the second type).

TEST CONSTRUCTION

Since we will be discussing personnel tests in this and the next chapter we first

145

will mention certain aspects of test construction, in particular, item analysis. In developing a test, the test developer first must select the content of items that are judged to treat whatever construct, field of knowledge, or whatever the test is supposed to measure. The next stage is actually developing items to incorporate into what usually is an experimental form of the test. Selecting the material to be included in test items and the actual development of items are important phases of test development and should be carried out on the basis of sound professional practice. Since an extensive treatment of test development is not within the scope of this text, we will not elaborate on these processes or on the statistical analyses that should follow. It is important to us, however, to acquire at least a passing acquaintance with item analysis.

In developing tests there are two aspects of item analysis, both of which are directed toward selecting those items for the final form of the test that would be most useful (meaning most valid) for measuring whatever is to be measured. One of these is the notion of internal consistency, and the other concerns the relationship of items to some independent criterion considered to reflect the "thing" the test is intended to measure.

The internal consistency of items within a test is concerned with the extent to which the individual items measure that which the total pool of items tends to measure. Internal consistency of the items can be measured in various ways. One of these is deriving a statistical index for each item that shows its relationship to the *total scores* on the experimental test of a sample of individuals. There are many indexes that can be used; one is called a "D" (standing for discrimination) value as presented by Lawshe (1942). In using the D value in the frame of reference of internal consistency a sample of subjects is divided into two groups on the basis of their total scores on

an experimental form of the test, namely, those with high scores and those with low scores (such as those above and below average). For each item, the percent who gave a correct response (or in some instances some specified response) is determined for those in each of the two criterion groups (high and low). These two percents then are used with a nomograph to derive a D value. The higher the D value is, the greater the discrimination of the item is in terms of the criterion. A few hypothetical examples are given below.

	Percent of Correct Responses		
Item No.	In High Group	In Low Group	D Value
1	90	60	1.1
2	60	60	0.0
3	65	40	.7
4	75	65	.3
5	95	85	.6

It should be added that the D value is influenced by the difference between the two percentages and by the difficulty of the item (that is, the combined percentage of those who give correct answers.) The selection of items with high D values tends to "purify" the test—that is, to form a final test with relatively homogeneous items. But internal consistency tells us nothing about the extent to which the test measures what it is intended to measure, other than whatever inferences can be drawn from a subjective evaluation of the items. To determine this one needs to administer the test to one or more groups for whom some external criterion can be obtained or inferred, a criterion considered to reflect variations in the quality that the test is intended to measure. Such a criterion might consist of scores on another test recognized as measuring the quality in question, or perhaps of groups of people considered to differ on the quality. For example, for a test that is supposed to measure arithmetic ability, one might use as criterion groups, high school students who have high grades in arithmetic courses and those who have low grades, or one might use a group of bookkeepers (who are considered to have substantial arithmetic ability) and a group of, say, receptionists (who would be expected on the average, to have less arithmetic ability). With "high" and "low" criterion groups so formed, it is then possible to administer the experimental form of the test to them and then carry out an item analysis to identify those items that discriminate adequately between the two groups. One could use the D value for this purpose.

The two-stage process of analyzing items against an internal criterion and then against an external criterion can assure that the items that survive both of these wringers presumably would comprise a reasonably adequate test of the quality the test is intended to measure. Repetition of these operations sometimes can contribute to even further "purification" of the test. After developing a final form of a test using such procedures, it is then usually sound practice to try it out as a total test with one or more additional groups of subjects as an additional validation step, as the basis for developing test-score norms.

BASIC HUMAN ABILITIES

We recognize full well that people differ in their capacities to be able to acquire specific skills and knowledges such as those needed for certain jobs and other activities. Such capacities conventionally are called *aptitudes*. These aptitudes (or capacities) actually are basic abilities, there being marked individual differences in each such ability. Measurements of these human abilities frequently are used in predicting job performance and other criteria.

The concept of basic human abilities is rather elusive. We all would agree that the ability to perform a heavy handling activity is different from the ability to add and subtract numbers. But is being able to remember numbers (such as telephone numbers) the same as being able to remember words (such as names or a set of directions)? Although there are arguments regarding the intrinsic nature of what we here refer to as basic human abilities, for our purposes Fleishman (1967) defined a basic human ability as " . . . a more general trait of the individual which has been inferred from certain response consistencies (e.g., correlations) on certain kinds of tasks" (1967, p.351).

Farina (1969) demonstrated that these basic abilities are fairly enduring traits which have both learning and genetic components underlying their development and that they derive their "conceptual existence"—that is, our concepts of them—from the prior existence of a *factor* as identified by factor analysis. Factor analysis (which we have discussed before) is the basic statistical procedure used to identify the "inventory" of constructs, as discussed before.

As used in this context, factor analysis consists of the following processes: (1) administering a variety of tests to a sample of people; (2) correlating each test with every other test: (3) identifying the various factors by means of statistical manipulations (essentially, this step is based on the identification of the several tests that tend to form individual "groups" or "clusters" on the basis of their correlations with each other); and (4) naming each factor on the basis of subjective judgment of the "common denominator" that characterizes those tests with high statistical "loadings" on each factor. Although some human abilities actually are quite separate from others (in the sense of having virtually no correlation with them), most abilities tend to have some correlation with one or more other abilities. In an effort aimed at identifying the spectrum of human abilities viewed in this way, Fleishman and his co-workers (Theologus and others, January 1970) identified an assortment of thirty-seven abilities (including both cognitive and physical abilities), some of which are mentioned later. In a somewhat similar, but later, effort Harman (1975) identified twenty-three cognitive abilities, which are also referred to later.

Interest in human mental—that is, cognitive or intellectual—abilities goes back to research by Sir Francis Galton (1883) and the development of the early tests by Binet (1895), specifically those for identifying mentally deficient children in schools. After years of discourse about the nature of intelligence, Spearman (1927) came forth with a postulated concept of a "g" (or "general") factor of *mental energy* available to an individual, plus a variety of "s" (or specific) factors. The next major stage in the analysis of intellectual abilities was the monumental work of Thurstone (1948), who by factor analysis sorted out seven primary mental abilities, as follows:

S—Spatial visualization

P—Perceptual speed

N—Number facility

V—Verbal comprehension

W—Word fluency

M—Memory

I—Inductive reasoning

Harman's research (1975) pulled together and integrated the results of many previous studies of cognitive (that is, mental) factors. His research was based on a series of studies carried out by the Educational Testing Service in which various combinations of tests were administered to large numbers of individuals. The end result of this effort was the crystallization of twenty-three cognitive factors that probably can be considered as representing the best current view of such factors.*

As one would expect, there are some similarities between and among the various "sets" of factors mentioned above. In particular there is considerable correspondence between Harman's factors and those identified by Fleishman and his associates (although there are some differences in titles of corresponding factors). In turn, these two sets of factors have certain factors that correspond with Thurstone's or that represent subdivisions of Thurstone's factors.

Tests of Mental Abilities

Mental abilities usually are measured by tests, although there have been instances in which mental abilities have been rated. In the case of Harman's twenty-three cognitive factors there are three, four, or five "factor-referenced" tests that are proposed for use in measuring each factor. Thurstone developed tests to measure each of his primary mental abilities. In addition there are literally thousands of tests that have been developed that purport to measure these and other mental ability factors. Many such tests (along with many others) are listed and described in the *Seventh Mental Measurements Yearbook* by Buros (1972), which also gives information about the source of the test, references to research with the test, and usually some evaluation of the test and data on validity and reliability. (Appendix D of this book lists certain

*The titles of these factors are as follows, along with their letter identifications: CF, flexibility of closure; CS, speed of closure; CV, verbal closure; FA, associational fluency; FE, expressional fluency; FF, figural fluency; FI, ideational fluency; FW, word fluency; I, induction; IP, integrative processes; MA, associative memory; MS, memory span; MV, visual memory; N, number; P, perceptual speed; RG, general reasoning; RL, logical reasoning; S, spatial orientation; SS, spatial scanning; V, verbal comprehension; VZ, visualization; XF, figural flexibility; and XU, flexibility of use.

tests used widely in industry, along with their publishers.)

Tests differ in various respects, such as mode of administration (group versus individual) and level (for children, teenagers, adults, and so forth). They also differ in their content—that is, in the aspect of mental ability covered. Some such tests are intended to measure specific facets of mental abilities, whereas others are broader or more heterogeneous in content, in that they cover a variety of aspects. In fact, a number of mental ability tests used in personnel selection are quite heterogeneous in their content and probably can be considered tests of general mental ability. The use of such broadly gauged tests probably can be justified on the grounds that certain of the specific mental ability factors discussed above are in fact correlated with each other and on the grounds that by empirical investigation of many job situations they have been found to have respectable validity. If there are hints, for individual jobs, that certain specific mental abilities are of substantial importance, it would be appropriate to use in a test validation study tests that are pinpointed to measure such mental ability factors.

Examples of Mental Ability Tests in Use

Mental ability tests have been used as the basis for selecting personnel for quite a wide variety of jobs, especially for those that require substantial decision making,

reasoning, or other cognitive activities. To illustrate them, a couple of examples of test validation studies with such tests will be given.

CLERICAL JOBS. In one study the Adaptability Test was administered to clerical employees in several departments of a paper company. The correlations of scores on the test with supervisors' ratings ranged from .40 to .65 in the various departments. The individual expectancy chart for the department in which the correlation was .65 is shown in Figure 8.1.

SUPERVISORS. Mental ability tests frequently have been found to have substantial validity as the basis for selecting supervisors. This was illustrated, for example, by the results of a study of seventy employees of a rubber company who had been promoted to supervisory jobs. During the first session of a training program for these men, they were given the Adaptability Test. The test results were filed for six months, at which time a follow-up analysis was made in relation to a criterion of being "still on the job." Approximately one-fourth of the men had not "survived" as supervisors for that period; they either had quit voluntarily or had been demoted, transferred, or dismissed. Figure 8.2 shows the percentage of men still on the job after these six months, in relation to their test scores. It is interesting to note that not a single man with a score of 4 or below was still on the job, and that of those with scores between 5 and 9 only 59 percent had survived (as contrasted

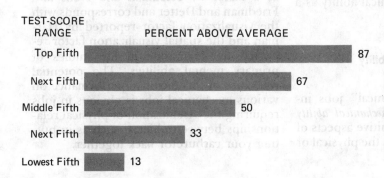

TEST-SCORE RANGE	PERCENT ABOVE AVERAGE
Top Fifth	87
Next Fifth	67
Middle Fifth	50
Next Fifth	33
Lowest Fifth	13

FIG. 8.1 Individual expectancy chart for the Adaptability Test as a predictor of job success for clerical jobs in a paper company. This chart is based on a correlation of .65 between test scores of job incumbents and supervisors' ratings of job performance.

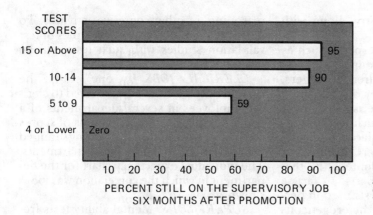

TEST SCORES

15 or Above	95
10-14	90
5 to 9	59
4 or Lower	Zero

PERCENT STILL ON THE SUPERVISORY JOB
SIX MONTHS AFTER PROMOTION

FIG. 8.2 Percent of men promoted to supervisory jobs in a rubber company who were still on the job six months later, as a function of score made on the Adaptability Test.

with 90 percent or more for those with higher scores).

DISCUSSION. The examples discussed are clearly instances in which mental ability tests have been found to be related to relevant criteria. There are many other types of jobs for which such tests also have been found to be valid predictors of job success. But it should be clearly understood that there are many other types of jobs for which such tests have little or no validity. Further reference to the level of validity of mental ability tests for various types of jobs will be made later in this chapter.

MECHANICAL ABILITY

The wide range of "mechanical" jobs that have been spawned by the mechanisms of our current world has increased the importance to jobs of mechanical ability as a human quality.

The Nature of Mechanical Ability

Although most "mechanical" jobs include physical activities, *mechanical ability* refers to the mental or cognitive aspects of such jobs as contrasted with the physical or motor aspects. Actually, as Tyler (1965) pointed out, there are two classes of such ability, which she called "mechanical aptitude." One of these is the comprehension of mechanical relations, the recognition of tools used for various purposes, and related cognitive abilities. This syndrome seems to agree with a statistically derived factor called *mechanical experience* that resulted from factor analyses by Friedman and Ivens (1954) and Friedman and Detter (1954). This factor appears to represent knowledge gained from experience with mechanical apparatus and tools. For convenience, it can be called *general mechanical aptitude.*

The other class of mechanical ability discussed by Tyler is the perception and manipulation of spatial relations— that is, the ability to visualize how parts or components fit together. This was also identified as a factor by Friedman and Ivens and Friedman and Detter and corresponds with the visualization factor reported by Harman and the spatial visualization factor reported by Thurstone in his studies of primary mental abilities. The potential relevance of this factor to performance on various mechanical jobs is obvious in jobs requiring the visualization of physical relationships between objects, such as in putting your carburetor back together.

Tests of Mechanical Ability

A few of the most commonly used tests of mechanical ability are listed in Appendix D. Examples of certain of these, or items from them, are shown in Figures 8.3, and 8.4. In addition, particular mention will be made of the Purdue Mechanical Adaptability Test, to illustrate the processes in developing standardized tests of this type.

The Purdue Mechanical Adaptabliity Test was developed to aid in identifying men or boys who are mechanically inclined and who, therefore, are most likely to succeed on jobs or in training programs calling for mechanical abilities and interests. The test measures one's experiential background in mechanical, electrical, and related activities. The test was constructed to measure experiential background because

there was reason to believe from a previous study that, other things being equal, those persons who have most profited in knowledge from previous mechanical experiences may do better on mechanical jobs than those persons who have not so profited may. The test is one of general mechanical aptitude.

The questions comprising Form A of the Purdue Mechanical Adaptability Test were selected by statistical methods designed to achieve maximum reliability of the final test and as low a correlation as possible with general intelligence. The effort to develop a mechanical ability test that would not depend very much on the general intelligence of the persons being tested payed off quite well, for the correlations of scores on this test with scores on various mental ability tests are generally rather low.

General mechanical ability and spatial

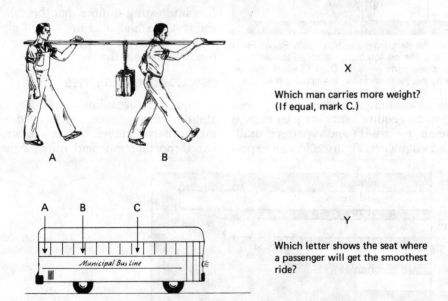

X

Which man carries more weight?
(If equal, mark C.)

Y

Which letter shows the seat where a passenger will get the smoothest ride?

FIG. 8.3 Two items from Forms S and T of the Bennett Test of Mechanical Comprehension (*Reproduced by permission. Copyright 1940, renewed 1967; 1941, renewed 1969; 1942, renewed 1969; © 1967, 1968 by The Psychological Corporation, New York, N. Y. All rights reserved.*)

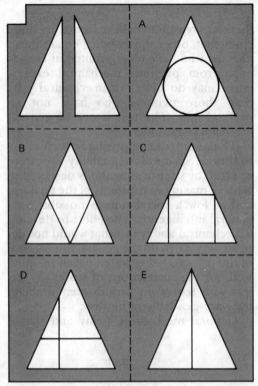

FIG. 8.4 An item from the Minnesota Paper Form Board Test. The person tested is asked to select the set of lettered parts (A, B, C, D, or E) which may be formed by the parts shown in the upper-left square.

visualization ability frequently have been found to be requirements for jobs such as craftsmen, mechanics and repairers, drafters, and engineers. Figure 8.5 is an expectancy chart based on a validation study with the Purdue Mechanical Adaptability Test for airplane engine mechanic trainees. The criterion used was instructor ratings. This figure illustrates the relevance of mechanical ability tests to successful performance in job activities of the type represented.

The use of mechanical ability tests for professional jobs is illustrated by the investigation of engineers conducted by Spencer and Reynolds (1961), who gave the Minnesota Engineering Analogies Test (MEAT) to twenty-eight recent mechanical and electrical engineering college graduates who had been employed by a manufacturer of business machines. Scores on this test were correlated with the three criteria listed below:

Criterion	Correlation
1. Training program class standing (at 6 mo.)	.40
2. Job performance ratings (at 6 mo.)	.58
3. Job performance ratings (at 18 mo.)	.64

It is interesting to note that the validity of the test was higher at the end of eighteen months of employment than at the end of the first six months.

PSYCHOMOTOR ABILITIES

Psychomotor abilities cover the range of abilities that we commonly call dexterity, manipulative ability, motor ability, eye-hand coordination, and other aspects of

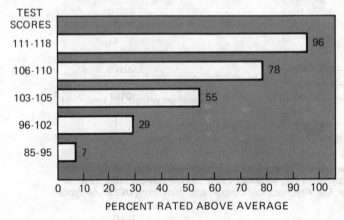

FIG. 8.5 Relation between scores on the Purdue Mechanical Adaptability Test and ratings of thirty-four airplane engine mechanic trainees.

relatively skilled muscular performance, frequently demanding some degree of visual control.

The Nature of Psychomotor Abilities

Substantial evidence indicates that there are various *kinds* of psychomotor abilities. Probably the currently most adequate representation of these was presented by Fleishman and his associates (Theologus and others, 1970) who extracted their account of psychomotor abilities from their more comprehensive taxonomy of human abilities. The following list of psychomotor activities is based in large part on several previous factor analyses by Fleishman and his associates.

Choice reaction time. This is the ability to select and initiate a response when the response is selected from two or more alternatives relative to two or more stimuli.

Reaction time. This is the speed with which a single motor response can be initiated relative to a single stimulus.

Speed of limb movement. This ability is the speed with which discrete movements of the arm or leg can be made.

Wrist-finger speed. This ability is the speed with which discrete movements of the fingers, hands, and wrists can be made.

Finger dexterity. This is the ability to make skillful, coordinated movements of the fingers in which manipulation of objects may or may not be needed.

Manual dexterity. This is the ability to make skillful, coordinated movements of the hand, or of a hand together with its arm.

Rate control. This is the ability to make timed, anticipatory motor adjustments relative to changes in the speed and/or direction of a continuously moving object.

Control precision. This is the ability to make controlled muscular movements necessary to adjust or position a machine or equipment control mechanism.

Relationships between Psychomotor Abilities

Although psychomotor abilities generally can be considered to be relatively separate types of abilities, there is still some question as to how accurate it would be to regard them as *completely* independent. The typical correlations between psychomotor tests are rather moderate, with some correlations being relatively low. Such correlations suggest that it is particularly important when using tests of such abilities to ensure that the test or tests used in a given situation are thoroughly validated for the job in question before they are used. A few typical psychomotor tests are listed in Appendix D. Illustrations of some of these are shown in Figures 8.6, 8.7, and 8.8.

Relationships between Psychomotor Abilities and Anthropometric Measures

There appear to be no across-the-board relationships between psychomotor abilities and various anthropometric measures, that is, the dimensions and other physical features of the body or body members, such as height, arm length, and hand width. However, Brady and others (1977) reported that certain anthropometric criteria (especially measures of body fat) are significantly related to three aspects of gross motor performance (specifically, dynamic strength, gross body coordination, and stamina) but not to six other aspects of gross motor performance.

Examples of Psychomotor Tests in Use

A typical job to which psychomotor abilities are of considerable importance is that of packer. In a test validation study of packers in a handcraft company, Wolins and MacKinney (1961) gave the Purdue Pegboard and the Minnesota Rate of Manipulation Test to twenty-seven employees. The job is packing handcraft kits in boxes or

FIG. 8.6 Bennett Hand-Tool Dexterity Test. (*Photograph courtesy of The Psychological Corporation.*)

envelopes. The packers were rated by their supervisor, who classified each in one of five rating categories. The correlations of the various parts of the two tests with these ratings are given below:

Test	Correlation*
Purdue Pegboard	
Right Hand	.19
Left Hand	.32
Both Hands	.19
Right + Left + Both	.27
Assembly	.47
Minnesota Rate of Manipulation Test	
Placing	.21

Turning	.40
Displacing	.16
1 hand turn and place	.26
2 hand turn and place	.27

* *The correlations for the Minnesota test were actually negative inasmuch as this test is a work-limit test with scores being based on the time taken to complete it. Because good performance on the test (low time scores) is related to good job performance (and vice versa), the correlations are shown here as positive.*

It can be seen from these data that all parts of both tests were correlated with the ratings, although certain parts had noticeably higher correlations than the others, espe-

FIG. 8.7 Purdue Pegboard.

FIG. 8.8 Stromberg Dexterity Test. (*Photograph courtesy The Psychological Corporation.*)

cially the Assembly Part of the Purdue test and the Turning Part of the Minnesota test.

VISUAL SKILLS

Most jobs use vision, but there are some jobs in which various types of visual skills are especially important to successful job performance, such as in some inspection operations, the operation of some machines, most office jobs, and the operation of vehicles.

The Nature of Visual Skills

Some of the more important visual skills are described, along with some observations regarding tests for measuring each.

VISUAL ACUITY. Visual acuity is the ability to discriminate black and white detail, usually measured as the minimum separable areas that can be distinguished. The ability to discriminate at near distances is relatively independent of the ability to do so at far distances. Therefore, tests should be given both for far visual acuity and for near visual acuity if both are relevant to job performance.

DEPTH PERCEPTION (STEREOPSIS). This function is an important phase of correct perception of spatial relationships. Of several measures for judging relative distances of objects, the most important to persons with normal vision, and the one that can be controlled and measured most reliably, depends on the slight difference in the position of the two eyes. The two eyes perform a geometric triangulation upon a distant object, and the distance of that object is perceived through an integration of the minute differences in appearance of the object to the two eyes. Other bases for perceiving distance in the third dimension may augment but cannot adequately substitute for this cue from two-eye functioning.

COLOR DISCRIMINATION. Although absolute color blindness is relatively rare, certain aspects of color deficiency are somewhat more common, such as the inability to discriminate between the reds and greens or between the blues and yellows. Even those who do not have distinct color deficiencies differ in the degree to which they can discriminate between and among various hues, shades, and tints of colors.

POSTURAL CHARACTERISTICS OF THE EYES (PHORIAS). Under normal seeing conditions the two eyes must move in relation to each other so that both converge symmetrically upon the object. It is this convergence that gives us a clear, single image of the object when it is viewed binocularly. Under certain testing conditions which eliminate the necessity for such convergence of the eyes on a single point, the eyes assume a posture that may converge or diverge from that required in normal seeing at the test distance. Such postures, called "phorias" in clinical terminology, are measured as angular deviation from the posture normally required for that distance. The deviation may be lateral or vertical and is measured separately in each direction. In addition, such deviations should be measured at the optical equivalent of both near and far vision. Many individuals have "learned" to overcome phoria conditions by controlling the muscles that direct both eyes to the point of visual regard, but in so doing they may have to maintain the eyes in a "strained" posture, thereby running the risk of muscular fatigue if the postures have to be retained for some time.

Examples of Vision Tests

Probably the most commonly used vision test is the Snellen letter chart that is a familiar sight on the walls of physicians' offices. The test consists of several rows of block letters in decreasing size, usually placed at a distance of twenty feet from the subject. The test is administered by determining, separately for each eye, the smallest letters that the subject can read. The smaller the letters the subject can read, the greater the visual acuity. The Snellen notation of acuity scores is in the form of a fraction—the smaller the fraction, the poorer the vision. In this fraction the numerator is constant and represents the distance of the test. Thus, visual acuity scored 20/20 is standard. A score of 20/40 means that the subject can read at twenty feet only a letter twice as large as standard, a letter that the "standard eye" can read at forty feet.

There are certain limitations of the usual Snellen type of vision test such as: It only measures visual acuity; it measures only far acuity (and not near acuity); and the visual targets used—namely, letters—vary in their level of difficulty. For vision testing in industry (and for that matter elsewhere), certain other tests have been developed, these testing people at the optical equivalent of both near and far distances. Four such instruments are the Ortho-Rater, the Sight-Screener, the Telebinocular, and the Vision Tester.[1] The Ortho-Rater is illustrated in Figure 8.9. This tests individuals at the optical equivalent of twenty-six feet (far distance) and thirteen inches (near distance). The Ortho-Rater includes the following twelve tests: far-distance tests of vertical phoria, lateral phoria, acuity both eyes, acuity left eye, acuity right eye, depth perception, and color discrimination; near-distance tests of vertical phoria, lateral phoria, acuity both eyes, acuity left eye, and acuity right eye.

[1]The Ortho-Rater is manufactured by Bausch & Lomb Optical Company, Rochester, New York; the Sight-Screener by American Optical Company, Southbridge, Massachusetts; the Telebinocular by Keystone View Company, Meadville, Pennsylvania; and the Vision Tester by the Titmus Optical Co., Petersburg, Virginia.

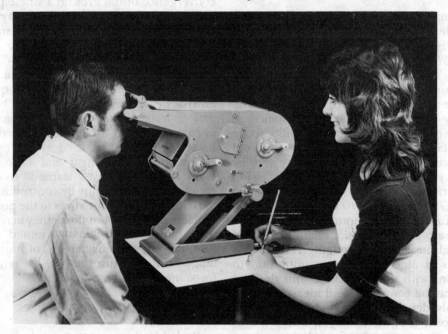

FIG. 8.9   The Ortho-Rater.

Vision Tests Used in Industry

Extensive research with the Ortho-Rater carried out over a period of years by Dr. Joseph Tiffin at Purdue University demonstrated conclusively that jobs differ in the visual demands they make upon the worker. These variations are both qualitative and quantitative. Some jobs, for example, require the ability to see at a distance, as in operating a crane or driving a truck, and others require the ability to see close at hand, as in watchmaking or fine assembly work. These are qualitative differences, inasmuch as they are predicated by different visual skills. In addition, jobs vary in the amount of a given skill that is required; some jobs, for example, require greater color discrimination than others do.

In the industrial vision research conducted at Purdue University, it was found that vision tests could be more effective if visual standards for jobs were set up in the form of "visual profiles," each profile specifying the minimum acceptable scores on the various Ortho-Rater tests. If a person had scores above the specified minimums, he "passed" the profile, and if he had one or more scores below any specified minimum, he "failed" the profile. Profiles for individual jobs were developed using various criteria such as quantity of work, quality of work, ratings, and accidents.

Additional research on the relationship between vision test scores and various criteria has shown that certain jobs in industry are similar to each other in terms of visual requirements. Jobs thus can be grouped according to their visual requirements, and the requirements of each group vary from those of the next group. Thus we have a series of job groupings, each representing a different pattern of visual requirements. This has led to the concept of "visual job families." A visual job family is a group of jobs whose visual requirements are similar. Six such visual job families have been identified: clerical and administrative, machine operator, inspection, laborer, vehicle oper-

ator, and mechanic. Research has shown that the vast majority of jobs fall into one or the other of these families. An example of the visual requirements for one of the job families is shown in Figure 8.10.

In order to investigate the relationship between visual skill test score requirements as represented by these six visual standards and success on industrial jobs, the method of cross-validation was used. A random sample of forty-three individual job studies was selected, representing 2,420 individuals. These jobs were categorized by job family, and the individuals on each job were divided into those whose visual skills "passed" or "failed" the visual performance profile for their job family. Because job performance criteria also were available for each individual, it was possible to determine the percentage of "high criterion" employees on the jobs among both those who had "adequate" and those who had "inadequate" vision, as measured by whether they passed or failed the vision profile standards. These results are summarized as follows:

It is obvious that there is generally a higher percentage of high criterion employees among those whose vision met the specified profiles than among those whose vision did not meet the profile standards, although this differs for the various job families. These differences occur in part because of the relative importance of different visual skills to the jobs in question.

JOB-SPECIFIC ABILITIES

As indicated earlier, job-specific abilities are those that have some particular relevance to particular jobs; such abilities typically are learned through experience, training, or education. The most common uses of tests of such abilities are for personnel selection and placement and for measuring performance in a training program, but they also are used for certain other purposes; for example, they may serve as the

VEHICLE OPERATOR

Visual Performance Profile

FAR

Phoria	Vertical	1	x	1	2	3	4	5	6	7	8				9	
	Lateral	2	x	1	2	3	4	5	6	7	8	9	10	11	12	13	14 15
Acuity	Both	3	0	1	2	3	4	5	6	7	8	9	10	11	12	13	14 15
	Right	4	0	1	2	3	4	5	6	7	8	9	10	11	12	13	14 15
	Left	5	0	1	2	3	4	5	6	7	8	9	10	11	12	13	14 15
	Unaided																
Depth		6	0	1	2	3	4	5	6	7	8	9	10	11	12	
Color		7	0	1	2	3	4	5	6	7	8	9	10	11	12	13	14 15

NEAR

Acuity	Both	1	0	1	2	3	4	5	6	7	8	9	10	11	12	13	14 15
	Right	2	0	1	2	3	4	5	6	7	8	9	10	11	12	13	14 15
	Left	3	0	1	2	3	4	5	6	7	8	9	10	11	12	13	14 15
	Unaided																
Phoria	Vertical	4	x	1	2	3	4	5	6	7	8				9	
	Lateral	5	x	1	2	3	4	5	6	7	8	9	10	11	12	13	14 15

FIG. 8.10 Visual performance profiles for an illustrative job family as based on the Ortho-Rater. An individual "passes" the visual requirements of a given profile if all scores fall in the shaded areas. He or she "fails" if one or more scores fall in an unshaded area.

basis for maintaining and updating performance levels (as with an airplane pilot) or as the basis for licensing and certification procedures (as with drivers' licenses and licenses to practice various occupations). The validity of job-specific tests frequently is of the *content* validity variety in which the appropriateness of the content (performance tasks, questions, and so forth) is determined by expert judgment. When an achievement test is to be used rather widely, however, as might be the case with a standardized test for commercial distribution, it is better to validate the test with an appropriate criterion. Usually this is done by using two or more job groups—such as a group of journeymen in a trade and a separate group of nonjourneymen (possibly apprentices)—as the criterion groups.

Types of Job-Specific Tests

Most job-specific tests are performance tests or written tests, although there are certain other types, such as in-basket tests. *PERFORMANCE WORK SAMPLE TESTS.* These tests provide for individuals

	Percent of "High Criterion" Employees among Those with:	
Visual Job Family	Adequate Vision	Inadequate Vision
1. Clerical and administrative	71	37
2. Inspection and close work	62	50
3. Vehicle operator	59	45
4. Machine operator	63	45
5. Laborer	67	34
6. Mechanic and skilled tradesman	69	57
Total	65	46

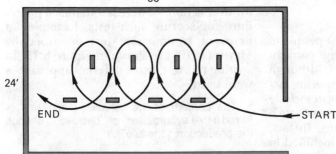

50'

24'

END

START

FIG. 8.11 Standard driving course diagram for performance test for fork-lift operator. (*Test prepared by U.S. War Dept., Office of Quartermaster General, Philadelphia Quartermaster Depot, Testing Station.*)

to perform specific job operations in a controlled testing situation, using actual or simulated equipment. A scoring procedure is developed, and norms of experienced and of inexperienced workers usually are developed in the test situation as a basis for evaluating scores.

An example of a performance work sample test is one that was developed by the Philadelphia Quartermaster Depot for fork-lift operators. A fork-lift truck is used for moving materials in a warehouse or around an industrial plant. The test consists of driving a loaded fork-lift truck around a standard driving course as shown in Figure 8.11. The "walls" and the obstacles are constructed from pallets thirty two by forty inches, painted yellow to contrast with the floor. Without going into detail, it should be pointed out that the equipment used and instructions should be standardized. The person giving the test has a check sheet on which to record observations. This checklist includes a listing of forty-two poor operating techniques such as "Did not start in low gear," "Started jerkily," "Scraped side walls of tires," "Lowered load too quickly," and "Number of pallets displaced." Scoring is based on the number

of errors made, as recorded on the checklist.

Although it might appear that many jobs would not lend themselves to work sample tests, it can be seen from an example such as this that the use of imagination and inventiveness can result in the development of tests that can be objectively scored for a wide variety of jobs.

Another area in which the work sample method of testing has had very satisfactory results is selecting employees for stenographic, clerical, and secretarial positions. Among the most commonly used work sample tests for office jobs are typing tests, such as the Typing Test for Business, the SRA Typing Skills Test, and the Thurstone Examination in Typing. Some of these tests are for typing from straight copy while others, such as the Thurstone Examination in Typing, also are for typing from corrected copy, as shown in Figure 8.12. Stenographic tests usually are recordings on tape or record from which the subject is to transcribe and then type. The Seashore-Bennett Stenographic Proficiency Test, for example, consists of five letters dictated by a typical business voice, and that vary in length and speed of dictation.

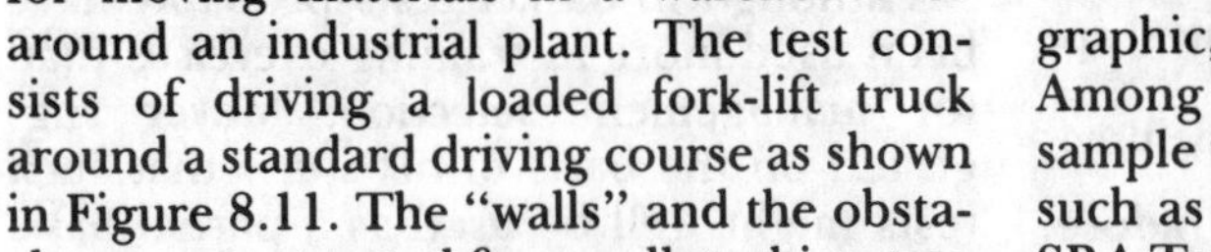

The typical business man is an optimist. For him, the future is full of possibilities that have never been realized in the past. He is not, however, a dreamer, but one whose imagination is used in formulating setting up purposes which lead to immediate action. His power of execution and planning often surpass that of his imagination, and he is often surprised to have realized his vision in less time than he had even dared hope.

FIG. 8.12 Part of the Thurstone Typing Test (part of the Thurstone Employment Tests). The person tested is required to copy this material, making the indicated corrections.

Written Work Sample Tests

Written work sample tests test people in certain job-related areas using conventional paper-and-pencil tests. Although most such tests contain items requiring factual knowledge, such tests can also include items that test the application of such knowledge to practical problems. In fact, the range of items that can be included in such tests is quite varied. The following is an example of an item from the Information Test of Engine Lathe Operation, one of the Purdue Vocational Tests.

> *Instructions.* In each of the multiple-choice statements to be listed below, there are four possible answers, but only one is correct. Read each statement carefully before making your choice of answers:
> When grinding a tool bit:
>   (A) It should be moved back and forth across the face of the tool
>   (B) It should be held on the wheel until the tool is blue
>   (C) It should be ground the same shape to cut all metals
>   (D) A tool rest should never be used

IN-BASKET TEST. As indicated before, certain tests—such as work samples, discussed earlier in this chapter—are, in effect, simulations of a job or of a part of a job. A type of simulation applicable to management performance that has received a fair amount of attention in recent years is the in-basket test. This has been used particularly in management training, but it also can be used as a selection technique. The name comes from the fact that the test consists of an assortment of items such as a manager might find in an in-basket—letters, reports, memoranda, notes, and related materials. Each subject taking such a test is confronted with these and must "do" something with each of the items or note down what action he would take about them if in a manager's job. For example, he may "answer" a letter, and in some instances may be asked to indicate the reason

for the "action." There is a standard procedure for scoring such tests. Examples of items of an in-basket test described by Meyer (1970) are shown in Figure 8.13. In scoring this test, three different approaches were used:

1. The *content* of the behavior (such as "referred it to a subordinate" or "decided to change the production schedule").

2. The *style* of behavior (such as "involves subordinates" or "makes a concluding decision").

3. Rating on *overall performance* by the scorer.

In this particular study, scores were given on twenty-seven specific categories. The split-half reliability of these scores ranged from .50 to .95. For a sample of forty-five managers there was a correlation of .31 between a composite score (based on certain in-basket test items) and criterion ratings made by their superiors on "planning-administrative" performance.

Although in-basket tests probably have been used more as training exercises than for management selection, Meyer suggested on the basis of his study that such tests might well be used as a partial basis for management selection. Brass and Oldham (1976) offered some substantiating evidence of the potential utility of in-basket tests for personnel selection of foremen. They emphasized the importance of developing appropriate scoring categories to reflect relevant leadership dimensions.

Job Sample Tests in Use

Job sample tests are most often used in the selection of individuals who have had—or claim to have had—some type of training or experience in the job-related field in question, such as typing or machine-shop work. A review by Asher and Sciarrino (1974) provided some inklings about the validity of such tests in actual use in various situations. They summarized validity data on the use of job sample tests (what they

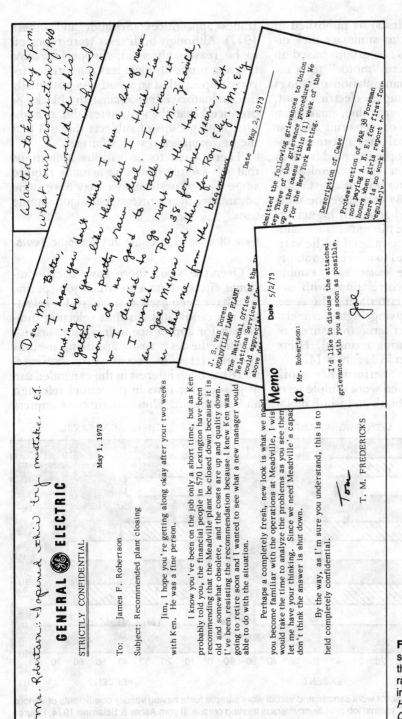

FIG. 8.13 Partial examples of some "items" of an in-basket test, these consisting of letters, memoranda, and the like, with which an individual is to deal. (*Courtesy H. H. Meyer and General Electric Company.*)

called work sample tests) as published in various sources. In this summary they divided the studies into two groups based on whether the tests were "motor" tests requiring a physical manipulation of things (such as tracing a complex electric circuit, operating a sewing machine, making a tooth from plaster, or repairing a gear box), or were "verbal" tests, either language-oriented or people-oriented (such as a test about farming, a test of chemical information, an in-basket test, or a test relating to police work). By and large the *motor* work sample tests had generally higher validity coefficients than the *verbal* work sample tests did. The criteria used in the various studies were found to affect the validity coefficients, with the *motor* work sample tests having higher correlations with on-the-job *job proficiency* criteria and the *verbal* work sample tests having higher correlations with *training* criteria (measures of learning obtained during training). These differences are shown in Figure 8.14.

In another study, performance work sample tests and written work sample tests were used with both black and white metal trades apprentices (Schmidt and others 1977). Although both tests were reported to be reasonably valid, the performance test was found to have less potentially adverse impact (that is, it had less potentially discriminatory effect against the black apprentices) than the written test did. In addition, both groups of subjects thought that the performance test was fairer.

There seem to be various indications that job sample tests that actually require some type of performance may have some advantages over written types of job sample tests.

New Directions in Using Job-Specific Tests

Over the years there have been occasional circumstances in which job-specific tests have been used as the basis for selecting job candidates, such as selecting individuals for apprentice training. In such instances, the tests really are being used as aptitude tests. In recent years, however, there has been interest in the expanded use of job-specific tests in personnel selection and placement. These stirrings of interest

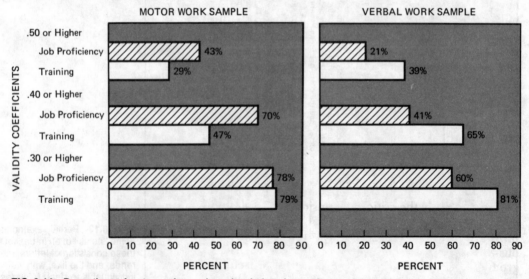

FIG. 8.14 Proportions of motor work sample and verbal work sample tests having validity coefficients of various magnitudes when validated against job proficiency versus training criteria. (From Asher & Sciarrino 1974, Figures 4 & 5, pp. 526, 527.)

arise in part because typical predictions of job success from conventional aptitude tests is relatively modest. In part this interest has been stimulated by the concern for ensuring equal employment opportunities for persons of various ethnic groups. There are indications that conventional aptitude tests may in some circumstances result in unfair discrimination. Because of court rulings and governmental equal opportunity policies that require evidence that tests used for personnel selection are "job-related," personnel people are increasingly turning to job-specific tests, which are more likely to fulfill the legal and policy requirements for such evidence.

In general, then, the current trend toward reexamination of the approaches to personnel selection appears to be encouraging the use of job-specific tests for this purpose.

THE CONCEPT OF BEHAVIORAL CONSISTENCY. One example of this search for new approaches appeared in the work of Werniment and Campbell (1968), who suggested the notion of behavioral consistency as a frame of reference. By consistency of behavior, they meant little more than the familiar bit of conventional wisdom, "the best indicator of future performance is past performance." They proposed that one should rely less on "signs" of future job performance than on "samples" of relevant behavior. "Signs" refer to the relatively conventional predictors such as aptitude tests and biographical data. They argued for the use of "samples" of behavior—that is, behaviors similar to the actual behaviors to be performed on the job.

Such an approach requires a systematic study of the job. The first step in this process is to identify the critical dimensions of job performance. This is followed by a thorough search of each applicant's previous work experience and educational background to determine if any behaviors (for example, "samples") relevant to these dimensions have been required of him or have been exhibited by him in the past. The adequacy of such "behaviors" then could be used as the basis for predicting performance in corresponding aspects of the job. If the person's past repertoire has not included such behaviors, one might then obtain a measure of such behaviors by using work sample or simulation exercises.

SUPPORT FOR THE BEHAVIORAL CONSISTENCY MODEL. Some support for the notion of behavioral consistency has been reported. For example, Asher and Sciarrino (1977) cited some evidence that background information about people reveals that their previous experience can better predict job performance than various tests can. On the basis of such evidence they postulated a point-to-point theory which stated that the more features there are in common between the predictor and the criterion the higher the validity will be.

As another example of a study that has implications for the behavioral consistency model, Campion (1972) used a performance work sample test for a group of thirty-four maintenance mechanics. From an analysis of the job, a work sample of four tasks was developed: installing pulleys and belts, disassembling and repairing a gearbox, installing and aligning a motor, and pressing a bushing into a sprocket and reaming to fit a shaft. These tests and a battery of paper-and-pencil tests were administered to the mechanics and paired comparison criterion ratings of the mechanics were obtained from the foremen. Scores on the work sample test had a correlation of .46 with the criterion, but none of the five paper-and-pencil tests had a significant correlation. Although one would feel more comfortable if the study had been carried out on a follow-up (that is, predictive validity) basis rather than on a present employee (that is, concurrent validity) basis, the findings nevertheless suggest that the behavioral consistency approach may be useful for the personnel selection arena.

In still another instance Gordon and Kleiman (1976) found that a work sample test for policemen with both "motor" and "verbal" components better predicted a criterion of trainability than an intelligence test did. (The trainability criterion was the sum of scores received on all graded exercises given during training.) Still further evidence comes from a laboratory study reported by Mount and others (1977) in which performance of a sample of subjects on a simple Gilbert Erector Set problem was found to be predictive on a more complex problem at a later date of performance.

Collectively, there appears to be substantial support for the behavioral consistency theory, which suggests that the closer one can come to getting some measure or indication of performance on *samples* of the work activities people might be expected to perform in a job, the better the predictions one would be able to make of the actual performance of individuals on the activities in question.

VALIDITY OF VARIOUS TYPES OF ABILITY TESTS

This chapter has included a few examples of test validation studies with certain ability tests used with specific jobs. Let us now take an overview of the validity of various types of ability tests for selecting people for various occupations and occupational groups. Ghiselli (1966) assembled and organized most of the published and some unpublished data on the validity of various types of basic ability tests (that he called aptitude tests) and personality tests. These data later were updated by the inclusion of data from published and unpublished sources that became available after his initial analyses (Ghiselli 1973). In both the initial and the updated studies the data from any given validity study were classified in terms of type of test used; the major categories in this classification were as follows:

Intellectual abilities

Spatial and mechanical abilities

Perceptual accuracy

Motor abilities

Personality traits

In turn, each job represented was put into an occupational category on the basis of two classification systems—(1) a General Occupational Classification system (GOC) with twenty-one categories developed for this purpose; and (2) certain categories of the classification system of the Dictionary of Occupational Titles (DOT) of the U.S. Department of Labor. A further distinction was made as to whether the criterion used in the validation study in question was a training criterion or a performance criterion.

Another source of related information is that reported by Asher and Sciarrino (1974). As discussed before and as illustrated in Figure 8.14, their survey of test validities was of work sample tests (both motor and verbal). However, they also presented data on the validity of such tests compared with the validity of certain types of aptitude tests, of personality tests(as originally summarized by Ghiselli), and of biographical data (as previously summarized by Asher, 1972).

Variability of Validity Coefficients

Some indication of the variability of validity coefficients of aptitude tests is given in Figure 8.15, which shows distributions of the coefficients for certain tests for particular job categories. The type of criterion is given for each. In discussing these coefficients, Ghiselli suggested that the variation may result from any of a number of factors such as sampling differences; differences in the kind of jobs within each group, the range of scores of the people on each job,

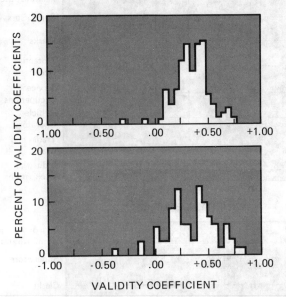

Jobs (N = 111): mechanical repairmen
Tests: mechanical principles
Criteria: training

Jobs (N = 72): general clerks
Tests: intelligence
Criteria: proficiency

FIG. 8.15 Examples of variation in the validity coefficients of given tests for certain job categories. (*From Ghiselli,* 1966 *Figures 2-4, p. 29.*)

and the conditions under which the tests were administered. Whatever the reasons, the variation is obvious. It should be noted that some of the coefficients hovered around zero, and a few were even negative.

Figure 8.14 shows some variability in the validity coefficients of work sample tests, although that figure does not show the complete range of such coefficients.

Mean Validity Coefficients

An impression of the average validity coefficients of the five types of tests summarized by Ghiselli for various occupation categories is given in Figure 8.16. The coefficients for training criteria are shown as part (*a*) and the coefficients for proficiency criteria as part (*b*). Scanning this figure produces the following conclusions: The validity coefficients of each class of test vary across the occupation categories (but for certain classes of tests the differences are greater than for other classes of tests);

training criteria generally are predicted better than proficiency criteria are; prediction for certain occupation categories is somewhat better than for others; the mean validity coefficients for the different classes of tests are rather different for certain occupation categories but are quite similar for others; and the general level of the coefficients is not particularly high, with most of the coefficients falling in the range from about .15 to .35 or .40. This last point implies that a very great amount of variability in the criteria is not explained by the types of tests covered in the study.

A partial comparison of the test validity data presented by Ghiselli with that for work sample tests and biographical data presented by Asher and Sciarrino (1974) is shown in Figure 8.17, these data being for job proficience criteria. (Note that the data from Ghiselli are on intelligence, mechanical aptitude, finger dexterity, and spatial relations, the last three of these representing subclasses of the categories of spatial

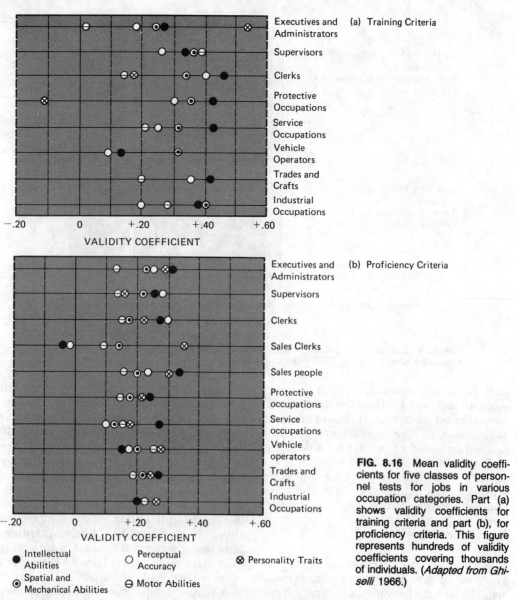

FIG. 8.16 Mean validity coefficients for five classes of personnel tests for jobs in various occupation categories. Part (a) shows validity coefficients for training criteria and part (b), for proficiency criteria. This figure represents hundreds of validity coefficients covering thousands of individuals. (*Adapted from Ghiselli* 1966.)

and mechanical abilities and of motor abilities.) The systematically highest correlations for biographical data will be discussed further in chapter 10, but such data, along with the good showing of motor work sample tests, also support the potential relevance of the concept of behavioral consistency already discussed.

Coefficients for Training and Proficiency Criteria

Ghiselli's summary of test validity data for aptitude tests reflected rather consistently higher validity coefficients for training criteria than for job proficiency criteria, although there are some inversions in this

166

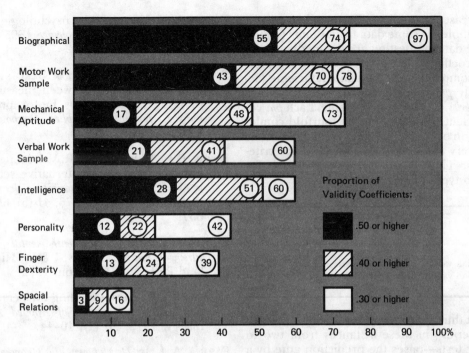

FIG. 8.17 Proportions of validity coefficients of various magnitudes with job proficiency criteria for eight types of predictors. (Adapted from Asher & Sciarrino 1974, Figures 1, 2, & 3. Data for item with * are from Ghiselli 1966.)

general pattern. The general pattern can be seen in the data shown in Figure 8.16 (a) as contrasted with 8.16 (b). The grand average of the validity coefficients for all tests for all jobs taken together is .39 for training criteria and .22 for proficiency criteria.

Bemis (1968) reported at least partially confirming evidence from an examination of 424 validity studies using the General Aptitude Test Battery of the United States Employment Service. He found that tests of "cognitive" aptitudes (general intelligence, verbal, numerical, and spatial) usually were correlated to a higher degree with training criteria than with job proficiency criteria. In moderate contrast with Ghiselli's findings of no appreciable difference between the two types of criteria with regard to motor abilities, Bemis found that manipulative tests (coordination and finger and manual

dexterity) tended to have slightly higher correlations with proficiency criteria than with training criteria.

Although validity coefficients for aptitude tests generally tend to be higher when the tests are validated against training criteria than against proficiency criteria, it will be recalled that in the motor work sample tests the reverse was true as shown in Figure 8.14.

Discussion

From the data summarized by Ghiselli (1966; 1973) and shown in Figures 8.15 and 8.16, it is obvious that the validity of individual aptitude tests generally is fairly moderate. Some additional predictability in using such tests frequently is possible if such tests are combined into batteries. This

167

increase in predictability is reflected, for example, by some data from Bemis (1968). The data in question are the median validity coefficients of all tests for all 424 jobs, as compared with median coefficients (actually *phi* coefficients) for jobs for which *batteries* of tests were available. Each *phi* coefficient was based on the fourfold combination of "pass" or "fail" on all tests in the battery and "high" or "low" on the criterion. These results are summarized, for both types of criteria used:

	Type of Criterion	
	Training	*Proficiency*
Median validity of individual tests	.22	.22
Median validity of test batteries	.42	.40

It thus appears that combining tests into batteries—in these instances from two to four tests—raises the prediction ante by a substantial amount.

In discussing the combining of tests into a battery, we should recall the discussion in chapter 7 of the two methods of doing this. One method uses composite scores in which the scores of individuals on two or more tests are added together, usually with statistically determined weights. The other method uses multiple cutoff scores, with a minimum cutoff score on each of the two or more tests.

REFERENCES

ASHER, J.J. The biographical item: Can it be improved? *Personnel Psychology*, 1972, *25* (2), 251–269.

ASHER, J.J., & SCIARRINO, J.A. Realistic work sample tests: A review. *Personnel Psychology*, 1974, *27* (4), 519–533.

BEMIS, S. E. Occupational validity of the General Aptitude Test Battery. *Journal of Applied Psychology*, 1968, *52* (3), 240–244.

BINET, A., & HENRI, V. La psychologie individuelle. *Année psychologie*, 1895, *2*, 411–465.

BRADY, J.I., KNIGHT, D.R., & BERGHAGE, T.E. Relationship between measures of body fat and gross motor proficiency. *Journal of Applied Psychology*, 1977, *62* (2), 224–229.

BRASS, D.J., & OLDHAM, G.R. Validating an in-basket test as an alternative set of leadership scoring dimensions. *Journal of Applied Psychology*, 1976, *61* (5), 652–657.

BUROS, O.K. (Ed.) *The seventh mental measurements yearbook.* (Vols. 1 & 2.) Highland Park, N.J.: Gryphon, 1972.

CAMPION, J. E. Work sampling for personnel selection. *Journal of Applied Psychology*, 1972, *56* (1), 40–44.

FARINA, A. J., Jr. *Development of a taxonomy of human performance: A review of descriptive schemes for human task behavior.* Silver Spring, Md: American Institutes for Research, Technical Report 2(R69–8), January 1969.

FLEISHMAN, E. A. Performance assessment based on an empirically derived task taxonomy. *Human Factors*, 1967, *9*, 349–366.

FRIEDMAN, G., & DETTER, H. M. Factor analysis of airman classification battery and selected air force and civilian tests. *Research Bulletin*, AFPTRC–TR–54–75.

FRIEDMAN, G., & IVENS, F. C. Factor analysis of the airman classification battery AC–1B; the USES General Aptitude Test Battery, experimental visualization and spatial tests, and psychomotor tests. *Research bulletin*, AFPTRC–TR–54–67, Air Force Personnel and Training Research Center, Lackland Air Force Base, San Antonio, Texas.

GALTON, F. *Inquiries into human faculty and its development.* London: Macmillan, 1883.

GHISELLI, E. E. *The validity of occupational aptitude tests.* New York: Wiley, 1966.

GHISELLI, E.E. The validity of aptitude tests in personnel selection. *Personnel Psychology,* 1973, *26* (4), 461–477.

GORDON, M.E., & KLEIMAN, L.S. The prediction of trainability using a work sample test and an aptitude test: A direct comparison. *Personnel Psychology,* 1976, *29* (2), 243–253.

GUILFORD, J. P. *The nature of human intelligence.* New York: McGraw-Hill, 1967.

HARMAN, H.H. Final report of research on assessing human abilities. Princeton, N.J. Educational Testing Service, PR–75–20, July 1975.

LAWSHE, C.H., JR. A nomograph for estimating the validity of test items. *Journal of Applied Psychology,* 1942, *26* (6), 846–849.

MEYER, H. H. The validity of the in-basket test as a measure of managerial performance. *Personnel Psychology,* 1970, *23* (3), 297–307.

MOUNT, M. K., MUCHINSKY, P. M., & HANSER, L. M. The predictive validity of a work sample: A laboratory study. *Personnel Psychology,* 1977, *30* (4), 637–645.

SCHMIDT, F.L., GREENTHAL, A.L., HUNTER, J.E., BERNER, J.G., & SEATON, F.W. Job sample vs. paper-and-pencil trades and technical tests: Adverse impact and examinee attitudes. *Personnel Psychology,* 1977, *30* (2), 187–197.

SPEARMAN, C.E. *The abilities of man.* New York: Macmillan, 1927.

SPENCER, G. M., & REYNOLDS, H. J. Validity information exchange, No. 14–04. *Personnel Psychology,* 1961, *14,* 456–458.

THEOLOGUS, G. C., ROMASHKO, T., & FLEISHMAN, E. A. *Development of a taxonomy of human performance: A feasibility study of ability dimensions for classifying tasks.* Silver Spring, Md.: American Institutes for Research, Technical Report 5 (R70–1), January 1970.

THURSTONE, L. L. *Primary mental abilities.* Chicago: Psychometric Laboratory, University of Chicago, Report No. 50, 1948.

TYLER, L.E. *The psychology of individual differences.* New York: Meredith, 1965, pp. 144–145.

WERNIMONT, P. F., & CAMPBELL, J. P. Signs, samples and criteria. *Journal of Applied Psychology,* 1968, *52* (5), 372–376.

WOLINS, L., & MACKINNEY, A. C. Validity information exchange, No. 15–04. *Personnel Psychology,* 1961, *15,* 227–229.

9
personality and interest factors

There is an almost universal assumption by personnel managers that the personality and interests of individuals can have a marked influence on their work performance and on the extent to which people adjust to their jobs. At the same time, however, the history of the use of personality and interest tests in personnel selection has been dismal. Assuming for the moment that such factors do affect job-related behavior, we can divide this argument into two segments. First, it is reasonable to assume that in some circumstances such factors do have an influence on job-related behavior via a motivational route. Hence one could expect that individuals with certain interest and personality patterns might be more inclined to look for certain types of jobs and that once on such jobs they would be expected to adjust better to them and perhaps to gain greater satisfaction from them than would people with other interest and personality patterns. Certainly vocational guidance pays much attention to such factors.

Second, it is reasonable to assume that, in *some kinds* of jobs, personality factors have a direct bearing on the adequacy with which people can fulfill the functions of their jobs. This is particularly true for jobs that require substantial amounts of personal contact with other people, as in some sales work, public relations work, some supervisory and management activities, interviewing, and the like. Even the success of some politicians depends on how well they interact with people.

Assuming the relevance of both of these assumptions of the implications of personality and interest factors as related to job behavior, the fact remains that using measures of these factors has been pretty bleak. We will discuss the problems associated with such measures later, but first we will discuss briefly the "structure" of personality and interest factors and will describe certain personality and interest tests.

THE STRUCTURE OF PERSONALITY AND INTERESTS

It is common to describe people in terms of various personal qualities or traits such as introversion-extroversion, sociability, dominance, or impulsiveness. This brings to mind our earlier discussion of constructs. On this subject Guion (1965) stated that the dimensions of personality and interest are fairly vague and ill defined. Although it is probably not yet possible to declare that there actually are certain distinct dimensions of personality, there are certain general syndromes that we can use in characterizing the outward behavior of people and that reflect our "conception" of personality dimensions or constructs. Perhaps the most current representation of such constructs is Harman's (1975), in the form of twenty-eight "temperament" factors. A few of these are agreeableness, alertness, dependability, dominance, emotional stability, gregariousness, and self-confidence.

The typical personality and interest tests measure constructs such as these, although it is probable that some of the constructs presumably measured by such tests are figments of the test developers' imaginations.

TYPES OF PERSONALITY TESTS

Personality tests generally fall into two categories—*projective techniques* and *questionnaire inventories.*

Projective Techniques

Examples of projective techniques are the Rorschach Ink Blot Test and the The-matic Apperception Test (TAT). In these tests, subjects are presented with an intentionally ambiguous stimulus (such as an ink blot or picture) and is asked to tell what they "see" in it. In other words, they "project" themselves into the stimulus. A trained administrator interprets the individual responses and patterns of responses and assesses the subjects. These tests are not used very commonly in industry, although they are used more for selecting executives than for other types of personnel. They are used rather widely in clinical practice.

Personality Inventories

The second class of personality tests consists of paper-and-pencil questionnaires. Although such questionnaires are commonly called tests, they are in a sense not really "tests" inasmuch as there are no right or wrong answers; the term *inventory* is more accurate.

CONVENTIONAL FORMAT AND SCORING OF INVENTORIES. Conventional personality inventories usually contain statements or questions relating to behavior, attitudes, feelings, or beliefs. Subjects are asked to respond to these as they apply to them. An example of such an item is given below:

I feel uncomfortable with other people

(a) Yes

(b) Don't know

(c) No

The responses to individual items usually are "scored" on each of several personality attributes or traits, such as dominance, sociability, or impulsiveness. Responses are scored for a particular attribute or trait after they have been identified—either by statistical analysis or on rational grounds—as the responses characteristic of individuals who possess that attribute or trait.

FORCED-CHOICE PERSONALITY IN-VENTORIES. Because of the possibility of what is labeled "faking" with conventional personality inventories, some inventories are based on the forced-choice technique. In the final form such inventories include blocks of two or more statements from which subjects are asked to select the one that is "most" or "least" like themselves. The items within any given block have been combined into that block because they are about equal on their "favorability." (This is based on a *favorability* index or *preference* index derived from the responses of a sample of subjects who were asked to make such judgments of the various items.) Of those with equal favorability within a block, however, one will have been selected because it has been found to discriminate statistically between a couple of criterion groups (for example, between introverts and extroverts). Because individuals presumably cannot select the "best" response (all responses being "equal" in favorability), they presumably would tend to select the one that really is most like themselves. Such a response "adds" to their score on the dimension on which the item has been found to discriminate. (In some variants of the forced-choice technique there are both favorable and unfavorable items. In such cases favorable ones are equally favorable, and unfavorable ones are equally unfavorable, and respondents are asked to select the response that is "most" applicable to them and the one that is "least" applicable.)

EXAMPLES OF PERSONALITY AND INTEREST INVENTORIES

Below are examples of a few personality and interest inventories used in personnel selection and placement.

Personality Inventories

A number of the personality inventories used for personnel selection and placement

are listed in Appendix D. Two of these will be described briefly.

CALIFORNIA PSYCHOLOGICAL IN-VENTORY (CPI). This inventory is essentially a spinoff of the Minnesota Multiphasic Personality Inventory (MMPI), except that whereas the MMPI was designed for use with "abnormal people," the CPI was developed for use with "normal individuals." It provides scores on eighteen components in four classes, as follows:

Class I. Measures of poise, ascendancy, and self-assurance.
Components: 1. Dominance; 2. Capacity for status; 3. Sociability; 4. Social presence; 5. Self-acceptance; 6. Sense of well-being.

Class II. Measures of socialization, maturity, and responsibility.
Components: 7. Responsibility; 8. Socialization; 9. Self-control; 10. Tolerance; 11. Good impression; 12. Communality.

Class III. Measures of achievement potential and intellectual efficiency.
Components: 13. Achievement via conformance; 14. Achievement via indepeodence; 15. Intellectual efficiency.

Class IV. Measures of intellectual and interest modes.
Components: 16. Psychological-mindedness; 17. Flexibility; and 18. Femininity.

GORDON PERSONAL INVENTORY. This inventory is based on the forced-choice technique discussed earlier in this chapter. The items consist of four descriptions of personal characteristics. Individuals are asked to indicate that statement which is *most* like themselves and the one which is *least* like themselves. Two of the statements are generally "favorable" (but about equally so) and the other two are generally unfavorable (but also equally so). Here is a sample set:

Prefers to get up early in the morning

Doesn't care for popular music

Has an excellent command of English

Obtains a poorly balanced diet

This inventory results in scores on the following four personality components:

Cautiousness (C)—reluctance to take chances

Original thinking (T)—enjoyment of creative or intellectual activity, curiosity

Personal Relations (P)—patience, understanding tolerance

Vigor (V)—ability to work rapidly and energetically

Interest Inventories

Interest inventories usually require the person being tested to indicate the strength of his interests in such things as hobbies, recreation, leisure-time activities, jobs, and other activities. Sometimes this is done by presenting groups of activities and asking the individual to indicate which one he likes most and which least, or by indicating for each stated activity how much he likes it. Brief descriptions of three interest inventories are given:

STRONG VOCATIONAL INTEREST BLANK (SVIB). This inventory has been developed primarily for vocational guidance counseling. It determines whether the subject's pattern of interests agrees with the interest pattern of persons in each of a number of professions and occupations. Other things being equal, a person choosing a profession or occupation is more likely to be happy and successful if his basic interests are similar to the interests of persons actually in that field. The scoring of the SVIB results in a standard score for each of a number of occupations, with corresponding letter grades of A, B+, B, B−, and C. The higher the score for any "occupation," the more nearly the person's pattern of interests jibes with that of successful people in that occupation. Part of a record form for the SVIB is shown in Figure 9.1 which illustrates the scores of one individual for a few of the many occupations. This example is based on the form for men, but there is a separate form for women.

KUDER INTEREST INVENTORIES. The items in the Kuder Interest Inventories consist of triads of activities, from each of which the individual chooses the most preferred and the least preferred. There are different forms of these inventories, the main one being the Kuder Preference Record (KPR)—Vocational (Form C). This form assesses interests associated with ten broad occupational areas: mechanical, outdoor, computational, scientific, persuasive, artistic, literary, musical, social service, and clerical. The Kuder Occupational Interest Survey (KOIS) (Form DD) provides for scoring on the basis of the interest patterns of people in various occupations who are satisfied with their work choices; in this respect it is much like the Strong Vocational Interest Bank (SVIB). Indeed, when Zytowski (1972) compared the scores on these two inventories for 332 individuals across fifty-two pairs of "identical" or "similarly named" occupational scales (for example, banker was correlated with banker, purchasing agent with buyer), he found that the median of the 332 correlations was .57. This is a fairly respectable, general level of relationship. Although the correlations for some individuals were much lower than this, the reason for those lower correlations could not be ascertained.

VOCATIONAL PREFERENCE INVENTORY (Holland). A more recent interest inventory, Holland's Vocational Preference Inventory (VPI) (Holland 1966), provides for scoring of interests for the following six categories: (R) Realistic; (I) Intellectual; (A) Artistic; (S) Social; (E) Enterprising; and (C) Conventional. An interesting elaboration is possible with this inventory by using these categories to assign occupations to different classifications consisting

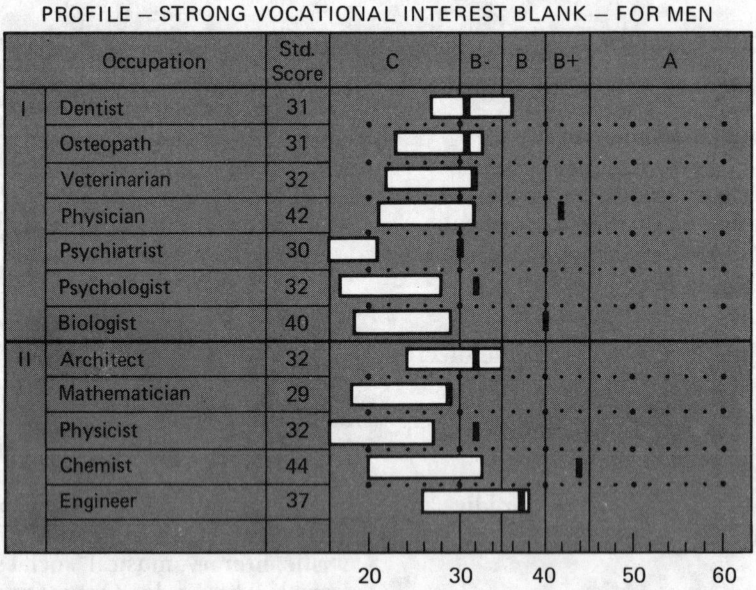

PROFILE — STRONG VOCATIONAL INTEREST BLANK — FOR MEN

	Occupation	Std. Score	C	B-	B	B+	A
I	Dentist	31					
	Osteopath	31					
	Veterinarian	32					
	Physician	42					
	Psychiatrist	30					
	Psychologist	32					
	Biologist	40					
II	Architect	32					
	Mathematician	29					
	Physicist	32					
	Chemist	44					
	Engineer	37					

20   30   40   50   60

FIG. 9.1 Part of the report form for the Strong Vocational Interest Blank for Men, showing the scores of one individual for a few of the occupation scales. The white area for any occupation represents the range of scores of the middle third of a sample of men-in-general. (*Reprinted with permission of the publishers, Stanford University Press.*)

of "combinations" of the above categories; for example, advertising agents and salesmen are in a category designated ESC (Enterprising, Social, Conventional).

LIMITATIONS OF PERSONALITY AND INTEREST INVENTORIES

As one might imagine, personality and interest inventories have rather serious limitations for personnel selection of which the most critical is the possibility of what is called "faking" by the individual taking the test.

Faking of Personality and Interest Inventories

People taking a personality or interest inventory for personal counseling or for vocational guidance usually will be moti-

vated to give relatively truthful answers for it is in their interest to find out all they can about themselves. If they are applying for a job, however, their motivation to get the job might consciously or unconsciously induce them to give responses that they *think* will make them appear to be the kind of persons for which the employer is looking. Various studies of faking have been carried out, some in simulated situations (as in classrooms) and others in real-life situations.

FAKING IN SIMULATED SITUATIONS. In a study of faking in a simulated situation Rusmore (1956) administered the Gordon Personal Profile to eighty-one college students in a simulated "industrial" situation (as though they were applying for a job) and also in a simulated "guidance" situation (as though they were being counseled). He found a significant difference in the scores on the *responsibility* component and on *total* scores. Evidence from other, similar studies generally has confirmed the suspicions that people can (and do) give somewhat different responses to personality inventories when given different instructions for the frame of reference they should assume when responding to the inventories.

FAKING IN REAL SITUATIONS. Although people can distort their responses to personality inventories if they wish to do so, to what extent, if at all, do people fake their responses in real situations, as when applying for a job? There is little evidence on this, but there are a few straws in the wind, though of mixed types. As an example of the tendency to "fudge" a bit when responding to personality inventories, Gordon and Stapleton (1956) compared the scores on the Gordon Personal Profile of 121 high school students who first took that inventory for their regular guidance program and who later took the inventory when applying for outside summer employment. The results revealed significant differences on the components of *responsibility* and *emotional stability* as well as on *total* scores. There have been other studies that also indicated that applicants for employment sometimes tend to give responses to personality and interest inventories that are somewhat different from those they would give under other circumstances.

On the other side of the coin, there are a few suggestions that the extent of faking in actual employment situations may not be as widespread and pervasive as it has generally been assumed to be. Some evidence, for example, comes from a study reported by Abrahams and others (1971) with the Strong Vocational Interest Blank (SVIB). The subjects used were applicants for Navy scholarships, and the inventory was given in a real-life situation. Scores obtained during this actual situation were compared with those taken under routine testing programs for two groups: (1) those who had

previously taken the SVIB when in high school, and (2) those who took the SVIB when in college—a year after applying for the scholarship. The mean scores (on a special scoring key) for these groups are given:

Test Condition	Group 1	Group 2
Routine test administration (mean)	102.7	98.9
Applying for scholarship (mean)	103.5	102.3
Correlation	.79	.71

The means reflect virtually no difference between the two test conditions for either group, and the correlations are reasonably acceptable. Further, the two profiles for the fifty-five occupational scales of the SVIB were virtually the same both for group 1 (a correlation of .95) and for group 2 (a correlation of .98).

As another example, Schwab and Packard (1973) administered the Gordon Personal Inventory and the Gordon Personal Profile to two groups of women who were employed by an electrical manufacturing firm. The firm decided to employ the individuals in both groups even before these inventories were given to them. One group of twenty-nine was given the inventories "as the final step in the selection process" but did not know that decisions had already been made to hire them, whereas the other group of thirty was given the inventories *after* they had been told that they had been hired (and were told that the data were simply being obtained for a university research project). There were no significant differences between the two groups in the mean responses on any of the scales for either inventory, and the investigators concluded that in this situation there was no evidence of distortion by applicants seeking employment.

DISCUSSION. In reflecting on the faking problem, it may be said with reasonable confidence that people *can* distort responses somewhat if they set their mind to it or if they are "coached" to do so by someone else. But it is *not* evident that there is a *generalized,* pervasive tendency for people actually to distort their responses in real-life situations in which they have (or think they have) something to gain by so doing. This is not to say that some individuals would not fake in virtually any situation, or that in certain circumstances they would not do so. It does suggest that faking may not be as great a factor in personality and interest inventories as has generally been suspected.

Methods of Minimizing Effects of Faking

The potential utility of personality and interest inventories is reduced by the extent— whatever it is—to which people distort their responses. However, there are ways and means of minimizing such effects.

FORCED-CHOICE TECHNIQUE. Even though it has been shown that some forced-choice inventories are vulnerable to faking, it probably is not possible to indicate the extent of this vulnerability in real-life situations. Although some unspecified amount of faking may be possible, it still seems that such inventories are somewhat preferable to conventional inventories that do not use this method.

IDENTIFICATION OF FAKERS. Some inventories have special scoring procedures for identifying individuals who tend to give faked responses. These scores are based on the responses to items which are seldom chosen by persons responding honestly but which are chosen frequently by those who deliberately try to fake the inventory. Such scores are provided for in such tests as the Minnesota Multiphasic Personality Inventory, the California Psychological Inventory, and the Kuder Preference Record. In fact, such scores themselves sometimes are predictive. For example, Ruch and Ruch (1967) found that such a score on the Minnesota Multiphasic Personality Inventory (the K score) had a correlation of .39 with rated performance of 182 sales representatives. The correlations of scores on the five scales of the inventory ranged from −.10 to −.41. Thus the K score was more predictive than all but one of the regular scores. Ruch and Ruch hypothesized that the good salesperson is more likely than the poor salesperson to have a clear conception of what the selling job's demands were in terms of personality and thus is better able to put the better foot forward. This insight may then also carry over into the responses the salesperson gives on the inventory, thus producing a higher K score. They refer to the hypothetical construct responsible for such behavior as "job-image discrepancy" (JID).

USE OF SPECIAL SCORING KEYS. Another scheme that can help to minimize the effects of faking is the development of a special scoring key for use in each circumstance, using the follow-up (that is, predictive) validation procedure. The steps are:

1. Administer a personality or interest inventory to a group of applicants for a particular type of job.

2. Select candidates in the usual way (*without* reference to the inventory).

3. Later obtain relevant criterion data for the personnel selected (such as measures of job performance, tenure, etc).

4. Item-analyze the responses to the inventory against the criterion in order to identify those responses which differentiate in terms of the criterion.

5. Incorporate these into a special scoring key.

In this procedure the responses that were given by individuals when they were candidates would have been influenced by whatever mental set the candidates had at the time. If some such responses—whether honestly given or not—do differentiate, they could be used in an empirically based scoring procedure.

A study by Tiffin and Phelan (1953) illustrated this approach. Personnel at a metal parts factory had been given the Kuder Preference Record (Vocational Form C-H) to applicants for hourly paid jobs for a period of fourteen months. The inventories, however, had not been used in the employment process. In a follow-up analysis, a criterion of job tenure was used. Of those who had originally taken the inventory two criterion groups were selected, namely, a "long-tenure" group of 250 present employees with eleven to fourteen months' job tenure, and a "short-tenure" group of 200 who had worked for three months or less. An item analysis as described in chapter 7 was carried out with these two criterion groups to identify the item responses that tended to discriminate between two groups, and a special scoring key was developed based on such responses.

This special scoring key was then used in scoring the inventories of other individuals who were likewise separated into long-tenure and short-tenure criterion groups. The results of this cross-validation are shown in Figure 9.2. With this type of cross-validated evidence an organization could use the spe-

cial scoring key for scoring the inventory with reasonable confidence that it would be useful in identifying the job candidates most likely to remain in the job.

PERSONALITY AND INTEREST INVENTORIES IN USE

Remembering the reservations about personality and interest inventories, let us cite a couple of validation studies in which such inventories were used and then take an overview of their use in personnel selection.

Examples of Inventories in Use

ARCHITECTS. As one example, Hall and MacKinnon (1969) used various personality and interest inventories as possible predictors of a criterion of creativity of architects. With one sample of architects who had been rated on creativity, they identified three components of the California Personality Inventory and three of the Strong Vocational Interest Blank (SVIB) most highly correlated with the criterion of creativity and determined the statistical weights that were optimum for such prediction. These weights then were used in deriving composite scores for another sample of architects who had also been rated on creativity. These composite scores were then corre-

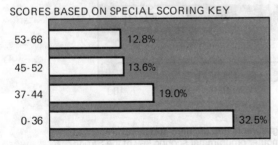

SCORES BASED ON SPECIAL SCORING KEY

53-66	12.8%
45-52	13.6%
37-44	19.0%
0-36	32.5%

PERCENT OF SHORT-TENURE EMPLOYEES

FIG. 9.2 Percent of short-tenure employees by test-score categories based on special scoring key as used with Kuder Preference Record. (*Adapted from Tiffin & Phelan 1953.*)

lated with the creativity ratings with the following results:

Inventory	Correlation
California Personality Inventory	.47
Strong Vocational Interest Blank	.55

COMPUTER PROGRAMMERS. The Strong Vocational Interest Blank (SVIB) usually is used by comparing the score of an individual on each of the many "occupation" scales (for example, optometrist, dentist, farmer) in order to identify the scores that differ noticeably from those of "men-in-general" and that are very close to those of people in specific occupations. When there is no scale or scoring key for a particular occupation, however, special scoring keys sometimes can be developed on the basis of statistical analysis. This was done, for example, by Perry and Cannon (1967) for computer programmers. In fact, they developed four such experimental keys using a sample of five hundred programmers and then cross-validated them on a second sample of five hundred. Figure 9.3 shows the percentage of computer programmers and of "men-in-general" receiving "grades" of A, B, and C on one of these computer programmer scoring keys. The differentiation is very clear.

General Predictiveness of Inventories

Chapter 8 referred to summarizations by Ghiselli (1966; 1973) of the validity of various kinds of tests for many different jobs. Although his summaries were primarily of aptitude tests, they also covered personality and interest inventories. Figure 8.16 in chapter 8 shows the mean validity coefficients for all five types of tests for jobs in various categories. In that figure the mean validity coefficients for personality tests (as measured against proficiency criteria) were highest for salesclerks and salespersons, with those for executives and administrators being the next highest. The predictiveness of personality tests for sales occupations is shown in greater detail in Figure 9.4, which gives the mean validity coefficients of personality and interest inventories for each of six more specific occupations. (These data are based on Ghiselli's 1966 summary.)

USING PROJECTIVE TECHNIQUES

The dreary history of using projective techniques in personnel selection probably justifies their restricted use in industry. In recent years, however, their use in assessment centers seems to offer some hint of increased utility. As discussed in chapter 6,

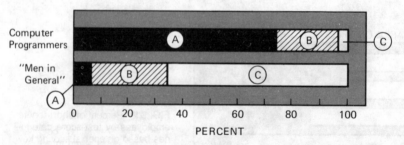

FIG. 9.3 Percentages of computer programmers and of "men-in-general" receiving "grades" of A, B, and C on a special computer programmer scoring key of the Strong Vocational Interest Blank (SVIB). (*Based on data from Perry & Cannon 1967, Table 4.*)

one feature of some assessment center programs is the clinical assessment of individuals by psychologists on the basis of observation of the individuals going through the assessment centers. In such circumstances, the use of projective techniques is reasonably feasible.

As a part of one assessment center program Grant and others (1967) administered three projective tests to 201 management personnel. These tests, one aspect of which was rating each candidate on nine variables (for example, achievement motivation, self-confidence), were used as the basis for clinical assessments of the men. Without going into details, these ratings, based on the test protocols, were correlated with a subsequent criterion of progress (as reflected by later salary increases), and it was found that ratings on several of the variables had significant (although moderate) correlations with the criterion. The correlations for these variables were somewhat higher than those of certain paper-and-pencil personality inventories. In brief, the results of this study indicate that there may be certain specific circumstances (as in assessment centers) for which projective tests have predictive potential, even though they have not been found to be generally useful in personnel selection. When they are used, however, they must be used by experienced psychologists.

DISCUSSION

As discussed at the beginning of this chapter, personality and interest variables can be relevant to work-related behavior in one or both of two ways: (1) as the basis for motivation, such as to perform effectively or to remain on the job; and (2) in the case of *certain* jobs, as the direct basis for effective job performance when job performance depends in part on "personality" (as in some sales positions). Although these variables have an obvious relation to work-related behavior, the use of measures of such variables is fraught with problems that might preclude these measures from having any practical utility. In view of this, the most defensible use of such tests is under circumstances in which their validity has been clearly demonstrated. In this regard the approach that normally would be the most defensible is to use a predictive validity strategy, since this strategy utilizes the responses to such inventories as given by candidates *at the time they are applying for a job* as the basis for the prediction of future job-related behavior. Using this procedure one can develop special scoring keys that may be more predictive than the standard scoring keys are.

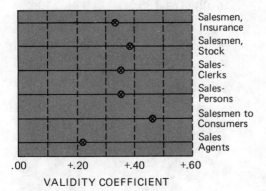

FIG. 9.4 Mean validity coefficients of personality and interest inventories for several sales jobs in each of certain sales occupation categories. (*Adapted from Ghiselli 1966; Figure 4-4, p. 79.*)

REFERENCES

ABRAHAMS, N. M., NEUMANN, I., & GILTHENS, W. H. Faking vocational interests: Simulated versus real life motivation. *Personnel Psychology*, 1971, *24* (1), 5-12.

GHISELLI, E. E. *The validity of occupational aptitude tests.* New York: Wiley, 1966.

————. The validity of aptitude tests in personnel selection. *Personnel Psychology*, 1973, *26* (4), 461-477.

GORDON, L. V., & STAPLETON, E. S. Fakability of a forced-choice personality test under realistic high school employment conditions. *Journal of Applied Psychology*, 1956, *40*, 258-262.

GRANT, D. L., KATOVSKY, W., & BRAY, D. W. Contributions of projective techniques to assessment of management potential. *Journal of Applied Psychology*, 1967, *51* (3), 226–232.

GUION, R. M. *Personnel testing.* New York: McGraw-Hill, 1965.

HALL, W. B., & MACKINNON, D. W. Personality inventory correlates of creativity among architects. *Journal of Applied Psychology*, 1969, *53*(4), 322-326.

HARMAN, H. H. *Final report on assessing human abilities.* Princeton, N. J., Educational Testing Service, PR-75-20, July 1975.

HOLLAND, J. L. A psychological classification scheme for occupations and major fields. *Journal of Counseling Psychology*, 1966, *13*, 278-288.

PERRY, D. K., & CANNON, W. M. Vocational interests of computer programmers. *Journal of Applied Psychology*, 1967, *51* (1) 28-34.

RUCH, F. L., & RUCH. W. W. The K factor as a (validity) suppressor variable in predicting success in selling. *Journal of Applied Psychology*, 1967, *51*(3), 201-204.

RUSMORE, J. T. Fakability of the Gordon Personal Profile. *Journal of Applied Psychology*, 1956, *40*, 175-177.

SCHWAB, D. P., & PACKARD, G. L. Response distortion on the Gordon Personal Inventory and Gordon Personal Profile in a selection context: Some implications for predicting employee turnover. *Journal of Applied Psychology*, 1973, *58* (3), 372-374.

TIFFIN, J., & PHELAN, R. F. Use of the Kuder Preference Record to predict turnover in an industrial plant. *Personnel Psychology*, 1953, *6*, 195-204.

ZYTOWSKI, D. G. Equivalence of the Kuder Occupational Interest Survey and the Strong Vocational Interest Blank revisited. *Journal of Applied Psychology*, 1972, *56* (2), 184-185.

10

biographical data and the interview

As discussed in the preceding chapters, those responsible for making personnel decisions generally seek to identify those individuals who best match the personnel specifications for the jobs in question (whether those specifications are formally stated or are conceptualizations in the minds of those responsible for personnel selection decisions). The matching is, of course, based on information—information about job candidates and about the job requirements implicit in the personnel specifications. The last two chapters dealt with test data about job candidates. This chapter deals with biographical data regarding job candidates and the information elicited during job interviews, as relevant to making personnel decisions.

BIOGRAPHICAL DATA

Biographical data about job candidates can cover a wide variety of information about individuals and their backgrounds including age, sex, place of birth, place(s) of residence, family background, numbers of brothers and sisters, education, work experience, marital status, number of children, physical characteristics (such as height and weight), medical history, hobbies, reading habits, use of leisure time, and sometimes history of the parents. Although most biographical data are factual, some may tap attitudes, feelings, and value judgments coming from experience, such as obtained by questions on enjoyment of various leisure activities.

Sources of Biographical Data

Biographical data (we will call them *biodata*) usually are obtained directly from job candidates on application forms or special questionnaires, such as biographical information blanks (BIB). In some circumstances such data might be obtained directly from individuals by an interviewer, and in some situations certain types of biodata are obtained from (or confirmed by) outside sources, such as former employers of educational institutions.

Biodata Items

In application forms and other questionnaires completed by job candidates, individuals may give responses to biodata "items." The nature and format of individual biodata items should be particularly suitable to the content, and their construction should follow acceptable professional practice. In this regard Owens (1976) and

Asher (1972) offered certain guidelines for constructing such items. Owens, for example, listed the following rules (along with others) for constructing biodata items:

1. Brevity is desirable.

2. Whenever possible, numbers should be used to graduate or scale and to define options or alternatives.

3. All response options or alternatives should be provided.

4. Items, particularly item stems, should have a neutral or a pleasant connotation for the respondent.

Examples of certain types of items follow (Owens 1976, p. 613):

Continuum, single choice

What is your weight?
(a) under 135 pounds
(b) 136 to 155 pounds
(c) 156 to 175 pounds
(d) 176 to 195 pounds
(e) over 195 pounds

Non-continuum, single choice

What was your marital status at college graduation?
(a) single
(b) married, no children
(c) married, one or more children
(d) widowed
(e) separated or divorced

Continuum, plus "escape option"

What was your length of service in your most recent full-time job?
(a) less than 6 months
(b) between 6 months and 1 year
(c) 1 to 2 years
(d) 2 to 5 years
(e) more than 5 years
(f) no previous full-time job

Non-continuum, plus "escape option"

When are you most likely to have a headache?
(a) when I strain my eyes
(b) when I don't eat on schedule
(c) when I am under tension
(d) January first
(e) never have headaches

Common stem, multiple continua

Over the past 5 years, how much have you enjoyed each of the following? (Use continuum 1 to 4 at right below.)
(a) loafing or watching TV
(b) reading
(c) constructive hobbies
(d) home improvement
(e) outdoor recreation
(f) music, art, or dramatics, etc.

(1) very much
(2) some
(3) very little
(4) not at all

The most comprehensive assortment of items has been compiled by a committee under the auspices of the Division of Industrial and Organizational Psychology of the American Psychological Association.[1] The purpose of this compilation was, in part, to provide standard formats of items that can be used by different organizations. Ultimately, a substantial body of data can be built up on the basis of such items so that comparisons can be made across jobs and across companies.

Accuracy of Biodata

In obtaining biodata from job candidates, it is natural to be curious about the accuracy of such data and whether candidates might tend to distort (that is, to "fake") their responses. Data on this issue are skimpy and somewhat inconsistent. We need to differentiate, however, between verifiable items (such as marital status, previous employment records, and residence) as contrasted with unverifiable items (such as opinions, attitudes, and beliefs). With regard to verifiable items Goldstein (1971) found substantial differences between responses given by applicants for unskilled labor jobs and data later verified. On the other hand, in an earlier study Keating and others (1950) reported remarkably close agreement among wages, duration of job, and job duties as learned during the inter-

[1] A catalogue of life history items. Prepared by Scientific Affairs Committee, Division of Industrial and Organizational Psychology (Division 14), American Psychological Association. Greensboro, N.C.: Creativity Research Institute, The Richardson Foundation, June 1966.

view (not from responses on the application form), as indicated in the following summary:

Drawing further on biodata reported during interviews, Weiss and others (1961) obtained information about the work histories of 325 physically handicapped individuals, who were interviewed at their homes after a structured interview procedure. For each job reported by each individual, a questionnaire was sent to the employer asking for information on job title, job duties, starting and ending dates, hours, pay rates, type and length of training, promotions, and reason for separation. Replies were received from 92 percent of the former employers to whom questionnaires were sent, covering 607 jobs.

These reports from former employers then made it possible to check the accuracy of the information given by the individuals. The results of some of the comparisons are summarized in Table 10.1. In deciding whether the information reported was or was not valid, a standard basis of comparison was used for each different item. In the case of quantitative data, for example, the information was considered valid if it was within 10 percent of the value given by the employer. It can be noted that the percentages of agreement for the various items cover quite a wide range from 83 to 38 but only two were below 60. It should be noted, however, that the four items with the lowest *percentages* of agreement (final pay, length of job, starting pay, and pay increases) still had high *correlations* between interview and employer data. These differences can be largely attributed to the distinct tendency of individuals to report "upgraded" or "in-

| | | Index of Agreement | |
Item	Type	Men	Women
Wages	Correlation	.90	.93
Duration of employment	Correlation	.98	.98
Duties of job	Per cent	96%	96%

TABLE 10.1   VALIDITY OF WORK HISTORY INFORMATION OBTAINED DURING
INTERVIEW AS COMPARED WITH DATA FURNISHED BY FORMER EMPLOYERS

Item and Basis for Accepting as Valid	Index of Validity	
	Percent	Correlation
1. Reason for separation (3 categories)	83	
2. Hours worked (± 10%)	78	.60
3. Starting date (± one month)	71	
4. Promotion (4 categories)	70	
5. Training (3 categories)	69	
6. Title and duties*	67	
7. Ending date (± one month)	66	
8. Final pay (± 10%)	60	.82
9. Length of job (± 10%)	60	.92
10. Starting pay (± 10%)	55	.78
11. Pay increases (± 10%)	38	.81

*Job titles were considered the same if they were within the same first three digits of the
Dictionary of Occupational Titles.
Source: *Adapted from Weiss and others 1961.*

flated" information about themselves. To
the extent that this is a general tendency, it
is possible for the percentage of accuracy to
be low but for the correlation to be high.

Although responses to verifiable items
fall somewhat short of perfect accuracy,
their accuracy nonetheless has generally
been considered to be adequate for use in
most circumstances (Keating and others
1950; Cascio 1975; Owens 1976). Responses to unverifiable items, however,
generally have been viewed with more
skepticism. Cascio, for example, stated that
the extent to which such information is
more prone to distortion is a subject for
further research.

As for faking biodata, Schrader and Osburn (1977) reported that students, when
given instructions to give responses to
make themselves "look as good as possible" (as though applying for a job (a "fake"
condition) did in fact give significantly
different responses than when asked a couple of weeks later to give "honest" answers.
These results do not tell us anything about
the extent of faking in real-life situations,
although the investigators did report some
evidence to suggest that students under

"faking" conditions tended to respond
differently than a nationwide sample of college recruits did, who were in fact applying
for jobs, thus implying (but not proving)
that faking in real-life situations may be less
frequent than in simulated job-application
circumstances in college classrooms.

As an interesting sideline to the topic of
faking, Cohen and Lefkowitz (1974) conducted an item analysis of eighty biodata
items as related to a separate criterion of
scores on the K Scale of the Minnesota
Multiphasic Personality Inventory (MMPI),
the K Scale being what is sometimes called
a "lie" scale that presumably indicates the
extent to which respondents to the MMPI
tend to give "socially desirable" responses.
They found that fourteen biodata items
were significantly related to scores on the K
Scale and interpreted the results as reflecting the personal attributes of individuals
who have a propensity to fake personality
inventory responses in a socially desirable
manner. They suggested the other possibility, however, that these fourteen biodata
items reflect the same socially desirable
"response set" of individuals as measured
by the K Scale.

Scoring of Biodata Items

Since there are no "right" or "wrong" responses to biodata items in the same sense that there are to, say, an arithmetic test, the responses should be scored in terms of their relevance to the prediction of the particular criterion in mind. In this regard there are two general strategies that can be used. One of these is a strictly empirical approach, treating each item separately. The other is based on deriving scores for groups of related items.

EMPIRICAL SCORING OF BIODATA ITEMS. In this approach, responses to individual items are subjected to item analysis against a job-related criterion such as tenure or job performance. Those responses found to discriminate significantly in terms of the criterion are then incorporated into a special scoring key that is then used in selecting future candidates. The individual items may be given equal, or differential, weights to the extent to which they contribute to the prediction of the criterion. One example of a differential weighting system is given in Table 7.3, based on the study by Fleishman and Berniger (1976).

Another example of differential weighting is the selection of retail-outlet dealers by an industrial concern.[2] A statistical analysis was made of various items of personal data of sixty dealers, in relation to ratings made by two regional management officials. The ratings were based on such fac-

tors as profitability, cleanliness, and efficiency of the retail outlets; the dealers were then divided into "high" and "low" groups. The type of statistical analysis is illustrated below. In order not to divulge the confidential scoring key, the items are not specifically identified. The weighting procedure used is one described by England (1971). The weight for any given response is based on the magnitude and direction of the difference in percentages of the two criterion groups. This procedure is illustrated in the following example for one particular item (here labeled item X):

Using this approach, there were nine items that differentiated significantly in terms of the criterion groups. These items were then used for a scoring key that was cross-validated with another sample of fifty-five dealers. The results of this study, shown in Figure 10.1, indicate quite clearly that the scores derived by this process could be used very effectively in the selection of potentially successful dealers. The odds of success for those with low scores (especially 8 and below) are quite limited. (Cross-validation is important to analyses of this type inasmuch as some personal data items might be found to be related to a criterion simply by chance and thus will not really be differentially discriminating in terms of the criterion. In other words, cross-validation provides something like a double check on the stability of the relationships.)

SCORING OF GROUPS OF BIODATA ITEMS. There is a growing body of data that suggests that groups or clusters of

[2]The company wishes to remain anonymous.

Item and Response	Percent of "High" Group	Percent of "Low" Group	Difference (Percent)	Weight
Item X				
Response a	15	37	−22	0
Response b	33	11	+22	2
Response c	36	41	− 5	1
Response d	15	7	+ 8	2
Response e	0	3	− 3	0

biodata items tend to reflect relatively basic patterns of previous experience. Owens (1976) suggested that such data can be regarded as presenting an historical view of the development of the individual. If we adopt this view of biodata as a measure of prior experience, we can gain some insight into the rationale for its possible use in predicting job-related criteria. This rationale is based on the axiom that what a person has done in the *past* is the best predictor of what he will do in the *future*. (This is the concept of behavioral consistency discussed in chapter 7.)

There are two methods for developing groups of biodata items, or what are sometimes called dimensions. The most common method is using factor analysis. One such example was reported by Morrison and others (1962). The subjects of their study were 418 petroleum research scientists employed by a large oil company. These men completed a questionnaire that included 484 biodata items. The responses to the questionnaires were subjected to a factor analysis that revealed the groupings or clusters of items that typically occur in combination—that have high intercorrelations. Five different factors emerged: (1) favorable self-perception; (2) inquisitive, professional orientation; (3) utilitarian drive; (4) tolerance for ambiguity; and (5)

general adjustment. Each factor can be characterized in terms of the biodata items that "hang together" to form it. For example, individuals who obtain high scores on the factor "utilitarian drive" characterize themselves generally as follows in their responses to pertinent items: desire extrinsic rewards (that is, from business and society); prefer urban dwelling; started dating before age twenty; feel free to express their views and perceive themselves as influencing others in group and individual situations; do not want to work autonomously; want to choose their own method but not necessarily the goal toward which they are working.

As another aspect of this study, information was obtained on the number of patents (patent disclosures) that had been submitted during the previous five years. It was then possible to determine the relationship of numbers of patents to each of the five factors. By and large, the most creative individuals (as reflected by number of patents) tended to be high in "inquisitive, professional orientation" and "tolerance for ambiguity," and to be low on "favorable self-perception," "utilitarian drive," and "general adjustment." Thus, an impression is given of the various dimensions that characterize creative research scientists.

Another example is a pair of studies by

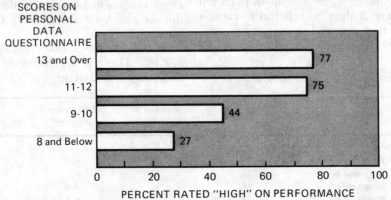

FIG. 10.1 Relationship between total scores based on nine items of personal data and successful performance of retail outlet dealers. (*Reproduced with permission of the company.*)

Baehr and Williams (1967; 1968). In the first study, they administered a personal history index[3] to a heterogeneous sample of 680 men and then subjected the responses to a factor analysis. This resulted in the identification of fifteen "first order" factors.[4] In the second study the personal history index was administered to 210 food products salesmen. A factor score was then derived for each man for each of the fifteen factors (by a statistical combination of responses to the personal history items), and these scores then were correlated with criterion measures obtained for each man. By using multiple regression analysis it was possible to identify the combination of factor scores that gave the highest (multiple) correlation with each criterion, with the following results:

The second approach to forming groups or dimensions of biodata items is sometimes called the development of homogeneous keys. This approach is represented by a study by Matteson and others (1970) in which they used data from 2,590 applicants for jobs in a petroleum refinery who had completed a biodata questionnaire. In developing the homogeneous keys, they started by grouping the biodata items into thirteen clusters on the basis of subjective

[3]Baehr, Melany E., Burns, R. K., & McMurry, R. N. Personal history index. (Rev. ed.) Chicago: Industrial Relations Center, University of Chicago, 1965.

[4]These were labeled as follows: (1) School achievement; (2) Higher educational achievement; (3) Drive; (4) Leadership and group participation; (5) Financial responsibility; (6) Early family responsibility; (7) Parental family adjustment; (8) Situational stability; (9) School activities; (10) Professional-successful parents; (11) Educational-vocational consistency; (12) Vocational decisiveness; (13) Vocational satisfaction; (14) Selling experience; and (15) General health.

judgments of item content. They then correlated these items with each other (using the applicants' responses) and selected the three items for each cluster with the highest correlations with each other, these then forming the nucleus of each cluster. They then added other items to each cluster, one at a time, based on how much they would add to the cluster. (This was done with a statistical index of "saturation," and the process was stopped when it was found that no additional item would add to the saturation.) Using data from another sample of 1,000 applicants, a computer program was used to derive a scoring key for each of the thirteen clusters.[5]

In a subsequent application of the scoring keys to another sample of 168 men who were actually employed, (but without the use of the biodata) it was found that there was a correlation of .43 between scores on a combination of the thirteen clusters and ratings on overall performance at the end of six months of employment.

In connection with biodata, there are some hints that the dimensions have reasonable generality, even across different cultural groups. Cassens (1966), for example, used a biodata questionnaire with 561 executives of a large international petrochemical corporation, who were divided into three groups: Americans in the United States, Americans working in Latin Amer-

[5]The clusters were academic ability, scientific interests, mechanical-electrical orientation, athletic involvement, paternal blue-collar background, maternal employment history, rural background, social aggressiveness, upper-middle class background, parental permissiveness, favorable self-perception, and musical interests.

Criterion	Factors Used in Correlation	Multiple Correlation
Performance rating	No. 1, 4, 5, 6, 7, 13	.42
Mean sales volume	No. 1, 2, 5, 8, 15	.50
Maximum sales volume	No. 5, 6, 7, 8	.36

ica, and Latin Americans working in their native country. Separate factor analyses of sixty-two items of biodata revealed substantially similar factors for the different cultural groups. In more general terms, Owens and Henry (1966) summarized the results of other studies that also indicated that there is substantial "structure" in the personal backgrounds of people—in other words, that certain types of personal background variables tend to exist in combination in the personal histories of people, thus reflecting different "dimensions" of life style.

For the biodata used in deriving scores on different dimensions (whether these are derived by factor analysis or by the homogeneous keys method), their validity in specific situations usually would have to be determined empirically by correlating scores of individuals on the various dimensions with relevant job-related criteria.

A New Look at Biodata

Now that we have discussed the nature of biodata and how they are scored, let us view their possible role in personnel selection. Although biodata have been used in personnel selection for several decades, they never have been a major factor. In fact, Dunnette and Borman (1979) admitted that these data have acquired a bad reputation among scientific industrial psychologists. However (as Dunnette and Borman stated) recent work by Owens (1976) and Schoenfeldt (1974) changed this image. Starting with the notion that biodata present a picture of where an individual "has been" as a reflection of what Dunnette and Borman called a person's "life path," Owens and Schoenfeldt argued that a person's past experiences can be useful in predicting what a person is likely to do in the future. A major source of data supporting this hypothesis comes from a study of nearly 2,000 students at the University of Georgia. Biodata obtained from the

students were subjected to factor analysis, and, in turn, scores on these factors (or dimensions) were used to identify clusters of individuals based on profile similarities of the factor scores. (There were twenty-three clusters of males and fourteen of females.) These clusters, in turn, were found to be related to such criteria as vocational interest, creativity, leadership activities, and even to drug usage.

Going one step further, to an admittedly speculative position, Schoenfeldt (1974) clarified what he and Owens had described as an assessment-classification model based on matching individuals in clusters of those with similar biodata profiles to jobs in job families that somehow had been determined to be reasonably compatible for individuals with such biodata profiles. This would include the analysis of jobs by a technique like the Position Analysis Questionnaire (PAQ) and the classification of jobs into homogeneous job families on the basis of job characteristics that would be relevant to matching individuals' biodata profiles. Although hard data on the tie-in between biodata and job data to support this notion still are rather skimpy, the concept seems to make sense. It remains for future investigators, however, to provide the research base to support—or conversely to pull the rug out from under—this possible approach for using biodata in personnel selection.

Validity of Biodata in Personnel Selection

Data from certain specific studies of biodata were given in earlier parts of this chapter. Perhaps the most comprehensive data on the validity of biodata for personnel selection, however, are those in Figure 8.17 as summarized by Asher and Sciarrino (1974). That figure represents the average validity coefficients from eleven previous studies (as summarized by Asher, 1972) in comparison with average validity coefficients for various types of tests and shows that, in general, biodata have been found to be more predictive of job proficiency criteria than various types of tests are. It should be noted that the eleven studies summarized by Asher used cross-validation with a second group, thus supporting these results. Schwab and Oliver (1974) pointed out, however, that some studies with biodata have not been cross-validated and that some studies with "negative" results do not find their way into published journals. Thus, the results given in Figure 8.17 may not be entirely representative of the overall utility of biodata for personnel selection. Any organization using such data therefore should cross-validate such data before using it for actual personnel selection.

Discussion of Biodata

There are certain constraints on using biodata imposed by the Uniform Guidelines on Employee Selection Procedures (1978) as discussed by Pace and Schoenfeldt (1977) and Cascio (1976). Despite such constraints, the potential use of biodata in personnel selection has acquired a bit of a renewed lease on life with the development of the assessment-classification model proposed by Owens (1976) and Schoenfeldt (1974). The concept underlying their model is that a person's past experiences can provide the best basis for predicting future behavior. Thus, biodata (which reflect a person's work experiences, hobbies, interests, use of leisure time, family background, etc.) should be a reasonably adequate basis for predicting what that person will do in the future. One should not become excessively enthusiastic about the possibility of such data solving all of the employment managers' problems, however, since the evidence on the practical use of such data still is rather mixed.

In attempting to "explain" some of the apparently conflicting evidence on the use of biodata for personnel selection, we would like to suggest a distinction that

might possibly account for some of the inconsistencies that have plagued the use of biodata. In particular we believe that biodata can be considered as falling into two general classes, *job-related* and *labor market–related* (although there undoubtedly would be substantial overlap between these two classes).

The job-related class contains those items that fit into the assessment-classification model and that have some stable implications (direct or indirect) for the human qualities required for successful performance on a job or group of jobs. The results of factor analysis studies tend to substantiate the notion that there are "dimensions" of personal background and experience that reflect relatively stable personal behavioral syndromes that in turn contribute to success (or failure) in certain classes of job activities. If this be the case, such *personal* dimensions would tend to predict job performance whenever performance on the given *job* dimensions is predicated on the human qualities implied by the personal dimensions in question. In this regard, Owens and Henry (1966) expressed the firm conviction that biodata potentially comprise the most valid measure of personality, broadly conceived, which we possess. (In fact they proposed the replacement of personality inventories by such data for prediction.)

The second group of biodata items are those that are more reflective of labor market conditions and the effects thereof on the kinds of people who present themselves as job candidates. (For example, in some communities more married women are available as job applicants than in other communities.) Labor market conditions are, of course, transitory, and as they change they can cause changes in the kinds of people who are available for work. In this regard, it is interesting to note that the analyses of some biodata items have been more predictive of criteria of tenure than of job performance. It is reasonable to expect that labor market conditions might well influence the kinds of people who make themselves available for work. As labor market changes occur, turnover on some jobs also might be affected. Thus, one might expect that biodata variables that are essentially a function of labor market conditions might be less stable and vary more with the shifting winds of the labor market than the "personal dimensions" that are more job-related and therefore more associated with job performance criteria than with tenure.

We have no substantive evidence to support this distinction. (Indeed, even if such a distinction does in fact exist, it would not be a neat dichotomy.) We have elaborated on this theme, however, in the hope that it may have some validity, or at least that it could lead to some further clarification of the sources of apparent inconsistency and ambiguity in dealing with biodata.

Before closing the discussion of biodata items, we should add some words of warning from Thayer (1977). In particular, he pointed out that organizational practices and policies can have an influence on the kinds of people who "make it" in organizations and therefore can influence the types of biographical backgrounds of those who do perform effectively and remain with the organization. Societal changes can influence the kinds of "experiences" people have during their developing years and thus can affect the biodata that might be characteristic of people of various age groups. The implication of these factors is that biodata predictors are "not forever," nor are they universally applicable to all organizations at all times. Thus, there is the need, in the analysis and use of biodata, to ensure that they are relevant to the particular situation.

As a postscript to the discussion of biodata for use in personnel selection, it might be added that some exploratory research has been carried out with "future autobiographies." These are statements written by individuals indicating what they expect to be doing at some time in the future, as in five or ten years. These can be scored in terms of different constructs or dimensions, and these scores can then be used as predictors of job-related criteria. An example of the use of future autobiographies as used in the prediction of success in a sales job was reported by Tullar and Barrett (1976). The autobiographies were written by thirty-six sales trainees at the time they first applied for a job (but were not used in the actual selection process). These were scored on three "dimensions," and the scores were correlated later with ratings on ten aspects of sales performance. The correlations of scores on one of the autobiography dimensions with the ratings on the ten sales performance areas ranged from .20 to .41 with an average of .31. Although the investigators acknowledge certain limitations of their study, they suggest that the use of future autobiographies offers reasonable promise for use in personnel selection.

REFERENCES

References are sometimes used in personnel selection, especially in the case of higher level positions. However, many people view references with some skepticism and probably with some justification. For references to be useful, at least four conditions must be fulfilled by those serving as references: (1) they must have had adequate opportunity to observe the individual in relevant situations (such as on the job); (2) they themselves must be competent to make the necessary assessments and evaluations; (3) they must be willing to give frank opinions; and (4) they must be able to express them so that the recipient interprets them as they were intended. All of these factors can be stumbling blocks to using references in personnel selection, but the willingness to convey one's real opinions is probably the most serious. There is abundant evidence that many people do not like to say negative things about others and tend to mention only their good sides.

To overcome some of these deficiencies, questionnaires offer some advantages over conventional letters of recommendation, inasmuch as questionnaires are able to solicit more specific information about candidates, in a more standardized (and therefore interpretable) form. Even such questionnaires, however, frequently fail to get information that would be useful in predicting future job performance, as reported by Mosel and Goheen (1958) in a study in which they analyzed data based on the Employment Recommendation Questionnaire (ERQ). The ERQ requires an evaluator to rate a job candidate on five factors, including occupational ability, character, and reputation. A statistical comparison was made between these ratings (obtained from former employers) and the performance of 1,-117 employees in twelve skilled trades, as rated by supervisors some time after the men were employed on a new job. Correlations were computed between the mean ratings of individuals on the five factors and the ratings on occupational ability, character, and reputation. The ranges and medians for the twelve trades are given below.

Although significant positive correlations were found for certain jobs, the general implication is that such questionnaires *do not necessarily* provide information useful in predicting future job success of candidates.

Browning (1968) reported equally discouraging correlations between pre-employment ratings of 508 candidates for teaching positions in a public school system and evaluations of teaching performance

made after a year of teaching in the system. The overall correlation was +.13.

Although letters of reference and reference questionnaires do have obvious limitations in personnel selection, it is probable that references are used most commonly in a negative fashion; that is, unfavorable information tends to be used to reject candidates. When some of the conditions mentioned above are fulfilled, however, especially when the information is received from persons who are known to the prospective employer, references can be used positively for affirmative decisions about candidates.

THE INTERVIEW

The interview, as a communication process, is used for various purposes in industry, such as employment counseling, attitude and opinion surveys, and market and consumer surveys. In this context, our interests are focused on the employment interview for personnel selection, although certain phases of our discussion may also be relevant to other contexts. The employment process is aimed at deciding whether or not to offer employment to individual job candidates.

Various people within an organization may interview job candidates, including employment interviewers, recruiters, personnel managers, executives, department heads, and supervisors. In some instances candidates may be interviewed by two or more individuals. If initial interviews are given by employment interviewers (or someone other than the person for whom the candidate would work), the role of the interviewers can be any one of the fol-

Rating Factor	Range of Correlations	Median Correlation
Occupational ability	+.03 to +.21	+.10
Character and reputation	+.03 to +.33	+.23
Mean (of 5 factors)	−.10 to +.29	+.10

lowing: (1) they can serve as "information gatherers" for job candidates and as "filters" to eliminate unlikely candidates (candidates who are not then eliminated are referred to other individuals for further interviewing); (2) they can make recommendations about candidates (with final employment decisions being made by others to whom the candidates are referred); or (3) they themselves can make employment decisions. The discussion later in this chapter on employment decisions would, of course, apply to anyone in the employment process who makes or recommends employment decisions about candidates.

As an almost universal ingredient in the employment process, however, the interview has been raked over the coals by many knowledgeable people (especially research workers) and in turn praised to the heavens by others (usually personnel people). In this connection Webster (1964) stated that reviews of the literature pertaining to the interview have stressed four principal points:

1. Judgments made by two or more interviewers examining the same applicants tend to differ markedly from one interviewer to another.

2. The validity of predictions tends to differ markedly from one interviewer to another.

3. Predictions made by clinicians tend to be no better than those made by actuarial methods (that is, those based on statistical data).

4. The interview is an important technique because of its widespread use. Compared to test procedures, the interview is simpler, more flexible, and evokes a greater degree of confidence in judgments.

Why Use the Interview?

In the light of quite widespread criticism about the interview, one might wonder why it is used so extensively. Why not do away with it? There are certain replies to this proposition. First, it is probable that the employment interview would not be used as widely as it is unless it were viewed as having more positive values than negative values. Although this is not an entirely rational argument, it must be inferred that at least it is generally *perceived* as having useful positive values. Second, some of the aspects of the interview that have been criticized are not necessarily beyond redemption. Just because the bathwater is a bit dirty, one does not necessarily throw the baby out with it.

Perhaps the best answer to questions about the usefulness of the interview came years ago from Dr. Walter V. Bingham (1949). He pointed out that skilled interviewers will always be at a premium in every well-run business. Even with the trend toward the use of computers in personnel decision making, Bingham suggested that there are four duties of the employment interviewer that will never be delegated to a computer:

1. He must answer fully and frankly the applicant's questions about your business, the job and the working conditions.

2. He must convince the man he is interviewing that the organization is a good firm to work for since it furnishes such and such opportunities for growth (if it does). In other words he must be skillful in selling the firm to the applicant.

3. He must steer the applicant toward a job for which he is better suited, if there is one somewhere, lest he later discover that job and shift to it only after the firm has spent a few hundred dollars in training him.

4. Finally, the interviewer should leave the prospect, in any case, with the feeling that he has made a personal friend. (1949, pp. 273, 274)

Because the interview appears to be a fixture in personnel selection, it behooves us to do whatever possible to make it effective. Toward this end, it may be useful to survey briefly some of the studies relating to the interview and to examine some of the possible methods of improvement.

Accuracy of Information Obtained from Interviewees

One of the responsibilities of those who interview job candidates is to obtain information about the candidates. It is natural to be curious about the reliability and accuracy of the information elicited from candidates. Although actual data on this are rare (and most of what are available are not very current), Kahn and Cannell (1957) suggested that there are persistent and important differences in interview data and corresponding data obtained from other sources. Some support for this pessimistic view was provided by a study by Weiss and Dawis (1960). On the other hand, the earlier discussion of biodata that could be verified, referred to certain reasonably accurate biodata obtained by interview (Keating and others 1950; Weiss and others 1961). The implications of the somewhat conflicting bits of evidence and opinions on the accuracy of data obtained from interviews are the following: That some types of data are probably more accurate than others; that interviewers should sharpen their interviewing techniques in order to elicit as accurate information as possible; and that, when particularly important data obtained from candidates should be verified, if possible.

Aside from obtaining information from candidates, interviewers also make judgments about candidates, and sometimes rate candidates on various qualities. In this regard Wagner (1949) made a very thorough survey of interview and interviewlike evaluations and summarized the information on the judgments that had been reported for ninety-six human traits or characteristics. For each trait or characteristic, he reported the number of studies in which it had been investigated and, when originally given, the reliability and/or the validity of the judgments. Note that the validity in this context refers to the accuracy of the judgment in characterizing that trait or characteristic itself, not the validity of predicting some separate, independent criterion such as job performance.

Some of the results of this survey are presented in Table 10.2, which shows the reliabilities or validities of each of twelve of

TABLE 10.2 RELIABILITY AND VALIDITY OF JUDGMENTS OF SELECTED HUMAN TRAITS AND CHARACTERISTICS IN INTERVIEW-LIKE SITUATIONS

Trait or Characteristic	Reliability			Validity		
Ability to present ideas	.42					
Alertness	.36					
Background, family and socio-economic				.20		
Energy	.64					
Initiative	.57					
Intelligence or mental ability	.96	.87	.77	.58	.82	.45
	.62	.90		.94	.51	.70
Personality				.21		
Self-confidence	.77					
Sociability	.87	.72		.37		
Social adjustment				.22		
Tact	.26					
Over-all ability	.71	.48	.24	.27	.21	.16
	−.20	.26	.43	.87	.23	
	.68	.61	.85			
	.55					

Source: Wagner 1949.

TABLE 10.3 CONVERGENT VALIDITY OF RATINGS ON THIRTEEN TRAITS OF THIRTY-FOUR INTERVIEWEES AS BASED ON THE CORRELATION BETWEEN THE RATINGS OF INTERVIEWERS AND OF POOLED RATINGS BY THREE MANAGERS AFTER VIEWING INTERVIEW VIDEOTAPES

Trait	Validity Coefficient
Attitude	.31*
Appearance	.46*
Interest	.51*
Intelligence	.25
Leadership	.60*
Maturity	.32*
Motiviation	.16
Persuasiveness	.32*
Self-confidence	.45*
Self-expression	.51*
Sociability	.44*
Potential	.42*
Overall	.10
Median	.42

*Statistically significant at the .05 level
Source: Moore & Lee 1974.

the ninety-six characteristics investigated. Because this information comes from a wide variety of situations, we must accept it with reservations, but nonetheless we can see that there are marked differences in the reliabilities and validities of the various traits and characteristics. For example, the reliability of ratings on "alertness" was .36, whereas for "sociability" the reliabilities (in two situations) were .87 and .72. The validities ranged from .20 for "background," to those in the .80s and .90s for "intelligence or mental ability." We also can see, however, that for a given characteristic, such as "overall ability," the range of validities and reliabilities varied a great deal. The validity coefficients for this characteristic ranged from .16 to .87, and the reliability coefficients ranged from –.20 to .85.

There are more recent data on interviewer ratings of interviewee traits from a study by Moore and Lee (1974) in which thirty-four graduate students in business school served as interview subjects, being interviewed by any one of six experienced

interviewers for a bank. The interviews were recorded on tape. The interviewers themselves rated the interviewees after the interview. Later, twenty-four bank managers viewed the tapes and rated the interviewees individually. Still later each interviewee received a rating based on the pooled judgments of three of the managers following a group discussion after viewing the videotapes. Here we will report the "convergent validity" of the ratings as based on the correlations of the interviewers' ratings and the pooled (group) ratings. The convergent validity can be considered in somewhat the same frame of reference as reliability can, since it is based on the correlation of two sets of ratings. These correlations for thirteen traits, given in Table 10.3, range from .10 to .60, with a median of .42, and collectively are not overly impressive.

Data from such sources as Wagner and Moore and Lee give the impression that there is much to be desired in interviewers' ratings of applicants, since evidence on the reliability and validity of such ratings is at best rather moderate and, in any event, rather mixed. In general, it is probably reasonable to expect that individual interviewers can form their own opinions about those characteristics or traits that are overtly obvious in the behavior of the interviewee during the interview or that can be inferred from such behavior. However, different individuals (including interviewers) have their own value systems, and (as we will see later) their own individual stereotypes undoubtedly account for some of the differences in interviewer ratings. Despite the differences, there is enough consistency in the ratings of some traits to make those ratings useful for personnel selection.

On the other hand, interviewers should not be expected to be able to form opinions about those traits or characteristics that typically would become manifest only over a period of time and perhaps only during the "normal" behavior of the individual but not during an interview situation. Thus, interviewers probably could not adequately form judgments of such characteristics as creativity, dependability, industriousness, honesty, originality, or punctuality. Neither can interviewers generally be expected to judge some of the acquired skills and abilities of interviewees, such as ability to diagnose mechanical disorders, add columns of numbers, spell words correctly, or assemble small parts. (Note, however, that inferences about some such abilities can be made from information about work experience.)

Determinants of Interview Outcome

The outcomes of an employment interview are the two-way decisions made by the person who makes the final decision about job candidates (the "interviewer") and by the interviewee. It is, of course, only when both parties make a "yes" decision that the outcome is the actual employment of the

candidate. A "no" decision on the part of either or both of course results in a negative outcome. The decisions on both sides are influenced by numerous variables. In this regard Schmitt (1976) summarized the major classes of variables that have been the object of most of the research on decision making in the interview. These variables provide us with a convenient framework within which to view the interview decision process and are illustrated in Figure 10.2. The direction of the arrows in the figure is intended to represent hypothesized causative effects, some of which were established from research evidence.

The following discussion of employment decisions touches on some of these variables and deals particularly with the interviewer's decision process, this treatment being one-sided partially because most of the relevant research has been from the interviewer's side of the desk.

Methods of Studying the Interview

Two principal approaches to the investigation of the interview have been named the *microanalytic* and the *macroanalytic* approaches. In the microanalytic approach, of which Mayfield (1964) and Mayfield and Carlson (1966) are the primary proponents, the interview is "dissected" into units for intensive probing and analysis in order to study interviewer bias, structuring of questions, and other aspects of the interview process as they might influence interview decisions. The macroanalytic approach treats the interview more as a complete entity and tends to focus on the variables that influence interview decisions based on the "overall" interview. Most of the research has been macroanalytic.

Another distinction regarding interview research should be made and that is among the types of subjects used. Some research has been carried out in the "real world" of industry, with actual interviewers and applicants. Perhaps more research has been done in simulated situations, usually within the ivy-covered walls of academe in which college students have been used as subjects, either as "interviewers" or as job "candidates." In the latter, the question of being able to generalize to the real world of course arises. Fortunately we have some evidence on this issue from a review by Bernstein and others from several studies in which the interview decisions made by college students in simulated interviews were compared with those of actual interviewers. In general, Bernstein and others concluded that "no important findings that would limit generalizability have been discovered, except that students are lenient relative to interviewers," and that " . . . interview decision-making processes appear to be similar for samples composed of students and employment interviewers" (1975, p. 267). These conclusions give substantial comfort to the generalization of research results to interview decisions based on research with college students.

Factors That Influence Interviewers' Decisions

Despite the murkiness of the interview decision process, research is beginning to clarify it. Certain variables that presumably influence this process are discussed below. In particular, this discussion covers: interviewer stereotypes, personal characteristics of candidates, type of information, temporal order of interview information, interviewer "set," contrast effects, and interview structure.

INTERVIEWER STEREOTYPES. One aspect of the decision process about which we seem to have fairly definite information is the stereotypes of "ideal" candidates that interviewers use as their "standard" in assessing actual candidates. One phase of a major research program sponsored by the Life Insurance Marketing and Research Association (formerly the Life Insurance Agency Management Association) deals with this problem (Mayfield & Carlson

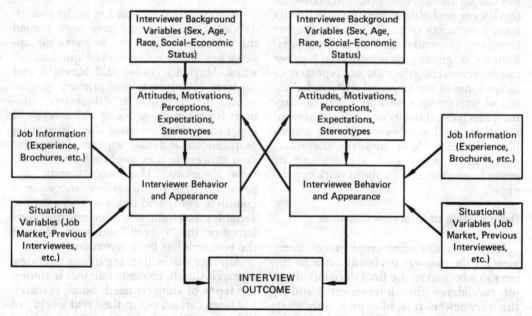

FIG. 10.2 Variables relating to the interviewer and the interviewee that are possible determinants of the interview outcome. (From Schmitt 1976, Figure 1, p. 93.)

1966). But before reporting the results let us describe the procedures used in this project, as an illustration of the microanalytic research approach.

To begin, a number of life insurance managers were asked to list the types of information about applicants that they as managers considered important to reaching a hiring decision. Using these sources, a list of 250 such items was developed and classified in three groups:

1. *Factual items* which might have been obtained from application blanks or from interviews, such as: "The applicant is twenty-four years old," or "The applicant has a net worth of $5,000." In constructing items of this type, a number of different items in each area were included, such as those indicating different ages or different levels of net worth.

2. *Statements* which an applicant might make during an interview, such as: "I will go out to be the best insurance agent in this area," or "I like work which requires considerable attention to detail."

3. *Descriptions of mannerism and appearance*, such as: "The applicant likes to walk around the room while talking."

Next, a number of life insurance managers were asked to rate each item on how favorable or unfavorable it would be if it were true of an applicant, these ratings being on a seven-point scale from "extremely favorable" to "extremely unfavorable," plus an eighth category "I would no longer consider this man." Each item was rated by over one hundred managers. As one would expect, these ratings showed very high agreement on some items, such as "earned all of his college expenses" (which was consistently rated as favorable) and "The ap-

plicant is separated from his wife" (which was consistently rated as unfavorable). More surprising was that the ratings on some items showed marked disagreement, such as "The applicant says he feels he's gotten nowhere for the last five years and it's change jobs now or never."

In the next phase of the research, seven "hypothetical" applicants were constructed, each consisting of six items of information. The items used were those on which there had been substantial disagreement on their favorability and unfavorability. An example of such an hypothetical applicant follows:

Has a net worth of $3,000.

Received a C average in college.

Is more satisfied than dissatisfied with his present job.

Owns $8,000 of life insurance (face value).

Has seven close friends in the community.

His favorite hobby is listening to music.

Sixty-nine managers then ranked these "applicants" in order of their suitability for the job of a life insurance agent, with the result that *each* applicant was ranked *best* by one or more managers, and *worst* by one or more, and at *each intervening rank* by one or more! Following are three examples:

With these differences in rankings of applicants by different raters, we can readily see how an applicant would fare if interviewed by different interviewers. For example, applicant 1 probably would be accepted by the ten interviewers who rated him "best," and rejected by the thirteen interviewers who rated him "worst."

Applicant No.	Number of Raters Ranking Applicant as:						
	Best	*2nd*	*3rd*	*4th*	*5th*	*6th*	*Worst*
1	10	5	12	8	8	13	13
4	16	17	12	7	9	7	1
7	8	8	10	9	10	12	14

To return to stereotypes, Schmitt (1976) summarized the results of some investigations (such as those by Rowe 1963, and Hakel 1971) that indicate quite strongly that many interviewers do hold stereotypes of idealized applicants against which real applicants are judged. Rowe, for example, in a study of the evaluation of hypothetical "applicants" for the Canadian Army reported that the interviewers who made the evaluations seemed to have a common stereotype of a "good soldier" that they used as a standard against which to judge each hypothetical candidate.

In pondering the results of their study, described above, Mayfield and Carlson (1966) also spoke of stereotypes. However, in interpreting the considerable inconsistency in the rankings of applicants by different raters (as shown in the data presented above) they concluded that the stereotypes have two parts. The first is the common stereotype of the ideal applicant which most interviewers share; this part is analogous to Rowe's "good soldier" stereotype. The other part is a "specific" stereotype that is different for different interviewers, the specific stereotypes of different individuals being represented by those items on which interviewers disagree as to favorability. The notion of there being a rather common stereotype of the ideal applicant seems to be fairly well established. If, in addition, individual interviewers tend to have their own individual stereotypes, this could account for at least a share of the inconsistencies characterizing decisions made by different interviewers.

PERSONAL CHARACTERISTICS OF CANDIDATES. It has been speculated that various personal characteristics of candidates might influence the decisions or judgments of interviewers, characteristics such as sex, ethnic group, age, and appearance. Data on such possible effects are fairly skimpy, and most are based on simulated studies rather than on data from actual interview situations. One rather interesting study is that reported by Dipboye and others (1975) in which they had thirty college recruiters rate the résumés of twelve hypothetical applicants for the position of head of the furniture department of a department store. The twelve résumés were systematically varied in terms of combination of three dimensions of information: applicant's sex (male and female)); scholastic record (high, average, and low); and physical attractiveness (attractive and unattractive). Photographs of the applicants were included, the photographs of the "attractive" versus "unattractive" applicants having been selected according to previous judgments of people not otherwise involved in the research.

The results of the study are summarized in Figure 10.3, showing the average ratings (on a nine-point scale with nine being high) given by the college recruiters who served as raters. Scholastic standing was clearly the most important determinant of the ratings. Assuming that scholastic standing was the most rational basis for the ratings, we can see rather systematic influences on the ratings of appearance and of sex, with appearance being the more dominant. These influences suggest the possibility of unfair discrimination, since persons with equal qualifications fared differently in the ratings, depending on their sex and appearance. (It should be noted that the differences in ratings of appearance might possibly have been based on the considered judgments of the raters that personal appearance might be relevant to "success" on the job of furniture department head, so the findings regarding appearance in this study do not necessarily reflect a generalized stereotype tendency to rate unattractive people lower, although this probably did have some influence on the ratings.)

A somewhat similar scheme was used by Haefner (1977) in which 286 managers (those in a position to make or to recommend hiring decisions) were asked to rate sixteen hypothetical job applicants for

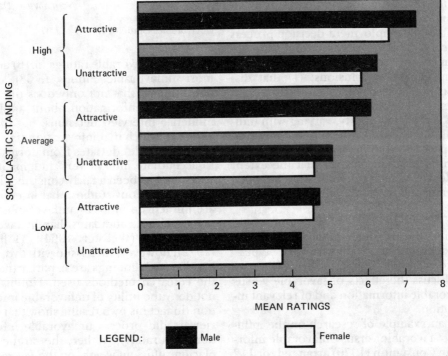

FIG. 10.3 Mean ratings by thirty college recruiters of résumés of twelve hypothetical applicants (six males and six females) with various combinations of scholastic standing and personal appearance. (Adapted from Dipboye and others 1975, Table 1, p. 41.) Copyright 1975 by the American Psychological Association. Reprinted by permission.

semiskilled jobs using a five-point scale ranging from "I would definitely recommend hiring" to "I would definitely not recommend hiring." The hypothetical applicants were "constructed" with various combinations of the following factors: age (twenty-five-year old or fifty-five-year old); competence (barely or highly competent); race (black or white); and sex (male or female). All applicants were also described as disadvantaged, having had limited education and having been raised in substandard living conditions. As in the study by Dipboye and others, competence was the dominant factor in influencing the ratings, but interestingly enough race did not enter into the recommendations. The managers did tend to recommend hiring males over females and younger persons over older

persons as shown by the following mean ratings (with 1=definitely recommend hiring, and 5=definitely not recommend hiring):

Race		Sex		Age	
Black	*White*	*Male*	*Female*	*25*	*55*
2.69	2.67	2.45	2.91	2.46	2.90

In another simulated study Terborg and Ilgen (1975) found some evidence of sex discrimination with respect to recommendations for work assignments and salary, but in contrast with some other studies they found that sex stereotyping may not have as much influence on "discriminatory behavior" in the employment decision process as previously believed.

After reviewing the potpourri of available information about possible discrimination in the employment decision process of such variables as sex, race, age, and appearance, we are inclined toward the following general conclusions: (1) that discrimination based on such factors still influence personnel actions, but that the effect is relatively spotty, varying with individual interviewers, the job in question, and perhaps the organization and geographical location; but (2) that the extent and degree of such discrimination has been declining and probably will continue to decline.

TYPE OF INFORMATION. One could envision the possible influence on interview decisions of a wide variety of "types" of information available to them. Here we will discuss the effects of favorable versus unfavorable information and of relevant information.

As an example of research on the influence of favorable versus unfavorable information Constantin (1976) arranged for 112 students in an organizational behavior and management course to rate an interviewee whose interview had been taped, the interviewee being an "applicant" for the job of laboratory assistant. Into the part of the tape dealing with academic achievement was inserted one of four, one-minute segments that varied in favorability and "normativity," as follows:

The normativity aspect reflected the degree to which the interviewee's grades were "normative" or "deviant" as compared with those of other students.

The mean ratings of the four interview tapes were as follows:

The favorable-deviant and unfavorable-deviant information, respectively, resulted

	Normative	Deviant
Favorable: Grade of A	4.39	5.18
Unfavorable: Grade of D	4.07	3.68

in the most favorable ratings (5.18) and the most unfavorable ratings (3.68). These data suggest that not only does the favorableness of information about applicants influence interview decisions, but that the extent to which that information (favorable or unfavorable) deviates from norms tends to accentuate interviewers' judgments.

There has been a fairly consistent belief, based on various studies, that interviewers are influenced more by unfavorable information about candidates than by favorable information (Webster 1964). Hollmann (1972), however, took issue with this, arguing that such findings are in part artifacts of the research methods used. Hollman did not deny the utility of unfavorable information (in fact his own results show that interviewers did process unfavorable information accurately); rather, he argued for placing sufficient weight on the *favorable* information about candidates. As a corollary he made a pitch for giving interviewers more information about what constitutes a good employee, and by inference, what the characteristics of a good applicant are.

As for the relevance to the job of information (favorable or unfavorable as the case may be) Weiner and Schneiderman (1974) reported on the basis of their investigation that information relevant to the job carried the greatest weight, but that information irrelevant to the job still had a moderate—but significant—effect on the ratings of job candidates. In a subsequent investigation Constantine (1976) also confirmed the importance of relevant information to the decision process but reported

Favorability	Normativity (grades of other students)	
	Normative	Deviant
Favorable: Grade of A	As and Bs	Cs and Ds
Unfavorable: Grade of D	Cs and Ds	As and Bs

somewhat different findings for irrelevant information. He found (as did Weiner and Schneiderman) that irrelevant, favorable information tended to contribute to higher applicant ratings. But in contrast, at the other end, he found that for unfavorable information the judges tended to differentiate between relevant and irrelevant. (They gave lower ratings to applicants with unfavorable, relevant information than to those with unfavorable, irrelevant information.) Regardless of the extent and direction of the influence of irrelevant information, adequate job information for interviewers presumably would contribute to its minimization.

TEMPORAL ORDER OF INTERVIEW INFORMATION. It has been found that interviewers typically make some tentative decisions about candidates early in the interview. In a study by Springbett (1958) (one of the several studies sponsored by Webster (1964) at McGill University), it was found that interviewers tended to make such decisions within the first four minutes of the typical fifteen-minute interview. This pattern of decision making is reasonably compatible with Bruner's (1957) concept of the "gating" phenomenon—a term referring to the process of selective attention in which the perceiver tends to attend to an increasingly narrower range of stimuli as the sequence of perceptual activities proceeds from initial to final stages. Webster suggested that, as applied to the interview, the gating or selective attention phenomenon implies that the effect of a particular item of information on a decision will depend on the time of the item's occurrence in the decision sequence. Thus, if "unfavorable" information bobs up early in the interview, it might lead to an early negative decision, and vice versa. In other words, the "first impression" may tend to persist, even to the extent of causing a later disregard of conflicting information.

An illustration of this effect is based on an investigation by Peters and Terborg (1975) in which they offered various items of favorable, unfavorable, and neutral information in a simulated interview and asked student judges to make two types of ratings of the "applicants" represented by the information. The various items of information were given in two sequences, one with the unfavorable information (U) presented early in the interview and the other with the favorable information (F) presented early. Certain items of neutral information (N) also were introduced. The two sequences were as follows:

1. Unfavorable information early:
U U U F N F N F

2. Favorable information early:
F F F U N U N U

Although the information presented collectively was the same, the judges tended to give lower ratings in terms of hiring decisions and salary recommendations to the interviewees for whom the unfavorable information was presented first, thus tending to confirm the "first impression" theory. Data from a study by Farr and York (1975), however, are a bit at odds with the implication that first impressions are dominant, thus advising caution on the generality of the assumed importance of first impressions.

INTERVIEWER "SET." The tendency of first impressions to affect interview decisions (especially when that information is unfavorable) led Springbett (1958) and Webster (1964) to suggest that the interviewer approaches applicant appraisal with a "set" of cautions that they describe as a search for *negative evidence.* In this search, however, they suggested that interviewers are influenced by the confidence they can place in the information at hand, indicating that there is a tendency to place more confidence in application form information (which is relatively objective and unambiguous) and less confidence in appearance or the personal history interview (which is more ambiguous). Thus, when application forms are presented and rated first, the ratings based on such information (whether favorable or unfavorable) are reflected quite consistently in the final ratings. When appearance or personal history interview are rated first, however, the effect depends more on whether the rating is favorable or unfavorable: if favorable, it tends to intensify the set of caution in the interviewer's search for negative evidence; if unfavorable, it tends to confirm the set of the interviewer to reject.

Some support for the existence and effects of such a "set" came from a study by Springbett (1958) in which he varied the order in which interviewers received three types of information—an application form, a physically present applicant, and a personal history interview. One part used actual industrial applicants, with an active interviewer and a passive interviewer (observer), and another part used descriptions of hypothetical army applicants. Without going into the specific procedures used, we may note that the interviewers rated each applicant (whether real or hypothetical) on the basis of the three types of information (the application form, appearance, and the total interview). The results generally agreed with the concept of such a set, and suggested that the review itself of an application form before or during the early part of an interview tends to generate a distinct frame of reference for acceptance or rejection of an applicant. The tendency of interviewers to seek negative evidence has been generally confirmed in various studies, such as by Miller and Rowe (1967), who found that when information contains both favorable and unfavorable evidence, the evaluation will be influenced more by the unfavorable evidence than by the favorable.

CONTRAST EFFECTS. The concept of contrast effects as applied to interviews refers to the possible effects of the interviewer's judgment of one candidate being influenced by the impression of the preceding interviewee(s). Thus, what might be a good "average" candidate might be judged as being a better candidate if interviewed after an interview with a very *poor* candidate than if interviewed after a very *good* candidate. Although there is something of a controversy over these effects, the evidence seems to indicate that there is such a tendency, such as shown by the results of a study by Wexley and others (1972). The subjects who served as raters of "applicants" watched videotaped interviews of applicants for the job of office system salesman. Each applicant was role played by a graduate student who gave predetermined responses to each of ten questions. From the information incorporated into the responses each applicant was categorized in terms of his suitability to the job as high (H), average (A), or low (L). Each rater watched three interviews and rated the applicant in the third interview. By planning for the first two applicants to be high, or low, in terms of suitability, it was possible to determine the effects of those applicants on the ratings of the third applicants (who were high, average, or low in their suitability).

Some of the results are shown in Figure 10.4. It can be seen that high-suitability applicants were systematically rated lower on the average following high-suitability applicants than when following low-suitability applicants. There also was the same general pattern for average- and low-suitability applicants. The general findings then tended to support the contrast effects theory.

INTERVIEW STRUCTURE. Interviews vary a great deal in their degree of structure. In what are called free interviews the content of the interview and the sequence of topics covered are not planned but rather depend upon the interaction of the interviewer and interviewee. Each interview then takes its own course. On the other hand, in a structured interview the

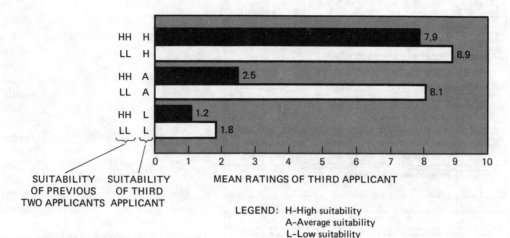

		MEAN RATINGS OF THIRD APPLICANT
HH	H	7.9
LL	H	8.9
HH	A	2.5
LL	A	8.1
HH	L	1.2
LL	L	1.8

SUITABILITY
OF PREVIOUS
TWO APPLICANTS

SUITABILITY
OF THIRD
APPLICANT

LEGEND: H–High suitability
A–Average suitability
L–Low suitability

FIG. 10.4 Mean ratings of third applicants (who varied in their "suitability" for a job following observed interviews with two previous applicants who were high (H) or low (L) in their job suitability. This demonstrates the contrast effect. (Adapted from Wexley and others 1972, Table 1, p. 46.) Copyright 1977 American Psychological Association. Reprinted by permission.

conversation is guided adroitly by the interviewer in order to cover a specified assortment of topics, but the interviewee is encouraged to speak freely about the topics considered relevant. As pointed out by Fear (1958), the control of the interview is maintained so that all important areas of the candidate's background can be covered systematically, but the information is obtained in an *indirect* manner. Although such an interview follows a logical pattern, its content is not automatic or stereotyped.

Usually a form is used, with provision for making notes and comments and for rating the candidate on each of several qualities. One such interview procedure, presented by Fear (1958) is referred to as *The Interview Guide.*[6] This particular interview procedure covers four background areas: work history, education and training, early home background, and current social adjustment. In addition, provision is made for rating the applicant on various qualities of personality, motivation, and character. For each area the interviewer rates the candidate on

[6]Copyright 1943, The Psychological Corporation, New York, N.Y.

a scale from above average to below average. He also provides an overall rating.

An example of part of the form used in another structured interview procedure is given in Figure 10.5. One feature of the typical structured interview is the provision for systematic rating of the candidate on various factors.

It is commonly believed that structured or patterned interviews generally are superior to less structured ones. Although there are bits and pieces of evidence that tend to confirm this assumption, on the whole the evidence is somewhat equivocal. As pointed out by Mayfield (1964), there have been no rigorously controlled studies on this question. One study has been directed to this problem (Schwab & Heneman, 1969). In this investigation, eighteen experienced interviewers interviewed the same five women who were "applicants" for the job of clerk-stenographer. A hypothetical description, which included a completed application form, was prepared for each woman, and each was instructed to play her hypothetical role and to provide consistent answers to similar questions when being interviewed by different interviewers.

SUMMARY OF APPLICANT'S QUALIFICATIONS

Use the following questions to help you analyze the various qualifications of your applicant. Determine, through unbiased consideration, whether or not you should employ. Don't jump to conclusions. Heed all "danger signals."

DOES THE APPLICANT QUALIFY FOR THE JOB?	1. Do the applicant's appearance and manner fit him for the work?	Yes ___ No ___ Maybe ___
	2. Does this applicant present himself well? (expression-voice-self-confidence)	Yes ___ No ___ Maybe ___
IS HIS RECORD CLEAN OF UNFAVORABLE FACTORS?	1. Is applicant's work record satisfactory?	Yes ___ No ___ Maybe ___
	2. Do reasons for leaving former jobs appear logical?	Yes ___ No ___ Maybe ___
WILL HE ADVANCE WITH McKESSON?	1. Does he have capacity for growth and advancement?	Yes ___ No ___ Maybe ___
	2. Do his stated business interests and ambitions seem to be in line with company possibilities?	Yes ___ No ___ Maybe ___
	7. Will he have the stamina for the job?	Yes ___ No ___ Maybe ___

CONCLUSION

You have now reached the point where it is necessary to decide whether or not the applicant should be employed. This can be done only through the exercise of judgment. You must recognize that no one is perfect. So, while you must compromise, be thorough. Weigh the answers you gave on each of the 20 questions in the above summary one against another for the solution.

1. Have you devoted sufficient time to arrive at conclusion?

Length of interview _____ Length of 2nd interview _____

Minutes _____   Minutes _____

2. What over-all rating do you give this applicant? Rating Scale Outstanding   Excellent   Good   Fair   Poor

3. Do you recommend his employment (Remember you should always replace one man with another as strong or stronger)   Yes _____ No _____

4. For what position _____ Starting Rate _____

1st Interviewer's Signature _____ 2nd Interviewer's Signature _____

Comments:

FIG. 10.5 Two sections of an interview guide used by one company. The first section provides for the interviewer to rate the applicant in response to a number of questions, but only a few illustrative questions are shown here. (*Courtesy of McKesson and Robbins, Inc., New York.*)

In turn, the interviewers were divided into three groups, one using structured interviews, one using semistructured interviews, and the third using unstructured interviews. Each interviewer subsequently ranked the five women as potential clerk-stenographers, and the consistency of their ratings was analyzed by the use of a coefficient of concordance that reflects the average of the rank orders of the ratings given by six raters. The coefficients are given below:

Interview Method	Coefficient
Structured	.79
Semistructured	.43
Unstructured	36

This study is not as convincing as one might wish, in part because it was carried out in a simulated context, but at least it supports the notion that more structured interviews tend to result in higher interviewer reliability (and hopefully validity).

DISCUSSION. We have seen that there are many factors that have been shown, or at least suspected, as influencing decisions based on interview procedures. The evidence on some of these factors is at best mixed. In reviewing the results of research investigations of the interview, it is somewhat disquieting to realize that most of it is based on simulated interview situations rather than on data from real, on-the-spot interviews as carried out in industry. In addition, one would wish that data on some aspects of the interview would have been updated by more current studies. But such are some of the constraints and limitations with which industrial psychologists have to live.

In connection with our discussion of decisions based on the interview we have only alluded to the validity of such decisions as related to actually selecting candidates. Although such decisions have been made millions of times by interviewers and placement officers, there is an abysmal absence of hard data on their validity as related to criteria of subsequent job performance of candidates actually selected according to such decisions. In fact, Ulrich and Trumbo (1965) made the bleak statement that, with the evidence at hand, it simply was not possible to determine the utility of the interview—in essence, its validity as a predictive procedure.

The evidence is perhaps not as negative as it is inconclusive. In fact, there are some hints that the interview is valuable as a predictive procedure. For example, Sydiaha (1958) compared the effect of two methods of arriving at selection decisions. One of these was a "clinical" method in which scores were assigned to candidates by interviewers on the basis of an interview. The other was an "actuarial" method in which the candidates received scores based on a statistical combination of personal data and test data. An analysis of the selection decisions that would have been made by these two methods indicated that the clinical approach presumably used more information than is contained in actuarial biographical and test data. Perhaps the interview, with its "clinical" approach, does add something new, supplying a dimension over and above that provided by actuarial data.

Current Guidelines

Pending the millenium, when such answers might become available, it behooves us to do the best we can based on what is now known. A number of source books include suggested interviewing techniques but in using them we should be mindful of Webster's (1964) observations that they typically have not taken into account some of the research findings actually available. For this reason, he suggested that the philosophies expressed in these source books and the suggestions they contain are more likely to be profitable if the structure of the interview is organized somewhat as follows:

1. Someone other than the person conducting the evaluation interview should do all of the preliminary screening. (This would minimize the possibility of "early" information about the applicant predisposing the evaluation interviewer to make a premature decision.)

2. This situation should be explained to the applicant.

3. The interview should commence by asking the applicant to talk about his early life.

4. Permit the examinee to bring his story up to date, including his reasons for wanting to change jobs.

5. The interview should become more systematic and probing.

6. Review the application form with the applicant.

7. Time should be taken following the interview to clarify impressions and to formulate a judgment.

8. Other information should be examined. (1964, pp. 112, 113)

Training Interviewers

It is unrealistic to expect that the various problems associated with the interview and the decisions based on it will simply "go away." The reduction of some of the problems lies in various directions, such as providing interviewers with realistic job information about the jobs, selecting individuals who would serve as good interviewers, using several interviewers, and training interviewers.

On the matter of training Wexley and others (1973, 1975) experimented with certain training methods to reduce the effects of such factors as the contrast effect, the "first impressions" effect, and the similarity effect (the tendency for interviewers to

react more favorably to persons like themselves than to those quite different from
themselves). In general they found that a
workshop training program using videotapes of interviews in which the various
types of errors were depicted and in which
certain relevant learning principles were
enunciated, was the most effective approach to minimizing such errors by subjects. A group-discussion approach was
also reasonably effective. Because of the
greater expense of the workshop (which
used the videotape), they suggested that
the choice between the two methods, in
most instances, would be contingent on the
particular organization's circumstances. In
any event, some form of training can aid in
minimizing the undesirable effects of certain factors that frequently plague the interview decision process.

A LOOK AHEAD

The decision processes in personnel selection preferably should be based on the
relevant information that can be obtained
about job candidates, including test data,
biodata, data from the interview (including
interviewers' evaluations), and other
sources. Combining the many "units" of
information about a single candidate and
making a corresponding prediction of success is indeed complex. In one employment
situation described by Smith (1968), the
combinations of the many different units of
information (such as individual test scores)
were computed to be in the order of 10^{76}—
nearly the estimated number of atoms in
the known universe! Smith proposed that
the complex thought processes required
for dealing with so much information could
be simulated reasonably well by computers.
He reported the results of one test of this
notion in which twenty-four female applicants were evaluated by both human and
machine methods. The procedures will not
be described except to say that the experience of the decision maker was organized

into graphic representations of thought
processes and subsequently was trans-
formed into a heuristic simulation of those
processes. (A heuristic approach is one in
which general decision rules or "rules of
thumb" make it possible to limit the area of
"search," thus limiting the number of possibilities to consider so that they are within
reasonable human and machine capabilities.) Smith found that such a computerized
simulation resulted in the same "decisions"
as those reached by human decision makers
in twenty-two of the twenty-four candidates. (The four decision categories were
to hire, reject, hire as a fair risk, or check
background further.)

A computerized approach to personnel
decision making will not be in widespread
use tomorrow, but it is not outside the
bounds of possibility to think in terms—
years away—of a synthesis of the decision
maker's thought processes and the decision
rules used by a computer as it grinds out
"decisions" about candidates.

REFERENCES

ASHER, J. J. The biographical item: Can it
    be improved? *Personnel Psychology,*
    1972, *25* (2), 251–269.

ASHER, J. J., & SCIARRINO, J. A. Realistic
    work sample tests: A review. *Personnel
    Psychology,* 1974, *27* (4), 519–523.

BAEHR, M. E., & WILLIAMS, G. B. Underly-
    ing dimensions of personal back-
    ground data and their relationship to
    occupational classification. *Journal of
    Applied Psychology,* 1967, *51* (6), 481–
    490.

————. Prediction of sales success from
    factorially determined dimensions of
    personal background data. *Journal of
    Applied Psychology,* 1968, *52* (2), 98–
    103.

BERNSTEIN, V., HAKEL, M. D., & HARLAN,
    A. The college student as interviewer:

A threat to generalizability? *Journal of Applied Psychology*, 1975, *60* (2), 266–268.

BINGHAM, W. V. Today and yesterday. *Personnel Psychology*, 1949, *2*, 267–275.

BROWNING, R. C. Validity of reference ratings from previous employers. *Personnel Psychology*, 1968, *21* (3), 389–393.

BRUNER, J. S. On perceptual readiness. *Psychological Review*, 1957, *64*, 123–152.

CASCIO, W. F. Accuracy of verifiable biographical blank responses. *Journal of Applied Psychology*, 1975, *60* (6), 767–768.

———. Turnover, biographical data, and fair employment practice. *Journal of Applied Psychology*, 1976, *61* (5), 576–580.

CASSENS, F. P. Cross cultural dimensions of executive life history antecedents. Greensboro, N.C.: Creativity Research Institute, Richardson Foundation, Inc., February 1966.

COHEN J., & LEFKOWITZ, J. Development of a biographical inventory blank to predict faking on personality tests. *Journal of Applied Psychology*, 1974, *59* (3), 404–405.

CONSTANTIN, S. W. An investigation of information favorability in the employment interview. *Journal of Applied Psychology*, 1976, *61* (6), 743–749.

DIPBOYE, R. L., FROMKIN, H. L., & WILBACK, K. The importance of applicant sex, attractiveness, and scholastic standing in evaluation of job applicant résumés. *Journal of Applied Psychology*, 1975, *60* (1), 39–43.

DUNNETTE, M. D., & BORMAN, W. C. Personnel selection and classification systems. *Annual Review of Psychology*, 1979, *30*, pp. 477–525.

ENGLAND, G. W. Development and use of weighted application blanks. Minneapolis: Industrial Relations Center, University of Minnesota, Bulletin *55*, 1971.

FARR, J. L., & YORK, C. M. Amount of information and primacy-recency effects in recruitment decisions. *Personnel Psychology*, 1975, *28* (2), 233–238.

FEAR, R. A. *The evaluation interview: Predictions of job performance.* New York: McGraw-Hill, 1958.

GOLDSTEIN, I. L. The application blank: How honest are the responses? *Journal of Applied Psychology*, 1971, *55*, 491–492.

HAEFNER, J. E. Race, age, sex, and competence as factors in employer selection of the disadvantaged. *Journal of Applied Psychology*, 1977, *62* (2), 199–202.

HAKEL, M. D. Similarity of post-interview trait rating intercorrelations as a contributor to interrater agreement in a structured employment interview. *Journal of Applied Psychology*, 1971, *55*, 443–448.

HOLLMANN, T. D. Employment interviewers' errors in processing positive and negative information. *Journal of Applied Psychology*, 1972, *56* (2), 130–134.

KAHN, R. L., & CANNELL, C. F. *The dynamics of interviewing.* New York: Wiley, 1956.

KEATING, E., PATERSON, D. G., & STONE, H. C. Validity of work histories obtained by interview. *Journal of Applied Psychology*, 1950, *34*, 6–11.

LATHAM, G. P., WEXLEY, K. N., & PURSELL, E. D. Training managers to minimize rating errors in the observation of behavior. *Journal of Applied Psychology*, 1975, *60* (5), 550–555.

MATTESON, M. T., OSBURN, H. G., & SPARKS, C. P. The use of non-empirically keyed biographical data for predicting success of refinery operating personnel. Washington, D.C.: Experimental Publication System, American Psychological Association, Issue No. 5, Ms. No. 118C, April 1970.

MAYFIELD, E. C. The selection interview: A re-evaluation of published research. *Personnel Psychology*, 1964, *17* (3), 239–260.

MAYFIELD, E. C., & CARLSON, R. E. Selection interview decisions: First results of a long-term research project. *Personnel Psychology*, 1966, *19* (1), 41–53.

MILLER, J., & ROWE, P. M. Influence of favorable and unfavorable information upon assessment decisions. *Journal of Applied Psychology*, 1967, *51* (5), 432–435.

MOORE, L. F., & LEE, A. J. Comparability of interviewer, group, and individual interviewer ratings. *Journal of Applied Psychology*, 1974, *59* (2), 163–167.

MORRISON, R. F., OWENS, W. A., GLENNON, J. R., & ALBRIGHT, L. E. Factored life history antecedents of industrial research performance. *Journal of Applied Psychology*, 1962, *46*, 281–284.

MOSEL, J. N., & GOHEEN, H. W. The validity of the employment recommendation in personnel selection: I. Skilled trades. *Personnel Psychology*, 1958, *11*, 481–490.

OWENS, W. A. Background data. In M. D. Dunnette (Ed.), *Handbook of industrial and organizational psychology* (Chap. 14). Chicago: Rand-McNally, 1976.

OWENS, W. A., & HENRY, E. R. Biographical data in industrial psychology: A review and evaluation. Greensboro, N.C.: The Creativity Research Institute, Richardson Foundation, February 1966.

PACE, L. A., & SCHOENFELDT, L. F. Legal concerns in the use of weighted applications. *Personnel Psychology*, 1977, *30* (2), 159–166.

PETERS, L. H., & TERBORG, J. R. The effects of temporal placement of unfavorable information and attitude similarity on personnel selection decisions. *Organizational Behavior and Human Performance*, 1975, *13* (2), 279–293.

ROWE, PATRICIA M. Individual differences in selection decisions. *Journal of Applied Psychology*, 1963, *47*, 304–307.

SCHMITT, N. Social and situational determinants of interview decisions: Implications for the employment interview. *Personnel Psychology*, 1976, *29* (1), 79–101.

SCHOENFELDT, L. F. Utilization of manpower: Development and evaluation of an assessment-classification model for matching individuals with jobs. *Journal of Applied Psychology*, 1974, *59* (5), 583–595.

SCHRADER, A. D., & OSBURN, H. G. Biodata faking: Effects of induced subtlety and position specificity. *Personnel Psychology*, 1977, *30* (3), 395–404.

SCHWAB, D. P., & HENEMAN, H. G., III. Relationship between interview structure and interviewer reliability in an employment situation. *Journal of Applied Psychology*, 1969, *53* (3), 214–217.

SCHWAB, D. P., & OLIVER, R. L. Predicting tenure with biographical data: Exhuming buried evidence. *Personnel Psychology*, 1974, *27* (1), 125–128.

SMITH, R. D. Heuristic simulation of psychological decision processes. *Journal of Applied Psychology*, 1968, *52* (4), 325–330.

SPRINGBETT, B. M. Factors affecting the final decision in the employment interview. *Canadian Journal of Psychology*, 1958, *12*, 13–22.

SYDIAHA, D. The relation between actuarial and descriptive methods in personnel appraisal. Unpublished doctoral dissertation, McGill University, 1958; reported in Webster 1964.

TERBORG, J. R., & ILGEN, D. R. A theoretical approach to sex discrimination in traditionally masculine occupations. *Organizational Behavior and Human Performance*, 1975, *13*, 352–376.

THAYER, P. W. Something old, Something new, *Personnel Psychology*, 1977, *30* (4) 513–524.

TULLAR, W. L., & BARRETT, G. V. The future autobiography as a predictor of sales success. Journal of Applied Psychology, 1976, *61* (3), 371–373.

ULRICH, L., & TRUMBO, D. The selection interview since 1949. *Psychological Bulletin*, 1965, *63* (2), 100–116.

Uniform guidelines in employee selection procedures. *Federal Register*. Vol. 43, No. 166, Friday, August 25, 1978, 38290–38309.

WAGNER, R. The employment interview: A critical summary. *Personnel Psychology*, 1949, *2*, 17–46.

WEBSTER, E. C. *Decision making in the employment interview*. Montreal, Canada: Industrial Relations Centre, McGill University, 1964.

WEISS, D. J., & DAWIS, R. V. An objective validation of factual interview data. *Journal of Applied Psychology*, 1960, *40*, 381–385.

WEISS, D. J., DAWIS, R. V., ENGLAND, G. W., & LOFQUIST, L. H. Validity of work histories obtained by interview. Minnesota Studies in Vocational Rehability: No. 12. Minneapolis: University of Minnesota, September 1961.

WEXLEY, K. N., SANDERS, R. E., & YUKL, G. A. Training interviewers to eliminate contrast effects in employment interviews. *Journal of Applied Psychology*, 1973, *57* (3), 233–236.

WEXLEY, K. N., YUKL, G. A., KOVACS, S. Z., & SANDERS, R. E. Importance of contrast effects in employment interviews. *Journal of Applied Psychology*, 1977, *56* (1), 43–48.

WIENER, Y., & SCHNEIDERMAN, M. L. Use of job information as a criterion in employment decisions of interviewers. *Journal of Applied Psychology*, 1974, *59* (6), 699–704.

11

equal employment opportunity

INTRODUCTION

It is generally accepted that in a free society every individual regardless of sex, race, or ethnic group has the right to fair consideration for any job for which he or she is qualified (Cascio 1978). Application of sound selection, placement, training, and appraisal practices can help to attain fair treatment for all individuals. These procedures also allow organizations to meet their staffing needs with qualified people who can contribute actively to organizational goals.

In the United States, increasing attention has been drawn to the fact that employment in many occupations is not proportionately representative of persons in various subgroups (such as sex and racial or ethnic minority groups). For example, the employees in certain occupations are dominantly males, or conversely, females.

And, in certain occupations, there are disproportionate numbers of whites or blacks, or members of other groups. This unequal distribution of subgroups to jobs is problematic particularly because lower level jobs in both status and pay tend to have a greater proportion of minority group members and women whereas the reverse tends to be true for higher level jobs.

Such disproportionate representation in some occupations and/or organizations has served as a basis for charges of unfair discrimination in employment. Undoubtedly, in several cases, racial, ethnic, and sexual biases did lead to employment practices that were intentionally discriminatory against certain subgroups. However, in many cases, unequal distribution of jobs across subgroups was either due to unintentional discrimination and/or to a complex mixture of causes. For example, word-of-mouth recruiting in organizations originally employing primarily white males unintentionally excludes minority group members. In other cases, the proportions of subgroup members were affected by cultural and other preference patterns. Women tend to enter the field of nursing more than men while the reverse is true for logging. It has been argued that these distributions are due, in part, to discrimination and the adaptation to such discrimination. For example, in the case of nursing, it is likely that some women attracted to a career in medicine gravitated toward nursing rather than toward a career as a medical doctor because they believed that they had little chance to become a doctor. Indirect evidence to support this conclusion is the fact that as medical schools attempted to attract more women, the number of women has increased. Although opportunities for women to become doctors may have restricted their entry into this field, such an interpretation is less likely for logging. In the latter case, attempts to attract women to jobs as loggers have not met with much success. This implies that preferences, cultural patterns, or a number of other factors other than discrimination against women tend to maintain unequal distributions of men and women in logging.

In the United States by the early 1960s public concern over apparent discrimination against minority group members and women had grown. This culminated in a series of legislative and executive actions and court decisions designed to ensure equal employment opportunity for all. These actions of the 1960s and 1970s have affected all aspects of employment from recruiting, screening, and selecting employees, to placement, evaluation, training, compensation, and promotion. The impact of these actions has been such that, in less than fifteen years, legal issues have become the most dominant concern of personnel management.

In the remainder of this chapter, we shall first address the legal developments in the United States which have shaped recent employment practices with respect to subgroup members. We shall attempt not only to describe the laws and court decisions which have evolved but also to place these in perspective by describing the social ends they were designed to attain. We then shall turn our attention to the impact of the laws upon personnel practices in organizations.

LEGAL CONSIDERATIONS

General Positions and Assumptions

In the United States two major foci guided development and implementation of public policy designed to ensure the development of fair employment practices. First and foremost was a desire to protect any individual minority group member or woman from unfair discriminatory practices. This led to descriptions of what constituted fair treatment and to the development of procedures to follow for those who believed they were unjustly treated. If these individuals were judged to be correct, various actions against the offending organization could be taken. The assumption underlying these actions was that if the legal framework protected each member of the groups in question, then the societal goal of an equal right to jobs for all individuals who were qualified for the jobs would be met.

A second less explicit aim was to right past wrongs to minority groups and women in regard to employment. This concern was directed toward groups as a whole rather than toward individuals. Starting from the observation that there exist differential distributions of subgroup members in job categories and/or organizations, it was often assumed that these unequal distributions were due to past or present discriminatory practices (regardless of whether they were intentional or unintentional). The assumption that this condition represented unfair discrimination against the group in question led to attempts to insure that the ratio of the number of subgroup members to the number of white males on the job (or in the organization) in question was equal approximately to the ratio of these groups in the appropriate comparison population. In many instances, the appropriate population is considered to be the group of potential employees in the locale who could reasonably be expected to consider employment at the organization under consideration.

Regardless of the causes of disproportionate representation in some occupations, the efforts to establish policies to correct for presumed injustice to the group or groups in question have led to many gains for minority groups and women over the last two decades in the United States. However, efforts to equalize employment in various occupations on an across-the-board basis have had at least two major drawbacks when attempts were made to implement them. First, as we have already indicated, disproportionate representation arises for many reasons. Therefore, in some cases, subgroup members may prefer to be underrepresented in a given career or job. Second, although the concern for minorities and women both at the individual and the group level led to legislative and court actions to establish equal employment opportunity, these actions also have had to be compatible with constitutional guarantees for *all* individuals. In theory, the individual and group aims are compatible with all individuals' rights. In practice, the government's decisions and policies and the organizations' responses as they focus on minority groups and women actually may deny majority groups' rights, also guaranteed (see *University of California Regents* v. *Bakke*, 1978).

Accompanying the belief in individual rights is the general acceptance that our society needs strong, healthy organizations in which the goods and services of the society are produced. To maintain this strength, it is assumed that organizations must be able to evaluate the qualifications of applicants and employees and to judge who will be hired, promoted, or placed on jobs.

With this assumption, along with the issue of individual rights, it is obvious that there will be some conflicts and that there will have to be compromises in order to meet all these requirements. One can only conclude that it is not easy to accomplish social goals through public policy. If one realizes that there are two overall goals (protect individuals and right past wrongs) and that the guarantee of individual rights and organizational needs for survival may conflict with these, in practice if not in theory, then it is easier to understand the problems during the recent years of personnel management. As public policy and organizational practices have evolved, often in an atmosphere of confrontation, it has been difficult for organizations to reach the goal of equal employment opportunity for all individuals in organizations and at the same time remain competitive by selecting, training, and promoting competent employees.

Legal Bases for Non-Discrimination

An overview of the legal process in the United States is beyond the scope of this book, but four areas of jurisdiction are particularly important to the requirement for nondiscriminatory actions by organizations. Each of these will be discussed with descriptions of the laws, orders, or decisions of that group which affect personnel practice.

FEDERAL LEGISLATIVE BRANCH. The legislative branch of the U.S. government enacts statutes which are the laws of the land. For personnel decisions, Title VII of the Civil Rights Act of 1964, as amended by the Equal Employment Acts of 1972, is by far the most significant legislation. Other acts, such as post-Civil War legislation on civil rights, the Equal Pay Act of 1963, and the Age Discrimination in Employment Act of 1967 have helped define and clarify fair employment, but none has had the impact of Title VII.

The central tenet of Title VII as amended is its declaration that it is illegal for employers to discriminate on the basis of race, sex, religion, or national origin. It states:

> It shall be an unlawful employment practice for an employer—
> (1) to fail or refuse to hire or to discharge any individual or otherwise to discriminate against any individual with respect to his compensation, terms, conditions, or privileges of employment, because of such individual's race, color, religion, sex, or national origin; or
> (2) to limit, segregate, or classify his employees or applicants for employment in any way which would deprive or tend to deprive any individual of employment opportunities or otherwise adversely affect his status as an employee because of such individual's race, color, religion, sex, or national origin.

Of most interest to us is the statement that employment may not be "designed, intended, or used" to discriminate against the same five classes mentioned above. In addition, the act describes some special conditions when race, color, sex, or national origin may be legitimate (for example, actors or actresses playing male or female parts) and addresses several other issues.

Similar statements outlawing discrimination apply to apprentice programs. The law affects private employers and labor organizations with fifteen or more employees (members), private employement agencies, and public organizations.

The second major tenet of Title VII is the establishment of the Equal Employment Opportunity Commission (EEOC), which in the EEO Act of 1972 was given considerable enforcement power. The commission is an independent regulatory agency which monitors compliance with Title VII by public and private employers and by labor organizations. It sets policy and determines whether there is reasonable cause to believe that discrimination has occurred in individual cases. These individual cases either may be brought to the commission by individuals or be initiated by the commission itself. By the mid-1970s the EEOC was processing approximately 70,000 such cases annually (Ash & Kroeker 1975).

FEDERAL EXECUTIVE BRANCH. Presidential executive orders directed at the discriminatory behavior of government contractors and federal employers (Executive Orders 11246, 11478, 11375) duplicate many of the Title VII regulations. For contractors, the Office of Federal Contract Compliance (OFCC) was established in 1965 under the Department of Labor to handle discrimination issues (now the Office of Federal Contract Compliance Programs, OFCCP). Before the EEO Act of 1972, the OFCC had considerably more power than the EEOC had because it could terminate or limit employers' contracts. Since approximately one-third of the labor force works for federal organizations or organizations having some form of government contracts, the OFCCP had considerable influence.

It should be noted that almost all companies with government contracts are subject to both the EEOC and the OFCCP. They must comply with the executive orders (OFCCP) because of the contract and to Title VII (EEOC) simply because all national companies are subject to federal law. Therefore, given the number of organizations having government contracts, it should come as no surprise that there was and is considerable pressure for the EEOC and the OFCCP to agree on practices related to fair employment. In 1978, there was a major step toward this goal when common guidelines, described later in this chapter were accepted.

FAIR EMPLOYMENT PRACTICES. In the United States, Fair Employment Practice (FEP) statutes are state rather than federal laws and date back to 1945. By the mid-1960s, over one-half of the states had such laws (Miner & Miner 1978). Although the laws vary from state to state, their existence is important to the total response of the government to alleged discrimination. Where they exist, state FEP commissions are the offices to which employees bring their initial complaints, or to which the EEOC refers cases. These complaints are reviewed at the state level and then either are acted on or referred to the appropriate federal agency. If there are discrepancies between state and federal statutes, the federal ones take precedence.

JUDICIAL BRANCH. The legislative and executive branches write laws and establish ways to enforce them, but the judicial branch interprets them and also determines how to enforce them (Cascio 1978). For issues of discrimination, the courts have interpreted the meaning and intent of Title VII and specified actions to be taken for noncompliance with the law. Much current policy has come from court decisions and the process is continuing with new cases being added every day.

The role of the courts is best understood by considering an example. Assume some group or individual feels that there has been discrimination by a private company with no federal contracts and that he or she wants to file a complaint. After the complaint is filed at a regional office of the EEOC, the EEOC refers the complaint to a state or local FEP commission, if it exists. The state agency may act or may refer it back to the EEOC. If it does not act after sixty days, the EEOC can begin its own investigation. From the EEOC investigation, decisions are made on whether there has been an infraction and, if it appears that

there has been, on what should be done about it. At this point, the most desirable conclusion is that the government, the company, and the one(s) who filed the complaint will agree on the conclusion, and the parties will voluntarily comply with the decision. If so, a mechanism for monitoring the compliance is established, and the case is closed. If, either the one who filed the complaint or the company does not accept the decision, the case will go to court. Assuming that it is not settled out of court, an eventual decision is reached by some court. Although this decision is for the particular case, it also provides a precedent for later decisions. This means that it may be necessary to change some of the EEOC guidelines to incorporate this decision. In this way, the courts are essential to evolving policy.

UNIFORM GUIDELINES

It was mentioned earlier that the EEOC and the OFCCP were established to set policy and to enforce laws or executive orders. Policies are prescribed by each agency as well as by the U.S. Civil Service Commission guidelines developed by each agency. In 1972, in order to decrease confusion caused by each agency having its own guidelines, efforts were initiated to develop a single set of guidelines. After much deliberation, the most recent Uniform Guidelines on Employee Selection Procedures were accepted in mid-1978 (*Federal Register,* August 25, 1978). These guidelines supercede all previous guidelines for employee selection and generally incorporate court decisions, previous guidelines, practical experience of the agencies, and test standards of the American Psychological Association. For the near future, the Uniform Guidelines will be the standards for fair employment. It must be kept in mind, however, that these are only guidelines and do not have the force of law. Also, as we have seen, decisions by the courts can always lead to modifications of these guidelines. In practice, however, the courts have given considerable weight to the guidelines.

FAIR EMPLOYMENT ISSUES

In the United States, through the interaction of the federal legislative and executive branches, state FEP acts, and the courts, fair employment practices have evolved. Although the overriding desire is to create conditions of equal employment opportunity for all, progress has been spotty. Often court decisions are made, policy is established, and laws are written by those who have had little direct experience with personnel practices. At other times, the issues are so complex that no firm solutions can be accepted by everyone. The result is that a whole set of issues and terms pertaining to fair employment have been born, which certainly were not central to personnel practices before 1964. The most important ones are discussed below.

Adverse Impact

Adverse impact refers to the effects of employment practices on members of groups protected by Title VII. The Uniform Guidelines state:

> The use of any selection procedure which has an adverse impact on the hiring, promotion or other employment or membership opportunities of any racial, ethnic, or sex group will be considered discriminatory and inconsistent with these guidelines, unless the procedure has been validated in accordance with the guidelines. . . .
> (Sec 3.A of the Uniform Guidelines, *Federal Register*, August 25, 1978, p. 38297.)

> A selection rate for any race, sex, or ethnic group which is less that four-fifths (4/5) (or eighty percent) of the rate of the group with the highest rate will generally be regarded by the Federal enforcement agen-

cies as evidence for adverse impact. Smaller differences in selection may nevertheless constitute adverse impact, where they are significant in both statistical and practical terms or where a user's actions have discouraged applicants disproportionately on grounds of race, sex, or ethnic group. Greater differences in selection rate may not constitute adverse impact where the differences are based on small numbers and are not statistically significant, or where special recruiting or other programs cause the pool of minority or female candidates to be atypical of the normal pool of applicants from the group. . . .
> (Sec. 4.D of the Uniform Guidelines, *Federal Register*, August 25, 1978, 38297–38298.)

The Uniform Guidelines demonstrate that regulatory agencies seldom question selection procedures unless adverse effects on protected groups are suspected. This means that organizations may use procedures with little or no validity as long as there is no adverse effect. Guion best described this as, ". . . organizations have the right even to be fairly stupid in their employment practices as long as they are stupid fairly" (1976, p. 818). It also explains why, in the short run, organizations fearful of litigation may turn to a quota-dominated selection procedure even though firm quotas are illegal (*University of California Regents* v. *Bakke*, 1978) and they limit the organization's options in selection decisions.

The 80 percent definition of adverse impact is new to the Uniform Guidelines. Previously, it has been left undefined. It should be noted that the exceptions listed to the 80 percent rule simply recognize that there may be extenuating circumstances making it an unreasonable standard. For example, without one of the exceptions, efforts to recruit more minority members would increase the denominator of the selection ratio and increase the probability of adverse impact. This, in turn, should decrease the incentive to recruit minorities actively

—an effect obviously not desired by those who developed the guidelines. Therefore, several exceptions are listed. The extent to which exceptions will be tolerated in practice remains to be seen as the EEOC interprets and applies the guidelines and the courts react to these interpretations.

Testing

The use of tests for making hiring and promotion decisions has become one of the most troublesome issues of Title VII (Miner & Miner 1978).[1] Testing is another issue on which most people agree in principle, but on which many disagree in practice. Title VII as amended accepts the use of tests as legitimate when the tests are related to performance on the job. Several Supreme Court decisions also have been made which explicitly deal with tests (such as *Griggs* v. *Duke Power Company* (1971), *Albemarle Paper Company* v. *Moody* (1975), and *Washington* v. *Davis* (1976). Although the latter cases place many restrictions on the test-to-performance relationship and the performance measure used, none denies that tests can be used or that they can be useful:

JOB ANALYSIS. On the use of tests, government policy and psychologists agree that the essential first step is a job analysis. The job analysis is necessary (1) to define the kind of test to be used, and (2) to decide how to judge the adequacy of criteria in a predictive validity study. The latter is critical from the psychologists' standpoint of developing good criteria. It is even more important as judges with limited experience in test validation must decide whether the criteria used are valid measures of job performance.

VALIDITY. The Uniform Guidelines specifically state that tests or other selection procedures may rely upon three methods of validation: criterion-related, content, and construct validity. In most cases criterion-related validity refers to predictive validity.

Without question, predictive validity, if feasible, is the preferred form of test validation. Government policy is difficult to understand, however, on several issues. One is the size of the validity coefficient. Psychologists have recognized for years that the usefulness of a test for making personnel decisions is directly related to the size of the validity coefficient, but that the *absolute* value of the coefficient depends upon the importance of the decision (Cronbach & Gleser 1965). For example, a low validity coefficient (e.g., .25) might be quite useful if it improves our ability to identify the best candidates on extremely important jobs when other procedures cannot identify such people at all. On the other hand such a low coefficient would be of no value on a simple job when most people selected without tests could handle the job. In spite of this fact, government policy tends to use a specific number on rather doubtful bases. At one time this was .30 or greater. Fortunately, more flexibility is beginning to be recognized as necessary.

A second issue is that government policy states that the criteria predicted by the test must be valid, job-related measures, but the judgment of whether criteria meet this requirement is very subjective. As a result, the judgment often must be made on a case-by-case basis, which can be very frustrating for those trying to meet a changing standard.

Issues of content and construct validity primarily concern the subjective judgment of the extent to which each is present. Unlike predictive validity, the techniques are less accepted for these two forms. Recently, psychologists have made some progress in specifying more precisely the nature of content validity (see Guion 1978; Lawshe 1976; Tenopyr 1976), but construct validity still remains equivocal. As a result, when

[1]By test we mean any standardized sample of behavior collected under standardized conditions, scored, and quantified.

judges, lawyers, government officials, and psychologists address a particular case, it is not surprising that they often disagree.

Linn (1978) raised another validity issue. He correctly stated that the emphasis on criterion-related validity has placed too great an emphasis upon the validity coefficient. We have already mentioned the need to consider the importance of the decision. We shall see in the next section that decisions on the presence or absence of discrimination depend on much more than the validity coefficient itself.

Although reasonable persons who are conscientiously trying to make a correct decision are bound to disagree at times, it is no wonder that there are conflicts in test validation. It is obvious from our description that, despite which form of validity is used, there are several subjective decisions that must be made. There are many opportunities for disagreement. When the stakes are as high as they are both for the individuals (loss of jobs, back pay, etc.) and for the organizations (settlements frequently cost thousands or millions of dollars), it is not surprising that the situation creates considerable anxiety.

In part because of these uncertainties, many organizations have stopped using standardized tests (Miner & Miner 1978). If this is done, two options are available. The first is to use some other source of information about job candidates. This has two drawbacks. First, all alternative methods are required to meet the same standards as tests. Yet, past research indicates that it is extremely unlikely that most alternatives will be as valid as the tests. The second option is to relinquish the organization's right to make decisions, by adopting a strategy that ensures the absence of adverse impact. Such a strategy concentrates almost exclusively upon keeping the proportions of subgroups in line to avoid adverse impact by using relatively rigid quotas. Although there may be short-term gains for this, in the long run it does not seem wise.

UNFAIR DISCRIMINATION. To many readers the subtitle, "unfair discrimination," may seem redundant. The fact that it is not has been one of the major problems related to testing.

Any effective predictor of job performance or behavior must discriminate in a *statistical* sense (Guion 1976). If the predictor is to be useful, it must be able to identify those who are likely to be successful and those who are likely not to be. To those concerned with testing, this means that the predictor must discriminate among those for whom predictor scores are available. For example, a test designed to measure color blindness must discriminate between those who are color-blind and those who are not. The test discriminates fairly if the differences between the groups defined by it (color-blind and normal color vision) are not caused by irrelevant factors associated with subgroup membership. Consider the case of the individual's sex and the color blindness test. If the color blindness test discriminates fairly, it should sort males and females into two groups—color-blind and normal color vison—regardless of the individual's sex. The test might discriminate unfairly if it used the technique of hiding colored numbers in a series of dots and if men were more likely to see numbers in the hidden figures than women were. In this case the "score" on the test would differ across sex groups for reasons totally unrelated to color blindness. The fact that the test will identify more men as color blind than women obviously does not mean that the test discriminates unfairly. It is well known that color blindness is a sex-linked characteristic which appears much more frequently among men than women. A fair test of color blindness should find many more color blind males than females.

Although to those familiar with testing, discrimination is a neutral term, to lay persons and to judges it is not. In a legal sense, to discriminate automatically implies unfairness (Guion 1976). Therefore, a major stumbling block in interpreting court cases and developing strategies of implementation is language. We shall use unfair discrimination as we have defined it, but we appreciate the fact that often "discrimination" is interpreted as *unfair* discrimination.

At a more technical level, the definition of unfair discrimination is not clear. This creates a second major problem for fair testing. Scholars have offered several different definitions of unfair discrimination, all of which seem reasonable at first glance, but many of which have very different implications. In Figure 11.1 we have listed a few of these in terms as non-technical as possible. Of these, the Cleary and Hilton one tends to be the most widely accepted. For an excellent technical discussion of the implications of several definitions, see Hunter, Schmidt, and Rauschenberger (1977).

In spite of the intuitive appeal of all of these definitions, their application has proven difficult. When the definitions are quantified through the application of measurement and statistical procedures appropriate to each, major differences result between them. These differences can lead to personnel decision strategies that result in the selection of a subset of minority group members in one case and the rejection of these same individuals in another. The selection or rejection of some of the individuals will depend, in part, upon the assumptions of the definition of fairness that is used.

Fortunately, the latest version of the Uniform Guidelines on Employee Selection Procedures recognizes that there is no specific definition of test fairness that is acceptable to all test experts or in all situations. In the guidelines, test fairness is de-

SOME DEFINITIONS OF TEST FAIRNESS

I. Cleary and Hilton (1968)
"A test is biased for members of a subgroup of the population if in the prediction of the criterion for which it was designed, consistent nonzero errors in prediction are made for members of the subgroup. In other words, the test is biased if the criterion score predicted from the common regression line is too high or too low for members of the subgroup."
(Cleary, 1968, p. 115)

II. Thorndike (1971)
"A test is fair if and only if the percentage of minoritiess selected with the test is equal to the percentage of minorities who would be successful if the selection were conducted on a perfectly valid test or on the criterion measure itself (corrected for unreliability)." (from Hunter *et al*, 1977, p. 245)

III. "Unfair discrimination exists when persons with equal probability of success on the job have unequal probabilities of being hired." (Guion, 1966, p. 16).

$\bar{Y}_b$ = criterion mean for blacks (minority)
$\bar{Y}_w$ = criterion mean for whites (majority)
$\bar{X}_b$ = predictor mean for blacks
$\bar{X}_w$ = predictor mean for whites
$\hat{Y}_b$ = predicted criterion score for blacks
$\hat{Y}_w$ = predicted criterion score for whites

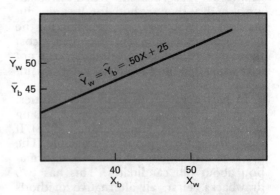

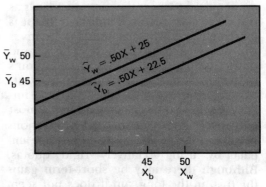

scribed as a "developing concept" that is not firmly delineated at the present time. With this recognition, it is possible to apply reasonable procedures to meet relatively well accepted criteria for fairness without having to demonstrate that the procedure is fair according to every possible definition.

DIFFERENTIAL VALIDITY. Concern about differential validity arose out of a commonly held belief that standardized tests unfairly discriminated against minority group members. It was assumed that tests either were predictive for majority group members but not for minority group members, or that the tests predicted each group's performance but in a different way. In the first case, if the test were used with minority group members, it would be unfair because the test simply did not relate to performance for them. In the second case, decisions using the test could be made if different cut-off scores were used for each group. In either case above, majority and minority group members should not be treated the same; different decision rules were needed for each group.

Differential validity exists when the validity coefficient for one subgroup differs significantly from that for another (Humpreys, 1973). In most cases in which differential validity exists, decisions based upon predictors which do not take into account group membership will produce unfair discrimination against members of one of the groups. The intuitive appeal of the belief that groups probably differ in their validities led the EEOC in their 1970 guidelines to state that, where feasible, organizations should validate their selection procedures for subgroups as well as for the whole group.

Linn (1978), after a thoughtful analysis of differential validity, concluded that to focus solely upon differences in validity coefficients is a mistake. He concurred with Bobko and Bartlett (1978) who stated that the real interest should be upon the differences in prediction systems between groups. That is, we should look at a number of different things which could differ when we try to predict performance from tests or other predictors. (For a discussion of the specific factors on which differences might exist, see Linn, 1978. Most of these are of a statistical nature beyond the scope of the present text.) Although we agree with this conclusion, we hasten to add that there is no reason to suspect that the direction of errors in predictive systems will be any different than it was for validity coefficients: minority group members more than likely are being overpredicted as frequently as underpredicted.

By now sufficient data are in to reach two conclusions. First, differential validity is far less common than originally assumed (Schmidt, 1977). Second, when differential validity does exist, the direction of the differences is such that the selection system is detrimental to the majority group approximately as often as it is to minority groups. Therefore, the failure in the past to carry out differential validity studies should have had little impact upon denying minority group members equal access to jobs.

We can only conclude from the extensive research on differential validity that it is a much less common phenomenon than originally expected by most people. When it does exist, its effects are beneficial to minority group members as frequently as they are detrimental. As a result of currently available data, the latest version of the Uniform Guidelines is less adamant about the need of employers to do differential validity studies than was the 1970 form of the EEOC guidelines. In fact, some individuals (Schmidt 1977) are questioning the utility of searching for differences in the face of what has been demonstrated by the research.

TECHNICAL FEASIBILITY. With regard to criterion-related validity, the Uniform Guidelines often refer to actions that employers should take where "technically feasible." Technical feasibility is defined as, ". . . conditions permitting the conduct of meaningful criterion-related validity studies." (See 16.V of the Uniform Guidelines, *Federal Register*, August 25, 1978, p. 38308). Conditions mentioned specifically as influencing technical feasibility are (1) adequate sample, (2) sufficient ranges of scores on predictors and criteria, and (3) unbiased, reliable, and relevant measures of job performance or other criteria of employee adequacy.

All three dimensions of technical feasibility involve some degree of subjectivity among professionals as to what is or is not sufficient. However, the issue of sample size has come under particular scrutiny in recent years. Schmidt, Hunter, and Ury (1976), focusing upon the statistical power of tests to detect differences in criterion scores, concluded that personnel psychologists have severely underestimated the size of the samples that were needed for meaningful criterion-related validity research. They point out that, in general, it has been assumed that samples of from 30 to 50 are adequate for criterion-related research. Schmidt and others show that this is a rather severe underestimate of the number needed for the research, and they provide tables to guide researchers in the selection of an adequate sample size. In the past, technical feasibility has been overestimated. The impact of this conclusion on future action is not clear at this time, but we would imagine that it should lead to a restriction in the number of situations in which criterion-related validity can be used and an expansion in the use of less direct and more inferential validation procedures such as content, construct, and job-component validation.

BUSINESS NECESSITY. The Uniform Guidelines recognize that, at times, the use of race, sex, color, religion, or national origin for selection may lead to adverse impact but also may be a requirement of the job. For example, it is legitimate to specify the sex and perhaps the race of applicants for a specific part in a play. Nevertheless, the government agencies and the courts have tended to define business necessity very narrowly. It is not legitimate to argue a business necessity on the basis of customer demands or that certain groups of individuals will fit better into the organization.

AFFIRMATIVE ACTION. We began the chapter by stating that the goal of equal employment opportunity was societal. We also stated that, to accomplish the goal of equal employment opportunity for all, government policy had focused on specific individuals and on specific subgroups in our society, which have been termed "protected classes" in reference to the protections guaranteed them by Title VII.

Affirmative action is an attempt to reach this goal by focusing on the protected groups rather than on individuals. It is also aimed at the future and is proactive rather than reactive (Cascio 1978). That is, affirmative action is an attempt by the organization to create conditions that will offer equal employment opportunity to all and will, over the long run, distribute members of protected groups among positions in the organization in approximately the same proportions as majority group members are distributed.

Guidelines for these practices have been developed for organizations to adopt affirmative action plans. The guidelines have required extensive analyses of the current labor force and of the labor market from which employees are drawn. Based on the race, ethnic background, and sex of current employees, the numbers of protected class members in the organization's labor market, and several other factors, goals are established for hiring and promoting members of protected classes. These goals have had substantial impact on recruiting, selecting, training, and promoting employees. Also, to form these goals and to evaluate progress toward them, the organization must keep extensive records. The reader is referred to other sources (such as Miner & Miner 1978) for a detailed description of what is needed to establish what is known as an Affirmative Action Plan.

Affirmative Action Plans must be filed by organizations subject to the OFCCP if they have government contracts. The EEOC or the courts also may require plans of organizations which have been found to be in violation of adverse impact guidelines. Finally, organizations voluntarily may set up such plans.

SUMMARY AND CONCLUSIONS

This chapter has had three goals. First we discussed the implications of EEO for personnel practice by briefly describing the U.S. government agencies involved in EEO issues, how they evolved, and their jurisdiction. Second, we selected what we consider to be the major problems in personnel practice that have developed out of the EEO emphasis. Finally, we have attempted to give a sufficient background of the development of EEO for the reader to realize its complexity.

The third goal is essential to remember. As should be apparent by now, one needs to be able to tolerate ambiguity in today's personnel management. This is not likely to change in the next few years as the United States attempts to meet the needs of protected groups as defined by Title VII, to maintain the right of individuals as defined by the U.S. Constitution, and at the same time to allow organizations the flexibility to make personnel decisions necessary to remain competitive.

Hopefully, sound personnel practices can be applied and developed to meet staffing needs in organizations if we realize (1) that there will be differences in opinion about how best to reach the goals of equal employment opportunity for all, at least in the short run, (2) that for any specific situation conflict between group, individual, and organization needs is likely, and (3) that the procedures developed for establishing the validity of personnel practices have a judgment component to them. The first step to dealing with complex problems is to recognize their complexity. Once this occurs, complex solutions are acceptable. Simple solutions, although appealing on the surface and often appealing to those who don't understand the problem very well, are not going to solve both organizational and societal needs for effective human resource management.

REFERENCES

ASH, P., & KROEKER, L. P. Personnel selections, classification, and placement. *Annual Review of Psychology*, 1975, *26*, 481–508.

BOBKO, P., & BARTLETT, C. J. Subgroup validities: Differential definitions and differential prediction. *Journal of Applied Psychology*, 1978, *63*, 12–14.

CASCIO, W. F. *Applied psychology in personnel management.* Reston, Va.: Reston Publishing Company, 1978.

CLEARY, R. A. Test bias: Prediction of grades of Negro and white students in integrated colleges. *Journal of Educational Measurement*, 1968, *5*, 115–124.

CRONBACH, L. J., & GLESER, G. C. *Psychological tests and personnel decisions* (2nd ed.). Urbana: University of Illinois Press, 1965.

DUNNETTE, M. D., & BORMAN, W. C. Personnel selection and classifications systems. *Annual Review of Psychology*, 1979, in press.

EQUAL EMPLOYMENT OPPORTUNITY COORDINATING COUNCIL. Uniform guidelines on employee selection procedures. *Federal Register*, August 25, 1978, 38290-38315.

GUION, R. M. Employment tests and discriminatory hiring. *Industrial Relations,* 1966, *5*, 20-37.

———. Recruiting, selection and job replacement. In M. D. Dunnette (Ed.), *Handbook of industrial and organizational psychology.* Chicago: Rand McNally, 1976.

———. Scoring of content domain samples: The problem of fairness. *Journal of Applied Psychology,* 1978, *63*, 499–506.

HUMPHREYS, L. B. Statistical definitions of test validity for minority groups. *Journal of Applied Psychology,* 1973, *58*, 1–4.

HUNTER, J. E., SCHMIDT, F. L., & RAUSCHENBERGER, J. M. Fairness of psychological tests: Implications of four definitions of selection utility and minority hiring. *Journal of Applied Psychology,* 1977, *62*, 245–260.

LAWSHE, C. H. A quantitative approach to content validity. *Personnel Psychology,* 1975, *28*, 563–575.

LINN, R. L. Single-group validity, differential validity, and differential prediction. *Journal of Applied Psychology,* 1978, *63*, 507–512.

MINER, M. G., & MINER, J. B. *Employee selection within the law.* Washington, D.C.: Bureau of National Affairs, 1978.

SCHMIDT, F. L. Are employment tests appropriate for minority group members? *Civil Service Journal,* October - December 1977, *18*, 10–11.

SCHMIDT, F. L., HUNTER, J. E., & URY, V. W. Statistical power in criterion-related validity studies. *Journal of Applied Psychology,* 1976, *61*, 473–485.

TENOPYR, M. L. Content-construct confusion. *Personnel Psychology,* 1977, *30*, 47–54.

THORNDIKE, R. L. Concepts of culture-fairness. *Journal of Educational Measurement,* 1971, *8*, 63–70.

U. S. SUPREME COURT, *Albemake Paper Company* v. *Moody, United States Reports,* 1975, 422, 405.

U. S. SUPREME COURT, *Griggs* v. *Duke Power, United States Reports,* 1971, 401, 424(a).

U. S. SUPREME COURT, *University of California Regents* v. *Bakke. United States Supreme Court Reports: Lawyer's Edition,* 1978, *57,* 750–853.

U. S. SUPREME COURT, *Washington* v. *Davis, Supreme Court,* 1976, *96,* 2040(c).

Training program. *(Courtesy A T & T)*

Discussion of design problem.
(Courtesy Duncan Electric Company)

Group leader instructing meter inspector.
(Courtesy Duncan Electric Company)

IV

the organizational and social context of human work

Working relationships are an important part of a person's life. Motivation and commitment to work and the satisfactions from it, are (or should be) the mutual concern of the organization and the individual. Thus, the interaction of motivation factors, value systems, attitudes, and the like with the working situation is part of the study of human behavior in industry. There has been increasing concern in recent years that many workers have expressed dissatisfaction with their work situations. Much of the current interest of industrial psychologists is with regard to this problem.

This part of the text covers some of the personal and situational variables that, in combination, create the organizational and social context within which people perform their work activities. The first chapter is on personnel training (since the training program of an organization usually provides new employees with their first "exposure" to the organization), followed by chapters on motivation, attitudes and job satisfaction, and leadership.

12

personnel training

Let us reflect for a moment on this question: What causes people to behave the way they do—in their personal and family lives or in their jobs? Within certain constraints imposed by hereditary factors, the answer to this question is simple: They have *learned* to behave as they do.

As individuals become employees within an organization or begin a new job, they bring with them their own assortment of previously learned "behaviors," including physical skills, acquired knowledge, language skills, temperament and interests, motivation, attitudes, habits, and idiosyncrasies, as well as other "types" of behavior. The additional learning that people acquire after they become employees or undertake a new type of work can take place in either of two ways: through everyday work experience or as the consequence of systematic training.

Day-to-day work experience probably is the most effective means of developing expertise in some jobs, or at least in some aspects of them. In fact, the "school of hard knocks" has a way of driving home some lessons that otherwise might not be learned. On the other hand, it has been demonstrated that for many jobs (or aspects thereof), some form of well planned and well executed training program provides the most practical way for people to develop job expertise—that is, "learning," since in some jobs learning on the job can be costly in terms of poor quality of work or of work injuries.

Depending upon the job and the purpose of the training program, the training may be directed toward: (1) the development of actual job knowledge and skills; (2) the transmission of information, as in orientation training; or (3) the modification of attitudes, for example, increasing the sensitivities of supervisors and management personnel to the feelings and reactions of others or influencing employees' attitudes toward the organization.

Whatever its purposes, a training program should be established on sound principles and practices conducive to human learning. Although many training programs have been established on such principles, some have been ill conceived and have failed to satisfy real needs.

THE NATURE OF LEARNING

Since training is essentially the management of learning, we will first look at the nature of learning and at some of the conditions that sometimes help people to learn. As we discuss learning, however, let us keep in mind that it is impossible to observe directly the process that we call learning. The fact that a person has "learned" something can be inferred only from a comparison of the individual's behavior before and after experiences of one kind or another, such as a person learning to drive a car as the result of driving lessons. This is not to say that there has been no learning following any given "experience" if there is no overt behavioral change, but this cannot be *known* unless there *is* a behavioral change. Incidently, an individual may learn, but because of lack of motivation may not manifest an improvement in behavior.

The Instigation of Behavior

Behavior of whatever form (starting a motor, dispatching a taxi, calling a meeting, or kicking the cat) is instigated; it is not fortuitous, even though it sometimes looks as though it is. In characterizing human behavior it is conventional to talk in terms of a stimulus (S) acting upon an organism (O) to bring about a response (R). The stimuli frequently are external to the individual (such as a part coming down a conveyor belt, the change in a traffic light, or instruc-

tions from a supervisor), but they may be internal (such as the completion of one operation that triggers another, as in a sequence of bookkeeping operations). Some external stimuli are very definite, such as a traffic light; others are very subtle and might be picked up only by those especially attuned to them—for example, the tone of a supervisor's voice, or slight differences in the appearance of tobacco leaves as perceived by a tobacco buyer.

In the job context there usually is, for each stimulus or syndrome of stimuli, some behavior or range of behaviors (that is, responses) that would be optimal (that is, most appropriate) for the objectives at hand. The purpose of training generally is to "establish the connection" between given stimuli and their optimum responses. This is a fairly straightforward proposition in the case of, say, routine assembly work, but it is a very complex affair in the case of jobs requiring complex decision making.

In many jobs, as well as in many circumstances in personal life, the "stimuli" are not identifiable individual stimuli; rather, they may be combinations of individual stimuli, such as one finds in complex traffic conditions. In turn, the response is not always a single discrete act, but may be composed of many separate acts, in some instances forming a predetermined routine and in other instances consisting only of behaviors generated on the spot.

The Learning Process

To say that training generally is directed toward establishing stimulus-response connections tells us nothing about what goes on in this process. "What goes on" can be discussed either at a descriptive level or at a more theoretical level.

DESCRIPTION OF LEARNING. The learning process can be described in various ways. One description that makes quite a bit of sense is that proposed by Gagné

(1977), which has two themes. One theme characterizes the *varieties of learning outcomes,* of which there are five: *intellectual skill* (with four subordinate types, namely, discrimination, concrete concept, defined-concept rule, and higher order rule), *cognitive strategy, verbal information, motor skill,* and *attitude.* These are really different types of capabilities that people can learn. In turn, the second theme deals with the factors that cause differences in learning these outcomes, that Gagné labels the *events of learning.* These "events" are both internal and external. The external events are the conditions outside the individual that contribute to learning the various types of learning outcomes. There are many of these conditions, such as the presentation of written or verbal information, the use of pictures or ôther representations, demonstrations, conditioning, practice, "modeling," and any of the principles of learning discussed below, such as reinforcement, knowledge of results, and distribution of practice. It should be emphasized that the conditions that facilitate one type of capability (that is, outcome) may be very different from those that facilitate another. For example, the learning of defined concepts (a subcategory of intellectual skills) depends in part on the presentation of relevant material in oral or printed form, whereas the learning of motor skills depends more on demonstrations, practice, and appropriate feedback, and the acquisition of attitudes depends in part on modeling (having other people in one's environment to use as a "model") and on reinforcement (Gagné 1977).

We might back up a moment to distinguish between two types of conditioning. *Classical* conditioning is the process of causing a *new* stimulus to bring about a natural or unconditioned response, as in Pavlov's early studies of conditioning a dog to salivate to a bell, by simultaneously presenting the dog with two stimuli—the bell and food. On the other hand, *operant* conditioning is somehow causing people or animals to make a response not in their "natural" repertoire of unconditioned responses, as when they operate the keyboard of a calculating machine while reading the numbers on a price list. When such responses are "reinforced" by some reward, the responses tend to be repeated later when the same stimuli are presented. When conditioning is dominant in learning job activities, it is typically operant conditioning.

One of the most important types of learning is learning from verbal presentations, both oral and written. Carroll (1968) made the point that learning "by being told" is not simply the learning of responses, but is in fact a process of acquiring knowledge through experience—although this experience is vicarious. This is sometimes called *cognitive* learning as contrasted with response learning. Verbal messages may or may not require an overt response. It remains true, however, that the *fact* of actual learning from verbal messages can be known only when a response is made.

LEARNING THEORIES. Various theories have been proposed to "explain" the learning process. A learning theory can be thought of as a way of explaining in conceptual terms what takes place when learning occurs, how the learning takes place, and what conditions aid the learning process. To date no single theory has been generally accepted as explaining the learning process. It is not within the province of this book to describe the various learning theories. From the welter of studies on learning, however, certain learning "principles" have emerged that are rather widely—but not universally—accepted as being relevant to the learning process.

PRINCIPLES OF LEARNING

There have been serious questions about the relevance of various learning "principles" to industrial training. We should be aware of Hinrich's (1976) caustic reference to repeating "the same tired list" of such principles. At the same time, one should at least be familiar with these conventional principles, since some of them may actually be applicable to certain specific training situations, even though they may not be applicable across the board to all training situations.

Reinforcement

Reinforcement in learning is some type of reward following the performance of an activity that leads to the likelihood of the activity being performed again. As shown by Goldstein (1974), there is a distinction between primary and secondary reinforcers. Primary reinforcers are considered to be innate or unlearned, such as food for a hungry person and water for a thirsty person. In turn, secondary reinforcers are those that have been learned (as by conditioning) to have some positive value to individuals. In job-learning situations most reinforcers are secondary, such as money, praise, attention, and prestige.

Knowledge of Results

The usefulness of knowledge of results —of feedback about the results of one's behavior—in learning has been accepted quite widely. There are some tasks for which such feedback is virtually mandatory for learning. A crane operator, for example, would have trouble learning to manipulate the controls without knowing how the crane responded to control actions.

An example of the effects of knowledge of results comes from a study by Alexander, Kepner, and Tregoe (1962). They had four thirteen-man crews of operators of a military information-processing system perform simulated military tasks twice a day, five days a week, for two months. Two crews were given the results and a de-

briefing session after each exercise. The other two groups received no such feedback. Pretests and posttests were used to provide thirteen different measures of performance. The average performance gains over all these functions are given below:

Groups with feedback:	A: 35.1%
	C: 49.6%
Groups without feedback:	B: 0.1%
	D: 4.6%

TYPES OF FEEDBACK. In considering feedback we should differentiate between different species. One distinction can be made between intrinsic and extrinsic feedback, and in extrinsic feedback we can differentiate between direct (or primary) and indirect (or secondary). Some examples are given below.

Intrinsic feedback (based on internal cues)
  Examples: body balance in walking; sensing by touch; hearing own speech; feel of steering wheel

Extrinsic (stimuli external to individual)
Direct (or primary)
  Examples: observing meter on gauge when controlling gasoline pump; clarity of sound when tuning radio; observing typed page while typing letter
Indirect (or secondary)
  Examples: acceptance or rejection of product by inspector

ROLE OF TRAINER IN PROVIDING FEEDBACK. The trainer has no direct opportunity to influence intrinsic feedback. However, as Holding (1965) pointed out, there are some tasks in which intrinsic feedback does *not necessarily* provide cues as to whether what the trainee does is correct (as in pronouncing a foreign word). In such cases the trainer should introduce appropriate extrinsic feedback in order to aid the trainee in recognizing and acting upon the intrinsic feedback. The trainer may or may not have the opportunity to influence the intrinsic or the direct extrinsic feedback since these depend on the task. When feedback is inadequate for the trainee, the trainer should go out of the way to provide indirect feedback. The trainer also should be sure to provide adequate secondary reinforcement for the trainee.

Motivation

There is evidence that learning is inhibited by a lack of desire to learn. The lack of motivation by trainees poses a problem for trainers. In some instances this lack of motivation can be counteracted by giving the trainees adequate reinforcement and knowledge of results. The topic of motivation is discussed in greater detail in chapter 13. For the moment, we will distinguish between intrinsic and extrinsic motivation. Intrinsic motivation is related to the task itself; there is some direct relationship between the task and the goal of the learner, as in the case of a mechanic who achieves satisfaction from a job well done. Extrinsic motivation is independent of the task, that is, the task is viewed as a possible means to some other end, such as the income the job might ultimately bring to the learner. Intrinsic motivation has an advantage over extrinsic motivation, for it can provide the trainee with a continuing job interest even after completion of training. But for new employees on many jobs in industry, there may be no initial basis for intrinsic motivation on the part of the trainees. If this is so, it is up to the trainer to do what is possible to generate the basis for the ultimate development of intrinsic motivation and also to provide incentives to stimulate external motivation. Some incentives were suggested by McGehee and Thayer (1961). These include: praise (sincere and from a valued person); good working conditions; pleasant relations with peers, supervisors, and subordinates; and status within the work group and community. Other incentives include earnings (or the prospects thereof), the recognition of the need for training, respect for the trainer, and job security.

Distribution of Practice

This principle pertains to the scheduling of training sessions over time. In the lingo of the experimental psychologists, the scheduling of learning sessions can be either "massed" or "distributed." If one has eight hours to train machine operators, should the eight hours be concentrated in one day, or should it be split up into two four-hour sessions on different days, or even spread out over eight days with a one-hour session each day? Although there is a commonly accepted notion that, for any given training situation, there is some "optimum" schedule, there are actually few data to support such a contention. McGehee (1979) found that most of the data on the distribution of practice come from studies on memorization of word tests or on the acquisition of simple manual skills and not from job-training situations. From the available evidence Bass and Vaughan (1966) did offer the following generalizations: distribution of learning has been more consistently beneficial to learning motor skills than to verbal learning and other complex forms of learning; the less meaningful the material to be learned and the greater its difficulty and amount are, the more distributed practice will be superior to massed practice; and material learned by distributed practice will tend to be retained longer than material learned in concentrated doses is. In addition, two or three other points might be made. First, it seems desirable to have each training period cover some cohesive segment of training content. Second, one should avoid the onset of excessive boredom or inattention by interspersing breaks in the training sessions. (Most trainers can get some hints of lack of attention by observing their captive audience.) Third, it has been found that even short breaks frequently facilitate the learning process.

Whole versus Part Learning

If a job has several "parts," such as various subtasks, it is possible to train people on the job as a complete entity (as a whole), or to train people separately on each part or subtask. Which is better in terms of efficiency of learning? The answer seems to depend on the *complexity* of the whole task and on the degree of *organization* of the subtasks, as based on a review of the research on this by Naylor (1962). *Organization* refers to the extent to which the subtasks are interrelated, as opposed to comprising separate, independent job activities. His review supported the following generalization: When a task has relatively *high organization,* an increase in task complexity leads to *whole* methods being more efficient than part methods are, and when a task has *low organization,* an increase in task complexity leads to *part* methods being more efficient.

Transfer of Learning

The circus tight-rope walker probably has a better chance of getting safely to the other end of an I-beam on a new skyscraper than you or I do. A pretzel twister probably could do a better job of tying bows on Christmas packages than the proverbial man on the street. These are examples of transfer of training, and such transfer is essentially what industrial training is. Much of the training in industry is carried out in "simulated" situations with the expectation that it will, in effect, transfer to the "real job" as such. Besides its relevance to training, the question of possible transfer of learning also comes up when an individual changes from one job to another, especially if there is some kind of similarity between the two jobs.

Psychologists have given a great deal of attention to the study of transfer of learning, beginning with the very early work of Thorndike and Woodworth (1901). Thorndike (1924) long ago concluded that transfer in a general way does not occur at all and that what is often regarded as transfer is simply the result of *identical elements* common to the two activities. The identical elements might be overt activities as such (for example, the operation of a spray painter, whether in painting automobile bodies or railroad cars), or methods or approaches (for example, the procedures used in balancing accounts, whether the accounts deal with girdles or dog whistles). In connection with this explanation of transfer of learning, some nagging questions have led to other possible explanations, some of which are predicated on the assumption of much more generalization than Thorndike implied.

The persisting ambiguity about the factors associated with transfer of learning raises questions about the degree of fidelity of the "simulation" provided during training. Although this question applies to virtually every facet of training, it is particularly relevant to the development of various types of training devices, equipment, and other physical facilities used in some training programs. In this connection, one needs to distinguish between the degree of *physical* fidelity and that of *psychological* fidelity. Psychological fidelity refers to the degree of similarity of the human operations and activities. Psychological fidelity is critical to the transfer-of-learning context.

PRINCIPLES OF TRAINING DESIGN

With these principles of learning two points alluded to previously should be emphasized: (1) Any given principle probably is pertinent to certain *types* of learning situations rather than being applicable on an across-the-board basis; and (2) there are conflicting opinions (and evidence) on the relevance of learning principles to industrial training situations. With regard to the conflicting points of view McGehee (1979) differentiated between what are called *connectionist* and *configurational* approaches to learning. We will not elaborate on this distinction, except to say that the "connectionist" approach assumes that learning occurs gradually and that correct responses or response patterns increase in probability through repeated instances in which reward or reinforcement follows the occurrence of the response. In turn, the configurational approach is based on the assumption that learning consists of the formation of "cognitive associations", and is intential and goal directed. Further, the configurationists feel that performance is not essential to learning.

McGehee, who is inclined toward the connectionist point of view, asserted that experimental data seem to indicate that such a point of view in designing training experiences can produce efficient and significant behavior modification. In turn he set forth certain principles that must be used if training is to be efficient. We should consider these as *principles of training design* as contrasted with the principles of learning that we have been discussing. The major principles are as follows:

1. Each subject to be learned or behavior to be acquired must be broken into small steps.

2. These steps must be defined in terms of outcomes expected in behavioral terms.

3. The learner must emit responses or otherwise actively engage in the learning sequence.

4. Contingencies of reinforcement of the desired responses must be established.

5. Cues must be used in instruction to elicit the desired responses, and then gradually fade out.

6. The concept of *shaping* must be used, involving the initial reinforcement of responses which approach the desired terminal responses and the gradual reinforcement only of the desired terminal behavior. (McGehee 1979, pp. 5–26, 5–27).

LEARNING CURVES

Although there still are many theoretical questions about the learning process and the principles relevant to learning, the fact is that people do learn. Job-related learning is depicted with learning curves that show the cumulative changes in criteria that occur over time. The form and length of learning curves vary considerably from one situation to another. The total period of training on some jobs, for example, may be months or even years, whereas on other jobs it may be only days or weeks. The shape of the curve also may vary. Figure 12.1 illustrates several generalized forms of learning curves. Most of these curves represent the curves of actual jobs, but the specific jobs are not particularly pertinent to the central point, which is to illustrate the differences in the curves from one job to another. These curves are averages for groups of employees, and the criterion scales for all of them have been converted to a common, arbitrary base.

With reference to learning and learning curves, generally the *relative* degree of improvement in learning is greater for more difficult jobs than for easier jobs. This is illustrated by the comparisons shown in Figure 12.2. Each part of this figure shows the production throughout training of employees on two pairs of related jobs in the manufacture of oscilloscope accessories; in each pair, one job had been judged by management representatives as "most difficult" and the other as "least difficult." The greater relative improvement in the most difficult job is evident in each pair. This difference generally can be attributed to the fact that an "easy" job is one for which most people already have the basic acquired skills and knowledge in ready-to-use form requiring little adaptation; thus they

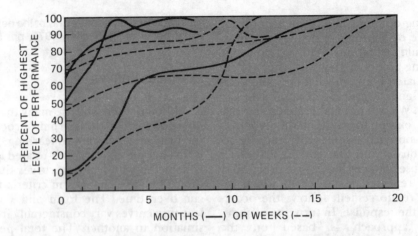

FIG. 12.1 Illustrations of generalized learning curves for several different jobs. Although the original curves were somewhat irregular, for illustrative purposes they have been smoothed.

start out closer to their ultimate ceiling. For more difficult jobs, initial performance is much lower relative to final performance, which leaves more "room" for improvement.

TYPES OF TRAINING PROGRAMS

Having had a brief overview of learning, let us now shift to the more specific matter of personnel training. Training generally is intended to provide learning experiences that will help people to perform more effectively in their present or future jobs; education, in contrast, generally is directed toward broader objectives. Training programs in organizations take on many forms, but in broad terms they fall into the following classes:

Orientation training. Typically used for orienting new employees to an organization by providing information about the organization, its history, products, policies, and so forth.

On-the-job training. Used in helping personnel to learn new jobs; may be on an organized, systematic basis, or on a catch-as-catch-can basis.

Off-the-job training. Covers a wide range of training activities given by an organization, such as vestibule training (training for specific jobs), supervisory and management training and development, some apprentice training, and job-improvement training. May be combined with on-the-job training, as in the case of apprentice training programs.

Outside training. Training arranged with outside organizations, such as universities or trade and professional associations.

TRAINING NEEDS

In his forthright manner McGehee (1979) stated that an organization should commit its resources to a training activity only if, in the best judgment of the managers, the training can be expected to *achieve some results other than modifying employee behavior.* It must support some *organizational end goal,* such as more efficient production or distribution of goods and services, reduction of operating costs, improved quality, or more effective personal relations. In other words, he said that the modification in employee behavior effected through

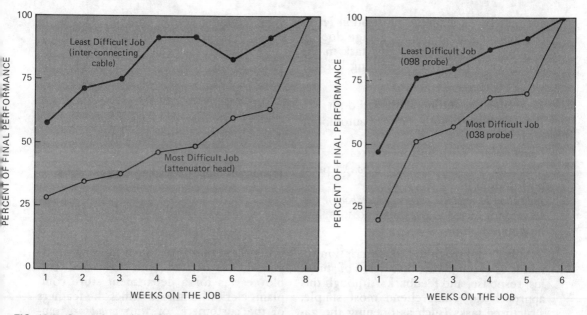

FIG. 12.2 Comparison of learning curves of two pairs of related jobs that differ in difficulty level. In each, productivity is shown relative to the productivity during the last week (equated to 100 percent). Note that the *relative* improvement is greater for the more difficult jobs (and, in fact, on those jobs was continuing to rise at the end of the period shown). (*Courtesy of Tetronix, Inc. and Dr. Guyot Frazier.*)

training should be aimed at supporting organizational objectives.

Keeping such organizational objectives in mind, the actual training needs of personnel tend to fall into two groups which more or less blend into each other. First is the need to provide specific job training, especially for new employees and sometimes for current employees deficient in job performance. Second is the need in most organizations to provide personal development training that will contribute to the longer range effectiveness of the individuals in question.

Training Needs: Job Training of New Employees

If inexperienced personnel are to be trained for new jobs, the training "needs" are fairly obvious—namely, the need to help individuals acquire the knowledge, skills, and attitudes required for the jobs.

Such training content, then, must be rooted in a detailed study of the job itself. Usually this is some method of identifying the tasks to be performed in the job.

TASK DESCRIPTION. The description of a task is a statement (or statements) of what Miller (1962) labeled the *requirements* of the task in question. In other words, the description usually describes the overt, observable activities in the task—the things a person "does." If a task requires some fairly standard cycle of activities, Miller suggested that task activity statements specify the *indication* or *cue* which calls for a response, the *object* to be used (such as a control device that is to be activated), the *activation* or *manipulation* to be made, and the *indication of response adequacy* or feedback. Thus, such a task description would specify *when* individuals are to do something, *what* they are to do it with, what *action* they are to take, and what *feedback* will indicate that the action has been performed adequately. As a simple illustration let us take opening an automatic garage door at a garage. An analysis of this task in the above terms might be something like the following:

Task: opening automatic garage door
Indication or cue (when): sound of automobile horn
Object (what): push-button control
Activation or manipulation (action): press push-button
Indication of response adequacy (feedback): observe door raised to overhead position and hear motor stop.

Miller's approach to task description reminds us of our earlier discussion of stimulus, response, and feedback. Although this approach can comprehend most simple, structured tasks (such as opening the garage door), the process can break down if the activity is unstructured and complex, as shown by Cunningham and Duncan (1967) and Annett and Duncan (1967).

A somewhat different approach to the description of tasks for the purpose of specifying training course content was proposed by Rundquist (1971). His scheme was predicated on a logical analytical process of identifying tasks at different and descending levels of scope. This produced a pyramidal hierarchy of task components in which a major task is subdivided into more specific tasks on as many as six or seven levels. In an analysis of the job of commanding officers of naval amphibious ships, Rundquist, West, and Zipse (1971) demonstrated that the technique can be used with complex jobs as well as with structured jobs.

A task description of the job to be learned specifies what a person must learn to do; these specifications in turn are based on specifications of the skills and knowledge that the learner must acquire. In effect, this process is one of building a bridge between tasks and their skill and knowledge requirements in order to de-

velop training course content. This is, in effect, the objective of Rundquist's scheme.

Despite the particular variant of task description that may be used to develop the training course material for a particular job, the actual training for individuals should, of course, be adapted to the individuals in question, taking into account their individual skills and abilities.

Training Needs: Upgrading Current Jobs

For current employees whose job performance is not satisfactory, it may be that some type of additional training can help to bring them up to par. Such training needs may be associated with *individual* employees (as for a department store complaint clerk who always ruffles the feathers of the customers) or with *groups* of employees (as for pickle sorters who cannot distinguish between good pickles and bad pickles). For individuals who need additional training, it is necessary to determine what training they need. This is what McGehee and Thayer (1961) called *man analysis.* Regular personnel appraisals may pinpoint individuals' training needs. But when there are indications of training deficiencies with groups of employees, a general approach to determining their training needs may be in order, looking toward the development of a training program to improve job performance.

There are many variants of the processes of determining such training needs. Johnson (1967), for example, described thirty-four specific procedures. Aside from those which derive from job analysis, most are predicated on the judgments and observations of people—the incumbents themselves, supervisors, managers, personnel officers, and so forth. For evaluating the training needs of first-line supervisors, professional and top-management personnel, and possibly other groups, Kirkpatrick (1977) proposed using one of these four methods: performance appraisals, survey of training needs, tests (paper-and-pencil tests for measuring knowledge and performance tests for measuring skills), and advisory committees. For survey procedures he proposed a questionnaire listing subjects (based on interviews with supervisors or available from other sources) that is completed by the job incumbents themselves and possibly by their supervisors. An example of such a questionnaire for office supervisors is given in Figure 12.3. In this particular instance the incumbents and their supervisors reported their judgments of the level of "need" by the incumbents for training in each of the areas listed. A simple scoring system is used to score the responses: great need $=2$; some need$=1$, and little need $=0$. Adding up the scores for several

OFFICE SUPERVISORS (Possible Subjects for First Line Supervisors and Foremen)					
	Please put an "x" after each topic to indicate the need as you see it.		Column Weights		
			2	1	0
			Great Need	Some Need	Little Need
Rank		Weighted Score			
3	1. The Supervisor's Job (Objectives, Activities, Authority, Responsibility)	48	20	8	2
3	2. Communication Principles & Approaches	48	16	16	2
9	3. Oral Communication	48	17	12	6
9	4. Written Communication (memos, reports)	48	15	12	7
12	5. Listening	45	17	11	6
16	6. Interviewing (employment, appraisal, etc.)	42	14	14	5
33	7. Conducting Departmental Meetings	28	9	10	12
1	8. Understanding & Motivating Employees	50	21	8	2
22	9. Selecting New Employees	36	11	14	8
22	10. Inducting New Employees	36	9	18	7
6	11. Training New Employees	47	16	15	3
28	12. Understanding the 20–30 year olds	32	11	10	11
14	13. Appraising Employee Performance	44	16	12	7
16	14. Preventing & Handling Complaints & Grievances	42	14	14	6

FIG. 12.3 Partial list of topics in a questionnaire used in surveying the training needs of office supervisors showing the weighted scores and rank orders of topics based on responses of one group of supervisors. (Adapted from Kirkpatrick 1977, Form 2, p. 24.) Reproduced by special permission from the February 1977 *Training and Development Journal.* Copyright 1977 by the American Society for Training and Development Inc.

individuals gives a total weighted score, as shown in Figure 12.3. These weighted scores, in turn, can be used to rank the various topics, thus establishing priorities in a training program.

Another procedure utilizes the critical incident technique. This method was used in a program reported by Folley (1969) for determining the training needs of department store sales personnel. The "critical incidents" were based on actual reports by regular customers who volunteered to prepare statements about the sales personnel who had served them in three department stores in a large city. The written statements by customers were analyzed to identify the critical incidents which differentiated both very effective and very ineffective performance. The two thousand resulting incidents were then categorized by content analysis into twenty-five categories of effective behavior and eleven of ineffective. These were then grouped into seven and six broader categories, respectively. Figure 12.4 shows the percentage of incidents in these categories. Although these percentages do not necessarily represent the relative importance of the categories, they do provide the trainer with some basis, during training, for ensuring that the sales personnel know the implications of these behaviors from the customers' point of view and that they know how to avoid the undesirable behaviors.

Training Needs: Personal Development

Training for personal development is generally directed toward providing learning experiences that will be useful to peo-

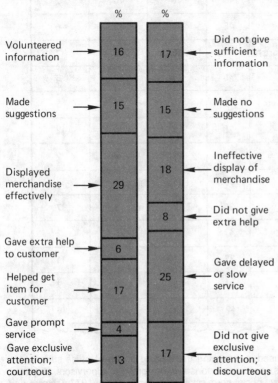

EFFECTIVE CATEGORIES   INEFFECTIVE CATEGORIES

%   %

Volunteered information — 16   17 — Did not give sufficient information

Made suggestions — 15   15 — Made no suggestions

Displayed merchandise effectively — 29   18 — Ineffective display of merchandise

8 — Did not give extra help

Gave extra help to customer — 6

Helped get item for customer — 17   25 — Gave delayed or slow service

Gave prompt service — 4

Gave exclusive attention; courteous — 13   17 — Did not give exclusive attention; discourteous

FIG. 12.4 Percent distribution by categories of 2,000 critical incidents regarding sales personnel as reported by customers. The critical incidents were divided into those representing effective performance and ineffective performance. (*Adapted from Folley 1969.*)

ple in their long-range effectiveness in their organizations, thus being useful both for themselves and for their organizations. Although personal development training programs generally have been limited to executives, the changing times are emphasizing the desirability of such training for other groups, to combat occupational obsolesence of professional and scientific personnel, to help disadvantaged groups adapt to the occupational world, and to help older people retain or strengthen their capacities to function effectively in the labor market. We will mention briefly the training needs of certain such groups.

MANAGERIAL AND SUPERVISORY TRAINING. The training needs of managerial and supervisory personnel usually have been studied within the confines of individual organizations. Occasionally, general surveys across industries have been made. Dubin, Alderman, and Marlow (1967), for example, made a statewide survey of managerial and supervisory training needs in Pennsylvania. Perhaps it would be more appropriate to say educational needs, for their intention was to adapt the "continuing education" program to the needs revealed by the study. Different questionnaires were sent to top management personnel, middle management, and first-line supervisors. For top and middle management personnel, the respondents were to report, for each of many topics, the following perceptions:

Your own training needs. Should have; could use; or don't really need.

Training needs of those you supervise. Should have.

The resulting tables and figures could fill the rest of this book, but we will confine ourselves to the example given in Figure 12.5.

OCCUPATIONAL OBSOLESCENCE. One of the prices we pay for a fast-moving technology is an increase in obsolescence in certain occupations, especially scientific and professional ones. There are different manifestations of this phenomenon. One such indication was reported by Zelikoff (1969) from an examination of the content of engineering curricula in five engineering institutions for five engineering specializations. The curricula were examined for changes in pedagogical material as reflected by course offerings dropped and added from 1935 to 1965. The results for civil engineering are shown in Figure 12.6. The figure shows the "erosion curves" for selected graduation classes and demonstrates rather dramatically the decline of courses in "applied" knowledge from 1935 to 1965. The implications of these and other hints of the extent of occupational obsolescence drive home the point that, in certain occupations, training is a continuous process. The training director needs to coordinate this continuing process.

DISADVANTAGED PERSONS. The problems of various disadvantaged groups (such as the hard-core unemployed, certain minorities, and the uneducated) have many dimensions—social, personal, economic and so forth. These problems have important implications for training, inasmuch as opportunities for gainful employment are predicated on the development of relevant job skills. Actual training is offered by various governmental agencies, school systems, and employing organizations. The training of such groups usually needs a scope of content that heretofore generally has been outside the baliwick of typical training activities. Byars and Schwefel (1969), for example, referred to the need to teach such prospective employees to be reliable, neat, and punctual, and in some instances to offer basic reading and arithmetic and to teach the moral obligations of citizenship. As for the skills contributing to "employability," Barbee and Keil (1973) found that a training program designed to enhance the interviewing skills of disadvantaged persons did in fact increase the chances of such person obtaining employment. The training consisted of different combinations of simulated interviews, viewing a videotape of one's initial interview, and behavior modification techniques (such as identifying behaviors to be altered, rehearsing roles, practicing, and reinforcing appropriate behaviors.)

The development and implementation of training programs for disadvantaged persons by organizations are admittedly difficult, and such efforts have had varying degrees of success. Some programs that have been reported as being reasonably successful are those of Lockheed, some of the automobile manufacturers, Southern Bell Telephone and Telegraph Company,

and International Harvester (mentioned by Byars and Schwefel), and Humble Oil and Refining Company (reported by Mahoney 1969).

In an overview of training the hard-core unemployed, Goodman and others (1973) surveyed a number of published studies on this topic, and Salipante and Goodman (1976) followed up the experiences of 130 programs directed toward hiring and training such individuals. The results of these overviews are admittedly somewhat mixed, and any generalizations need to be taken with some reservations. A few of the inferences drawn by Goodman and others are that: Trained individuals are more likely to value work, to have positive attitudes to-

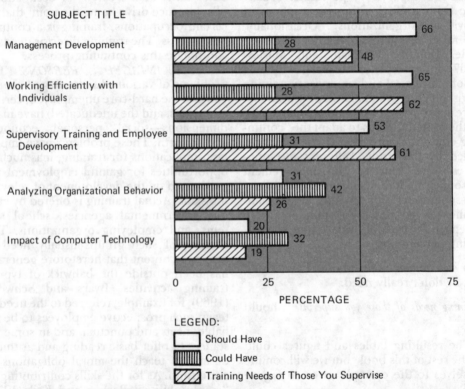

FIG. 12.5 Illustrative results of survey of managerial and supervisory educational needs resulting from survey by Pennsylvania State University. This particular figure shows those relating to "general management," as reported by 1,093 top managers. (*From Dubin, Alderman, & Marlow 1967, Figure 11.*)

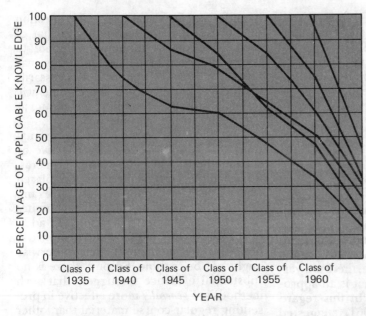

FIG. 12.6 "Erosion" curves showing occupational obsolescence in chemical engineering as reflected by an analysis of curriculum content of five engineering universities for selected graduating classes since 1935. (*From Zelikoff,* op. cit.)

ward time schedules, and to show increased feelings of personal efficacy concerning achievement and that, although training can have positive values, it can also have dysfunctional consequences, such as leading to greater expectations than the job situation can fulfill. Although they also reported that training was unlikely to affect the retention of trainees on their jobs, the later survey by Salipante and Goodman raised questions of the generality of this conclusion. In particular, Salipante and Goodman found a tendency for retention to be somewhat higher for training programs that emphasized job-skills content as contrasted with those that emphasized role playing (to sensitize trainees to themselves and others). They hastened to state that these results should not imply that training programs for the disadvantaged should be devoted completely to job-skills training (as opposed to "attitudinal" training) but rather, implied that job-skills training should be a major focus of such programs. They also found that the longer the training program was, the less the trainees retained *unless* the program was accompanied

by counseling to provide direct reinforcements to strengthen beliefs in the desirability of coming to work.

There are no simple rules to ensure success of training programs for the disadvantaged, but available materials suggest that the greatest emphasis on job-skills training with moderate emphasis on "attitudinal" training, accompanied by counseling, may enhance the likelihood of success. Petty (1974) provided evidence that the best way to present job-related information to disadvantaged trainees is orally; if written materials are to be distributed, they should be preceded by an oral version of the same material.

TRAINING METHODS AND TECHNIQUES

A wide spectrum of training methods and techniques, each with its own uses and constraints, is available for the various training programs sponsored by training organizations. Some of these are: lecture, audio-visual aids, simulators and training aids, conference methods, laboratory training, case method, role playing, behavior modeling, management games, programmed instruction (PI), and computer-assisted instruction (CAI). It is not appropriate here to attempt an exhaustive analysis of the various methods and techniques and their uses.[1] Instead, we will describe a few briefly and a few more extensively.

Lecture

The lecture has been severely criticized as a method of training, primarily because it normally does not allow for active participation by the trainees; this lack of participation, in turn, usually precludes any feedback. Although such criticisms argue against its indiscriminate use, there are various circumstances in which it is an appropriate method of training. In this regard Proctor and Thornton (1961) suggested that the lecture method be used in the following circumstances: when presenting completely new material to a group, when working with a large group, when introducing another instruction method, when classroom time is limited, and when summarizing material developed by another instruction method. It also can be useful in reducing anxiety about upcoming training programs, job changes, and other changes.

Audio-Visual Aids

Technology has enabled the use in training of a variety of audio-visual aids such as motion pictures, slides, filmstrips, overhead and opaque projectors, and television.[2] This equipment also enables the presentation of a wide range of subject matter in audio and/or visual form. The question of the use of these techniques is that of their effectiveness in helping people to learn; Hollywood-type presentations may be very impressive but are not necessarily instructive. In this regard, three points will be made with respect to these techniques as they relate to the learning process.

First, there are certain kinds of presentations that can be made more effective by such methods than by any other. Cameras, for example, can sometimes be placed where a learner cannot be—as, for example, in demonstrating surgical techniques or certain mechanical operations. In addition, these techniques facilitate demonstrations (as by animation) that otherwise might not be feasible. Second, there is no substantial evidence to suggest that such methods are *generally* more effective in presenting regular course material than other methods, but in some *individual* circumstances they have been found to be. Brightman (1975), for example, reported that a Sound-on Slide system (a product of the 3M Company) was found to be very effective (and relatively inexpensive) in training aviation mechanics of Continental Airlines. Although the system can be used with groups, the company encourages its individualized use to give mechanics the opportunity to learn at their own pace.

Third, a disadvantage of some audiovisual methods is that they do not allow for participation by the trainees. Certain specific systems are exceptions, such as the system discussed above.

Simulators and Training Aids

Simulators and training devices are used to give trainees physical equipment that resembles to some degree the equipment to be used on the job. Usually such devices are used when it is impractical for some reason (such as possible injury to the trainees or others) to use the actual equipment or

[1]The interested reader is referred to such sources as: Craig, R. L., & Bittel, L. R. *Training and development handbook.* New York: McGraw-Hill, 1967.
[2]For an excellent discussion of the equipment available and techniques in the use of audio-visual aids, the reader is referred to Otto, C. P., & Glaser, O. (Eds.). *The management of training.* Reading, Mass.: Addison-Wesley, 1970.

when the cost of the actual equipment is excessive.

As indicated earlier, the transfer of training from some type of physical simulator to the actual job depends more on the degree of "psychological" fidelity than on the degree of physical fidelity. Psychological fidelity is the extent to which the various stimuli and responses in the simulation and in the intervening mental operations and decisions correspond to those of the actual job. Although there undoubtedly are some circumstances in which the degree of psychological fidelity depends on the degree of physical fidelity, Weitz and Adler (1973) found that the results of various studies suggested that much beneficial training can result from the use of devices with low physical fidelity. On the basis of their own research with simulation, there are indications that, in a training situation on a simulator, trainees should not be trained beyond the point at which they have reached some minimal criterion of performance. They asserted that such overtraining could not only be wasteful in time and money, but that it might be detrimental to performance on the real task.

It is generally accepted that training aids add to the effectiveness of training, and there is experimental evidence to support this belief. There is however, a danger in using training aids, for the instructor may become "training-aid happy," relying on them to the detriment of the effectiveness of the training. In other words, they should be used judiciously, and when used, they should be appropriate to the purpose.

Conference Methods

In the training context the conference method allows for the participants to pool ideas, to discuss ideas and facts, to test assumptions, and to draw inferences and conclusions. This method, intended to improve job performance and personnel development, is most appropriate for such

purposes as: (1) developing the problem-solving and decision-making faculties of personnel, (2) presenting new and sometimes complicated material, and (3) modifying attitudes.

Probably the most important psychological principle is the active participation of those taking part in the conference. In addition, the conference permits "reinforcement" of such participation by the trainer, as pointed out by McGehee and Thayer (1961). Reinforcement should be for the participation as such and should not be verbal rewards or punishments for the *nature* of the participation; otherwise the conference leader would lose his neutrality.

Laboratory Training

There are a number of variations of what is sometimes called laboratory training or sensitivity training. Some programs are called T-group training (T for training).

The most common applications of such a method in industry are to the development of supervisory and management personnel, but they have also been used to develop other groups of personnel. In some instances training is given by an individual organization to its own personnel, and in other instances the individuals to be trained are sent to some facility specializing in such training, such as the National Training Laboratories (NTL). In either case, the trainees form a group with a trainer in which they interact in a very unstructured manner for a period of two or three days, or a week or more. There are no established agendas for the sessions, nor are there any established membership or leadership roles, thus creating an environment in which anxieties and tensions almost inevitably arise. Within this unstructured, ambiguous, and tension-generating environment, the interaction among the participants is intended to bring about greater self-awareness of the individual participants and increased sensitivity to, and understanding of, others and thus to improve their facility in interpersonal relationship skills. Bradford and Mial (1967) explained that laboratory training is designed to facilitate the development of such skills by providing the following conditions of learning:

(1)exposure of one's own behavior to others, (2) feedback from others about one's own behavior, (3) a "supportive" climate or atmosphere (which reduces defensiveness), (4) knowledge as a "map" (to provide for growth and change), (5) experimentation and practice, (6) application (how to maintain changed behavior back on the job), and (7) learning how to learn.

It should be noted that the experience of undergoing laboratory training is indeed traumatic for some individuals. There have been instances of breakdowns following such training, for example. In some instances the leaders or members have failed to protect some individuals from aggressive members of the group.

EVALUATION OF LABORATORY TRAINING. The problem of evaluating the effectiveness of laboratory training is, to use a British phrase, a sticky wicket. One can get testimonials from the participants as well as other measures linked directly to the content and processes of the training (such as measures of attitude change and performance in simulated problem-solving situations). These are what Campbell and Dunnette (1968) called internal criteria. Such changes are not themselves indicative of actual behavioral changes on the job. In one sense, the proof of the pudding should be in the changes in job behavior; such changes, which Campbell and Dunnette called external criteria, can be reflected by ratings from superiors, subordinates, or peers, by changes in production or other aspects of job performance, by turnover, or by other indices.

In adding up the black and red sides of the ledger for laboratory training, let us paraphase the observations of Campbell and Dunnette: the assumption that such training has positive utility for organizations must necessarily rest on shaky ground, for it has been neither confirmed nor disproved; on the other hand, it should be emphasized that utility for an organization is not necessarily the same as utility for the individual.

For those individuals who have undergone such training, it is undoubtedly true that many have gained useful personal insight into and understanding of themselves. But it should be added that such training programs have been criticized because some participants may feel pressured into participating when in fact they would rather not, and because their personal privacy may be invaded either during the training or by the subsequent feedback that they may be asked to give. Further, the traumatic aftermath of such training in the case of some individuals must be considered as one of the liabilities of this method.

Case Method

The case method is one in which an actual or hypothetical problem is presented to a training group—usually of supervisors or management personnel—for discussion and solution. The cases usually are some human relations problem and may be presented in writing, "live" (with individuals playing different roles), on film, or by recordings. There are a number of variations in the techniques and procedures, but they have the same constituent elements, including a case report (in some form), a case discussion (of some sort), case analysis (systematic or otherwise), and the current situation (the interaction of the group members and course director in learning to work together). The case method is intended to help the participants analyze problems and to discover underlying principles. Because most do not have any "single" answers, as is the case with most problems in the real world, the method helps to demonstrate that many problems have multiple causes and effects, thus aiding the participant to recognize that simple answers are few and far between.

Proctor and Thornton (1961) proposed that the case method is especially appropriate under the following circumstances: when employees need to be trained to identify and analyze complex problems and to frame their own decisions; when employees need to be exposed to a variety of approaches, interpretations, and personalities (to be shown, in short, that there are very few pat answers to business problems); when the personnel are sufficiently sophisticated to draw principles from actual cases and to formulate solutions to problems themselves; and when a challenge is needed for overconfident individuals. On the other hand, the procedure should be avoided with "beginners" or immature persons or when internal jealousies and tensions make people reluctant to air their opinions and ideas freely.

Role Playing

In role playing each participant plays the "part" (role) of someone in a simulated situation. There are many variations of role playing, but generally they are either preplanned or spontaneous. In the preplanned format the (hypothetical) situation is structured by setting forth the "facts" of the situation, such as the job situation in question, the events that led up to the "current" situation, and other information. It is in these respects much like the case method. In role playing, however, individuals are designated to play the roles of persons in the "case." The cases used can be built up around many different kinds of problems that can generate conflicting interests, such as unscheduled coffee breaks, work assignments, or vacation schedules. Once the case has been stated and the individuals assigned to their roles, they "play" those

roles as though the situation were real. Thus, a supervisor might play the role of a subordinate, a salesperson the role of a customer, and a nurse's aide the role of a hospital patient. Having to put one's self in someone else's place and play the part of that person generally increases one's empathy for the other person and one's understanding of his behavior.

In spontaneous role playing, the participants play the roles of different individuals in discussing some problem without a prepared script.

Role playing can be used in any training situation involving interaction between two or more people, such as in counseling, interviewing, performance review, supervision, job instruction, or selling. In whatever context it is used, the intent of role playing is to teach principles or skills or to provide a tool for changing attitudes and behavior in interpersonal relationships.

BEHAVIOR MODELING

Behavior modeling is a relatively recent addition to the training techniques available for supervisory and management training in interpersonal skills. These programs have four features: 1. modeling, 2. behavior rehearsal, 3. feedback, and 4. transfer of training.

Features of Behavior Modeling

The descriptions of these features as given by Moses are given below.

Modeling. This is the foundation of the program. A short film or videotape is presented to participants. The modeling display typically shows a supervisor-subordinate interaction dealing with a management problem (poor work quality, excessive absenteeism, discrimination complaints, etc.). The supervisor models a number of key behaviors which result in a successful resolution of the problem.

While the modeling display is necessary for learning to occur, it is not sufficient.

Behavior rehearsal. Each participant is provided an opportunity to rehearse and practice the behaviors demonstrated by the model. Although often confused with role playing, behavior rehearsal does not require the participant to play a role. Rather, he or she rehearses the actual behaviors which will be used on the job, by following the action steps demonstrated by the trainer.

Feedback. This is provided by the trainer and other participants for applying the principles modeled. Social reinforcement plays an important role in the initial acceptance on the part of participants. As the participant becomes confident with his or her new skills, considerable feedback is received from subordinates, and as importantly, by the participant as well.

Transfer of training. A variety of strategies are used to facilitate transfer. The term "applied learning" is an apt description. The problem situations selected reflect real problems with real solutions. Training schedules, job aids, and management support systems all facilitate transfer of skills from classroom to the job. While modeling approaches vary depending on program intent, the following features enhance transfer: 1. A pretraining needs analysis to identify real problem situations; 2. Sequencing of training from simple to complex problems; 3. Training schedules designed for distributed rather than massed practice; and 4. Follow up and reinforcement of acquired skills. (1978, p. 226)

The behavior modeling training method is a systematic procedure for applying what is a fairly well recognized principle that people do, to some extent, tend to "model" their behavior, for better or for worse, after that of other people with whom they are associated, such as children modeling their behavior after that of their parents, teachers, or peers, and employees tending to behave as their supervisors or peers do.

Evaluation of Behavior Modeling

As one example of an evaluation study of the effectiveness of behavior modeling, Moses and Ritchie (1976) evaluated the performance of ninety supervisors in the A. T. & T. Company who participated in a behavior modeling program, compared to that of ninety-three supervisors in a control group who had not undergone such training. The evaluation was made two months after the trained group had completed its training, this being done in an assessment center setting in which each of the supervisors (both trained and untrained) held a discussion with a specially trained individual who played the role of the subject's subordinate. Each supervisor handled three discussion problems in this simulated situation, being evaluated on how well he could transfer and apply training concepts to discussion problems not specifically covered in the training. Neither the person playing the role of the subordinate nor the evaluator knew whether the individual supervisors had or had not been in the behavior modeling program. The mean performance ratings of the two groups are shown in Figure 12.7, which shows higher ratings for all three discussion problems in the trained group. The distribution of overall performance ratings for the two groups shown below also reflects the superior ability of the trained group to deal with the supervisory problems covered in the study.

Overall Rating	Trained Group	Control Group
Above average	84%	32%
Average	10	35
Below average	6	33

In reviewing this and other investigations of the effectiveness of behavior modeling, McGehee and Tullar (1978) raised questions on the design of such studies and

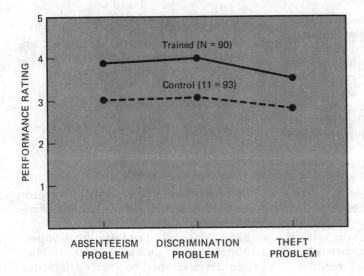

FIG. 12.7 Mean performance ratings of two groups of supervisors in three simulated problem-solving discussions with role-playing subordinates. The trained group had been through a behavior modeling training program two months before. (Adapted from Moses & Ritchie 1976, Table 3.)

the interpretation of some of the results. (In the case of the Moses and Ritchie study, for example, they pointed out that the two *groups* of subjects, not *individual* subjects, were randomly assigned to the trained and control groups, and suggested that the results may have been because the trained supervisors simply became more effective role players.) Recognizing the possible sense of such criticism, it is our opinion that behavior modeling does offer considerable promise as a training method but at the same time urge further evaluation of it.

Business Games

A business game (or management game) is a form of simulation in which separate teams of participants are presented with a typical management "problem," such as one concerned with production scheduling, retailing operations, personnel assignment, or product development. Whatever the problem the team is given appropriate information. Depending on the problem, this information can cover such factors as

assets, inventories, labor costs, storage costs, demand curves (the demand for a product as it varies with price), and interest charges. The team then organizes itself (perhaps by selecting a president and other officials) and proceeds to make decisions about its policies and operations. The effects of these decisions can be computed in quantitative terms, such as profits; this may be done either by computers or by hand. At the end it is possible to determine which team "won." Whether the game takes hours, days, or even months, it actually represents a longer time span, for the theoretical total time is compressed into the time spent on the game itself. The game is then followed by a critique in which the actions of the teams are analyzed.

Goldstein (1974) stated that such games provide practice in decision making and experience in interacting with others and that the feedback provisions and the dynamic quality of the play are seen as being intrinsically motivating to the participants. However, there have been some questions about the effectiveness of such games as a training method. Bass and Vaughan (1966), for example, believe that the participants may become so involved in the competitive features of the game that they lose sight of the principles and the evaluation of consequences that the games are intended to emphasize. There also are questions as to how well such games simulate the "psychological fidelity" of actual business decision-making processes.

Although business games have a certain intuitive appeal as a training method and generally are viewed favorably by participants, there is little hard evidence of their effectiveness as a management training method. This is not to say that the method is not useful but rather, that there has been little rigorous evaluation of the method.

Programmed Instruction (PI)

In programmed instruction (frequently referred to as PI), the material to be learned is presented in a series of steps or units that generally progress from simple to complex. At each step learners make a response and receive feedback in some way so that they know whether their response was correct or not. If the response was incorrect the trainees back up and are guided in some way to learn the correct response (and why it is correct) so that they can proceed further in the program. The features of this method are rooted in certain psychological principles of learning, which Hawley gives as follows:

Features: What the learner does

1. Works way through material by series of small steps.

2. Active response by answering questions, solving problems, etc.

3. Confirms correctness, or is provided with additional information to correct response.

4. Proceeds at own pace.

Principles: The effect on the learner

1. Minimizes risk of error. Errors are believed to interfere with learning.

2. People learn best by doing.

3. Immediate reinforcement.

4. Because of individual difference, people learn best at their own rate. (1967, p. 226)

Of particular importance to programmed instruction is the principle of reinforcement.

BACKGROUND. The forerunner of programmed instruction was a simple mechanical device developed by Pressy (1926) for testing students. It contained a window through which a multiple-choice test item was presented and a keyboard with four keys corresponding to the four possible responses. Only when the key of the correct answer was pressed did the next question appear. Thus, feedback was made available immediately.

Although Pressey laid the groundwork for programmed instruction, it was the later research of Skinner (1954) on operant conditioning that probably sparked the recent flurry of interest in this technique.

VARIATIONS IN PROGRAMMED INSTRUCTION METHODS. Most of the essential features of programmed instruction can be embodied in any of a number of different methods of presentation. These include elaborate teaching machines (some of which are tied in with computers) that present material visually, on films, or on sound tapes; more simple machines (still using electronic or mechanical features); simple devices that hold the paper on which the "program" is printed (some with a manual procedure for uncovering the "frames" successively); programmed books; and, at the simplest level, illustrations, diagrams, and other printed material.

Whatever method of presentation is used—elaborate or simple as the case may be—it performs at least three functions: (1) its presents information and/or questions or problems to the learner; (2) it provides an opportunity for him or her to respond; and (3) it provides feedback as to whether the response is right or wrong.

PROGRAMMING. The typical instructional program used in programmed instruction consists of a series of "frames" (also referred to as "images," "items," or "pages"). Each frame contains a small segment of information that is intended to elicit some sort of response from the learner. The frames vary from one program to another; examples are given in Figure 12.8. The frames are ordered in sequence, and usually one frame builds upon the preceding frame. As the learners progress from frame to frame (receiving feedback in each case), they then build up, bit by bit, the complete subject matter of the program.

Certain variations in approaches to programming should be noted. First, the responses can be "constructed" or "multiple-choice." A constructed response is one in which the learner actually writes in the response; it requires recall, or the formation of an answer based on what he has learned. A multiple-choice response is one in which the learner selects one of several possible responses; this requires recognition rather than recall. The evidence regarding the pros and cons of these two approaches generally has shown no systematic superiority of one over the other. Another distinction is between "linear" and "branching" programs. With linear programs, each subject goes through all frames in sequence and must master each one in turn. This is the form proposed by Skinner (1958). A "branching" program is one that can be adapted to the level of achievement of the learner. This is done by providing, at specific frames in the program, "branches" to be followed by those who have not adequately mastered the material to the point in question. This is the practice followed by Crowder (1959).

Use of Programmed Instruction

As programmed instruction methods developed in the 1950s they were used initially in educational institutions, most of the programs covering classroom subjects. Since then, as Goldstein (1974) found, there has been an astonishing increase in the number and kinds of programs available, including programs for industry and government as well as for educational institutions. For example, a U.S. Civil Service Commission survey (1970) identified over 2,300 programs being used in various government organizations. The topics of such programs extend far beyond classroom subjects, some programs covering such varied subjects as air-traffic control, blueprint reading, day-and-night storm signals and their meanings, food-borne disease in-

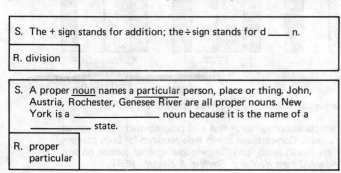

S. The + sign stands for addition; the ÷ sign stands for d ____ n.

R. division

S. A proper <u>noun</u> names a particular person, place or thing. John, Austria, Rochester, Genesee River are all proper nouns. New York is a _____ noun because it is the name of a _____ state.

R. proper
particular

FIG. 12.8 Illustrative programmed instruction frames from various programs. Only one or two frames are shown from each program; thus, these examples do not illustrate the sequence of frames within a single program. The correct response (shown as R) is not in view of the respondent until he has entered his response. (*From Lysaught & Williams 1963.*)

vestigation, magnetic amplifiers, analysis of tax returns, and even how to develop programmed instruction programs. Although the dominant use of programmed instruction is still in educational institutions, this method is being used by some industrial organizations.

Programmed Instruction in Industry

In evaluating programmed instruction as a training procedure in industry let us first summarize the results of a study carried out in an insurance company by Hedberg, Steffen, and Baxter (1965). They compared the effectiveness of programmed instruction with a conventional text as the basis for instructing new life insurance agents, the comparison being based on time required and amount learned (as measured by a test). Some of these comparisons are shown in Figure 12.9. There was no appreciable difference in the test scores of

trainees a month later, but the programmed instruction procedures took less time and thus resulted in more "knowledge" (as measured by test scores) per unit of time. For some general evaluation of its practical effectiveness, Nash, Muczyk, and Vettori (1971) analyzed the results of over a hundred empirical studies in which programmed instruction had been used either in academic or industrial circumstances. In about half of these, programmed instruction was reported to be of "practical effectiveness" (meaning that the differences in results between it and conventional instruction were statistically significant and exceeded 10 percent of the criterion values in question). Figure 12.10 shows a comparison among these for several studies in industry. This comparison and other data show that programmed instruction almost always reduces training time to a significant extent; the average saving in time is about one-third. Such a procedure usually does

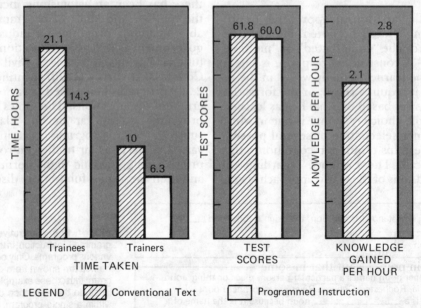

FIG. 12.9 Comparison of effects of conventional text and programmed instruction as used by new life insurance agents. Comparisons are in time required (of both trainees and trainers), test scores (one month later), and "knowledge" gained (based on test scores) per hour of time. (*Adapted from Hedberg, Steffen, & Baxter 1965.*)

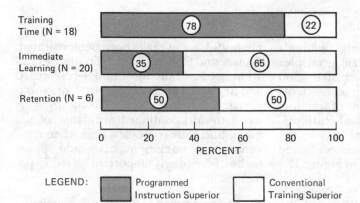

Training
Time (N = 18)   78   22

Immediate
Learning (N = 20)   35   65

Retention (N = 6)   50   50

0   20   40   60   80   100
PERCENT

LEGEND: Programmed   Conventional
Instruction Superior   Training Superior

FIG. 12.10 Percent of training programs in industry in which programmed instruction (PI) was "practically superior" to conventional training methods for three criteria. (Adapted from Nash and others 1971, Table 3.)

not improve training performance in terms of immediate learning or retention, for the studies show no significant difference in favor of either method. Thus, the primary advantage of programmed instruction seems to be in term of training time. This suggests that economic considerations are important to considering programmed instruction, specifically a comparison between the savings in instruction costs and time of the trainees and the cost of developing programmed instruction materials (which can run into many thousands of dollars).

Although programmed instruction seems not to have any general advantage over conventional training in amount or retention of learning, Goldstein (1974) called attention to certain other advantages, such as that the materials are easily packaged and can be sent to various training centers, that individual students can take the training when it is most convenient and appropriate, and the possibility that the individualization of the method may be particularly advantageous to high-and low-ability learners (who might benefit especially from the self-pacing aspect). On the other side of the ledger (and aside from the expense), Goldstein pointed out that in some school systems, student reaction has indicated that PI by itself may not be an acceptable mode of instruction and suggested that for adults in industry it may also be important to combine it with other methods allowing for human interaction in the training situation.

Computer Assisted Instruction (CAI)

Computer assisted instruction (CAI) is essentially a sophisticated descendent of programmed instruction. A major advantage of computers is their memory and storage capabilities which make possible various types of interactions with the learner not possible with programmed instruction procedures. These capabilities permit drill and practice, problem solving, simulation, and gaming forms of instruction, and certain forms of individualized tutorial instruction. To date, computer-assisted instruction procedures have been used mostly in educational institutions. Although they can be used in personnel training, the limitations probably are associated with cost factors. Although long-range, future developments (especially in reduced costs) may cause computer-assisted instruction to blossom as a training procedure in industry, its use within the foreseeable future would probably be limited to special circumstances in which computer facilities are available and in which costs can be spread over many trainees.

Discussion

As implied throughout much of this chapter, there is considerable queasiness about the generality of various principles of learning and about the relevance and effectiveness of certain training methods. Despite this doubt, it is still reasonable to believe that individual training methods would be predicated on certain principles of learning. In this connection, Bass and Vaughan (1966) set forth their assessments of the use, by various methods of training, of at least a few "principles of learning" and also indicated the typical uses of the various methods. These assessments and judgments are shown in part in Figure 12.-11.

THE EVALUATION OF TRAINING

Any discussion of the evaluation of training should be forthright in stating that the state of affairs of such evaluation is desultory. The number of training programs that have been evaluated is indeed miniscule, and the results of even some of the evaluations leave much to be desired in terms of experimental rigor. It is evident in the previous discussion of certain training methods that the actual effectiveness of some

methods has not really been demonstrated. Bunker and Cohen stated: "Training evaluation is one of the most under-researched and neglected areas of industrial/organizational psychology." ... "Ironically, this trend toward continued avoidance of the evaluation issue comes at a time when measurement of training impact would appear to be increasingly important" (1977, pp. 525, 526).

Validity as Applied to Training Evaluation

The concept of validity as applied to the evaluation of training usually has been viewed as being in two classes, namely, internal validity and external validity. Internal validity refers to the effects of a particular training treatment or program on the individuals who undergo the training. External validity refers to the extent to which one can generalize from the results of training in a given situation to other training

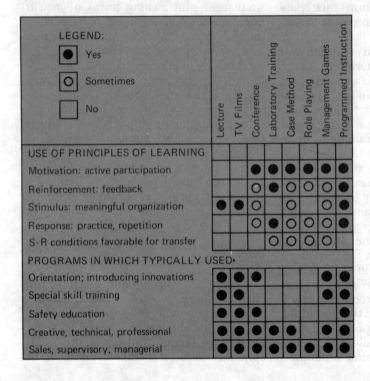

LEGEND: ● Yes ○ Sometimes □ No	Lecture	TV Films	Conference	Laboratory Training	Case Method	Role Playing	Management Games	Programmed Instruction
USE OF PRINCIPLES OF LEARNING								
Motivation: active participation			●	●	●	●	●	●
Reinforcement: feedback			○	●	○	○	○	●
Stimulus: meaningful organization	●	●	○		○		○	
Response: practice, repetition			○	●	○	○	○	●
S-R conditions favorable for transfer				○	○	○	○	
PROGRAMS IN WHICH TYPICALLY USED:								
Orientation; introducing innovations	●	●	●				●	●
Special skill training	●	●					●	●
Safety education	●	●	●					●
Creative, technical, professional	●	●	●	●	●		●	●
Sales, supervisory, managerial	●	●	●	●	●	●	●	●

FIG. 12.11 Extent to which selected training methods utilize certain principles of learning and indications of typical use of training methods. (*Adapted from Training in industry: The management of learning by Bernard M. Bass and James A. Vaughan, Tables 7-3 and 7-4. Copyright 1966 by Wadsworth Publishing Company, Inc. Adapted by permission of the publisher, Brooks/Cole Publishing Company, Monterey, Cal.*)

situations. However, Goldstein (1978) proposed the following classification scheme:

1. Training validity. Training validity is determined by the performance of trainees on criteria established for the training program.

2. Performance validity. This refers to the validity of the training program as measured by performance in the transfer setting or on the job.

3. Intraorganizational validity. This concept refers to the performance of a new group of trainees within the same organization that developed the training program.

4. Interorganizational validity. This refers to the question as to whether a training program validated in one organization can be utilized in another organization.

Goldstein's definition of training validity is clearly a form of internal validity. Although performance validity usually has been considered a form of internal validity, Goldstein considered it as an external validity concept along with intra- and interorganizational validity. Thus Goldstein's concepts of performance validity as related to training is a bit at odds with the more commonly recognized concepts of internal and external validity.

Experimental Design in Training Evaluation

The demonstration of the utility (that is, the validity) of a training program or method is by no means simple. For example, if the performance of a sample of people as measured before and after training is different, one cannot be sure that the difference is due to the training as such. Maybe the trainees would have improved anyway because of the intervening time. Maybe the assignment to the training increased their motivation. Or maybe the performance test taken before training helped to improve their performance. These and other variables can adversely affect the conclusions and inferences one can draw from a train-

ing evaluation study, *unless* the design of the study has been carefully planned and executed. Although this book is not the place to discuss experimental design, we will at least mention certain aspects relevant to training evaluation.

We will illustrate what is called the Solomon design, which is based on the use of four groups of subjects, with individual subjects being assigned randomly to the four groups. In this representation the following codes are used: T-1 represents a pretest, T-2 a posttest, and X the training given. The four groups are then as follows:

	Time $\longrightarrow$		
Group 1	T–1	X	T–2
Group 2	T–1		T–2
Group 3		X	T–2
Group 4			T–2

The use of a single group (as group 1) offers no assurance that the training (X) caused any difference between the pretest and the posttest, since other variables (such as those referred to) might have had an influence. The use of a second group as a control group at least equalizes the possible effects of the pretest for the two groups but still leaves dangling the question of the possible effects of the pretest. The use of three groups gets around the possible effects of the pretest (since there is none for the third group) but does not make it possible to compare what would have happened without either a pretest or the training. The use of the fourth group helps to make that kind of comparison. There are a number of variables that can influence the results of evaluation studies in addition to the ones we have mentioned, but the use of four groups as illustrated quite well controls for those that could influence internal validity and would control for certain variables that could influence external validity (especially if the criterion tests T-1 and T-2 are appropriate). As McGehee (1979) pointed out, the four-group design does not eliminate all sources of external invalidity.

It must be acknowledged that the practical problems in training evaluation frequently preclude the use of a four-group experimental design like that illustrated. One of the extremely rare instances in which such a design was used was in a study of electronics training conducted by Bunker and Cohen (1977). They found that the failure to have used such a design in their study would not have resulted in catastrophic distortion of the major evaluation results, but only because of certain factors unique to their subjects. They made a strong pitch for using "extended control designs" like that illustrated, stating that

industry can no longer afford to bypass or conserve expenses in training evaluation because of the investments in training and the risks and costs associated with erroneous evaluations. We strongly endorse such an objective. At the same time the practical problems will undoubtedly continue to preclude the possibility of truly rigorous evaluation in many circumstances. It is urged that the evaluation be as rigorous as the circumstances will permit.

A Survey of Evaluation Practices

Some reflection of the actual practices of companies in the evaluation of training programs comes from a survey by Catalano and Kirkpatrick (1968). They queried 110

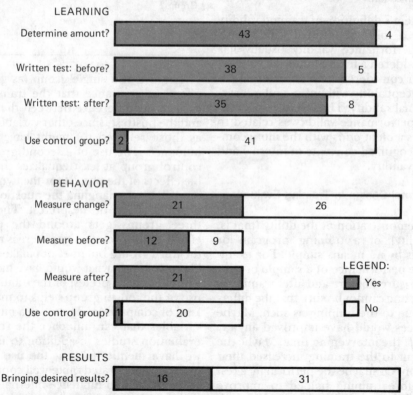

FIG. 12.12 Responses of forty-seven selected companies to questionnaire regarding their practices in measuring learning, behavior, and results in relation to human relations training programs. (*Adapted from Catalanello & Kirkpatrick 1968.*)

organizations known to be concerned with human relations training about their training evaluation practices. Of these, about 78 percent reported that they attempted to measure trainee *reactions,* and about half said they attempted evaluation in terms of *learning, behavior,* and/or *results.* More detailed questionnaires were sent subsequently to the "half" just referred to, with forty-seven companies responding. Replies to certain questions are summarized in Figure 12.12. We can see that a large portion did attempt to measure learning both before and after the training programs but that less than half attempted to measure changes in behavior as such, and about a third attempted to measure results. Those that did measure results reported that they did so on the basis of observation, interviews, analysis of production reports, turnover figures, and other indices. It might be noted that the number using control groups was virtually negligible; collectively, then, the companies would not stack up very well in terms of acceptable standards of experimental design!

Examples of Training Evaluation

A couple of examples of training evaluation are presented to illustrate evaluation studies that have been reported, but (as with most reported studies) these would not fulfill all the requirements of rigorous experimental design.

SKILL TRAINING. A comparison of the learning curves of employees in a cotton weaving mill is shown in Figure 12.13. Both of these curves are expressed in wages earned (directly related to productivity on the job), but one shows the average earnings during a period in which there was no organized training, whereas the other shows earnings for those who went through a specialized training program. It can be observed that those who received the specialized training reached the "shed average" within about twenty-six weeks, as opposed to the previous full year required to reach par.

ANXIETY-REDUCTION TRAINING. A rather unusual approach to operator training was taken at Texas Instruments Incor-

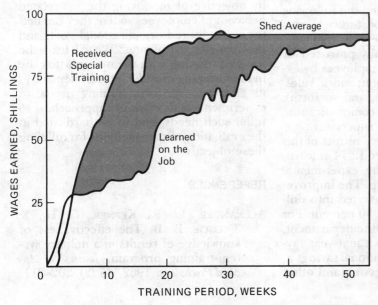

FIG. 12.13 Learning curves (shown in wages earned) for two groups of employees in a cotton-weaving mill. One group learned "on the job" without any organized training effort; the other group went through a specialized training program. The study was carried out by the Cotton Board Productivity Centre, Ltd. of Great Britain. (Originally published by Fielded House Productivity Centre, Ltd., as presented by Singer & Ramsden 1969, Figure 3.2.)

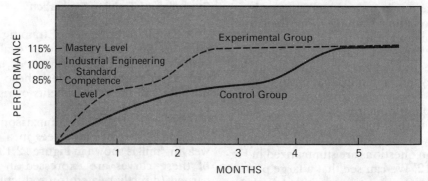

FIG. 12.14 Performance during training period of a control group of assemblers (who received conventional job training) and of an experimental group (who in addition received a day of "anxiety-reduction" training). The performance scale shows a "competence" level, the industrial engineering standard, and a "mastery" level. (*From Gomersall & Myers 1966.*)

porated, as reported by Gommersall and Myers (1966). On the basis of interviews with over four hundred operators, it was suspected that a major impediment to learning during training arose from the anxieties of the trainees. So, in addition to the regular orientation training for the various groups of operators, a special one-day program was worked up specifically to help the trainees overcome the anxieties not sloughed off during the regular training. This orientation emphasized the following four points: (1) Your opportunity to succeed is very good; (2) Disregard "hall talk" (that is, the hazing typically practiced by older employees on new employees by exaggerating allegations about work rules, work standards, discipline, and so forth); (3) Take the initiative in communication; and (4) Get to know your supervisor.

The "before" and "after" results of this training are shown in Figure 12.14 as learning curves for one of the experimental groups and a control group. The improvement in performance, converted into dollars and cents, was almost 50 percent. For one hundred new hires in the department, the gain was equivalent to a first-year saving of at least $50,000; additional savings in reduced turnover, absenteeism, and other factors would result in additional savings of $35,000.

DISCUSSION

Much of the training in industry has been based on faith and hope. This is not to say that it has not been effective but rather, indicates that, generally, it is not known whether much of the training fulfills its objective of modifying the job-related behavior of employees so that they can better serve desired organizational goals and in a cost-effective manner. We will leave the topic of training with the opinion that the field of training must be more systematic in its efforts to set forth training needs, to experiment with various approaches to fulfill such needs, and to be hardfisted in the evaluation of such methods for fulfilling these objectives.

REFERENCES

ALEXANDER, L. T., KEPNER, C. H., & TREGOE, B. B. The effectiveness of knowledge of results in a military system-training program. *Journal of Applied Psychology*, 1962, *46* (2), 202–211.

ANNETT, J., & DUNCAN, K. D. Task analysis and training design. *Occupational Psychology,* 1967, *41,* 211–221.

BARBEE, J. R., & KEIL, E. Experimental techniques of job interview training for the disadvantaged. *Journal of Applied Psychology,* 1973, *58* (2), 209–213.

BASS, B. M. & VAUGHAN, J. A. *Training in industry: The management of learning.* Belmont, Calif.: Wadsworth, 1966.

BRADFORD, L. P., & MIAL, D. J. Human relations laboratory training. In R. L. Craig & L. R. Bittel (Eds.), *Training and development handbook* (Chap. 12). New York: McGraw-Hill, 1967.

BRIGHTMAN, C. E. Improving maintenance training of Continental Airlines. *Training and Development Journal,* December 1975, *29* (12), 46–48.

BUNKER, K. A., & COHEN, S. L. The rigors of training evaluation. A discussion and field demonstration. *Personnel Psychology,* 1977, *30* (4), 525–541.

BYARS, L. L., & SCHWEFEL, L. Training the hard-core unemployed. *Training and Development Journal,* July 1969, *23* (7), 48–51.

CAMPBELL, J. P., & DUNNETTE, M. D. Effectiveness of T-group experiences in managerial training and development. *Psychological Bulletin,* 1968, *70* (2), 73–104.

CARROLL, J. B. On learning from being told. *Educational Psychologist* (Newsletter of Division 15, American Psychological Association), March 1968, *5* (2), 1 & 5–10.

CATALANO, R. E., & KIRKPATRICK, D. L. Evaluating training programs: The state of the art. *Training and Development Journal,* May 1968, *22* (5), 2–9.

CRAIG, R. L., & BITTEL, L. R. (Eds.). *Training and development handbook.* New York: McGraw Hill, 1967.

CROWDER, N. A. Automatic tutoring by means of intrinsic programming. In Galanter, E. (Ed.). *Automatic teaching: the state of the art.* New York: Wiley, 1959.

CUNNINGHAM, J. D., & DUNCAN, K. D. Describing non-repetitive tasks for training purposes. *Occupational Psychology,* 1967, *41,* 203–210.

DUBIN, S. S., ALDERMAN, E., & MARLOW, H. L. *Managerial and supervisory educational needs of business and industry in Pennsylvania.* University Park: Pennsylvania State University, 1967.

FOLLEY, J. D., JR. Determining training needs of department store sales personnel. *Training and Development Journal,* July 1969, *23* (7), 24–26.

GAGNÉ, R. M. *The conditions of learning* (3rd ed.). New York: Holt, Rinehart & Winston, 1977.

GOLDSTEIN, I. L. *Training: Program development and evaluation.* Monterey, Calif.: Brooks/Cole, 1974.

GOLDSTEIN, I. L. Pursuit of validity in the evaluation of training programs. *Human Factors,* 1978, *20* (2) 131–144.

GOMMERSALL, E. A., & MYERS, M. S. Breakthrough in on-the-job training. *Harvard Business Review,* July–August 1966, *44* (4), 62–72.

GOODMAN, P. S., SALIPANTE, P., & PARANSKY, H. Hiring, training, and retraining the hard-core unemployed: A selected review. *Journal of Applied Psychology.* 1973, *58* (1), 23–33.

HAWLEY, W. E. Programmed instruction. In R. I. Craig & S. L. R. Bittel (Eds.),

Training and development handbook (Chap. 12). New York: McGraw-Hill, 1967.

HEDBERG, R., STEFFEN, H., & BAXTER, B. Insurance fundamentals—A programmed text versus a conventional text. *Personnel Psychology,* 1965, *18* (2), 165–171.

HINRICHS, J. R. Personnel training. In M. D. Dunnette (Ed.), *Handbook of industrial and organizational psychology* (Chap. 19). Chicago: Rand McNally, 1976.

HOLDING, D. H. *Principles of training.* Oxford: Pergamon Press, 1965.

JOHNSON, R. B. Determining training needs. In R. I. Craig & L. R. Bittel (Eds.), *Training and development handbook* (Chap. 2). New York: McGraw-Hill, 1967.

KIRKPATRICK, D. L. Determining training needs: Four simple and effective approaches. *Training and Development Journal,* February 1977, *31* (2), 22–25.

LYSAUGHT, J. P., & WILLIAMS, C. M. *A guide to programmed instruction.* New York: Wiley, 1963.

MCGEHEE, W. Training and development theory, policies, and practices. In D. Yoder & H. G. Honenman, Jr. (Eds.), *ASPA Handbook of personnel and industrial relations* (Chap. 5.1). Washington, D.C.: Bureau of National Affairs, 1979.

MCGEHEE, W., & THAYER, P. W. *Training in business and industry.* New York: Wiley, 1961, p. 132.

MCGEHEE, W., & TULLAR, W. L. A note on evaluating behavior modification and behavior modeling as industrial training techniques. *Personnel Psychology,* 1978, *31* (3), 477–484.

MAHONEY, F. X. New approaches for new employees. *Training and Development Journal,* January 1969, *23* (1), 22–28.

MILLER, R. B. Task description and analysis. In R. M. Gagné (Ed.), *Psychological principles in system development.* New York: Holt, Rinehart & Winson, 1962.

MOSES, J. L. Behavior modeling for managers. *Human Factors,* 1978, *20* (2), 225–232.

MOSES, J. L., & RITCHIE, R. J. Supervisory relationships training: A behavioral evaluation of a behavior modeling program. *Personnel Psychology,* 1976, *29* (3), 337–343.

NASH, A. N., MUCZYK, J. P., & VETTORI, F. L. The relative practical effectiveness of programmed instruction. *Personnel Psychology,* 1971, *24,* 397–418.

NAYLOR, J. C. Parameters affecting the relative efficiency of part and whole practice methods: A review of the literature. United States Naval Training Devices Center, Technical Report No. 950–1, February 1962.

PETTY, M. M. Relative effectiveness of four combinations of oral and written presentations of job related information to disadvantaged trainees. *Journal of Applied Psychology,* 1974, *59* (1), 105–106.

PRESSEY, S. L. A simple apparatus which tests and scores—and teaches. *School and Society,* March 20, 1926, *23* (586), 373–376.

PROCTOR, J. H., & THORNTON, W. M. *Training: A handbook for line managers.* New York: American Management Association, 1961.

RUNDQUIST, E. A. *Job training course design and improvement* (2nd ed.). San Diego:

Naval Personnel and Training Research Laboratory, Research Report SRR 71–4, September 1970.

RUNDQUIST, E.A., WEST, C. M., & ZIPSE, R. I. *Development of a job task inventory for commanding officers of amphibious ships.* San Diego: Naval Personnel and Training Research Laboratory, Research Report SRR 72–2, August 1971.

SALIPANTE, P., JR., & GOODMAN, P. Training, counseling, and retention of the hard-core unemployed. *Journal of Applied Psychology,* 1976, *61* (1), 1–11.

SINGER, E. J., & RAMSDEN, J. *The practical approach to skills analysis.* London: McGraw-Hill, 1969. (Published and distributed in the United States by Daniel Davey & Co., Inc., Hartford, Connecticut.)

SKINNER, B. F. Teaching machines. *Science,* 1958, *128,* 969–977.

THORNDIKE, E. L. Mental discipline in high school studies. *Journal of Educational Psychology,* 1924, *15,* 1–22, 83–98.

THORNDIKE, E. L., & WOODWORTH, R. S. The influence of improvement in one mental function upon efficiency of other functions. *Psychological Review,* 1901, *8,* 247–261, 384–385, 553–564.

U.S. Civil Service Commission. *Programmed instruction: A brief of its development and current status.* Washington, D.C.: U.S. Government Printing Office, 1970.

WEITZ, J., & ADLER, S. The optimal use of simulation. *Journal of Applied Psychology,* 1973, *58* (2), 219–224.

YODER, D., & HENEMAN, H. G., JR. *ASPA Handbook of personnel and industrial relations.* Washington, D.C. Bureau of National Affairs, 1979.

ZELIKOFF, S. B. On the obsolescence and retraining of engineering personnel. *Training and Development Journal,* May 1969, *23* (5), 3–14.

13
work motivation

Why do people work? Work is so pervasive in our society that almost all people wrestled with this question at some time during their lives. If they have not asked it about others, they at least have wondered about their own work behavior.

Over a seven-year period, Studs Terkel interviewed hundreds of workers about their work. His book, *Working* (Terkel 1972), is a fascinating glimpse of what people see in their work. Figure 13.1 has some brief excerpts from the book. Reading through these, one immediately is struck by their diversity. People work for *many* reasons. Some work only for money; some work because they love what they are doing; others work because of the status they receive. The list goes on and on.

ABILITY VERSUS MOTIVATION

Understanding why people work is the domain of work motivation. To clarify what is meant by motivation let us start with an observed behavior and work backwards to possible causes of it. Assume that we have just observed a bank teller who has handled approximately three hundred transactions a day for five days and, at the end of each day, his or her transactions check out perfectly the first time they are totaled. Two general classes of explanatory concepts usually are used to describe behaviors such as this. The first is *ability*. Abilities represent the individual's capability of handling the job at a certain time. For a teller, the ability to add and subtract as well as to operate the equipment for entering transactions certainly would be critical to being able to perform as well as was indicated. The abilities represent certain minimum conditions necessary for completion of the work. In a sense, we can think of them as the "can do" factors associated with the behavior. They are necessary but not sufficient precursors of the behavior.

FIG. 13:1 Selected quotes from Studs Terkel's *Working*, New York: Pantheon Press, 1972.

Hots Michaels, player at piano bar in New York hotel

"... because I enjoy the action. I enjoy people. If I were suddenly to inherit four million dollars, I guarantee you I'd be playin' piano, either here or at some other place. I can't explain why. I would miss the flow of people in and out."

Cathleen Moran, nurse's aid

"I really don't know if I mind the work as much as you always have to work with people, and that drives me nuts. I don't mind emptying the bed pan, what's in it, blood, none of that bothers me at all. Dealing with people is what I don't like. It just makes everything else blah."

Nora Watson, editor

"Jobs are not big enough for people. It's not just the assembly line worker whose job is too small for his spirit, you know? A job like mine, if you really put your spirit into it, you would sabotage immediately. You don't dare. So you absent your spirit from it. My mind has been divorced from my job, except as a source of income, it's really absurd."

Elmer Ruiz, gravedigger

"Not anybody can be a gravedigger. You can dig a hole any way they come. A gravedigger, you have to make a neat job. I had a fella once, he wanted to see a grave. He was a fella that digged sewers. He was impressed when he seen me diggin' this grave—how square and how perfect it was. A human body is goin' into this grave. That's why you need skill when you're gonna dig a grave ... I start early, about seven o'clock in the morning, and I have the part cleaned before the funeral. We have two funerals for tomorrow, eleven and one o'clock. That's my life ...

I enjoy it very much, especially in summer. I don't think any job inside a factory or an office is so nice. You have the air all day and it's just beautiful. The smell of the grass when it's cut, it's just fantastic. Winter goes so fast sometimes you just don't feel it."

The second set of explanatory concepts for the behavior often is labeled *motivation.* Motivation is the individual's *desire* to show the behavior and might be thought of as the "will do" factors influencing the display of work-related behaviors. Knowing that a teller can perform arithmetic operations flawlessly and can operate the machines by no means ensures that that teller will perform as well as the one in our example. He or she must want to perform accurately and efficiently and direct his or her effort toward doing a good job.

DEFINITION OF WORK MOTIVATION

Steers and Porter (1975) in their text entitled *Motivation and Work Behavior* identified three major components of motivation.

The first is an *energizing* component. This is the force or drive present in the organism which leads to some behavior. Second, there is some *directing* function that guides the behavior in a particular direction. For example, for the person who is hungry, behaviors are likely to be directed toward obtaining food. Finally, motivation is *maintaining* or *sustaining* behavior once it has occurred. The latter is particularly important to work settings in which job incumbents once hired and placed on jobs are expected to maintain high attendance, good performance, and the like, as long as they remain with the organization.

Emphasizing these three factors, work motivation is defined as *conditions which influence the arousal, direction, and maintenance of behaviors relevant in work settings.* The inclusion of behaviors *relevant* to work settings emphasizes that not all behaviors at work are of interest. In the past, relevant behaviors were defined as productivity-oriented activities—absenteeism, turnover, and performance. Yet, other behaviors also are important, such as political maneuvering of executives for attractive positions in the organization or scientists' conflict and rivalry for scientific information. Behaviors such as leaning back in one's chair or writing with the left versus the right hand, are irrelevant to most jobs and, therefore, are not of interest.

PROBLEMS FACING THE UNDERSTANDING OF WORK BEHAVIOR

To limit our search for reasons for work behavior to those labeled motivational influences would seem to simplify the task of understanding people's behavior. Unfortunately, it does not. At least four factors complicate our understanding of work motivation. The first already has been mentioned—the *diversity of reasons* for which people work. The others need to be explained.

A second stumbling block in understanding work behavior is *stereotypes* abound. Everyone has his or her pet theory for why people do what they do on the job. Managers and workers alike have their own views and, without hesitation, can cite numerous examples which "prove" their "theory." Two of these "theories" are worth noting because they are so pervasive. The first assumes that motivation to work is a basic human characteristic. Some have it; some do not. Perhaps more accurately, it should be said, a few ("like me") have it and most do not. Motivation, according to this view, is seen as a personal trait just as is height or weight. Since it is part of the person, individuals who hold this view tend to feel that having high work motivation is a matter of finding the right people—those who possess this trait. We shall label this

view the "internal state" view of motivation.

Another widely accepted stereotype of why people work emphasizes the conditions of the work environment and the job. Stress is placed upon pay, supervision, working conditions, geography of the area, and so on. It can be considered "carrot and stick" motivation. The emphasis is on "external states" which are assumed to influence most individuals, regardless of their personal orientations.[1]

These two stereotype points of view are held to various degrees by managers and workers and have some interesting twists. For example, people tend to attribute good performance to internal states if it is their own performance more often than if it is someone else's performance. Also, on some jobs, it is expected that people will be motivated by internal states more than by external conditions, and on other jobs it is the reverse. As a result, it is assumed that college professors work because they love their work and grave diggers work only because they need the money. Complaints among college professors about pay, teaching loads, class size, as well as publication pressures, and statements such as the one in Figure 13.1 from the grave digger vividly illustrate the fallacies of such theories. Nevertheless, these "theories" of motivation are well entrenched and cannot be ignored.

A third factor that complicates understanding why people behave the way they do is that there are *different reasons for behaviors at different times.* For example, the bank teller introduced earlier may have worked very hard to do well when he or she first took the job, in order to avoid being reprimanded by the supervisor and to improve his or her chances for promotion. After several months on the job, having done well during this time, it would probably be apparent to the teller that he or she was very

[1]Landy and Trumbo (1976) described a similar system which they labeled trait and environment approaches.

well respected by the supervisor and that his or her position was quite secure. At the same time, it may be equally apparent that there is no chance for any promotion in the job. Does this mean that the teller's performance will drop off? Perhaps, but also, perhaps not. In most banks, at the end of the work day, tellers must stay at their work area until their daily transactions balance. When their records balance they may go home. The teller, in this case, may maintain high performance simply in order to be able to leave soon after the bank closes. The reasons for the same observed behavior may have changed.

Finally, work motivation is complicated because there are many *different behaviors* in the work setting that are of interest. Number of units produced per hour, attendance, quitting, drinking on the job, listening to a supervisor, taking night school courses, accidents, and so forth all are types of behaviors considered relevant work behaviors for various jobs. The causes or reasons for these behaviors may be very different. Their diversity attests to the difficulty of understanding work motivation.

APPROACH TO MOTIVATION

Vroom (1964) and Landy and Trumbo (1976) correctly concluded that work motivation does not differ extensively from other kinds of motivation. The focus is limited only because the subset of behaviors of interest are those relevant to a work environment. Yet, these are still behaviors, and, if we can understand the reasons for behaviors in general, we shall be able to understand work behavior in particular.

The remainder of the discussion will concentrate first on theories of work motivation. Some theories apply to all behavior, not just to work behavior. Others are adaptations of general theories of human motivation to behavior at work. In either case, the emphasis of the following section on theories is not on specific applications of techniques to improve work performance but rather on understanding why people do as they do in work settings. Following the theoretical views, we will turn to practices within organizational settings which have motivational emphases. These practices either explicitly or implicitly have their roots in one or more of the theoretical positions.

THEORIES OF WORK MOTIVATION

The theoretical treatment of work motivation was a latecomer to the study of work behavior. Before the mid-1950s it was generally assumed that people worked for either economic or social reasons. Personnel practices and policies reflected these assumptions. Today the situation has changed. There now are several theories which have a substantial impact on the way work behavior is conceived. Mitchell, in his 1979 chapter for the *Annual Review of Psychology,* found almost 25 percent of the articles on behavior in organizations were concerned with motivation.

The upsurge of theoretical interest is both a blessing and a curse. On the one hand, the theoretical orientations do offer a better understanding of work behavior and an appreciation for its complexity. On the other hand, several very diverse theoretical orientations have evolved. Ideally, we would offer an integration and evaluation of all theories that lead to a single, accepted position on work motivation. Unfortunately, such a definitive conclusion is beyond the knowledge of work motivation at the present time. There are several theoretical positions that provide some useful insights into why people behave as they do in work settings. With a good knowledge of the theories that do exist and the support or lack of support for them, intelligent decisions can be made about the design of jobs and the development of personnel practices to facilitate desirable job behaviors.

Need Theories

Motivational theories which emphasize needs posit the existence of some internal state of the individual, labeled a need or a motive. This internal state usually is described in terms of the conditions that will satisfy the need. Thus, a need for food is identified by the fact that individuals will seek out objects classified as food when the individual is believed to be hungry. The need for food, or hunger, is inferred from the behaviors of seeking food. Let us now turn to the description of several need theories relevant to work motivation.

NEED HIERARCHY THEORY. Perhaps the most widely discussed theory of motivation is Maslow's (1954, 1970). Although Maslow did not develop the theory specifically for work motivation, the implications of the theory for work were quickly recognized and received extensive attention (see for example, Porter 1962).

Maslow proposed that sound motivational theory assumes that people are continuously in a motivational state, but that the nature of the motivation is fluctuating and complex. In addition, human beings seldom reach a state of complete satisfaction except for a short time; as one need or desire becomes satisfied, another rises to take its place. This never-ending sequence produces a hierarchy of needs. The theory has two goals. First, it is concerned with identifying the needs, which are the basis of motivation. These needs provide the content of the theory. The second goal is explaining how the needs are related to each other.

Maslow proposed that the needs were ordered in a hierarchical fashion with all needs lower in the hierarchy having *prepotence* over those higher. As lower needs were satisfied, the individual shifted his or her concern to higher order needs. The hierarchy of needs was often misconstrued to mean that the lower level needs had to be satisfied before higher order needs began

to operate. Maslow clarified this misinterpretation (Maslow 1970), stating that lower order needs are, in general, satisfied to a greater extent than are higher order ones. This did not preclude the possibility of more than one need operating at a time. He also recognized individual exceptions to the theory, such as individuals who would give up everything including life for their ideals (Locke 1976).

Some modifications of Maslow's original categories (especially of labels) were made by McGregor (1957, 1960). These are described and discussed briefly.

Physiological needs are taken as the starting point and are conceived to be the most prepotent. These include the basic needs for food, water, and the like. These needs cannot be ignored for long and must be met before all others. To the person in a state of virtual starvation or water deprivation, matters other than food or water are of little concern.

Once the physiological needs are relatively well met, there emerges a new set of needs which are categorized generally as *safety needs.* These are concerned with protection against danger, threat, and deprivation. Protection against physical dangers is of less consequence now, in our civilization, than it was in the past. On the other hand, in an industrial society the safety needs may be important to the dependent relationship between employees and employers. As pointed out by McGregor, the safety needs may serve as motivators in such circumstances as arbitrary management actions, behavior which arouses uncertainty of continued employment, and unpredictable administration of policy.

Once the physiological and safety needs are reasonably well fulfilled, the *social needs* become important motivators of behavior. These include needs for belonging, for association, for love, for acceptance by one's fellows, and for giving and receiving friendship.

Next in the hierarchy are the *ego needs.*

McGregor distinguished two kinds: (1) those needs that relate to one's self-esteem —needs for self-confidence, for achievement, for competence, for knowledge; and (2) those that relate to one's reputation— needs for status, for recognition, for appreciation, for the deserved respect of one's fellows. In contrast with the lower needs, the ego needs are seldom fully satisfied. These needs usually do not become dominant until the lower needs have been fulfilled.

Highest among the needs is that of self-fulfillment or *self-actualization*—the need for realizing one's own potentialities and for continual self-development. This need is seldom fully met by human beings.

Keeping constantly in mind that the above hierarchy represents the *general* order of relative potency of the various needs and does not apply invariably to all individuals, remember that Maslow (1970) believed that the hierarchy was characterized by some supporting aspects or features, a few of which are given below:

1. The higher needs are a later evolutionary development.

2. The higher the need, and the less imperative it is for sheer survival, the longer gratification can be postponed, and the easier it is for the need to disappear permanently.

3. Living at the higher need level means greater biological efficiency, greater longevity, less disease, better sleep, better appetite, and so forth.

4. Higher needs are less urgent, subjectively.

5. Higher need gratifications produce more desirable subjective results, that is, more profound happiness, serenity, and richness of the inner life.

6. Pursuit and gratification of higher needs represent a general trend toward good health.

7. Higher needs require better outside conditions (economic, educational, etc.) to make them possible.

8. Satisfaction of higher needs is closer to self-actualization than is the satisfaction of lower needs.

Maslow suggested that the various need levels are interdependent and overlapping, each higher level need emerging before the lower level need has been completely satisfied. In addition, he noted that individuals may reorder the needs. The latter obviously violates a strict adherence to the hierarchy.

Although widely accepted because of its intuitive appeal, the empirical support for the theory is less than impressive. For many years supposed tests of the theory relied upon cross-sectional data. Comparisons among work groups such as workers versus managers generally found that managers reported better satisfied lower order needs than workers did and more concern for higher order needs. These data were seen as generally supportive of Maslow's position. However, such comparisons across groups do not represent strong tests of the theory. To adequately test it, longitudinal research must demonstrate that the same individual progresses through the hierarchy changing from one need level to the next as lower needs are satisfied. Two studies in which changes over time were addressed provided no support for the theory. Hall and Nougaim (1968) followed A.T.&T. executives over several years and hypothesized that as a need became satisfied its importance should drop, according to Maslow's theory. In fact, just the opposite occurred for the executives; the more satisfied they were with a particular need, the more important it was seen to be. Similar findings by Lawler and Suttle (1972) using causal correlational analyses must lead us to conclude that the hierarchical nature of the theory simply does not hold.

In addition, Miner and Dachler (1973) concluded from their review that there is no support for the contention that Maslow's list of five needs is somehow inherent in or basic to man. Factor analytic research as well as other research, fails to reproduce a set of five and only five needs that match Maslow's set. Finally, Locke criticized the theory on logical grounds. The most telling of his criticisms is that it is impossible to find an intelligible definition of self-actualization. Locke said:

> For example, to "become more and more what one is" is self-contradictory. To become "everything one is capable of becoming" is impossible if taken literally, since every person is metaphysically capable of becoming almost an unlimited number of things. A person who tried to become self-actualized in this sense would probably become neurotic due to unsolvable conflicts among the thousands of choices open to him. (1976, p. 1308)

ERG THEORY. Alderfer (1969, 1972) offered an alternative theory closely related to Maslow's that addresses some but not all of the criticisms raised. He termed his theory *Existence, Relatedness, Growth (ERG)* theory. The name reflects the three basic needs postulated by the theory. They are:

1. *Existence Needs:* These are needs concerned with the physical existence of the organism. They include basics such as food, clothing, and shelter and the means provided by work organizations to attain these factors, for example, pay, fringe benefits, safe working conditions, and job security.

2. *Relatedness Needs:* These needs are those interpersonal needs that are satisfied through interactions with others both on and off the job.

3. *Growth Needs:* These are needs for personal development and improvement. They are met by developing whatever abilities and capabilities are important to the individual.

As can be seen from this description, for growth needs, Alderfer's definition is "as slippery as ever and . . . represents no major conceptual breakthrough" (Campbell & Pritchard 1976, p. 77). A direct comparison of Maslow's needs to Alderfer's is presented in Figure 13.2.

Although Alderfer's list of needs may be neither more complete nor more conceptually clear than Maslow's, the processes he proposed do offer some definite improvements. First of all, ERG theory places less emphasis on the hierarchical order. More than one need may operate at one time, and satisfaction of a need may or may not lead to a progression to the next higher need.

The second major change in orientation is that frustration of higher needs may lead to *regression,* with an increased concern for lower level needs rather than, as Maslow predicted, continued efforts to satisfy the frustrated need. The regression effect has some particularly interesting ramifications for work behavior. Alderfer (1969) suggested that if relatedness needs are frustrated and if individuals are not able to feel that they are able to make the close inter-

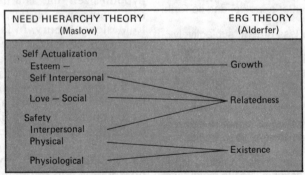

FIG. 13.2 A comparison of Maslow's needs to those of Alderfer

personal associations they need from their job, rather than trying to obtain these factors, they may become more concerned with meeting their existence needs. Therefore, they may show more concern for salary, working conditions, vacations, and other fringe benefits as a result of frustrated social needs. Alderfer wondered if perhaps the high concentration of existence issues in union contracts may be due, in part, to frustrated social needs which have led to the regression effect. His original data suggested such an effect but, to our knowledge, this interesting hypothesis has not been properly tested to date.

A final process difference in ERG theory is the statement that some needs, specifically relatedness and growth, may *increase* in strength when individuals have been presented with relatively high levels of conditions to meet the need. For example, having a very challenging job may increase rather than decrease the growth needs of an individual. This is directly opposite to what Maslow predicted; yet it is consistent with results of Hall and Nougaim (1968) and others, who found satisfaction of a need positively related to its importance.

All in all, Alderfer's ERG theory appears to be the most promising version of the need hierarchy theory available at this time (Miner & Dachler 1973). Research is needed to explore it in more detail, but unfortunately, little has been done with it recently (Mitchell 1979).

NEED FOR ACHIEVEMENT. In separate studies of one aspect of motivation, McClelland (1961) and Atkinson (1957) addressed achievement-oriented activity. McClelland formulated the concept of the need to achieve (n-Achievement, sometimes abbreviated *n-Ach*), postulating that this seemed to be a relatively stable personality trait rooted in experiences of middle childhood. McClelland's interest in this construct is related especially to entrepreneurial activities in developing countries (McClelland & Winter 1969). The pos-

sible implications of this construct cover a wide range of occupations in industry and business.

The theory is concerned with predicting the behavior of those who have either high or low needs for achievement. It has been postulated that those who have high *n-Ach* tend to "approach" those tasks for which there is a reasonable probability of success and to avoid those tasks which either are too easy (because they are not challenging) or are too difficult (because of fear of failure). Thus, the opportunity for success associated with a task can affect the tendency to "approach" it. These relationships have been worked into a theoretical formulation by Atkinson and Feather (1966). Their theory postulates that achievement-oriented activity is undertaken by an individual with the expectation that his or her performance will be evaluated in terms of some standard of excellence. Further, it is presumed that any situation which presents a challenge to achieve (by arousing an expectation that action will lead to success) also must pose the threat of failure (by arousing an expectation that action may lead to failure). Thus, achievement-oriented activity is influenced by the result of a conflict between two opposing tendencies—the tendency to achieve success (*n-Ach*) and the tendency to avoid failure (*n-AF*).

Achievement-oriented activities also are influenced by other extrinsic *motivational* tendencies. Atkinson and Feather proposed that the tendency to approach or continue a task depends both on the difficulty of the situation and on the individual's motivation. A generalized model of their predictions is presented in Figure 13.3. Those with high *n-Ach* are shown as having the strongest tendency to approach tasks of intermediate difficulty; those with low *n-Ach* tend also to approach tasks of intermediate difficulty, but the curve is much flatter. Those with high fear of failure (the *negative* aspect of *n-Ach*) tend to avoid such tasks, preferring either easier tasks, in

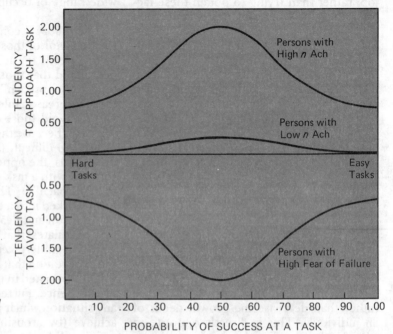

FIG. 13.3 The interaction of type of motive and probability of success in influencing the tendency to approach or to avoid, a task, as based on the theory of Atkinson & Feather, 1966. (*Adapted from McClelland & Winter, 1969, Fig. 1-1, p. 17.*)

which they are almost certain to succeed, or harder tasks (because failure at such tasks is clearly "not their fault").

Atkinson and Feather (1966) presented evidence from a number of studies that tends to support the basic premise of their theory. McClelland and Winter (1969) summarized the results of studies that reflect relationships between *n-Ach* and various indices of entrepreneurial success. For example, Koch (1965) reported correlations ranging from .27 to .63 between the *n-Ach* scores of executives at fifteen Finnish knitwear factories and several indices of business expansion (such as increase in number of workers and gross investments). Such data tend to suggest that the success of the companies is related to the high achievement motivation of their executives. McClelland and Winter also found that achievement motivation apparently can be learned and is not exclusively predeter-

mined by childhood experiences. Such learning has been brought about through special training programs and, in some instances, presumably as a result of being placed in a position in which achievement-motivated behavior is in some measure expected and rewarded.

The learned aspect of the need brings up the issue of whether staffing an organization with people who have high achievement needs leads to highly competitive and successful organizations as McClelland suggested, or whether the placement of people in highly competitive jobs or organizations leads to achievement-related behavior. Obviously both occur, but McClelland implied that it is more the former than the latter. On the other hand, the weight of the data seems to be in favor of the reverse (Klinger & McNelly 1969).

Regardless of the order of causation, achievement motivation does seem to be related to important work behaviors. For example, it has been found that high achievers stay on the job longer than low achievers do (Rhode, Sorensen, & Lawler 1976). Also when criticized, high achievers tend to respond better and to improve their performance more than low achievers do (Greenberg 1977). Finally, achievement-oriented managers tend to display the types of behaviors considered desirable for managers: being candid, open, and receptive to new ideas, offering subordinates more opportunity to participate in decisions, and having more respect for others (Hall 1976).

DISCUSSION OF NEED THEORIES. There are several other need-oriented theories that could be discussed at this point. We have chosen to conclude our treatment of the topic for three reasons. First, there is no end to the number of needs that can be conjured up to explain behavior. As a result, where one stops the search for new needs is arbitrary. We felt that those presented are sufficiently representative to cease our search at this point.

More importantly, two crucial controversies have developed which seriously question the utility of need-oriented approaches (Mitchell 1979). First, the existence of a relatively permanent need structure within an individual has been seriously questioned in the area of personality psychologist by Mischel (1973). Citing past research, he questioned the extent to which it has been demonstrated that people show relatively stable behavior patterns over a wide variety of settings. That is, if some person has a high need for achievement, then he or she should show achievement orientation in a wide variety of situations which require performance. Mischel's point is that individuals do not show the stability in behavior that we would hope to see, if needs are relatively permanent characteristics. As a result, emphasis in the field of personality, long dominated by an individual difference focus, is shifting to an interactionist position (Ekehammer 1974).

The latter strikes a balance between characteristics of 1) the individual, 2) the situation, and 3) the specific interaction between the particular individual and the setting in question.

The second and more telling criticism, from a pragmatic standpoint, is that personality traits such as needs explain far less of the variance in behavior than do the characteristics of the situation. This may be partially because measures of needs tend to be less reliable and valid than measures of situations. However, even with statistical corrections for unreliability, often situations are more important. Since our task is to understand and explain work behavior, our efforts may be better directed at assessing situations than trying to measure one or more needs. Although the needs have intuitive appeal, the empirical support for some relatively permanent set is weak and the measures are shaky. As a result, the recent trend has been away from an emphasis on needs and toward the cognitive processing of information available in situations.

Balance Theories

Throughout the late 1950s and most of the 1960s social psychological research and thought was dominated by what is known as balance or consistency theories of behavior. The best known of these is Festinger's (1957) theory of cognitive dissonance; yet there are several others. For those interested in a comprehensive collection of these theories see the book by Abelsen, Aronson, McGuire, Newcomb, Rosenberg, and Tannenbaum, entitled Theories of Cognitive Consistency (1968).

Although the theories vary somewhat, they all share the following tenets. First, individuals are said to possess some set of beliefs. Beliefs can be about almost anything—oneself, friends, the physical environment, political candidates, and the like. In addition, these beliefs (or cognitions) are not isolated. They often are associated with each other, and the association can vary from being very consistent to very inconsistent. An example of a consistent set of beliefs would be that you are a very ambitious and competent person and that you were promoted much more quickly than were others. Two inconsistent beliefs are the belief that you are ambitious and competent and the knowledge that you have just been fired because of laziness. According to balance theories, inconsistent beliefs are dissatisfying and create tension within the individual. The tension, in turn, leads to attempts by the individual to reduce the tension and to return to a consonant state. Therefore, from a motivational standpoint, the tension is the source of the motivational force that pushes the individual to action. What action is taken is another matter. We shall address this issue in detail later.

For behavior in organizations, two balance theories have been influential. These are the *Equity Theory* originally formulated by J. Stacy Adams (1965) and Abraham Korman's (1970, 1976) *Consistency Theory*. Each is discussed below.

EQUITY THEORY. Equity theory as constituted by J. Stacy Adams (Adams 1965; Adams & Jacobson 1964; Adams & Rosenbaum 1962) combines the notions of cognitive dissonance with those of social exchange to address the issue of the effects of money on behavior in work settings. It has two major process emphases. According to Adams (1965), people hold certain beliefs about the *outputs* they get from their jobs and the *inputs* they bring to bear in order to obtain certain outcomes. The outcomes of a job situation include actual pay, fringe benefits, status, intrinsic interest in the job, or other factors that the individuals perceive to have utility or value to them and that result from their job relationship. In turn, the inputs include any and all of the factors that individuals perceive as being their "investment" in the job or that they perceive as something of value that they bring or put into their job. The inputs

could include a person's general qualifications for a job, his or her skill, education level, effort, and other similar factors. The various specific outcomes and inputs as they are perceived by an individual are weighted according to his or her judgment of their relative importance to form a total outcome and a total input. These two totals combine to form an outcome/input ratio.

According to Adams' theory, a person is said to consciously or unconsciously compare his or her outcome/input ratio with that of other persons or other classes of persons whom he or she perceives as relevant to such comparative purposes. Equity is said to exist when an individual perceives his or her own outcome/input ratio to be equal to that of other persons; inequity exists if the person's ratio is *not* the same as that of other persons. All of these comparisons are subjective, not objective. Inequity can be in either direction and of varying magnitudes. Let us use Pritchard's (1969) notation to illustrate these ratios and to illustrate those combinations which, according to the theory, result in equity and inequity. Let H indicate that the individual perceives his or her input or outcome to be high and L mean that it is seen as low. The basic ratio is:

$$\text{Equity ratio} = \frac{\text{Outcome (H or L)}}{\text{Input (H or L)}}$$

In the following, the first ratio is that of the individual himself or herself, the second (following v for *versus*) is that of the persons used for comparison. The comparisons are thus described by Pritchard (1969).

The dissonance formulation enters into the comparison process to explain the degree of affect (or tension) associated with a comparison. If a comparison is equitable, no tension exists; the individual is satisfied and should have little desire to change the outcome/input ratio. If, on the other hand, the comparison of the two ratios results in

Equity	L/L v L/L	H/H v H/H	L/L v H/H
	H/H v L/L	L/H v L/H	H/L v H/L
Over-reward Inequity	L/L v L/H	H/L v L/L	H/L v L/H
	H/L v H/H	H/H v L/H	
Under-reward Inequity	L/L v H/L	L/H v L/L	L/H v H/L
	L/H v H/H	H/H v H/L	

a perception of inequality between them, inequity results. The inequity creates tension and, with it, a desire by the individual to reduce the tension by altering one or more elements of the ratios to bring the comparison back to equality.

There can be two types of inequity with regard to pay. *Underpayment* is the more common by far. Here the individual believes that, in comparison to others, he or she is not receiving a sufficient amount of pay (the outcome) for the input invested in the job. In other words, the amount of money is not high enough. Dissatisfaction results, and the individual is motivated by a desire to improve his or her outcome/input ratio and bring it in line with the ratio of the comparison other.

Overpayment is less common but more interesting for it predicts that the individual will be dissatisfied because he or she receives *too much* money. Therefore, there is tension, and the individual is motivated to reduce it. Adams (Adams & Rosenbaum 1962) did recognize that there was a much greater tolerance of overpayment inequity than of underpayment!

Equity theory generated considerable interest and research (see Campbell & Pritchard 1976; Goodman 1977; Goodman & Friedman 1971; Miner & Dachler 1973; and Pritchard 1969, for major reviews of equity theory.) Interest was piqued primarily because of the overpayment condition. The idea so opposed the accepted notion of economic people who seek to maximize rewards that many sought to research it carefully. Underpayment inequity, on the other hand, led to the same behavioral predictions as did already existing theories.

Adams's and Rosenbaum's study (1962) is a good example of the equity phenomenon. The authors assumed that feelings of equity or inequity could be manipulated in a controlled setting by telling employees that they were either qualified or not qualified for a job. Presumably, those told they were qualified for a job would use as their comparison group others like themselves. Those told they did not have the necessary qualifications would assume others did have them and, therefore, what they brought to the job in terms of qualifications was less than what others brought. The result would be that they would have lower inputs than those who were qualified.

Students who answered a newspaper advertisement conducted interviews for a company. Half were led to believe they were qualified for the job and half, unqualified. One of two bases for pay were established. Those employed in one condition were paid a fixed amount per hour (hourly pay). The others were paid a certain amount per interview that they completed (piece rate). The interview task itself allowed the individuals to vary performance on two dimensions, quantity and quality. Quantity was the number of interviews completed, and quality was the completeness and detail in each interview report turned in after a work session.

The two pay systems offered an excellent test of equity effects. Overpaid people who believed they were not qualified for the job and who were paid by the hour could increase their effort and do more interviews and/or increase the quality of their interviews. Both behaviors should increase their perceived inputs and produce a more equitable comparison. On the other hand, overpaid people who were paid on a piece-rate system could not increase quantity to bring their outcome/input ratio back into line because increasing the number of interviews also increased the amount of money received, both numerator and denominator changed leaving the ratio still inequitable.

For the most part, the data supported the theory. Overpaid employees conducted significantly more interviews than equitably paid ones only when paid by the hour. The quality of the interviews was higher for those overpaid as compared to those equitably paid when a piece-rate pay system was used. Quality was not as predicted under hourly pay, but this, more than likely, was because the nature of the job made it extremely difficult, if not impossible, to increase both quantity and quality.

The original research generated considerable interest and was supported in replications. However, it was pointed out that the results may have been caused by many factors other than equity. A number of studies eliminated most of the alternative explanations, save one. It was argued that underqualified people who had just been told they were unqualified might have worked in order to save face or prove themselves; the observed behaviors may not have had anything to do with a feeling of equity. In attempts to create overpayment inequity without threat or manipulation, the researchers found it extremely difficult to replicate the overpayment effect. Only one study was able to generate moderate support for it. In this case, employees were hired to do a catalogue-order task for one week (Pritchard, Dunnette, & Jorgenson

1972). Overpaid employees tended to process more catalogue orders than equitably paid employees who received the same amount of pay.

With respect to equity theory, two conclusions seem justified. First, people do make social comparisons, and these comparisons are important. To understand why people behave as they do we must get outside the individual and look at how that individual compares himself or herself to others. Second, with respect to pay, an equity notion often does seem to operate. However, individuals' tolerance of overpayment inequities are *much* greater than of underpayment inequities. With respect to overpayment, the effect on behavior does not seem to be very significant in most settings. There are many reasons for this. It may be that in most organizational settings the range in possible amounts of inequity is so controlled because of salary schedules that it seldom is great enough to have an effect. It also may be that the types of conditions necessary to evoke equity concerns often do not exist. Finally, it may be that the individuals reduce inequity in ways other than altering performance. The last two of these issues will be addressed after the other balance theory is presented.

CONSISTENCY THEORY. In 1970 Korman outlined a theory of work behavior and in 1976 updated and extended it. The theory has two foci. First is the balance notion. The theory states that individuals will engage in and find satisfying those behaviors which maximize their sense of cognitive balance or consistency. More specifically, they will be motivated to perform in a manner consistent with their self-image. The latter statement clarifies what individuals are to use as a standard to bring their behavior into balance—their self-image. The self-image standard, often described as one's self-esteem, is the second focus of the theory.

In order to understand the theory, we must understand self-esteem. Basically, it is a perception of self-worth. This usually means that the person has some idea of how well he or she will do in a performance setting. The individual, based upon several factors discussed below, in a sense anticipates how his or her own behavior will be evaluated in some setting. This evaluation represents self-esteem. One's self-esteem is estimated using two major inputs. First, there is *chronic* self-esteem. This is a general evaluation of oneself based upon past experience in a wide variety of settings over a lifetime. If the individual generally has been successful at most things undertaken in the past, it is reasonable to expect that the individual will have a relatively high chronic self-esteem. Second, there is *situational-specific* self-esteem which is based upon performance in the particular setting or settings very similar to the one in question. Although the two types often are highly consistent in their evaluations, they need not be. For example, a person who is generally successful in many areas but cannot swim may have a high chronic self-esteem but low specific self-esteem with regard to swimming.

The consistency notion predicts that high self-esteem people will choose to perform highly, will choose high prestige careers, and the like, in order to maintain a consistent and, therefore, satisfying state. As Korman's (1976) reevaluation of the theory implied, the data generally support this position; high self-esteem people tend to perform better than those with low self-esteem and to prefer higher status careers. Also, those with high self-esteem who are already launched on a career tend to rate their own careers as more important.

The most interesting yet the most controversial prediction occurs at the low end of the self-esteem continuum. Here it is predicted that low self-esteem individuals will prefer to behave in a manner consistent with their low self-image. For example, they will prefer low performance over high. One reason Korman gives for this is that

they (low self-esteem people) may fear that if they perform well at one time, others will expect high performance of them and they feel they will not be able to live up to the others' expectations.

Dipboye (1977) distinguished between the strong and the weak version of consistency theory. The weak version predicts high self-esteem people will perform better than low self-esteem ones will. The data generally support this. It is not necessary to assume that this results because those with low self-esteem *prefer* or *like* low performance. For example, low self-esteem people may be such because of poor performance in the past, perhaps because of low ability. If so, this does not mean they like to be low performers or prefer low to high performance. Dipboye (1977) reconsidered the literature that Korman (1970, 1976) took as support for his theory and concluded that only the weaker interpretation is consistently supported. Ilgen and Gunn (1976) reached a similar conclusion. Therefore, although the notion of a self-image as an important source of influence of work behavior is very compelling and contributes to the understanding of work behavior, the strength of the consistency interpretation, in the strictest sense, is still in doubt, with the scales tipped against it at the present time. There are, however, some very interesting notions of self-esteem and their effects on personal growth and other changes over time, raised by Korman in his 1976 revision and extension of the theory, which offer intriguing possibilities for future research.

DISCUSSION OF BALANCE THEORIES. The evidence from social psychological research as well as from the two theories discussed here does support the notion that human beings do strive for some kind of balance or consistency among beliefs. They also may display behaviors designed to make previously inconsistent conditions more consistent. The role of others in the comparison process is important particularly in organizational settings and is stressed in both equity and consistency theory. In Adams's equity theory others are central as the comparison object; in Korman's consistency theory, others are more peripheral.

Despite this, there are some major questions about balance theories, which greatly affect their use in understanding work behavior. In many cases, the questions place rather stringent limitations on the ability of the theories to explain work behavior. It is our conclusion, at this time, that because of several limitations, balance theories will play only a minor role in the understanding of work behavior in the near future. This is not to say that the concepts are not reasonable and do not influence behavior; they are and they do. But other motivational constructs seem to explain a greater proportion of the variance in work behavior over a wider variety of settings than do either equity or consistency constructs. A few of the issues are outlined below.

1. Do behaviors or cognitive distortions usually create balance? Exactly how balance will be restored has always been a problem. It may be through behaviors which change inputs and/or alter performance, but it also may be a simple cognitive distortion without action. For example, the overpaid person may reduce inequity by simply rationalizing that the other's inputs really were not that great. Or the low self-esteem person who performs well may devalue the high performance and conclude that he or she did not do that well. In either case there is no change in behavior. It would be good if more guidelines could be offered for whatever resolution is chosen.

2. What conditions evoke comparisons? Some settings evoke comparisons more than others do. Both Korman (1976) and Pritchard (1969) pointed this out. Yet, we need to know more about when people will or will not be responsive to comparisons.

3. How quickly does self-esteem change? Perhaps low self-esteem is easily raised—especially

situational self-esteem. If so, the problematic case of low self-esteem persons "desiring" low performance, if it occurs at all, may be very temporary and not very significant over the long range in suppressing the performance of people who perform well on occasion.

4. How are others chosen for comparison?

5. Can inputs and outcomes really be kept separate? For example, one person may consider a challenging job to be an outcome while another may see it as an imput requiring more time and effort from him or her.

Two-Factor Theory

Herzberg (Herzberg, Mausner, & Snyderman 1959) proposed a theory of job satisfaction that was adopted to a motivational theory by Herzberg in his 1966 book. Its motivational implications have received the most attention so we shall discuss them here. As we shall see, the theory has had considerable influence on job design. Let us summarize the basic study from which the theory arose and then turn to the contributions and controversies related to the theory.

The original study (Herzberg and others 1959) was an intensive analysis of the experiences and feelings of two hundred engineers and accountants in nine different companies. During structured interviews, employees were asked to describe a few previous job experiences in which they felt "exceptionally good" or "exceptionally bad" about their jobs. Some of the most significant results are shown in Figure 13.4. High and low job attitude events are the events which were described as leading to feeling good or feeling bad about their work, respectively.

The major inferences of these and other data from the study relate to the distinction between what are called *motivator* factors and *hygiene* factors. The events that are associated with high job attitudes generally

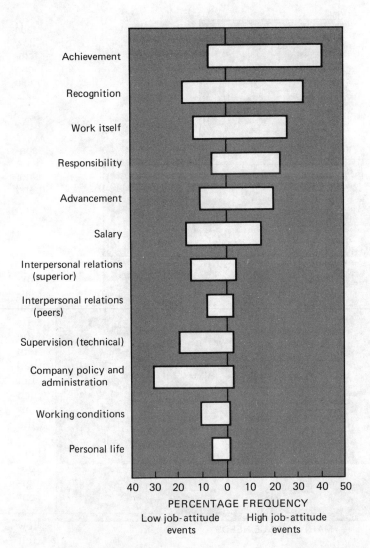

FIG. 13.4 Percentage of "high" and of "low" job-attitude sequences in which each of the categories appeared. (*Adapted from Herzberg and others 1959, p. 72.*)

are linked directly or indirectly with the *job activities;* these categories are achievement, recognition, the work itself, responsibility, and advancement. These factors are related to job content, which means that they are intrinsic to the job itself. Because positive expressions of these factors generally are associated with high job attitude situations, they have been called *motivators, satisfiers, intrinsics,* or *content* factors. The events predominately associated with low job attitude situations are those extrinsic to the

work itself and are associated with the job context rather than with job activities. These have been called *hygiene factors, dissatisfiers, extrinsics,* or *context* factors.

From a motivational standpoint, Herzberg (1966) distinguished between two sets of human needs. The second set stems from people's animal nature and their need to avoid pain; this set consists of the needs to which the hygiene factors are relevant. Because these factors serve only to reduce pain, they cannot contribute to positive sat-

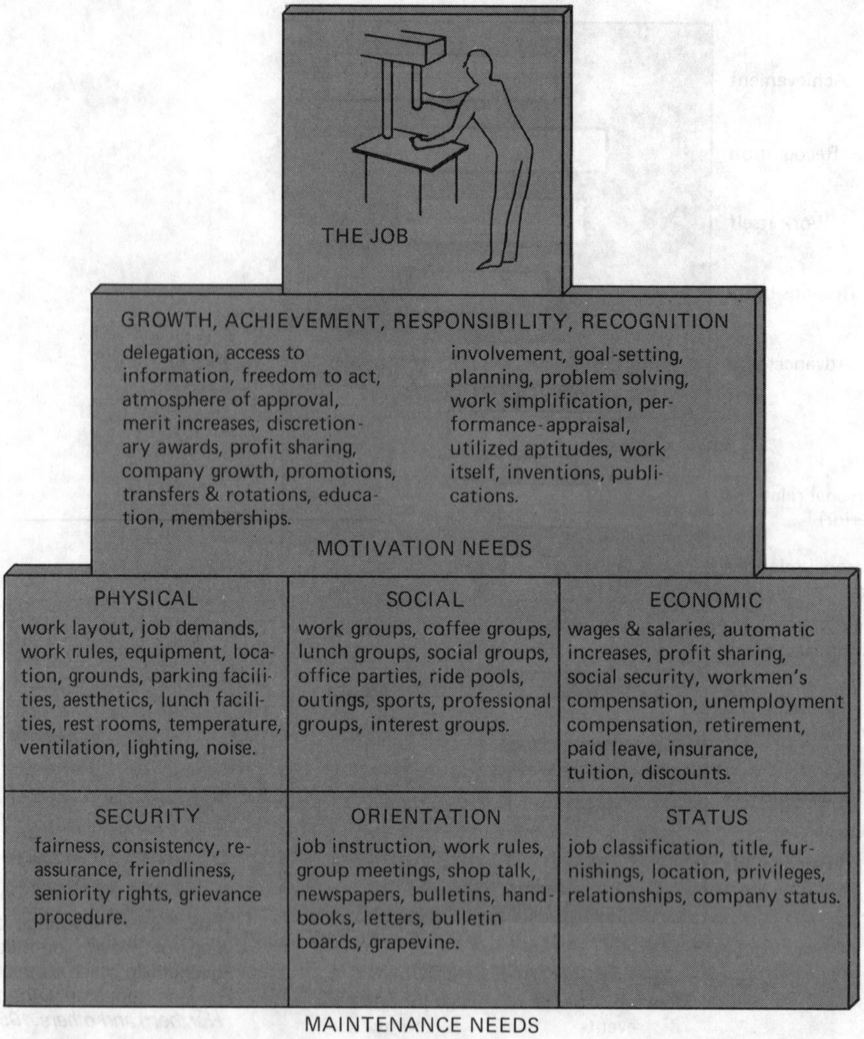

THE JOB

GROWTH, ACHIEVEMENT, RESPONSIBILITY, RECOGNITION

delegation, access to
information, freedom to act,
atmosphere of approval,
merit increases, discretion-
ary awards, profit sharing,
company growth, promotions,
transfers & rotations, education, memberships.

involvement, goal-setting,
planning, problem solving,
work simplification, per-
formance-appraisal,
utilized aptitudes, work
itself, inventions, publi-
cations.

MOTIVATION NEEDS

PHYSICAL	SOCIAL	ECONOMIC
work layout, job demands, work rules, equipment, loca- tion, grounds, parking facili- ties, aesthetics, lunch facili- ties, rest rooms, temperature, ventilation, lighting, noise.	work groups, coffee groups, lunch groups, social groups, office parties, ride pools, outings, sports, professional groups, interest groups.	wages & salaries, automatic increases, profit sharing, social security, workmen's compensation, unemployment compensation, retirement, paid leave, insurance, tuition, discounts.
SECURITY	ORIENTATION	STATUS
fairness, consistency, re- assurance, friendliness, seniority rights, grievance procedure.	job instruction, work rules, group meetings, shop talk, newspapers, bulletins, hand- books, letters, bulletin boards, grapevine.	job classification, title, fur- nishings, location, privileges, relationships, company status.

MAINTENANCE NEEDS

FIG. 13.5 Illustration of the motivation and maintenance needs of employees as formulated by one organization, (*Adapted from Myers 1964.*)

isfaction but only to the avoidance of dissatisfaction according to Herzberg (1966).
One set of needs within this framework relates to the human drive toward self-realization, that is, essentially the self-fulfillment need as postulated by Maslow.
According to the theory, self-realization
can be achieved only through the fulfillment of factors intrinsic to the work itself,
in other words, the motivator factors. Figure 13.5 depicts one individual's view of
the motivational and hygiene needs of
workers.

From its inception, the theory has been
surrounded by controversy. Throughout
the 1960s and into the early 1970s, there
were multiple attacks and sometimes even
a counterattack, at least at the early stages.

Most of the shots were directed at the theory as it relates to job satisfaction. We shall address these issues later, under job satisfaction. The distinction between satisfaction and motivation often is not clear, so there will be some overlap.

The major criticism of the theory was directed at the assumed independence of motivator and hygiene factors. According to the theory, the presence of hygiene factors led *only* to the absence of dissatisfaction rather than to satisfaction. Likewise only motivators could lead to satisfaction. Assuming a hedonic model of motivation in which individuals seek satisfaction, the implication of the theory was that true motivation could be obtained only through the provisions of motivators in work settings.

Neither the satisfaction nor the motivation conclusion following from it held up to empirical test. (For a review of the satisfaction data see King, 1970, and our discussion in the following chapter.) Suffice it to say that work behavior can be maintained for extended periods of time with hygiene factors as well as with motivators.

DISCUSSION OF TWO-FACTOR THEORY. Although virtually every major tenet of the theory is unsupported, it did have and still does have a major impact on organizational psychology. When it appeared, the time was right for some fresh ideas, and the two-factor theory stimulated work in two major and interrelated areas. First, for many, it served as a basis for the design of jobs in order to provide more interesting and absorbing work. Concern for expanding the content of jobs led to several early quasi-experiments in large corporations such as Texas Instruments (Myers 1964) and American Telephone and Telegraph (Ford 1969) and formed the basis for what has become known as *job enrichment* or *job enlargement.* The early work in job enrichment used as its theoretical springboard Herzberg's two-factor theory. Although it has been argued that there certainly are more sound bases for job enrichment than

the two-factor theory (Hulin 1971), it cannot be denied that the theory did provide the impetus for important research.

A second contribution of the theory was to create an interest in what has been termed intrinsic motivation. Those concerned with intrinsic motivation recognize that the features of a job itself can provide an environment in which the individual can gain satisfaction from doing the job, without receiving any external reinforcement such as money, praise, or recognition. It is said that individuals are motivated to do such jobs simply because of the characteristics intrinsic to the jobs themselves. Although the two-factor theory did not develop the notion of intrinsic motivation very well, the existence of the theory and the controversy surrounding it created interest in intrinsic motivation.

Behavior Modification

Behavior modification (also termed operant conditioning or Skinnerian approaches in recognition of the monumental impact of B. F. Skinner on this approach) focuses upon the individual's environment. The tenets of behavior modification are few and clear. Simply stated, it posits that behavior is controlled by its consequences. The consequences of interest are *reinforcers.* A reinforcer is anything that follows a behavior and influences the probability that that behavior will be repeated in the future. Reinforcers can be positive, such as a raise, or negative, such as a verbal reprimand. For example, the employee who receives a warm smile and a friendly "Good morning" after saying "Good morning" to another employee is reinforced for the behavior and is more likely to repeat the friendly greeting in the future. The reinforcer, in this case, is the friendly response from the person greeted.

The second major variable is the *contingency* or degree of association between the response and the receipt of the reinforcement. The connection between a response and the receipt of the reinforcement varies on two dimensions. One dimension is *time*. The length of the time interval between the response and the reinforcement can vary from almost immediately to weeks or months. With few exceptions, the shorter the interval the more likely it is that the reinforcer will influence behavior at least in rather simple tasks. The second dimension is the *ratio* of responses needed before the reinforcer is administered. For example, considering pay as a reinforcer, a salesperson may be paid by the company only after selling one hundred cases of a product. Such a schedule would require one hundred responses (assuming each sale is for only one case) before the reinforcer is administered. In this example, the time between sales of one hundred cases may vary considerably. Therefore, the reinforcement schedule cannot be described in units of time.

With (1) the assumption that the behavioral response of interest can be made by the individual, (2) the principle of contingency, and (3) the notion of reinforcement, behavior modification proposes that all behavior can be understood. Internal characteristics of the individual such as needs, values, and beliefs are considered totally unnecessary for understanding behavior, according to this view. In fact, taken literally, internal states are not only unnecessary, they have no causal effect on behavior (Locke 1977).

USE OF BEHAVIOR MODIFICATION IN ORGANIZATIONS. The popularity of behavior modification techniques in industry was given a real shot in the arm by the widely publicized work of Feeney at Emery Air Freight (*Business Week,* December 18, 1971; *Business Week,* December 2, 1972). Discouraged by the lack of success of sales training programs based on testimonials from "super-salespeople," Feeney instituted a new program which emphasized programmed learning procedures with fre-

quent feedback. Annual sales increases jumped from 11 percent to 27.8 percent and, rightly or wrongly, were credited largely to the application of behavior modification techniques. Dramatic changes in customer service and shipping container use also were associated with newly installed systems of feedback and positive reinforcement. Considerable improvements backed by a vocal and visable spokesman has led to heightened interest in behavior modifications in industry since the early 1970s. Although the effects observed at Emery Freight can be questioned because of the weaknesses in experimental design, the effects were so strong that it did appear that something was happening and that behavior modification techniques deserved a further look.

Research conducted under more controlled conditions has been limited in scope, but its conclusions are generally as predicted by behavior modification. Reinforcement increases behavior more than non reinforcement does (Jablonsky & De Vries 1972; Komaki, Waddell, & Pearce 1977), and schedules of reinforcement can influence behavior (Pritchard, Leonard, Von Bergen, & Kirk 1976).

DISCUSSION OF BEHAVIOR MODIFICATION. It is clear that reinforcers influence behavior and so do the contingencies between behavior and reinforcement. What is not clear is the extent to which behavior modification adds anything to what already exists (Locke 1977). Other theories stress rewards (reinforcements) and contingencies without denying or downplaying the importance of the organism's internal states as behavior modification does. Clearly, people think, hold values, and have different needs and feelings. Granted, these factors may have been overemphasized at times, but to deny their existence or relegate absolutely no importance to them flies in the face of what is known (Locke 1977). Therefore, according to Locke, the tenets of the behavior modification position appear to add little that is new and something that is false.

Another criticism of applied behavior modification has been from an ethical standpoint. It is argued that controlling the behavior of others denies them control over their own actions. Criticism has been particularly severe when the individuals involved are confined to total control institutions such as prisons and hospitals and, to some extent, military organizations. In work organizations, the criticism is less justified because of the freedom to leave the organization. Even denying this, the attack on ethical grounds is rather weak. A wide range of behaviors by organizational members could be seen as attempts to influence others. Behavior modification represents just one of many ways in which one might attempt to influence others. The fact that it works better than many other more subtle attempts does not mean that it is unethical.

A final criticism of behavior modification is made on an empirical basis. Mewhinney (1975) remarked that much of the research purporting to apply behavioral modification procedures in organizational contexts had not done so because of a misunderstanding of behavior modification. As a result, some of the purported support remains to be demonstrated. Along a different line, there is some evidence that implies that when money is used as a reinforcer and is highly contingent upon performance, the frequency of the behavior may decrease instead of increase as would be predicted by behavior modification (Deci 1972, 1975). According to Deci, linking external rewards too closely to behavior in jobs that originally are very interesting to the individuals can decrease motivation because these people no longer are doing the job out of interest; they are doing it for the pay. We shall address this issue to a greater extent later, but it suffices to say at this point that, to the extent that this does occur, schedules of reinforcement with pay predictions made from a behavior

modification position may need to be modified.

In spite of the criticism, behavior modification makes at least two contributions to the understanding of human behavior in organizations. First, although its focus on the individual's environment rather than on internal states of the organism may be overstated, it offers a healthy counterposition. Industrial/organizational psychologists and managers often tend to overemphasize individual characteristics to the exclusion of environmental ones. Behavior modification emphasizes the need to look outside the individual for explanation. Second, it offers a series of terms and technologies for dealing with individual behavior. Classes of reinforcers, schedules of reinforcement, and well researched, descriptive terminologies relating to changes in behavior are useful. Applications of the techniques have been particularly useful in programmed learning for training. The procedures and technology have had some real benefits.

Expectancy Theory

The historical roots of expectancy theory go back to Tolman (1932), Lewin (1938), and Peak (1955), but Vroom's version of the theory presented in 1964 in *Work and Motivation* introduced it to industrial/organizational psychology. Since that time, the theory has been modified and expanded by Campbell, Dunnette, Lawler, and Weick (1970), Dachler and Mobley (1973), Lawler (1971), and Porter and Lawler (1968), to name a few. Without a doubt, the theory has been extremely influential in the field over the last ten years.

The theory is a cognitive one based upon a rational-economic view of people. It is assumed that people are decision makers who choose among alternative courses of actions by selecting the action that, at that time, appears most advantageous. The choice need not actually be the most advantageous one, however. It is recognized that individuals are limited in their rationality and their ability to recognize alternatives. They are limited also by habits and other factors which may inhibit decision making. Nevertheless, the theory assumes that individuals cognitively consider alternatives and make choices within the limits of their capabilities. The theory is concerned with (1) the elements of cognitions that go into the decision and (2) the way in which individuals process these elements to reach a decision. The exact nature of each of these factors depends upon which particular version of the theory is considered. But they have much in common. We first shall address the elements of the theory and then the process by which they are said to combine.

VALENCE. An individual's "affective" orientation toward particular outcomes is called the valence of the outcome. Put another way, the valence is a person's desire for the outcome or the attractiveness of the outcome to him or her. When the outcome is actually received it may or may not be as satisfying as anticipated. From the standpoint of the valence, at any one time the degree to which the actual and anticipated satisfaction agree does not matter. For example, consider the valence of a promotion to a specific position. An individual may find the possibility of receiving the promotion and working in the position very attractive, yet if he or she is promoted to it, the position may not look nearly as attractive. At a time before the promotion, the individual's behavior would be based not on what actually will be but on what he or she thinks will be. The term valence refers to this anticipation of the attractiveness of the position.

Valence does not exist in the abstract. It is associated with some object or state called an outcome. The outcomes may be tangible objects such as money or clean work settings, intangible factors such as recognition or feelings of accomplishment,

or they may be levels of performance. Frequently, behaviors and performance levels are termed first-level outcomes and all others second-level ones (Campbell and others 1970).

Theoretically, the number of second-level outcomes is almost limitless. However, within work settings, individuals share a relatively small set that really influences their behavior. In fact, Parker and Dyer (1976) found that a set of only eight outcomes did a better job than a set of twenty-five for predicting reenlistment decisions of naval officers.

INSTRUMENTALITY. The outcomes we discussed before all are considered to have some degree of association with the individual's performance. Instrumentalities represent this association. Vroom defined instrumentalities as subjective correlations between two outcomes. Usually one outcome is performance. For performance, a positive subjective correlation means that the individual believes that as his or her performance increases so will the amount of the outcome in question. A negative subjective correlation is the reverse of this, and a zero subjective correlation means that the amount of the outcome received is unrelated to performance.

EXPECTANCY. The final element in the theory links an individual's act to an outcome. Again the outcome in this link usually is considered to be performance. Vroom considered this link to be a subjective probability held by the individual that an act (a behavior) would lead to the outcome. As is the case with all probabilities, the values ranged from 0.00 probability to +1.00. A subjective probability of zero means the person is absolutely certain that the act will *not* lead to the attainment of the outcome; +1.00 is certainty that the act *will* lead to the outcome, and other levels of certainty lie between. Figure 13.6 shows the three terms.

MOTIVATION MODEL. Motivation is seen as a function of the combination of the

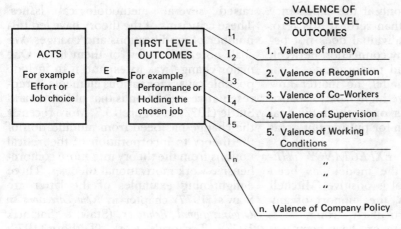

FIG. 13.6 Expectancy Theory Terms

VALENCE OF
SECOND LEVEL
OUTCOMES

1. Valence of money
2. Valence of Recognition
3. Valence of Co-Workers
4. Valence of Supervision
5. Valence of Working Conditions

"
"
"

n. Valence of Company Policy

E = Expectancy
= Subjective probability that an act will lead to an outcome
$0.00 \leq E \leq +1.00$

I_j = Instrumentality of the first level outcome for the attainment of second level outcome j
= Subjective correlation between attainment of the first level outcome and outcome j
$-1.00 \leq I_j \leq +1.00$

V_j = Valence of outcome j
= Subjective judgment about the attractiveness of outcome j

three elements. Mitchell (1974) presented what is perhaps the most generally accepted of the models for the combination of valence, instrumentality, and expectancy. Note that, as presented, it treats the act of committing effort to work. It would function the same way for committing an act of choosing a job or engaging in any other behavior or act. The model is as follows:

$$W = E \left(\sum_{j=1}^{n} I_{ij} V_j \right)$$

in which

W = effort

E = the expectancy that effort leads to performance

I_{ij} = the instrumentality of performance level i for the attainment of second level outcome j

V_j = the valence of second level outcome j

n = the number of second level outcomes

Look more closely at the model in the preceding paragraph. The summated product of the I_{ij}s multiplied by the V_js represents the valence of performance. If the sum of these products is very high, it means that the individual perceives a high degree of association between performance and the attainment of valued (that is, highly valent) outcomes. If the value is near zero, the individual does not perceive much of value to be associated with performance, and if it is negative, he or she believes that increases in performance lead to more and more undesirable conditions.

At first glance one might think that individuals would strive to attain high performance if they believed that performance led to valued outcomes. According to the model, this is true only if the expectancy term (E) is greater than zero. If it is zero, which means the individual does not believe that there is any connection between his or her effort and performance, then, according to the model, no matter how much more attractive higher performance levels are than lower ones, the individual should see no reason for putting out great effort.

DISCUSSION OF EXPECTANCY THEORY. Support for the model has been mixed but in general is positive (Mitchell 1974). Nevertheless, the support of any one study is not particularly strong.

Criticisms of the theory have been leveled at the assumptions of the theory and at methodological issues. It is most severely criticized for assuming that humans are too calculative in their decision processes (Behling & Starke 1973; Korman 1977). We already have mentioned that the theory recognized that people are limited in their capability of making decisions on such a complex basis as the theory requires. The critics say such recognition is not enough. People simply cannot and do not use such a complicated process. All types of simplification strategies are used to process information according to people's cognitive limits. The theory does not give sufficient weight to these limits.

A second assumption of the theory which has been attacked is its assumption that people are basically hedonic—that is they seek to attain more and more pleasant conditions and avoid painful ones. Both Locke (1976) and Korman (1976) took issue with this assumption on both logical and empirical grounds. Although we may believe that these criticisms are valid at the extremes—that is, hedonic principles are not sufficient for all people or, for that matter, for any one person all of the time—we still believe that for a vast majority of behaviors under consideration at work, the assumption is better than any others.

Empirical results using the theory have raised several methodological issues. These criticisms of the theory have led to a number of modifications and changes. We shall note only a few of them here. One major change was to expand it to include possible causes for various elements. A representative expansion is that of Lawler and Suttle (1973) in Figure 13.7. More recently the change has been from modification of the theory to incorporation of theoretical notions from the theory into more comprehensive work motivational theories. Three enlightening examples of the latter are Staw's (1977) chapter in *New Directions in Organizational Behavior* (Staw & Salancik 1977), Terborg's work (Terborg 1977; Terborg & Miller 1978), and Naylor, Pritchard, & Ilgen 1980. The latter two have concentrated on predicting specific behaviors rather than on effort and have incorporated such factors as goal setting, role expectations, and judgment into the whole process.

In summary, expectancy theory has generated high interest and considerable controversy. The result, in most cases, is modifications and extensions that have been incorporated into broader theories of work behavior. Clearly, the concepts introduced by the theory are useful in understanding behavior. People do seem to weigh alternatives and select courses of action based on some judgment of the value of alternatives. Yet, there is also more to behavior than can be predicted by such a rational decision model. Therefore, the theory has contributed, and we believe will continue to contribute, when viewed as only part of how behaviors at work are chosen.

Intrinsic Motivation

Intrinsic motivation is not a "full-blown" theory on the same level of development as are the other theories. Yet, it is a topic that recently has received considerable attention in organizational behavior and, given the trends in work values and thinking

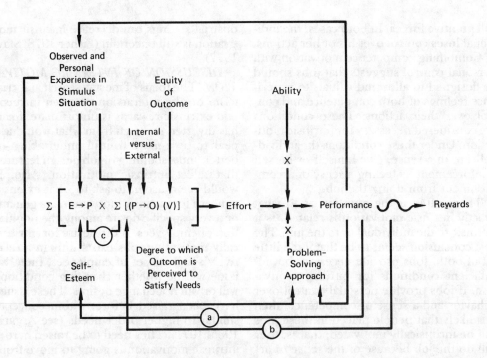

$$\Sigma \left[E \rightarrow P \ X \ \Sigma \left[(P \rightarrow O) \ (V) \right] \right]$$

FIG. 13.7 An Expanded Expectancy Theory of Work Performance

about the role of organizations in the work-life of their employees, it will continue to receive more attention over the next few years.

In many ways, intrinsic motivation is not much different from the concern for higher order needs in Maslow's hierarchy (1954) or for growth needs in Alderfer's ERG theory (1969, 1972). Given the current interest and the "catchy" nature of the topic to date, we have decided to risk redundancy and present it as separate.

Intrinsic motivation as currently conceived is championed by Deci (1975). His construal of intrinsic motivation stems from two sources. The first is White's (1959) notion of competence motivation. He assumed that in performance settings people are motivated to do well in order to experience a sense of competence. Experiencing a sense of competence is satisfying and, as a result, individuals will strive to attain it. The second concept of intrinsic

motivation, according to Deci, stems from De Charms' (1968) notion of personal causation. This assumes that people need to feel responsible for their own actions. Responsibility for action is the freedom to choose among alternative courses of action. This occurs in the absence of pressure, either positive or negative, to select one course of action over another. Negative pressure to display some behavior could be created by the threat of punishment for not doing it; for example, the threat of losing one's job for not coming to work prevents absenteeism. Positive coercion is less intuitively obvious. Here, the individual loses freedom to choose to reject a behavior because of the positive inducements. "Golden handcuffs" created by pension plans with lucrative profit-sharing contributions from the organizations, new cars provided at company expense, and other benefits will restrict an executive's freedom to leave an organization just as surely as will punitive forces. In both cases, the individual loses control over his or her actions.

Combining competence motivation with personal control suggests that jobs should be designed to allow individuals to experience feelings of both competence and control over their actions. These conditions are considered necessary for intrinsic motivation. Under these conditions the individual can, in a sense, give himself or herself reinforcement by feeling a sense of accomplishment from doing the job.

There often is the question as to what exactly intrinsic motivation is related. Is it intrinsic to the individual or to the job? The best conclusion seems to be that it is a little bit of both. Jobs provide necessary but insufficient conditions for intrinsic motivation. If jobs provide personal control over behavior and a sense of competence, then it is likely that people placed in these jobs will be intrinsically motivated; that is, they will do the job because of the sense of accomplishment and enjoyment they feel while doing it. On the other hand, since individuals in a sense must give to themselves the rewards of accomplishment and enjoyment of the task, the task conditions alone are not sufficient for intrinsic motivation.

Most of the research on intrinsic motivation has concentrated on the interaction between intrinsic and extrinsic rewards. Deci (1975) in a series of intriguing studies concluded that money, an extrinsic reward, under certain conditions could *decrease* intrinsic motivation because it would decrease personal control. This led to the intriguing conclusion that perhaps interesting jobs would be less stimulating and enjoyable if one were paid too much to do them. Although the validity of this conclusion is uncertain because of some questions about Deci's methodology (Calder & Staw 1975), there is some evidence that the phenomenon does occur when these problems are controlled (Pritchard, Campbell, & Campbell 1977). Nevertheless, whether pay practices normally experienced in in-

dustrial settings can decrease intrinsic motivation is still uncertain (Fisher 1978; Staw 1977).

DISCUSSION OF INTRINSIC MOTIVATION. The focus of most research and criticism on the interaction between intrinsic and extrinsic rewards is unfortunate, for it has diverted research from what would appear to be a more fruitful undertaking—a better understanding of job design features that affect intrinsic motivation. Also, it would seem useful to ask to what extent a concern for intrinsic motivation is a general or a very specific desire among the population of employees. If the desire for intrinsically motivating jobs exists only in a relatively small subset of employees, then the issue will be whether changing conditions will or will not change desires. These issues have been raised before, within concepts similar to higher order needs (see Argyris 1965, 1971). They need to be raised here if intrinsic motivation is going to move from a trendy term to a lasting concern.

Conclusion about Theories

After a review of the most prominent theories of work motivation, we have two general impressions. First, the theoretical positions are quite different. Diversity seems to be the rule with little convergence upon one global, all-encompassing theory. Second, none of the theories is without problems. All have been quite thoroughly researched but none has held up under all conditions.

Despite the diversity of the area in general and the moderate support for any theory in particular, there are several useful generalizations. First, the theories have identified three general processes which influence people's behavior. The first is some attempt by individuals to judge the value of courses of action and to select behaviors that seem to be most beneficial, based on their limited rationality. People think and in many instances try to do what they think is best for themselves. Expectancy theory addresses these issues most directly. Second, individuals compare themselves to others around them, and their behavior is based, in part, on the results of these comparisons. Finally, people may limit their desires, based on some judgment of what is a "proper" amount. More is not always better. Equity theory and consistency theory speak most directly to these last two processes. Although no single one of these processes is sufficient to explain all people's behavior or any one person's behavior all of the time, all three do seem to operate for various behaviors at any one time for all persons.

Besides the process of work motivation, we have learned something about its content. People do differ in what they desire or value from work. These differences occur among individuals and within individuals across time and across situations. During certain stages in a person's development, some factors are more important than others. For example, the social needs of adolescents may dominate all others, whereas older workers may be more concerned with security issues. Our review of motivation theories has identified several content issues. For example, achievement-oriented concerns and an individual's self-concept seem to be very important. We also have seen that environmental issues may influence content factors in the interaction between intrinsic and extrinsic outcomes. All of these issues illustrate that theories of motivation do offer some cues to issues to consider when attempting to understand behavior at work.

MOTIVATIONAL PRACTICES IN ORGANIZATIONS

The Place of Theory

The theories presented here are the major ones influencing industrial/organizational psychology today. Yet, as we have seen, all have their weaknesses as well as their strengths. There are no quick and easy answers to the question, "What motivates people to work?" Some may claim to have this answer but we, and now you, know better.

The absence of simple answers does not mean that the theories have nothing to offer. On the contrary, they have contributed the basis for the design and structure of work settings as well as guidelines for personnel practices. The link between theories and practice in motivation (Figure 13.8) can be construed as a three-step process. The theories are the most general level of analysis. They provide a basis for a second level which we have termed General Practices for Influencing Behavior in Organizations. Here, theoretical issues have identified important sets of variables related to work behavior. These variables have, for the most part, been researched extensively, and their impact on behavior has been relatively well understood. Finally, specific programs are developed and implemented within organizations which may incorporate one or more of the general procedures. An example of the latter is *Management by Objectives* (MBO). This rather popular management procedure incorporates goal setting into individual participation in decision making in order to establish individual work goals to which the employee feels reasonably committed.

A discussion of the specific programs is beyond the scope of this book; they are far too diverse and eclectic for our consideration. But, the general practices are very important to psychologists and others concerned with work behavior. Of the four general practices listed in Figure 13.8, we shall address three; the fourth will be treated in a later chapter.

Goal Setting

According to Locke (1968), the most direct antecedent to performance-related work behavior is the employee's performance goal or goals. These goals represent

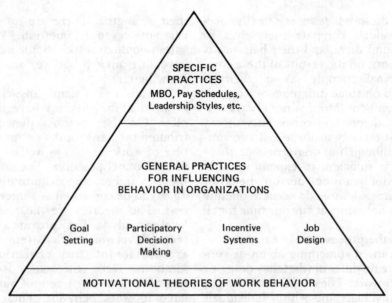

SPECIFIC
PRACTICES
MBO, Pay Schedules,
Leadership Styles, etc.

GENERAL PRACTICES
FOR INFLUENCING
BEHAVIOR IN ORGANIZATIONS

Goal   Participatory   Incentive   Job
Setting   Decision   Systems   Design
              Making

MOTIVATIONAL THEORIES OF WORK BEHAVIOR

FIG. 13.8 Levels of Consideration for Work Motivation

what the employee intends to do at some time in the future. For example, the salesperson's goals may be to sell x number of units in the next six months, establish y number of new accounts, and/or decrease the number of customer complaints by z amount. Note that all these goals are related to the performance of a salesperson and pertain to future rather than to past or present behavior. It should also be noted that, although the goals refer to the employee and will be discussed in terms of the employee, others may have similar goals for him or her. In the example above, the salesperson's supervisor may have similar types of goals for him or her.

Our knowledge of the effects of goals on past behavior is well grounded in theory and in empirical research. The seminal work of E. A. Locke (see Locke 1968, for a statement of his theory and his early research) provided a theoretical framework for understanding goal-setting effects, and research since that time has substantiated most of his propositions. Latham and Yukl (1975) reviewed goal-setting research done

only in the field and found over twenty-five studies, almost all of which substantiated Locke's earlier propositions.

FUNCTIONS OF GOALS. Goals have two major functions; they provide a basis for motivation, and they guide behaviors. Motivationally, a goal offers guidelines for deciding how much effort to put into the work. If the individual receives feedback about how he or she is doing with regard to a goal, this provides information on whether the individual should work harder, continue at the same pace, or relax a bit. It also might persuade the individual to reject the goal by deciding it is just too difficult or easy and therefore not worth the effort. Either way, the effect is motivational.

Goals guide behavior in conjunction with feedback. By guiding the behavior we mean that they provide the individual with cues about the specific behaviors that need to be accomplished. For example, consider a goal of writing ten letters by tomorrow afternoon. This goal tells the individual that sitting at a desk is more appropriate behavior than talking on the telephone if

286

the goal is to be met. Both behaviors may be relevant to the job, but the goal offers a cue to which behaviors are more appropriate if the goal is to be met.

NECESSARY CONDITIONS FOR GOALS. Goals are, to the individual, his or her intended behaviors. Yet, when it comes to goals which are set or held by others for a specific individual, we all know from experience that the other's goal for the individual may not be the behavior toward which the individual intends to work. Therefore, we must ask what the most basic conditions are that a goal must meet. We suggest that there are two conditions. First, the individual must be aware of the goal and know what it is that is supposed to be accomplished. The combination of awareness and knowledge of action can be considered the goal's *information value.* Second, the individual must *accept* the goal for himself or herself. Acceptance of it implies that the individual must intend to use the behavior(s) necessary to accomplish the goal. Most of our discussion of goals is on their effects on awareness or on acceptance.

DIMENSIONS OF GOALS. Goals can vary along several dimensions, but two of these stand out as by far the most significant. These are *specificity* and *difficulty.* The effects of these are quite clear; in general, work performance increases as goal specificity increases and as goal difficulty increases (Steers & Porter 1974; Latham & Yukl 1975).

The specificity of a goal provides information for the individual. The more specific the goal, the more the individual knows what is required of him or her. Therefore, the goal serves to route behavior in a specific direction (Terborg 1977). In an informational sense, specific goals may also improve the value of performance feedback (Ilgen, Fisher, & Taylor 1979). Often feedback from others is quite general, such as "You're doing a good job." Such feedback is of little value if the individual is not sure what is to be done. If the communicator of the general feedback has expressed specific goals, then the general feedback takes on specific meaning in terms of those goals.

There is no reason to expect that, under most conditions, the degree of acceptance of the goal is affected by its specificity. People should be just as likely to be committed to specific goals as to general ones. There is indirect evidence for this in a study of the production of logging crews (Ronan, Latham, & Kinne 1973). Setting specific goals for the crews influenced the behavior only when the supervisors stayed around to encourage their crews to meet the goals. In this setting the specificity of the goal was not sufficient to influence performance. Only when acceptance or commitment was enforced by the supervisor did behavior improve with specific goals.

One recent study of truck drivers who drove loads of logs to lumber mills demonstrated the complexity of trying to understand how specific goals work. Latham and Baldes (1975) created two groups by randomly selecting truck drivers for one of two treatments. One group was told to do its best in loading its trucks. Another group was told to set a goal of trying to load its trucks up to 94 percent of the legal limit. (The closer to legal limit, the fewer trips needed, and the more economical per unit of logs). Figure 13.9 shows that specific goals were superior, but why? The most likely reason is informational—when they received feedback about how close they came to the goal they learned how to load their trucks to their limits (Terborg 1977). Commitment also may have been responsible. The authors reported that it became a "game" among the truckers to see who could do better. Therefore, the competition, not the specificity per se, may have fostered improved performance. Regardless of what was the actual cause, the data illustrate that specificity of goals can improve performance but that the nature of exactly how is often difficult to isolate.

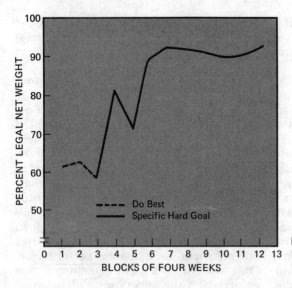

FIG. 13.9 Percent legal net weight of 36 logging trucks across blocks as a function of a specific hard goal. (Latham & Baldes 1975, p. 122.)

Turning to goal difficulty, the effect seems to be through commitment more than through information increase. There is no reason to believe that the commitment to the easier goal of typing twenty words per minute would be any stronger than typing sixty words per minute. However, if rewards (such as pay, promotions, or supervisory approval) were associated with reaching the goal, we would expect greater commitment to the goal of sixty versus twenty words per minute.

The commitment effect is quite clear when the goal becomes too difficult, that is, when it becomes perceived as impossible. At that point, performance drops off to a point lower than with no goal at all. Stedry and Kay (1966) had foreman set goals that were easy, difficult, or impossible with respect to production and to rework orders. Their data showed that performance under the impossible condition was significantly lower than under the other two conditions.

GROUP VERSUS INDIVIDUAL GOALS.
Goals can be set for a given individual or for a whole group. Since most people in

organizations function in groups, an interesting question is whether goals set for individuals or for groups are more effective. The effects depend on the information value of the goal and on commitment to the goal. For the first, group goals often dilute the information value of the goal. If the goal is stated in terms of group performance and if feedback is also in terms of the group, frequently the individual is not sure of his or her contribution to the group product and, therefore, is unsure of what the goal means to him or her. Similarly, commitment may be less to group goals, for there is some evidence that people tend to blame others rather than themselves for a group's failure to meet a goal and thus do not take responsibility for it (Johnston 1967; Schlenker, Soraci, & McCarthy 1976). On the other hand, commitment may be higher if there is strong group pressure for goal compliance.

The alternative possibilities given above suggest that to ask whether group or individual goals are better is to ask the wrong question. The data simply do not allow for a simple answer. It seems to us, if one were interested in choosing between setting group or individual goals, one would need to ask two questions. What is the effect of each type on the information about performance available to the individual under each condition? And, what effect will each have on the individual's commitment to the goal? The answers will vary according to conditions, but they should be more constructive than remaining at the more global level of individuals versus groups.

Participation in Decision Making (PDM)

Participation in decision making is a highly complex and controversial topic because it is the *cause célèbre* of many, for reasons varying from moral, to political, to pragmatic. The humanist argues that people must be allowed to decide about factors related to work because, to do anything less, is inhuman. Communist and socialist political philosophies see it as a way to avoid domination by a capitalist minority. Pragmatists support PDM for they believe that employees who participate in making decisions will be more committed to their decisions and will work harder to accomplish them. The result is a widely diverse set of conditions, all of which are labeled PDM, but many of which have little in common. Therefore, we first shall consider what is meant by PDM and then turn to a description of some of its effects as well as an evaluation of it.

DESCRIPTION OF PDM. At the individual level, PDM means that the person participates in the decisions that need to be made about the work he or she does. This seems quite simple, but it is not, because the nature of the participation can vary along several dimensions. Locke and Schweiger (1978) pointed out that PDM can vary in *degree, content,* and *scope.* Degree refers to a continuum ranging from no participation to full participation. In the middle ranges PDM is more on the basis of consultation with those who have the power to either accept or reject the participant's inputs. The content of the issues on which one participates can vary in several respects, but Locke and Schweiger concluded that there are four categories usually encountered in organizations. These are: I. routine, personnel functions (training, payment, etc.), II. work itself (task assignments, work methods, speed of work, etc.), III. working conditions (number and nature of rest pauses, lighting, placement of equipment, etc.), and IV. company policy (layoffs, profit sharing, general wage level, etc.).

The scope of PDM is the total system in which it occurs and the involvement of individuals in the issues faced by the system. High scope PDM is exemplified by the workers' councils in Yugoslavia where employees at the rank-and-file level of production in the company are elected and serve on a council responsible for all the major management decisions involving that company. Low scope PDM might limit the decisions to issues of the specific job and work area of the individuals.

EFFECTS OF PDM. Possible psychological effects of PDM are best illustrated by Figure 13.10 from Locke and Schweiger (1979). Note that the initial impact of PDM on the individual can be classified into three major areas—values, cognitions, and motivation. At the motivational level, it is hypothesized that resistance to change is decreased if individuals participate in decisions regarding change and that individuals accept and are more committed to decisions in which they have participated. From the standpoint of the motivational theories discussed earlier in this chapter, PDM borrows from many but tends to have its roots more in the humanistic theories of Maslow and Alderfer. Cognitively, it is assumed that better ideas are generated by those who are closest to the task to be done.

Let us consider two field experiments in which the motivational effects of PDM were

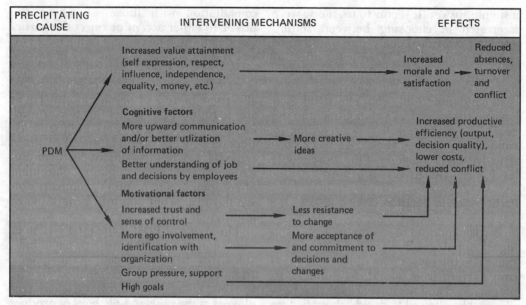

FIG. 13.10 Proposed Effects and Mechanisms of PDM. (From Locke & Schweiger 1978.)

clearly demonstrated. A study by Coch and French (1948) found large decreases in resistance to change among production workers who were allowed to participate in decisions about production changeovers. Before Coch's and French's intervention, there was high turnover and severe production losses whenever the company changed procedures for jobs at a pajama manufacturing plant. Four groups were created by the experimenters. The first continued to use the old method of having managers inform the workers of needed changes and then implement them. The second group elected a representative to be on the management team that laid out the changeover procedures. The other two groups had total participation among all members in designing the change. Results of the research impressively supported PDM. Production and other indicants of performance were far superior in the PDM groups and were highest under the total participation conditions.

In the Coch and French study the PDM effects could have been from either motivational, cognitive, or value factors and, most likely, were a combination of all three. For example, PDM groups may have discovered better ways to make the change, and the improved methods, not motivation, may have influenced production.

Lawler and Hackman (1969) eliminated the latter effect and still found improvements in attendance under PDM. A certain company had many small teams assigned to offices and businesses throughout the city to provide janitorial services. Absenteeism was high among these teams, so several were allowed to devise ways to handle absenteeism in their team. The solution the team reached was then implemented for that team *and* for another team which did not participate in designing their own procedure. In this way, the change was controlled. Any difference between the teams should have been due primarily to participation. The results showed much stronger effects on attendance in the participation groups than in the other groups.

An interesting follow-up to the above study was reported by Scheflen, Lawler, and Hackman (1971). After implementing the changes for a short time, the company decided to withdraw them. The follow-up showed that once the old methods were restored, absenteeism in the participation groups dropped to a level well below the prechange conditions, whereas the control group's attendance varied little before, during, or after the changes. These two sets of data clearly indicated that PDM can affect behavior, but that its presence or absence cannot be taken lightly.

EVALUATION OF PDM's EFFECTIVENESS. The euphoric reaction to PDM following the Coch and French experiment should have been short lived. Yet, faith more than fact led to its continued advocacy from diverse points to view. From very comprehensive reviews of PDM first by Lowin (1968) and more recently by Dachler and Wilpert (1978) and by Locke and Schweiger (1979), there have been two general conclusions:

1. PDM usually has either a positive effect or no effect on the attitudes (satisfaction) of those who have the degree of their decision-making possibilities increased. Rarely does it decrease satisfaction.[2]

2. Positive behaviors result from PDM at about the same frequency as do negative ones, and both of these occur less frequently than no observable effect of PDM on behavior.[2]

There are many explanations for the mixed support. Yet, all explanations lead to the conclusion that effective PDM depends upon many complex factors in the particular *setting,* the *nature of the decision,* and the *individuals* in the setting. These factors are too complex and numerous for us to outline here. A few examples should illustrate some of these issues. With regard to the participants, they must possess knowledge of the topics or issues in which they are to participate. This seems obvious but is often

ignored. Second the decisions to be made must be ones that do not have to be made quickly. We would not want a truckload of fire fighters to sit down and discuss the advantages and disadvantages of entering the front door versus a second-story window of a burning building upon arriving at the fire. Suffice it to say, PDM is no panacea for all ills facing organizational members. Yet, there are conditions in which it can be highly effective. Some of these conditions are addressed in the reviews we have cited as well as in a recent approach to leadership by Vroom and Yetton (1973) developed according to the description of conditions to which various forms of PDM should be applied.

Incentive Systems

Work for organizations is an exchange between the employee and the employer. The employee agrees to exchange time and effort to produce goods or services for the employer. In exchange for the employee's inputs, the employer agrees to exchange various items or outcomes (either tangible or intangible) for his or her contributions. A subset of the total set of items in this exchange and the rules of the exchange form the incentive system of the organization.

Incentives are those items given to individuals that are designed to influence future behavior. The future orientation is important, for it means that an incentive serves as an anticipated reward for behavior to be accomplished. The individual may have received the reward in the past for some behavior, but it serves as an incentive for continued behavior only to the extent that he or she anticipates that continuing the behavior will lead to more of the reward.

Incentive systems are concerned with (1) identifying the items to be included as incentives and (2) establishing rules and procedures for disbursing the items to mem-

---

[2]Our conclusions are based primarily on the summary tables in Locke and Schweiger (1979).

bers of the organization. The motivational issues associated with these factors are most closely associated with the tenets of the expectancy theory, reinforcement approaches, and equity theory discussed earlier.

IMPORTANCE OF REWARDS. Identifying items valued by employees is extremely important to establishing effective incentive systems, but there has been surprisingly little good research on this, perhaps because most managers, union leaders, and industrial psychologists think they already know what people want. It stands to reason that people differ in what they want from work, and effective incentive systems should consider these differences.

The value of pay is an interesting case, illustrating the lack of understanding that can and does result from misunderstanding employees' views. For the most part, managers and union leaders view pay as the single most important reward overshadowing all others. Psychologists, on the other hand, have conducted numerous surveys and find pay ranked from third to sixth in importance behind such items as a steady job and being able to do the type of work wanted.

There is sufficient reason to believe none of these estimates is very accurate for most groups. Pay is not the most important characteristic of work for many people, but it depends on how pay is treated. If by pay we mean pay or no pay at all, pay probably would be *the* most important. It is the incremental change or difference in pay level on which people differ in their evaluation and on which more pay is often not the most important issue.

Just as pay is probably not the most important item to employees, as managers and union leaders assume it is, it probably is not as low in importance as psychologists' ratings seem to indicate. Values frequently expressed which could be summarized by "money isn't everything" may make individuals who rate the importance

of pay either reluctant to state its real importance when they feel it is very high or unwilling to admit to themselves that they value it so highly.

The research by Nealey (1964) was an exception to not fully studying the value of rewards to a group to which a set of rewards is to be applied. He assessed the preferences of a large sample of electrical trade union members for six benefit options. All options were approximately equal in cost to the employer. The six options were: (1) an additional $50.00 per month contribution to the retirement fund by the employer, (2) a 6 percent raise, (3) reduction in the work week from forty to thirty-seven and a half hours with no drop in pay, (4) full-hospitalization insurance for the employee and his or her family, (5) a union shop, and (6) an extra three weeks of paid vacation. Figure 13.11 shows the preferences of the employees. Figure 13.12 shows that employees of different ages had very different preferences. The differences across age groups clearly indicate that the application of one set of incentives and one incentive system to all employees in a given job class may not be best from a motivational standpoint.

Jurgensen (1978) capitalized on his position in a large metropolitan utility to gather data on over 57,000 job applicants from 1945 to 1975 to assess the preferences of men and women of various ages for different work-related factors. The data in Table 13.1 are preferences by age and sex. Not presented here were ranks over time. For the most part, preferences have stayed relatively stable over the last thirty years, but differences between age groups and sex are evident in his data (See Table 13.1).

REWARD CONTINGENCIES. To influence behavior, the rewards must be associated with the behavior of interest (Lawler 1971). Both expectancy theory and reinforcement approaches emphasize the connection between behavior and reward. The degree of association can vary from none at

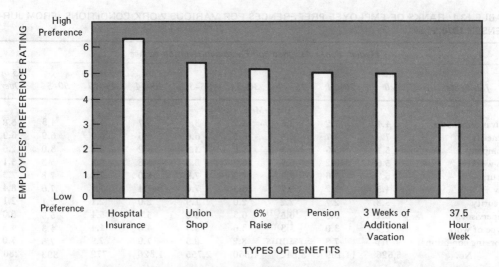

FIG. 13.11 Relative Preference for Benefits Equated to Their Cost to the Organization. (Adapted from S. M. Nealey 1964.)

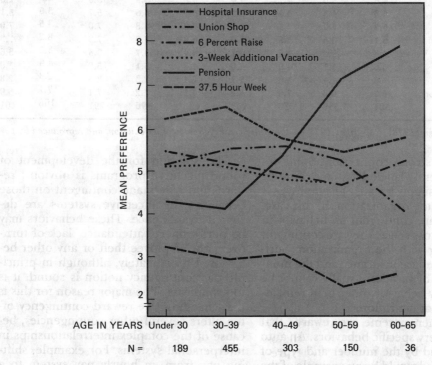

FIG. 13.12 Benefit preference by age. (From S. M. Nealey. Determining worker preference among employee benefit programs. *Journal of Applied Psychology,* 1964, 48(1), 7–12.)

TABLE 13.1 RANKS OF EMPLOYEE PREFERENCES FOR VARIOUS WORK CONDITIONS (FROM JURGENSEN 1978, P. 271

Job Factor	Median Ranks Assigned Job Factors in Relation to Age								
	Under 20	20–24	25–29	30–34	35–39	40–44	45–49	50–54	55 or Over
Men									
Advancement	4.4	3.2	3.0	3.2	3.5	3.7	4.1	4.3	5.8
Benefits	7.9	6.7	6.5	6.5	6.6	6.6	6.9	6.9	6.9
Company	5.7	5.0	4.3	3.9	3.3	3.2	2.8	3.0	2.6
Co-workers	5.6	6.2	6.3	6.2	5.8	5.8	5.8	5.3	5.1
Hours	6.2	7.6	7.9	7.9	7.9	8.0	7.8	7.8	7.3
Pay	4.5	5.2	5.7	6.3	7.0	7.4	7.4	7.6	8.4
Security	3.8	2.7	2.2	2.0	1.9	2.0	2.1	2.1	2.1
Supervisor	6.1	6.5	6.5	6.3	6.0	5.8	5.4	5.5	5.0
Type of work	2.7	3.0	3.3	3.6	3.9	4.0	4.4	4.3	4.5
Working conditions	7.1	7.8	8.2	8.2	8.3	7.9	7.9	7.5	7.0
No.	6,626	14,109	8,842	4,560	2,755	1,326	779	393	280
Women									
Advancement	5.4	5.0	5.1	4.7	5.1	5.6	5.4	6.1	6.7
Benefits	8.4	8.0	7.7	7.5	7.6	7.1	7.0	7.0	7.8
Company	4.6	5.0	4.7	4.4	3.8	3.9	3.0	2.3	2.8
Co-workers	5.3	4.8	5.1	5.7	5.5	5.6	5.7	5.5	5.1
Hours	6.5	7.2	7.1	7.3	7.3	6.8	7.0	7.5	7.0
Pay	6.1	5.5	5.8	6.0	6.7	7.0	7.3	8.2	7.3
Security	4.8	5.2	4.9	4.1	3.4	3.7	3.5	3.5	3.6
Supervisor	5.6	5.1	4.9	5.0	4.9	5.1	5.2	4.9	5.0
Type of work	1.5	1.4	1.6	2.1	2.4	2.3	2.5	2.3	2.8
Working conditions	5.9	6.8	7.0	7.2	7.3	7.2	7.1	7.1	6.9
No.	7,501	5,535	1,633	709	495	396	291	168	101

Source: Jurgensen (1978). Copyright 1978 by the American Psychological Association, and reproduced by permission.

all to a very strong connection. Some rewards, frequently labeled systems rewards, are available simply because an employee is a member of the organization. In this case, the rewards are contingent on behavior in only a very gross sense; they are contingent on remaining with the organization. Such rewards as medical insurance and the number of weeks of vacation usually cannot be influenced by behavior other than remaining with the organization.

At the other extreme are rewards that depend on very specific behaviors. An auto mechanic paid by the number and type of jobs completed would be an example of the latter.

The solution for the development of sound incentive programs is obvious; rewards must be made contingent on those behaviors the incentive systems are designed to influence. These behaviors may be performance, attendance, lack of turnover, low employee theft or any other behavior. Unfortunately, although in principle the contingency notion is sound, it is too simplistic. The major reason for this is that changing one reward contingency often alters several other contingencies, because of the complex interrelationships in interpersonal systems. For example, shifting pay from an hourly pay system to a piece-rate system theoretically should lead pay to be more closely tied to behavior and should increase the influence of pay on performance. The individual piece-rate system, however, may increase tension among group members if it creates large differences in performance among group members and makes these differences obvious. For example, older workers with more seniority may not be able to keep up with younger, less senior workers. The net result could be a decrease in performance across the group with the piece rate as compared to the hourly condition because of the tension it creates. Obviously, in this case, a simple change in pay procedures would not lead to the predicted results, because of the complexities of the pay and social system. Regardless of the reward under consideration, it is rare when a change in the contingency between that reward and a behavior does not influence other reward-behavior contingencies in the work setting. Often the effects on other contingencies are unexpected and work against the desired effects of the change in the reward under investigation.

EXTRINSIC REWARDS AND INTRINSIC MOTIVATION. The contingency between pay and task performance recently has come under particular scrutiny because of its alleged effect on intrinsic motivation. Recall that intrinsic motivation is the extent to which the individual works on the job because of the intrinsic enjoyment he or she gets from doing it. Deci (1972, 1975) has argued that pay that is closely associated with (contingent on) performance *decreases* intrinsic motivation because the person is controlled by the pay and no longer can choose to do or not to do the task. The controlling nature of pay decreases the intrinsic motivation.

The ramifications of this effect for incentive programs are obvious. The ideas of intrinsic motivation question the practices originally thought to be useful. Absorbing and interesting jobs usually carry more re-

sponsibility *and pay more.* These findings imply that perhaps pay for these types of jobs should not be related very closely to performance.

Deci's findings have not gone unquestioned. They have been criticized methodologically (Calder & Staw 1975) as well as for their limited ability to generalize the laboratory research from which most of these conclusions were drawn (Fisher 1978; Staw 1977). It looks as if this effect is not very likely in work settings in which pay is an integral part of the employment contract (Fisher 1978). Nevertheless, the jury is still out on this issue; further work is needed. Until we know more, the effects of pay on intrinsic motivation should at least be considered when incentive systems are designed.

DISCUSSION

Our treatment of work motivation has been long and extensive. It should be obvious to you that the topic of work motivation is complex and diverse. There are no panaceas. None of the theories incorporates all we need to know about work behavior. Each offers a perspective which can be useful for understanding why and how people work.

The general practices which were discussed (goal setting, participatory decision making, and incentive systems) all had as their basis one or more of the theoretical frameworks discussed in the earlier part of the chapter. These general practices are then incorporated into specific organizational policies and practices. We did not discuss this final step because of the diversity of ways to accomplish this. One cannot prescribe, a priori, a particular system without a thorough understanding of the particular organization and its functioning. We have tried to show that psychologists and others concerned about the behavior of individuals in organizations have considered the motivational bases for work behavior and have developed some general strategies with reference to a particular theory or theories.

REFERENCES

ABELSON, R. P., ARONSON, E., McGUIRE, W. J., NEWCOMB, T. M., ROSENBERG, M. J., & TANNENBAUM, P. H. (Eds.). *Theories of cognitive consistency: A source book.* Chicago: Rand McNally, 1968.

ADAMS, J. S. Inequality in social exchange. In L. Berkowitz (Ed.), *Advances in experimental psychology* (Vol. 2). New York: Academic Press, 1965.

ADAMS, J. S., & JACOBSON, P. R. Effects of wage inequities on work quality. *Journal of Abnormal and Social Psychology,* 1964, *69,* 19–25.

ADAMS, J. S., & ROSENBAUM, W. E. The relationship of worker productivity to cognitive dissonance about inequities. *Journal of Applied Psychology,* 1962, *46,* 161–164.

ALDERFER, C. P. Effects of task factors on job attitudes and job behaviors. II. Job enlargement and the organizational context. *Personnel Psychology,* 1969, *22,* 418–426.

ALDERFER, C. P. *Existence, relatedness, and growth: Human needs in organizational settings.* New York: Free Press, 1972.

ARGYRIS, C. *Organization and innovation.* Homewood, Ill.: Irwin-Dorsey, 1965.

ARGYRIS, C. *Management and Organizational Development: The Path from Xa to Yb.* New York: McGraw-Hill, 1971.

ATKINSON, J. W. Motivational determinants of risk-taking behavior. *Psychological Review,* 1957, *64,* 359–372.

ATKINSON, J. W., & FEATHER, N. T. *A theory of achievement motivation.* New York: Wiley, 1966.

BEHLING, O., & STARKE, F. A. *Some limits on expectancy theories of work effort.* Proceedings of the Midwest Meeting of the American Institute of Decision Sciences, 1973.

CALDER, B. J., & STAW, B. M. Self-perception of intrinsic and extrinsic motivation. *Journal of Personality and Social Psychology,* 1975, *31,* 599–605.

CAMPBELL, J. P., DUNNETTE, M. D., LAWLER, E. E., & WEICK, K. E., JR. *Managerial behavior, performance and effectiveness.* New York: McGraw-Hill, 1970.

CAMPBELL, J. P., & PRITCHARD, R. D. Motivation theory in individual and organizational psychology. In M. D. Dunnette (Ed.), *Handbook of industrial and organizational psychology.* Chicago: Rand McNally, 1976.

COCH, L., & FRENCH, J. R. P. Overcoming resistance to change. *Human Relations,* 1948, *1,* 512–532.

DACHLER, H. P., & MOBLEY, W. H. Construct validation of an instrumentality-expectancy-task-goal model of work motivation: Some theoretical boundary conditions. *Journal of Applied Psychology,* 1973, *58,* 397–418.

DACHLER, H. P., & WILPERT, B. Conceptual dimensions and boundaries of participation in organizations: A critical evaluation. *Administrative Science Quarterly,* 1978, *23,* 1–39.

DeCHARMS, R. *Personal causation: The internal affective determinants of behavior.* New York: Academic Press, 1968.

DECI, E. L. The effects of contingent and noncontingent rewards and controls on intrinsic motivation. *Organizational Behavior and Human Performance*, 1972, *8*, 217–229.

DECI, E. L. *Intrinsic motivation*. New York: Plenum Press, 1975.

DIPBOYE, R. L. A critical review of Korman's self-consistency theory of work motivation and occupational choice. *Organizational Behavior and Human Performance*, 1977, *18*, 108–126.

EKEHAMMER, B. Interactionism in personality from a historical perspective. *Psychological Bulletin*, 1974, *81*, 1020–1048.

FESTINGER, L. A. *A theory of cognitive dissonance*. Evanston, Ill.: Row, Peterson, 1957.

FISHER, C. D. The effects of personal control, competence, and extrinsic reward systems on intrinsic motivation. *Organizational Behavior and Human Performance*, 1978, *21*, 273–288.

FORD, R. N. *Motivation through work itself*. New York: American Management Association, 1969.

GOODMAN, P. S. Social comparison processes in organizations. In B. M. Staw & G. R. Salancik (Eds.), *New directions in organizational behavior*. Chicago: St. Clair Press, 1977.

GOODMAN, P. S., & FRIEDMAN, A. Adams' theory of inequity. *Administrative Science Quarterly*, 1971, *16*, 271–288.

GREENBERG, J. The protestant work ethic and reactions to negative performance evaluations on a laboratory task. *Journal of Applied Psychology*, 1977, *62*, 682–690.

HALL, D. T., & NOUGAIM, K. E. An examination of Maslow's need hierarchy in an organizational setting. *Organizational Behavior and Human Performance*, 1968, *3*, 12–35.

HALL, J. To achieve or not: The manager's choice. *California Management Review*, Summer 1976, *15*(3), 5–18.

HERZBERG, F. *Work and the nature of man*. Cleveland: World Publishing, 1966.

HERZBERG, F., MAUSNER, B., & SNYDERMAN, B. B. *The motivation to work*. New York: Wiley, 1959.

HULIN, C. L. Individual differences and job enrichment—The case against general treatments. In J. R. Maher (Ed.), *New Perspectives in Job Enrichment*. New York: Van Nostrand, 1971.

ILGEN, D. R., FISHER, C. D., & TAYLOR, M. S. Motivational consequences of individual feedback on behavior in organizations. *Journal of Applied Psychology*, 1979, *64*, 349–371.

ILGEN, D. R., & GUNN, J. Affective consequences of disconfirming performance expectations. *Journal of Social Psychology*, 1976, *100*, 245–255.

JABLONSKY, S. F., & DeVRIES, D. L. Operant conditioning principles extrapolated to the theory of management. *Organizational Behavior and Human Performance*, 1972, *17*, 340–358.

JOHNSTON, W. A. Individual performance and self-evaluation in a simulated team. *Organizational Behavior and Human Performance*, 1967, *2*, 309–328.

JURGENSEN, C. E. Job preferences (what makes a job good or bad?) *Journal of Applied Psychology*, 1978, *63*, 267–276.

KING, N. Clarification and evaluation of the two-factor theory of job satisfaction. *Psychological Bulletin*, 1970, *74*, 18–31.

KLINGER, E., & McNELLY, F. W., JR. Fantasy need achievement and performance: A role analysis. *Psychological Review*, 1969, *76*, 574–591.

KOCH, S. W. *Management and motivation*. Summary of doctoral dissertation presented at the Swedish School of Economics, Helsigfors, Finland, 1965.

KOMAKI, J., WADDELL, W. M., & PEARCE, M. G. The applied behavior analysis approach and individual employees: Improving performance in two small businesses. *Organizational Behavior and Human Performance*, 1977, *19*(2), 337–352.

KORMAN, A. K. Toward a hypothesis of work behavior. *Journal of Applied Psychology*, 1970, *54*, 31–41.

KORMAN, A. K. Hypothesis of work behavior revisited and an extension. *Academy of Management Review*, 1976, *1*, 50–63.

KORMAN, A. K. *Organizational behavior*. Englewood Cliffs, N.J.: Prentice-Hall, 1977.

LANDY, F. J., & TRUMBO, D. A. *Psychology of work behavior*. Homewood, Ill.: Dorsey Press, 1976.

LATHAM, G. P., & BALDES, J. J. The practical significance of Locke's theory of goal setting. *Journal of Applied Psychology*, 1975, *60*, 122–124.

LATHAM, G. P., & YUKL, G. A. A review of research on the application of goal setting in organizations. *Academy of Management Journal*, 1975, *18*, 824–845.

LAWLER, E. E., III. *Pay and organizational effectiveness: A psychological view*. New York: McGraw-Hill, 1971.

LAWLER, E. E., III, & HACKMAN, J. R. Impact of employee participation in the development of pay incentive plans: A field experiment. *Journal of Applied Psychology*, 1969, *53*, 467–471.

LAWLER, E. E., III, & SUTTLE, J. L. A causal correlational test of the need hierarchy concept. *Organizational Behavior and Human Performance*, 1972, *7*, 265–287.

LAWLER, E. E., III, & SUTTLE, J. L. Expectancy theory and job performance. *Organizational Behavior and Human Performance*, 1973, *9*, 482–503.

LEWIN, L. *The conceptual representation and the measurement of psychological forces*. Durham, N. C.: Duke University Press, 1938.

LOCKE, E. A. Toward a theory of task motivation and incentives. *Organizational Behavior and Human Performance*, 1968, *3*, 157–189.

LOCKE, E. A. The nature and causes of job satisfaction. In M. D. Dunnette (Ed.), *Handbook of industrial and organizational psychology*. Chicago: Rand McNally, 1976.

LOCKE, E. A. The myths of behavior mod in organizations. *The Academy of Management Review*, 1977, *2*(4), 543–553.

LOCKE, E. A., & SCHWEIGER, D. M. Participation in decision-making: One more look. In B. M. Staw (Ed.), *Research in organizational behavior* (Vol.1). Greenwich, Conn.: JAI Press, 1979.

LOWIN, A. Participative decision making: A model, literature critique, and prescriptions for research. *Organizational Behavior and Human Performance*, 1968, *3*, 68–106.

MASLOW, A. H. *Motivation and personality*. New York: Harper & Row, 1954.

MASLOW, A. H. *Motivation and personality* (2nd ed.). New York: Harper & Row, 1970.

MCCLELLAND, D. C. *The achieving society*. Princeton, N.J.: Van Nostrand, 1961.

McClelland, D. C., & Winter, D. C. *Motivating economic achievement.* New York: Free Press, 1969.

McGregor D. M. The human side of enterprise. *Management Review,* 1957, *46,* 22–29, 88–92.

McGregor, D. *The human side of enterprise.* New York: McGraw-Hill, 1960.

Mewhinney, T. C. Operant terms and concepts in the description of individual work behavior: Some problems of interpretation, application and evaluation. *Journal of Applied Psychology,* 1975, *60,* 704–712.

Miner, J. B., & Dachler, H. P. Personnel attitudes and motivation. *Annual Review of Psychology,* 1973, *24,* 379–422.

Mischell, W. Toward a cognitive social learning reconceptualization of personality. *Psychological Review,* 1973, *80,* 252–283.

Mitchell, T. R. Expectancy models of job satisfaction, occupational preference, and effort: A theoretical, methodological, and empirical appraisal. *Psychological Bulletin,* 1974, *82,* 1053–1077.

Mitchell, T. R. *People in organizations; understanding their behavior.* New York: McGraw-Hill, 1978.

Mitchell, T. R. Organizational behavior. *Annual Review of Psychology.* Palo Alto, Calif.: Annual Reviews, 1979, *30,* 243–282.

Myers, M. S. Who are your motivated workers? *Harvard Business Review,* January-February 1964, *42,* 73–88.

Naylor, J. C., Pritchard, R. D., & Ilgen, D. R. *A theory of behavior in organizations.* New York: Academic Press, in press.

Nealey, S. M. Determining worker preferences among employee benefit programs. *Journal of Applied Psychology,* 1964, *48,* 7–12.

Nebeker, D. M., Dockstader, S. L., & Shumate, E. Predictions of key entry performance using the reconceptualized expectancy model. NPRDC TR 78–11, January 1978.

New Tool: "Reinforcement" for good work. *Business Week,* December 18, 1971, pp. 76–77.

Parker, D. F., and Dyer, L. Expectancy theory as a within-person behavioral choice model: An empirical test of some conceptual and methodological refinements. *Organizational Behavior and Human Performance,* 1976, *17*(1), 97–117.

Peak, H. Attitude and motivation. In M. R. Jones (Ed.), *Nebraska Symposium on Motivation.* Lincoln: University of Nebraska Press, 1955.

Porter, L. W. Job attitudes in management: I. Perceived deficiencies in need fulfillment as a function of job level. *Journal of Applied Psychology,* 1962, *46,* 375–384.

Porter, L. W., & Lawler, E. E., III. *Managerial attitudes and performances.* Homewood, Ill.: Dorsey Press, 1968.

Pritchard, R. D. Equity theory: A review and critique. *Organizational Behavior and Human Performance,* 1969, *4,* 176–211.

Pritchard, R. D., Campbell, K. M., & Campbell, D. J. The effects of extrinsic financial rewards on intrinsic motivation. *Journal of Applied Psychology,* 1977, *62,* 9–15.

Pritchard, R. D., Dunnette, M. D., & Jorgenson, D. O. Effects of perceptions of equity and inequity on worker performance and satisfaction. *Journal of Applied Psychology,* 1972, *56,* 75–94. (Monograph No. 1).

PRITCHARD, R. D., LEONARD, D. W., VON BERGEN, C. W., JR., & KIRK, R. J. The effects of varying schedules of reinforcement on human task performance. *Organizational Behavior and Human Performance*, 1976, *16*, 205–230.

RHODE, J. G., SORENSEN, J. E., & LAWLER, E. E., III. An analysis of personal characteristics related to professional staff turnover in public accounting firms. *Decision Sciences*, 1976, *7*, 771–800.

RONAN, W. W., LATHAM, G. P., & KINNE, S. B. Effects of goal setting and supervision on worker behavior in an industrial situation. *Journal of Applied Psychology*, 1973, *58*, 302–307.

SCHEFLEN, K. C., LAWLER, E. E., III, & HACKMAN, J. R. Long-term impact of employee participation in the development of pay incentive plans: A field experiment revisited. *Journal of Applied Psychology*, 1971, *55*, 182–186.

SCHLENKER, B. R., SORACI, S., & MC-CARTHY, M. Self-esteem and group performance as determinants of egocentric perceptions in cooperative groups. *Human Relations*, 1976, *29*, 1163–1187.

STAW, B. M. Motivation in organizations: Toward synthesis and redirection. In B. M. Staw & G. R. Salancik (Eds.), *New Directions in Organizational Behavior*. Chicago: St. Clair Press, 1977.

STAW, B. M., & SALANCIK, G. R. (Eds.). *New directions in organizational behavior*. Chicago: St. Clair Press, 1977.

STEDRY, A. C., & KAY, E. The effects of goal difficulty on performance. *Behavioral Science*, 1966, *11*, 459–470.

STEERS, R. M., & PORTER, L. W. The role of task-goal attributes in employee performance. *Psychological Bulletin*, 1974, *81*, 434–452.

STEERS, R. M., & PORTER, L. W. (Eds.). *Motivation and work behavior*. New York: McGraw-Hill, 1975.

TERBORG, J. R. Validation and extension of an individual differences model of work performance. *Organizational Behavior and Human Performance*, 1977, *18*, 188–216.

TERBORG, J. R., & MILLER, H. E. Motivation, behavior, and performance: A closer examination of goal setting and monetary incentive. *Journal of Applied Psychology*, 1978, *63*, 29–39.

TERKEL, S. *Working: People talk about what they do all day and how they feel about what they do*. New York: Pantheon, 1972.

TOLMAN, E. C. *Purposive behavior in animals and men*. New York: Century, 1932.

VROOM, V. H. *Work and motivation*. New York: Wiley, 1964.

VROOM, V. H., & YETTON, P. W. *Leadership and decision-making*. Pittsburgh: University of Pittsburgh Press, 1973.

Where Skinner's theories work. *Business Week*, December 2, 1972, pp. 64–65.

WHITE, R. W. Motivation reconsidered: The concept of competence. *Psychological Review*, 1959, *66*, 297–333.

14

job satisfaction, attitudes, and opinions

INTRODUCTION

As human beings, members of work-oriented organizations have thoughts and feelings which strongly influence their behavior on the job. These thoughts and feelings are part of their conscious state and provide the inputs used by them to make decisions about their actions and reactions to their jobs. Therefore, it is necessary that we understand more about these conscious states. In everyday language these are loosely termed thoughts and feelings. By those who study human behavior these conscious states are labeled attitudes and beliefs.

Our discussion first will define what we mean by beliefs or opinions and attitudes and then discuss, in detail, job satisfaction as a particular subset of attitudes. Both the nature of job satisfaction and its relationship to several aspects of work-related be-

havior will be explored. Following this discussion we shall turn our attention to the measurement of satisfaction, attitudes, and opinions.

BELIEFS OR OPINIONS[1]

Beliefs are cognitions held about some object, concept, or event or the relationship between these things. "My cash register is jamming," "The pressure in the tank is up to 150 pounds per square inch," "You are working harder than she is" all are beliefs. Note that all are subjective states of the individual. Most are very concrete and, more than likely, represent true states of

[1] The terms beliefs and opinions tend to be used interchangeably. We shall do the same. For example, psychologists who study attitudes tend to talk about beliefs. However, when sample surveys are constructed to ask people about what they believe, these surveys tend to be labeled opinion surveys.

301

affairs, but they may not. For example, the pressure in the tank might not be 150 pounds per square inch; the individual may have misread the dial or the pressure gauge may be incorrect. Regardless of the inaccuracy of the belief, to the individual it represents the basis on which he or she responds.

One final point should be made about beliefs. They are theoretically affect-free. That is to say, they do not necessarily convey any information about goodness or badness, liking or disliking by the belief holder. For example, consider the belief that my cash register is jammed. In and of itself, this does not say anything about whether the person who holds this belief sees it as good or bad. If he or she is the store manager and customers are backed up waiting to check out, this is probably bad. However, if the person is the cashier who has not had a break in six hours, he or she may be delighted to have the cash register break down.

ATTITUDES

Definition

Attitudes, like beliefs, are conscious states. Unlike beliefs, they do represent the degree of affect felt by the individual. They are the feelings the individual has toward some object, and these feelings are manifested in some judgment about the goodness or badness of the attitude object from the individual's point of view.

We shall define an attitude as *the affective orientation toward a particular attitude object.* This definition is consistent with much of major research on attitudes at the present time (Fishbein & Ajzen 1975). Note two things about this definition. First, attitudes are toward some attitude object. They do not exist in a vacuum. The object may be very specific, such as an attitude toward the letterhead on the stationery or may be very general, such as an attitude toward big business, but there is some object toward which the affective response is directed. Second, the term attitude as used in the statement, "She has a good attitude," has no meaning as it will be used in this chapter. As used in this statement, the term attitude really has no specific attitude object. It is a very general description incorporating much more than is usually included in more precise treatments of attitudes.

Importance

The attitudes of employees are important to the employees themselves and to those who manage organizations. Employees' attitudes have several functions. They provide information about employees' reactions to other individuals, events, or objects. For example, an individual who does not like being in or around water knows that he or she would not like to be a skin diver without first trying skin diving. The attitude toward a whole class of activities provides a knowledge base for judging specific elements within that class.

Attitudes may also guide behavior. If we assume that, other things being equal, employees will seek to approach or obtain attitude objects toward which they hold positive attitudes and avoid those for which they hold negative ones, then they should intend to behave in order to attain positive and to avoid negative attitude objects. Whether the behavior actually occurs depends, of course, on many factors which aid or inhibit the behavior. Nevertheless, the attitude does reflect an *intended* behavior if the behavior is feasible.

As a final example, it should be pointed out that attitudes are related even to the physical health of employees. Sales (1969) found a significant negative correlation between serum cholesterol level while working on a one-hour laboratory task and the degree of enjoyment of the task. Sales and

House (1971) found that job satisfaction was negatively correlated with the rate of deaths from arteriosclerotic heart disease across groups of employees. Although the Sales and House data are correlational, they certainly deserve further attention.

Employees' attitudes are important to employers for at least two reasons. As mentioned earlier, attitudes indicate intended responses. Therefore, knowledge of those attitude objects on the job to which employees respond favorably and to which they respond unfavorably can provide a basis for job design, policy, and practice decisions. When possible, positive features should be strengthened and negative ones altered or removed. At a more general level, employees' attitudes are important to employers for philosophical reasons. Today it is not sufficient to be content simply with providing work for employees. It is well accepted that employers should provide meaningful and satisfying work, to the extent that it is possible to do so. Although it is often argued that it is not technically possible to provide satisfying jobs, the technical limits are not quite as restrictive as many employers had once believed. It is perfectly reasonable for employers to be concerned with positive employee attitudes as an end in itself rather than simply as a means to some end such as lower turnover.

JOB SATISFACTION

Job satisfaction is a specific subset of attitudes held by organization members. It is the attitude one has toward his or her job. Stated another way it is one's affective response to the job.

Job satisfaction has been the primary attitude of interest to both practitioners and researchers over the years. In 1976, Locke reported that there had been well over three thousand published studies on job satisfaction, between the early work of Hoppock in 1935 and Locke's review and critique in 1976. Because of the interest and importance of the topic we shall devote most of the remainder of the chapter to discussing it.

Dimensions of Job Satisfaction

SPECIFIC JOB DIMENSIONS. The concept of a job is very complex. It has many facets, such as the nature of the work, the supervisor, the company, pay, or promotional opportunities. The job itself seldom serves as a unitary attitude object. Rather, the attitude, in this case the satisfaction that the individual associates with his or her job, is really the degree of satisfaction with a number of different dimensions of the job.

Over the years considerable time and effort has been devoted to discovering the dimensions of job satisfaction. The best conclusion to draw from this work is that, although there are many very specific and diverse job dimensions which have been shown to relate to job satisfaction at one time or another, there is a set of dimensions common to most jobs that is sufficient to describe most of the predictable variance in job satisfaction. This set varies roughly from five to twenty job dimensions, but seldom is it necessary to assess the degree of satisfaction using more than ten. The number in this set may vary somewhat depending upon the nature of the job and the purpose for which job satisfaction is being investigated. As we shall see, a common core of job dimensions is a good index of job satisfaction over a wide variety of jobs.

Locke (1976) presented a summary of the dimensions of jobs that consistently had been found to contribute significantly to employees' job satisfaction. Figure 14.1 illustrates his discussion by organizing specific job dimensions according to the classification scheme introduced by Locke in 1973. The specific dimensions listed in Figure 14.1 represent those job characteristics typically used to assess job satisfaction.

They are relatively specific attitude objects for which the organizational members have some position on a like-dislike continuum. They are also work characteristics salient to most people. For example, consider work itself and pay. Job incumbents quickly form very definite attitudes about the work they do. After very little experience on the job, they have definite feelings about how interesting the work is, how routine, how well they are doing, and, in general, how much they enjoy doing whatever it is they do. Likewise, feelings about pay are quite clear. The same amount of pay may lead to quite different feelings about how good it is, but, nevertheless, almost all will have formed for themselves some feeling about that amount.

The general categories of job dimensions depicted on the left-hand side of Fig-

General Categories	Specific Dimension	Dimension Descriptions
I. Events or Conditions		
1. Work	Work Itself	Includes intrinsic interest, variety, opportunity for learning, difficulty, amount, chances for success, control over work flow, etc.
2. Rewards	Pay	Amount, fairness or equity, basis for pay, etc.
	Promotions	Opportunities for, basis of, fairness of, etc.
	Recognition	Praise, criticism, credit for work done, etc.
3. Context of Work	Working Conditions	Hours, rest pauses, equipment, quality of the workspace, temperature, ventilation, location of plant, etc.
	Benefits	Pensions, medical and life insurance plans, annual leave, vacations, etc.
II. Agents		
1. Self	Self	Values, skills and abilities, etc.
2. Others (In-Company)	Supervision	Supervisory style and influence, technical adequacy, administrative skills, etc.
	Co-Workers	Competence, friendliness, helpfulness, technical competence, etc.
3. Others (Outside Company)	Customers	Technical competence, friendliness, etc.
	Family Members*	Supportiveness, knowledge of job, demands for time, etc.
	Others	Depending upon position, e.g. students, parents, voters

*not included in Locke's discussion

FIG. 14-1 Job Dimensions Typically Considered Relevant to Job Satisfaction and Classified as to Events and Agents According to Locke (Adapted from Locke 1976, p. 1302).

ure 14.1 are not addressed by most researchers who attempt to identify the job dimensions important to job satisfaction. Locke (1973, 1976) introduced the general categories in order to cluster common dimensions into more theoretically meaningful groups. We feel his system is useful for it provides some basis for considering the adequacy of the set of dimensions as well as a basis for better understanding how and why some dimensions are liked or disliked. For example, according to Locke, "every Event or Condition ultimately is caused by someone or something, and . . . every Agent is liked or disliked because he is perceived as having done (or failed to do) something . . ." (1976, p. 1302). To the extent that this is so, it is clear that in some settings in which supervisors have considerable control over the work done by their subordinates and over their pay, we should expect to find satisfaction with supervision closely related to satisfaction with the work itself and the pay. In other settings in which supervisors influence the work done by subordinates very little, and subordinates' pay is based upon some companywide scale, we should expect less covariation among satisfaction with work itself, pay, and supervision.

SINGLE OR MULTIPLE DIMENSIONS. Should job satisfaction be considered a single entity or should satisfaction with each of the dimensions of interest be considered separately? The answer depends on the reason or reasons for being concerned about job satisfaction. If job satisfaction measures are used to diagnose potential problem areas in the job setting, then separate dimensions are more valuable than an overall measure. The individual job facets can be considered in order to learn which ones seem to be producing positive and which ones negative feelings on the part of employees. If, on the other hand, the interest is in the relationship between a general response to the job such as quitting, a measure of overall job satisfaction may be more appropriate.

COMBINING DIMENSIONS OF JOB SATISFACTION. It seems intuitively obvious that all of a job's dimensions are not equally important to all people in determining overall satisfaction with their jobs. Some people may consider their pay very important and working conditions less so; for others it may be the reverse. Therefore, when combining measures of satisfaction with several dimensions of the job, it is tempting to weight the dimensions by their relative importance to the individual. The data are very clear for this issue; it does *not* work (Ewen 1967). It is much better to select a set of job dimensions that have been found to apply to most jobs and then simply to weight each dimension score equally to calculate overall satisfaction.

Several reasons have been suggested for why importance ratings do not work. The most compelling is that when individuals rate their satisfaction with any single dimension of the job, they also indirectly indicate the dimension's importance (Dachler & Hulin 1969; Locke 1976). To have either strong positive or strong negative feelings indicates that the dimension is important enough to feel strongly about it. On the other hand, neutral feelings of satisfaction usually mean that the factor really does not matter much. Therefore, weighting satisfaction ratings by importance is redundant and adds nothing.

Theoretical Views of Job Satisfaction

Often job satisfaction is treated as if it were the same as or very similar to work motivation. For example, it is not uncommon to treat both topics in a single chapter. It should be clear from our discussion so far that we consider the two topics quite distinct. Job satisfaction is concerned with the *feelings* one has toward the job, and work motivation is concerned with the *behaviors* that occur on the job. Nevertheless, it is not surprising that the two topics are not clearly differentiated. This occurs for two reasons. First, satisfaction is a hedonic response of liking or disliking the attitude object. Also, it is often assumed that individuals will approach those things with which they are satisfied and avoid those things with which they are dissatisfied. As a result, job satisfaction is frequently associated with job behaviors just as motivation is. Second, most theories of motivation have an underlying hedonic assumption that individuals are motivated to seek that which is pleasant to them. As a result, many theories of motivation are also considered, at least in part, theories of job satisfaction.

In the discussion that follows we have not addressed all of the individual theories of job satisfaction. If interested, the reader should consult Locke's 1976 review. We will suggest five general orientations toward job satisfaction, all of which describe the processes by which job satisfaction is determined for individuals.

COMPARISON PROCESSES. The most widely accepted view of job satisfaction assumes that the degree of affect experienced results from some comparison between the individual's standard and that individual's perception of the extent to which the standard is met. The amount of satisfaction that results is a function of the size of the discrepancy between the standard and what is believed to be received from the job. Vroom (1964) labeled this view a *subtractive* theory of job satisfaction.

There is one issue with regard to the comparison process view of job satisfaction. This is the specification of what is used as the standard to which the job is compared. Some have argued that the individual's needs serve as a standard (Morse 1953; Porter 1962, 1963). Locke (1976) believes that the individual's values, rather than needs, serve as a standard. Smith, Kendall, and Hulin (1969), in their devel-

opment of a popular job satisfaction measure, the Job Descriptive Index (JDI), considered the cognitive state of an individual's frame-of-reference as the standard to which the job is compared. The evidence seems to show that both values and frames-of-reference serve as standards more than needs.

INSTRUMENTALITY THEORY. A second view of job satisfaction is that individuals calculate the degree to which the job is satisfying by considering the extent to which the job leads to valued outcomes. It is assumed that the individuals have a set of judgments about how much they value certain outcomes such as pay, a promotion, or good working conditions. They then estimate the extent to which holding the job leads to each of these outcomes. Finally, by weighting the perceived value or attractiveness of each outcome and considering all outcomes in the set, the individual arrives at an estimate of the satisfaction he or she feels will come from the job. This process, labeled instrumentality theory for its emphasis on the extent to which the job is instrumental to producing satisfaction, is illustrated in Figure 14.2.

Although the notion of instrumentality appears to be important to motivation, as discussed earlier under expectancy theory in the chapter on motivation, its use for job satisfaction seems limited. First, it tends to focus on the future rather than on the present or on the past. Most of the concern is with anticipated satisfaction using an instrumental view, whereas job satisfaction is a present- or past-oriented concept. Second, weighting each outcome by its instrumentality is a very complicated cognitive process which may be more complex than the process that human beings usually apply. Finally, one still is left with the question of how the valences were formed by the individual. Because of its future orientation, complexity, and need to explain issues of valences, it has not received widespread acceptance as a view of satisfaction.

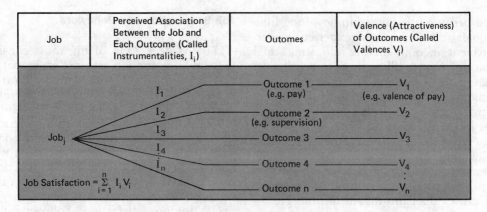

Job	Perceived Association Between the Job and Each Outcome (Called Instrumentalities, I_i)	Outcomes	Valence (Attractiveness) of Outcomes (Called Valences V_i)
	I_1	Outcome 1 (e.g. pay)	V_1 (e.g. valence of pay)
	I_2	Outcome 2 (e.g. supervision)	V_2
Job_j	I_3	Outcome 3	V_3
	I_4	Outcome 4	V_4
Job Satisfaction = $\sum_{i=1}^{n} I_i V_i$	I_n	Outcome n	V_n

FIG. 14.2 Instrumentality Theory of Job Satisfaction

SOCIAL INFLUENCE. Salancik and Pfeffer (1977) questioned comparison theories of job satisfaction and suggested that perhaps people decide how satisfied they are with their job not by processing all kinds of information about it but by observing others on similar jobs and making inferences about others' satisfaction. In a similar vein Weiss and Shaw (1979) suggest that an individual simply infers a level of his or her own satisfaction from observing others. In a sense they are saying that individuals may come into a new job not knowing how satisfied they will be with it. They look around, see others like themselves who are satisfied (or dissatisfied) with it, and these observations influence how satisfied (or dissatisfied) they are with their job.

Research by White and Mitchell (1979) and Weiss and Shaw (1979) showed that people indeed are influenced by their perceptions of others' satisfaction. Weiss and Shaw had people first view a training film showing others working on an electrical assembly task. The films showed others either working on an interesting or on a boring task. While working on the task, those in the film made incidental comments which indicated that they liked the task (for example, "This task is OK" or "I don't mind doing this at all") or that they held a neutral position toward the task. Following the film, the participants in the study worked on the same task they saw demonstrated in the film (either the interesting one or the boring one) and rated their degree of satisfaction. The results clearly showed that the feelings about the task were influenced by others' reactions as well as by properties of the task itself.

Social influence theory of job satisfaction is interesting because it recognizes the social nature of work and suggests a way of determining job satisfaction that has been ignored for a long time. It seems obvious that social factors do influence satisfaction and that they deserve more attention than they have received in the past.

EQUITY THEORY. Equity theory also contains a social element in which the individual compares his or her inputs and outcomes to those of others. The theory was discussed in detail in chapter 13. For job satisfaction the same process is hypothesized. It differs from that presented thus far in that it predicts that too much of a good thing is dissatisfying. That is, receiving more than is equitable will produce less satisfaction.

The evidence seems to indicate that equity norms do operate and that overpayment inequity can exist (for example, Pritchard and others 1972). Because the conditions occur relatively infrequently

307

and because it is uncertain how long individuals will continue to experience overpayment inequity before adjusting their point of view to allow them to receive the same returns without feeling overcompensated, it does not appear to us that an equity framework controls a major portion of the job satisfaction variance.

TWO-FACTOR THEORY. Herzberg (Herzberg, Mausner, & Snyderman 1959; Herzberg 1966) proposed that job satisfaction stemmed from an entirely different set of causes than job dissatisfaction. He argued that "satisfiers," which were such work-related dimensions as recognition, autonomy, and responsibility, and the work itself could affect only satisfaction and not dissatisfaction, whereas the opposite effect occurred for "dissatisfiers," such as pay, working conditions, and human relations behaviors of supervisors or co-workers. This position generated considerable research and debate during the 1960s. By now it is clear that the position has no support (see King 1970; Locke 1976; Miner & Dachler 1973, for reviews). Both facets contribute to both satisfaction and dissatisfaction, although satisfiers seem, in general, to contribute more to both than dissatisfiers do. The two-factor theory no longer deserves consideration.

CONCLUSIONS ABOUT THEORIES. Of the five theories presented, comparison process views seem to be the most important. That is, they appear to explain more variance in job satisfaction than other points of view do. Neither the social influence nor equity views should be overlooked, however. These seem to influence job satisfaction over and above the comparison process. Also, in settings in which social comparisons are quite prominent, these processes may in fact dominate. Comparative research on different theories is sorely lacking and is needed for firm conclusions.

Job Satisfaction and Behaviors

TURNOVER. One of the most consistent findings for job satisfaction is that it correlates negatively with turnover (Porter & Steers 1973). Some of the most interesting research in this area was done by Hulin (1966; 1968). In his 1966 study, clerical workers who subsequently quit were compared to a matched sample, who did not quit, on their responses to a job satisfaction survey taken before the former group resigned. Turnover was clearly related (negatively) to job satisfaction. Following the 1966 study, changes were made in the jobs to correct some of the factors mentioned by those who had quit as unsatisfactory. These changes led to a significant decrease in turnover (Hulin 1968).

ABSENTEEISM. Absenteeism also tends to show a negative correlation with job satisfaction, but the strength of the correlations is not high. More than occasionally the relationship is zero, and there are cases in which it is positive. (For example, the latter has occurred when conditions allow increased absences to create a need for more overtime work.)

Absenteeism frequently may not be associated strongly with job satisfaction, because absence behavior is determined by other factors even when there is dissatisfaction (Ilgen & Hollenbeck 1977). Smith (1977) demonstrated this quite clearly. Smith surveyed many managers in the Chicago headquarters of a large organization shortly before a crippling snowstorm. Smith argued that on the day after the snowstorm the managers had a built-in excuse not to come to work. This should have removed constraints on attendance behavior so that attendance should have been more a function of attitudes than under other conditions. His data clearly show job satisfaction negatively correlated with absenteeism under this condition. For a control group in New York, where there was no snow, there was no correlation between attendance on the same day and job satisfaction.

PERFORMANCE. Although it is intuitively appealing to conclude that satisfied employees are better performers, the data simply do not support such a position. Major reviews by Brayfield and Crockett (1955), Herzberg, Mausner, Peterson, and Capwell (1957), and Vroom (1964) refuted this view. Clearly, it is no longer acceptable to hold such a position.

What is less clear is why the two are unrelated. At one extreme it could be argued that job attitudes are unrelated to performance behavior. A more moderate and more appealing position to us is that the two may be related, but only under certain conditions. These conditions are ones in which performance behavior is not constrained or controlled. For example, performance on a machine-paced job is influenced much more by the speed of the machine than by job satisfaction. Similarly, the sales representative's dollar volume in sales may be more a function of the quality of the district than of his or her satisfaction. Therefore, Herman (1973) argued that job satisfaction should relate to performance (and to any other behavior) only when other influences on behavior have been removed. Complex behaviors, such as those represented by work performance, frequently are influenced by other factors; therefore, we would suggest that they often would not be strongly related to job satisfaction. This is much different from saying that, across the board, job satisfaction is unimportant to performance.

BEHAVIORS IN GENERAL. Two final comments about job satisfaction and behaviors need to be made before we leave the topic. First, as we have already mentioned, one must ask if the behavior in question could possibly be related to job satisfaction. Frequently behavior is constrained by outside factors not related to job satisfaction. In addition, the dimensions on which satisfaction is measured may be only weakly related to the behavior in question. Ilgen and Hollenback (1977) raised this issue with regard to absenteeism. If employees do not believe that company policies give much weight to absenses in making pay and promotional decisions and if supervisors and co-workers accept absenteeism as a way of life, then satisfaction with company policies, supervision, and co-workers should not be expected to be negatively correlated with absenteeism.

A second comment questions the adequacy of the set of behaviors most frequently related to job satisfaction. The focus has been on a narrow set closely associated with productivity goals of the organization, for example, absenteeism, turnover, and individual performance. Nord (1977) castigated researchers for their myopic focus and challenged them not to abandon the old as wrong but to expand the domain of concern. He stressed that research on job satisfaction must consider existing social, political, and economic variables which will allow us to place job satisfaction in a more realistic perspective, given today's organizational climates and attitudes toward work. His position is well taken and deserves attention.

The Measurement of Job Satisfaction

It should not be surprising that with the hundreds of studies on job satisfaction over the last thirty to forty years, there have been many different scales used to measure it. These scales fall into two general categories. One is called *tailor-made* scales. These are constructed for a particular setting or project. The second set is comprised of *standardized* scales which, before their use, have been developed to establish group norms on the scales and to ensure the reliability and validity of the measuring instruments. With the present level of knowledge of job satisfaction and the availability of good measures of it, there is almost no reason to use tailor-made scales. Unfortunately, tailor-made scales still are being used quite frequently.

We shall devote all our attention to standardized scales. Below we briefly describe two such measures. The first, the Job Description Index (JDI) has been well developed and is used widely. The second, the Kunin faces scale, is presented for its uniqueness. Several other good scales are available. We shall leave it up to those who are interested to check the literature on them.

JOB DESCRIPTION INDEX (JDI). The Job Description Index (JDI), [2] was developed by Smith and some of her associates over the years and reported by Smith, Kendall, and Hulin (1969). In earlier versions of the scale, individuals were asked to describe the job they would most like to have (their "best" job) and the one they would least like to have (their "worst" job). Responses thus elicited were used in an item analysis to identify those items which tended to be most discriminating; such items were then included in the final scale. In its final form the scale measures attitudes in five areas: work, supervision, pay, promotions, and co-workers. The scale consists of a series of adjectives or statements for each of these categories, and the individual is asked to mark each one as yes (Y), no (N), or cannot decide (?) as it relates to his or her job. A few examples are given:

Work
____Fascinating
____Routine
____Frustrating

Supervision
____Hard to please
____Praises good work
____Stubborn

Pay
____Adequate for normal expenses
____Less than I deserve

Promotions
____Promotion on ability
____Dead-end job

Co-workers
____Stimulating
____Talk too much

Although the scale actually "describes" one's job, the "description" implies the individual's evaluation of it. Scores based on this scale have been found to be related to other measures of job satisfaction.

The internal consistency reliability of the JDI, derived by correlating scores of random split-halves of the items for eighty men, ranged from .80 to .88 for the five separate scales. The intercorrelations of the five scales for a sample of 980 men ranged fron .28 to .42. These intercorrelations reflect only moderate relationships, thus implying that the five scales were tapping somewhat separate facets of job satisfaction. Schneider and Dachler (1978) replicated the low intercorrelations among dimensions in a large utility companv and also showed that the test-retest reliabilities of the subscales were good (r = .57) when compared over a sixteen-month period.

"FACES" JOB SATISFACTION SCALE. A rather different scheme for measuring job satisfaction was developed by Kunin (1955). This consists of a series of drawings of people's faces with varying expressions, including variations in the curvature of the mouth ranging from a broad smile to a deep frown, as illustrated in Figure 14.3. The respondent simply marks that face which best expresses how he feels about his "job in general." Dunham and Herman

[2]The Job Description Index is copyrighted by Dr. Patricia C. Smith, Bowling Green State University. Inquiries about it should be addressed to her at Bowling Green State University, Bowling Green, Ohio 43403.

Put a check under the face that expresses how you feel about your job in general, including the work, the pay, the supervision, the opportunities for promotion and the people you work with.

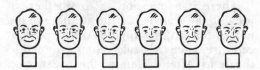

FIG. 14.3 Illustration of the "Faces" scale for measuring job satisfaction (*From Kunin 1955*).

(1975) found that such a scale could also be used with faces of women for women.

Conclusions About Job Satisfaction

Job satisfaction is an interesting concept which has received much attention in the past and deserves to receive more in the future. There are good instruments for measuring it and well formulated theoretical explanations of it. By periodically measuring job satisfaction in organizations, it should be possible to understand better the extent to which organizations are meeting employees' needs and expectations. This information provides a valuable input into decisions about the design and implementation of the human resource systems within organizations.

ATTITUDE AND OPINION MEASUREMENT

Frequently there is an interest in measuring employees' attitudes toward and opinions about a range of items or concepts than is typically tapped by job satisfaction questionnaires. For example, with the growing number of dual-career couples, one might be interested in assessing employees' attitudes toward and opinions about the organization's transfer policies associated with promotions, particularly as they relate to transfers requiring relocation. The information from an attitude and

opinion survey could be very useful for formulating policy on transfers. To get such information, it would be necessary to tailor-make a survey instrument to obtain the types of information desired. We shall discuss some typical ways of contructing scales for such an instrument.

Attitude Scales

Typically, an "attitude score" for any given individual is based on the summation of responses to individual questionnaire items. In turn, it is usual to average all the individual attitude scores of the members of a group, such as a job group, department, or company. Various types of scales are used for this; a few of these will be discussed here.

THURSTONE SCALES. The Thurstone attitude scale goes back to the early work of Thurstone and Chave (1929). An example of such a scale, developed by Uhrbrock (1934) is given in Table 14.1. This particular scale is intended to measure the attitudes of employees toward the companies in which they worked. Table 14.1 gives the scale values of the items, but these are not shown on the questionnaires filled out by the employees.

The development of the Thurstone scale is essentially the same as the development of the weighted check list type of performance appraisal system illustrated earlier. In this process the first step is to write out a large number of statements, perhaps a hundred or more, each of which, if endorsed by a respondent as reflecting his or her attitude, would imply a viewpoint—favorable or unfavorable—toward the attitude "object" (for example, the organization or some aspect of it). An effort should be made to have these statements express all possible viewpoints from extremely favorable to extremely unfavorable. Each of these statements is typed on a separate slip of paper, and a judge is asked to place each statement in one of several piles (usually seven, nine, or eleven), ranging from statements judged to express the *least* favorable viewpoints (placed in pile 1), to statements judged to express the *most* favorable viewpoints (placed in the top pile, 7, 9, or 11). Statements judged to express varying degrees of favorableness between these extremes are placed in the piles that characterize their judged degrees of relative favorableness. Usually many judges are used in this process.

The objective here is to identify a limited number of statements to use in a final scale. The selection is made on the basis of two primary considerations. The first is the consistency of the judgments of each statement; those statements that tend to be concentrated by the judges in one or a limited number of categories reflect greater agreement than those spread across several categories. From those that have been judged with reasonable agreement, several statements are then selected to represent varying positions along the scale. For each statement that is kept for the final scale, a

scale value is computed; usually this is the mean or median of the numerical identifications of the categories in which the statement was placed by several judges.

There is a question as to whether, in judging the scale items, the attitudes of the judges toward the stimulus object or concept prejudice the scale values assigned to the items. After examining the evidence on this, Shaw and Wright (1967) concluded that this is not the case, although there are still some questions.

As indicated above, the scale, as it is presented to respondents, does not include the scale values. Further, the items are presented in jumbled order. Each respondent checks those statements with which he or she agrees. An "attitude score" is then based either on the average or the median scale value of the statements that the person checked. Chapter 6 mentioned a possible fallacy in using the median value as related to using the Thurstone type of scale in a weighted checklist appraisal system. The solution to this problem was discussed in Chapter 6.

TABLE 14.1 STATEMENTS USED IN UHRBROCK'S SCALE FOR MEASURING ATTITUDE OF EMPLOYEES TOWARD THEIR COMPANY

Statement	Scale Value
I think this company treats its employees better than any other company does	10.4
If I had to do it over again I'd still work for this company	9.5
They don't play favorites in this company	9.3
A person can get ahead in this company if one tries	8.9
The company is sincere in wanting to know what its employees think about it	8.5
On the whole the company treats us about as well as we deserve	7.4
The workers put as much over on the company as the company puts over on them	5.1
The company does too much welfare work	4.4
I do not think applicants for employment are treated courteously	3.6
I believe many good suggestions are killed by the bosses	3.2
My boss gives all the breaks to his lodge and church friends	2.9
You've got to have "pull" with certain people around here to get ahead	1.5
In the long run this company will "put it over" on you	1.5
An honest person fails in this company	0.8

Source: Uhrbrock, 1934. Copyright by the American Psychological Association, and reproduced by permission.

LIKERT SCALE. Soon after Thurstone brought out his scale, Likert (1932) experimented with certain other varieties of attitude scales and ended up proposing a scale that is illustrated below:

My supervisor is consistently fair in dealing with his subordinates.

5 Strongly agree
4 Agree
3 Undecided (neither agree nor disagree)
2 Disagree
1 Strongly disagree

The numbers (which may or may not be included in the questionnaire) are the numerical values in scoring. An individual's score is derived by a simple addition of the numerical values of the responses he or she selects for the several items.

COMPARISON OF LIKERT AND THURSTONE SCALES. There has been some controversy over the relative virtues of the Likert and Thurstone scales. Seiler and Hough (1970) in recapping several studies, referred specifically to Likert's hypothesis that the Likert scale was (1) equally or more reliable than the Thurstone, (2) faster, and (3) equally or more valid. They stated that two of these issues seem to have been resolved. First, comparisons of the reliability coefficients, which usually are derived by the alternate forms or split-halves methods, tended to give Likert the edge; of several such coefficients—for various scales dealing with different attitude objects—the median coefficients for the Likert scales were around .90 and for the Thurstone scales, in the lower .80s. Second, in terms of time required, it appeared that a Likert scale of twenty to twenty-five items was usually enough to produce a reliability coefficient of .90 or more, whereas it would take a scale of about fifty items in a Thurstone scale (and presumably proportionately more time) to achieve comparable reliability. The third issue, relating to relative validity, remains something of an open question.

Opinion Surveys

Attitude scales, such as those mentioned above, typically are used to derive an attitude index for each individual (usually anonymously), which in turn can be averaged for individuals within a unit, department, or organization. In contrast, opinion surveys elicit opinions of specific matters. An example of part of such a questionnaire is shown in Figure 14.4. The usual practice in opinion questionnaires is to obtain a single response to each item or question which will indicate the degree of satisfaction with, or an opinion about, some specific aspect of the total work situation. Opinion items are not limited to evaluative judgments of goodness and badness as are attitude scales. Just about any topic can be addressed with an opinion scale.

Combination Questionnaires

Aside from questionnaires mentioned above for measuring attitudes, job satisfaction, opinions, and so forth, there also are certain other questionnaires for these and related purposes, including some that might be called combination questionnaires—that is, questionnaires that tap a couple of different facets.

CONCLUSION

The attitudes and opinions of employees are important and measurable. Most large organizations recognize their importance and systematically survey employees' attitudes and opinions to aid in forming organizational policies and practices. As we have seen here, measures for such surveys are neither complicated not particularly expensive, although care must be taken to develop scales with good psychometric

```
EMPLOYEE SURVEY QUESTIONNAIRE

 4.  Do you feel you would rather be doing some
     other type of work?                                  Yes ☐    No ☐
     If yes, have you discussed it with the
     Personnel Office?                                     Yes ☐    No ☐
 6.  Does your foreman "know his stuff"?                   Yes ☐    No ☐
 7.  Does your foreman play favorites?                     Yes ☐    No ☐
 9.  Does your foreman keep his promises?                  Yes ☐    No ☐
22.  Do you feel that you are receiving
     considerate treatment here?                           Yes ☐    No ☐
     If not, why? _____

     _____

23.  Do you feel top management is interested
     in the employees?                                     Yes ☐    No ☐
26.  Are you interested in Company athletic
     activities?                                           Yes ☐    No ☐
28.  Do you feel you have a good future with
     this Company?                                         Yes ☐    No ☐
32.  Are you getting the kind of information
     about the Company that you want?                      Yes ☐    No ☐
33.  What do you think of working conditions
     here as compared with other plants?
        Above average ☐   Average ☐   Below average ☐
34.  How do you think your average weekly earnings (gross earnings
     before deductions) compare with that paid in other companies
     for the same type of work?
        Better here ☐   About the same ☐   Lower here ☐
```

FIG. 14.4 Selected items from a questionnaire used in an employee survey conducted by the Victor Adding Machine Co. (*Courtesy Victor Adding Machine Co., Chicago, Ill.*)

properties. It would behoove most organizations to measure them.

Attitudes toward and opinions about work and/or related issues relevant to work have changed over the last decade or so in ways that emphasize the need for greater awareness of them. Some, such as the well publicized study entitled *Work in America* (U.S. Department of Health, Education, & Welfare, 1973), suggested that people today are much less satisfied with work than they were in the past. Given the data available today, this conclusion appears to be an overreaction. There is some evidence of a slight decline in job satisfaction, as evidenced by Smith, Scott, & Hulin's (1977) comparison of employee responses to an

attitude survey administered at Sears Roebuck over the past twenty-five years.

Organ (1977) showed, however, that when a similar downward trend in job satisfaction was corrected for employees' ages, job satisfaction stayed relatively constant. He argued that the work force is simply getting younger, and younger employees, in general, tend to be less satisfied. He hypothesized that when the "baby boom" of the 1940s and early 1950s moves through the work force, job satisfaction will reflect the age changes of this group.

Regardless of the mean level of job satisfaction, there have been major changes in the value and meaning of work in a large enough segment of the working population to make these issues relevant to many organizations. The desire to share one job between two individuals and the emergence of a large number of dual-career families among managerial and professional staff are just a few of these changes. Such changes simply emphasize the need to become more aware of the attitudes and opinions of the work force in order to maintain effective human resource systems within organizations. These issues demand attention and attention that focuses on job satisfaction and opinions from a broader perspective than simply trying to correlate attitudes and opinions with performance or attendance. Exploring the impact of families, group norms, and other factors of attitudes or opinions as suggested by Nord (1977) appears to be a good start for a more in-depth analysis of these issues.

REFERENCES

BRAYFIELD, A. H. & CROCKETT, W. H. Employee attitudes and employee performance. *Psychological Bulletin*, 1955, *52*, 396–424.

DACHLER, H. P., & HULIN, C. L. A reconsideration of the relationship between satisfaction and judged importance of environmental and job characteristics. *Organizational Behavior and Human Performance*, 1969, *4*, 252–266.

DUNHAM, R. B., & HERMAN, J. B. Development of a female faces scale for measuring job satisfaction. *Journal of Applied Psychology*, 1975, *60*, 629–632.

EWEN, R. B. Weighting components of job satisfaction. *Journal of Applied Psychology*, 1967, *51*, 68–73.

FISHBEIN, M. (Ed.). *Readings in attitude theory and measurement.* New York: Wiley, 1967.

FISHBEIN, M., & AJZEN, I. *Belief, attitude, intention, and behavior: An introduction to theory and research.* Reading, Mass.: Addison-Wesley, 1975.

HERMAN, J. B. Are situational contingencies limiting job attitude-job performance relationships? *Organizational Behavior and Human Performance*, 1973, *10*, 208–224.

HERZBERG, F. *Work and the nature of man.* New York: Van Nostrand, 1966.

HERZBERG, F., MAUSNER, B., PETERSON, R. O., & CAPWELL, D. F. *Job attitudes: Review of research and opinion.* Pittsburgh: Psychological Service of Pittsburgh, 1957.

HERZBERG, F., MAUSNER, B., & SNYDERMAN, B. B. *The motivation to work.* New York: Wiley, 1959.

HULIN, C. L. Job satifaction and turnover. *Journal of Applied Psychology*, 1966, *50*, 280–285.

HULIN, C. L. Effects of changes in job satisfaction levels on employee turnover. *Journal of Applied Psychology*, 1968, *52*, 122–126.

ILGEN, D. R., & HOLLENBACK, J. H. The role of job satisfaction in absence behavior. *Organizational Behavior and Human Performance*, 1977, *19*, 148–161.

KING, N. Clarification and evaluation of the two-factor theory of job satisfaction. *Psychological Bulletin*, 1970, *74*, 18–31.

KUNIN, T. The construction of a new type of attitude measure. *Personnel Psychology*, 1955, *8*, 65–78.

LIKERT, R. A technique for the measurement of attitudes. *Archives of Psychology*, 1932, No. 140.

LOCKE, E. A. Satisfiers and dissatisfiers among white and blue collar employees. *Journal of Applied Psychology*, 1973, *58*, 67–76

LOCKE, E. A. The nature and causes of job satisfaction. In M. D. Dunnette (Ed.), *Handbook of industrial and organizational psychology*. Chicago: Rand McNally, 1976.

MINER, J. B., & DACHLER, H. P. Personnel attitudes and motivation. *Annual Review of Psychology*, 1973, *24*, 379–422.

MORSE, N. C. *Satisfaction in the white-collar job.* Ann-Arbor: University of Michigan Press, 1953.

NORD, W. R. Job satisfaction reconsidered. *American Psychologist*, 1977, *32*, 1026–1035.

ORGAN, D. W. Inferences about trends in labor force satisfaction: A causal-correlational analysis. *Academy of Management Journal*, 1977, *20*, 510–519.

PORTER, L. W., & STEERS, R. M. Organizational, work, and personal factors in employee turnover and absenteeism. *Psychological Bulletin*, 1973, *80*, 151–176.

PRITCHARD, R. D., DUNNETTE, M. D., & JORGENSON, D. O. Effects of perceptions of equity and inequity on worker performance and satisfaction. *Journal of Applied Psychology*, 1972, *56*, 75–94.

SALANCIK, G. R., & PFEFFER, J. An examination of need satisfaction models of job satisfaction. *Administrative Science Quarterly*, 1977, *22*, 427–456.

SALES, S. M. Organizational role as a risk factor in coronary disease. *Administrative Science Quarterly*, 1969, *14*, 325–336.

SALES, S. M., & HOUSE, J. Job dissatisfaction as a possible risk factor in coronary heart disease. *Journal of Chronic Diseases*, 1971, *28*, 861–873.

SCHNEIDER, B., & DACHLER, H. P. A note on the stability of the Job Descriptive Index. *Journal of Applied Psychology*, 1978, *63*, 650–653.

SEILER, L. H., & HOUGH, R. L. Empirical comparisons of the Thurstone and Likert techniques. In G. F. Summers (Ed.), *Attitude measurement.* Chicago: Rand McNally, 1970.

SHAW, M. E., & WRIGHT, J. M. *Scales for the measurement of attitudes.* New York: McGraw-Hill, 1967.

SMITH, F. J. Work attitudes as predictors of attendance on a specific day. *Journal of Applied Psychology*, 1977, *62*, 16–19.

SMITH, F. J., SCOTT, K. D., & HULIN, C. L. Trends in job-related attitudes of management and professional employees. *Academy of Management Journal*, 1977, *20*, 454–460.

SMITH, P. C., KENDALL, L. M., & HULIN, C. L. *The measurement of satisfaction in work and retirement.* Chicago: Rand McNally, 1969.

THURSTONE, L. L., & CHAVE, E. J. *The measurement of attitude.* Chicago: University of Chicago Press, 1929.

UHRBROCK, R. S. Attitudes of 4,430 employees. *Journal of Social Psychology*, 1934, *5*, 365–377.

U.S. DEPARTMENT OF HEALTH, EDUCATION, AND WELFARE. *Work in America.* Cambridge, Mass.: M.I.T. Press, 1973.

VROOM, V. H. *Work and motivation.* New York: Wiley, 1964.

WEISS, H. M., & SHAW, J. B. Social influences on judgments about tasks. *Organizational Behavior and Human Performance,* in press.

WHITE, S. E., & MITCHELL, T. R. Job enrichment versus social cues: A comparison and competitive test. *Journal of Applied Psychology,* in press.

15

leadership

In this chapter we shift our emphasis from the individual to groups of individuals. Organizations, by definition, are composed of more than one individual. Usually individuals are clustered into groups, either formally or informally, and often they must interact with others to accomplish their tasks. In fact, any particular individual in an organization may be a member of several groups all within the same organization. Whereas traditional bureaucratic organization guidelines minimized multiple group memberships, modern organizational theory encourages them. (See Likert's 1961, 1967, notion of linking pins and descriptions of matrix organizations as described in French, 1978.) Whether individuals are members of one or more groups, it is reasonable to conclude that members of organizations are members of groups. Therefore, social factors do influence human behavior at work.

Even the most cursory view of the behavior of people in groups leads to the conclusion that there are differences in power and influence among group members. These differences evolve quite quickly after a group is formed, even without any formalized structural demands. In organizations, the status differences among participants in groups is apparent because there are specific policies and practices which state the formal power relationships among group members. Because of felt needs for establishing accountability for individuals' actions in the organization, lines of authority are established. At the primary group level, this means that usually one person is held responsible for the group's goal-directed behavior and is designated the supervisor or manager.

Individuals in supervisory or managerial positions are expected to plan, coordinate, direct, and control the task-relevant activities of those individuals for whom they have responsibility, so as to accomplish the goals established for their group. In other words, they are expected to demonstrate "leadership" by influencing group members to contribute to the group's task. Since it is so essential to the organization that work group members direct their activities toward organizational goals and since the extent to which they do this is often credited, rightly or wrongly, to the supervisor's or manager's ability to lead, it is not surprising that leadership has been studied so extensively.

We wish that we could say that all this effort has led to a clear understanding of leadership and to a concise set of principles for those in leadership positions. Unfortunatly, we cannot. Nevertheless, there has been progress in understanding leadership, which is worth noting. In the remainder of the chapter, we first shall consider definitions of leadership, then discuss the need for leadership in organizations. Next, we shall consider theoretical approaches to leadership and, when appropriate, applications of these theories to improving leader effectiveness.

POSITION, PERSON, OR PROCESS?

Leadership is an illusive concept because it often is used to mean very different things. Three viewpoints are considered below.

Position

To some, leadership resides in a position within the organization. From this point of view, a position is a set of prescribed behaviors for the person assigned to it. Persons in this position acquire a certain set of behaviors expected of them. These behaviors may be those normally considered leadership behaviors. Thus, the individual in this position may be expected to direct the behavior of others and to reward and to reprimand others according to the quality of their performance. In a strict sense, leadership, according to this view, is little more than exercising the role or roles defined as part of the position. Taken to its extreme, little credit for leadership is given to the individual who occupies the position. Most of the behavior is seen as coming from the power, authority, and other aspects delegated to the position. Historians who place most of the causal emphasis on the events and the conditions of the times rather than praising the accomplishments of the leaders exemplify this view. Although the positionist view of leadership recognizes that interaction between leaders and their position requirements influences leadership, the emphasis is on the position and the role or roles defined by it.

Person

A second view of leadership focuses on the person. The answer to the historical question in this case is that a person contributed more to events than did the conditions of the times. The search for an understanding of leadership from this point of view has addressed the leader's personal characteristics. Abilities, personality variables, interests, and values have been investigated as possible explanations of differences among effective and ineffective leaders.

Process

A third focus is on the process by which leaders lead. The question is what do they do to lead. At the most general level, leaders influence others; they must achieve group goals by soliciting the aid and commitment of those under them to contribute time and effort toward the accomplishment of group goals. Yet, as Katz and Kahn (1978) explained, this influence must be more than merely routinely exercising the power of the role or position. The prison guard who "influences" the prisoner to move from the exercise yard by pointing his gun could hardly be considered to be demonstrating leadership. Therefore, leadership is influence, but it must be some degree of influence that can be attributed to the individual in the leadership position. If everyone in the same position always had the same degree of influence, regardless of what he or she did, then this would not be leadership.

In many ways, the process orientation toward leadership combines the position and the person by recognizing that the major component of what is called leadership is the leader's ability to influence his or her subordinates. The influence process obviously is affected by the situation which is primarily composed of properties of the leader's position. For example, some leadership positions make available to individuals in them the ability to control valued rewards of the subordinates; other positions offer little in the way of rewards for the position-holder to use. Similarly, some individual characteristics affect the person's ability to influence others. For example, a leader's own skill will influence his or her ability as an expert and guide the behavior of subordinates by the use of expert power. Mainly, process approaches to leadership recognize the separate contributions of situational and individual factors as well as the interaction between the two as they impact on the influence process.

We view leadership in organizations as influence, exerted by individuals in leadership positions, that is not entirely determined by the position itself. Thus, ours is a process orientation. We limit our discussion to those in leadership positions. These positions may be identified from organization charts or may be positions within other organizations concerned with behavior in that organization. An example of the latter is a union steward. Although we recognize

that any number of individuals in a group may emerge and serve leadership functions, we shall ignore these possibilities in our discussion.

It should be noticed that we accept the incremental influence notion of Katz and Kahn (1978). That is, the degree of influence must be more than just applying standard operating procedures. Graen and his colleagues (Dansereau, Graen, & Haga 1975; Graen 1976) distinguish this quite clearly by differentiating leadership from supervision. Supervision is influencing subordinates to do nothing more than simply fulfill the minimum requirements of their jobs to avoid being fired. Leadership is influencing them to participate actively in the group's activities. Furthermore, leadership is knowing who within the workgroup needs merely to be supervised and who needs to be stretched beyond the minimum requirements of his or her job.

THEORIES OF LEADERSHIP

Many diverse theories of leadership have been presented over the years. Most of these theories can be grouped into three categories based upon the primary emphasis of the theory. In this section, we shall address each of the three major orientations. These are labeled *trait, behavior,* and *situational moderator* theories.

Trait Theories

Systematic research on leadership often has been focused on the leader's personal traits or characteristics. Explanations of leader effectiveness were thought to be his or her aggressiveness, intelligence, or other personal characteristics such as age or physical attractiveness. The typical research strategy measured personal characteristics, then correlated them with evaluations of leader effectiveness.

Although a large number of studies were

made to discover the traits that distinguished leaders from nonleaders and good leaders from bad, the results were rather disappointing. No traits clearly identified leaders, especially effective ones. In general, leaders tended to be somewhat stronger than nonleaders in such characteristics as intelligence, social skills, or task skills, but the differences were small and the number of nonleaders who had the same characteristics was large. As a result several reviews of leadership by the mid-1950s (for example, Gibb 1954) concluded that there was little reason to pursue leader traits.

Opinion has changed somewhat in the past few years. Reviews directed at managerial positions in organizations have offered some hope for trait concerns (Campbell,

Dunnette, Lawler, & Weick 1970; Stogdill 1974). This change can be credited to at least two factors. First, Ghiselli (1971) demonstrated that through careful consideration of a specific leadership position— that of manager in formal work organizations—a set of relevant traits can be identified and measured which relate to managerial effectiveness. Figure 15.1 describes several of the traits and their relationship to managerial success in a national sample of managers. Some similar traits also were identified as important by Campbell and others, 1970.

A reconsideration of the information gained by understanding leader traits also may have influenced the tendency to evaluate trait theories more carefully. Although it is true that traits do not show extremely

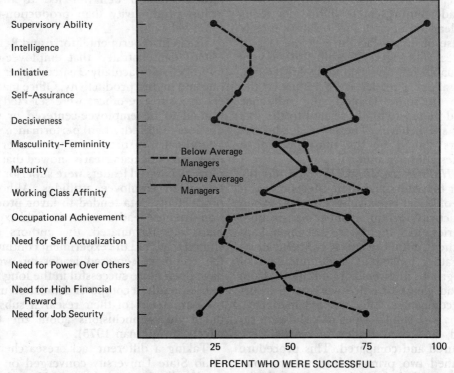

FIG. 15.1 Mean Scores for Managers High or Low on Job Success Across the Thirteen Traits Measured By Ghiselli's Self-Description Inventory (Adapted from Figures 2, 6, & 10 in Ghiselli 1971). (N in each group equals approximately 122.)

strong associations with managerial effectiveness, given the high degree of importance of many managerial jobs to the effectiveness of the organization, even modest relationships between managerial traits and success can be useful. From this standpoint, smaller degrees of association between the trait or construct under consideration and effectiveness can be tolerated as the importance of being effective increases. Therefore, it is safe to conclude that, although leadership traits are not strongly associated with leader effectiveness, some generalizations can be made about a number of traits and can be useful for understanding and identifying leaders, particularly for managerial jobs.

Behavior Theories

Leadership research shifted its focus from leader traits to leader behavior mostly because of dissatisfaction with the lack of progress with traits. This shift also was very reasonable for understanding leadership. After all, if a leader is to influence the group in some fashion, the influence should be most closely related to the way he or she behaves. Therefore, leader behaviors should be the most immediate manifestations of influence.

BEHAVIOR DIMENSIONS. To identify leader behaviors and their effects on measures of leader effectiveness, such as group productivity, group member satisfaction, and grievances, there were two general approaches. At the University of Michigan investigators looked at large numbers of work groups in diverse organizations, from railroad gangs to office workers in insurance companies. Effective and ineffective groups with similar types of tasks were selected, and then leader behaviors were measured and compared. This procedure identified two primary leader behaviors. One was labeled employee-centered, the other, production-centered supervision. The former covered behaviors directed to-ward the social and emotional needs of group members, whereas the latter were behaviors directed toward task accomplishment. Although the early work tended to see these two as dependent, in the sense that leaders who were strong in one should be weak on the other, later work recognized that the two dimensions were relatively independent.

When the behaviors were related to group performance, there was clear support for the belief that employee-centered behaviors led to improved social and emotional responses. For example, leaders strong in this dimension usually had more satisfied group members than leaders weak in this dimension. Although somewhat less clear, the Michigan research also supported the human relations position that employee-centered behavior led to higher group productivity than production-centered behavior.

In a field experiment, Morse and Reimer (1956) demonstrated that employee-centered behavior actually created higher morale and higher productivity. Office managers in insurance offices were selected and trained to be employee-centered or production-centered; then performance and attitudinal measures were taken over the next year. The data clearly showed that employee-centered leaders were superior with regard to employee attitudes. Although productivity data tended to favor production-oriented leaders when the field experiment was terminated, the authors concluded that, had the experiment continued, the employee-centered leadership would have been more successful in the long run. Subsequently, a computer simulation using the parameters of their research substantiated their conclusions about the time effects (Brightman 1975).

Taking a different tack, researchers at Ohio State University converged on two very similar leader behaviors. Here the focus was on developing an instrument to measure leader behavior with relatively independent dimensions of leader behavior when the scale was subjected to factor analyses. There were two scales. One asked group members to describe leader behaviors (the Leader Behavior Description Questionnaire, LBDQ) and the other had leaders describe their own behavior (the Leader Opinion Questionnaire, LOQ).[1]

Two relatively independent dimensions of leader behavior emerged, labeled Initiation of Structure and Consideration. Table 15.1 lists the items that describe each. It is obvious from these that they describe behaviors very similar to those found by the University of Michigan group. Subsequent research from a variety of perspectives

[1]Actually there were two versions of the LBDQ. See Halpin & Winer 1957, Fleishman 1957, and Stogdill 1963, for descriptions of this work; and Fleishman 1973, Korman 1966, and Stogdill 1974, for evaluations of leadership as defined by the LBDQ.

tends to support the conclusion that leader behaviors can be categorized into two major classes, one for social-emotional behaviors, the other for task-related ones.

Unlike the Michigan research, conclusions about the relationship of leader behavior to leader effectiveness were less clear. It was found that consideration was positively related to social-emotional factors, such as member satisfaction with the leader and the group, but its relationship to productivity was not consistent. Initiation of structure, on the other hand, was not consistently related to either social-emotional behavior or performance. Therefore, at this time, the best conclusion we can reach about leader behavior is that person-oriented behaviors usually are positively correlated with the social-emotional responses of subordinates, but whether person-oriented or production-oriented be-

TABLE 15.1 ITEMS FROM THE LEADER BEHAVIOR DESCRIPTION QUESTION-AIRE (FORM XII) USED TO DEFINE CONSIDERATION AND INITIATION OF STRUCTURE

Consideration Items
1. Is friendly and approachable.
2. Does little things to make it pleasant to be a member of the group.
3. Puts suggestions made by the group into operation.
4. Treats all group members as equals.
5. Gives advance notice of changes.
6. Keeps to himself or herself.
7. Looks out for the personal welfare of group members.
8. Is willing to make changes.
9. Refuses to explain actions. (Reverse scored)
10. Acts without consulting the group. (Reverse scored)

Initiation of Structure Items
1. Lets group members know what is expected of them.
2. Encourages the use of uniform procedures.
3. Tries out ideas on the group.
4. Makes attitude clear to the group.
5. Decides what will be done and how it shall be done.
6. Assigns group members to particular tasks.
7. Makes sure that role in the group is understood by the group members.
8. Schedules the work to be done.
9. Maintains definite standards of performance.
10. Asks that group members follow standard rules and regulations.

Source: The Leader Behavior Description Questionnaire is copyrighted by Ohio State University.

haviors are related more closely to other types of criteria of leader effectiveness depends on several other considerations. Some of these are addressed in the following section.

CONCERNS ABOUT LEADER BEHAVIORS. As researchers began to look closely at leader behavior and to conclude that there were two major dimensions of leader behavior, several reservations developed. First, it was obvious that there was no simple relationship between leader behavior and effectiveness other than that of consideration and social-emotional responses. It was apparent that there were no specific behaviors that were going to be best for all situations. Therefore, leadership research shifted from the behaviors to an attempt to discover the conditions under which certain leader behaviors were or were not effective. We shall discuss this issue more extensively later in the chapter.

Second, Schreisheim, House, and Kerr (1976) suggested that the inconsistent findings related to initiation of structure behavior may have been because the behavior was described by different items on different questionnaires. Three questionnaires had been used over the years to measure initiation of structure. Although the items on each were similar, there were some notable exceptions. In particular, the earliest measure contained items on punitive behaviors designed to persuade members to exert more effort, whereas later scales did not contain such items. In addition, later scales contained more items on organizing the leader's work and the work of others than earlier scales did. Schreisheim and others found that in considering these differences, several of the inconsistencies among findings from different research studies could be explained by the measures they used. Nevertheless, there still are many differences in conclusions about which behaviors are more effective.

A third issue is the direction of causality between leader behaviors and effectiveness. Up to now we have been assuming that when leader behaviors were related to group effectiveness, the behaviors caused effectiveness. Morse's and Reimer's (1956) field experiment demonstrated that leader behaviors can cause group responses. However, it is possible that the causal sequence may go the other way in many work settings. For example, consider that consideration behavior correlates positively with group performance in some settings. Perhaps, in these cases, the leader did not show consideration behaviors until the group was performing well. At that time the leader may have decided that he or she could afford to show more considerate behaviors. It is not possible to tell from field research whether a positive correlation between consideration and group performance is because leader behavior causes performance or the other way around.

Lowin and Craig (1969) in a laboratory experiment studied just this issue. They had leaders assigned to groups but manipulated the group's performance independent of what the leader did. They found that through these manipulations the group could cause leader behaviors which paralleled the findings in field settings. Therefore, although Lowin's and Craig's findings did not exclude the possibility that leader behavior affects group effectiveness, they did emphasize that the direction of causation may be reversed and that the interaction patterns between leaders and group members are complex, with the direction of influence going both ways.

Finally, the efficacy of reducing all leader behavior to two dimensions has been questioned. Bowers and Seashore (1962), for example, although recognizing that two factors can be used, suggested that a four-category system may be more useful. These four were supportive behavior, in which the leader addresses interpersonal, supportive matters in the group; goal emphasis, which stresses goal accomplishment; work facilitation, which is specific behavior designed to help subordinates with their particular tasks; and interaction facilitation, which is directed toward aiding interactions among group members as well as between group members and others in the organization. Hammer and Dachler (1975) went even farther. They suggested that the two major dimensions are so general that they do little to specify guidelines for leaders. For the latter, a much more particularistic behavior taxonomy is needed, which may vary from situation to situation.

The concerns about leader behaviors question the assumption of general behaviors effective in all situations. This we feel is legitimate. The researchers also found that much more particularistic behavior descriptions might be more useful to leaders. Yet, the concerns still lead to the conclusion that what a leader does (that is, how he or she behaves) is important and needs to be understood in order to improve leadership effectiveness and management in organizations. After a brief digression in the next section, we shall examine some current leadership approaches which maintain behavioral concerns while emphasizing situational influences on leadership.

AN APPLICATION OF LEADER BEHAVIORS. Blake and Mouton (1964, 1969) established an elaborate commercial program for training leaders based on the two leader dimensions. In their model, these are labeled *concern for people* and *concern for production.* They treated the two dimensions as independent and concluded that the most effective leaders in organizations are those strong in both dimensions.[2] Therefore, their program first assesses the current style of managers in the two-dimensional leader-behavior space (known

as the managerial grid) and then attempts to move them to the desired state of strong in both (cell 9, 9 in their two-dimensional grid with nine points for each dimension).

The procedure for accomplishing the training is an elaborate one that involves the entire managerial staff of the whole organization in a multistep, self-evaluation of their leadership styles. The program attempts to change participants in the direction suggested by the grid. The process is really a complete organizational development package of which the leadership training is a central part but certainly not the only part. Since contribution of the leadership portion is nested within the whole program, it is impossible to evaluate the effectiveness of the leadership training per se.

Situational Moderators of Leader Effectiveness

The evidence seems clear; the same leaders and/or the same leader behaviors are not equally effective in all situations. In some situations some people do better than others; likewise, certain behaviors are effective in some settings but not in others. With this realization, the task seems simple enough; all that is needed is a description of what works best under what conditions.

Unfortunately, the problem is not so simple. It is complex because there are no well-accepted taxonomies of situations. The only real standard for describing situations is that the classification scheme be useful for the purpose at hand. Within the area of leadership are several systems which are quite reasonable in their own right, yet quite different from each other. Furthermore, there has been no attempt to integrate all into a single system. Therefore, we have selected three approaches from among many. They were chosen because they represent a range of possible situational views and, to some extent, because of the current interest in them.

[2]Note we have already indicated that it is very unlikely that one style fits all situations. This conclusion opposes Blake's and Mouton's assumption.

THE CONTINGENCY MODEL. The contingency model of leadership, developed by Fred E. Fiedler (Fiedler 1964, 1967, 1971) is by far the best known model to explain situations. The model posits a motivational style for leaders, defines situations, and describes the relationship between different leadership styles and situations as they relate to the effectiveness of the group.

According to Fiedler (1972), leaders can be described as having one of two motivational orientations which create a leadership style for them. Some leaders are *task-oriented.* These leaders prefer to accomplish group goals by structuring and working with the task. Other leaders are *person-oriented.* For them, group goals are seen as best accomplished by working closely with the interpersonal relations in the group. Although these are very similar to the two behavior dimensions discussed earlier, there are two exceptions. First, the preferred style does not mean that the leader will use behaviors consistent with the preferred style. For example, a person-oriented leader may want to be considerate but may feel he or she needs to work with the task. Therefore, style and behavior are not the same. The second difference is that Fiedler feels that leader style is relatively permanent and unchanging. He would not advocate trying to change leader style.

Leader style is measured by the Least Preferred Coworker (LPC) scale. Respondents are asked to think of all the persons with whom they have worked, then to describe the person with whom they have had the most difficulty working. The scale contains bipolar adjectives such as "friendly . . . unfriendly" and "cooperative . . . uncooperative." Those who score high on the scale are said to have a relationship-oriented style (and are termed high LPC leaders), and those with low scores are described as having a task-oriented style (low LPC leaders).

Turning to the situation, the model focuses upon the extent to which it facilitates or inhibits the leader's ability to influence his or her subordinates. A single dimension is created, termed situational favorability, which is said to index the leader's ease of influence in a particular setting. It has three factors; (1) leader-member relations, (2) task structure, and (3) position power. Each of these is then dichotomized and combined so that good leader-member relations, a highly structured task and a position with great power define the most favorable conditions for influence and the opposite on all three, the least favorable. The top two-thirds of Figure 15.2 shows how the dimensions are combined by the model.

Figure 15.2 also illustrates how leader style relates to situational favorability. Based on a review of many studies in a variety of settings, such as high school basketball teams, voluntary church groups, tank crews, and supermarket employees, Fiedler (1964, 1967) concluded that low LPC leaders outperformed high LPC leaders in either very favorable or very unfavorable settings. High LPC leaders, on the other hand, were better in moderately difficult situations.

Since its introduction, the contingency model has generated considerable research and controversy. (See, for example, Ashour 1973; Evans & Dermer 1974; Graen, Alvarez, Orris, & Martella 1969; Korman 1973; Mitchell, Biglan, Onken, & Fiedler 1970.) Several are worth noting. First, there still is considerable doubt as to what is measured by the LPC scale. Fiedler's (1972) description of motivational orientation is interesting but lacks strong empirical support. Research that has concentrated exclusively on the LPC scale still has not provided definitive results (Evans & Dermer 1974; Mitchell 1969).

Also worth noting is that the relationship between leader style and situational favorability depicted in Figure 15. 2 often is not empirically demonstrated. Fiedler and his colleagues frequently attributed the lack of empirical support to some moderating variable such as the intelligence or experience of the leader. Others, such as Graen and others (1970), simply have doubted the validity of the model in accordance with the disconfirming data.

At present the issues are not resolved. The criticisms of the LPC measure and of the degree to which leaders and situations interact as the model says they do are well taken. Nevertheless, Fiedler made a significant contribution to the study of leadership by focusing attention on the leader-situation interaction and by attempting to describe that interaction. In addition, research using the LPC scale and the concepts of the model continues to find enough for further investigation.

AN APPLICATION OF THE CONTINGENCY MODEL. Recently Fiedler, Chemmers, and Maher (1976) advocated applying the model through a self-paced training program entitled *Leader Match.* The idea of the program is that, although leader style is relatively unchangeable, leaders can be trained to diagnose the situation and perhaps alter it to better fit their own style.

The training consists of a self-paced programmed learning text which presents the leader with a series of cases or incidents to which he or she responds by choosing from a set of alternative answers. If the correct answer is chosen, the individual advances to the next problem. Incorrect choices are explained, and the individual chooses again until correct. Before the presentation of incidents, the individual is presented with the notion of leadership styles and situational favorability according to the contingency model. In addition, the participant takes the LPC scale and scores it himself or herself. The purpose of the training is to teach the person how to diagnose situations and to alter them to fit leader styles in general and his or her own style in particular. This text takes three to four hours to complete.

In the one published study that used *Leader Match,* Csoka and Bons (1978) found that leaders trained with the manual outperformed those who did not have access to it. The differences in performance between trained and untrained leaders, although not large, was statistically significant and occurred in two independent samples. One was a laboratory sample and the other a field sample of West Point cadets who were assigned leadership positions in Army units for two to four weeks. Csoka and Bons noted that the group differences may have been due to factors other than the knowledge of the model,

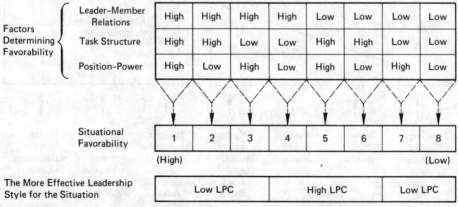

FIG. 15.2   The Relationship between Leadership Style and Situational Favorability According to the Contingency Model (Adapted from Fiedler 1967.)

such as an increase in self-confidence for those who had completed the training. Nevertheless, the differences that were found were sufficient to warrant further research and evaluation of *Leader Match*.

VROOM-YETTON MODEL. To Vroom and Yetton (1973), the most important aspect of leadership was the leader's actions related to distributing the decison-making functions within the group. As is illustrated in Figure 15.3, leaders have a number of options for distributing decision making in the group. According to Vroom and Yetton, which options they choose depend on several situational factors. Factors such as the amount of time that can be allowed to make the decision, the subordinates' knowledge of the issues, and the degree to which subordinates must be committed to the final decision all influence leaders' choice of decision-making strategies.

Vroom and Yetton emphasized that the proper choice of a decision-making strat-

egy is critical to two major components of leader effectiveness—the quality of actions reached from the decision and the degree to which subordinates are motivated to work toward the chosen course of action. To aid the leader in choosing decision strategies and thus improve his or her effectiveness, the model describes a series of conditions, then advocates one or several decision-making strategies that fall along the continuum of Figure 15.3. It is a normative model because the strategies prescribed for a given set of conditions are based on a compilation of research and practice prior to 1973. On the basis of the literature, Vroom and Yetton then concluded which decision-making procedure(s) was best for each setting.

The model is used to train leaders by asking them a series of questions about their own situation. The questions can be answered either yes or no, so the series represents a flow-chart with branches that

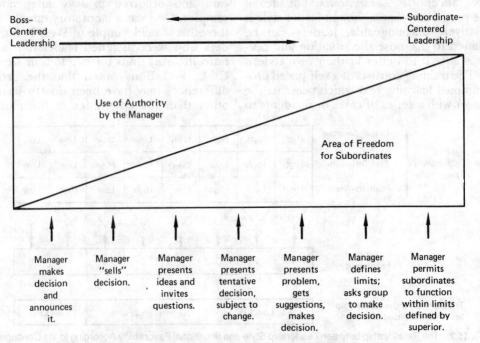

Boss-Centered Leadership ← → Subordinate-Centered Leadership

Use of Authority by the Manager

Area of Freedom for Subordinates

| Manager makes decision and announces it. | Manager "sells" decision. | Manager presents ideas and invites questions. | Manager presents tentative decision, subject to change. | Manager presents problem, gets suggestions, makes decision. | Manager defines limits; asks group to make decision. | Manager permits subordinates to function within limits defined by superior. |

FIG. 15.3 Possible Distributions of Decision-Making in Groups

eventually lead to a statement of which decision-making style should be best in their setting. In essence, the training's primary goal is to train leaders to diagnose their own leadership situation. If the diagnosis is correct (that is, diagnosed as the model says it should be), then the leader should know what decison-making style to use.

The model and its application are relatively new, so there are few data on which to judge either the model's validity or the training's effectiveness. What data do exist are on the model and not on the training. Vroom and Jago (1978) had ninety-six managers who were unaware of the model describe two actual problem-solving situations that they had encountered on their jobs. One problem was to be one in which they felt their handling of the problem had been effective, and one was to be an ineffective one. Once the managers had described the situations, they were trained on the model. They then reanalyzed the problems they had described in the first session, according to the model. The result was a set of problem descriptions in which the managers either did or did not do what the model recommended. In addition, the manager described his or her degree of success in each situation. It was argued that if the model really did describe the proper

way to make decisions, then when the managers' actions matched the model's prescribed set of actions, the actions should have been successful. When there was not a match, the actions should not have been successful. Table 15.2 supports this point of view.

The Vroom and Jago (1978) study has two major limitations. First, it would have provided more support for the model if it had been a predictive rather than a concurrent study. That is, a stronger test would have consisted of observations of actual behaviors followed by a waiting period in which actual behaviors would have been observed and evaluated. If the model is correct, the behaviors that fit the model should be the more successful ones. Second, by having managers code their own responses after they had been trained on the model, there may have been a tendency for them to bias their descriptions in favor of matching the model. Nevertheless, the data do offer an initial attempt at validation of the model and suggest that it does have some validity. Therefore, it definitely seems worth further exploration as a guide for training managers.

SUBORDINATE-FOCUSED SITUATIONAL MODELS. Our final set of approaches to leadership emphasizes the in

TABLE 15.2 THE FREQUENCY WITH WHICH DESCRIPTIONS OF SUCCESSFUL AND UNSUCCESSFUL ACTIONS BY MANAGERS AGREE WITH THE VROOM AND YETTON MODEL

		Degree of Agreement between the Manager's Course of Action and the Model's Recommended Course of Action	
		Agree	*Disagree*
Manager's judgment of	*Successful*	80	14
the quality of his/her	*Unsuccessful*	37	50
course of action		$x^2 = 34.00$	$p \leqslant .01$

(Adapted from Vroom & Jago 1978, Table 3, p. 115)

teraction between the leader and the situation by focusing on the subordinate as the key situational component. Two models have taken this perspective. They were labeled the *Path-Goal* model and the *Vertical Dyad Linkage* (VDL) model by their proponents.

The path-goal model of leadership concentrates on the leader's role in the motivation of his or her subordinates (Evans 1974; House 1971; House & Mitchell 1974). Leaders have a major impact on their subordinates' work goals and goal-directed performance through their management of positive and negative rewards for goal accomplishment and through their assignment of tasks to subordinates. Since within any workgroup, members have different desires and needs as well as different skills and abilities, leaders must be attuned to the differences among their group members to be able to influence and guide their behaviors most effectively.

House and Mitchell (1974) reviewed leadership research according to the path-goal model. Their review identified four general leadership styles or patterns of behaviors—(1) directive, (2) supportive, (3) achievement-oriented, and (4) participative. The styles then were seen to interact with situational characteristics defined as those characteristics that influence subordinate motivation. The two situational features were (1) the environment which affected the leader's freedom to assign tasks and give rewards, as well as the quality of the tasks he or she had to assign; and (2) subordinate individual characteristics, such as their needs. Leadership effectiveness, according to the model, is matching the proper style with the task requirements and individual needs of subordinates so that the subordinates will be motivated to facilitate accomplishment of group goals.

The Vertical Dyad Linkage Model, developed by Graen and his colleagues (Graen, Dansereau, & Minami 1972; Dansereau, Graen, & Haga 1974) also emphasized the individual subordinates. The VDL model confutes the commonly held belief that leaders should treat all their subordinates alike. According to VDL, leaders must form dyadic relationships between themselves and each of their subordinates. Leaders also must identify those subordinates who are capable of expanding their roles by sharing the decision-making and other leadership functions technically delegated to the leader. In one sense, these capable subordinates become informal assistants. Other subordinates who cannot or do not want expanded roles also must be identified by effective leaders. These individuals are assigned the more routine tasks of the group. The result is that the leader must tailor his or her responses according to subordinate capabilities and limitations, then must establish effective dyadic relationships with each so that two subgroups are formed. These are labeled "informal assistants" and "hired hands" in the VDL model.

Although the path-goal model emphasizes positive and negative rewards and the VDL model emphasizes task assignment, each model pertains to some extent to both rewards and task assignment, and therefore the two models are complimentary. Unlike Fiedler and Vroom and Yetton, individuals associated with situational models with the subordinate focus have not developed programs to train leaders. Nevertheless, the implications of the models are clear. Leaders must evaluate the needs and capabilities of their subordinates and then modify their own behaviors to meet those needs and abilities. This means that leaders will need to treat differentially individuals within their groups both in the subtasks they assign to them and in the positive and negative rewards they administer in response to each subordinate's behavior.

CONCLUSION

Leadership is one of the few topics in which there is a systematic flow in research and thought (Calder 1977). We have seen how an initial concern with leader traits shifted to the study of leader behaviors when there was little progress with traits. When behaviors were reliably identified and measured, but the relationship between the behaviors and leader effectiveness was unclear, the notion of an interaction between leader behaviors and situational conditions began to dominate thinking about leadership. Although there still are many questions about the impact of leaders on groups, much has been learned. Each of the three major emphases listed has contributed some guidelines for management practice. The work with managerial traits by Ghiselli demonstrated that mangers have some stable characteristics. These may not account for a large portion of the variance in managerial behavior, but given the great value of identifying managerial talent, knowledge of such personal characteristics can be useful for selecting and managing managerial staff.

The emphasis on leader behaviors and leadership situations has been useful training for leader behaviors and/or for skills in determining the requirements of various situations. Unfortunately, there still is a considerable lack of consensus on which leader behaviors are most important and on how leader situations should be viewed. We presented several points of view. All represent reasonable approaches; yet none has emerged as clearly superior. Nevertheless, with a few exceptions (for example, Calder 1977; Korman 1973), most would agree that there have been advances in our knowledge of the leader-situation interaction and that those in leadership positions must learn more about this interaction in order to improve leader effectiveness.

REFERENCES

ASHOUR, A. S. The contingency model of leadership effectiveness: An evaluation. *Organizational Behavior and Human Performance*, 1973, *9*, 339–355.

BLAKE, R. R., & MOUTON, J. S. *The managerial grid.* Houston: Gulf, 1964.

BLAKE, R. R., & MOUTON, J. S. *Building a dynamic corporation through grid organization development.* Reading, Mass.: Addison-Wesley, 1969.

BOWERS, D. G., & SEASHORE, S. E. Predicting organizational effectiveness with a four-factor theory of leadership. *Administrative Science Quarterly*, 1966, *11*, 238–263.

BRIGHTMAN, H. J. Leadership style and worker interpersonal orientation: A computer simulation study. *Organizational Behavior and Human Performance*, 1975, *14*, 91–122.

CALDER, B. J. An attribution theory of leadership. In B. M. Staw & G. R. Salancik (Eds.), *New directions in organizational behavior.* Chicago: St. Clair Press, 1977.

CAMPBELL, J. P., DUNNETTE, M. D., LAWLER, E. E., III, & WEICK, K. E. *Managerial behavior, performance, and effectiveness.* New York: McGraw-Hill, 1970.

CSOKA, L. S., & BONS, P. M. Manipulating the situation to fit the leader's style: Two validation studies of leader match. *Journal of Applied Psychology*, 1978, *63*, 295–300.

DANSEREAU, F., JR., GRAEN, G. B., & HAGA, W. J. A vertical dyad linkage approach to leadership within formal organizations: A longitudinal investigation of the role-making process. *Organizational Behavior and Human Performance*, 1975, *13*, 46–78.

EVANS, M. G. Extensions of a path goal theory of leadership. *Journal of Applied Psychology*, 1974, *59*, 172–178.

EVANS, M. G., & DERMER, J. What does the least preferred co-worker scale really measure? *Journal of Applied Psychology,* 1974, *59,* 202–206.

FIEDLER, F. E. A contingency model of leadership effectiveness. In L. Berkowitz (Ed.), *Advances in experimental social psychology* (Vol. 1). New York: Academic Press, 1964.

FIEDLER, F. E. *A theory of leader effectiveness.* New York: McGraw-Hill, 1967.

FIEDLER, F. E. Validation and extension of the contingency model of leadership effectiveness: A review of empirical findings. *Psychological Bulletin,* 1971, *76,* 128–148.

FIEDLER, F. E. Personality, motivational systems, and behavior of high and low LPC persons. *Human relations,* 1972, *25,* 391–412.

FIEDLER, F. E., CHEMMERS, M. M., & MAHER, L. L. *Improving leadership effectiveness: The leader match concept.* New York: Wiley, 1976.

FLEISHMAN, E. A. The leader opinion questionnaire. In R. M. Stogdill & A. E. Coons (Eds.), *Leader behavior: Its description and measurement.* Columbus: Bureau of Business Research, Ohio State University, 1957.

FLEISHMAN, E. A. Twenty years of consideration and structure. In E. A. Fleishman & J. G. Hunt (Eds.), *Current developments in the study of leadership.* Carbondale: Southern Illinois University Press, 1973.

FRENCH, W. L. *The personnel management process.* Fourth Edition. Boston: Houghton Mifflin Co., 1978.

GHISELLI, E. E. *Explorations in managerial talent.* Pacific Palisades, Calif.: Goodyear, 1971.

GIBB, C. A. Leadership. In G. Lindzey (Ed.), *Handbook of social psychology* (Vol.

2). Reading, Mass.: Addison-Wesley, 1954, pp. 877–920.

GRAEN, G. B. Role-making processes within complex organizations. In M. D. Dunnette (Ed.), *Handbook of industrial and organizational psychology.* Chicago: Rand McNally, 1976, pp. 1201–1248.

GRAEN, G. B., ALVAREZ K., ORRIS, J. B., & MARTELLA, J. A. Contingency model of leadership effectiveness: Antecedent and evidential results. *Psychological Bulletin,* 1969, *74,* 285–296.

GRAEN, G. B., DANSEREAU, F., & MINAMI, R. Dysfunctional leadership styles. *Organizational Behavior and Human Performance,* 1972, *7,* 216–236.

HALPIN, A. W., & WINER, B. J. A factorial study of leader behavior descriptions. In R. M. Stogdill & A. E. Coons (Eds.), *Leader behavior: Its description and measurement.* Columbus: Bureau of Business Research, Ohio State University, 1957.

HAMMER, T. H. & DACHLER, H. P. A test of some assumptions underlying the path goal model of supervision: some suggested conceptual modifications. *Organizational Behavior and Human Performance,* 1975, *14,* 60–75.

HOUSE, R. J. A path-goal theory of leader effectiveness. *Administrative Science Quarterly,* 1971, *16,* 321–338.

HOUSE, R. J., & MITCHELL, T. R. Path-goal theory of leadership. *Journal of Contemporary Business,* Autumn 1974, *3,* 81–97.

KATZ, D., & KAHN, R. L. *The social psychology of organizations* (2nd ed.). New York: Wiley, 1978.

KORMAN, A. K. Consideration, initiation of structure, and organizational criteria—A review. *Personnel Psychology,* 1966, *19,* 349–361.

KORMAN, A. K. On the development of contingency theories of leadership: Some methodological considerations and a possible alternative. *Journal of Applied Psychology*, 1973, *58*, 384–387.

LIKERT, R. *New patterns of management.* New York: McGraw-Hill, 1961.

LIKERT, R. *The human organization.* New York: McGraw-Hill, 1967.

LOWIN, A., & CRAIG, J. R. The influences of level of performance on managerial style: An experimental object-lesson in the ambiguity of correlational data. *Organizational Behavior and Human Performance*, 1968, *3*, 440–458.

MITCHELL, T. R., BIGLAN, A., ONKEN, G. R., & FIEDLER, F. E. The contingency model: Criticism and suggestions. *Academy of Management Journal*, 1970, *13*, 253–268.

MORSE, N. C., & REIMER, E. The experimental change of a major organizational variable. *Journal of Abnormal and Social Psychology*, 1956, *52*,, 120–129.

SCHREISHEIM, C. A., HOUSE, R. J., & KERR, S. Leader initiating structure: A reconciliation of discrepant research results and some empirical tests. *Organizational Behavior and Human Performance*, 1976, *15*, 297–321.

STOGDILL, R. M. *Manual for the leader behavior description questionnaire—Form XII.* Columbus: Bureau of Business Research, Ohio State University, 1963.

STOGDILL, R. M. *Handbook of leadership.* New York: Free Press, 1974.

TANNENBAUM, R., & SCHMIDT, W. H. How to choose a leadership pattern. *Harvard Business Review*, 1958, *36*, 95–101.

VROOM, V. H., & JAGO, A. On the validity of the Vroom-Yetton model. *Journal of Applied Psychology*, 1978, *63*, 151–162.

VROOM, V. H., & YETTON, P. W. *Leadership and decision-making.* Pittsburgh: University of Pittsburgh Press, 1973.

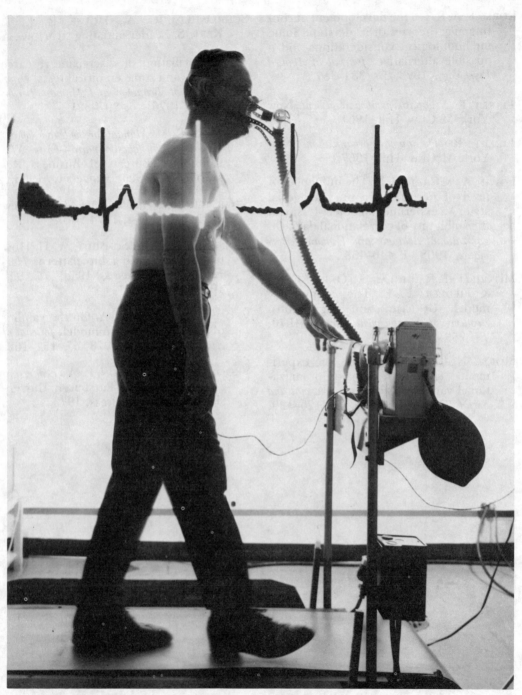

Measuring energy cost of activity. *(Courtesy Eastman Kodak Company)*

V

the job and work environment

For approximately forty hours a week an individual performs the work activities assigned in the working environment. In recent decades there has been increased interest in the "design" of the jobs people are expected to perform and the environments in which they are to work. For job design human factors and job enlargement approaches are used, which at times are at odds with each other. This part of the text studies these approaches as they relate to job design, along with the processes of job evaluation to establish wages and salary rates for jobs. In addition there are chapters on working conditions (including illumination, noise, atmospheric conditions, and work schedules) and on accidents and safety (which are integrally related to the job and working conditions).

16
human factors in job design

In large part this text is concerned with some of the factors that might affect job performance, job attendance, job satisfaction, and other criteria of human behavior in industry. In this context, we have discussed and illustrated the implications of individual differences and of certain social and organizational factors. Many pages ago we also explained that the specific nature of a job and the working conditions related to it also can influence such criteria, for better or for worse. To the extent that jobs and at least certain working conditions are created by people, they can be created so as to achieve certain possible advantages in terms of relevant criteria. But before touching further on these criteria, let us reflect for a moment on the processes or factors that influence the nature of jobs.

The nature of jobs—that is, their "content," methods, procedures, activities, and so forth—can be the consequence of any of

several influences, some intentional and others unintentional. It is true that over the centuries people have improved methods of doing work and improved tools and devices to carry out work activities. This has been essentially an *evolutionary* process, with succeeding generations benefitting from the experiences of past generations. It is probably only in this century, however, that *systematic* efforts have been made to change or to improve work methods, equipment, and environments—the factors that influence the nature of jobs. Such efforts sometimes are referred to as job design.

MAJOR APPROACHES TO JOB DESIGN

In the twentieth century there have been three major types of efforts that have had some impact on the nature of jobs and that can be viewed as approaches to job design. Although these approaches overlap each other, each tended to emerge as a major influence on job design at a different time. These approaches are methods analysis, human factors, and job enlargement.

Methods Analysis

What has become known as methods analysis emerged from industrial engineering. The developments of industrial engineering during the early part of the century were dominated by Frederick W. Taylor (1903), who introduced time-study methods, and by Frank and Lillian Gilbreth (1921), who introduced motion study. These and related developments ultimately formed what is now commonly called methods analysis, focusing on the development of efficient work methods, thus having a significant impact on the nature of jobs.

Human Factors

The second effort that has had a major influence on job design is what is now commonly called human factors. It has also been called human engineering and human factors in engineering. In most other countries it is called ergonomics. This field is concerned generally with the design of physical equipment and facilities people use and the environments in which they work and live so they are more suitable for human use. Various disciplines are concerned with human factors, including engineering, architecture, industrial design, physiology, biology, anthropology, sociology, and psychology. The phase of human factors that is rooted in psychology is sometimes called engineering psychology. In 1974 the Society of Engineering Psychologists adopted a new statement of the purpose of engineering psychology as follows: "... to promote research, development, application, and evaluation of psychological principle relating human behavior to the characteristics, design, and use of the environments and systems within which human beings work and live...." This reflects a broadening of human factors from its earlier focus. The field received its first major impetus during World War II from problems in operating and maintaining complicated military equipment. Alluisi and Morgan (1976) trace the evolution of human factors from its original emphasis on military and man-machine systems to the present broad view concerned with the design, maintenance, operation, and improvement of all kinds of operating systems in which humans are components. Today the human factors field has relevance to the design of industrial equipment, transportation systems, communication systems, automobiles, health care systems, recreation, buildings, consumer products, and the general living environment.

Our particular interests in human factors in this text are in its implications in influencing the nature of jobs. Such influence arises from two sources: first from the design of the machines, tools, equipment, and other devices that are used by people in their jobs since their design features affect the work activity demands of jobs; and second from the manner in which such physical items are integrated into operational systems. The integration aspect (and in some instances the design aspect) frequently is carried out by industrial engineers using methods analysis techniques. Thus, to a considerable degree, the methods analysis approach of the industrial engineers and the human factors fields have merged, with many industrial engineers concentrating on both areas of application in job design.

Job Enlargement

The third major approach to job design is called job enlargement or job enrichment. This effort has some of its roots in the work of Herzberg and others (1959) as discussed in chapter 14. It will be recalled that, according to Herzberg's two-factor theory of job satisfaction, positive job satisfaction could occur only when the *job content* could provide intrinsic rewards, and that *job context* factors (even though fully adequate) could not be expected to produce satisfaction but only could avoid dissatisfaction. Although his work was concerned with job satisfaction (and the factors that might influence it), it was perhaps more the cultural climate that propelled the notion of job enlargement to public attention. In the 1960s and 1970s there were strong undercurrents of concern in the United States and in some other countries (especially in Europe) about the "dehumanization" of some work and the "quality of work life" that gave the major impetus to the job enlargement movement.

Discussion

The methods analysis and human factors approaches to job design often result in the simplification of work activities. The methods analysis approach in particular has resulted sometimes in highly specialized jobs such as typified by the automobile assembly line jobs. On the other hand, job enlargement has been aimed more at expanding jobs, thereby increasing job complexity, decision making, and responsibility. As McCormick points out (1976), these apparently opposite objectives in job design create a possible dilemma for those concerned with job design. However, the distinction between these apparently opposite directions is not nearly as clear-cut as it might at first appear. There is also a definite trend on the part of methods analysts and human factors personnel to recognize the importance of creating jobs that offer greater opportunities for job satisfaction to more

people. This is reflected, for example, by Corlett (1973), Swain (1973), Chapanis (1974), and Christensen (1973). The theme enunciated by these and others is that jobs should be designed to fulfill two objectives, those of efficiency and of providing, and greater opportunity for job satisfaction and general improvement in the quality of work life. It must be acknowledged, there have not been, as of now, many practical guidelines for designing jobs to fulfill these two objectives, although some are beginning to emerge.

In designing jobs one should know the importance of individual differences. One person's meat is another person's poison. There are indeed some individuals who thrive on jobs that would drive other people up the wall. Thus, job enlargement is not for everyone. It probably can be added that some people have prevailing attitudes that predispose them to react favorably—or unfavorably—to virtually any job situation. Thus, some people probably are allergic to virtually any kind of work and would find much to complain about, even about the best job in the world. In turn, others might react positively to virtually any job situation.

In summary, it must be recognized that a large piece of unfinished business for those concerned with job design is to develop realistic guidelines for creating jobs that fulfill the dual objectives of work efficiency and improvement in the quality of work life. Realizing that such guidelines must integrate methods analysis, human factors, and job enlargement, our discussion in this chapter will be largely on human factors (including some discussion of methods analysis), and the next chapter will be on job enlargement. The discussion of human factors will consist of an overview of that field, but we should keep in mind that the design of the physical equipment and facilities people use usually influences the nature of their jobs.

CRITERIA FOR EVALUATING
HUMAN FACTORS

In chapter 5 we discussed some of the criteria that may be pertinent to some aspects of industrial psychology. Of the types of criteria mentioned, those particularly relevant to evaluating human factors principles and data are performance criteria, physiological criteria, certain subjective criteria, and accident and injury criteria. (Accidents are discussed in chapter 20.) These types of criteria can be useful for comparing the appropriateness of one design of equipment to another, of one job design to another, of one set of working conditions to another, and of other job-related variables. Because of the significance of criteria for such purposes, let us take a minute to discuss them further.

Performance Criteria

Probably the most common type of criterion used for such purposes is some measure of performance, such as work output, time to complete some job activity, quality of performance, or performance decrement over time. In some circumstances, however, performance measures of more basic human processes, such as visual, motor, or mental performance, may be important. Such criteria generally are most relevant to research in performance measurement.

Physiological Criteria

Human work is accomplished by certain physiological processes. As a person performs work, especially physical work, there are various changes in his physiological condition. If the work is taxing enough or long enough, an individual's physical ability to perform the task deteriorates. The energy used in any muscular task comes from potential energy stored in chemical form in the muscles. As this energy is expended, the muscles become less and less able to perform their task. This reduction in potential energy available in the muscles is caused by two processes: (1) the consumption, during muscle activity, of the contractile material or the substances available to supply potential energy to this material; and (2) the accumulation of the waste products of muscle contraction, especially lactic acid; such waste products are the chemical result of muscle activity.

Muscle activity triggers, directly or indirectly, quite an assortment of physiological reactions, each of which can be considered an index of the muscle activity itself. These include changes in heart rate, energy expenditure, blood pressure, oxygen consumption, breathing rate, blood composition, and electrical resistance of the skin. The heart rate recovery curve is a particularly good example of a physiological criterion. This measure, which has been used especially by Brouha (1960) in some of his research, is obtained by counting the pulse rate at one-minute intervals during the first three minutes of the recovery period after terminating work and while the subject is sitting quietly. The curve based on such readings indicates the actual value of the pulse and the rate of recovery toward resting level. Figure 16.1 shows the heart rate recovery curves resulting from one, two, and three repetitions of a strenuous physical operation. The differences in the levels of these curves indicate differences in the physiological stress of performing the operation once, twice, and three times.

Energy expenditure of the total organism frequently is measured in terms of kilocalories per minute (kcal/min). Some examples of this measure for various work activities are given below (McCormick 1976, p. 173).

Activity	kcal/min
Light assembly	1.6

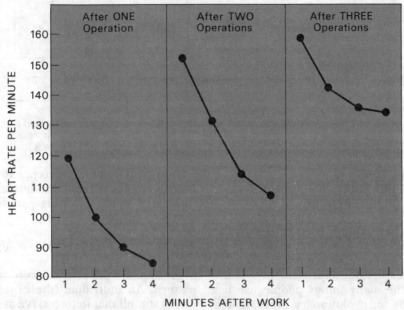

FIG. 16.1 Change in heart rate recovery curves after one, two, and three repetitions of a strenuous physical operation. (*From Brouha 1960, p. 91.*)

Brick laying	4.0
Sawing	6.8
Lawn mowing	7.7
Chopping down a tree	8.0
Stoking furnace	10.2

Edholm (1967) suggested that work loads preferably should be kept below about 2000 kcal/day (per eight-hour day), this being equivalent to an average of about 4.2 kcal/min.

For measuring the muscular effort in local muscle groups (as opposed to measuring total body energy expenditure), electromyographic recordings are sometimes used, those being recordings of the electrical output of the muscles. Khalil (1973) suggested that this technique lends itself quite well for use with industrial jobs. Examples of such recordings are shown in Figure 16.2, for four muscles of a subject while maintaining a constant torque of sixty foot pounds and of fifteen foot pounds. The difference in the recordings for these two work loads is quite evident.

Subjective Criteria

Work may be accompanied by some subjective (psychological) reactions to it. There are various dimensions of such reactions, such as boredom and job satisfaction. Job satisfaction was discussed in chapter 14 and is discussed further in chapter 17 on job enlargement. In the more restricted framework of human factors, other types of subjective responses are sometimes used as criteria, in particular expressions of opinions of various design features, such as expressions of preference for one design feature over others, judgments of design features, and expressions of comfort (as in seating design or temperature conditions).

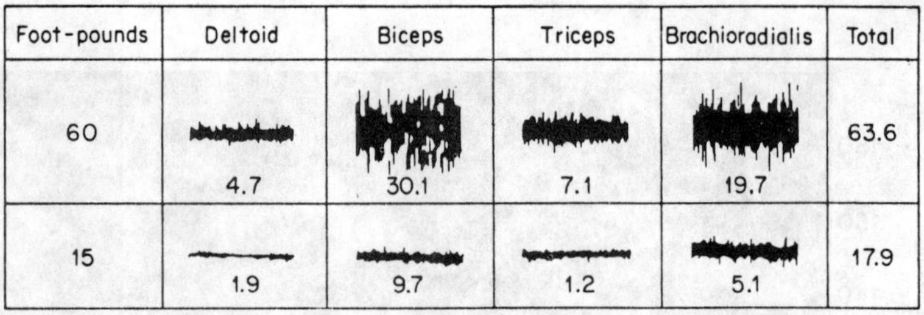

Foot-pounds	Deltoid	Biceps	Triceps	Brachioradialis	Total
60	4.7	30.1	7.1	19.7	63.6
15	1.9	9.7	1.2	5.1	17.9

FIG. 16.2 Electromyograms recorded for four muscles of a subject maintaining a constant torque of 60 ft-lb and of 15 ft-lb. The sum of the four values is an index of the total amount of energy expended. [Adapted from Khalil 1973, Figure 3.]

HUMAN FACTORS: BACKGROUND AND A FRAME OF REFERENCE*

People have always tried to design the things they use so they can use them more effectively and require minimum effort. As indicated earlier, the improvement over the years of the many things people use has been really an evolutionary process until recent times. This evolutionary process, however, has been predicated on trial and error and has become incompatible with the fast-moving technology of the recent decades. The development of complex equipment and systems has concentrated on the need to consider human factors early in designing such equipment and systems in order to ensure that they can be used effectively when they are produced. This has placed greater emphasis on the need for research to produce data that in turn can be used in designing items for human use. Although the entire human factors field has potential applications to virtually all of the man-made features of our world, including many aspects of our daily lives, our current interest in human factors is in its relevance to the design of the physical facilities people use in their work, and that therefore can influence the nature of the jobs people do.

*Readers interested in human factors are referred to McCormick, E. J., *Human factors in engineering and design.* New York: McGraw-Hill, 1976.

A helpful frame of reference for viewing human factors as related to human work is illustrated in the following paradigm:

S →O →R
(Stimulus) (Organism) (Response)

Many human work activities conform to this pattern: An individual (the organism) receives stimuli that in turn serve as the instigation of responses.

Using somewhat more operational terms, we can express this paradigm in terms of *information input, mediation* (that is, mental) *processes,* and *action processes.* A generalized schematic diagram of these functions is given in Figure 16.3. Consider, for example, an electric power station operator. He receives information from the instruments of his control panel, and on the basis of this information (and of what he has learned), he decides what to do and takes corresponding action, such as opening one switch and closing another.

Many of the stimuli that impinge on the organism come from the external environment and are sensed by the sense organs. But many of the stimuli that trigger human activity are generated internally, as the result of mediation processes (such as recalling that a particular chore is to be done at a particular time) or of physiological processes (such as hunger pangs).

The stimulus-organism-response frame of reference is useful in designing physical equipment, because it reminds us con-

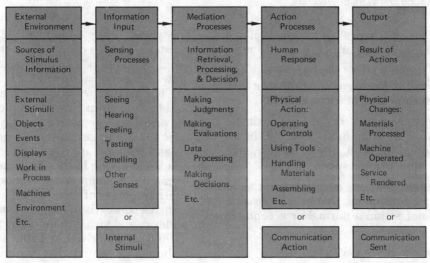

External Environment	Information Input	Mediation Processes	Action Processes	Output
Sources of Stimulus Information	Sensing Processes	Information Retrieval, Processing, & Decision	Human Response	Result of Actions
External Stimuli: Objects Events Displays Work in Process Machines Environment Etc.	Seeing Hearing Feeling Tasting Smelling Other Senses	Making Judgments Making Evaluations Data Processing Making Decisions Etc.	Physical Action: Operating Controls Using Tools Handling Materials Assembling Etc.	Physical Changes: Materials Processed Machine Operated Service Rendered Etc.
	or		or	or
	Internal Stimuli		Communication Action	Communication Sent

FIG. 16.3 Schematic diagram of basic functions of human beings in performing work and other activities. For each basic function a few examples are given in the lower part of the figure.

stantly of the three factors that must be considered in designing the features that will influence, for better or for worse, the effectiveness with which people can perform these basic functions. Thus, well designed road signs can help drivers receive the information they need, and well designed control mechanisms (the accelerator, brake, and steering mechanisms) can help drivers to control their vehicles better. Because this basic frame of reference is important to human factors, we will examine each of these aspects separately. Since we cannot cover each of these aspects thoroughly, we will use examples of research in these areas to illustrate how such research can provide guidelines for presenting data that can be applied to the design of the things people use in their jobs.

INFORMATION-INPUT PROCESSES

The sensory organs of the body are the avenues through which individuals receive information about their environment, including the information available in performing their jobs. We commonly think that there are five senses—seeing, hearing, touch, taste, and smell. There are, however, other senses, such as sensations of heat and cold, of body movement, of body posture, of position of body members (such as arms and legs), and probably some others not yet identified. Seeing and hearing are the senses used most frequently in work or in our everyday lives, although some of the other senses are important in certain specific circumstances. We sense many things in our environment directly, but in some circumstances information is presented *indirectly* by the use of some manmade *display,* such as the many types of visual instruments on control panels, machinery, and testing equipment; labels and instructions; blueprints and diagrams; hazard symbols and signs; and various sound signals like those from horns and bells.

Types and Uses of Displays

In general, displays can be described as either *static* (signs, printed material, labels, and so forth) or *dynamic* (speedometers, clocks, radios, and so forth). These can be used for different purposes—that is, to

343

present various "types" of information—of which the following are perhaps the most common:

Quantitative information, i.e., quantitative values such as weight, pressure, etc.

Qualitative information, i.e., the approximate value of some continuous variable, or an indication of its trend, rate of change, etc., such as approximate speed.

Check information, i.e., and indication as to whether a continuous changeable variable is or is not within a normal or acceptable range.

Alphanumeric or symbolic information.

Selection of Sensory Modality

In designing a display to present information to people, the designer *may* have a choice of the sensory modality to use, although in many circumstances the sensory modality is virtually predetermined by the nature of the case. When there is some option, there are two factors to consider—(1) the relative advantages of one sensory modality over another for the purpose at hand, and (2) the relative demands already made on the different senses.

The visual sense undoubtedly is used most extensively as a display input channel, followed by audition. The other senses are not now used very extensively for such purposes. The tactual sense is being used by some blind persons (for example, with Braille print) and seems to offer reasonable promise for use in circumstances in which vision and audition are overloaded. When there is some option in choosing one channel over another, some consideration of the relative advantages of each can aid in selection. Such a comparison has been made for the auditory and visual channels by Singleton (1969), and is given in Table 16.1.

It should be noted that the auditory channel is best for transmitting simple and short messages, whereas the visual channel can be used more effectively with complex and long messages.

Use of Coding in Displays

Displays present stimuli that in turn convey information indirectly to people. (For example, we can read an outdoor thermometer through the window without having to stick our head outside to find that the temperature is down around zero.) The stimuli presented by displays usually are in

TABLE 16.1 RELATIVE ADVANTAGES OF THE AUDITORY AND VISUAL SENSORY CHANNELS IN INFORMATION INPUT

Basis of Comparison	Auditory (Hearing)	Visual (Seeing)
Reception	Requires no directional search	Requires attention and location
Speed	Fast	Slowest
Order	Most easily retained	Easily lost
Urgency	Most easily incorporated	Difficult to incorporate
Noise	Not affected by visual noise	Not affected by auditory noise
Accepted symbolism	Melodious Linguistic	Pictorial Linguistic
Mobility	Most flexible	Some flexibility
Suitability	Dominantly time information For rhythmical data For warning signals	Dominantly space information For stored data For routine multichannel checking

Source: Singleton 1969, p. 525.

the form of codes that *represent* the basic information in question. In designing displays (that is, the stimuli), there are certain guidelines that must be followed and others that may be useful in some circumstances. These guidelines are given below (adapted from McCormick 1976).

DETECTABILITY. Any stimulus used in coding information *must* be detectable by the relevant sensory mechanism, like those in seeing, hearing, feeling, and the like.

DISCRIMINABILITY. In addition, every code symbol, even though detectable, needs to be discriminable from other symbols of the same class, such as different letters or numerals or different tones.

COMPATIBILITY. The notion of compatibility is discussed in a later section of this chapter but generally refers to one's expectations, such as the numbers on a clock face increasing in a clockwise direction. When relevant, stimuli used in displays should be compatible.

SYMBOLIC ASSOCIATION. This is a special case of compatibility, referring to the desirability (when relevant) of using stimuli that are symbolic representations of the basic information in question.

STANDARDIZATION. When coding systems are to be used by different people in different situations, it is desirable to use the same codes.

USE OF MULTIDIMENSIONAL CODES. In some circumstances two or more coding dimensions can be used, such as color and shape of signs.

Design Features of Displays

There has been considerable research on the effectiveness of various design features of displays in transmitting information. Although we will not summarize this research, a few examples will illustrate the nature of such research.

NUMERICAL VISUAL SCALES. Among the more common visual displays are those that represent some numerical scale, for use either in quantitative reading tasks (to determine the actual numerical value) or qualitative reading (to determine an approximate value, direction, or other variable). Some examples of such scales are shown in Figure 16.4. These include instruments with *moving pointers* and fixed scales and instruments with *moving scales* and fixed pointers. These designs are typically used for quantitative reading tasks but in some instances may also be used for qualitative reading or a combination of both. The features of these illustrations generally reflect acceptable design practice as based on research, particularly the preferable relationships of moving pointers with fixed scales and of moving scales with fixed pointers.

Research on these visual displays reflects the principle that such displays should be designed or selected for a specific purpose. For example, there are bits and pieces of evidence indicating that if the only purpose of a display is to obtain a quantitative value (*and* if the values do not fluctuate very much), a counter (that is, a digital display) usually is preferable. This was demonstrated, for example, by van Nes (1972) in an experiment with a conventional clock such as (a) in Figure 16.4 and a counter such as (i), in which the subjects were to rate time differences between pairs of displays of one type or the other. The following are the average times taken by ten subjects in performing the task, along with their errors, when using circular and counter displays:

	Average Time	Average Errors
Circular (clock) display	118 sec.	15%
Counter (digital) display	51 sec.	5%

Although the absolute values given are not meaningful if the details of the task are not known, the relative differences clearly show the superiority of the counter display in this general type of task.

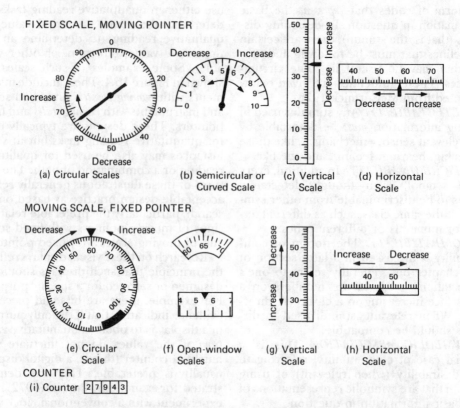

FIXED SCALE, MOVING POINTER

(a) Circular Scales

(b) Semicircular or Curved Scale

(c) Vertical Scale

(d) Horizontal Scale

MOVING SCALE, FIXED POINTER

(e) Circular Scale

(f) Open-window Scales

(g) Vertical Scale

(h) Horizontal Scale

COUNTER

(i) Counter | 2 | 7 | 9 | 4 | 3 |

FIG. 16.4 Some examples of visual displays that present numerical values. Such displays are typically used for quantitative reading tasks but in certain situations may also be used for qualitative reading tasks. (*Adapted from* Human factors in engineering and design (4th ed.), p. 68 by E. J. McCormick, Copyright © 1976 by McGraw-Hill, Inc. Used with permission of McGraw-Hill Book Company.)

SYMBOLIC DESIGNS. For some purposes, symbols are used as codes to represent various concepts. When symbols are so used it is preferable that they represent the concept as realistically as possible, as in the international road signs that include depictions of pedestrians, deer, bicycles, and the like. In some instances it is not possible to use a depiction of a concept, so we have to learn the association between a symbol and its meaning, such as a diagonal slash through a circle that indicates that entry is forbidden.

Easterby (1967, 1970) urged that, when feasible, symbols should have some direct association with what they symbolize and explained that the effective use of such displays is predicated on perceptual processes. In this regard he offered a number of principles from perceptual research that generally would enhance the use of such displays. Some of these principles are summarized below, and examples of their application to machine displays are shown in Figure 16.5.

Figure/ground. The important features of a display should be clearly discriminable from the "ground" (the background), as shown in (a) of Figure 16.5.

Figure boundary. A contrast boundary

346

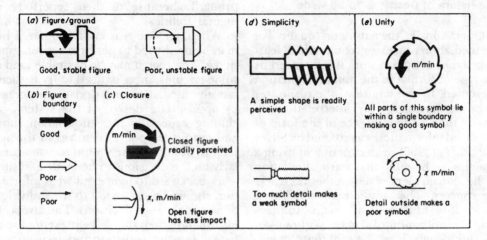

FIG. 16.5 Examples of certain perceptual principles relevant to the design of visual code symbols. These particular examples relate to codes used with machines. [Adapted from Easterby 1970, by McCormick 1976.]

(essentially a solid shape) is preferable to a line boundary, as illustrated in (b) of Figure 16.5.

Closure. An enclosed figure, such as shown in (c), usually is preferable to one not so enclosed, unless there is some particular reason for doing otherwise.

Simplicity. Symbols should be as simple as possible, as long as they include all essential features, as shown in (d).

Unity. Symbols should be as unified as possible. For example, when solid and outline figures are used together, the solid figure should be within the line outline figure, as shown in (e) of Figure 16.5.

Discussion

We have given only a few examples of design features of visual displays that could improve the reception of relevant information by workers, these features having been supported by behavioral research. As a generalization, however, it can be said that whenever job-related information is to be transmitted indirectly to workers, the likelihood of the information being received can be increased by improving the design of whatever man-made displays are to be used.

MEDIATION PROCESSES

As indicated earlier, nearly every human activity requires some mediation processes. The grist for these operations consists of input information and information retrieved from storage—that is, from memory. The nature of these mediation functions naturally varies with the situation but can include judgments and evaluations, reasoning, computations, and other mental operations. Whatever their nature, however, the end result usually is some decision or choice of action. It should be noted, however, that these mediation operations cannot be neatly differentiated from the preceding information input and the succeeding output (that is, response) functions. For example, the process of perception is inextricably intertwined with both sensation functions and mediation processes, because perception, as a psychological process, includes the attachment of meaning to that which is sensed.

347

The Nature of Decisions to be Made

Operationally, the nature or "quality" of the mediation processes required in at least some types of human work is influenced by the type or format of the input information presented, by the nature of the responses to be made, and by the interrelationship among them. The influence of the form of displayed information was studied by Silver and others (1966) in an experiment using a "gaming technique" that was a simulation of the management of a hypothetical trucking concern. The "traffic managers" used three different formats of "maps" in planning the utilization of trucks. Without going into details, it can be said that the efficiency of such utilization, as measured by mean "profit" per load, was significantly influenced by the format of the maps used.

Given certain informational input (stimuli), the mediation processes should lead to a decision which, when implemented by a human response, should produce the most appropriate end result (output). In repetitive operations the decision as to what to do is virtually predetermined, and the human response to a given stimulus is essentially a conditioned response. Such operations, of course, are best mechanized or automated; however, economic factors, the state of the art, or other considerations may argue for retaining human beings in some such operations. In less structured, less predictable circumstances, people's mental capacities are more effectively utilized. In fact, as pointed out by Singleton (1969), the reason for incorporating a human operator into a system is that certain required functions cannot be defined or predicted accurately. In a sense, the human being is needed most when there is an inherent uncertainty in or vagueness about the problem at hand, which requires indeterminate responses at indeterminate times. Although human beings certainly have their shortcomings (some more than others), they generally are more adaptable than machines, primarily because of their repertoire of mental abilities.

When, for one reason or another, a human being is used to perform a given function in a system, it may be desirable (and in some circumstances critical) to try to facilitate the mediation and decision processes by appropriate design of the system, including especially the information input and output (response) features of the system. In doing so, one should focus particularly on the decisions to be made and then work backward to figure out what information should be presented to the individual to help make such decisions. The displayed information then should be presented so as to facilitate the mediation and decision processes.

Facilitating Mediation Processes

We cannot here explore the various ways of facilitating the mediation functions in systems, but a couple of aspects will be discussed briefly as examples.

DECISION TIME. In fairly well structured job situations in which specific responses are to be made to specific stimuli, the decision time (or response time) is clearly a function of the number of possible alternatives. This was illustrated, for example, by Hilgendorf (1966) in an experiment with a key-punching task in which he examined the relationship between information input (as measured by the number of equally probable alternative stimuli which could occur) and response time (RT). The stimuli consisted of numerals, letters, and other typewriter symbols, and the subjects responded by activating corresponding keys on a specially prepared typewriter on which only specified sets of keys were displayed. There were six sets of stimuli and corresponding keys, these consisting of 2, 4, 10, 26, 100, and 1000 symbols.

The results, summarized in Figure 16.6, indicate that response time varied directly with the logarithm of the number of alternatives for values up to 1,000. This gener-

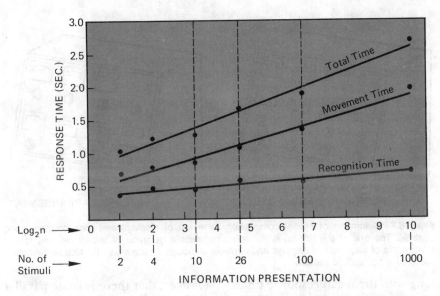

FIG. 16.6 Average response times plotted as a function of $\log_2 n$ (that is, the number of "bits" of information) and as the number of possible stimuli. (*Adapted from Hilgendorf 1966, FIG. 1.*)

ally confirmed the results of previous studies except that it extended the range of application to the larger number of one thousand alternatives. It should be noted that the total response time was made up of two values—*recognition time* (the time the subject took to identify the stimulus and raise his hand from a resting position) and *movement time* (the actual time taken to make the response).

The implications of such findings probably are particularly pertinent to circumstances in which a premium is placed on the time to choose, from among various possible reactions, the one that is specifically indicated. In such circumstances, a reduction of the number of possible actions (if feasible) would tend to bring about a more rapid response.

Compatibility

The concept of compatibility in the human factors field refers to the spatial, movement, or conceptual features of stimuli and responses, individually or in combination, which are most consistent with human expectations. It has been demonstrated time and again that the use of compatible relationships definitely improves human performance in terms of time, accuracy, and other criteria. Some examples will illustrate the concept.

SPATIAL COMPATIBILITY. Spatial compatibility refers to the compatibility of the physical features, or arrangement, of items such as displays and controls. Figure 16.7, for example, shows two arrangements of a set of eight displays and their corresponding controls. Of these two, the first is the more compatible because of the closer one-to-one relationship of each control to its corresponding display, although the second arrangement also is acceptable.

In one study of spatial compatibility, Chapanis and Mankin (1967) tried out ten different linkages between four displays (arranged in a square) and four controls (arranged vertically). The subject's task was to push the appropriate control button as soon as a light appeared in one of the displays. The ten linkages are shown in Figure

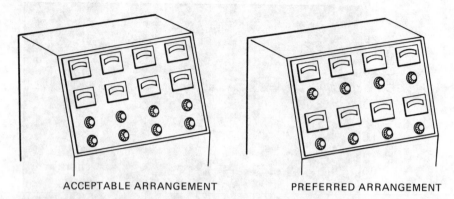

ACCEPTABLE ARRANGEMENT   PREFERRED ARRANGEMENT

FIG. 16.7 Illustration of spatial compatibility of a set of displays and their corresponding controls. The one at the left (a) is the more compatible because of the closer, one-to-one relationship of each pair of displays and controls, although arrangement (b) also represents a reasonably compatible pattern.

16.8, along with the mean response times. The first two or three arrangements are clearly the most compatible.

MOVEMENT COMPATIBILITY. There are several variants of movement compatibility, but they all pertain to the relationship between the direction of some physical movement (usually of a control device) and the direction of response of the system. Frequently the response of the system is shown by a display. It should be noted,

however, that there is some parallel to the chicken-and-egg conundrum here inasmuch as in some circumstances the control action is to correspond with some indication such as a display, whereas in others the indication reflects the consequence of the control action. In general, those linkages most consistent with human expectations result in superior human performance. Some examples of compatible control-display relationships are shown in Figure 16.9.

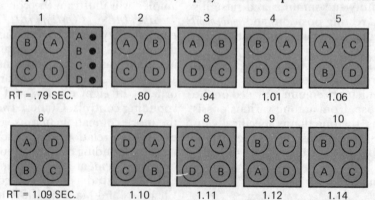

FIG. 16.8 Linkages of four displays and their corresponding controls used in study of spatial compatibility by Chapanis and Mankin. The mean reaction time (RT) for eight subjects (ninety-six trials for each) is shown for each linkage. The first shows the basic arrangement of the controls and displays (except that the displays were four inches in size within a thirty-inch panel); the remaining nine figures show only the variations in the display arrangements, since the control arrangement was always the same. (*Adapted from Chapanis & Mankin 1967.*)

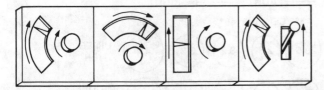

CONCEPTUAL COMPATIBILITY. Conceptual compatibility probably can be better illustrated than defined. Some examples are: the use of red for danger and the use of symbolic codes such as those illustrated in Figure 16.12, these particular examples dealing with control knobs.

Discussion

Not all mediation and decision processes are contingent on the design features of the physical things people use. But there are indeed some activities—including jobs—on which these processes are so contingent. When this is the case there should be efforts to create design features which facilitate these functions. Although some directions have been discussed briefly, such as taking advantage of compatibility relationships, reducing short-term memory demands, and so forth—there are also other avenues that will suggest themselves in specific circumstances.

ACTION PROCESSES

For a decision to be implemented, some action must be taken by the individual. This may be some physical action or a communication action. For our brief discussion here, we will be concerned with physical actions. In designing equipment and in developing methods, it is desirable to provide for those human physical actions and responses that will result in the desired output. This can be done through the design, location, and arrangement of control devices, by the use of tools and other devices, and through the methods established for carrying out work activities.

Psychomotor Skills

The human being is capable of performing a wide variety of psychomotor activities. Some of these were discussed in chapter 8. The relevance of the psychomotor skills of people to work and equipment design perhaps can be viewed from two frames of reference—(1) performance on variations of a given basic activity; and (2) individual differences in performance of a given activity.

VARIATIONS OF A GIVEN ACTIVITY. To optimize performance of some basic psychomotor activity, one can examine the efficiency of *variations* in that activity as related to *people in general.* Depending on the basic activity, variations may be related to parameters such as direction of movement or location of body members. A classic study by Fitts (1947) illustrated this. The study was on making "blind-positioning" movements such as reaching for a control device while not looking. The subjects were seated in an enclosure with targets arranged from left to right in three tiers, the middle tier being at approximately shoulder height, with the others being about forty-five degrees above and below. The subjects were blindfolded and were asked to use a marker in making movements to the various targets. They were scored on accuracy, with low scores indicating greater accuracy.

The results are shown in Figure 16.10. The size of each circle indicates the relative error-scores of the movements to the target at that particular location. The average error scores are given inside the circles. Figure 16.10 indicates that accuracy was greatest in the positions straight ahead and was

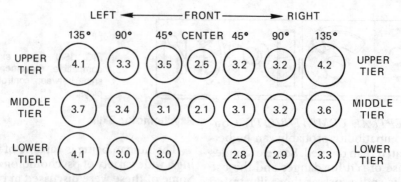

FIG. 16.10 Accuracy of blind-positioning movements in different directions. Each circle represents the location of a target (left to right and in upper, middle, and lower tiers). The average error-score for each target is given inside the circle, and the size of the circle is proportional to the error-score. (*Adapted from Fitts 1947, Courtesy Psychology Branch, Aero-Medical Laboratory.*)

least in the extreme side positions. For target level, the accuracy was greatest for the lowest tier and least for the highest tier.

The results of this and other studies of human performance on variations of a basic psychomotor activity naturally can have implications for equipment design and layout—in this particular instance in locating, say, control devices that might be used under blind-positioning conditions.

INDIVIDUAL DIFFERENCES IN PERFORMANCE. The second frame of reference in considering the human factors implications of psychomotor activities relates to the range of individual differences in performance on any *given* activity. Let us consider a hypothetical example. Suppose, according to the above discussion, a comparison has been made of the performance of people generally on the speed of activating a control mechanism in each of various locations and that the optimum location has been identified as a result. We might now consider the individual differences in speed of activating the device in that specific location. As a general practice, one should consider the level of performance of the *poorest* individuals who would be likely to use the facility—in general, perhaps the fifth percentile. The resulting design should be such that the performance of

such individuals would be satisfactory in terms of ultimate output. (If the system cannot be designed to be operable by such individuals, a program of careful personnel selection would be required to select those who would be superior in such performance.) One could apply this same general reasoning to situations requiring other kinds of psychomotor activities and to other kinds of criteria, such as strength, endurance, or accuracy.

Control Devices

Three points should be discussed with respect to the many types of control devices that we use, each of which can affect their use. These are: (1) correct identification, essentially a coding problem; (2) specific design features; and (3) location.

CODING OF CONTROL DEVICES. When a number of control devices of the same general class are to be used, mistakes may occur because of failure to distinguish one from another. Under such circumstances, some form of coding usually can reduce such errors. Different methods of coding can be used, such as shape, size, location, texture, and color. In coding control devices the same guidelines for coding of displays are applicable. For control de-

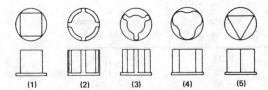

Scale in inches

vices, however, the tactile and kinaesthetic senses frequently are most important. The tactile sense is relevant to being able to discriminate individual controls from each other if they are to be used without visual control, and the kinaesthetic sense is relevant if people are to reach for controls in various locations without visual control.

For ability to discriminate among control knobs, Hunt (1953) experimented with various designs of three classes of knobs in order to identify those that could be identified accurately by touch alone. The subjects who tried to identify the various designs did so under conditions in which they could not see them. Examples of a few of the designs that could be accurately identified are shown in Figure 16.11, that particular figure showing the designs of so-called fractional rotation knobs (those that in use are not rotated beyond one full turn). In some circumstances knobs with symbolic associations can be used, such as those shown in Figure 16.12.

DESIGN FEATURES OF CONTROL DEVICES. There are many types of control devices, including cranks, handwheels, knobs, levers, pedals, push buttons, and se-lector switches. Recommendations of the suitability of various controls for different situations are given in other sources, such as the *Applied Ergonomics Handbook* (1974) and will not be repeated here. It should be noted, though, that variations in the design of any given type of control device can influence its effectiveness in actual use. For example, it has been found that hand-wheels should have diameters in the range of 7 to 21 inches, and that their maximum displacement usually should not be more than about 90° to 120° (McCormick 1976).

LOCATION OF CONTROL DEVICES. As an example of the effects of location of control devices on their use, we will draw upon the results of a study by Snyder (1976) on relative locations of the brake and accelerator in motor vehicles. In a mockup of a vehicle cab, three combinations of relative locations of the brake and accelerator were used, these characterized by the lateral and vertical separation between the two, as given below. The mean movement times from the accelerator to the brake also are given.

The mean movement times were least for conditions 2 and 3 in which the brake and accelerator were even with each other (zero vertical separation). Under emergency conditions the saving in time of even a few milliseconds in applying the brake could be important.

Tool Design

As an example of the application of human factors considerations to the design of tools, we will refer to the redesign of cutting pliers as reported by Yoder and others (1973). These pliers are used in cutting in-

LANDING FLAP | LANDING GEAR | FIRE EXTINGUISHER

FIG. 16.12 Illustration of shape-coded control knobs. Although they can be differentiated by touch, they also have symbolic association with their uses.

Condition	Lateral Separation (cm)	Vertical Separation (cm)	Mean Movement Time (msec)
1	6.35	5.08	202
2	10.16	.00	152
3	15.24	.00	168

jection-molded parts for boxes used in a pharmaceutical plant. With the conventional pliers the operators complained of muscle fatigue and a condition called wrist tenosynovitis, presumably caused by an angle at which the wrist was bent, as illustrated in Figure 16.13. The use of these pliers depended most on the third and fourth fingers of the hand. A redesigned pair of pliers is also shown in Figure 16.13, along with the cutting position when using it. On the basis of an electromyographic analysis it was found that the redesigned pliers utilized a greater portion of the muscles of all of the fingers (which, along with the wrist position, had caused the fatigue and tenosynovitis). Many other types of hand tools likewise could be redesigned in order to minimize physiological stress or to make them more efficient for human use.

WORK SPACE DESIGN

Fixed work stations should be so designed that the individuals can perform their tasks effectively, comfortably, and safely. Three of the major aspects of this design problem are concerned with the total work space, the arrangement of facilities and features of that work space, and the design of the seats individuals are to use.

Workspace Envelope

The workspace envelope can be viewed as a three-dimensional space around an in-

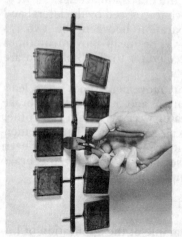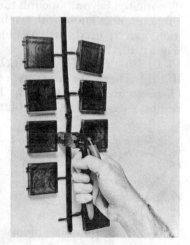

FIG. 16.13 Cutting pliers used in cutting parts for injection-molded plastic boxes. The original design (shown in use in *a*) caused fatigue and wrist tenosynovitis. The redesigned pliers (*b* and *c*) improved wrist posture and better distributed the work load across all the fingers, thus basically correcting the problem with the original design. (From Yoder and others 1973, Figures 7 & 8.)

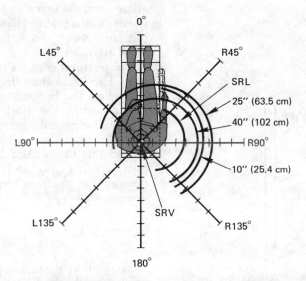

FIG. 16.14 Distances of reach of the fifth percentile of a sample of Air Force personnel in grasping a knob at various angles at the seat reference level (SRL) and at 10", 25", and 40" above the SRL. Such data can define the work space envelope within which most people can conveniently work. (Adapted from Kennedy 1964.)

dividual which can be used for the physical activities he will be expected to perform. For a seated individual this typically consists of whatever space he can reach conveniently by hand. Of course, this leads to the problem of individual differences, and the types of actions people are to take with their hands. An example of research relating to the workspace envelope is Kennedy's (1964). The subjects were presented with a vertical rack of measuring staves, each pointing toward the right shoulder and each with a knob on the end. Each subject grasped each rod between the thumb and forefinger and moved it out until the arm was fully extended without pulling the shoulder away from the back. This was done with the racks at 15° intervals around an imaginary vertical line, beginning at a seat reference point behind the subject. The distances for the fifth-percentile subjects are given in Figure 16.14 for three vertical levels, namely 10", 25" and 40" above the seat reference level and for the seat reference level (SAL).

Data like these can, of course, be used for creating the immediate work space for seated personnel. The fifth-percentile values frequently are used for setting the outer limits that individuals would be expected to reach, since those beyond the fifth percentile (95 percent of the population) would be able to reach the location that those of the fifth percentile can reach.

Arrangement of Facilities

When people use various things in their job (such as displays, controls, tools, materials, parts, and so forth) these usually should be arranged within the work space according to some guiding principle or principles, such as *importance* (putting the most important things where they are most easily used), *frequency of use, functional relationships,* or *sequence of use.* Figure 16.15, for example, illustrates the principle of functional relationships by clearly separating the displays and their corresponding controls into functional groups.

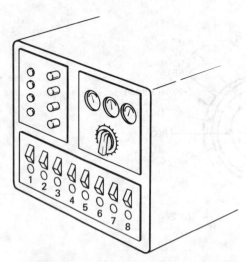

FIG. 16.15 Example of controls and displays grouped by function, in which the different groups are clearly indicated. (Adapted from McCormick 1976, Figure 11.12.)

Seating and Posture

For people who are seated at their work for extended periods of time, the type of seat provided can have an effect on comfort, physiological conditions, and work performance. This is a special concern to physical anthropologists. Based on research, various specifications have been made for seats for different situations. For our purposes, we will simply refer to certain aspects of seating to illustrate its relevance to the design of satisfactory work situations.

In most situations seats should be designed with the following guidelines in mind: the weight of the body should be borne primarily by the bony structure of the buttocks (the ischial tuberosities); the seat height should be such as to avoid pressure of the underside of the thigh (toward the front of the seat); the trunk should be stabilized (this can be facilitated by having the seat at an angle, and the back at an

angle); and the seat should make it possible for the individual to change or adjust posture to relieve discomfort or to change work activities.

For postural changes Mandal (1976) designed an office chair that tilts forward (to 15° below the horizontal) to improve the posture when the work activity requires that the individual lean forward (as over a desk). Incidentally, a sloping work surface also can be useful. Mandal's concept is illustrated in Figure 16.16, along with the posture that would be required with a conventional chair.

METHODS ANALYSIS

Methods analysis is in part aimed at improving methods of work. Amrine and others defined this field (that they call methods engineering) as "that body of knowledge concerned with the analysis of methods and the equipment used in performing a job, the design of an optimum method, and the standardization of the proposed method" (1975, p. 116).

Various techniques are used to analyze work activities toward accomplishing the objectives of methods analysis, including those that are called process charts, operation charts, man and machine charts, simocharts, and micro-motion study. We will not go into the details of these procedures, but the data resulting from them are used in developing improved methods of work. In this regard a number of principles of motion economy have been developed, most of these going back to Gilbreth's early work. These principles, as set forth by Amrine and others are as follows:

1. The movements of the two hands should be balanced and the two hands should begin and end their motions simultaneously.

2. The hands should be doing productive work and should not be idle at the same time except during rest periods.

Conventional chair with 5° backward inclination

Chair with tilting seat and inclining desk top

FIG. 16.16 Illustrations of postures required in a bent-forward position with a conventional office chair and with one with a forward-tilting seat and inclined desk top. (Adapted from Mandal 1976, Figures 10 & 11.)

3. Motions of the hands should be made in opposite and symmetrical directions and at the same time.

4. The work should be arranged to permit it to be performed with an easy and natural rhythm.

5. Momentum and ballistic-type movements should be employed wherever possible in order to reduce muscular effort.

6. There should be a definite location for all tools and materials, and they should be located in front of and close to the worker.

7. Bins or other devices should be used to deliver the materials close to the point of use.

8. The workplace should be designed to insure adequate illumination, proper workplace height, and provision for alternate standing and sitting by the operator.

9. Wherever possible, jigs, fixtures, or other mechanical devices should be used to relieve the hands of unnecessary work.

10. Tools should be pre-positioned wherever possible in order to facilitate grasping them. (1975, p. 130)

It is primarily by applying these principles that the results of methods and analysis are implemented. It should be added, however, that there are some questions about the generality of such principles for work improvement.

DISCUSSION

Although the human factors and methods analysis approaches to job design are viewed by some as being at odds with the objectives of job enlargement, we should not, on the basis of such assertions, conclude that there is an irreconcilable cleavage between these approaches to job design. Rather, we should view this as a challenge to the behavioral scientists and the industrial engineers to work toward developing integrated guidelines for job design that will fulfill the dual objectives of contributing to the efficient production of goods and services and of providing jobs that offer reasonable opportunities for people to gain some satisfaction from their work activities. In this chapter we have discussed the human factors and methods analysis approaches. The next chapter deals with the job enlargement approach.

REFERENCES

ALLUISI, E. A., & MORGAN B. B., JR. Engineering psychology and human performance. *Annual Review of Psychology,* 1976, *27,* pp. 305–330.

AMRINE, H. T., RITCHEY, J. A., & HULLEY, O. S. *Manufacturing organization and management.* Englewood Cliffs, N.J.: Prentice-Hall, 1975.

BROUHA, L. *Physiology in industry.* New York: Pergamon Press, 1960.

CHAPANIS, A. *What does ergonomics have to do with job satisfaction?* Paper presented at international symposium on ergonomics, Bucharest, Rumania, September 1974.

CHAPANIS, A., & MANKIN, D. A. Tests of ten control-display linkages. *Human Factors,* 1967, *9* (2), 119–126.

CHRISTENSON, J. M. *Limitless man.* Presidential address presented at the Annual meeting of the Division of Military Psychology, American Psychological Association, Montreal, Canada, September 1974.

CORLETT, E. N. Human factors in the design of manufacturing systems. *Human Factors,* 1973, *15* (2), 105–110.

EASTERBY, R. S. Perceptual organization in static displays for man/machine systems. *Ergonomics,* 1967, *10,* 195–205.

EASTERBY, R. S. The perception of symbols for machine displays. *Ergonomics,* 1970, *13,* 149–158.

EDHOLM, O. G. *The biology of work.* New York: World University Library, McGraw-Hill, 1967.

FITTS, P. M. A study of location discrimination ability. In P. M. Fitts (Ed.), *Psychological Research on Equipment Design.* Superintendent of Documents, USAF, Aviation Psychology Program, Research Report No. 19, 1947.

GILBRETH, F. B., & GILBRETH, L. M. First steps in finding the one best way to do work. Paper presented at the annual meeting of the American Society of Mechanical Engineers, New York, New York, December 5–9, 1921.

HERZBERG, F., MAUSNER, B., & SNYDERMAN, B. B. *The motivation to work.* New York: Wiley, 1959.

HILGENDORF, L. Information input and response time. *Ergonomics,* 1966, *9* (1), 31–37.

HUNT, D. P. *The coding of aircraft controls.* U.S. Air Force, Wright Air Development Center, Technical Report 53–221, August 1953.

KENNEDY, R. W. *Reach capability of the USAF population: Phase 1. The outer boundaries of grasping-reach envelopes for the shirt-sleeved seated operator.* U.S. Air Force, Aerospace Medical Research Laboratory, TDR 65–59, 1964.

KHALIL, T. M. An electromyographic methodology for the evaluation of industrial design. *Human Factors,* 1973, *15* (3), 257–264.

McCORMICK, E. J. Ergonomics: Future perspectives. Opening address at the annual convention of the Psychological Institute of the Republic of South Africa, Johannesburg, September 1975. *Perspectives in Industrial Psychology* (University of Stellenbosch), 1976, *2* (1), 1–27.

MANDAL, A. C. Work-chair and tilting seat. *Ergonomics,* 1976, *19* (2), 157–164.

SILVER, C. A., JONES, J. M., & LANDIS, D. Decision quality as a measure of visual display effectiveness. *Journal of Applied Psychology,* 1966, *50* (2), 109–113.

SINGLETON, W. T. Display design: Principles and procedures. *Ergonomics,* 1969, *12* (4), 519–531.

SWAIN,, A. D. Design of industrial jobs a

worker can and will do. *Human Factors,* 1973, *15* (2), 129–136.

SNYDER, H. L. Braking movement time and accelerator-brake separation. *Human Factors,* 1976, *18* (2), 201–204.

TAYLOR, F. W. Shop management. *Transactions of the American Society of Mechanical Engineers,* 1903, *XXIV,* pp. 1337–1481.

VAN NES, F. L. Determining temporal differences with analogue and digital time displays. *Ergonomics,* 1972, *15* (1), 73–79.

YODER, T. A., LUCAS, R. L., & BOTZUM, G. D. The marriage of human factors and safety in industry. *Human Factors,* 1973, *15* (3), 197–205.

17

job enlargement

Over the years, the application of methods analysis and human factors principles often led to the creation of jobs more and more limited in scope. That is, the jobs required fewer skills and abilities from the job-holder for successful performance. Technological advances also influenced the general trend. More highly automated production processes often demanded little from those whose jobs were associated with the automated process.

As the number of low-scope jobs expanded, so did the resistance to them. On the one hand, job simplification was criticized for failing to meet the same criterion (efficiency) that had led to limiting job scope in the first place. Frequently, as the jobs were simplified to the point at which almost anyone could perform them with little or no training, lack of involvement, boredom, and frustration lowered performance.

Job simplification also was criticized from a philosophical standpoint. It was argued that, since work occupied a major part of most people's lives, the dissatisfaction with work assumed to accompany simple jobs adversely affected the quality of life available to those with simple jobs.

Both criticisms attributed reactions to simple jobs to similar factors, and both recommended similar changes. In particular, both assumed a humanistic orientation. Humans were seen as needing to grow and develop throughout life. To do this it was necessary to provide opportunities for growth and development at work. Therefore, regardless of the initial reasons for questioning the design of jobs with limited scope, the suggested solutions were the same—increase the complexity of jobs.

Increasing job scope, that is job enlargement, is a motivational concern. This is in contrast to methods analyses and human factors analyses discussed in the previous chapter. These do not ignore motivation, but their emphasis is more on an individual's requisite skills, abilities, and capabilities. Job enlargement concentrates on motivational issues. In this chapter we shall describe and evaluate job enlargement principles and practices.

JOB ENLARGEMENT: A DEFINITION

Job enlargement has been used to describe the expansion of the number of duties and responsibilities associated with a particular job. This expansion can occur along two dimensions. One, frequently called "horizontal loading," increases the number of subtasks required in jobs without increasing their responsibility or complexity. For example, the job of cashier at a supermarket could be expanded horizontally by requiring the cashier to bag groceries as well as to operate the cash register and perhaps to require him or her to change prices on sale goods on the shelves when there were no customers checking out. Similarly, job enlargement using job rotation often represents horizontal loading. In this case, the cashier could check and bag groceries in the morning and price goods in the afternoon.

Jobs also can be enlarged vertically by expanding ability and skill requirements as well as the amount of responsibility and autonomy required from job-holders. Changes which require job-holders to complete more complex tasks, make decisions about various aspects of the work, and so forth, are vertical job enlargement.

The literature has tended to use job enlargement to refer to both vertical and horizontal changes. Recently the primary concern has been with vertical ones. Therefore, our use of job enlargement will refer to vertical job changes unless otherwise indicated. Job enlargement as used here is called job enrichment by many writers.

EARLY SUCCESSES

In the mid-1960s job enlargement received considerable attention from several highly publicized job redesign projects in some major American industries. Some of the most visible projects were at American Telegraph and Telephone (A.T.&T.) (Ford 1969) and Texas Instruments (TI) (Myers 1964, 1966; Weed 1971). For an example of the job enlargement research typical of that period, let us consider one of several projects at TI, as reported by Weed (1971).

Enlarging a Job at TI: An Example (from Weed 1971)

Before 1967, cleaning and janitorial services at Texas Instruments were performed by four contract cleaning companies. Three hundred-forty people were employed for this, and a company-developed rating scheme rated cleanliness at 65 percent, with 100 percent theoretically perfect. Turnover ranged from 100 percent to 400 percent, and the average education of the employees was lower than the third-grade level.

A decision was made to drop the contract service and develop an in-house staff to handle cleaning services. In setting up the new staff, the goal was to change several factors associated with the job. Specifically, it was decided to improve the cleaning technology and equipment, to improve selection and training of employees, to increase pay over 40 percent, and to increase the scope of the jobs to allow all individuals more control over planning their own activities and over their own behavior on the job. The focus of the project was on the latter issues, those involving job scope.

Weed (1971) reported that the program was very successful. Teams of cleaning services staff were given areas of responsibility and the freedom to design their own ways of doing the tasks. These teams took the responsibility and developed more efficient ways to do their jobs. Following the introduction of the program the cleanliness rating of the facilities improved from 65 percent to around 80 percent, turnover dropped to below 20 percent, and the total number of cleaning personnel dropped over 30 percent. Weed concluded that these changes demonstrated the strong effects of job enlargement.

Evaluation of Early Research

The TI study is typical of many of the early studies. Certainly very impressive changes accompanied the change in job scope. There was reason to believe that enlarging jobs may be very beneficial, but the support was not nearly as strong as the proponents advocated. This was because the job enlargement changes were always accompanied by many other changes. The TI study is a good example. True, the scope of the job was enlarged. Also however, pay was raised significantly, orientation programs were added, and selection improved as evidenced by the fact that the education level of employees was somewhat higher. Any of these factors either alone or in combination with the job enlargement may have caused the observed changes in cleanliness, turnover, and amount of work done. This study or the other studies could not conclude unequivocally that job enlargement improved satisfaction and performance. Nevertheless, the results were enticing, and the issue deserves further attention.

Besides the difficulty of isolating the job enlargement effect, early research was not very clear on what constituted a change that involved an increase in job scope. Most investigators used Herzberg's two-factor theory (Herzberg and others 1959) as the theoretical underpinning for selecting job-scope dimensions. Remember from our earlier discussions in chapters 13 and 14 that the theory considered motivators to

be those features of the job that were intrinsic to the work—recognition, achievement, responsibility, and the work itself. Therefore, increases in job scope attempted to vary one or more of these characteristics of the job.

Remember also that the two-factor theory itself was under considerable attack during this time; in fact, it had received little or no support. As a result job enlargement research was on the horns of a dilemma: desirable effects were found, but the theoretical foundation leading to the research in the first place was crumbling.

THE JOB CHARACTERISTICS MODEL

The void created by the collapse of the two-factor theory was filled by Hackman and his colleagues (Hackman & Lawler 1971; Hackman & Oldham 1975). A field study of job enlargement by Hackman and Lawler (1971) leaned heavily on the work of Turner and Lawrence (1965) and identified seven core dimensions of jobs. Of particular interest to job enlargement were the dimensions of variety, feedback, autonomy, and identity. The last is the extent to which the individual is allowed to complete some identifiable part of the task and therefore claim some responsibility for it. A field study obtained ratings of these dimensions by incumbents and outside investigators for 208 employees in thirteen jobs with an eastern telephone company. With some possible exceptions (feedback in particular), these dimensions correlated significantly with job satisfaction, performance, and withdrawal measures. Furthermore, higher order needs for achievement and growth moderated the observed correlations so that job-scope correlations with satisfaction and performance were stronger for those with greater higher order needs.

Hackman and Oldham (1976) refined and supplemented the concepts explored by Hackman and Lawler (1971). The result

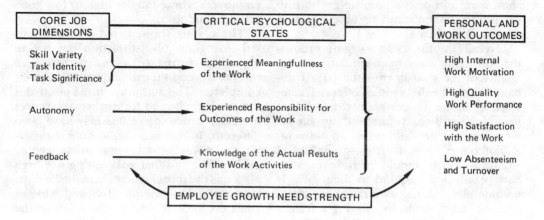

```
CORE JOB                          CRITICAL PSYCHOLOGICAL              PERSONAL AND
DIMENSIONS                               STATES                       WORK OUTCOMES

Skill Variety                                                         High Internal
Task Identity                     Experienced Meaningfullness         Work Motivation
Task Significance                 of the Work
                                                                      High Quality
                                                                      Work Performance
Autonomy                          Experienced Responsibility for
                                  Outcomes of the Work                High Satisfaction
                                                                      with the Work

Feedback                          Knowledge of the Actual Results     Low Absenteeism
                                  of the Work Activities              and Turnover

                        EMPLOYEE GROWTH NEED STRENGTH
```

FIG. 17.1. The job characteristics model of work motivation. (From Hackman & Oldham, 1976.)

was the model presented in Figure 17.1. In the model, five basic dimensions of jobs are identified which affect psychological states of the employee. These psychological states then act as the bases of various responses to the job. Finally, employee differences in "growth-need strength" moderate the links between the job and the psychological states as well as the psychological states and reactions to the job.

The five core dimensions are described as follows:

(1) *Skill Variety* is the degree to which the job requires a variety of different activities in carrying out the work. These activities vary in the number of *different* skills and talents of the individual needed on the job. Simply an increase in the number of activities without increasing skill demands is not sufficient to affect skill variety.

(2) *Task Identity* is the degree to which the job requires the completion of a whole unit of work. This unit of work should be obvious to the job holder so that he or she is aware of the unit and accepts credit or blame for its quality.

(3) *Task Significance* is the extent to which the job has a substantial impact on the lives and work of other people.

(4) *Autonomy* is the freedom the job holder has to schedule his or her activities on the job and

determine the procedures to be used to carry them out.

(5) *Feedback* is the degree to which the individual obtains direct and clear information about the effectiveness of his or her performance.

Besides describing the job dimensions and the psychological processes involved in them, Hackman and Oldham specified how the dimensions should be combined to establish a unidimensional measure of job scope. This dimension was termed the *Motivation Potential Score (MPS)* of a job and was defined as:

$$MPS = (\frac{SV+TI+TS}{3}) \times A \times F$$

in which

MPS = Motivational Potential Score
SV = Skill variety
TI = Task identity
TS = Task significance
A = Autonomy
F = Feedback

In order to test the theory, an instrument was developed to study jobs, called the Job Diagnostic Survey (JDS) (Hackman & Oldham 1975). This instrument or a short form of it was administered both to the job incumbents and to supervisors of the job incumbents.

Overall, the theory looks quite promising. Criticisms have been primarily of the quality of the instrument—the JDS (Dunham 1976). The theory itself offers a framework for future job design, recognizes that individuals will react differently to similar job characteristics, and posits an individual difference characteristic—growth-need strength—which should provide cues to how people will respond to their jobs. If nothing else, the theory already has made a major contribution by offering a framework within which to consider job enlargement. Before this such a framework was lacking.

RECENT JOB ENLARGEMENT RESEARCH

With a clearer conceptualization about what is meant by job scope from the job enlargement point of view, numerous research studies have been conducted. Katzell and his colleagues made an excellent summary and review of much of this work (See Katzell, Yankelovich, and others 1975; Katzell, Bienstock, & Faerstein 1977). Two studies not reviewed by Katzell are particularly worth noting, for one directly tested the Hackman and Oldham model, and the other illustrates some of the problems confronted when enlarging jobs.

An Experimental Simulation with Job Enlargement

Umstot, Bell, and Mitchell (1976) hired individuals to work for four days on a job of identifying and coding parcels of land with appropriate zoning codes. The job was one which had been subcontracted to the researchers by a county government in the Seattle area. The actual jobs for particular employees were constricted so as to be either high or low on MPS as defined by the Hackman and Oldham model. In addition

employees worked under high or low goal-setting conditions.

The results showed that enlarged jobs led to higher job satisfaction but not to higher performance when performance was measured in terms of quantity of items completed. The authors pointed out that if the job had allowed for quality differences in performance the results may have been different. It is interesting to note that performance was most strongly influenced by goal setting and that goal setting *and* high MPS was the most favorable condition. Furthermore, jobs low on MPS and without goals created conditions which led to the lowest level of performance. In sum, under well-controlled conditions job enlargement alone not only influenced employee satisfaction but also tended to interact with the performance goals to influence performance.

An Experimental Field Study in the Civil Service

Locke, Sirota, and Wolfson (1976) applied job enlargement in the headquarters of a large federal agency to a number of groups of employees in relatively low-level jobs. After extensive pretesting to diagnose how the jobs might be changed, agency supervisory personnel were instructed in the nature of the changes. Then specific changes were made in some units while control units were selected to which no change was introduced. Nearly eleven months were required to prepare to implement change.

Following the change the enlarged job groups and controls were observed and compared for seven months. The results are summarized in Table 17.1. On the surface there seemed to be strong support for job enlargement with the exception of attitude changes. Yet, Locke's and others' elaboration of these findings were instructive. First, they showed that much of the performance change probably was due to

TABLE 17.1 SUMMARY OF RESULTS OF JOB EN-
LARGEMENT EXPERIMENT

Measure	Group	
	Experimental Units	Control Units
Productivity	+23%	+2%
Absenteeism	−5%	+7%
Turnover	−6%	+20%
Complaints and disciplinary actions	0	4
Attitudes	no change	no change

*Source: Locke and others (1976). Copyright 1976 by
the American Psychological Association and copied by
permission.*

more efficient work procedures. The same
changes that led to a change for more responsibility led to better methods for doing
the job. Therefore, a by-product of job enlargement had a positive effect but could
not be credited to responsibility per se.

Second, the lack of any attitude differences was attributed to the fact that employees initially responded quite positively.
They also felt that if they were to do more
work they should be paid more and get promotions which reflected their new levels of
responsibility. Not receiving the extrinsic
rewards soon led to disappointment and
even lower attitudes than before the
change, by the time the study ended. This
effect has been observed by others or has
been avoided by increasing extrinsic rewards when jobs are enlarged, which supports the idea that simply enlarging the job
usually is not sufficient for improved responses to the job. These results also emphasize the complex interrelationships
among many facets of the job.

QUALIFYING CONDITIONS
FOR JOB ENLARGEMENT

Katzell, Yankelovich, and others (1975)
drew three conclusions from their review of
job design research, which emphasized job
scope issues. These conclusions are quite
appropriate to the work between 1975

and the present as well as to the work they
reviewed. First, in most cases enlarging
jobs does lead to higher levels of job satisfaction and other job attitudes. When the
predicted attitude shifts are not observed,
the result is no difference, rather than
lower attitudes for high scope than low
scope jobs. Seldom are there negative
effects unless other extraneous factors enter into the picture, such as raising levels of
expectations for pay without being able to
raise pay itself.

Their second conclusion was that the
performance changes in response to job
enlargement are equivocal. Sometimes
there are improvements and sometimes
there are not. In addition, many of the improvements may be simply because of better procedures rather than of increases in
motivation. Often work processes before
the job scope change are less efficient than
those used after the increase in job scope.

Their third conclusion was that the effectiveness of job enlargement is affected by
conditions in the job environment and by
the individuals who experience it. Clearly
job enlargement is not for all people, nor is
it appropriate to all situations. Therefore, it
behooves us to understand with whom and
under what conditions job enlargement is
effective. These issues now are addressed.

Individual Differences

The case for individual differences was
made early in the study of job enlargement
(Hulin 1971; Hulin & Blood 1968). Hulin
and Blood (1968) concluded from a review
of the literature that for those who identified with the Protestant work ethic, job enlargement led to greater satisfaction with
the job, but for those alienated from the
work ethic, it led to greater dissatisfaction.
This position has been slightly modified
since Hulin's and Blood's review with regard to higher order needs (Hackman &
Lawler 1971; Hackman & Oldham 1976;
Stone 1975). Those with strong higher or-

der needs (needs for esteem and self-actu-alization) respond favorably to job enlarge-ment, whereas those with low higher order needs do not. There is little evidence to indicate that the latter group becomes more dissatisfied on high scope jobs; they simply do not find such jobs more satisfy-ing (Stone 1976).

Skills and abilities of job holders moder-ate the use of job enlargement. Obviously one would not want to increase the scope of the job to such an extent that the job-hold-ers were unable to perform the new job effectively. In an interesting twist to this issue, Katz (1978) found that employees' responsiveness to challenging, unstruc-tured jobs varies according to the degree to which they feel they have adapted to the work setting. New employees who are at-tempting to "get their feet on the ground" prefer more structure and guidance. Once established, the preferences shift toward challenge and involvement.

Job Context Issues

The data seem clear that job enlarge-ment must take place in an environment in which other contextual factors are rela-tively well met. Oldham, Hackman, and Pierce (1976) took what might be termed a distractor view of job enlargement. They argued that only if other issues of pay, secu-rity, relationships with co-workers and su-pervisors, and so on, are quite well met will people become concerned with issues of job enlargement. The study by Locke and others (1976) of civil service jobs substan-tiated this position. Workers whose jobs were enlarged were initially satisfied but quickly became dissatisfied because they were receiving a very low level of pay and felt that for doing more demanding work they should receive higher pay. In the same vein, Fein (1973) felt that the positive effects observed from job enlargement may not have occurred in companies with long histories of labor strife and dissatisfaction before the introduction of job changes.

Non-Participating Groups

In some instances job redesign inadver-tently may have negative effects upon other employees who observe and/or interact with those on enlarged jobs (Katzell, Yan-kelovich, and others 1975). The most com-mon difficulty is with supervisors on rede-signed jobs, rather than on new jobs. In the former case, the jobs are often expanded by relegating some of the responsibility and decision-making power formerly held by the supervisor to the employees in the re-designed jobs. The result is a supervisor in a position described as responsible for the behavior of the employees under him or her but without the authority to influence the employees. These circumstances can be avoided when the enlarged job is a com-pletely new one, perhaps by eliminating one level of supervision.

Employees less directly involved with those on the enlarged jobs, other than their supervisors, may also be dissatisfied with the changes. Feelings of jealousy and of being left out of the action have been ob-served in some settings among those whose jobs were not involved.

Job Design: A Systems Perspective

These qualifying issues all point to a need for a systems perspective in the rede-sign of jobs with regard to job enlarge-ment. Changing one element of the orga-nization, in this case a job, is never done in isolation. The change is bound to have rip-pling effects felt in all those subsystems to which the job in question is interrelated. Therefore, if job enlargement is consid-ered, these other subsystems must be con-sidered in order to integrate effectively the change into the total system.

CONCLUSIONS

Redesigning jobs in order to enhance job scope can be effective, but careful consideration must be given to the process. Fortunately, it is an area for which a theoretical foundation has been established and for which there is a data base for guiding application. It is clear that sweeping changes in large numbers of jobs in order to meet social values related to the quality of working life and/or in order to increase productivity is not possible and, furthermore, probably not desirable given the differences in individuals' values and desires. Nevertheless, it is equally clear that there exists a sizable number of jobs that could be improved through some form of job enlargement in a way that would affect positively the individuals in those jobs. Our task is to identify these jobs and to consider such changes. Already there are some bases for these changes; yet more research is needed to understand the process better. Given the present level of interest in job enlargement, it seems likely that the needed research will follow.

REFERENCES

DUNHAM, R. B. The measurement and dimensionality of job characteristics. *Journal of Applied Psychology,* 1976, *61,* 404–409.

FEIN, M. The real needs and goals of blue collar workers. *The Conference Board Record,* February 1973, 26–33.

FORD, R. N. *Motivation through the work itself.* New York: American Management Association, 1969.

HACKMAN, J. R., & LAWLER, E. E., III. Employee reactions to job characteristics. *Journal of Applied Psychology,* 1971, *55,* 259–286. (Monograph)

HACKMAN, J. R., & OLDHAM, G. R. Development of the Job Diagnostic Survey. *Journal of Applied Psychology,* 1975, *60,* 159–170.

HACKMAN, J. R., & OLDHAM, G. R. Motivation through the design of work: Test of a theory. *Organizational Behavior and Human Performance,* 1976, *16,* 250–279.

HERZBERG, F., MAUSNER, B., & SNYDERMAN, B. *The motivation to work.* New York: Wiley, 1959.

HULIN, C. L. Individual differences and job enrichment—The case against general treatments. In J. R. Maher (Ed.), *New perspectives in job enrichment.* New York: Van Nostrand, 1971.

HULIN, C. L., & BLOOD, M. R. Job enlargement, individual differences and worker responses. *Psychological Bulletin,* 1968, *69,* 41–55.

KATZ, R. Job enrichment: Some career considerations. In J. van Maaner (Ed.), *Organizational Careers.* New York: Wiley, 1977.

KATZELL, R., BIENSTOCK, P., & FAERSTEIN, P. *A guide to worker productivity experiments in the United States 1971–1975.* New York: New York University Press, 1977.

KATZELL, R. A., & YANKELOVICH, D., with M. FEIN, O. A. ORNATI, & A. NASH, assisted by J. A. Berman, R. A. Deliberto, I. J. Morrow, & H. M. Weiss. *Work, productivity, and job satisfaction: An evaluation of policy-related research.* New York: Psychological Corporation, 1975.

LOCKE, E. A., SIROTA, D., & WOLFSON, A. D. An experimental case study of the successes and failures of job enrichment in a government agency. *Journal of Applied Psychology*, 1976, *61*, 701–711.

MYERS, M. S. Who are your motivated workers? *Harvard Business Review*, January–February 1964, *42*, 8–16.

MYERS, M. S. Conditions for manager motivation. *Harvard Business Review*, January–February 1966, *44*, 1–17.

OLDHAM, G. R., HACKMAN, J. R., & PIERCE, J. L. Conditions under which employees respond positively to enriched work. *Journal of Applied Psychology*, 1976, *61*, 395–403.

STONE, E. F. The moderating effect of work-related values on the job scope–job satisfaction relationship. *Organiza-*

tional Behavior and Human Performance, 1976, *15*, 147–167.

TURNER, A. H., & LAWRENCE, P. R. *Industrial jobs and the worker: An investigation of responses to task attributes.* Boston: Graduate School of Business Administration, Harvard University, 1965.

UMSTOT, D. D., BELL, C. H., Jr., & MITCHELL, T. R. Effects of job enrichment and task goals on satisfaction and productivity: Implications for job design. *Journal of Applied Psychology*, 1976, *61*, 379–394.

WEED, E. D. Job enrichment "cleans up" at Texas Instruments. In J. R. Maher (Ed.), *New perspectives in job enrichment.* New York: Van Nostrand Reinhold, 1971.

18
job evaluation

Although the motivation for people to work is indeed complex, we find virtually unanimous agreement that money is a dominant factor in such motivation. In the labor market individuals have certain potentialities, skills, or other qualities that they seek to "sell" to prospective employers. In turn, the intent of employing organizations is to offer wages that will attract personnel who can perform the available jobs. Thus, the proffered wages are intended to serve as an incentive to accept employment. But there is more to it than that. Lawler (1971) for example, stated that pay is typically thought of as performing a number of functions that contribute to organizational effectiveness; in particular, it serves as a reward to make employees satisfied with their jobs, to motivate them, to gain their commitment to the organization, and to keep them in the organization.

To meet these ends, pay, of course, must serve as an incentive that is perceived as fulfilling certain needs of individuals. In this regard it is obvious that for most people money does provide the wherewithall to keep body and soul together—in effect to fulfill what Maslow described as the individual's physiological needs. Its instrumentality for the satisfaction of other needs depends on the need in question. For example, Lawler indicated that it generally is perceived primarily as satisfying the need for esteem, secondarily as being instrumental in satisfying the autonomy and security needs, and being only marginal for satisfying the social and self-actualizing needs. In effect, he suggested that the importance of pay to any given individual is the combined effect of the importance of the various needs to the individual and the extent to which the individual perceives pay as being "instrumental" in satisfying those needs.

Granting that money is a very dominant

facet of the employment relationship, Opsahl and Dunnette (1966) remarked that we know amazingly little either about how money interacts with other factors or about how it acts individually to affect job performance of people—and, we might add, about how it causes people to accept or reject employment at given rates of pay.

Some of the motivational aspects of pay, including equity theory, were discussed in the chapter on motivation (chapter 13) and will not be repeated here. The primary purpose of this chapter is to discuss the process of job evaluation, which is the dominant procedure for establishing rates of pay for various jobs. Before getting into the different methods of job evaluation, however, we will touch briefly on legal matters relating to pay, different bases for paying people, and labor market influences on compensation.

LEGAL ASPECTS IN JOB COMPENSATION

There are certain laws in the United States on rates of pay for employed workers. The Fair Labor Standards Act, for example, sets minimum hourly wages for those covered by the act. Beginning January 1, 1978, the minimum rate for those covered by the act was $2.65, with provision for subsequent increments at specified dates. In turn, the Equal Pay Act of 1963 requires that there be "equal pay for equal" work, meaning that men and women are to be paid the same if they are doing "equal work." In particular, the act specifies that if work requires equal *skill, effort,* and *responsibility,* performed under similar *working conditions,* employees of both sexes must be paid the same. (It should be added, however, that the question as to what constitutes equal work is still open to question and probably to later legal clarification.) The Civil Rights Act of 1964 specifies in Title VII that it is unlawful for an employer to discriminate against individuals with regard to compensation (as well as with regard to hiring) because of race, sex, color, religion, or national origin. These acts establish the primary legal boundaries for establishing compensation practice in the United States.

BASES FOR COMPENSATION

There are different bases on which people are paid for their work, some of these being associated with certain specific types of jobs. The primary bases are as follows:

Salary. Salaries are paid to people for many types of jobs. Salaries can be specified by the week, month, or year.

Hourly wage rate. Hourly rates are commonly paid to workers in many blue-collar jobs, some office jobs, and certain other types of jobs.

Incentive pay. Workers in many jobs are paid in relation to their productivity, particular incentive systems ranging from simple piece rates to complex systems in which increasing productivity is rewarded by differing ratios.

Commission. Commissions are basically the same as incentive systems except that they apply largely to sales jobs.

Tips. In the case of some jobs, especially service jobs involving direct service to individuals, tips are a form of payment, in some instances over and above a basic salary or hourly rate, and in other instances as virtually the exclusive basis of earnings.

Other forms of compensation. There are certain other forms of compensation, usually supplementary, such as profit-sharing schemes and bonuses.

Regardless of the basis on which compensation for any given job is established, it is necessary to determine "how much" the job is to pay. In some organizations, especially small ones, the rates for specific jobs may be in terms of the "going rate" for the job in question (if the job exists in other organizations in the labor market). In many organizations, however, especially larger organizations, rates of pay are established by some type of job evaluation system. Such systems set pay rates for all the jobs to be covered using the same guidelines or factors.

WAGES AND THE LABOR MARKET

An organization obtains its employees from one or more labor markets. A labor market comprises that general pool of people who are prospective candidates for employment in some type of occupation. For example, the labor market for hourly paid and office jobs usually is the local community, whereas that for certain types of professional and managerial jobs may be regional or national in scope, comprising those who have the particular qualifications required, wherever they may be. Whatever the labor market in question, an organization that expects to obtain its employees from that market must be able to compete with other organizations in the market, and wage rates are one of the important bargaining ingredients.

The general wage level in any given labor market depends on a number of different factors. (We will use here the terms *wage* and *wage level* in a general sense, to include not only hourly wages but also salaries and other forms of financial compensation.) These factors include supply and demand, government wage controls, contract negotiations, general economic conditions (including the cost of living), general regional and industrial factors (wages are higher in certain regions or industries than in others), and productivity. In the long run, of course, "real" wages—that is, how much people can buy with their earnings—depend very much on the productivity of industry. It is only by increasing general productivity that the general level of real wages can be raised.

OBJECTIVES IN WAGE ADMINISTRATION

Let us now crystallize what appear to be the two dominant factors that an organization must take into consideration in establishing its wage administration policies. On the one hand, there is the organization's economic situation. Most organizations have continuing pressures for economy in their operations for economic survival and for profit, although these pressures differ in various organizations and industries. On the other hand, there is the competition of other organizations in the same labor market. An organization needs to be in a reasonably competitive position, with regard not only to wages as such but also to the "package" of related incentives if it is to be able to employ people in its labor market.

The labor market is not a vague, ethereal concept. Rather, it is comprised of live people with motivations and sets of values which are reflected—in the labor market—by their behavior in offering their services and accepting or rejecting employment under specified conditions.

This inescapable fact reminds us of our earlier discussion of equity theory in chapter 13. Granting some question about certain aspects of this theory, we can nonetheless see how individual members of the labor market might, in a general way, think in terms of an outcome/input ratio applied to themselves, based on their perceptions of the combination of the various types of outcomes and what they would put into the work situation. Further, we can see that individuals might view this "ratio" as applied to themselves in relationship to their perceptions of the corresponding factors as related to *others* in the labor market. Thus, individuals would be most likely to consider proferred employment as "equitable" if the perceived outcomes and inputs are reasonably in line with those of *others* in a similar line of work. (Of course, people probably tend to be more perceptive of in-equity of the "under-reward" variety than of the "over-reward" variety.)

Thus, we probably can say that the "go-ing rate" for a particular type of work is a very rough-and-ready reflection of the no-tion of "equity," in that it reflects the ap-proximate level of (at least) the financial "outcomes" for the typical "inputs" in the type of work in question. It thus provides individuals with a basis for their percep-tions of the outcome/input ratios of *other* people whose inputs into a job (that is, their job-related skills and other factors) might be comparable to their own.

The wage administration policy of an or-ganization, then, needs to provide for offer-ing wages that will attract and retain a com-petent work force (meaning, in effect, that the wages offered must be within the gen-eral range of going rates for similar work in the labor market), and at the same time it needs to keep its total wage payments rea-sonably in line with going rate levels in or-der to remain competitive in the sale of its products or services. In attempting to achieve these objectives, many organiza-tions use some type of job evaluation sys-tem. A job evaluation program provides a systematic basis for establishing compensa-tion rates for jobs so that they are in rea-sonable alignment with going rates for cor-responding jobs in the labor market. Most job evaluation systems incorporate system-atic procedures for deriving indices of rela-tive job values for the jobs within the orga-nization, usually on the basis of judgments of the jobs or of their characteristics. In turn, these indices are used as the basis for setting wage rates for the jobs covered by the system. Usually this conversion to wage rates is made on the basis of a wage survey to determine the going rates for a sample of jobs. The relationship for this sample of jobs between their job evaluation values and their going rates in the labor market

then serves as the basis for converting the job evaluation values of all the other jobs to wage rates.

INSTALLING A JOB EVALUATION SYSTEM

Although it is not appropriate here to go into the details of the development, instal-lation, and operation of a job evaluation program, let us at least get an overview of these processes, which typically include the following steps:[1]

1. Establishing responsibility. Usually a job eval-uation committee is set up to be responsible for a job evaluation program, although in some cir-cumstances this responsibility will be assigned to one individual.

2. Development or selection of the job evalu-ation system to be used.

3. Preparing job descriptions.

4. Evaluation of jobs.

5. Converting evaluations to money values. This process frequently includes carrying out a wage or salary survey of going rates in the labor mar-ket.

6. Providing for evaluation of new jobs.

METHODS OF JOB EVALUATION

The four rather traditional job evalu-ation methods are based on individuals' judgments of job characteristics. In addi-tion, a more statistical approach to job eval-uation, based on structured job-analysis data, seems to offer considerable promise for establishing rates of pay. The first

[1]The reader interested in further discussion of com-pensation administration is referred to such texts as: Belcher, D. W., *Compensation administration,* Englewood Cliffs, N. J.: Prentice-Hall, 1974; Berg, J. G., *Managing compensation,* New York: AMACOM, American Man-agement Associations, 1976; Henderson, R., *Compen-sation Management,* Reston, Va.: Reston Publishing Company, 1976; and H. G. Zollitsch & A. Langsner, *Wage and salary administration,* Cincinnati: South-West-ern Publishing, 1970.

four of the methods listed require judgments of job characteristics; the fifth is based on structured job-analysis data.

1. Ranking method

2. Classification method

3. Point method

4. Factor comparison method

5. Job-component method

Ranking Method

In the ranking method, jobs are compared with each other, usually on the basis of judged overall worth. Most typically, these judgments are obtained by a simple ranking of jobs—hence the name *ranking method.* Because jobs can be judged relative to others by other procedures, such as the paired comparison procedure, this method could more appropriately be called the *job comparison* method. The reliability of the evaluations usually is increased by having several individuals—preferably people already familiar with the jobs—serve as evaluators. When there are many jobs to be evaluated, however, it usually is impossible to find individuals familiar with all of them. Although there are ways of combining evaluations when each rater evaluates only some of the jobs, this method is usually most suitable to small organizations with limited numbers of jobs.

Classification Method

The classification method consists of several categories of jobs along a hypothetical scale. Each such classification usually is defined and sometimes is illustrated. The General Schedule (GS) of the Civil Service System of the federal government is essentially a classification system. In using this method, each job is assigned to a specific classification on the basis of its judged overall worth and its relation to the descriptions of the several classifications.

The classification method is rather simple to develop and use. Unless special care is taken, however, it tends to perpetuate possible inequalities in existing rates of pay if it is used to evaluate existing jobs with already designated rates.

Point Method

The point method is without question the most common. It is characterized by the following: (1) the use of several job evaluation factors; (2) the assignment of "points" to varying "degrees" or levels of each factor; (3) the evaluation of individual jobs in terms of their "degree" or level on each factor, and the assignment to each job of the number of points designated for the degree or level on the factor; and (4) the addition of the point values for the individual factors to derive the total point value for each job. This total point value then is converted to corresponding wage or salary rates. The following illustration taken from the system of the National Electric Manufacturers Association NEMA, shows how one of the factors used in this system (experience) is converted into points for the various degrees of this factor.

Degree	Amount of Experience	Points
1	Up to three months	22
2	Over three months up to one year	44
3	Over one year up to three years	66
4	Over three years up to five years	88
5	Over five years	110

Similar "degree definitions" are included for the various degrees of the remaining factors, of which there are eleven in this particular system. The eleven factors and the point values assigned to the various degrees of those factors are given in Table 18.1. This particular system was designed

TABLE 18.1 JOB CHARACTERISTICS AND POINT VALUES CORRESPONDING TO VAR-
IOUS DEGREES OF EACH USED IN THE NATIONAL ELECTRICAL MANUFACTURERS
ASSOCIATION JOB EVALUATION SYSTEM

	Points Assigned to Factors and Key Grades				
Factors	First Degree	Second Degree	Third Degree	Fourth Degree	Fifth Degree
Skill					
1. Education	14	28	42	56	70
2. Experience	22	44	66	88	110
3. Initiative and ingenuity	14	28	42	56	70
Effort					
4. Physical demand	10	20	30	40	50
5. Mental or visual demand	5	10	15	20	25
Responsibility					
6. Equipment or process	5	10	15	20	25
7. Material or product	5	10	15	20	25
8. Safety of others	5	10	15	20	25
9. Work of others	5		15		25
Job Conditions					
10. Working conditions	10	20	30	40	50
11. Unavoidable hazards	5	10	15	20	25

Source: NEMA Job Rating Plan for Hourly Rated Jobs.

for hourly paid jobs. The system used by the National Metal Trades Association is essentially the same. Different systems usually are used for different major types of jobs, such as hourly paid jobs, salaried jobs, and so forth.

Factor Comparison Method

The factor comparison method was initially developed and described by Benge, Burk, and Hay (1941). The system must be tailor made for the organization for which it is to be used. The development is time consuming and complex, this probably accounting in part for its somewhat limited use. Once the system is developed, however, its implementation is relatively straightforward. Our discussion of the system focuses on the procedures used in its development.

In this method, fifteen or twenty tentative "key jobs" first are selected. These are jobs that have current rates not subject to

controversy and that are considered by the job evaluation committee to be neither underpaid nor overpaid. These jobs then are compared to others in terms of factors common to all jobs. The factors used in the Benge, Burk, and Hay system are:

Mental requirements

Skill requirements

Physical requirements

Responsibility

Working conditions

The "key jobs" are first *ranked* on each of the factors mentioned, with all of the jobs appearing on each of the factor lists. The rankings usually are made independently by several people, with differences in rankings being resolved by consensus. Next, the jobs are subjected to a *rating* process in which the going rate (hourly or salary) is "allocated" to the individual factors according to the judgments of the job evaluation committee members of how much of the going rate is being "paid" for each factor. This is done independently by the various raters, and the averages of these values are then used as the final "rate" for each job for each factor. In turn, these money rates for the key jobs are then assigned rank orders.

From these two procedures two rank orders of the key jobs on each of the factors result, the first based on the direct ranking of the key jobs on each factor, and the second, the rank order of the money values resulting from the rating process. A hypothetical example of the results of these processes is given in Table 18.2 for six jobs (usually fifteen or twenty or more key jobs are used). This table shows the going rate for each job, the money value for each job "allocated" to the five factors (identified by the dollar sign "$"), the rank order for each factor of these money values for the six jobs (Rank order—$), and the rank order for each factor as assigned by the direct ranking procedure (rank order—D).

A major objective in deriving these two sets of rank orders is to identify any inconsistencies between them. In the examples given, such inconsistencies are shown for the jobs of poleman and rammer on the factor of physical requirements. When such inconsistencies are identified they must be reconciled, or one or both of the jobs in question must be eliminated from the key jobs that are to represent the system. Once such inconsistencies are thus resolved, the remaining key jobs are formed into five scales, one for each factor, in which the money values of those jobs represent points along the scale as shown below for the factor of mental requirements for the four key jobs that would be retained after eliminating the two for which inconsistencies were found.

In the actual application of the system, other jobs are evaluated on each individual factor by comparing them with the jobs that

Job	$ Value on Mental requirements
Patternmaker	$1.85
Substation operator	1.35
Machinist	1.15
Laborer	.30

represent the scale for that factor, each job being assigned a value for each factor. The sum of these values for the five factors for any given job is then the total value for the job. These are actually money values, relative to the rates of pay for the key jobs, but because of the now rather persistent inflation that would cause such values to become obsolete there are procedures for adjusting for inflation effects.

Job-Component Method

Behind what we will call the job-component method of job evaluation is the implicit assumption that similarities in job content impose similar job demands on the incumbents and should therefore warrant corresponding rates of pay. One could then argue that any given job component carries its own "value," regardless of the combination of other job components with which it might occur in any given job. The application of this rationale in job evaluation leads to structured job analysis procedures that make it possible to identify and measure the level of each of many job components as they occur in jobs.

One illustration of this approach is the Clerical Task Inventory[2] (originally called the Job Analysis Check List of Office Operations) as reported by Miles (1952). In this task inventory, the analyst rates the importance to the job of each of many office operations. In this study it was found that a weighted combination of the five most important office operations resulted in total

[2]The Clerical Task Inventory (CTI) is copyrighted by C. H. Lawshe, Jr., and is available through the Village Book Cellar, 308 West State Street, West Lafayette, Indiana, 47906.

TABLE 18.2 ILLUSTRATION OF DATA FOR A HYPOTHETICAL SAMPLE OF KEY JOBS AS USED IN THE FACTOR COMPARISON METHOD OF JOB EVALUATION

Key Job Title	Going Rate of Pay	Mental Requirements			Skill Requirements			Physical Requirements			Responsibility			Working Conditions		
		$	Rank Order	D	$	Rank Order	D	$	Rank Order	D	$	Rank Order	D	$	Rank Order	D
Pattern maker	$6.30	1.85	1	1	2.30	1	1	.70	5	5	1.05	2	2	.40	5	5
Machinist	5.35	1.15	3	3	1.70	2	2	.95	4	4	1.00	3	3	.55	4	4
Poleman	5.20	.55	4	4	.90	4	4	1.85	(2)	(1)	.70	4	4	1.20	2	2
Substation operator	4.50	1.35	2	2	1.60	3	3	.15	6	6	1.25	1	1	.15	6	6
Rammer	4.20	.25	6	6	.40	5	5	1.90	(1)	(2)	.40	5	5	1.25	1	1
Laborer	3.50	.30	5	5	.25	6	6	1.60	3	3	.30	6	6	1.05	3	3

Note: Titles and rates are illustrative and for comparison purposes only.

Legend:
Going rate of pay: Prevailing hourly rate for the job.
$_: Amount of pay judged to be paid for the factor in question as based on rating process.
Rank order-$: Rank order of these amounts for the jobs.
Rank order-D: Rank order of jobs as based on the "direct" ranking process.

Source: *Adapted from Zollitsch & Langsner, 1970, Table 7.5, p. 183.*

values that were highly correlated with going rates for jobs.

In a more generalized application of the job-component method, McCormick, Jeanneret, and Mecham (1972) used the Position Analysis Questionnaire (PAQ)[3] with a sample of 340 jobs of various kinds in various industries in various parts of the country. As indicated in chapter 4, the PAQ is a structured job analysis questionnaire that provides for analyzing jobs in terms of 194 "worker-oriented" job elements. In this particular study, job dimension scores were derived statistically for the thirty-two factors resulting from a previous factor analysis of the PAQ. A statistically weighted combination of scores on nine of these job dimensions produced correlations in the upper .80s with actual rates of pay for two subsamples consisting of 165 and 175 of the jobs as well as for the total sample of 340. With a larger sample of over eight hundred varied jobs, the correlation with actual rates of pay was .85, as reported by Mecham (1972). For a sample of seventy-nine jobs in an insurance company, Taylor (1971) reported a correlation of .93 between a weighted combination of job dimension scores and actual rates of pay.

In the job component approach, indices of relative job values are derived statistically by using equations that weight job dimension scores in proportion to how much the dimensions contribute to the prediction of going rates for jobs. Thus, one can derive job evaluation point values for jobs directly from quantitative job analysis data (specifically job dimension scores) without the conventional evaluation of jobs by a job evaluation committee. Actually there are

two approaches that can be used to derive weights for the individual job dimensions with the PAQ. The first is based on data from a large number of varied jobs in various industries, producing a "generalized" equation with rather broad applicability. The other approach is based on the use of going rate data for a sample of jobs within the organization or within the labor market from which the organization obtains its employees. In this instance the statistical analysis produces a unique equation that incorporates weights for the job dimensions that, collectively, best predict the going rates for the sample of jobs used in the analysis. This unique equation is an example of what has been named a policy-capturing approach in that it "captures," statistically, the prevailing pay policy reflected in the pay rates of the jobs in the sample.

A slight variation of this approach is represented by a study by Robinson and others (1974) of jobs in a medium-sized municipality. The investigators obtained data on the going rates for a sample of jobs from twenty-one cities of similar size and used the medians of these rates for the individual jobs as the rates to be "captured" in the statistical analysis. The correlation coefficient between the predicted rates (based on the derived equation) and the actual median rates was .945. In addition, four other job evaluation methods were used to derive estimated compensation rates. The intercorrelation coefficients between the various methods ranged from .82 to .95. The job component method of job evaluation in this instance resulted in values for the sample jobs that were as highly correlated with the going rates of jobs as were the values derived by the other, more traditional, methods, and more highly correlated than some of the methods. In another study by these investigators using data relating to jobs in a major utility in the mountain states, it was found that an equation derived with a sample of jobs in the orga-

---

[3]The Position Analysis Questionnaire (PAQ) is copyrighted by the Purdue Research Foundation. The PAQ and related materials are available through the University Book Store, 360 West State Street, West Lafayette, Indiana 47906. Further information about the PAQ is available through PAQ Services, Inc., P.O. Box 3337, Logan, Utah 84321.

nization resulted in predicted job values that had a correlation of .90 with going rates for the jobs in the sample.

In these and other organizations, the use of the PAQ in the framework of the job component job evaluation method has been demonstrated as being a practical method for establishing compensation rates for jobs. In addition it may have a particular importance to the current concern for ensuring equal pay for men and women for equal work. This possibility is based on the fact that, for practical purposes, the various job dimensions have their own "values" in the labor market, so by deriving job dimensions scores for any given job, and by assigning the appropriate weights to the job dimensions, one can "build up" the total value for the job. This would virtually eliminate the possibility of bias based on the sex of the job incumbent having an influence on the final job value. As an aside, it might be mentioned that Arvey and others (1977) provided data from a well-controlled study that indicate that analyses of jobs with the PAQ are not influenced appreciably by the sex of the job incumbent. Data from a few organizations in which the PAQ has been used strongly supported the contention that the job component approach to job evaluation may be the most promising one to ensure equal pay for equal work.

Discussion

It should be noted that, among the four traditional methods of job evaluation (that

is, ranking, classification, point, and factor comparison), there are differences both in the *techniques* of evaluation and in the *bases* of evaluation. These differences are illustrated below:

CONVERTING JOB EVALUATION RESULTS TO PAY SCALES

Most job evaluation systems result in jobs being placed at varying positions along a hypothetical scale of job values, as reflected by point values, rank orders, job classifications, or other measuring systems. In some applications of the factor comparison and job component methods, the resulting evaluations actually are expressed in money terms, but most evaluations are expressed as point values which need to be converted to actual money values in order to establish the rates of pay for the jobs in question. This typically requires developing a "going rate" curve and an "organization rate" curve.

Developing a Going Rate Curve

At some stage of developing a wage or salary administration program, it is necessary to determine the relationship between evaluations, usually of a sample of key jobs, and rates of pay for corresponding jobs in the labor market. If data on the going rates of such jobs are not available, a wage or salary survey is made. For our purposes, data on the median "going" rates of pay of a sample of jobs have been drawn from a survey by the Bureau of Labor Statistics

		Technique of Evaluation	
		By Comparison with Other Jobs	By Evaluation Against a "Standard"
Basis of Evaluation	Whole job	Ranking method	Classification method
	Job factors	Factor comparison method	Point method

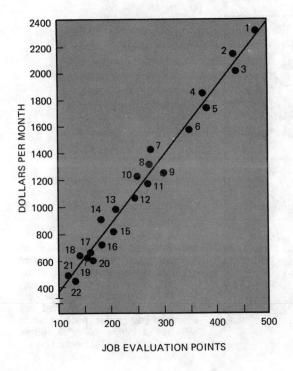

FIG. 18.1 Relationship between job evaluation points and median monthly pay rates for 22 jobs. The going rates are the median rates for a sample of jobs as reported by the Bureau of Labor Statistics. The line of best fit (in this case a straight line) is the going rate curve; it reflects the relationship of the job evaluation points to going rates. (From McCormick 1979, Figure 12–4.)

(1975). (We could consider these going rates as the median rates for a sample of companies in any given labor market.) These going rates, along with evaluation points for the jobs, are shown in Figure 18.1 to illustrate the establishment of a going wage curve. Although this particular relationship is linear, with some job evaluation systems the relationship is curvilinear.

Setting an Organization Rate Curve

The next stage is to establish a wage or salary curve for the specific organization. (In private companies this is called the company wage or salary curve.) This curve is set so it has some predetermined relationship to the going rate curve, being the same as the going rate curve or a bit above

or below it. This curve is then used by the organization for establishing rates of pay for all of the jobs covered. This assures that all the jobs covered will have their rates of pay established on the same basis.

Figure 18.2 shows an "organization" wage curve for the same jobs illustrated in Figure 18.1. In this case it is shown as slightly below the going rate curve of the labor market. Where this curve is actually set with respect to the going wage curve in any given case, however, is a function of various considerations, including economic conditions, contract negotiations, and fringe benefits. Thus, it can be at the level of the going wage curve as such, or at various levels above or below.

In converting job evaluation points to actual rates of pay, different practices may be followed. It would be possible to take

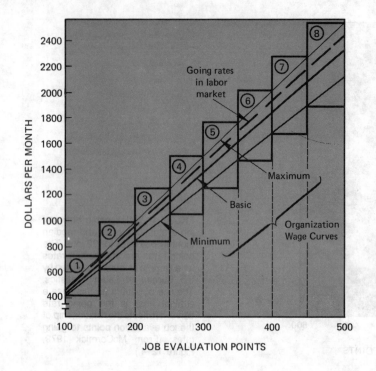

FIG. 18.2 Illustration of an "organization" wage curve and of one pattern of conversion of job evaluation points into rates of pay. In this particular example, the point values are converted into nine pay grades, each of which has a range of rates. (From McCormick 1979, Figure 12-3.)

the evaluated points for a given job and derive the corresponding exact rate that would be applicable. Thus, every slight difference in points would result in some difference in hourly rate. In practice most organizations (and unions) feel that the inherent lack of perfect accuracy in the judgments that underlie a set of job evaluations makes it desirable to bracket together jobs of approximately the same point value and to consider these jobs as equal in setting up the wage structure. This bracketing results in so-called *labor grades*. The number of labor grades found in specific wage structures varies from around eight or ten to twenty or twenty-five. The tendency of most current union demands in wage contract negotiations is to favor a relatively small number of labor grades.

When the jobs have been bracketed in labor grades, provision is usually made for

wage increases within each labor grade, as illustrated in Figure 18.2 Various procedures have been used in granting wage increases within labor grades, as well as in upgrading employees to higher categories. Some organizations use an automatic acceleration schedule under which specified increases automatically become effective after a specified period of time on the job. This principle is used most frequently in the lower labor grades and with new employees, but it is sometimes used in higher levels in the wage structure as well. Regular personnel evaluations are also used by some organizations as a means of identifying employees who are eligible for a pay increase under the prevailing pay structure.

As already mentioned, there are various policies for converting points to rates of pay. Although these will not be discussed here, two or three variations will be mentioned. Figure 18.2 shows an increasing range of rates with higher pay grades; in actual practice the range may be constant, or may be greater or less than that illustrated. In some systems the width of the pay grades (in terms of job evaluation points) increases with higher rates; these increases may be systematic or adapted in some way to the concentration of jobs along the evaluation scale.

FACTORS IN JOB EVALUATION SYSTEMS

The most common type of job evaluation system is the point system, which provides for the evaluation of jobs on various factors. In selecting or developing a job evaluation system for some general class of jobs, the question naturally arises as to what factors to include. In this regard, although there are indeed differences in the factors actually used for jobs of a given general class, there is still a fairly substantial degree of similarity between and among various systems. (The fact that there are certain commonly used systems contributes to the similarity.)

In practice, the selection of factors usually is made by the job evaluation committee. The committee also usually determines the weights to be given to the individual factors, frequently following the practice of other organizations. Such weights are reflected by the point values assigned to the various factors and the degrees of the factors, as shown for the NEMA system in Table 18.1. (The first column, which adds up to 100, reflects the intended weights for the individual factors.)

In discussing such weights, however, let us hark back to the discussion in chapter 6 of the weighting of factors in performance evaluation systems. The point was made there that the *actual* or *effective* weights of factors (as opposed to the *intended* weights) are in part influenced by the variability (specifically the standard deviations) of the values assigned on the various factors to

different cases in the sample. Thus, if the values on a given job evaluation factor which are assigned to different jobs show little variation, then that factor would have relatively nominal effective weight—*unless* appropriate statistical steps are taken to give it its intended weight.

Optimum Combinations of Factors and Weights

As stated above, the usual practice in developing a job evaluation system is for the job evaluation committee to select the factors and to designate their intended weights. The optimum combination of factors and weights, however, can be determined by statistical procedures. The use of such procedures, however, forces us to ask: What is the *standard* (that is, the criterion) by which we would determine that jobs have their own appropriate values? The criterion implicit in our previous discussions is that of going rates in the labor market, for the reasons previously expressed.

If one is willing to accept this criterion, it naturally follows that the combination of factors and weights used in a job evaluation system should be one that maximizes the correlation between total point values for jobs *within* the organization and for those *outside* the organization (that is, in the labor market). Such factors and their optimum weights can be identified with data on a sample of jobs within the organization that also are in this labor market. The scheme to follow has the following steps: (1) developing an "experimental" job evaluation system with several factors; (2) evaluating the sample of jobs using this system; (3) determining the going rates for the jobs in the labor market (by a wage or salary survey); (4) and applying appropriate statistical procedures (specifically some form of regression analysis). The factors and their statistically determined weights could then be used in the organization with reasonable assurance that the rates of pay based on the system would have a reasonable relationship with rates in the labor market.

DISCUSSION

Wage and salary administrators must feel that they are continuously walking a tightrope because of the conflicting pressures on them. A wage and salary program simultaneously must provide positive work incentives for the employees, must be generally acceptable to employees, must be reasonably competitive with conditions in the labor market, and must keep the organization solvent. Obviously, there are no pat and simplistic resolutions to meet these various objectives. The note on which we would like to close this discussion is that insight into and knowledge relevant to the problem, derived through research, can aid in developing a satisfactory program.

REFERENCES

ARVEY R. D., PASSINO, E. M., & LOUNS-BURY, J. W. Job analysis results as influenced by sex of incumbent and sex of analyst. *Journal of Applied Psychology,* 1977, *62*(4), 411–416.

BENGE, E. J., BURK, S. L. H., & HAY, E. N. *Manual of job evaluation* (4th ed.). New York: Harper & Row, 1941.

LAWLER, E. E. *Pay and organizational effectiveness: A psychological view.* New York: McGraw-Hill, 1971.

McCORMICK, E. J., JEANNERET, P. R., & MECHAM, R. C. A study of job characteristics and job dimensions as based on the Position Analysis Questionnaire (PAQ). *Journal of Applied Psychology,* 1972, *56*(4), 347–368.

MECHAM, R. C. Personal communication, 1972.

MILES, M. C. Studies in job evaluation: A. validity of a check list for evaluating office jobs. *Journal of Applied Psychology,* 1952, *36,* 97–101.

National survey of professional, administrative, technical, and clerical pay. Bulletin 1891, Bureau of Labor Statistics, March 1975.

OPSAHL, R. L., & DUNNETTE, M. D. The role of financial compensation in industrial motivation. *Psychological Bulletin,* 1966, *66*(2), 94–118.

ROBINSON, D. D., WAHLSTROM, O. W., & MECHAM, R. C. Comparison of job evaluation methods: A "policy-capturing" approach using the Position Analysis Questionnaire (PAQ). *Journal of Applied Psychology,* 1974, *59*(5), 633–637.

TAYLOR, L. R. Personal communication, 1971.

ZOLLITSCH, H. G., & LANGSNER, A. *Wage and salary administration* (2nd ed.). Cincinnati: South-Western Publishing, 1970.

19
working conditions

The working conditions in the United States and in many other industrial countries have improved markedly over the last century or so, probably because of such things as increased social concern by management, pressures from employees and unions, improved technology, and tighter legal and regulatory requirements. In the United States, the Occupational Safety and Health Administration (OSHA) of the Department of Labor is charged with administering the Occupational Safety and Health Act (OSH Act) that sets certain standards for working conditions. Granting significant improvements over the years, there still are improvements that can be made in working conditions for some types of jobs, or in certain industries or in specific establishments.

Our discussion of working conditions covers two general categories. The first is on the physical environment with particular reference to illumination, noise, and atmospheric conditions. The second is on various aspects of time, such as hours of work, work schedules, and rest pauses.

ILLUMINATION

We all would agree that reading the fine print in a contract requires more illumination than, say, dumping trash cans into a truck. The problem is determining how much illumination should be provided for any given task. As the basis for making such determinations, the Illuminating Engineering Society in the *IES Illuminating Handbook* (1972) proposed that illumination levels for various tasks should be prescribed according to two classes of criteria—visual performance and visual comfort. Of these, greater attention has been given to the former.

Factors That Influence Visual Performance

Of course, the visual performance of people in tasks with significant visual components is in part the consequence of the visual abilities of the individuals, as discussed in chapter 8. Our present interests, however, are more concerned with the task-related factors that may affect visual performance and thus should be considered in prescribing the levels of illumination for various tasks. The IES points out that there are two aspects of this question: the intrinsic characteristics of the task and the characteristics of the luminous environment. The intrinsic characteristics of the task that affect the ability to make visual discriminations include the brightness contrast of the "details" to be discriminated against their backgrounds, the size of the details to be discriminated, and the time available for seeing.

A couple of sets of data relating to task variables will be given to illustrate the effect of such variables on visual performance. One example, from a much broader study by Blackwell (1959), shows the relationship between brightness contrast and visual performance. The details of this study will not be discussed here, but the results are shown in general terms in Figure 19.1. An example of low brightness contrast is gray printing on a slightly lighter gray paper; an example of high contrast is black printing on very white paper. Another example, also from Blackwell, shows the interaction between viewing time and brightness contrast, as related to illumination level. The data, shown in Figure 19.2, indicate that for any given time curve (such as a one-second viewing time), the various combinations of illumination level and brightness contrast produce the *same level* of visual discriminability. (The level of discriminability depicted in this figure was 50 percent detection of the particular visual stimuli used.) For any given level of illumination, it can be seen that if viewing time is *decreased*, the

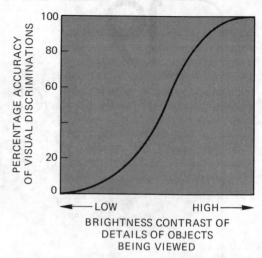

FIG. 19.1 Generalized relationship between brightness contrast of visual detail and accuracy of visual discriminations. (*Adapted from Blackwell 1959, Figure 4.*)

brightness contrast must be increased in order to maintain the same level of visual discriminability.

Prescribing Illumination Standards

The specification of illumination standards—for kumquat inspectors, doughnut-hole punchers, pin-ball machine assemblers, or any other job—involves an intricate process that we cannot cover in detail here. But we will at least touch on one or two aspects of it. The basis for such prescriptions is the research of Blackwell (1959, 1972), which has been supported largely by the IES. His procedure in part is predicated on the concept of a visibility reference function, shown in Figure 19.3. The curve showing this function (the solid curve) represents the task contrast (C) required at different levels of task background luminance (in footlamberts) for equal threshold visibility of a specified visual task. (The reference task is to identify a visual target four minutes of visual angle in diameter, exposed for one-half of a second.) The contrast is the ratio of the re-

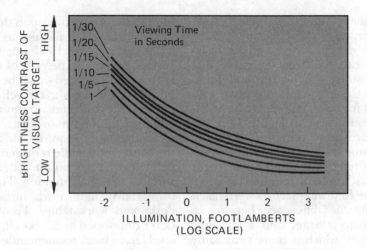

FIG. 19.2 Illumination and brightness contrast relationships for each of six viewing times. The curve for any viewing time represents the combinations of illumination and brightness required for equal visual discriminability. (*Adapted from Blackwell 1959, Figure 33.*)

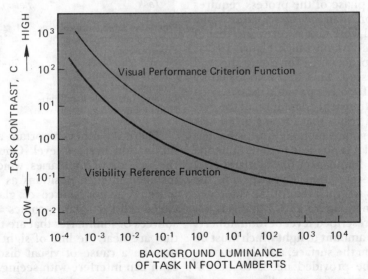

FIG. 19.3 Task contrast (C) required at different levels of background luminance in footlamberts for equal threshold visibility of a specified visual task. The solid line (the visibility reference function) relates to the identification (with 50 percent certainty) of a visual target that is 4-minutes of visual arc in diameter exposed for 1/2 second. The dotted curve (the visual performance criterion function) relates to the same task adjusted for other factors (such as movement, location, and 99 percent certainty of detection). (*From IES lighting handbook 1972, Figure 3–24.*)

flectance of the features of the visual target —that is, the ratio of the reflectances of the target to be discriminated and its background. We can see from the curve that with low contrast the background luminance needs to be much higher than with high contrast for equal visibility to be possible. The second curve in Figure 19.3, the visual performance criterion function, shows the same basic relationship, except that it is adjusted to account for differences in contrast that would be required for equal visibility if the following factors were taken into account: the difference between a static (stationary) target and a dynamic (moving) target, which is more commonly found in practice; the difference between not knowing and knowing where and when the target will appear in the visual field; and the difference between being 99 percent sure of detecting the target and being 50 percent certain.

A second phase of the process requires the estimation of an *equivalent contrast* value for the actual work task as related to that of the reference task on which Figure 19.3 is based. The procedures for doing this will not be discussed. This step is followed by adjustments for other possible factors, such as glare and transient adaptation of the eye, with the end result that for any given task for which the equivalent contrast value has been derived it is possible to determine the background luminance (in footlamberts) that must be provided if visibility on the actual task is to equal that of the reference task as shown in Figure 19.3. But this is not all, for the prescribed level of footlamberts indicates the amount of light which must be reflected from the surface, and the amount of light to be provided needs to be expressed in terms of footcandles.

A footlambert can be thought of as the brightness of *reflected* light that is equivalent to a perfectly diffusing, perfectly white surface which is illuminated by one footcandle of light. The number of footcandles (fc) required to produce any specified level of footlamberts depends upon the reflectance of the surface. Let us take, as an example, a task that requires 100 footlamberts. If the surface reflects 80 percent of the light, the footcandles required would be 100 fc ÷ .80, or 125 fc. If the surface reflects only 25 percent, the footcandles required would be 100 fc ÷ .25, or 400 fc. Thus, for any level of footlamberts required for a given task, the actual footcandle requirements will depend very largely on the reflectance of the surfaces of visual attention. This argues for using fairly light work surfaces such as desks and work tables. From the procedures developed by Blackwell, illumination levels have been recommended for various types of tasks. A few examples of these recommendations are give below (these are from the *IES Lighting Handbook*, 1972, pp. 9-81 to 9-95):

Task	Recommended Illumination, Footcandles
Operating table (surgical)	2500
Very difficult inspection	500
Proofreading	150
General office work	70–150
Food preparation	70
Wrapping and labeling	50
Loading (materials handling)	20
Hotel lobby	10

There are other important aspects of illumination besides level. One of these is the location of luminaries, which should be installed in such positions as to minimize glare. A major source of glare—what is called direct glare—comes from light sources or luminaries that are too bright or that are near the line of sight. Such glare may be a cause of visual discomfort and even can interfere with seeing.

A somewhat related aspect of illumination is the distribution of light throughout the work area. Not only should the immediate work area be illuminated at the level prescribed for the visual tasks in question, but there also should be a reasonably adequate level of general illumination.

ATMOSPHERIC CONDITIONS

Different kinds of variables can be considered aspects of our atmosphere. Besides temperature and humidity there also are air flow, barometric pressure, composition of the atmosphere, and sometimes toxic conditions. There also is the temperature of objects in the environment, which is not strictly an "atmospheric" condition but certainly relates to this subject. Our discussion will deal largely with the more common aspects of the atmosphere, especially temperature and humidity.

The Metabolic Process

The body continually generates heat by a chemical process called metabolism, based on the oxidation of the food we eat by the oxygen we breathe. It is estimated that in a state of rest the body generates heat at a rate equivalent to the power consumption of a sixty-watt electric bulb. During physical work the muscles of the body convert only about 20 percent of the chemical energy used into mechanical power; the remaining 80 percent is converted into heat (*Applied ergonomics handbook* 1974, p.60).

The Heat-Exchange Process

The body continuously attempts to maintain a condition of thermal equilibrium with its environment. Thus, under conditions that we call hot, the body tries to dissipate heat to the environment, and under cold conditions it tries to preserve its heat. There are four ways in which this heat exchange process can take place. *Convection* is the transmission of heat by a fluid that occurs when there is a temperature difference between an object and the fluid. In the case of people, the body typically transmits heat to the air (which is technically a fluid), although when the air temperature rises above body temperature the transmission is reversed. *Evaporation* is another method

of heat exchange; this consists primarily of evaporation of perspiration, and to some degree of vapor that is exhaled from the lungs in breathing. *Radiation* is the process of transmission of thermal energy (either with or without an atmosphere) between objects such as the sun and the earth. When such transmission occurs, the warmer object loses heat to the cooler. Usually people transmit heat to other objects by this method, but occasionally they may be in a situation in which objects, such as boilers or heated metal, transmit heat to them. *Conduction* is the transmission of heat by direct contact, such as with chairs or the floor. Our clothing usually insulates us so that this is a very unimportant method of heat exchange.

Environmental Factors That Influence Heat Exchange

The heat exchange process is, of course, affected very much by certain environmental conditions, in particular, air temperature, humidity, air flow, and the temperature of objects in the environment (such as the walls, ceilings, windows, furnaces, or the sun). The interaction of these conditions is very complex and cannot be covered in detail here. But we can point out that under conditions of high air temperature and high wall temperature, heat loss by convection and radiation is minimized, so that heat *gain* to the body may result. Under such circumstances the only remaining means of heat loss is by evaporation. But if the humidity also is high, evaporative heat loss will be minimized, with the result that body temperature rises. In winter high humidity and wind have an unhappy cooling effect. The wind-chill index, frequently given in weather reports, is based on the cooling effects of the combinations of low temperatures and wind.

INDICES OF ENVIRONMENTAL EFFECTS. Various indices of the effects of combinations of environmental factors have been developed. Two of these—to be referred to later—are described here. One of these, the Wet-Bulb Globe Temperature (WBTG), used in enclosed environments, is a weighted average of dry-bulb and wet-bulb temperatures. (Wet-bulb temperature takes into account the effects of humidity in combination with air temperature and is especially useful when the human body is near its upper limits of temperature regulation by sweating.) The other index, Effective Temperature (ET), has undergone a change in its derivation in recent years, but in the sense in which it is referred to later in this section (the original formulation), it was intended to equate varying combinations of temperature and humidity, in terms of equal sensations of warmth or cold. For example, an ET of 70° characterized the thermal sensation of a 70° temperature in combination with 100 percent humidity, but that value also characterized other (higher) temperatures and other (lower) humidities that gave the same thermal sensations (such as 81° temperature and 10 percent humidity). (Although research has indicated that it tended to overemphasize the importance of humidity at lower temperatures, it still is often used to measure comfort).

Effects of Heat on Performance

The effects of heat on the performance of people performing heavy physical activities have been rather well documented. But heat also can affect performance on cognitive tasks, as demonstrated by the results of a study by Fine and Kobrick (1978). Their subjects performed various cognitive tasks under conditions of 95°F (35°C) and 88 percent humidity over a period of seven hours. The mean errors (in percent) during the work period are shown in Figure 19.4 with those of two control groups working under conditions of 70 °F (21.1 °C) and 25 percent humidity. The increased errors

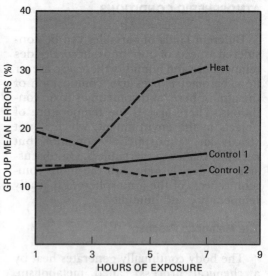

FIG. 19.4 Group mean percent errors on four cognitive tasks over a period of seven hours for men working under conditions of heat (95°F. and 88% humidity) and for two control groups. (Adapted from Fine & Kobrick 1978, Figure 2.)

with the long hours of exposure are quite obvious.

Heat Exposure Limits

We all are familiar with the effects of a hot, humid day even when we are not physically active. Physical work makes the situation even less tolerable. Since heat stress, heat stroke, and even death can be caused by excessive heat, it is desirable to provide working conditions that are within reasonable tolerance limits. Such limits, however, need to take into account the work load (such as in terms of kcal/hr) and duration of work. If a particular work load performed continuously were excessive in terms of physiological tolerance, rest periods should be provided to bring the total work load down to acceptable limits. Figure 19.5 gives the permissible heat exposure limits for various WBGT values for continuous work (over an eight-hour day) and for

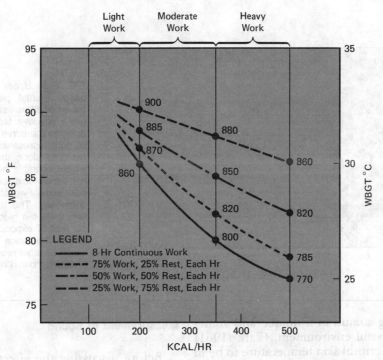

FIG. 19.5 Permissible heat exposure limits for various work loads and combinations of work and rest predicted by the Wet-Bulb Globe Temperature Index (WBGT). (From Dukes-Dobos & Henschel 1971, as presented in the *ASHRAE 1977 fundamentals handbook,* Figure 13, p. 8.18.)

various combinations of work and rest. In particular, this figure gives the amount of rest that must be provided for various work loads and WBGT values. For heavy work of 500 kcal/hr, for example, if the WBGT is as high as 86°F, people should work only 25 percent of the time (and rest 75 percent), whereas if the WBGT is as low as 77 the same work can be carried on continuously.

For tolerance limits for carrying out mental activities, Wing (1965) summarized the results of fifteen different studies, presenting the generalized results shown in the lower line of Figure 19.6. The environmental conditions of the various studies were characterized in terms of ET. The lower line shows the tolerance limits (in terms of time) for carrying out mental activities without impairment of the work activity under different ET conditions. Work beyond the indicated time limits typically

suffered some degradation. The upper line, in turn, shows the recommended upper limit of exposure in terms of heat tolerance as based on other data.

Effects of Cold

Exposure to cold is accompanied by a number of physiological changes, including the vasoconstriction of the peripheral blood vessels, which reduces the flow of blood to the surface of the skin and results in reduced skin temperature. This is a protective response of the body to minimize heat loss (although it numbs the fingers and toes). With reference to the performance of manual work under conditions of cold, Fox (1967), in summarizing many studies, found that performance decrements appear to stem from this physical lowering of the hand skin temperature (HST) and the

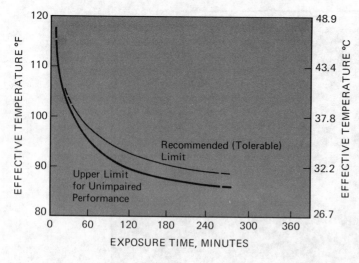

FIG. 19.6 Upper limit for unimpaired mental performance as based on fifteen studies. For any given effective temperature, the point on the curve horizontally to its right represents the time limit (as read along the base) within which mental activity typically is not impaired; a longer period of work usually would result in work decrement. The upper curve, in turn, gives the recommended upper limit of exposure in terms of human tolerance to heat, as based on other research findings. (*Adapted from Wing 1965, Figure 9.*)

competing stimuli in a unique and sometimes stressful environment. Clark (1961) found the critical skin temperature to be in the 55° to 60° range. Manual performance is not affected by skin temperatures above 60°, but decrements may be expected with skin temperatures below 55°.

Although there have been very few studies of the effects of cold on higher mental processes, available evidence suggests that such processes are not markedly affected by cold.

NOISE

There has been serious concern, over a period of years, about noise in industry and in communities, but in recent years this concern has taken on a more urgent note and has become more widespread. As we talk about various forms of environmental pollution, the term "noise pollution" has become a household word. It is, of course, human technology that has created this problem, with the creation of machines, trains, airplanes, automobiles, motors, and other mechanisms of our lives.

Measurement of Sound

Before discussing the effects of sound, let us mention the primary physical characteristics of sound. These are *frequency* and *intensity*. The psychological counterparts of these are *pitch* and *loudness*. Vibrating objects (such as tuning forks and machines) cause fluctuating changes in air pressure to spread out away from them. This is something like the waves in a pond that are generated by a pebble thrown into it, except that sound waves travel in all directions. For an object that has a *single* frequency, these waves, if shown graphically, form a sine (sinusoidal) wave, with the number of repetitions per second being the frequency. Frequency is expressed in terms of cycles per second (cps), or in terms of Hertz (Hz); the two terms are synonymous. Actually, most vibrating sources generate complex waves rather than pure waves; thus, although middle C on the piano and on a trumpet have the same dominant frequency (256 Hz), their "qualities" are different because of the differences in the *other* frequencies also generated. Incidentally, one octave has twice the frequency of the one below it.

The intensity of sound is usually measured by decibels (dB). The decibel scale is actually a logarithmic scale, which accounts for the fact that a ten decibel difference in intensity actually reflects a tenfold difference in sound energy. Figure 19.7 shows a decibel scale with several sounds to illustrate it.

Effects of Noise on Performance

The evidence from noise studies indicates that noise does not *generally* cause deterioration in work performance. In fact, Broadbent (1957) stated that a review of available reports showed no experiments in which there were statistically significant effects of noise at noise levels less than 90 decibels, although there have been some studies of noise levels at about 90 decibels that showed significant decrements. (It should be noted, however, that there is no proof that lower levels will *not* impair performance.

Broadbent points out further that there is no clear-cut and obvious distinction between tasks on which performance *is* affected and those on which performance is *not* affected. There are some hints, however, discussed by Cohen (1968) that suggest that some simple, repetitive types of tasks are relatively insensitive to the effects of noise, but that performance on vigilance (that is, monitoring) tasks may be adversely affected. Further, there are some hints (but not fully confirmed data) that noise may cause degradation in such tasks as complex mental tasks, tasks that call for skill and speed, and tasks that demand a high level of perceptual capacity.

In reflecting on the effects of noise on performance, however, it is probably safe to say that, in general, if noise levels are kept within reasonable bounds in terms of

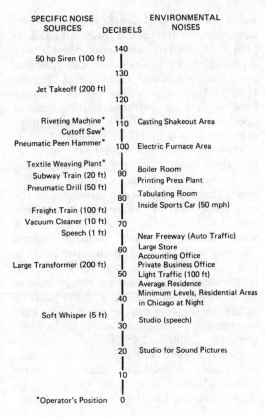

FIG. 19.7 Decibel levels (dB) and sound power ratios for various sounds. Decibel levels are weighted sound levels measured with a sound-level meter. [Examples from Peterson & Gross 1972, Figure 2–1, p. 4.]

other criteria (especially in terms of avoiding hearing loss), such levels typically would not have a serious effect on work performance as such.

Effects of Noise on Hearing

The effects of noise on hearing are much less controversial than are the effects of noise on work performance. Such effects have been demonstrated time and again in people exposed to intense noise levels over a period of years. One such example was presented by LaBenz, Cohen, and Pearson (1967). Their survey was on the hearing loss of sixty-six earthmoving equipment operators, the noise levels of such equipment ranging from 90 to 120 dB.

Hearing tests were given to the men before their work shift, and the results were compared with estimates of the hearing losses that typically occur through age for individuals of comparable age. A comparison of these data is given in Figure 19.8 which shows, for each of three groups differing in years of exposure, the hearing loss corrected for age. In other words, the figure shows what could be considered as the hearing loss associated with the noise to which the subjects were exposed. The loss is especially pronounced at the higher frequencies (2,000 and 4,000 Hz).

Hearing loss is a function of various factors, both individual and situational. Some individuals, for example, are more susceptible to hearing loss than others are. Situational factors include the intensity of noise, its duration, its continuity, and the number of years of exposure. Although it is not possible to specify definitive tolerance limits for noise (because of the various factors that can affect hearing loss), several noise level criteria have been proposed as guidelines.

Hearing Loss Criteria

Regarding exposure to continuous noise, the Occupational Safety and Health Administration of the U.S. Department of Labor has established a set of permissible noise exposures for persons working on jobs in industry (*Federal Register* 1971). These permissible levels depend on the duration of exposure, as given below (the sound levels are reported in terms of the "A-scale," which is adjusted somewhat for the fact that the ear is not particularly sensitive to the lower frequencies):

Discussion

We have discussed the possible effects of noise in terms of human performance and

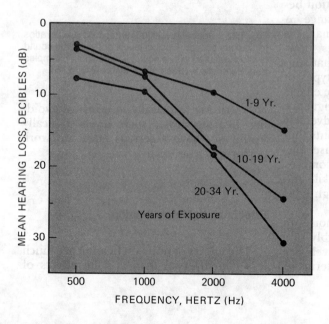

FIG. 19.8 Hearing loss of three groups of earth-moving equipment operators varying in length of exposure. These data are corrected for age, that is, the hearing loss shown is that over and above the normal hearing loss for men of corresponding age. (*Adapted from LaBenz, Cohen, & Pearson 1967, Table 6.*)

Duration per day (hours)	Sound level dB-A
8	90
6	92
4	95
3	97
2	100
1½	102
1	105
½	110
¼ or less	115

hearing loss. But noise can have other effects as well, such as being a source of annoyance (in communities and homes, as well as on the job) and interfering with communications. There also are some hints that there may be some long-term physiological effects. For example, Cohen (1972) reported that a five-year, follow-up study of five hundred workers subjected to noise levels of 95 dB or above revealed a higher incidence of somatic complaints of illness and diagnosed disorders than another group of workers not subject to such noise levels. He also reported a higher absence rate for those working in high noise levels, which may indicate greater psychological stress.

The control of noise is very much an engineering problem. Generally, it can include the following approaches: reduction of noise at the source (such as by proper machine design, lubrication, mounting); enclosing the noise; and the use of baffles and soundproofing materials. If these steps still do not bring the noise level within acceptable limits, the use of ear protection devices is in order.

WORK SCHEDULE

An important condition of work from the worker's point of view is that of the work schedule. Work schedules have various aspects, including the total number of hours worked per week, the distribution of hours throughout the work week, shift work, and provision for rest periods. We will discuss briefly some of these aspects.

Hours of Work

The sixty-, seventy-, and eighty-hour work weeks of past years are virtually bygones, and for many kinds of work, schedules have settled down at somewhere around the conventional forty-hour week. In general, then, the total hours worked by people on their jobs is not now a major issue. For what interest it might have, however, a survey was carried out by Kossoris and others (1947) after World War II of the experiences of thirty-four plants with various work schedules used during the war. The survey included seventy-eight "cases" in these plants (covering 2,445 men and 1,060 women) in which there had been some change in hours of work and in which it was possible to obtain some indication of work "efficiency" (as productivity per hour), injuries, or absenteeism. Generally, the results indicated that, everything else being equal, the forty-four-hour week was best in terms of efficiency and absenteeism. With few exceptions, longer hours did result in greater output, but the increased output generally was not proportional to the increased hours. This was particularly the case with heavy work. Injuries also increased as hours increased, not only in absolute numbers but also in the rate of increase.

Although the forty-hour week has now become fairly standard (this being, below the forty-four-hour week common then), the results of that study probably still have implications for overtime work and the rather common practice of moonlighting (in which people have two jobs).

Four-Day Work Week

Given the fairly standard forty-hour work week, there is next the matter of its distribution over the week. The most common is the five-day, eight-hour per-day schedule (5/40). In recent years there has been a flurry of interest in other work schedules, in particular the four-day, ten-hour per-day schedule (4/40). A major argument for such a schedule has been that it would permit three days each week of leisure (usually weekends). The idea of a 4/40 work week (and other variations) has caught on quite quickly, both with employees and employers, with a number of organizations adopting such plans (Poor 1973).

Following the fanfare that typically accompanies various personnel innovations, it is reasonable to wonder how such plans have actually worked out. Although it probably will take a few more years of experience with such plans for a thorough evaluation, there now are at least a few straws in the wind to report.

From a questionnaire survey of 434 clerical and 40 supervisory employees who had been on a 4/40 schedule for a year, Goodale and Aagaard (1975) reported "mixed and somewhat inconsistent reaction" to the schedule. In reply to a general question, 80 percent reported they did not want to revert to a traditional five-day work week. Replies to more specific questions, however, were more mixed. For example, 62 percent felt they were making better use of their leisure time, and 53 percent had not adopted an earlier bedtime to compensate for an earlier starting time. In another survey of workers in a 4/40 schedule, Fottler (1977) interviewed employees of the food and nutrition department of a large hospital and found that about 56 percent were in favor of continuing the schedule. This percentage is at the low end of the range of responses reported from other studies.

In synthesizing the results of various studies, Dunham and Hawk (1977) indicated that the 4/40 schedules are viewed most favorably by younger workers with low job levels, with low income levels, and with low satisfaction with job-related com-

ponents. The results from various studies (including their own survey) led these authors to concur with certain other investigators that the 4/40 schedule may be viewed most favorably when it is considered as a partial escape from negative work and work-related factors.

In summary, it appears that data on employees' attitudes toward the 4/40 schedule represent something of a mixed bag and do not support some of the early enthusiastic claims that the 4/40 schedule is the wave of the future. This is not to say that such a schedule should not be considered but rather, to suggest that it should not be viewed as a panacea for employee discontent and to urge that consideration of such a program take into account the attitudes of the employees toward it, along with the practical feasibility of scheduling work.

Flexible Work Hours

Another innovation in work scheduling is the adoption of flexible work hours (sometimes referred to as Flexi-time, F-T). Such programs have been adopted by some companies in the United States, Europe, and Canada. There are many variations of the flexible work hours scheme, but in general they provide that employees work for a specified number of hours (such as thirty-five or forty hours per week) but permit flexibility in terms of individuals reporting for work each day. Most plans permit individuals to vary the hours worked per day within certain limits as long as the total number of hours worked per week (or month) fulfills the specified weekly hours. For an individual who works the same number of hours per day (like seven and a half or eight), the beginning time determines the closing time. Virtually all plans require that all individuals be at work during certain "core" hours, these ranging from about three hours to six or seven hours per day. There are certain specified hours before and after which people cannot work. The flexible work week scheme was devised primarily to enable individuals to accommodate their working schedule to such things as commuting and traveling schedules, family considerations, school schedules of children, and shopping.

One's curiosity about the results of the flexible work week includes interest in the attitudes of employers toward it and whether it has had any effect on work-related behavior. In this regard Golembiewski and Proehl (1978) summarized the results of sixteen studies from which we can draw some conclusions about both types of criteria.

Although we cannot present all of the results of the attitude data from these studies, in the nine studies in which people were asked if they wanted the program continued, the percentages who urged continuation were as follows: 80, 83, 85, 96, 98, 98, 99, 100, and 100. Although data on other attitude factors reflected some variability, the pattern of attitudes is very definitely on the plus side, or, as expressed by the authors, " . . . the attitudinal data summarized . . . provide major motivation for (flexible workweek) applications" (Golembiewski & Proehl 1978, p. 849).

On the behavioral side, the "hard" data available from the studies were skimpy but included, in some instances, data on sick leave and absenteeism, tardiness, turnover, overtime, and trends in costs. Although such data were limited Golembiewski and Proehl concluded that, by and large, the benefits of flexible work schedules far outweigh their costs and indicated that such schedules do not seem to induce negative or managerially undesirable behaviors at work. Some support from such conclusions came from a study by Schein (1977) of 246 clerical-level employees in a large financial institution. She concluded that in this situation flexible working hours did not appear to have any adverse impact on productivity, adding that it may be a benefit to employees that can be introduced at little cost to the organization.

In discussing flexible work hours two points should be added. First, the research results available are still rather sparse, and there needs to be more research before more definitive conclusions and recommendations can be made. Second, flexible work hours probably would not be practical in some organizations in which the operations require full staffs during scheduled hours of work. But the results to date regarding flexible work hours are definitely on the plus side.

SHIFT WORK

Having evolved in a world with a twenty-four hour, day-night schedule, the human being has developed a temporal "program" called circadian rhythm. As Aschoff (1978) remarked, this system is characterized by its persistence under a variety of conditions and by a certain rigidity against manipulations. One of the factors that affects the adaptability of individuals to shift work (either permanent or rotating) is their circadian rhythm. There presumably are differences in how much individuals' circadian rhythms enable them to adapt to shift work. As Reinberg and others (1978) reported, it appears that in a population of healthy adults only a limited number are able to sustain shift work, and that, to date, there has been no procedure available (other than personal experience) to determine whether or not a given individual will be able to adjust to shift work. (It might be added that Reinberg and others have developed certain physiological indices that may make this possible.)

In common parlance, we talk about "morning" and "evening" types, and there seem to be some indications that these "types" differ somewhat in their circadian phase "positions." In this regard, Breithaupt and others (1978) reported that the predominantly morning types react to late shift work with sleep deficiency and its accompanying pathological symptoms. They added that evening types have constitutions inherently less vulnerable than those of morning types to delayed sleep, simply because of their delayed circadian rhythm phase position. Recognizing that the underlying physiological factors are indeed complex, it is probable that such factors have a significant effect on how much individuals can adapt to shift work (and, incidentally, on whether they tend to be morning or evening types.)

Attitudes toward Shift Work

As one would expect, most people take a dim view of shift work. But this is by no means a universal attitude. For example, in a survey by de la Mare and Walker (1968) the following expressions of preference were reported:

Preference	Percent
Permanent day work	61
Rotating shift work	12
Permanent night work	27

From a survey of 315 shift workers in the British steel industry, Wedderburn (1978) reported the following responses to the question: "On the whole how do you feel about working shifts?"

Response	Percent
I like it very much	18
I like it more than I dislike it	29
I neither like it nor dislike it	22
I dislike it more than I like it	23
I dislike it very much	8

Although these results indicated more favorable than unfavorable attitudes toward the "general" question used, this does not mean that those who do like shift work are completely enthralled by it, for responses of the same individuals indicated considerable dislike of it for certain reasons, such as effects on social life, 61 percent; irregular sleeping times, 47 percent; working at night, 44 percent; irregular meal times, 38 percent; and early rising, 35 percent.

Some indications of the opinions of people on the perceived advantages and disadvantages of the conventional three shifts are given in Table 19.1, based on the responses of the 315 steel workers. The regular day shift is valued because it "gives me more spare time," is "quickly over," is "good for family life," and does not "restrict my social life." But over half also reported that it "starts too early." Substantial percentages of responses to the evening shift were reported for "restricts my social life," and "wastes the day," but it is also perceived as "being the least tiring." The night shift was characterized by such items as "tiring," "restricts my social life," "is not good for family life," and "disturbs my sleep" but was favored by many because it "gives me more spare time."

Individuals' attitudes toward shift work probably are influenced in part by how much their circadian rhythms adjust to such a schedule, but their perceptions of various features of shift work presumably also influence their overall attitudes toward it. It is clear from the studies cited, as well as others, that there are rather noticeable differences in the attitudes of individuals toward shift work, these presumably reflecting different value systems as well as one's status in life (such as whether the person is married or not). These differences seem to suggest that when shift work is necessary, individuals should be given their preference for shift insofar as this is feasible. In one company the employees with the longest seniority were given their choice of shifts.

TABLE 19.1   REPORTED PERCEPTIONS OF 315 STEEL MILL WORKERS REGARD-
ING VARIOUS DESCRIPTIONS OF WORK ON DAY, EVENING, AND NIGHT SHIFTS

| | Percentage of "Yes" Responses About | | |
Descriptive Item*	Day Shift	Afternoon Shift	Night Shift
Quickly over	84	38	29
Seems a longer shift	12	40	64
Gives me indigestion	7	4	21
Tiring	58	15	80
Disturbs my sleep	36	2	52
More friendly atmosphere	48	51	21
Makes me irritable	25	18	48
Peaceful	49	62	58
More responsibility at work	28	16	24
More independent	35	26	42
Good for family life	73	19	17
Gives me more spare time	88	15	49
Wastes the day	10	68	55
Starts too early	53	7	20
Restricts my social life	17	79	77
Sexless	13	11	44

*Note: Responses were to this question: "Think of work on . . . shift. How well does
each of the above words describe what it is like for you on . . . shift?"
Source: Wedderburn 1978, Table 4, p. 830.

Effects of Shift Work on Health and Well-being

The evidence on the effects of shift work
on general well-being is sparse and somewhat ambiguous, and most of what evidence is available comes from self-reports.
Mott and others (1965) reported that the
results of several surveys suggested that
shift work tends to affect the time-oriented
body functions such as sleep, digestion,
and elimination. In turn, Akerstedt and
Torsvall (1978) reported that for Swedish
steel mill workers, a change in shift work
from one that included night work to one
without night work was accompanied by an
improvement in physical, mental, and social "well-being." In turn, Meers and others (1978) found that the "subjective
health" of a sample of shift workers decreased during the first six months of shift

work and was somewhat more pronounced
after four years. Although the pattern is not
entirely systematic, it appears that shift
work tends to be accompanied by some
modest effects on health and well-being, at
least for some individuals.

Effects of Shift Work on Work-Related Behavior

For the possible effects of shift work on
people's work-related behavior, Mott and
others (1965) reported that there was some
evidence indicating that errors tend to be a
bit higher and output a bit lower on shift
work, especially on the night shift, but
these effects were not consistent and may
be attributable to certain characteristics of
the workers. Therefore, we probably
should be wary of any bland generalizations.

REST PERIODS

Rest breaks during scheduled work sessions are becoming rather common practice, providing time to have coffee, soft drinks, tea, and other refreshments. Although such breaks tend to be predicated on the assumption that the breaks are "good" in terms of various criteria (such as productivity and employee reactions), it must be stated that there are actually not much hard data available to support such an assumption, although there has been a lot of fuzzy speculation about the accumulation of "fatigue" during the work period.

For rest during work it should be noted first that for work that is physically demanding or that is done under extremely hot conditions, rest periods should be provided in order to compensate for adverse physiological effects. Figure 19.5 earlier in this chapter illustrated this.

Employee Reactions throughout Work Period

Among the few surveys of employees' reactions to their work schedules is one in which Nelson and Bartley (1968) surveyed seventy-five female office workers, asking each to report, for the hours of each half of each work day, the hour during which she had become "most tired," "most bored," and "most rested." The average responses are shown in Figure 19.9. The investigators suggested that the "personal dimensions" of work were not the result of some simple and continuous "fatigue" variable, for if this were so the "tired" curve would have built up continuously after some point, instead of actually dropping from the beginning of the work period. Rather, they maintained that the reactions of individuals depended on how they "cognitively structured" the demands placed on them. From the figure it can be seen that the first hour is a period in which work demands are eas-

ily met by most workers (as shown by the high percentage who reported feeling most "rested"), but that some workers actually reported this as the period in which they were most "tired." The middle period is less likely to be accompanied by extreme states of any quality, but the last hour seems to be one in which there frequently is considerable adjustment to work.

Data from other studies indicate that the greatest feelings of "fatigue" tend to occur during the fourth and eighth hours of the eight-hour work shift, thus tending to jibe with the results shown in Figure 19.9 for the "most tired" and "most bored" responses.

Rest Periods and Work Performance

Although there are few hard facts about the effects of rest periods, the bits and pieces of evidence available suggest that rest periods typically do not reduce output even though there is less time worked and in fact sometimes increase output. For example, the effects of rest pauses in a typical production job were analyzed in a very early study in Great Britain by Farmer and Bevington (1922). Figure 19.10 shows the production of a group of employees before and after the introduction of scheduled rest periods.

Scheduling of Rest Periods

Some work is so irregular that an individual has occasional or frequent periods of inactivity. When work activity does not provide such breaks, however, it is rather widely granted that people should have some breaks during work periods; there is, then, a question as to whether they should be scheduled or taken at the discretion of the employee. There can be no single answer to this question, inasmuch as administrative considerations, the nature of the work, and other factors must be taken into

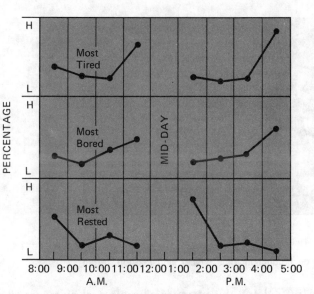

PERCENTAGE

H
Most
Tired
L

H
Most
Bored
L

H
Most
Rested
L

MID-DAY

8:00 9:00 10:00 11:00 12:00 1:00 2:00 3:00 4:00 5:00
A.M.   P.M.

HOURS OF WORKDAY

FIG. 19.9 Percentage of female office workers reporting hours during each half-day when they felt most tired, bored, or rested. Data points are plotted at midpoints of the hours. (*Adapted from Nelson & Bartley 1968, Figure 1.*)

account. In this connection, however, McGehee and Owen (1940) found that in one office, the introduction of two short rest pauses during the day reduced unauthorized rest periods and increased the speed of work.

As far as scheduling is concerned, it is reasonable to believe that there would be some optimum for any given type of work which—if circumstances permit, but they usually do not—could be ascertained experimentally. As an example of such an exercise, Bhatia and Murrell (1969) experimented with two rest period schedules with an admittedly small group of twelve female operatives who had no previous rest schedule. A summary of some of the results is given below.

These results are not dramatic, but they do show that the introduction of rest pauses did not reduce productivity, even though the rest pauses reduced actual work from eight to seven hours. Further, there is a hint that six ten-minute pauses resulted in a slight increase in efficiency over four fifteen-minute pauses; what is more, there was overwhelming preference for the six ten-minute rest periods.

It is probable, as an unconfirmed hypothesis, that in the case of most sedentary and light physical activities, the possible gains from rest periods are more from "psychological" factors, such as boredom or some vague desire for change, than from any significant change in the individual's physical or physiological condition. For

Condition	No. of Weeks	Mean Efficiency Index	Mean Earnings (£)
Control	9	100.2	14.60
Six 10-min. pauses	18	104.4	15.42
Four 15-min. pauses	7	102.5	14.40
Six 10-min. pauses	5	103.1	15.59

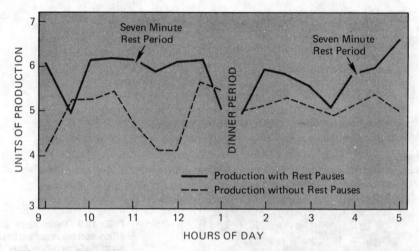

FIG. 19.10 Effect of rest pauses on production for a typical industrial job. (From Farmer & Berington 1922.)

heavy or highly repetitive physical activity, however, physical wear and tear enters the picture. Especially for heavy physical work, the schedule of work and rest should preclude the accumulation of physiological stress. Perhaps the most objective way of doing this is to use physiological measures as guidelines, as proposed by Davis, Faulkner, and Miller (1969). They compared the effects on heart rate of two different rest breaks (one for two minutes, the other for seven minutes) interspersed between ten-

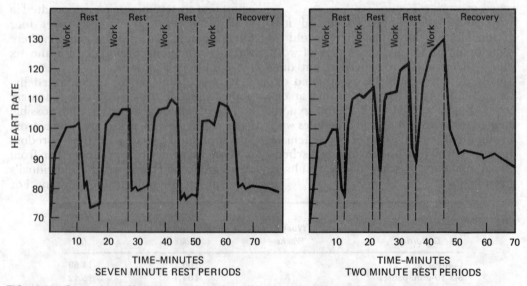

FIG. 19.11 Comparison of heart-rate patterns for a lifting task carried out under two-minute and seven-minute rest-break schedules. The two-minute break is clearly inadequate in that it permits continued increase in the heart rate during successive work periods. (*From Davis, Faulkner, & Miller 1969, Figures 2 & 3.*)

minute work periods of a lifting task. The heart-rate patterns in the case of these two rest-break schedules are shown in Figure 19.11. It can be seen that the seven-minute rest breaks kept the heart rate at a fairly steady state, as contrasted with the two-minute schedule. If it is not feasible to measure physiological conditions, such as heart rate, to use as the basis for scheduling of rest breaks, in the case of heavy physical work, it may well be that the workers should be encouraged to take rest breaks when they feel they need them.

In discussing the scheduling of rest breaks, particular mention should be made of vigilance (or monitoring) tasks requiring continual attention to detect infrequent stimuli or signals. Performance on such tasks tends to deteriorate after twenty to thirty minutes. Thus, for monitoring activities rest periods, or changes in work, should be provided at twenty- or thirty-minute intervals.

REFERENCES

AKERSTEDT, T., & TORSVALL, L. Experimental changes in shift schedules: Their effects on well-being. *Ergonomics*, 1978, *21* (10), 849–856.

Applied ergonomics handbook. Guilford, Surrey, England: IPC Science and Technology Press Ltd., 1974.

ASCHOFF, J. Features of circadian rhythms relevant for the design of shift schedules. *Ergonomics*, 1978, *21* (10), 739–754.

ASHRAE 1977 Fundamentals handbook. New York: American Society of Heating, Refrigerating and Air-Conditioning Engineers, 1977.

BHATIA, N., & MURRELL, K. F. H. An industrial experiment in organized rest pauses. *Human Factors*, 1969, *11* (2), 167–174.

BLACKWELL, H. R. Development and use of a quantitative method for specification of interior illumination levels. *Illumination Engineering*, June 1959, *54* (6), 317–353.

BLACKWELL, H. R. A human factors approach to lighting recommendations and standards. Proceedings of the Sixteenth Annual Meeting of the Human Factors Society, October 1972. Santa Monica, California: The Human Factors Society.

BREITHAUPT, H., HILDEBRANDT, G., DÖHRE, D., JOSCH, R., SIEBER, U., & WERNER, M. Tolerance to shift of sleep, as related to the individual's circadian phase position. *Ergonomics*, 1978, *21*, (10), 767–774.

BROADBENT, D. S. Effect of noise on behavior. In C. M. Harris (Ed.), *Handbook of noise control* (Chap. 10). New York: McGraw-Hill, 1957.

CLARK, R. E. *The limiting hand skin temperature for unaffected manual performance in the cold.* Natick, Mass.: Quartermaster Research and Engineering Command, Technical Report EP-147, February 1961.

COHEN, A. Noise effects on health, production, and well-being. *Transactions of the New York Academy of Sciences*, May 1968, Series II, *30* (7), 910–918.

COHEN, A. The role of psychology in improving worker safety and health under the Occupational Safety and Health Act. Paper given at the meetings of the American Psychological Association, Honolulu, Hawaii, September 1972.

DAVIS, H. L., FAULKNER, T. W., & MILLER, C. I. Work physiology, *Human Factors*, 1969, *11* (2), 157–166.

DE LA MARE, G., & WALKER, J. Factors influencing the choice of shift rotation. *Occupational Psychology*, 1968, *42* (1), 1–21.

DUKES-DOBOS, F., & HENSCHEL, A. The modification of the WBGT Index for establishing permissible heat exposure limits in occupational work. Washington, D. C.: U. S. Public Health Service, ROSH, TR-69, 1971.

DUNHAM, R. B., & HAWK, D. L. The four-day/forty-hour week: Who wants it? *Academy of Management Journal*, 1977, *20* (4), 656–668.

FARMER, E., & BEVINGTON, S. M. An experiment in the introduction of rest pauses. *Journal of the National Institute of Industrial Psychology*, 1922, *1*, 89–92.

Federal Register, May 29, 1971, Vol. 36, No. 105.

FINE, B. J., & KOBRICK, J. L. Effects of altitude and heat on complex cognitive tasks. *Human Factors*, 1978, *20* (1), 115–122.

FOTTLER, M. D. Employee acceptance of a four-day work week. *Academy of Management Journal*, 1977, *20* (4), 656–668.

FOX, W. F. Human performance in the cold. *Human Factors*, 1967, *9* (3), 203–220.

GOLEMBIEWSKI, R. T., & PROEHL, C. W., Jr. A survey of the empirical literature on flexible workhours: Character and consequences of a major innovation. *The Academy of Management Review*, October 1978, *3* (4), 837–853.

GOODALE, J. L., & AARGAARD, A. K. Factors relating to varying reactions to the 4-day work week. *Journal of Applied Psychology*, 1975, *60* (1), 25–38.

IES lighting handbook. (5th ed.) New York: Illuminating Engineering Society, 1972, pp. 3–14.

KOSSORIS, M. D., KOHLER, R. F., and others. *Hours of work and output*. U.S. Department of Labor, Bureau of Labor Statistics, Bulletin No. 917, 1947.

LABENZ, P., COHEN, A., & PEARSON, B. A noise and hearing survey of earth-moving equipment operators. *American Industrial Hygiene Association Journal*, March-April 1967, *28*, 117–128.

McGEHEE, W., & OWEN, F. B. Authorized and unauthorized rest pauses in clerical work. *Journal of Applied Psychology*, 1940, *24*, 605–614.

MEERS, A., MAASEN, A., & VERHAAGEN, P. Subjective health after six months and after four years of shift work. *Ergonomics*, 1978, *21* (10), 857–859.

MOTT, P. E., MANN, F. C., McLAUGHLIN, Q., & WARWICK, D. P. *Shift Work*. Ann Arbor: University of Michigan Press, 1965.

NELSON, T. M., & BARTLEY, S. H. The pattern of personal response arising during the· office work day. *Occupational Psychology*, 1968, *42*(1), 77–83.

PETERSON, A. P. G., & GROSS, F. E., Jr. *Handbook of noise measurement* (8th ed.). New Concord, Mass.: GenRad, Inc., 1978.

POOR, R. (Ed.). *Four days forty hours*. New York: Mentor, 1973.

REINBERG, A., VIEUX, N., GHATA, J., CHAUMONT, A. J., & LAPORTE, A. Circadian rhythm amplitude and individual ability to adjust to shift work. *Ergonomics*, 1978, *21* (10), 763–766.

SCHEIN, V. E., MAURER, E. M., & NOVAK, J. F. Impact of flexible working hours on productivity. *Journal of Applied Psychology,* 1977, *62* (4), 463–465.

WEDDERBURN, A. A. I. Some suggestions for increasing the usefulness of psychological and sociological studies of shiftwork. *Ergonomics,* 1978, *21* (10), 827–833.

WING, J. F. *A review of the effects of high ambient temperature on mental performance.* Technical Report AMRL-TR-65-102, USAF, Aerospace Medical Research Laboratories, Wright-Patterson Air Force Base, September 1965.

ASHRAE 1977 Fundamentals handbook. New York: American Society of Heating, Refrigerating and Air-Conditioning Engineers, 1977.

20
accidents and safety

There is evidence of dramatic improvements in safety in American industry over the past half-century or century. Such evidence is in the reductions in death rates, injury frequency rates, and severity rates (*Accident Prevention Manual for Industrial Operations,* 1974, p. 9). But such improvements should not bring a sigh of relief, because the human and economic costs of accidents and injuries still are of major proportions. The National Safety Council, for example, estimated that work accidents result in annual deaths of over 14,000 individuals, injuries of more than 2,400,000 persons, and monetary costs of more than $11.5 billion.

DEFINITIONS

The term *accident* has been used with various shades of meanings. For certain purposes the National Safety Council considers an accident to mean "any unexpected event that interrupts or interferes with the orderly progress of the production activity or process." In this frame of reference, an accident may cause damage to equipment or materials or may delay production, without resulting in an injury or fatality. For our purposes, however, we will generally consider accidents to be events in which injuries or fatalities occur.

In 1971 a new procedure for recording and reporting occupational injuries and illnesses was promulgated under the Occupational Safety and Health Act of 1970. This procedure, described in the Federal Register (1971), records injuries and illnesses that result in:

Fatalities

Lost workday cases (these sometimes are called disabling injuries)

404

Nonfatal cases without lost workdays (cases without lost workdays which result in transfer to another job or termination of employment or require medical treatment other than first aid.)

In turn, we will consider *accident behavior* (or unsafe behavior) in the sense proposed by Whitlock and others (1963), as that behavior which might result in injury to the individual himself or herself, or to someone else; but we will stretch this concept to include possible physical damage (as in automobile driving) in addition to personal injury. Accident behavior, of course, does not necessarily result in personal injury or physical damage but can be considered as being a precipitating factor in by far the majority of accidents.

THE "CAUSES" OF ACCIDENTS

The objective of accident research is to ferret out data that can be used as the basis for taking action which will reduce the possibilities of subsequent accidents. Thus, one would wish to determine the "causes" of accidents. As Haddon and others (1964) showed, however, the "cause" of accidents frequently is used as a synonym for the mechanics of injury (for example, "piercing instruments") without recognizing that this often contributes little to the understanding of the behaviors leading up to the accident. Knowledge of the relationships of different variables to accidents—such as accident rates in different circumstances or for people of different ages—certainly can be useful, but one would hope ultimately to be able to "explain" the accident behavior that contributes to accident occurrence—or, to accentuate the positive—to isolate and describe the patterns of behavior which, as McGlade (1970) explained, *consistently* produce *safe* performance.

Because such explanations continue to elude us, we still have to deal largely with empirical relationships. Recognizing that

human behavior that contributes to accidents is the focus, it is logical for us to discuss such behavior in terms of two classes of variables—namely, *situational* and *individual.* One could hypothesize that the occurrence of all accidents is associated, at least theoretically, with some combination of one or both of these factors.

A MODEL OF THE ACCIDENT PHENOMENON

In discussing industrial accidents Surry (1968) proposed a model that seems to offer a reasonable frame of reference for viewing the occurrence of accidents.

Principal Stages of Model

The model has three principal stages, as shown in Figure 20.1 with two similar "cycles" linking them. Each intervening cycle is characterized by a series of six questions that can be answered by "yes" or "no."

Stage 1. The first stage is the *environment* in question, both spatial and temporal, with potential injury agents (moving equipment, machines, tools, hazards, etc.). It is out of this environment that a dangerous situation can arise, thus setting the stage for a possible accident (such as walking under an overhead crane, driving an automobile, or walking along a passage with a puddle of oil on the floor).

The link between this stage and the next is the *danger build-up cycle* with its sequence of events reflected by the six questions in Figure 20.1. If there is a negative response to anyone of the questions during this cycle, the danger is imminent. If all replies are affirmative, the danger will not grow and no injury or damage will ensue.

Stage 2. This is the stage of *hazard-imminent danger* caused by a condition or circumstance (a "release of energy") that, if unchecked, will lead to inevitable injury or damage (such as a bucket falling from the

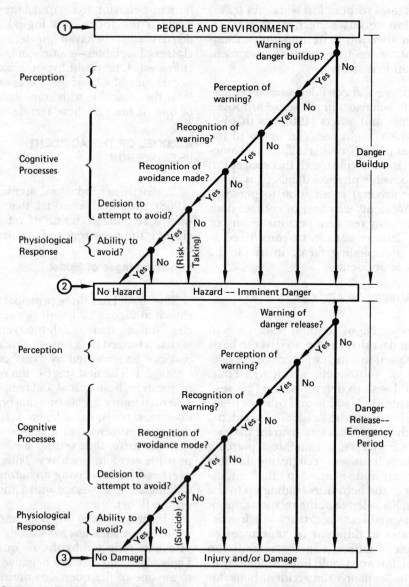

FIG. 20.1 A decision model of the accident process. (From Surry 1968, Figure 12, p. 41.)

overhead crane, an automobile crossing the lane immediately ahead of another car, or starting to slip on the oil on the floor). The cycle that links this stage to the third stage is the *danger release–emergency period* cycle, with its sequence of events also re-flected by the questions in Figure 20.1 (the same questions as for the danger build-up cycle). Any negative response to one of these questions will lead inevitably to injury or damage.

Stage 3. The third stage, *injury and/or*

damages (an "accident"), would develop if there is *any* negative response to one of the questions in the cycle leading to this stage. If the responses all are affirmative, no injury or damage will occur.

Needless to say, the time involved in this sequence of stages can vary tremendously. In some circumstances only seconds (or even split seconds) may separate them; thus the implied decisions to the sequences of questions (and the associated perceptual and cognitive processes and physiological responses) therefore may occur almost instantaneously. However, Surry showed that there was a definite distinction between the behaviors (really the decisions) implied by the two cycles of questions: people often court danger by taking risks in the face of *probable* danger build-up. (In some factories, mines, and other work situations, and in driving an automobile, one is continuously in a danger build-up stage). But if a condition of hazard (imminent danger) develops, and if a person continues to court danger in face of inevitable injury or damage, his actions are not risky but willful.

We can see in this model some distinction between situational and individual factors as they might influence accident liability. The situational factors are particularly associated with stage 1 (people and the en-

vironment), and the individual factors are primarily associated with the decision (and action) processes that occur during the danger build-up and danger release cycles.

SITUATIONAL FACTORS IN ACCIDENT OCCURRENCE

Figure 20.2 presents a conceptualization of situational factors and the way in which they might influence the liability of any given work situation. The *general characteristics of situations* and the *predisposing characteristics of situations* set the stage by establishing the probability of accident-inducing circumstances. In any given situation such a probability in combination with the *incidence of accident behavior* by people in the situation, determine the *liability (risk)* of accidents in the situation. The incidence of people's "normal" accident behavior can be thought of as the consequence of the combinations of decisions and actions (responses) of typical people to the situation that result in accidents. Although there are many different situational factors that can be related to frequency rates, a few examples will illustrate that such relationships exist.

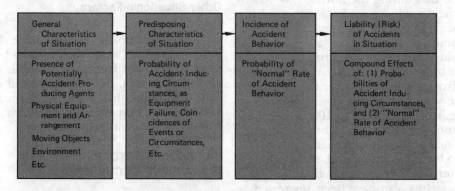

FIG. 20.2 Generalized illustration of the manner in which situational factors can influence the accident liability rate. This illustration is based on the incidence of some "normal" rate of accident behavior, such as might be expected by well-qualified, well-trained personnel.

Job Factors

The differences in injury rates as related to different jobs are illustrated in the following tabulation of the average number of hospital visits per year for employees on each of a few jobs in a steel mill:

Job	Average Number of Hospital Visits
Crane operator	3.55
Reckoner	2.96
Sheet inspector	2.54
Potman	2.10
Supervisor	1.16
Roll turner	.47

Closely associated with differences in rates for various jobs are the differences associated with various departments. In this regard, the average number of hospital visits of personnel in eleven departments of the steel mill ranged from .55 to 1.26.

In many job situations, appropriate human factors principles applied to the design of equipment can reduce the probabilities of accidents.

Work Schedule

From a review of research relating accidents to work schedules Surry (1968) concluded that during the normal day schedule, their incidence tends to increase from the beginning of the morning work period, reaching a peak during the later part of the morning, but tends to drop before the lunch break. The increase in the accident rate from the low period at the beginning of the work period and the peak tends to range from 50 percent to 100 percent. After lunch the rate tends to be low but rises until mid-afternoon and then tends to decline a bit or to remain level. Although such a pattern has been attributed to "fatigue," other factors also have been suggested as causes, such as reduced motivation (especially since in anticipation of lunch the rate sometimes goes down) and the possibility of generally increased activity in the work situation. But it would be risky to attribute the pattern to any single factor. For night shift work there is a different tendency. The rate tends to be high at the beginning of the shift but then drops, increasing slightly after work breaks but then dropping again. Here, again, there is no clear explanation. Although these patterns of accidents as related to work schedules have been found in certain work situations, we should not assume that they are universal.

Atmospheric Conditions

In certain studies of atmospheric conditions, an inverted ∪ shaped curve has been found to characterize the relationship between temperature and accidents, with the accident rate being lowest near an "optimum" temperature and higher in lower and higher temperatures (Surry 1968). The optimum temperature in any given circumstance would depend upon the nature of the task work, the clothing worn, the degree of acclimatization of the workers, and even the age of the individuals, but in one study of British industrial workers to which Surry refers, the optimum was in the upper sixties.

Other Situational Factors

Other situational factors have been found in various work situations to be related to accident frequency, including sociological factors, but the above will illustrate the point that many work-situation variables can, in specific job situations, contribute to accident frequency.

INDIVIDUAL FACTORS IN ACCIDENT OCCURRENCE

Figure 20.3 presents a conceptualization of how individual (personal) factors may influence the incidence of an individual's

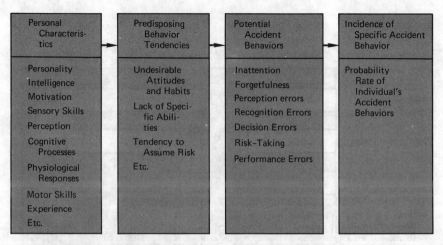

Personal Characteristics	Predisposing Behavior Tendencies	Potential Accident Behaviors	Incidence of Specific Accident Behavior
Personality Intelligence Motivation Sensory Skills Perception Cognitive Processes Physiological Responses Motor Skills Experience Etc.	Undesirable Attitudes and Habits Lack of Specific Abilities Tendency to Assume Risk Etc.	Inattention Forgetfulness Perception errors Recognition Errors Decision Errors Risk-Taking Performance Errors	Probability Rate of Individual's Accident Behaviors

FIG. 20.3 Generalized formulation of the manner in which individual factors may influence the incidence of accident behaviors of individuals.

accident behaviors. An individual's *personal characteristics* give rise to one's *predisposing behavior tendencies* that in turn influence *potential accident behaviors,* thus in a sense contributing to the *incidence of specific accident behavior* of an individual in any given situation. Surry's formulation (shown in Figure 20.1) specifically refers to the human functions of perception, cognitive processes, and physiological responses as contributing to the decisions and resulting actions implied in her model. Errors in such functions are the behaviors that contribute to accident causation (as indicated in the third block of Figure 20.3). Referring specifically to motor vehicle driving, the Indiana University Institute for Research in Public Safety (IRPS) (1973) and Fell (1976) categorized the "causes" of accidents in somewhat corresponding terms, as follows:

Those (and perhaps other) errors can then be regarded as behaviors that, in combination with situational factors, can cause

accidents. It should be noted that the specific *types* of behaviors that can contribute to accidents in any *given* circumstances depend on the nature of the circumstance. For motor vehicle accidents, a study of 150 collisions by the IRPS (1973) included a careful, in-depth analysis of the "direct cause" of the accidents in terms of the categories listed above. The allocation of direct causes were made according to decisions of *definite* involvement and *probable* involvement. The results, shown in Figure 20.4, indicate that decision errors and recognition errors were dominant.

More conclusive evidence that accident behaviors do contribute to accident occurrence came from a study by Whitlock and others (1963) on industrial workers. They arranged for supervisors of 350 employees on similar production jobs to record employees' "unsafe behaviors," using the critical incident technique, over a period of about eight months. The number of unsafe

Surry	IRPS	Fell
Perception	—	Perception failure
—	Recognition	Comprehension failure
Cognitive processes	Decision errors	Decision failure
Physiological response	Performance errors	Action failure
—	Critical non-performance (blackout, etc.)	

409

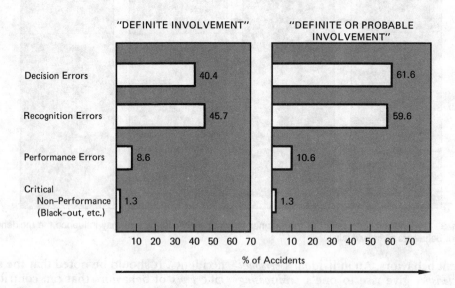

	"DEFINITE INVOLVEMENT"	"DEFINITE OR PROBABLE INVOLVEMENT"
Decision Errors	40.4	61.6
Recognition Errors	45.7	59.6
Performance Errors	8.6	10.6
Critical Non–Performance (Black–out, etc.)	1.3	1.3

% of Accidents

FIG. 20.4 Summary of types of errors determined as definite or probable causes of 150 automobile accidents. (From study by the Institute for Research in Public Safety, Indiana University—DOT HS 800 850, 1973—as presented by Fell 1976, Figure 2.)

behaviors served as an "accident-behavior" score for each individual. (The average score was 3.01). These scores, in turn, were correlated with injuries recorded during the eight-month period and for as long as five years after the study. The correlations, for 284 employees for whom injury records were available for various periods of time, are given below:

Time period: 1 2 3 4 5

(years)

Correlation: .35 .49 .29 .51 .56

These correlations, along with data from other sources, strongly support the contention that accidents are in part the consequence of unsafe behaviors and that people (in at least some situations) tend somewhat to maintain over time a somewhat consistent pattern of such behaviors—a high, average, or low rate as the case may be.

Granting that we all perform unsafe acts

and all have accidents, the central questions for accident research as related to individuals are these:

1. Are there *significant differences* among people in the incidence of accident behaviors (and of accidents)—within specific situations and/or across different situations?

2. If so, what personal differences (if any) are there among individuals in terms of accident behavior or accidents?

Accident Behavior and Accidents within Specific Situations

One cannot say that there are significant, individual differences in accident behaviors and accidents among personnel in each of the many types of jobs or in each of the many other situations in life, but one can say that in *some* jobs and in *some* situations, people do differ significantly in both of these respects.

CONSISTENCY OF ACCIDENT-RE-LATED BEHAVIOR. Although people in any given situation might differ in the frequency of their accident behaviors and accidents, the mere fact of such differences should not per se delude us into concluding that those with high frequencies are "accident prone." The accident literature is strewn with instances in which individuals with above average numbers of accidents during *one* period of time have been erroneously labeled as "accident prone." Some years ago Mintz and Blum (1949) called attention to the fact that if *only* chance factors were "causing" accidents, individuals would not be equally lucky or unlucky during given periods of work. If chance factors alone were operating, the situation would be analogous to tossing coins. If 1,000 individuals were each to toss ten coins, the average number of heads per person would be very close to five. But the individuals would vary in number of heads from very few (perhaps none) to many (perhaps ten). If we simply identify those who tossed heads eight or more times, and call these "heads-prone," we would be making the same error that is made when individuals who have more than the average number of accidents for one period of time are called "accident-prone."

Given any specified number of individuals (with equal liability) and a specified number of accidents, it is possible to determine, statistically, the "expected" distribution of accidents *if* they were distributed by chance. Such an expected distribution is illustrated in Figure 20.5, this being the expected distribution of 1,470 minor injuries suffered by 1,060 individuals over a specified period of time. From this we can see that 51 individuals (42 + 6 + 3) would be *expected* (by chance) to have 4 or more accidents, even though the average would be only 1.4. We can see that 170 individuals (16 percent) would be expected (by chance) to have 600 (40 percent) of the accidents.

Granting that chance factors can (and typically do) result in some people having more accidents than others do, there are indeed specific situations in which some individuals have more accidents than can reasonably be attributed to chance. To determine if some individuals do have more accidents than can be attributed to chance, however, one needs to carry out some type of statistical analysis. One procedure is to compare the *actual* distribution of accidents

NUMBER OF ACCIDENTS (N)	NUMBER OF MEN SUFFERING N ACCIDENTS				TOTAL NUMBER OF ACCIDENTS			
0			266			0		
1			368			368		
2			256			512		
3			119			357		
4	170	51	42	16% / 75%	600	168	40% / 100%
5			6			30		
6 or more			3			35		

FIG. 20.5 Estimated "chance" distribution of 1,470 accidents among 1,060 individuals all equally liable. (From Froggatt & Smiley, 1964, as adapted by Surry 1968, Table B.4, p. 189.)

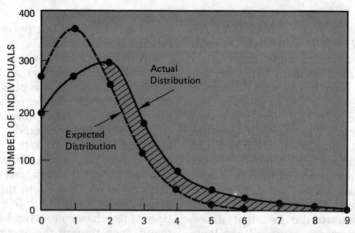

FIG. 20.6 Comparison of an expected (chance) distribution of 1,470 accidents (as based on data in Figure 20.5) and a hypothetical actual distribution to illustrate tendency toward accident repetitiveness on the part of some individuals (illustrated by the shaded area).

(for people with similar liability) with the (chance) *expected* distribution (such as the expected distribution shown in Figure 20.-5). If the actual distribution differs significantly from the expected distribution, it then can be inferred that some individuals do in fact have more accidents than can be accounted for by chance. This is illustrated by a hypothetical example in Figure 20.6. The expected distribution in that figure is the one represented in Figure 20.5, but the "actual" distribution is hypothetical and is exaggerated in order to illustrate the point. The shaded area between the two curves represents the extent to which the actual distribution stretches beyond the expected distribution and thus indicates the probable influence of individual factors on accident occurrence.

Another statistical procedure that can be used is comparing the number of accidents of individuals over time, such as for two periods of time. In this regard Maritz (1950) urged using the technique of correlating accident records for consecutive periods of time as the basis for determining if there is such a pattern. Such correlations, of course, would have to be statistically significant to demonstrate this.

Statistical evidence developed by either

of these (or other) methods can support the hypothesis of what we will call *accident repetitiveness* in the situation, that is, the systematic tendency for some individuals to have more accidents than can be attributed to chance. (Note that we are avoiding the term *accident proneness.*)

EVIDENCE OF ACCIDENT REPETITIVENESS. Such statistically confirmed evidence has been presented for many different jobs and other situations, indicating that—in such circumstances—there is a tendency for individuals to maintain their accident rates over time. Such evidence was presented by Mintz (1954), for example. In a study by one of the authors, an injury index was derived for employees on three jobs. This index, based on the frequency of accidents per thousand hours worked, was derived separately from two six-month periods, and these were then correlated. The correlations are given below:

Job	Correlation
Drill press	.86
Assembler	.88
Machine operator	.74

Such a pattern of accident repetitiveness

is also evident from accident records for about nine thousand employees in a steel mill, as shown in Figure 20.7. The solid line of this figure shows the relationship between number of hospital visits (which reflect injuries) for two successive years for the employees. These data cover eleven departments, and although the accident rates for the various departments varied (indicating varying liability), the relationship within each department was relatively the same as that shown in the figure.

Because of different accident liability for the various jobs included in these data, it is possible that that relationship might be accentuated or distorted to some extent. An adjustment was made to eliminate this possible distortion and the corrected curve in Figure 20.7 (the dotted line) turned out to be substantially the same, thus essentially confirming the implication that the employees tended to maintain their "individual" accident rates over time. Further examples come from the study by Whitlock and others (1968). The correlation between the numbers of unsafe behaviors between the odd-numbered weeks and the even-numbered weeks for the eight-month period was .74 (The corresponding correlation for a sample of workers in a chemical plant was .93.) In turn, correlations of numbers of injuries for odd-numbered months and even-numbered months also were derived; these were computed separately for personnel for whom data were available for the different periods of time. The resulting correlations were .63 for one year of data, .58 for two years, .75 for three years, .66 for four years, and .67 for five years. Data from this study thus reflect a distinct tendency for the personnel to maintain their own rates of accident behaviors and of injuries over time, regardless of whether these rates are high, average, or low.

Accident Behavior and Accidents across Situations

As we shift to the discussion of accident behavior and accidents across situations,

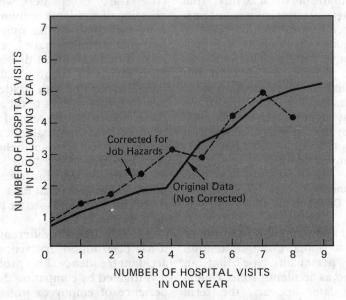

FIG. 20.7 Relationship between number of hospital visits for two successive years among about 9,000 steelworkers. The solid line represents the original data, while the dotted line represents the same data "corrected" for differences in job hazards.

we can no longer stave off a discussion of the notion of accident proneness. The concept of accident proneness has been discussed since roughly the 1920s, with various implied meanings. Of these various meanings, Suchman and Scherzer stated what is perhaps the most common one: "Accident proneness . . . implies the existence of a particular personality type which is predisposed toward having repeated accidents. This predisposition is regarded as a psychological abnormality due to some underlying neurotic or psychopathic condition" (1960, p. 7). They then showed that the evidence in support of this concept of accident proneness is not conclusive and therefore argued against the use of the term in this sense.

Another possible interpretation of accident proneness is that it is a generalized pattern of accident repetitiveness reflected by a tendency of some people to be accident repeaters in virtually any situation. In this sense, the concept of accident proneness merely describes such a tendency, but does not explain the personal factor(s) that induce the pattern. At present it is not possible to produce any substantial body of data that unequivocally confirms this generalized repetitive pattern. This is not to say that such a pattern does *not* exist, but rather that it has not been demonstrably confirmed. Actually, there are some straws in the wind that suggest there may be such a tendency, but even if it is confirmed, it probably will not "account" for a large portion of our many accidents.

Accident Proneness: An Operational Concept

As discussed above, there is no substantive evidence to support the contention that there is a "personality type" that can be characterized as accident prone. Unless such evidence later appears, the term should not be used in this frame of reference. If the term is used at all, we urge that

it be used *strictly* in a statistical, descriptive sense, to refer to the *consistent* tendency of some individuals to have more accidents than reasonably can be attributed to chance. By and large, this implies that this tendency should be viewed as *situational*, for there is not yet convincing evidence that the accident repeaters in one situation are also accident repeaters in other circumstances (although this ultimately may prove to be the case).

Specific Personal Factors Related to Accidents

If, in any given situation with a given situation liability, there is confirmed evidence of accident repetitiveness, it is logical to wonder what personal qualities differentiate between those individuals with high accident rates and those with low rates. Analyses of such possible relationships are carried out in essentially the same manner as the validation of tests and other predictors as related to job performance criteria are, except here we would use a criterion of accidents or injuries. It appears from such analyses that quite a number of personal attributes have been found to be related to accidents in different situations. Such variations suggest that the personal factors associated with accident occurrence may be rather specific to the situation itself; these factors may be related to the specific types of behaviors that contribute to accidents (that is, accident behaviors) or the converse (that is, the "safe" behaviors). A few examples will illustrate the range of personal variables that have been found— in specific situations—to be related to accident frequency.

VISION. In many different types of jobs, it has been found that vision is related to accident frequency. This problem has been investigated by comparing the accident experience of empoyees whose visual skills meet certain statistically determined standards with the corresponding accident ex-

TABLE 20.1 RESULTS OF VISUAL SKILL TESTS IN RELATION TO INJURIES

| N | Group | Percent who had not over two injuries during the period of the investigation among those who: | |
		Pass Visual Standards	*Fail Visual Standards*
59	Passenger car drivers	71	42
116	Mobile equipment operators	74	71
65	Machine operators	67	50
15	Machine operators	67	44
29	Sheet metal workers	58	41
105	Maintenance men	81	75
63	City bus drivers	44	33
66	Intercity bus drivers	54	30
68	Supervisors	65	57
125	Machine operators	56	32
102	Laborers	82	89
15	Skilled tradesmen	45	33
828	All groups combined	65	57

perience of employees whose vision does not meet these standards. Table 20.1 summarizes the data from a study by Kephart and Tiffin (1950) on the relationship between injuries and visual skills for twelve groups of people—passenger car drivers and employees on eleven different jobs. This table shows, for those who passed and those who failed the visual standards, the percentage who had no more than two injuries during the specified time period. In all but one of the groups those who passed the visual standards had better accident records than those who failed.

The results of another study on vision and accidents are shown in Figure 20.8; this particular example was of paper machine operators.

AGE AND LENGTH OF SERVICE. A number of accident surveys have revealed relationships between age and accident data. As might be expected, these surveys do not reveal entirely consistent results, and one could hypothesize that different patterns might be found for different jobs or activities. Data from a steel mill on hospital visits for men of varying ages and lengths of service on their present jobs are shown in Figure 20.9. Both of these sets of data show a sharp rise and then a constant tapering off.

The age curve in this figure has the same

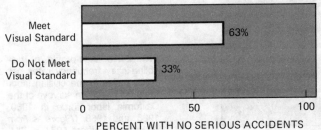

PERCENT WITH NO SERIOUS ACCIDENTS
IN ONE YEAR*

* A "serious" accident is one requiring the attention of the plant physician.

FIG. 20.8 Vision in relation to serious accidents among 104 paper machine operators.

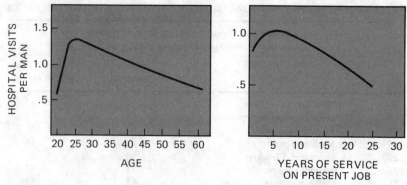

FIG. 20.9 Hospital visits per man per year in relation to age and years of service on present job among 9,000 steel workers.

general form as one based on three age-injury surveys carried out by the California Division of Labor Statistics and Research, covering 135,000, 153,000, and 169,000 men. The consolidated data are shown in Figure 20.10, as presented by Gordon and others (1971). Granting the similarities of the age curves in Figures 20.9 and 20.10, both of which are based on large numbers of cases, one needs to interpret these with some caution, particularly because they do not control for accident liability. It is conceivable that, say, very young workers and older workers might be placed in jobs not as hazardous as those in which men in their twenties are placed. Despite this possible

source of distortion, however, the impression remains that accident rates tend to be associated with age across a variety of jobs in the labor market, with the most susceptible ages being in the early twenties. Why this is so is not clear, but the fact of such a relationship is important to the management of a safety program.

PERCEPTUAL-MOTOR RELATION-SHIPS. As implied above, the specific behavior tendencies that predispose people to having high accident rates might well be different in different circumstances because of the special activities in the various circumstances. Some years ago Drake (1940) turned up some interesting data in a study

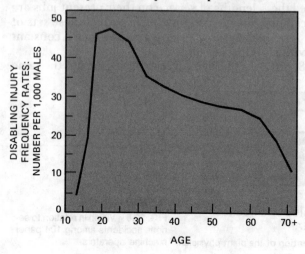

FIG. 20.10 Age-profile of disabling-injury frequency rates per 1,000 males in the civilian labor force, as based on surveys of the California labor force in 1960, 1965, and 1968. (*Figure is from Gordon and others 1971, p. 211, as based on California work injury surveys.*)

of accidents in relation to perceptual speed and motor (that is, muscular) speed in one industrial operation. He administered tests to measure these two variables to thirty-eight employees for whom an "accident index" was available. While examining his data he noted that those with accident records tended to have motor speed scores relatively better than their scores on the perceptual speed tests. Conversely, the accident-free individuals tended to have scores on the perceptual speed tests that were relatively better than their motor speed test scores were. By a procedure that need not be described here, he derived a composite score that indicated the relative difference between each person's perceptual speed and his motor speed. The relationship of these scores to the accident indexes of the thirty-eight employees is shown in Figure 20.11. The general trend of the relationship is clear. Though it is not a straight line or linear relation, individuals with negative composite scores show a definite tendency to be among those with the high accident indexes, whereas those with the positive composite scores are relatively free from accidents. Drake's statement of the principle, as illustrated in Figure 20.11, is that:

> Individuals whose level of muscular reaction is above their level of perception are prone to more frequent and more severe accidents than those individuals whose muscular actions are below their perceptual level. In other words, the person who reacts quicker than he can perceive is more likely to have accidents than is the person who can perceive quicker than he can react. (1940, p. 339)

More recently, investigation of perceptual-motor relationships was revived by Babarik (1968) in the context of automobile accidents. Suggesting the possibility that *specific* "refined" patterns of component perceptual-motor factors might be associated with *specific* driving acts, Babarik explored such a pattern in connection with rear-end or struck-from-behind accidents, which are quite common. Relative to emergency stopping in traffic, he argued that drivers who make up for long "initiation" time with fast movements (that is, have short movement time and thus stop their vehicles more abruptly after applying the

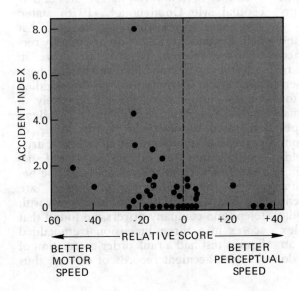

FIG. 20.11 Relationship between accident frequency of thirty-eight industrial workers and the relative difference between their motor (that is, muscular) speed and perceptual speed. (*From Drake 1940.*)

brake) would be expected to have more rear-end accidents than drivers who—in the same time—initiate a movement more rapidly but make a less abrupt stopping movement. A ratio of these was found to be significantly related to rear-end accidents with a sample of 104 taxi drivers. Those with the most markedly different such ratios were referred to as having "desynchronizing" reaction patterns, whereas the others were referred to as "normal." The results are summarized briefly below, in particular showing the percentage of drivers in these two groups who had two or more rear-end accidents.

Reaction-pattern Group	*Drivers with Two or More Rear-end Accidents*
Normal	10 percent
Desynchronizing	38 percent

Although certain other findings from this study left the water a bit murky, the fact that in both this study and Drake's a combination of perceptual-motor factors was related to accidents in the specific situations under examination suggests that how such factors are related to the *specific* activities of people may contribute to accident occurrence—and, conversely, to safety.

PERCEPTUAL STYLE. Aside from the perceptual-motor relationships mentioned above as related to accidents, there are some clues that what is referred to as "perceptual style" is another personal factor that can contribute to driving accidents. Barrett and Thornton (1968) were especially interested in the perceptual style concept of field-dependence versus field-independence (Witkin and others 1962). This construct is viewed as a continuum along which individuals may be differentiated with respect to their perceptual abilities to discriminate figures in a complex background (or to "pull" a figure from an embedded context). Those who do not do this well are referred to as field-dependent (that is, the visual "field" somehow inhibits their perception of the "embedded figure" in the field); those who are better at "seeing" a figure in an embedded background are referred to as field-*in*dependent.

Using this distinction, Barrett and Thornton tested a group of fifty men in a driving simulator. They were particularly concerned with the response of the drivers to an "emergency" created by a "dummy" figure appearing in the simulated model. Various measures of subject response were obtained, including reaction time and deceleration rate. These, in turn, were related to a measure of field-dependence and field-independence. The results as related to the deceleration rate criterion are shown in Figure 20.12. Although these results were obtained in a simulated situation, Harano (1969) provided some data based on twenty-seven "no accident" subjects and twenty-eight "accident" subjects which indicated that the relationship may hold up in actual driving, inasmuch as he found that field-independent individuals had had better accident records for three years than field-dependent individuals had had.

From a review of relevant studies of perceptual syle Goodenough (1976) stated that there was evidence to suggest that field-dependent drivers do not quickly recognize developing hazards, are slower in responding to embedded road signs, have difficulty in learning to control a skidding vehicle, and fail to drive defensively in high-speed traffic. As Williams (1977) demonstrated, however, the various studies of perceptual style as related to vehicular driving have met with varying degrees of success. But such mixed results might be because the tests typically used are two-dimensional. In a follow-up study with telephone company drivers, he found that scores in a three-dimensional embedded figures test had a rank order correlation of .77 with accident records of drivers, thus

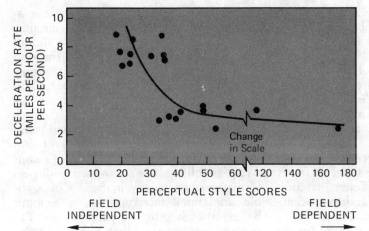

FIG. 20.12 Relationship between perceptual style and deceleration rate of fifty subjects in an "emergency" during a simulated driving task. (*From Barrett & Thornton 1968, Figure 3.*)

emphasizing the possible importance of stereoscopic vision to the testing of field-dependence versus field-independence.

Certainly more data are necessary to nail down the relevance of perceptual style to vehicular driving, but the current cues suggest that this may be important to minimizing vehicular accidents and probably especially so when using a three-dimensional test using stereoscopic vision.

OTHER FACTORS. In some job situations various other personal factors have been found to be related to accident occurrence, some of these having been measured by tests of one sort or another. For example, Kunce (1967) reported that a certain combination of scores on the Strong Vocational Interest Blank (SVIB) that he re-

ferred to as an "accident proneness" index was related to the accident rates of employees of a food processing plant, as shown in Figure 20.13. In some circumstances personality factors have been found to be related to accident occurrence. Spangenberg (1968), for example, reported a correlation of .53 between scores in the Thematic Apperception Test (TAT)—a projective personality test—and accident records for a sample of seventy-five bus drivers in South Africa. The results of this study, however, are in rather marked contrast with an analysis by Goldstein (1964) of the results of several studies in which personal, emotional, and attitudinal factors were generally rather miserable predictors of traffic accidents.

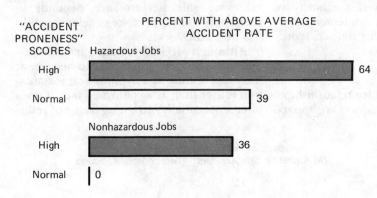

FIG. 20.13 Relationship between an "accident proneness" index (based on the Strong Vocational Interest Blank) and accident rates of sixty-two male employees on jobs rated hazardous and nonhazardous in a food processing plant. (*Adapted from Kunce 1967.*)

With regard to other types of tests Ruch (1965) reported that a combination of two paper-and-pencil tests did a good job of differentiating between "accident-free" and "accident prone" patrol car officers in a large metropolitan police department. The tests were the Space Visualization test of the Employee Aptitude Survey and the McGuire Safe Driver Scale. The results are recapped below.

DISCUSSION. In an overview, we can see that many different personal variables have been found, in different circumstances, to be related to accident occurrence. Surry (1968) summarized many other investigations of this type, including some concerned with personal factors other than those discussed above. But Surry's survey, and some of the above studies, revealed that some factors that one might *expect* to be related to accident frequency have *not* been found to be so related. Such inconclusive findings may in part be because of the limited reliability of criteria. As Goldstein explained, accident records themselves do not measure a very stable human performance characteristic, and accident repeaters account for only a very small part of the total traffic accidents on record. This is because the number of accidents per individual in the usual reporting periods is small, and because "chance" factors probably contribute to some of these, thus partially masking whatever underlying "accident repeating" pattern there may be. Although Goldstein referred specifically to automobile driving, the statement has some relevance also to industrial accidents.

ADJUSTIVE BEHAVIOR

In those situations in which relationships of personal factors and accidents are apparent, we have argued for viewing these relationships in the context of the specific situation at hand. Conversely, we also should argue for persistent efforts in tracking down any patterns of relationships that may be more generally applied between and among various accident situations or classes of such situations.

In this regard, McGlade proposed using the construct of *adjustive behavior* in relation to safe performance. He defined this construct as follows: *Consistent* successful performance of an activity, in the face of possible unplanned interruptions, is *adjustive* behavior leading to safe performance. Expressed another way, such behavior is the capacity to "mesh" a person's "abilities, skills, and tasks into a meaningful whole which brings about successful performance of an activity in virtually all situations and under almost all conditions" (1970, p. 33). McGlade envisioned the construct of adjustiveness as being more or less related to perceptual style or life style.

Of course, the specific "form" of adjustive behavior in any given situation would have to be appropriate to that situation and could consist of varying combinations of both "unguided" behavior (automatic, habituated responses) and of "guided" behavior (intentionally performed responses). Such specific behaviors, however, are rooted in the individual's general abilities and skills. Thus, it seems that the effectiveness of one's adjustive behavior in achieving safe performance depends in part upon one's repertoire of relevant abilities and skills.

Although McGlade's construct of adjustive behavior probably needs to be seen at the present time as a hypothetical formulation rather than as a confirmed fact, it does offer a potentially intriguing frame of refer-

	Number of Patrol Officers with:		
	No Accidents	*One Accident*	*Two or More Accidents*
Passed tests	40	15	8
Failed tests	6	8	13

ence to explain at least some of the accidents that can be attributed to personal factors. Taking some license in interpreting the construct, we may conclude that the "adjustive behavior" of those whose "life style" includes such adjustiveness tends to contribute to their more consistent *exercise* of those abilities and skills which—*in the specific situation*—are required for safe performance. Without the required skills, individuals with such an adjustive "life style" might encounter accidents, but perhaps not to the extent experienced by others who also lacked the requisite skills but whose life styles did not incline them toward "adjustive behavior."

Adjustive behavior, then, can be viewed as a consistent predisposition toward safe behavior—essentially an attitude. One is thus led to speculate about the possibility that *if* there is in fact any general tendency for some people to perform more safely—wherever they may be—the underpinnings of that tendency might well be an attitudinal proclivity toward behaving in a safe manner. The actual *effectiveness* of such a tendency to engage in "adjustive behavior" would depend, of course, upon the possession of the requisite skills.

THE REDUCTION OF ACCIDENTS

From our previous discussion, it follows that efforts to reduce accidents must be in the direction of (1) reducing the liability of the situation or (2) minimizing the possible influence of any relevant personal factors. The wares of the safety engineers cover a spectrum of techniques, procedures, and guidelines directed toward reducing situational liability. These include the installation of protective guards on machines, changes of method, arrangement of materials and equipment, use of protective clothing and gear, improvements in the environment, and a wide range of other techniques aimed at minimizing specific types of hazards. As indicated in chapters 16 and 19, the design of equipment and the nature of

the physical environment can affect the accident liability of specific situations. In fact, a major part of the field of human factors engineering is directed toward the design of equipment and work environments for improved safety.

In our discussion we will touch on at least a few of the possible approaches to reducing accidents from the human liability side of the coin, rather than from the situational side.

Personnel Selection and Placement

When it has been demonstrated that some personal factor is *significantly related* to accident frequency on a given job or in some other circumstance, it is then possible to select those individuals with characteristics associated with good accident records. In some circumstances biographical data might be relevant, such as age. In other circumstances certain tests might be appropriate, such as vision tests, psychomotor tests, and job sample tests. In using job sample tests, for example, Leslie and Adams (1973) used a simulated punch press in a job training program. (The variations in training included programmed instruction methods with audio-visual and videotape presentations, as well as "classical" training methods.) The simulated punch press was rigged up with electric eyes to detect errors (which, in a normal operation, could result in accidents) that prevented the operators from having holes punched in their fingers. One recommendation made by the investigators was that a simulator could be used effectively in personnel selection to weed out individuals who, because of their lack of proper safety attitudes or their deficiencies in manual skills, are not suitable to be punch press operators. This recommendation is in line with the concept of behavioral consistency discussed in chapter 8 and is rooted in the notion that *samples* of performance similar to the activities one is supposed to learn to do generally are better predictors of future performance than *signs* (such as aptitude tests) are that are less like the activity one is supposed to learn to do.

Safety Training

Surry (1968) has pointed out that past experience greatly reduces accidents and that training can provide certain aspects of this experience. Especially for new employees, it may be appropriate to set up training programs before they begin their jobs, in order to acquaint them with possible hazards and with those practices and methods that will minimize the likelihood of their having accidents, and to develop proper attitudes toward safety practices. Training programs sometimes also are appropriate for current employees. In such training programs it is, of course, important to apply sound principles of learning, as discussed in chapter 12.

For the communication media used in safety training programs, the *Accident Prevention Manual for Industrial Operations* of the National Safety Council ranks the methods on a scale of concrete to abstract experience, showing that the more concrete the method is, the more effective it is. The ranking of the methods is as follows:

DO—Actual experience (most effective)

DO—Acting role

TELL AND SHOW—Demonstration

SHOW—Live on spot

SHOW—Display or exhibit

TELL AND SHOW—Sound film, TV

TELL—Lecture

SHOW—Charts

TELL—Recordings (1974, Figure 14-1, p. 316)

One needs to accept such a ranking with a few grains of salt since the effectiveness of communications depends very much on the type of material to be communicated, and some safety training material might best be transmitted by methods not near the top of such a list, but such a list can provide some general guidance in selecting training methods.* In considering techniques of training, safety training might use programmed instruction which Leslie and Adams (1973) found to be reasonably effective in training with the simulated punch press referred to above.

The dramatic reduction in accidents since the turn of the century has been, of course, because of many factors, including the improvement of the machines and equipment people use in their jobs, the use of safety devices, and the improvement of working conditions. Among these, however, one should include safety training. An excellent example of a reduction in lost-time injuries which followed an intensive training program on safety teamwork was reported by Ewell (1955). His report covers the experience of the Proctor and Gamble company with its safety program—one aspect of which consisted of safety training—in twenty of its plants over a span of twenty-five years. Figure 20.14 shows the lost-time accident rates during that period, starting out at over 30 per million working hours and dropping to about 1.01. In the last year, incidentally, eleven of the twenty plants had perfect records. It should be added that this dramatic reduction was the consequence of the complete safety program, including efforts to minimize hazards, publicity, training, and so forth, so that it cannot be entirely attributed to training alone. But the results do reflect what a comprehensive safety program can accomplish in an organization.

*For the use of various visual aids for safety training the *Accident Prevention Manual for Industrial Operations* (1974) presents information on the major features and limitations of several such aids in Table 14-B, p. 318.

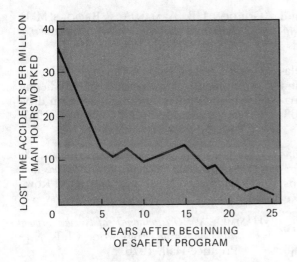

FIG. 20.14 Lost-time injury reduction following a safety program (including safety training) in twenty plants of the Proctor and Gamble Company. (*From Ewell 1955.*)

Persuasion and Propaganda

Various forms of persuasion and propaganda—posters and placards, for example—are used in most safety programs. The effect of such techniques is sometimes difficult to assess. In one investigation, however, Laner and Sell (1960) surveyed the effects of safety posters in thirteen steel plants in Great Britain during a six-week period and reported that in seven of the plants "safe behavior" increased by more than 20 percent. In the use of posters and placards both common sense and sound psychological principles argue for writing their messages in terms of specific actions and practices that contribute to safe performance, or conversely to accidents, rather than simply using general platitudes such as "Be Careful."

Surry (1968) offered certain suggestions for developing propaganda campaigns, including the following: (1) use sound premises based on known cause-and-effect relationships; (2) use various media of information exposure; (3) use a direct (as opposed to a diffuse) approach in which the campaign is aimed at specific points, rather than a more general appeal; and (4) make sure the appeal pertains to the persons to whom it is directed.

Discussion

The occurrence of accidents is a major concern of many organizations and their employees. The Occupational Safety and Health Act of 1970, one hopes, will serve as the impetus to improve working conditions in some industries toward reducing accidents. But accidents pervade areas of human life in addition to work situations, as in driving, using consumer products, working around the home, mowing the yard, or mountain climbing. The point on which we will terminate this discussion is that in efforts to reduce accidents in any kind of situation one needs to be fortified with relevant research data in order to know what specific approaches and programs would be most appropriate to the specific situation.

REFERENCES

Accident prevention manual for industrial operations (7th ed.). Chicago: National Safety Council, 1974.

BABARIK, P. Automobile accidents and driver reaction pattern. *Journal of Applied Psychology,* 1968, *52* (1), 49–54.

BARRETT, G. V., & THORNTON, C. L. Relationship between perceptual style and driver reaction to an emergency situation. *Journal of Applied Psychology,* 1968, *52* (2), 169–176.

California work injuries, 1960, 1965, and 1968. San Francisco: State of California, Department of Human Relations, Division of Labor Statistics and Research, November 1961, December 1966, and September 1969, Tables 16.

DRAKE, C. A. Accident proneness: A hypothesis. *Character and Personality,* 1940, *8,* 335–341.

EWELL, J. M. *1955, a yardstick for '56.* Proctor and Gamble Safety Bulletin, January 1956.

Federal Register, Friday, July 2, 1971, *36* (128), 12612–12616.

FELL, J. C. A motor vehicle accident causal system: The human element. *Human Factors,* 1976, *18* (1), 85–94.

FROGGATT, P., & SMILEY, J. A. The concept of accident proneness. *British Journal of Industrial Medicine,* January 1964, *21,* 1–12.

GOLDSTEIN, L. G. Human variables in traffic accidents: A digest of research. *Traffic Safety Research Review* (National Safety Council), March 1964, *8* (1), 26–31.

GOODENOUGH, D. R. A review of individual differences in field dependence as a factor in auto safety. *Human Factors,* 1976, *18* (1), 53–62.

GORDON, J. B., AKMAN, A., & BROOKS, M. L. *Industrial accident statistics: A re-examination.* New York: Praeger, 1971.

GREENSHIELDS, B. D., & PLATT, F. N. Development of a method of predicting high-accident and high-violation drivers. *Journal of Applied Psychology,* 1967, *51* (3), 205–210.

HADDON, W., JR., SUCHMAN, E. A., & KLEIN, D. *Accident research: Methods and approaches.* New York: Harper & Row, 1964.

HAMMER, W. *Occupational safety management and engineering,* Englewood Cliffs, N.J.: Prentice-Hall, 1976.

HARANO, R. M. *The relationship between field dependence and motor vehicle accident involvement.* American Psychological Association, Experimental Publication System. October 1969, Issue No. 2, Ms. No. 065B.

Institute for Research in Public Safety (IRPS), Indiana University. A study to determine the relationship between vehicle defects and failure, and vehicle crashes, Vol. 1. Study findings, part 1, regarding accident causes. Washington, D.C.: Department of Transportation, DOT HS 800 850, 1973.

KEPHART, N. C., & TIFFIN, J. Vision and accident experience. *National Safety News,* 1950, *62,* 90–91.

KUNCE, J. T. Vocational interest and accident proneness. *Journal of Applied Psychology,* 1967, *51* (3), 223–225.

LANER, S., & SELL, R. G. An experiment on the effect of specially designed safety posters. *Occupational Psychology,* 1960, *34,* 153–169.

LESLIE, J. H., JR., & ADAMS, S. K. Programmed safety through programmed learning. *Human Factors*, 1973, *15* (3), 223–236.

MARITZ, J. S. On the validity of inference drawn from the fitting of Poisson and negative binomial distributions to observed accident data. *Psychological Bulletin*, 1950, *47*, 434–443.

McGLADE, F. S. *Adjustive behavior and safe performance.* Springfield, Ill.: Charles C. Thomas, 1970, pp. 10–16.

MINTZ, A. The inference of accident liability from the accident record. *Journal of Applied Psychology*, 1954, *38*, 41–46.

MINTZ, A., & BLUM, M. L. A re-examination of the accident proneness concept. *Journal of Applied Psychology*, 1949, *33*, 195–211.

RUCH, W. W. Identification of accident proneness through paper and pencil tests. Paper presented at the meetings of the American Psychological Association, Chicago, September 4, 1965.

SPANGENBERG, H. H. The use of projective tests in the selection of bus drivers. *Traffic Safety Research Review* (National Safety Council), December 1968, *12* (4), 118–121.

SUCHMAN, E. E., & SCHERZER, A. L. *Current research in childhood accidents.* New York: Association for the Aid of Crippled Children, 1960.

SURRY, J. Industrial Accident Research: A Human Engineering Approach. University of Toronto, Department of Industrial Engineering, June 1968.

WHITLOCK, G. H., CLOUSE, R. J., & SPENCER, W. F. Predicting accident proneness. *Personnel Psychology*, 1963, *16* (1), 35–44.

WILLIAMS, J. R. Follow-up study of relationships between perceptual style measures and telephone company vehicle accidents. *Journal of Applied Psychology*, 1977, *62* (6), 751–754.

WITKIN, H. A., DYK, R. B., FATERSON, H. F., GOODENOUGH, D. R., & KARP, S. A. *Psychological differentiation: Studies of development.* New York: Wiley, 1962.

A

elementary descriptive statistics

DESCRIPTIVE VERSUS SAMPLING STATISTICS

Statistical methods have two purposes. One is to describe a body of data. This is done using *descriptive statistics,* which reduces a body of data by graphic methods, computational methods yielding numerical measures, and tabular methods. The sole aim of *descriptive statistics* is to reduce the original data to charts, graphs, averages, and the like so that the facts concerning the data will be more apparent.

The second purpose of statistical methods is to enable experimenters to learn how safely they can generalize from *descriptive statistics* obtained from a sample. This approach is known as *sampling statistics.* It applies the mathematics of probability and is very important to industrial psychology.

This appendix will deal with only certain concepts of *descriptive statistics,* but the importance of *sampling statistics* should not be underestimated, and every serious student of industrial psychology should become familiar with these methods.

Descriptive statistics in industrial psychology are used to summarize various types of raw data, such as test scores, attitude measures, and criterion values.

GRAPHIC REPRESENTATION OF DATA

In discussing various types of descriptive statistics, let us use as an example a set of data like that shown in Table A.1. These data represent the number of defects identified by each of sixty inspectors during a week.

Frequency Distribution

A frequency distribution shows the number of cases in each of various *class intervals*

426

TABLE A.1   NUMBER OF DEFECTS DETECTED BY EACH OF 60 INSPECTORS
DURING ONE WEEK OF WORK

15	36	40	37	32	13	35	20	33	36	33	16	38	19	33	34	24
36	25	29	27	39	42	31	21	26	28	53	23	51	21	26	39	28
30	31	32	30	29	49	39	30	44	34	37	35	38	35	41	37	43
42	38	45	22	46	41	47	48	34								

of the value in question; in this case it would be the number of inspectors for each of the various class intervals of numbers of defects detected. The steps in constructing a frequency distribution are as follows:

1. Determine the range of the values in the raw data. Quickly glance through the data to determine the *highest* and the *lowest* values. The range is the difference between these values. For the sixty inspector records, the highest figure is 53 and the lowest is 13. The range is therefore 53 – 13 = 40.

2. If we find that the range of the data is large (that they are widely spread), it usually will be more convenient to group them by class intervals (abbreviated c.i.) with a range in each c.i. of more than 1 unit. A simple rule of thumb helpful in deciding on the correct size of the c.i. is to divide the range by 15 (because, on the average, this is the most desirable number of c.i.'s), and take as the c.i. the whole number nearest to the quotient. In our problem, the range divided by 15 would be 40 ÷ 15 = 2.66. As 3 is the whole number nearest to 2.66, 3 would be the size of the c.i. to be used.

3. Arrange the adjacent c.i.'s in a column, leaving a blank space immediately to the right of this column. The arrangements of the c.i.'s preparatory to constructing a frequency distribution are illustrated in the first column of Table A.2.

4. Place a tally mark for each value in the original list of raw data opposite the appropriate class interval. As the first value

TABLE A.2   ILLUSTRATION OF DATA RELATING TO A FREQUENCY DISTRIBUTION AND OF DATA
USED FOR COMPUTING THE ARITHMETIC MEAN AND MEDIAN

1	2	3	4	5	6	7	8
Class Interval (c.i.)	Tally Marks	Frequency (f)	Calculation of Percentage	Percentage	d	fd	Cumulative f
51–53	//	2	2/60 = .033	3	6	12	60
48–50	//	2	2/60 = .033	3	5	10	58
45–47	///	3	3/60 = .050	5	4	12	56
42–44	////	4	4/60 = .066	7	3	12	53
39–41	₦₦ /	6	6/60 = .100	10	2	12	49
36–38	₦₦ ////	9	9/60 = .150	15	1	9	43
33–35	₦₦ ////	9	9/60 = .150	15	0	0	34
30–32	₦₦ //	7	7/60 = .117	12	–1	–7	25
27–29	₦₦	5	5/60 = .083	8	–2	–10	18
24–26	////	4	4/60 = .066	7	–3	–12	13
21–23	////	4	4/60 = .066	7	–4	–16	9
18–20	//	2	2/60 = .033	3	–5	–10	5
15–17	//	2	2/60 = .033	3	–6	–12	3
12–14	/	1	1/60 = .017	2	–7	–7	1
	Total = 60			100		$\Sigma fd = -7$	

among the sixty listed in Table A.1 is 15, the first tally mark should be in the 15–17 c.i. The second value, 36, is represented by a tally mark in the 36–38 c.i. Usually it is advisable to tally the fifth entry in each c.i. with a line across the preceding four tally marks. When all the tallies have been made, they will appear as in column 2 of Table A.2 Column 3 simply reflects the count of the tally marks for each.

In some circumstances it may be desirable to show the percentage of cases in each class interval instead of (or in addition to) the frequency. This may be done by dividing each f value (in the third column) by the total number of cases in the distribution. Each quotient thus obtained indicates the percentage of the total number of cases that fall in the respective c.i.'s. These computations are shown in column 4 of Table A.2 and the computed percentages in column 5.

Frequency Polygon

A frequency polygon is a graphic representation of the frequency data—in this case, the data in column 3 of Table A.2. In making a frequency polygon, first lay off appropriate units on cross-section or graph paper in such a manner that the midpoints of the c.i.'s can be plotted on the base line as shown in Figure A.1 and the frequencies plotted on the vertical axis as shown by the

left-hand vertical scale of that figure. Then place a dot representing each frequency and connect these dots as shown in the figure. When it is desirable to compare a frequency polygon with other polygons, it usually is desirable to plot the *percentages* (as given in column 5 of Table A.2) rather than the actual *frequencies* (as shown in column 3). Such a polygon would have the same form as that based on frequencies, but the vertical scale would be shown as percentages, as illustrated by the right-hand vertical scale of that figure. In either form (whether based on frequencies or percentages), a frequency polygon gives a graphic impression of the data represented.

The Normal Distribution

The shape of the frequency polygon shown in Figure A.1 is typical of the kind of distribution usually found when data obtained from a group of people are plotted. It will be noted that the curve is approximately "bell-shaped," that is, it is high in the center and tapers off toward the base line at both ends. If we were to divide the area under this curve by drawing a perpendicular line from the central high point to the base line, the two parts would be approximately equal in area and would be bilaterally symmetrical in shape. It is generally recognized that all, or nearly all, measurements of human traits and abilities re-

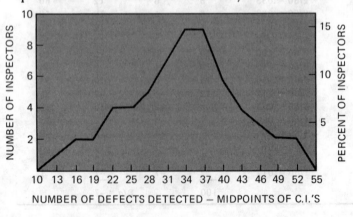

FIG. A.1 Frequency polygon of data given in Table 21.2. The figure as characterized by the left-hand scale illustrates a polygon based on *frequencies,* and that characterized by the right-hand scale illustrates one based on *percentages.*

sult in distributions of approximately this form. These distributions are called *normal distributions*. A strictly normal distribution conforms to a symmetrical bell-shaped curve defined by a mathematical equation, the basis of which is beyond the scope of this discussion. It will suffice for the beginning student to know that:

1. A normal distribution is bell-shaped—that is, it is high in the center and low at both ends. Its two halves are symmetrical.

2. Measurements obtained from a group of persons usually approximate this type of distribution.

MEASURES OF CENTRAL TENDENCY

For some purposes it is desirable to have a single numerical value called a measure of central tendency that "represents" a set of data. A measure of central tendency may be defined as a single figure or value representative of the entire set of data. Three such measures in common use are the *arithmetic mean,* the *median,* and the *mode.*

The Arithmetic Mean

The arithmetic mean, sometimes simply called the mean, may be defined as the sum of the measures divided by the number of measures. For the sixty values previously discussed from which a frequency polygon was constructed, the mean is obtained by finding the total of the sixty measures and dividing this total by 60, thus:

$$\text{Arithmetic Mean } (A.M.) = \frac{\text{Sum of measures}}{N}$$

$$= \frac{2016}{60} = 33.6$$

This is the procedure for computing the exact value of the arithmetic mean of any set of values. In practice, a shorter method of computation utilizing data as tabulated

in a frequency distribution and yielding an approximation (rather than the exact value) of the mean often is used. This shorter method assumes that each score as tabulated in a frequency distribution has the same value as the midpoint of the c.i. in which it falls. For further convenience in calculation, the mean is first computed in c.i. units from an arbitrary base selected near the center of the distribution at the midpoint of one of the c.i.'s. The base selected is entirely arbitrary—it may be taken as any point in the distribution. We have chosen one near the center of the distribution to simplify computation.

If this method is used, columns such as 6 and 7 in Table A.2 should be prepared. Column 6(d) represents the number of c.i. units of each c.i. above or below the c.i. that has been arbitrarily chosen as the base for the calculations. (For example, the c.i. 51–53, which has two scores, is 6 c.i. units above the arbitrary base.) The values in column 7(*fd*) are derived by multiplying for each class interval the *f* value by the *d* value. (For the 51–53 c.i. this value is 12, which is the product of the *f* of 2 multiplied by the *d* of 6.) The scores tabulated in c.i.'s below the arbitrary base are represented by negative values in the *fd* column. The arithmetic mean (*A.M.*) is computed with the following formula:

Formula for Computing *A.M.*
$A.M. = M° + c.i.(c)$
$M° = $ assumed mean
$c.i. = $ size of *c.i.*

$c = \dfrac{\Sigma fd}{N} = $ summation of deviations from assumed mean divided by N

$A.M. = 34 + 3 \left(\dfrac{-7}{60}\right) = 34 - .35 = 33.65$

In this formula the *fd* value is the algebraic sum of the values in the *fd* column (column 6). This sum divided by the number of cases indicates how far the computed mean will deviate from the assumed mean (base) in terms of c.i. units. From the tabulation, this deviation in c.i. units from the arbitrary base (assumed mean) is defined as:

$$\text{Deviation in c.i. units from base} = \frac{\Sigma fd}{N}$$

This computation for the data under consideration shows that:

$$\text{Deviation in c.i. units from base} = \frac{\Sigma fd}{N}$$

$$= \frac{-7}{60} = -.117$$

This is interpreted to mean that the *A.M.* is .117 of a class interval below the midpoint of the arbitrary base (see formula in illustrative problem). In order to transmute this deviation (–.117) into raw score units, we would multiply it by 3 (the size of the class interval). Thus, in raw score units, the deviation is –.35. The mean, as computed by this method, is therefore .35 raw score units below the midpoint of the 33–35 c.i. As the midpoint of this is 34, the mean is 34 – .35 = 33.65. This approximation does not agree exactly with the exact method in which all raw data are added and the sum is divided by the number of cases, but the approximation is sufficiently close to justify its use in many cases.

The Median

The median is a measure of central tendency defined as that score (or value) that exceeds, and is exceeded by, half the measures; that is, it is that point in the distribution above and below which 50 percent of the values lie. A logical (though laborious) method to determine the median consists in arranging all the raw data in rank order from lowest to highest and counting off the bottom half of the measures. The value at this point is the median. If this method is followed for the data in Table A.1, the following arrangement of the scores is obtained:

53	45	41	38	36	34	32	29	26	21
51	44	40	38	36	34	31	29	25	20
49	43	39	37	35	33	31	28	24	19
48	42	39	37	35	33	30	28	23	16
47	42	39	37	35	33	30	27	22	15
46	41	38	36	34	32	30	26	21	13

Counting from the lowest score up, we find that the thirtieth from the low end is 34, and the thirty-first from the low end also is 34. The median score would therefore be 34. If there had been a difference between the thirtieth and the thirty-first scores, the median would be the value halfway between these scores. If an odd number of cases were included in the original set of scores (sixty-one instead of sixty), the median would be the value of the middle score.

In practice, the median as well as the mean may be conveniently approximated from a tabulated frequency distribution. This requires the preparation of a *cumulative f* column, shown in column 8 of Table 21.2. This column shows the cumulative frequencies by c.i., starting with the lowest c.i. The median value in this distribution is that value which separates the lower thirty from the upper thirty, which is within the c.i. of 33–35. There is a procedure for determining the specific value within this c.i. that characterizes the median, but that procedure will not be discussed here.

The Mode

A third measure of central tendency is the mode, defined as the measure appearing most frequently. This value, as well as the mean and the median, may be determined directly from the raw data (if one value appears more often than any other) or may be approximated from a frequency distribution of the data. In computing the mode directly from the raw data, the values are inspected to determine which one appears most frequently.

Sometimes, as in the values shown in Table A.1, several of the measures appear an equal number of times. In this case, each of the values 30, 33, 34, 35, 36, 37, 38, 39 appears three times. In such an instance, an approximation of the mode may be obtained from a frequency distribution using the following empirical formula:

Mode = 3(Median) − 2(Mean)

For the data we have been discussing, this formula gives the following value for the mode:

Mode = 3(34.2) − 2(33.65) = 35.30.

When to Use the Mean, Median, and Mode

Why is it necessary to have three different measures to indicate the central tendency of a set of data? The answer is that each is best adapted to certain uses; that is, in some cases one may be most representative of a set of data, but in other cases another measure may be most suitable. The mean is ordinarily used if the distribution is approximately normal. (If the distribution is perfectly normal, the three measures of central tendency have the same value.) If, on the other hand, there is a preponderance of extreme cases at either end of the distribution, the mean may give an incorrect impression of the central tendency of the data. Under these circumstances, the median or mode is more suitable. Consider, for example, the following monthly incomes of five persons:

$800 $900 $850 $750 $5,000

The mean for these five incomes is

$$\frac{\$800 + \$900 + \$850 + \$750 + \$5,000}{5} =$$

$1,660.

This figure, though an accurate statement of the mean, is not typical of the group as a whole because it is so markedly affected by the one income of $5,000. The median income is $850, and this value is more typical for the group as a whole than is the mean income of $1,660. We may generalize in the above illustration by saying that if a distribution is very much *skewed* (that is, contains more cases at one extreme than at the other), the median or mode is more likely to be representative of the typical score than the mean is.

MEASURES OF VARIABILITY

Besides a measure or value to represent the central tendency of a set of data, there is also quite frequently a need for some measure of the spread, or variability, of the data. The need for a measurement of this type may be seen by comparing the data shown in Table A.1 (the mean of which, computed from the frequency distribution, was found to be 33.65) with another set of data that, as an example, we might assume to consist of twenty-one scores of 33 and thirty-nine scores of 34, making sixty scores in all. The mean of these sixty scores is 33.65.

$$\frac{(21)(33) + (39)(34)}{60} = 33.65$$

Although both distributions have the same mean, they differ markedly in variability or spread. The former is made up of scores varying from 13 to 53, and the latter consists entirely of scores of 33 and 34. A quantitative measure of variability is therefore valuable. There are statistical procedures that yield a single value describing this variability; as in means and medians, these measures tell us something about the group as a whole.

The Standard Deviation

The standard deviation is the most widely used measure of variability. It is defined as the square root of the mean square deviation. Defined by formula:

$$\text{Standard Deviation} = S.D. = \sigma = \sqrt{\frac{\Sigma D^2}{N}}$$

in which ΣD^2 is read "the sum of the squared deviation of the scores from their mean," and N is the number of cases. S.D. and σ are abbreviations for the standard deviation and are used interchangeably.

Although the standard deviation may be computed directly from a set of raw data by means of the formula

$$S.D. = \sqrt{\frac{\Sigma D^2}{N}},$$

this process is laborious. For example, for the set of data we have been using as an example (tabulated in Table A.1), we would proceed by determining the difference between each raw score and the mean of the sixty scores, squaring these differences, summing the sixty squared differences, dividing by 60, and extracting the square root of the quotient. The first score tabuled is 15. The difference between this value and the mean of the sixty scores (as computed directly from the raw data) is $D = 33.6 - 15.0 = 18.6$. D^2 would therefore be $(18.6)^2 = 345.96$. This process must be repeated for every one of the sixty scores before the sum of the squared deviations can be obtained.

Because it is tedious to compute the S.D. directly from the raw data, a simple process that approximates the true value of the S.D. has been developed. This is used in the computations shown in Table A.3, in which is computed the standard deviation of the data shown previously in Table A.2.

The standard deviation is the most commonly used measure of variability. Usually when the mean value of a set of data is given, the S.D. also is given to indicate the variability of the data.

TABLE A.3 COMPUTATION OF THE STANDARD DEVIATION FROM A FREQUENCY DISTRIBUTION*

c.i.	f	d	fd	fd²	
51–53	2	6	12	72	
48–50	2	5	10	50	
45–47	3	4	12	48	
42–44	4	3	12	36	
39–41	6	2	12	24	$\text{Mean} = M^\circ + c.i. \left(\frac{\Sigma fd}{N}\right)$
36–38	9	1	9	9	
33–35	9	0	0	0	$\text{Mean} = 34 + 3 \left(\frac{-7}{60}\right) = 33.65$
30–32	7	-1	-7	7	
27–29	5	-2	-10	20	$S.D. = \sqrt{\frac{\Sigma D^2}{N}} = c.i. \sqrt{\frac{\Sigma fd^2}{N} - \frac{\Sigma fd}{N}^2}$
24–26	4	-3	-12	36	
21–23	4	-4	-16	64	$= 3\sqrt{537/60 - (.117)^2}$
18–20	2	-5	-10	50	$= 3\sqrt{8.950 - .014}$
15–17	2	-6	-12	72	$= 3\sqrt{8.936}$
12–14	1	-7	-7	49	$= 3(2.99)$
Total = 60			$\Sigma fd = -7$	$\Sigma fd^2 = 537$	S.D. = 8.97

*The data used in this table are from Table A.2.

COMPARABLE SCORES

The S.D. also can be used in comparing individual scores from different distributions. For example, suppose that two inspectors from departments *A* and *B,* who are working at different inspection jobs, detect respectively 45 and 89 defects during a week of work. How can we compare the efficiency of these two employees? It will be seen immediately that a direct comparison of the figures 45 and 89 is not valid because the two inspection jobs may be very different. It will also be seen that we can say little about the position of these inspectors in their respective groups without knowing their relation to the mean of their group in inspection work. To make a comparison, then, we must first compute the mean number of defects spotted by all inspectors in Department A, and the mean number spotted by all inspectors in Department *B*. Suppose that those means are respectively 38 and 95. We thus see that the inspector from Department *A* is $45 - 38 = 7$ pieces *above* the mean for that department and that the inspector from Department *B* is $89 - 95 = -6$, or 6 pieces *below* the mean of inspectors from that department. We thus can say, at this point, that the inspector from Department *A* is above average in ability on the job and that the inspector from Department *B* is below average. But how about their relative distance from the average? To answer this we must compute the S.D.s of the two distributions and determine how many S.D.s each inspector is above or below average.

Suppose we find the S.D. of the operators in Department *A* to be 5.5 pieces. Our first inspector is therefore

$$\frac{45 - 38}{5.5} = 1.27 \text{ S.D.s}$$

above average. If the S.D. of the inspectors in Department *B* is 9.5, the inspector from the group who detected 89 pieces is

$$\frac{89 - 95}{9.5} = -.63 \text{ or } .63 \text{ S.D.s}$$

below average. *The deviation of a score from the means of the distribution expressed in S.D. units results in a measurement comparable with similarly determined measurements from other distributions.* Thus, we may say that out first inspector is about *twice* as far above average, in terms of comparable scale units, as the second operator is below average. Scores computed in this manner are known as *z*-scores. The formula for a *z*-score is as follows:

$$z\text{-score} = \frac{\text{Raw Score} - \text{Mean of Raw Scores}}{\text{S.D. of Raw Scores}}$$

The *z*-score is helpful not only when comparing scores from one distribution to another but also when, for any reason, it is desirable to combine scores with the same or differential weighting. An example of an industrial situation that requires this technique is combining factors in a personnel evaluation system, such as those illustrated in chapter 6. Let us suppose, as an example, that we want to combine the evaluations of each person on these two factors into an overall rating. (If more than two factors are included in the system, as is usually the case, the procedure is identical.) Suppose that an employee, Mr. A, has received 40 points on industriousness and 30 points on knowledge of job, making a total of 70 points if the ratings are added directly. Suppose that another employee, Mr. B, has received 30 points on industriousness and 40 points on knowledge of job, which also results in a total of 70 points if the ratings are added directly. It is clear that such direct and immediate combination of ratings would result in identical overall ratings for these two employees. The question we may raise is whether such a statement of equal ratings is justified. The answer is that it is not. If the mean rating of all employees on industriousness was 33 with a S.D. of 3, then A's rating would be

$$\frac{40 - 33}{3} = 2.33, \text{ or } 2.33 \text{ S.D.s}$$

above the mean, and B's would be

$$\frac{30 - 33}{3} 1 = -1.00, \text{ or } 1.00 \text{ S.D.}$$

below the mean on this trait. If the mean rating for all employees on knowledge of job were 25, with a S.D. of 6, A would be

$$\frac{30 - 25}{6} = +.83, \text{ or } .83 \text{ S.D.s}$$

above average in knowledge of job and B would be

$$\frac{40 - 25}{6} = 2.50 \text{ or } 2.50 \text{ S.D.s}$$

above average in this respect. Now, the proper combination of the two factors, if we wish to weight them equally, would be:

Changing ratings into z-scores and adding the z-scores show that the two employees A and B are not equal in rating (as we would infer if the raw ratings were added) but rather, that A is definitely higher than B. The procedure described is based on the assumption that the two factors should receive equal weights and shows how they can be combined with equal weight into a composite score. One might think that conversion of raw scores to z-scores is not necessary if the raw scores are to be given equal weight in the combination score. Actually, if we do not give the

raw scores equal weight by converting them into z-scores, the scores will weight themselves according to the size of their respective standard deviations. In other words, if combined directly, the raw scores will be weighted too much or too little, depending on their position relative to the means of their respective distributions and on the variability of the distribution of which they are a part. When scores are combined, they *always* are weighted in some manner, whether we deliberately weight them or not. It is important, therefore, to weight them deliberately (either with equal weight or otherwise) by converting them into z-scores and then combining them.

It does not follow from this discussion that combined scores should always be weighted equally. Indeed, it is often desirable to weight various scores according to some plan that has been decided before the scores are combined. When this is desired, such weighting can be done easily by multiplying each z-score by the appropriate weight before they are combined. In our example, suppose that we have decided that *industriousness* should be given twice as much weight as *knowledge of job* is in determining the total rating. This would be done as follows:

The combined ratings so obtained show a still greater difference between employees A and B that was obtained when the scores were equally weighted. If, on the other hand, it is desired to give the rating on *knowledge of job* twice as much weight as the rating on *industriousness,* the following computations would be made:

Essentially the same procedures can be followed when combining other sets of data

Employee	z-Score in Industriousness	z-Score in Knowledge of Job	Weighted z-Score in Industriousness	Weighted z-Score in Knowledge of Job	Combined Weighted z-Scores
A	+2.33	+.83	-4.66	+.83	+5.49
B	-1.00	+2.50	-2.00	+2.50	+.50

Employee	Rating in Industri- ousness	Rating in Knowledge of Job	z-Score in Industri- ousness	z-Score in Knowledge of Job	Sum of Scores for Both Units
A	40	30	−2.33	+.83	+3.16
B	30	40	−1.00	+2.50	+1.50

with specified weights, as in combining various subcriteria, job evaluation factors, or test scores. As an example, in selecting candidates for electrical apprentice training in one company, it was desirable to assign differential weights to four factors according to the judged importance of these factors to apprentice training. These weights were as follows:

General intelligence   40%
Knowledge of electricity   30%
Merit rating   20%
Seniority of service with the company   10%

To score the candidates according to this plan, each was given a general intelligence test and a test covering technical phases of electricity. Merit ratings and seniority were obtained from the company records. Each of the four scores for each candidate was converted into a z-score, and the four resulting z-scores were respectively multiplied by 40, 30, 20, and 10. For each candidate the sum of the weighted z-scores was used to indicate whether or not he was selected for apprenticeship training.

PERCENTILES

The discussion of comparable scores should have made clear that a raw score on any test is relatively meaningless unless it is interpreted in relation to its location in a distribution of other scores made by other people. If a test has seventy-five very easy questions, a score of 65 might be near the bottom of the distribution and hence should be interpreted as a very low score. On the other hand, if a test has seventy-five very difficult questions, a score of 65 might be at or near the top of the distribution and should therefore be considered a very high score. In other words, a raw score of 65 might be a low score or a high score, depending on the distribution of scores from which it is drawn.

One convenient and widely used method of interpreting a raw score is by using *percentile ranks*. A percentile rank may be defined as the number showing the percentage of the total group equal to or below the score in question. Thus, on a certain test, if 65 percent of the total group scored 129 or below, the score of 129 would be at the sixty-fifth percentile or would have a percentile rank of 65. The fiftieth percentile, it will be noted, is the same as the median as previously defined.

A convenient, practical method of determining by close approximation the percentile equivalents of a set of raw scores uses a cumulative frequency distribution like that tabulated in Table A.4. This tabulation

Employee	z-Score in Industri- ousness	z-Score in Knowledge of Job	Weighted z-Score in Industri- ousness	Weighted z-Score in Knowledge of Job	Combined Weighted z-Scores
A	+2.333	+.833	+2.333	+1.666	+4.0
B	−1.000	+2.500	−1.000	+5.000	+4.0

is based on the same distribution previously used in Table A.2.

The percent values in column 4 of Table A.4, are obtained by dividing each of the values in the cumulative f column (column 3) by the total of column 2, in this instance 60. The percent values in column 4 are then plotted against the upper limits of the class intervals, as shown in Figure A.2. From Figure A.2 the percentile ranks of the raw scores may be read directly, with sufficient accuracy for most purposes.

The manual published with standardized tests usually includes percentile tables enabling the conversion of raw scores into percentile ranks. Because the percentile rank of a given raw score is dependent on the nature of the group used in constructing the conversion table, several raw-score-to-percentile-rank conversion tables, based on different groups, are often published with standardized tests.

CORRELATION

For quantitative data on a sample from a population (such as a sample of people),

TABLE A.4   CUMULATIVE FREQUENCY DISTRIBUTION USED IN DETERMINING PERCENTILE RANKS OF RAW SCORES

(1) Class Intervals	(2) f	(3) Cumulative f	(4) Percent
51–53	2	60	100
48–50	2	58	96
45–47	3	56	93
42–44	4	53	88
39–41	6	49	81
36–38	9	43	71
33–35	9	34	56
30–32	7	25	42
27–29	5	18	30
24–26	4	13	22
21–23	4	9	15
18–20	2	5	8
15–17	2	3	5
12–14	1	1	2
Total = 60			

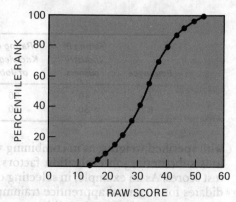

FIG. A.2 Chart for converting raw scores into percentile ranks for illustrative data in Table 21.4.

there may be two items of data for each of the several cases so related that they vary, or tend to vary, with each other. An obvious example would be the height and weight of people—two variables that are somewhat related. A correlation is a statistical index of the degree of relationship between two such variables. A correlation can range from +1.00 (a perfect positive relationship) through to –1.00 (a perfect negative relationship). Graphic examples of correlations are shown in Figure A.3.

In discussing correlations, let us use data for eight punch-press operators for whom we have two items of data, as follows: (1) production for a given period of time and (2) pounds of waste (material wasted by mispunching or otherwise). The following are these data for the eight operators:

Operator	Production	Waste
1	95	3.0
2	103	4.5
3	88	3.5
4	98	4.0
5	93	3.0
6	107	4.5
7	114	4.0
8	106	5.0

A graphic representation of these data can be presented as in Figure A.3. This is made

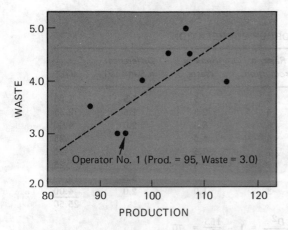

FIG. A.3 A plot of the production and waste records for the eight punch-press operators shown above.

by plotting the values on coordinate axes, with one variable (production) being represented on the x or horizontal axis and the other (waste) on the y or vertical axis. Such a representation gives a better indication of the relationship between the two variables than the data in the columns above do, and it is even possible to draw in by inspection, a line or curve that represents this relationship in an approximate form.

Although this simple method of studying the relationship between two variables is sometimes adequate for very simple problems or for those using only a small amount of data, it is not adequate for an exact study because it does not give a quantitative statement of the degree of relationship. The slope of the dotted line cannot be considered a quantitative statement because: (1) this line is drawn in by inspection, and (2) its slope depends on the units of measurement on both the x and y axes. Two commonly used quantitative methods for measuring the degree of relationship between two paired sets of data are rank-order correlation and product-moment correlation.

Rank-Order Correlation

This method may be described by applying it to the data for the eight punch-press operators.

In Table A.5 the two columns headed *Rank* give, respectively, the rank of the operators on the two measures (production and waste). The highest producing operator (in this case the seventh in the list) is given a rank of 1, the second highest a rank of 2, and so on. In like manner, the rank of each operator in wastage is placed in the waste-rank column. If two or more operators are tied for a given rank (as in the case of the second and sixth operators, who are tied at 4.5 pounds of waste each), the tied scores are all given the same rank, the average of the ranks that would have been assigned to the tied scores if they had not been tied. The values in the D^2 column are obtained by squaring each D value. The sum of the D^2 column is determined and the correlation computed using the formula:

$$\text{Rho} = 1 - \frac{6\Sigma D^2}{N(N^2 - 1)}$$

in which N is the number of cases entering into the computation.

This formula for the rank-order correlation is empirical. It yields a value of +1.00 if the data are in exactly the same rank order. (The reason for this is that if all ranks are the same, all D's are zero, all D^2 values are zero, ΣD^2 is zero, and the formula becomes $1 - 0 = 1$.) If the data are in exactly reverse order (that is, if the individual who ranks highest on one series is lowest on the

437

TABLE A.5   COMPUTATION OF RANK-ORDER CORRELATION

Operator	Production	Waste	Rank in Production	Rank in Waste	Difference in Rank (D)	(D)²
1	95	3.0	6	7.5	1.5	2.25
2	103	4.5	4	2.5	1.5	2.25
3	88	3.5	8	6.0	2.0	4.00
4	98	4.0	5	4.5	.5	.25
5	93	3.0	7	7.5	.5	.25
6	107	4.5	2	2.5	.5	.25
7	114	4.0	1	2.5	3.5	12.25
8	106	5.0	3	1.0	2.0	4.00
						25.50

$$Rho = 1 - \frac{6\Sigma D^2}{N(N^2 - 1)} = 1 - \frac{153}{504} = .70$$

other, and so on), the formula will yield a value of −1.00, but if there is no relationship between the two sets of data, a correlation of zero will be found.

If there are an appreciable number of cases, however, the rank-order method of computing the degree of relationship is extremely laborious. For this reason—and for other reasons of a mathematical nature—it ordinarily is used only when the data are limited to a very few cases (less than thirty).

The Product-Moment Coefficient

This is the most widely used measure of relationship. Like the rank-order correlation, it may vary from +1.00 (indicating perfect positive relationship) through zero (indicating no relationship) to −1.00 (indicating perfect negative relationship). The product-moment correlation, represented by the symbol r, may be defined in several ways. One of the simplest definitions is that r is the slope of the straight line that best fits the data after the data have been plotted as z-scores on coordinate axes; that is, it is the tangent of the angle made by this line with the base line.

Several terms in this definition require further definition. *Slope* means the steepness with which the line rises. The slope of a straight line drawn in any manner across

coordinate paper is defined as the distance, y, from any given point on the line to the x intercept, minus the distance, a, from the origin to the y intercept, divided by the distance, x, from the point on the line to y intercept. Thus the slope, which we will call b, is defined in Figure A.4 as follows:

$$b = \frac{y - a}{x}$$

It should be remembered that, on coordinate axes, distances above and to the right of the origin are positive, but distances measured below and/or to the left of the origin are negative. The slope of any line that *rises* as it goes from left to right will

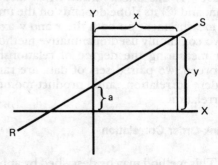

FIG. A.4   The slope of the line RS is defined as $b = \frac{y - a}{x}$.

TABLE A.6   PRODUCTION AND WASTE FOR EIGHT PUNCH-PRESS OPERATORS
WITH CORRESPONDING Z-SCORES OF THE PRODUCTION AND WASTE FIGURES

Operator	Production	Waste	z-Score in Production	z-Score in Waste
1	95	3.0	-.69	-1.38
2	103	4.5	+.31	+.82
3	88	3.5	-1.56	-.65
4	98	4.0	-.31	+.09
5	93	3.0	-.94	-1.38
6	107	4.5	+.81	+.82
7	114	4.0	+1.69	+.09
8	106	5.0	+.69	+1.56
Mean	100.5	3.94		
S.D.	8.0	.68		

therefore be positive (the greater the rise in a given distance to the right, the larger the positive value of the slope), and the slope of any line that *falls* as it goes from left to right will be negative (the greater the fall in a given distance to the right, the greater the negative value of the slope).

The line of *best fit* in the definition is a line so drawn that the sum of the squared deviations in a vertical direction from the original points to the line is less than the sum would be for any other straight line that might be drawn.

A rough approximation of the value of r may be obtained by plotting the z-scores of the two variables, fitting a straight line to these points by inspection and graphically measuring the slope of this straight line. Although this method is never used in practical computation (because it is both inaccurate and laborious), the application of it to a set of representative data may clarify the meaning of the correlation coefficient, r. Returning to the data for which we have previously computed the rank-order correlation (see Table A.5), we first compute the z-scores for each measure as shown in Table A.6.

These pairs of z-scores are used as the x and y values for eight points plotted on coordinate axes as in Figure A.5. The straight line that seems best to fit these points is then determined (as with a stretched string that is moved about until the desired location is obtained) and drawn on the graph. The correlation, r, as determined by this crude method, is obtained by measuring the slope of this line. The procedure applied to Figure A.5 gives a value of $r = .61$, but it should be emphasized that this value is affected by:

1. The accuracy with which the straight line has been located, and

2. The accuracy with which the slope of the line has been measured after it has been drawn.

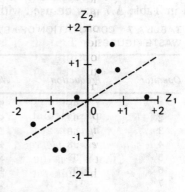

FIG. A.5   A plot of the z-scores for production and waste records of the eight punch-press operators shown above.

Points 1 and 2 both eliminate the possibility of complete accuracy in this method of determining a correlation coefficient. Therefore, a mathematical method has been devised to make the computation, so that no plotting of points or graphic measurements are required. This method requires the derivation of the equation of the straight line that, if plotted, would best fit the point and computing the slope of this straight line of best fit from the equation.

It may be proved mathematically that the slope of the straight line of best fit is given by the following equation:

$$\text{Slope} = r = \frac{\Sigma Z_x Z_y}{N}$$

in which $\Sigma Z_x Z_y$ is read "the sum of the products of the z-scores for the pairs of points or values."

Applying the formula to the data in Table A.6, we may compute the correlation as in Table A.7. The value of r thus obtained by computation, .67, differs from the value of .61 obtained by plotting and inspection. The plotting and inspection method yielded a value that was somewhat incorrect for the data in question.

Although the z-score method of computing a correlation coefficient as illustrated in Table A.7 may be used with any

number of cases and will yield the correct mathematical value of r, this method when many pairs of data are to be correlated is very laborious. It is therefore recommended, under such circumstances, that a modification of the fundamental formula

$$r = \frac{\Sigma Z_x Z_y}{N},$$

which makes it possible to compute r from raw score values rather than z-score values, be used. One convenient formula for determining the coefficient of correlation directly from the raw data is:

$$r = \frac{N\Sigma XY - \Sigma X \Sigma Y}{\sqrt{N\Sigma X^2 - (\Sigma X)^2}\sqrt{N\Sigma Y^2 - (\Sigma Y^2)}}$$

When we apply this formula to the data tabulated in Table A.7, the computations shown in Table A.8 result.

When many pairs of data are to be correlated, the use of a chart will further simplify the computations. Several forms of such a chart have been prepared. One convenient form is shown in Figure A.6. This chart shows the computation of the correlation between time used in inspecting three hundred pieces of material and the number of defective pieces detected. In using this

TABLE A.7 COMPUTATION OF r BY Z-SCORE METHOD BETWEEN PRODUCTION AND WASTE FIGURES

Operator	Production	Waste	z-Score in Production	z-Score in Waste	$(z_1 z_2)$
1	95	3.0	−.69	−1.38	+.95
2	103	4.5	+.31	+.82	+.25
3	88	3.5	−1.56	−.65	+1.01
4	98	4.0	−.31	+.09	−.03
5	93	3.0	−.94	−1.38	+1.30
6	107	4.5	+.81	+.82	+.66
7	114	4.0	+1.69	+.09	+.15
8	106	5.0	+.69	+1.56	+1.08
					+5.38

$$r = \frac{Z_x Z_y}{N} = \frac{+5.38}{8} = .67$$

chart the following steps should be followed:

1. Decide upon appropriate class intervals for one of the variables (using the rules given on p. 000), and write these in on either the x or the y axis.

2. Decide upon appropriate class intervals for the other variable, and write these in on the axis not used in (1) above.

3. Place 1 tally mark on the scattergram for each pair of values being correlated. For example, if an inspector spotted 33 defects in 16.5 minutes, the tally mark would go in the cell that is found at the intersection of the *row* containing 33 defects and the *column* containing 16.5 minutes.

4. After all tally marks have been placed on the chart, the rows should be added horizontally and the sum of the tally marks in each row written opposite this row in the f_y column (column *l*).

5. The tally marks in each column should be added and the sum written at the bottom of each column in the row (*A*), the f_x row.

6. The f_y column should be added and the sum written opposite N at the bottom of this column. *The value of N thus obtained may be checked by adding the values in the f_x row. The sum of these values also should give the value of* N.

7. Each value of f_y in the column so headed should be multiplied by the value of d_y opposite it and the resultant product written in column *3*, headed $f_y d_y$. *The sum of column 3 is the value of* ΣY *used in the formula.*

8. Each value in column *3*, the $f_y d_y$ column, should be multiplied by the corresponding value in column 2, the d_y column, resulting in the values for column *4*, or the $f_y d_y{}^2$ column. *The sum of column 4 is the value of* ΣY^2 *which is used in the formula.*

9. The values going into column *5*, the fd_x column, are determined by finding, for each row, the sum of the products of the number of cases in each cell times the x value of that cell. For example, in the first row in which a tally mark appears, there is only a single case, which appears in the cell under an x value of 13. The value to go into the blank in column *5* is therefore $(1)(13) = 13$. In the next row no tally marks appear; therefore, this row is blank. In the next row, 1 tally mark appears in the cell under an x value of 11, 2 in the cell with an x value of 12, and 1 in the cell with an x value of 13. The value to go into the blank cell in column *5* is therefore $(1)(11) + (2)(12) + (1)(13) = 48$. The remaining cells in column *5* are filled in a similar manner.

10. The cells in column *6*, the $fd_x d_y$ column, are filled with values obtained by multiplying each

TABLE A.8   COMPUTATIONS OF r DIRECTLY FROM RAW DATA

Operator	Production (X)	Waste (Y)	X^2	Y^2	XY
1	95	3.0	9,025	9.00	285.0
2	103	4.5	10,609	20.25	463.5
3	88	3.5	7,744	12.25	308.0
4	98	4.0	9,604	16.00	392.0
5	93	3.0	8,649	9.00	279.0
6	107	4.5	11,449	20.25	481.5
7	114	4.0	12,996	16.00	456.0
8	106	5.0	11,236	25.00	530.0
	$\Sigma X = 804$	$\Sigma Y = 31.5$	$\Sigma X^2 = 81,312$	$\Sigma Y^2 = 127.75$	$\Sigma XY = 3,195.0$

$$r = \frac{N\Sigma XY - \Sigma X \Sigma Y}{\sqrt{N\Sigma X^2 - (\Sigma X)^2}\ \sqrt{N\Sigma Y^2 - (\Sigma Y)^2}}$$

$$r = \frac{8(3,195) - (804)(31.5)}{\sqrt{8(81,312) - (804)^2}\ \sqrt{8(127.75) - (31.5)^2}}$$

$$r = .67$$

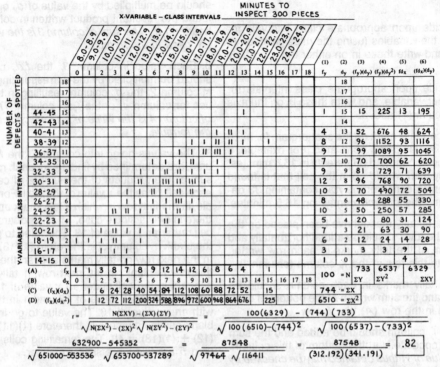

FIG. A.6 A chart used to compute a product moment coefficient of correlation.

value in column *2*, the d_y column, by the value in that same row appearing in column *5*, the *fd $_x$* column. The value in the first cell in column *6* is therefore (15)(13) = 195. *The sum of column 6 is the value of ΣXY used in the formula.*

11. The values in row *C* are obtained by multiplying each value in row *A*, the f_x row, by the value directly below it in row *B*, the d_x row. The values appearing in row *A* have already been obtained (see Step *5* above). The resultant values are entered in row *C*, the $f_x d_x$ row. *The sum of the values appearing in row C is the value of ΣX used in the formula.*

12. Each value in row *B*, the d_x row, should be multiplied by the value directly below in row *C*, the $f_x d_x$ row. The resultant values should be entered in row *D*, the $f_x d_x{}^2$ row. *The sum of the values in row D is the value of ΣX^2 used in the formula.*

13. The value for N (see Step *6*), ΣY (see Step *7*), ΣY^2 (see Step *8*), ΣXY (see Step *10*), ΣX (see Step *11*), and ΣX^2 (see Step *12*) are now entered in the formula. The indicated arithmetic computations are then performed, yielding the value of *r*.

This method assumes that each measure has the value of the midpoint of the class interval in which it falls. The computations indicated on the chart produce not only the value for *r* but also the mean and the standard deviations of both the *X* and Y arrays.

B
taylor-russell tables (institutional prediction)

Tables[1] of the Proportion who will be Satisfactory among those Selected for Given Values of the Proportion of Present Employees Considered Satisfactory, the Selection Ratio, and r

PROPORTION OF EMPLOYEES CONSIDERED SATISFACTORY = .05
SELECTION RATIO

r	.05	.10	.20	.30	.40	.50	.60	.70	.80	.90	.95
.00	.05	.05	.05	.05	.05	.05	.05	.05	.05	.05	.05
.05	.06	.06	.06	.06	.06	.05	.05	.05	.05	.05	.05
.10	.07	.07	.07	.06	.06	.06	.06	.05	.05	.05	.05
.15	.09	.08	.07	.07	.07	.06	.06	.06	.05	.05	.05
.20	.11	.09	.08	.08	.07	.07	.06	.06	.06	.05	.05
.25	.12	.11	.09	.08	.08	.07	.07	.06	.06	.05	.05
.30	.14	.12	.10	.09	.08	.07	.07	.06	.06	.05	.05
.35	.17	.14	.11	.10	.09	.08	.07	.06	.06	.05	.05
.40	.19	.16	.12	.10	.09	.08	.07	.07	.06	.05	.05
.45	.22	.17	.13	.11	.10	.08	.08	.07	.06	.06	.05
.50	.24	.19	.15	.12	.10	.09	.08	.07	.06	.06	.05
.55	.28	.22	.16	.13	.11	.09	.08	.07	.06	.06	.05
.60	.31	.24	.17	.13	.11	.09	.08	.07	.06	.06	.05
.65	.35	.26	.18	.14	.11	.10	.08	.07	.06	.06	.05
.70	.39	.29	.20	.15	.12	.10	.08	.07	.06	.06	.05
.75	.44	.32	.21	.15	.12	.10	.08	.07	.06	.06	.05
.80	.50	.35	.22	.16	.12	.10	.08	.07	.06	.06	.05
.85	.56	.39	.23	.16	.12	.10	.08	.07	.06	.06	.05
.90	.64	.43	.24	.17	.13	.10	.08	.07	.06	.06	.05
.95	.73	.47	.25	.17	.13	.10	.08	.07	.06	.06	.05
1.00	1.00	.50	.25	.17	.13	.10	.08	.07	.06	.06	.05

1 Source: Taylor, H. C. & Russell, J. T., The relationship of validity coefficients to the practical effectiveness of tests in selection: Discussion and tables. Journal of Applied Psychology, 1939, 23, 565–578.

PROPORTION OF EMPLOYEES CONSIDERED SATISFACTORY = .10
SELECTION RATIO

r	.05	.10	.20	.30	.40	.50	.60	.70	.80	.90	.95
.00	.10	.10	.10	.10	.10	.10	.10	.10	.10	.10	.10
.05	.12	.12	.11	.11	.11	.11	.11	.10	.10	.10	.10
.10	.14	.13	.13	.12	.12	.11	.11	.11	.11	.10	.10
.15	.16	.15	.14	.13	.13	.12	.12	.11	.11	.10	.10
.20	.19	.17	.15	.14	.14	.13	.12	.12	.11	.11	.10
.25	.22	.19	.17	.16	.14	.13	.13	.12	.11	.11	.10
.30	.25	.22	.19	.17	.15	.14	.13	.12	.12	.11	.10
.35	.28	.24	.20	.18	.16	.15	.14	.13	.12	.11	.10
.40	.31	.27	.22	.19	.17	.16	.14	.13	.12	.11	.10
.45	.35	.29	.24	.20	.18	.16	.15	.13	.12	.11	.10
.50	.39	.32	.26	.22	.19	.17	.15	.13	.12	.11	.11
.55	.43	.36	.28	.23	.20	.17	.15	.14	.12	.11	.11
.60	.48	.39	.30	.25	.21	.18	.16	.14	.12	.11	.11
.65	.53	.43	.32	.26	.22	.18	.16	.14	.12	.11	.11
.70	.58	.47	.35	.27	.22	.19	.16	.14	.12	.11	.11
.75	.64	.51	.37	.29	.23	.19	.16	.14	.12	.11	.11
.80	.71	.56	.40	.30	.24	.20	.17	.14	.11	.11	.11
.85	.78	.62	.43	.31	.25	.20	.17	.14	.12	.11	.11
.90	.86	.69	.46	.33	.25	.20	.17	.14	.12	.11	.11
.95	.95	.78	.49	.33	.25	.20	.17	14	.12	.11	.11
1.00	1.00	1.00	.50	.33	.25	.20	.17	.14	.13	.11	.11

PROPORTION OF EMPLOYEES CONSIDERED SATISFACTORY = .20
SELECTION RATIO

r	.05	.10	.20	.30	.40	.50	.60	.70	.80	.90	.95
.00	.20	.20	.20	.20	.20	.20	.20	.20	.20	.20	.20
.05	.23	.23	.22	.22	.21	.21	.21	.21	.20	.20	.20
.10	.26	.25	.24	.23	.23	.22	.22	.21	.21	.21	.20
.15	.30	.28	.26	.25	.24	.23	.23	.22	.21	.21	.20
.20	.33	.31	.28	.27	.26	.25	.24	.23	.22	.21	.21
.25	.37	.34	.31	.29	.27	.26	.24	.23	.22	.21	.21
.30	.41	.37	.33	.30	.28	.27	.25	.24	.23	.21	.21
.35	.45	.41	.36	.32	.30	.28	.26	.24	.23	.22	.21
.40	.49	.44	.38	.34	.31	.29	.27	.25	.23	.22	.21
.45	.54	.48	.41	.36	.33	.30	.28	.26	.24	.22	.21
.50	.59	.52	.44	.38	.35	.31	.29	.26	.24	.22	.21
.55	.63	.56	.47	.41	.36	.32	.29	.27	.24	.22	.21
.60	.68	.60	.50	.43	.38	.34	.30	.27	.24	.22	.21
.65	.73	.64	.53	.45	.39	.35	.31	.27	.25	.22	.21
.70	.79	.69	.56	.48	.41	.36	.31	.28	.25	.22	.21
.75	.84	.74	.60	.50	.43	.37	.32	.28	.25	.22	.21
.80	.89	.79	.64	.53	.45	.38	.33	.28	.25	.22	.21
.85	.94	.85	.69	.56	.47	.39	.33	.28	.25	.22	.21
.90	.98	.91	.75	.60	.48	.40	.33	.29	.25	.22	.21
.95	1.00	.97	.82	.64	.50	.40	.33	.29	.25	.22	.21
1.00	1.00	1.00	1.00	.67	.50	.40	.33	.29	.25	.22	.21

Source. Taylor, H. C., & Russell, J. T. The relationship of validity coefficients to the practical effectiveness of tests in selection: discussion and tables. Journal of Applied Psychology, 1939, 23, 565–578.

PROPORTION OF EMPLOYEES CONSIDERED SATISFACTORY = .30
SELECTION RATIO

r	.05	.10	.20	.30	.40	.50	.60	.70	.80	.90	.95
.00	.30	.30	.30	.30	.30	.30	.30	.30	.30	.30	.30
.05	.34	.33	.33	.32	.32	.31	.31	.31	.31	.30	.30
.10	.38	.36	.35	.34	.33	.33	.32	.32	.31	.31	.30
.15	.42	.40	.38	.36	.35	.34	.33	.33	.32	.31	.31
.20	.46	.43	.40	.38	.37	.36	.34	.33	.32	.31	.31
.25	.50	.47	.43	.41	.39	.37	.36	.34	.33	.32	.31
.30	.54	.50	.46	.43	.40	.38	.37	.35	.33	.32	.31
.35	.58	.54	.49	.45	.42	.40	.38	.36	.34	.32	.31
.40	.63	.58	.51	.47	.44	.41	.39	.37	.34	.32	.31
.45	.67	.61	.55	.50	.46	.43	.40	.37	.35	.32	.31
.50	.72	.65	.58	.52	.48	.44	.41	.38	.35	.33	.31
.55	.76	.69	.61	.55	.50	.46	.42	.39	.36	.33	.31
.60	.81	.74	.64	.58	.52	.47	.43	.40	.36	.33	.31
.65	.85	.78	.68	.60	.54	.49	.44	.40	.37	.33	.32
.70	.89	.82	.72	.63	.57	.51	.46	.41	.37	.33	.32
.75	.93	.86	.76	.67	.59	.52	.47	.42	.37	.33	.32
.80	.96	.90	.80	.70	.62	.54	.48	.42	.37	.33	.32
.85	.99	.94	.85	.74	.65	.56	.49	.43	.37	.33	.32
.90	1.00	.98	90	.79	.68	.58	.49	.43	.37	.33	.32
.95	1.00	1.00	.96	.85	.72	.60	.50	.43	.37	.33	.32
1.00	1.00	1.00	1.00	1.00	.75	.60	.50	.43	.38	.33	.32

PROPORTION OF EMPLOYEES CONSIDERED SATISFACTORY = .40
SELECTION RATIO

r	.05	.10	.20	.30	.40	.50	.60	.70	.80	.90	.95
.00	.40	.40	.40	.40	.40	.40	.40	.40	.40	.40	.40
.05	.44	.43	.43	.42	.42	.42	.41	.41	.41	.40	.40
.10	.48	.47	.46	.45	.44	.43	.42	.42	.41	.41	.40
.15	.52	.50	.48	.47	.46	.45	.44	.43	.42	.41	.41
.20	.57	.54	.51	.49	.48	.46	.45	.44	.43	.41	.41
.25	.61	.58	.54	.51	.49	.48	.46	.45	.43	.42	.41
.30	.65	.61	.57	.54	.51	.49	.47	.46	.44	.42	.41
.35	.69	.65	.60	.56	.53	.51	.49	.47	.45	.42	.41
.40	.73	.69	.63	.59	.56	.53	.50	.48	.45	.43	.41
.45	.77	.72	.66	.61	.58	.54	.51	.49	.46	.43	.42
.50	.81	.76	.69	.64	.60	.56	.53	.49	.46	.43	.42
.55	.85	.79	.72	.67	.62	.58	.54	.50	.47	.44	.42
.60	.89	.83	.75	.69	.64	.60	.55	.51	.48	.44	.42
.65	.92	.87	.79	.72	.67	.62	.57	.52	.48	.44	.42
.70	.95	.90	.82	.76	.69	.64	.58	.53	.49	.44	.42
.75	.97	.93	.86	.79	.72	.66	.60	.54	.49	.44	.42
.80	.99	.96	.89	.82	.75	.68	.61	.55	.49	.44	.42
.85	1.00	.98	.93	.86	.79	.71	.63	.56	.50	.44	.42
.90	1.00	1.00	.97	.91	.82	.74	.65	.57	.50	.44	.42
.95	1.00	1.00	.99	.96	.87	.77	.66	.57	.50	.44	.42
1.00	1.00	1.00	1.00	1.00	1.00	.80	.67	.57	.50	.44	.42

445

PROPORTION OF EMPLOYEES CONSIDERED SATISFACTORY = .50
SELECTION RATIO

r	.05	.10	.20	.30	.40	.50	.60	.70	.80	.90	.95
.00	.50	.50	.50	.50	.50	.50	.50	.50	.50	.50	.50
.05	.54	.54	.53	.52	.52	.52	.51	.51	.51	.50	.50
.10	.58	.57	.56	.55	.54	.53	.53	.52	.51	.51	.50
.15	.63	.61	.58	.57	.56	.55	.54	.53	.52	.51	.51
.20	.67	.64	.61	.59	.58	.56	.55	.54	.53	.52	.51
.25	.70	.67	.64	.62	.60	.58	.56	.55	.54	.52	.51
.30	.74	.71	.67	.64	.62	.60	.58	.56	.54	.52	.51
.35	.78	.74	.70	.66	.64	.61	.59	.57	.55	.53	.51
.40	.82	.78	.73	.69	.66	.63	.61	.58	.56	.53	.52
.45	.85	.81	.75	.71	.68	.65	.62	.59	.56	.53	.52
.50	.88	.84	.78	.74	.70	.67	.63	.60	.57	.54	.52
.55	.91	.87	.81	.76	.72	.69	.65	.61	.58	.54	.52
.60	.94	.90	.84	.79	.75	.70	.66	.62	.59	.54	.52
.65	.96	.92	.87	.82	.77	.73	.68	.64	.59	.55	.52
.70	.98	.95	.90	.85	.80	.75	.70	.65	.60	.55	.53
.75	.99	.97	.92	.87	.82	.77	.72	.66	.61	.55	.53
.80	1.00	.99	.95	.90	.85	.80	.73	.67	.61	.55	.53
.85	1.00	.99	.97	.94	.88	.82	.76	.69	.62	.55	.53
.90	1.00	1.00	.99	.97	.92	.86	.78	.70	.62	.56	.53
.95	1.00	1.00	1.00	.99	.96	.90	.81	.71	.63	.56	.53
1.00	1.00	1.00	1.00	1.00	1.00	1.00	.83	.71	.63	.56	.53

PROPORTION OF EMPLOYEES CONSIDERED SATISFACTORY = .60
SELECTION RATIO

r	.05	.10	.20	.30	.40	.50	.60	.70	.80	.90	.95
.00	.60	.60	.60	.60	.60	.60	.60	.60	.60	.60	.60
.05	.64	.63	.63	.62	.62	.62	.61	.61	.61	.60	.60
.10	.68	.67	.65	.64	.64	.63	.63	.62	.61	.61	.60
.15	.71	.70	.68	.67	.66	.65	.64	.63	.62	.61	.61
.20	.75	.73	.71	.69	.67	.66	.65	.64	.63	.62	.61
.25	.78	.76	.73	.71	.69	.68	.66	.65	.63	.62	.61
.30	.82	.79	.76	.73	.71	.69	.68	.66	.64	.62	.61
.35	.85	.82	.78	.75	.73	.71	.69	.67	.65	.63	.62
.40	.88	.85	.81	.78	.75	.73	.70	.68	.66	.63	.62
.45	.90	.87	.83	.80	.77	.74	.72	.69	.66	.64	.62
.50	.93	.90	.86	.82	.79	.76	.73	.70	.67	.64	.62
.55	.95	.92	.88	.84	.81	.78	.75	.71	.68	.64	.62
.60	.96	.94	.90	.87	.83	.80	.76	.73	.69	.65	.63
.65	.98	.96	.92	.89	.85	.82	.78	.74	.70	.65	.63
.70	.99	.97	.94	.91	.87	.84	.80	.75	.71	.66	.63
.75	.99	.99	.96	.93	.90	.86	.81	.77	.71	.66	.63
.80	1.00	.99	.98	.95	.92	.88	.83	.78	.72	.66	.63
.85	1.00	1.00	.99	.97	.95	.91	.86	.80	.73	.66	.63
.90	1.00	1.00	1.00	.99	.97	.94	.88	.82	.74	.67	.63
.95	1.00	1.00	1.00	1.00	.99	.97	.92	.84	.75	.67	.63
1.00	1.00	1.00	1.00	1.00	1.00	1.00	1.00	.86	.75	.67	.63

PROPORTION OF EMPLOYEES CONSIDERED SATISFACTORY = .70
SELECTION RATIO

r	.05	.10	.20	.30	.40	.50	.60	.70	.80	.90	.95
.00	.70	.70	.70	.70	.70	.70	.70	.70	.70	.70	.70
.05	.73	.73	.72	.72	.72	.71	.71	.71	.71	.70	.70
.10	.77	.76	.75	.74	.73	.73	.72	.72	.71	.71	.70
.15	.80	.79	.77	.76	.75	.74	.73	.73	.72	.71	.71
.20	.83	.81	.79	.78	.77	.76	.75	.74	.73	.71	.71
.25	.86	.84	.81	.80	.78	.77	.76	.75	.73	.72	.71
.30	.88	.86	.84	.82	.80	.78	.77	.75	.74	.72	.71
.35	.91	.89	.86	.83	.82	.80	.78	.76	.75	.73	.71
.40	.93	.91	.88	.85	.83	.81	.79	.77	.75	.73	.72
.45	.94	.93	.90	.87	.85	.83	.81	.78	.76	.73	.72
.50	.96	.94	.91	.89	.87	.84	.82	.80	.77	.74	.72
.55	.97	.96	.93	.91	.88	.86	.83	.81	.78	.74	.72
.60	.98	.97	.95	.92	.90	.87	.85	.82	.79	.75	.73
.65	.99	.98	.96	.94	.92	.89	.86	.83	.80	.75	.73
.70	1.00	.99	.97	.96	.93	.91	.88	.84	.80	.76	.73
.75	1.00	1.00	.98	.97	.95	.92	.89	.86	.81	.76	.73
.80	1.00	1.00	.99	.98	.97	.94	.91	.87	.82	.77	.73
.85	1.00	1.00	1.00	.99	.98	.96	.93	.89	.84	.77	.74
.90	1.00	1.00	1.00	1.00	.99	.98	.95	.91	.85	.78	.74
.95	1.00	1.00	1.00	1.00	1.00	.99	.98	.94	.86	.78	.74
1.00	1.00	1.00	1.00	1.00	1.00	1.00	1.00	1.00	.88	.78	.74

PROPORTION OF EMPLOYEES CONSIDERED SATISFACTORY = .80
SELECTION RATIO

r	.05	.10	.20	.30	.40	.50	.60	.70	.80	.90	.95
.00	.80	.80	.80	.80	.80	.80	.80	.80	.80	.80	.80
.05	.83	.82	.82	.82	.81	.81	.81	.81	.81	.80	.80
.10	.85	.85	.84	.83	.83	.82	.82	.81	.81	.81	.80
.15	.88	.87	.86	.85	.84	.83	.83	.82	.82	.81	.81
.20	.90	.89	.87	.86	.85	.84	.84	.83	.82	.81	.81
.25	.92	.91	.89	.88	.87	.86	.85	.84	.83	.82	.81
.30	.94	.92	.90	.89	.88	.87	.86	.84	.83	.82	.81
.35	.95	.94	.92	.90	.89	.89	.87	.85	.84	.82	.81
.40	.96	.95	.93	.92	.90	.89	.88	.86	.85	.83	.82
.45	.97	.96	.95	.93	.92	.90	.89	.87	.85	.83	.82
.50	.98	.97	.96	.94	.93	.91	.90	.88	.86	.84	.82
.55	.99	.98	.97	.95	.94	.92	.91	.89	.87	.84	.82
.60	.99	.99	.98	.96	.95	.94	.92	.90	.87	.84	.83
.65	1.00	.99	.98	.97	.96	.95	.93	.91	.88	.85	.83
.70	1.00	1.00	.99	.98	.97	.96	.94	.92	.89	.85	.83
.75	1.00	1.00	1.00	.99	.98	.97	.95	.93	.90	.86	.83
.80	1.00	1.00	1.00	1.00	.99	.98	.96	.94	.91	.87	.84
.85	1.00	1.00	1.00	1.00	1.00	.99	.98	.96	.92	.87	.84
.90	1.00	1.00	1.00	1.00	1.00	1.00	.99	.97	.94	.88	.84
.95	1.00	1.00	1.00	1.00	1.00	1.00	1.00	.99	.96	.89	.84
1.00	1.00	1.00	1.00	1.00	1.00	1.00	1.00	1.00	1.00	.89	.84

PROPORTION OF EMPLOYEES CONSIDERED SATISFACTORY = .90
SELECTION RATIO

r	.05	.10	.20	.30	.40	.50	.60	.70	.80	.90	.95
.00	.90	.90	.90	.90	.90	.90	.90	.90	.90	.90	.90
.05	.92	.91	.91	.91	.91	.91	.91	.90	.90	.90	.90
.10	.93	.93	.92	.92	.92	.91	.91	.91	.91	.90	.90
.15	.95	.94	.93	.93	.92	.92	.92	.91	.91	.91	.90
.20	.96	.95	.94	.94	.93	.93	.92	.92	.91	.91	.90
.25	.97	.96	.95	.95	.94	.93	.93	.92	.92	.91	.91
.30	.98	.97	.96	.95	.95	.94	.94	.93	.92	.91	.91
.35	.98	.98	.97	.96	.95	.95	.94	.93	.93	.92	.91
.40	.99	.98	.98	.97	.96	.95	.95	.94	.93	.92	.91
.45	.99	.99	.98	.98	.97	.96	.95	.94	.93	.92	.91
.50	1.00	.99	.99	.98	.97	.97	.96	.95	.94	.92	.92
.55	1.00	1.00	.99	.99	.98	.97	.97	.96	.94	.93	.92
.60	1.00	1.00	.99	.99	.99	.98	.97	.96	.95	.93	.92
.65	1.00	1.00	1.00	.99	.99	.98	.98	.97	.96	.94	.92
.70	1.00	1.00	1.00	1.00	.99	.99	.98	.97	.96	.94	.93
.75	1.00	1.00	1.00	1.00	1.00	.99	.99	.98	.97	.95	.93
.80	1.00	1.00	1.00	1.00	1.00	1.00	.99	.99	.97	.95	.93
.85	1.00	1.00	1.00	1.00	1.00	1.00	1.00	.99	.98	.96	.94
.90	1.00	1.00	1.00	1.00	1.00	1.00	1.00	1.00	.99	.97	.94
.95	1.00	1.00	1.00	1.00	1.00	1.00	1.00	1.00	1 00	.98	.94
1 00	1.00	1.00	1.00	1 00	1.00	1.00	1.00	1.00	1.00	1.00	.95

C

lawshe expectancy tables (individual prediction)

PERCENT OF EMPLOYEES CONSIDERED
SATISFACTORY = 30%

r	INDIVIDUAL PREDICTOR CATEGORIES				
	Hi 1/5	Next 1/5	Middle 1/5	Next 1/5	Lo 1/5
.15	38	32	30	28	22
.20	40	34	29	26	21
.25	43	35	29	24	19
.30	46	35	29	24	16
.35	49	36	29	22	14
.40	51	37	28	21	12
.45	55	38	28	20	10
.50	58	38	27	18	09
.55	61	39	27	17	07
.60	64	40	26	15	05
.65	68	41	25	13	04
.70	72	42	23	11	03
.75	76	43	22	09	02
.80	80	44	20	06	01
.85	85	45	17	04	00
.90	90	46	12	02	00
.95	96	48	07	00	00

1 Source: Lawshe, C. H., Bolda, R. L., & Auclair, G.
Expectancy charts, III: Their theoretical development.
Personnel Psychology, 1958, 11, 545–599.

PERCENT OF EMPLOYEES CONSIDERED
SATISFACTORY = 40%

	INDIVIDUAL PREDICTOR CATEGORIES				
r	Hi 1/5	Next 1/5	Middle 1/5	Next 1/5	Lo 1/5
.15	48	44	40	36	32
.20	51	45	40	35	30
.25	54	44	40	34	28
.30	57	46	40	33	24
.35	60	47	39	32	22
.40	63	48	39	31	19
.45	66	49	39	29	17
.50	69	50	39	28	14
.55	72	53	38	26	12
.60	75	53	38	24	10
.65	79	55	37	22	08
.70	82	58	36	19	06
.75	86	59	35	17	04
.80	89	61	34	14	02
.85	93	64	32	10	01
.90	97	69	29	06	00
.95	100	76	23	02	00

PERCENT OF EMPLOYEES CONSIDERED
SATISFACTORY = 50%

	INDIVIDUAL PREDICTOR CATEGORIES				
r	Hi 1/5	Next 1/5	Middle 1/5	Next 1/5	Lo 1/5
.15	58	54	50	46	42
.20	61	55	50	45	39
.25	64	56	50	44	36
.30	67	57	50	43	33
.35	70	58	50	42	30
.40	73	59	50	41	28
.45	75	60	50	40	25
.50	78	62	50	38	22
.55	81	64	50	36	19
.60	84	65	50	35	16
.65	87	67	50	33	13
.70	90	70	50	30	10
.75	92	72	50	28	08
.80	95	75	50	25	05
.85	97	80	50	20	03
.90	99	85	50	15	01
.95	100	93	50	08	00

PERCENT OF EMPLOYEES CONSIDERED
SATISFACTORY = 60%

r	Hi 1/5	Next 1/5	Middle 1/5	Next 1/5	Lo 1/5
			INDIVIDUAL PREDICTOR CATEGORIES		
.15	68	64	60	57	52
.20	71	63	60	56	48
.25	73	65	60	55	48
.30	76	66	61	54	44
.35	78	68	61	53	40
.40	81	69	61	52	37
.45	83	71	61	51	34
.50	86	72	62	50	31
.55	88	74	62	48	28
.60	90	76	62	47	25
.65	92	78	63	45	21
.70	94	80	64	43	18
.75	96	83	65	42	14
.80	98	86	66	39	11
.85	99	90	68	36	07
.90	100	94	71	31	03
.95	100	98	77	24	00

PERCENT OF EMPLOYEES CONSIDERED
SATISFACTORY = 70%

r	Hi 1/5	Next 1/5	Middle 1/5	Next 1/5	Lo 1/5
			INDIVIDUAL PREDICTOR CATEGORIES		
.15	77	73	69	69	62
.20	79	75	70	67	59
.25	81	75	71	65	58
.30	84	76	71	65	54
.35	86	78	71	64	52
.40	88	79	72	63	49
.45	90	80	72	63	46
.50	91	82	73	62	42
.55	93	83	73	61	39
.60	95	85	74	60	36
.65	96	87	75	59	32
.70	97	89	77	58	29
.75	98	91	78	57	25
.80	99	94	80	56	20
.85	100	96	83	55	16
.90	100	98	88	54	10
.95	100	100	93	52	04

D

representative personnel tests

This appendix lists some of the more commonly used personnel tests. This list includes most of the tests mentioned in this text and also includes some not mentioned there. The most comprehensive source of information about commercially available tests is *The Seventh Mental Measurements Yearbook,* vols. 1 and 2, edited by O. K. Buros (Highland Park, N.J.: The Gryphon Press, 1972). This book, and its earlier editions, gives information about publishers of tests and usually reviews of individual tests by one or more competent authorities.

The list of tests below is divided into various classes. For each test listed is a code for the publisher.

Name of test　　　　　　*Code to publisher*
　　　　　　　　　　　　　(see p. 000)

Mental Ability Tests

Adaptability Test	13
Alpha Examination, Modified Form 9	11
Army General Classification Test (AGCT)	13
California Test of Mental Maturity	5
D.A.T. Abstract Reasoning	11
D.A.T. Numerical Ability	11
D.A.T. Verbal Reasoning	11
Otis Self-Administering Tests of Mental Ability	19
Primary Mental Abilities	13
PTI-Oral Directions Test	11
Purdue Non-Language Personnel Test	17
Revised Beta Examination (nonverbal)	11
SRA Nonverbal Form	13
SRA Verbal Form	13
Thurstone Test of Mental Alertness (TMA)	13
Wonderlic Personnel Test	18

Purdue Trade Information Test in Engine
Lathe Operation   17
Purdue Trade Information Test in
Welding   17

General Tests

Purdue Creativity Test   17
Purdue Industrial Supervisors
Word-Meaning Test   17
Purdue Reading Test for Industrial
Supervisors   17

Industrial Test Batteries

Employee Aptitude Survey (EAS)   12
Flanagan Aptitude Classification Tests
(FACT)
(Aptitude Tests for sixteen on-the-job
skills)   13
Flanagan Industrial Tests (FIT) (Tests of
eighteen aptitudes; adaptations of the
Flanagan Aptitude Classification Tests)
                                                   13

TEST PUBLISHERS

1. American Optical Company
   Safety Products Division
   Southbridge, Massachusetts 01550
2. Bausch & Lomb Optical Company
   635 Saint Paul Street
   Rochester, New York 14602
3. Brown & Associates
   252 Pleasantburg Building
   Box 5092 Station B
   Greenville, South Carolina 29606
4. Consulting Psychologists Press, Inc.
   577 College Avenue
   Palo Alto, California 94306
5. CTB/McGraw-Hill
   Del Monte Research Park
   Monterey, California 93940

6. Harcourt Brace Jovanovich, Inc.
   757 Third Avenue
   New York, New York, 10017
7. Human Engineering Laboratory, Inc.
   347 Beacon Street
   Boston, Massachusetts 02186
8. Humm Personnel Service
   1219 West 12th Street
   Los Angeles, California 90015
9. Keystone View Company
   Meadville, Pennsylvania 16335
10. Lafayette Instrument Co.
    Sagamore Parkway
    P.O. Box 1279
    Lafayette, Indiana 47902
11. Psychological Corporation
    304 East 45th Street
    New York, New York 10017
12. Psychological Services, Inc.
    4311 Wilshire Boulevard
    Suite 600
    Los Angeles, California 90005
13. Science Research Associates
    259 East Erie Street
    Chicago, Illinois 60611
14. Sheridan Psychological Services,
    Inc.
    P.O. Box 837
    Beverly Hills, California 90213
15. C. H. Stoelting Company
    424 North Homan Avenue
    Chicago, Illinois 60624
16. Titmus Optical Company
    Petersburg, Virginia 23804
17. University Book Store
    360 State Street
    West Lafayette, Indiana 47906
18. Wonderlic Personnel Test Co.
    P.O. Box 7
    Northfield, Illinois 60093
19. World Book Co.
    Cross Country Medical Hospital
    Yonkers, New York 10704

index

NAME

456

SUBJECT

464